Families

in Context

Families
in Context

Gene H. Starbuck
Mesa State College

WADSWORTH

™

THOMSON LEARNING

Australia • Canada • Mexico • Singapore • Spain
United Kingdom • United States

WADSWORTH

THOMSON LEARNING

Sociology Editor: Bryan Leake
Development Editor: Margaret McAndrew Beasley
Editorial Assistant: Danette Cross
Technology Project Manager: Sarah Davis Packard
Marketing Manager: Laura Brennan
Marketing Assistant: Lisa Huebner
Project Editor: Laura Webb
Print/Media Buyer: Lisa Kelley
Permissions Editor: Charlotte Thomas

Production Manager: Diane Gray
Art Designer: Linda Beaupré
Photo Researcher: Lili Weiner
Copy Editor: Leon Unruh
Cover Image: Kevin Tolman
Cover Printer: Lehigh Press, Inc.
Compositor: Progressive
Printer: Courier Kendallville

1 2 3 4 5 6 7 073 05 04 03 02 01

For more information about our products, contact us at:
Thomson Leaning Academic Resource Center
1-800-423-0563

For permission to use material from this text, contact us by:
Phone: 1-800-730-2214   **Fax:** 1-800-730-2215
Web: http://www.thomsonrights.com

Library of Congress Catalog Card Number: 2001095364
ISBN: 0-15-507136-X

Asia
Thomson Learning
60 Albert Street, #15-01
Albert Complex
Singapore 189969

Australia
Nelson Thomson Learning
102 Dodds Street
South Melbourne, Victoria 3205
Australia

Canada
Nelson Thomson Learning
1120 Birchmount Road
Toronto, Ontario M1K 5G4
Canada

Europe/Middle East/Africa
Thomson Learning
Berkshire House
168-173 High Holborn
London WC1 V7AA
United Kingdom

Latin America
Thomson Learning
Seneca, 53
Colonia Polanco
11560 Mexico D.F.
Mexico

Spain
Paraninfo Thomson Learning
Calle/Magallanes, 25
28015 Madrid, Spain

This book is dedicated to the memory of father, son, and mentor.

Paul F. Starbuck
(1911–1994)

Scott F. Starbuck
(1969–1983)

Howard Higman
(1915–1995)

started this project because I had in mind a particular kind of book about the family that I wanted to make available to college students. That book would be scholarly yet readable. It would excite students about the subject matter and about the promise of social science so that they would want to learn more.

The book I wanted to write would have a broader approach than most. The title, *Families in Context,* summarizes its main theme: families exist in a context that must be understood before families will be fully understood. This context is economic, political, religious, educational, historical, theoretical, and methodological.

The textbook I wanted to write would be inclusive. Virtually all available family textbooks promote their coverage of diversity. By that they usually mean diversity of *topics:* diverse family types, issues of race, class, and gender, and same-sex relationships. Some texts accomplish topical diversity, but remain singular in their theoretical, political, or methodological perspective. *Families in Context* goes beyond topical diversity, and explores differing perspectives. I feel strongly that it is the responsibility of authors of textbooks at this level to introduce students to the field and the subject matter as a whole. Competing theories often interpret data very differently, and even look for different sets of facts. It is important for students to see, understand, and evaluate those differences. Some sections of this book explain such differences directly; and in other sections, students, with the help of their instructors, can work out their own connections between facts and theories. This approach should help students develop critical thinking skills.

I am a sociologist, and wanted to write a book that could open the students' eyes to this fascinating discipline. But sociology is a broad tent, able to cover other fields of study, and I wanted to include those where relevant. The book thus includes topics and research findings from economics, anthropology, history, political science, and psychology. It also draws from the area of family studies, which is often rightfully considered a field in itself.

For four semesters, my students used some version of the manuscript. One semester, the publisher furnished the manuscript to students in my classes. In return, the students critiqued each chapter. They made a number of suggestions that helped shape and refine the final book. They alerted me to sections they found too difficult or unclear, and they let me know, with a certain amount of glee, when they found a misspelled word or a grammatical error.

As a result of the feedback from class testing and many professional reviews, *Families in Context* has evolved, but I have, in essence, written the book I wanted to write.

Plan of the Book

The first part of *Families in Context* is primarily macrosociological. Later chapters then put microsociological coverage into the "big picture" context. The book ends with a brief chapter that helps pull all the material together.

The text is organized into sixteen chapters. Chapter 1 plays with the origin and implication of various definitions of family. The introduction of family-related terms makes family diversity real. Gendered variables and the "family decline" debate are also introduced.

Every student has some experience with families, but courses for which this text will be used attract students with different levels of exposure to sociology and other social sciences. For students with little prior knowledge, Chapter 2 provides an introduction to key theories and methods. Students with a strong sociology background will benefit because the concepts discussed here are specifically applied to the field of family sociology.

Chapters 3 and 4 provide historical analysis, using modes of production as the unifying analytic tool. These chapters emphasize the theme that the family institution is part of a society, and must be understood in that larger context. The relationships between the institution of the family and the institutions of economics, politics, religion, and education are explored. Chapter 3, which incorporates material from the field of anthropology, focuses on preindustrial families. Chapter 4 considers the impact of industrialization on the family and other institutions.

The next three chapters provide an overview of contemporary families. The postindustrial work-family context is the focus of Chapter 5. Chapter 6 explores the concepts of social class and stratification, then puts the American family into that context. Chapter 7 adds analysis of racial and ethnic family diversity.

Chapters 8, 9, and 10 include micro-level analysis that draws some material from psychology. Chapter 8 explores the process of forming intimate relationships. Chapter 9 looks more closely at the mate selection process. Chapter 10 puts the scripting model to its original use in an analysis of human sexuality.

Chapters 11, 12, and 13 examine how families are constructed and maintained. Chapter 11 provides both macro- and micro-level analysis of demographic variables related to families. Chapter 12 covers marital adjustment and power, while Chapter 13 explores parent-child interactions.

Chapter 14 applies a social-movement perspective to problems in families, especially those involving violence. Macro- and micro-level analyses of divorce, remarriage, and stepfamilies are found in Chapter 15. Finally, Chapter 16 projects into the future and explores policy issues as a way of synthesizing and concluding the textbook.

Special Features

Students are generally most interested in topics that appear to affect their own lives directly. Family experiences affect all of us, so textbook authors in this area have something of an advantage over authors in other disciplines. However, there are many topics in the academic study of families that appear to have only a remote connection to students' everyday lives. Several of the features developed for *Families in Context* help make those subtle connections more visible.

- **Finding Out.** Just as many undergraduates are less than enthusiastic about abstract theories, they generally have little initial interest in research methods. I try to demonstrate that understanding how researchers define and measure concepts is key to understanding results. Chapter 2 introduces the methods most commonly used by social scientists. Each remaining chapter includes a Finding Out box that discusses methods in some way. In most cases, a particular well-known study will be discussed. Other Finding Out features compare various ways of studying a particular topic. Still others focus on how a concept can be operationalized for research purposes. All include critical comments about methodology.

- **Prelude.** Each chapter begins with a personal vignette that brings the chapter topic to an

individual level. The preludes involve issues and experiences that will likely seem familiar to students, but may also encourage them to think about those topics in a new way. The Prelude in Chapter 4 is biographically true; remaining Preludes are fictionalized accounts.

- **Thinking Ahead** sections at the chapter openings help sensitize students to the upcoming material. Considering these pre-reading questions will encourage students to begin forming some ideas that can be tested by or compared with chapter material.

- **Rethinking in Context** questions fall at the end of each chapter. These questions can help students to place their pre-reading answers in the context of the material they have just read. The two companion features work best when the "Thinking Ahead" questions are answered before the student has even scanned the chapter or heard lectures on chapter content and the "Rethinking in Context" questions are answered after study of the chapter content.

- **Families in the News.** These boxed items consist of recent news accounts—many with which the students will be familiar—that relate to the chapter topics. This feature highlights family-related topics found in the newspapers, magazines, and television stories every day. Students may find the news a bit more interesting when they are able to connect it to their own lives through a field of study.

- **Running Glossary.** In addition to an end-of-book glossary, important terms in this text are identified and defined at the bottom of the page on which the term is introduced.

- **Suggested Resources.** Additional print and online resources are listed at the end of each chapter for those students who wish to explore specific topics beyond the text.

Supplements

STUDENT RESOURCES

Study Guide
ISBN: 0-15-506250-6
By Wanda Clark, South Plains College
This text-specific study guide contains learning objectives, chapter outlines, multiple-choice, true-false,

matching, short essays, and critical thinking questions. In addition, crossword puzzles provide an entertaining way to approach the important concepts and terms for each chapter.

Student Guide to InfoTrac® College Edition for Sociology

http://sociology.wadsworth.com
ISBN: 0-534-58766-6
By Michele Adams, University of California, Riverside
This unique supplement features exercises that utilize InfoTrac® College Edition's huge database of articles. These exercises, based on 23 subjects vital to the study of sociology, help students narrow down the search of articles related to each subject, and ask questions that enable students to see the concepts more clearly.

Researching Sociology on the Internet

http://sociology.wadsworth.com/socnet.html
ISBN: 0-534-56894-7
By D. R. Wilson and David L. Carlson
This useful guide assists sociology students when doing research on the Internet. From general information necessary to get started to a more focused look at each main discipline in Sociology, this guide is the ideal companion to your students' Internet travels.

Marriage and Family: An Introduction Using MicroCase® ExplorIt, Second Edition

ISBN: 0-922914-35-4
By Kevin Demmitt, Clayton College and State University
This software-based workbook is an exciting way to get students to view marriage and family from the sociological perspective. With this workbook and accompanying *MicroCase® ExplorIt* software and data sets, students use national and cross-national surveys to examine and actively learn marriage and family topics. This inexpensive workbook will add an exciting dimension to your marriage and family course.

INSTRUCTOR RESOURCES

Instructor's Manual and Test Bank

ISBN: 0-15-506284-0
By Gene H. Starbuck, Mesa State College
I insisted on authoring the Instructor's Manual and Test Bank myself because I have found the quality of such productions to be somewhat uneven. I hope that my knowledge of the material, along with almost three decades of teaching experience, will help produce a

valuable instructor's tool. The test item file, printed in the Instructor's Manual, is also available as a computerized ExamView® file. For each chapter, the Instructor's Manual provides suggestions for lectures, assignments, and discussions. These suggestions have been class-tested with my students and, in many cases, by other instructors as well.

A unique feature of the Instructor's Manual is inclusion of an opinion and experience questionnaire that can be given to students early in the term. Instructors can tabulate and reveal the results when related material is covered in class. Because most of the questions are common ones asked by the likes of the GSS or Gallup Polls, I have collated and included national-level results for each of the questions on the student questionnaire. Interesting comparisons between responses from the students and those from a nationally representative sample can be discussed in class. I have found the questionnaire discussions quite useful in helping students think in terms of "social facts" and not solely in personal experiences.

ExamView® Computerized Test Bank

Cross-platform ISBN: 0-15-506276-X
Create, deliver, and customize tests and study guides (both print and online) in minutes with this easy-to-use assessment and tutorial system. **ExamView®** offers both a Quick Test Wizard and an Online Test Wizard that guide you step-by-step through the process of creating tests, while its unique *"WYSIWYG"* capability allows you to see the test you are creating on the screen exactly as it will print or display online. You can build tests of up to 250 questions using up to 12 question types. Using **ExamView®**'s complete word processing capabilities, you can enter an unlimited number of new questions or edit existing questions. **ExamView®** and **ExamView® Pro** are trademarks of FSCreations, Inc. Windows is a registered trademark of the Microsoft® Corporation and used herein under license. Macintosh and Power Macintosh are registered trademarks of Apple Computer, Inc. used herein under license.

PowerPoint® Presentation Slides

http://sociology.wadsworth.com
By Paul Lamy of the University of Ottawa, Canada
These text-specific PowerPoint slides provide lecture aids such as graphs, charts, and tables corresponding to the material in each chapter. The presentation includes approximately 20 slides per chapter plus auxiliary images, allowing professors to customize their own presentation. The slides are available to download from the Web site.

InfoTrac® College Edition

FREE! The latest news and research articles online—updated daily and spanning four years! **InfoTrac® College Edition** is automatically packaged with every new student copy of this text. Students receive four FREE months of real-time access to **InfoTrac® College Edition's** online database of continuously updated, full-length articles from hundreds of journals and periodicals, including *Journal of Family Practice, Society, Family, and Community Health, Family Planning Perspectives, Sex Roles: A Journal of Research,* and more. Contact your Wadsworth/Thomson Learning representative for more information.

Available to North American college and university students only. Journals subject to change.

SocLink 2002 CD-ROM: A Microsoft® PowerPoint® Presentation Tool

ISBN: 0-534-55592-6

SocLink is an easy-to-use interface that instructors can use to create customized lecture presentations for their students. SocLink includes a searchable database of thousands of pieces of art and media, including a photo-gallery of all Wadsworth Introduction to Sociology, Marriage & Family, and Social Problems titles; unique CNN Video clips; and Sociology PowerPoint® slides. SocLink gives instructors the ability to post their presentations on the Web and import information from their own lecture notes. SocLink is FREE to adopters.

Virtual Society: The Wadsworth Sociology Resource Center

http://sociology.wadsworth.com

Combine Starbuck's text with Virtual Society's exciting range of Web resources and you have expanded your students' learning opportunities to the Web. Access to this powerful online resource center is FREE to text adopters and their students. The Virtual Society features a wealth of text-specific resources, forums, links to news groups, surfing lessons, a career center, and more. For instructors, a password-protected Instructor Resource Center offers the Instructor's Manual online, Power-Point® presentations, e-mail access to Wadsworth editors, and more. For students, hyper-contents and chapter-by-chapter resources (chapter quizzes, online self-quizzes, and more) take studying to a new level.

CNN® Today: Marriage and Family Video Series

Volume I ISBN: 0-534-55257-9
Volume II ISBN: 0-534-55258-7;
Volume III ISBN: 0-534-55268-4
Volume IV ISBN: 0-534-55270-6

Now you can integrate the up-to-the-minute programming power of CNN and its affiliate networks right into your course. Updated yearly, the CNN Today course-specific videos can help you launch a lecture, spark a discussion, or demonstrate an application—using the top-notch business, science, consumer, and political reporting of the CNN networks. Produced by Turner Learning, Inc., these 45-minute videos show your students how the principles they learn in the classroom apply to the stories they see on television. Special adoption conditions apply.

Wadsworth Marriage and the Family Transparency Acetates

ISBN: 0-534-58919-7

A selection of quality acetates from Wadsworth's marriage and family texts. Free to qualified adopters.

Acknowledgments

I was surprised to learn how many specialized professionals are involved in the writing and publishing processes for a book like this, and I am thankful for all of them. First, there are the roughly 8,500 students I have taught over the last 27 years. I can't say that each and every one of them contributed to my learning experience or to the book, but collectively they have been invaluable. The four classes that read and critiqued versions of the manuscript were especially helpful.

Since I wanted to include voices from disciplines outside of sociology, it was especially helpful that I am in a multidisciplinary department. My colleagues in sociology, anthropology, political science, history, economics, and psychology were all supportive. They were quite helpful when I wandered the halls late in the afternoon seeking information. In particular, anthropologists Barry Michrina and Clare Boulanger were patient in pointing me in the right direction. The former, as well as sociologist Adele Cummings and historian Doug O'Roark, read portions of the manuscript and helped to improve it. Historian Lewis Chere is a treasure chest of arcane information. To these and all the other wonderful folks in my department: party at my house at a time to be determined.

Mesa State College, in Grand Junction, Colorado where I have loved my work for 27 years, also deserves my thanks. I received a sabbatical, followed by a leave of absence, to complete most of the first draft of the book. I spent those two years at Utah State University, reading, writing, and teaching. Gary Kiger and the rest of the Department of Sociology, Anthropology, and Social Work, were gracious and helpful.

Because of corporate mergers in the publishing industry, my emerging manuscript passed through three different publishers before assuming its current form. Thanks to Robert Jucha (then at West Publishing) and Lin Marshall (then at Harcourt Brace) for having faith enough to acquire the book. Working with senior developmental editor Margaret McAndrew Beasley at Harcourt was a real joy. It was under her guidance that the project transformed from a rough manuscript to a finished product. Along the way, help came from Laura Webb, project editor; Diane Gray, production manager; Linda Beaupré, creative director; Charlotte Thomas, photo editor; Sarah Davis-Packard, Web editor; Lili Weiner, freelance photo researcher, and others whose names I will never know.

Several colleagues around the country read drafts of the textbook and provided valuable suggestions. The most helpful were often the ones who objected most strongly to elements of the manuscript. Frankly, their comments sometimes hurt or temporarily angered me. It was a bit like hearing a stranger criticize my children. But in a day or two, I was able to more objectively consider their comments and to make the necessary changes. My thanks to the following reviewers: Barbara Bearnson, Utah Valley State College; Jon P. Block, Southern Connecticut State University; Henry Borne,

Holy Cross College; Lee Frank, Community College of Allegheny County; Norval D. Glenn, University of Texas at Austin; Theodore N. Greenstein, North Carolina State University; Joanna Grey, Pikes Peak Community College; Ron J. Hammond, Utah Valley State College; David M. Klein, University of Notre Dame; Barbara M. Lazarus, California State University, Northridge; Rudy Ray Seward, University of North Texas; Hasan Shahpari, Villanova University; Toni Terling-Watt, University of Oklahoma; and those whose names I do not know.

Both David Klein of Notre Dame and Norval Glenn of the University of Texas went beyond the help normally expected of reviewers. Although I didn't know them personally when I started this project, they each helped by providing encouragement and offering advice about how to navigate the ever-changing landscape of college publishing. They are true scholars and gentlemen, and it has been an honor to make their acquaintance.

It is not simply out of tradition that I want to publicly thank my mother, Ethel Starbuck. She is one of the most thoughtful, intelligent people I have ever known, and she has supported me even through all the mistakes I've made. She and her partner, Joe Sullivan, read an earlier version of the text, commented helpfully, and gave their approval.

Gene H. Starbuck
Mesa State College

Gene H. Starbuck received a BA in Psychology from the University of Colorado in 1969. He earned his MA in Sociology in 1971 from a program jointly sponsored by the Oglala Sioux Tribe, Volunteers in Service to America, and the University of Colorado. Upon completing coursework for a PhD in Sociology, he accepted a teaching position at Mesa College, Colorado. Dr. Starbuck completed the doctorate in 1985, and he continues to teach at what has become Mesa State College.

Dr. Starbuck has dedicated his professional life primarily to teaching, and has won several awards in the field. His preparation to teach such classes as Sex and Gender, Social Stratification, Methods of Social Research, Crime and Delinquency, Social Problems, and others, gives him the broad background with which he approaches his favorite class—Marriage and Families.

Dr. Starbuck has published and presented papers at professional conferences in the areas of human sexuality, gender, and families. He has a particular interest in the study of domestic violence. He belongs to the American Sociological Association and the National Council on Family Relations, and currently serves as the Sociology Section Coordinator for the Western Social Science Association.

Dr. Starbuck enjoys the great outdoors by riding on one of the many great mountain bike trails a few miles from his home.

Brief Table of Contents

Contents

Chapter 3 — Families in Preindustrial Context

Chapter 4 — Industrialization and Families

Chapter 5   Gender, Work, and Postindustrial Families   107

Chapter 6   Social Class and Families   135

Chapter 7   Race/Ethnicity and Families   161

Chapter 8   Forming Intimate Relationships   193

Chapter 9   Mate Selection   219

Chapter 12   Negotiating Marriages   305

Chapter 13   Parents and Children   335

Chapter 14   Crisis and Violence in Families   369

Chapter 15   Divorce and Rescripted Families   397

Chapter 16 Family Perspectives, Policy, and the Future   427

Features

Chapter 1

Defining Family Variation

Prelude

Throughout our lives, many of our deepest sorrows, our most profound joys, and our most mundane moments are associated with family relationships we have had or hope to have someday. We experience these as intensely personal, unique, individual events. We seldom stop to think about the influence our society has on these family experiences.

Yet, the makeup of our family, who we include as family members, and what shape we expect our families to take are all subject to significant social influence. Out of the extensive menu imaginable for constructing families, our society supports only a few possibilities. As individuals, we select from this limited menu only a few possibilities for ourselves. This chapter is about the broader universe of cultural choices that might be possible.

Would all these options be feasible in American society today?

The study of marriage and the family is complicated by the fact that we each have a somewhat different image of what a family is. When asked about their families, one person might think of his mother, father, sister, and two brothers. Another might have her own husband and children in mind. Someone else might immediately think of a grandmother, mother, and brother. In some cultures, a man might think of his 4 wives, 26 children, and 65 grandchildren.

This book is primarily about families in the United States today, but it puts those families in historical and cultural context. To do this requires definitions that apply to all types of families, from the earliest groups of people who survived solely by hunting and gathering their food to today's complex postindustrial societies.

This chapter will explore various types of definitions of family, using symbolic human groups as illustrations. In the process, several terms that refer to diverse family forms will be introduced, and a variety of analytic tools for studying families will be presented.

> **Thinking Ahead** Write a definition of the family. Make sure that your definition includes all those groups of persons you think of as being a family, while ruling out all groups that you think do not constitute a family.

Basic Considerations

Social scientists have developed a set of symbols for describing different kinds of family relationships. These symbols (see Figure 1.1) can help define types of families and provide models of groups that might or might not be called families. To get the most out of this section of the text, students can refer to their own definition of family as they consider each symbolic group of people.

What Is a Family?

Figure 1.2 represents a man and woman we will call John and Jennifer. They are married to each other and have a son and daughter we will call Kyle and Kayla. By anyone's definition, this group is a family. In fact, it is an important enough type that it has a specific name: the **nuclear family**. As the word "nuclear" implies, this is the nucleus, or central unit of the family. It is not, however, the smallest kind of family unit.

In Figure 1.3 John and Jennifer are married to each other but have no children. This group, too, has a specific term because of its importance to the family. The husband-wife pair is called the **conjugal unit**. A family containing this unit would be called a **conjugal family**. The term derives from the Latin word that means "to join," as does the word "conjunction." Thus, conjugal implies the bringing together of previously unrelated units.

Figure 1.4(a) represents a more complicated, three-generation, group. Jennifer is labeled Ego in the diagram, indicating that she is the reference point for defining relationships. She and her husband, John, are parents of Kyle and Kayla, and her brother and parents are also represented in the diagram. This entire unit is an example of an **extended family**; it extends, or goes beyond, a nuclear family. While extended families typically include three generations, they can include a variety of other arrangements (for example, see Figure 1.4b).

Jennifer in Figure 1.4(a) is actually part of several family units. In addition to the extended family, she and

---

Nuclear family: A two-generation group that includes parents and their children.   **Conjugal unit:** The husband-wife pair.
Extended family: A family composed of the nuclear family plus additional relatives, usually a third generation.

<figure>**Figure 1.1**   Relationship Symbols

Family Symbols
O means female
| means descendant or ancestor

Δ means male
— means same generation

= means marriage
</figure>

John constitute a conjugal unit. She is also a member of two nuclear family units: one involves her parents and brother, the other includes her husband and children.

To avoid confusion, the two nuclear units to which Ego belongs are sometimes given separate names. The family that includes her parents and siblings is the one in which she is "oriented" into the world. For that reason it is called her **family of orientation.** The other family is the one into which she married and had children. This is called her **family of procreation.**

Now, unfortunately, John and Jennifer get a divorce, as depicted in Figure 1.5. From Kyle and Kayla's perspective, John and Jennifer each maintain their family-related terms; they remain mother and father. The relationship terms in the former conjugal unit of John and Jennifer, however, now become ex-husband and ex-wife. This unit as a whole might no longer be called a family, although the children/father unit could be, as could the children/mother unit. In either case the children would be part of a single-parent family, even though they still have two parents.

Figure 1.6 depicts Jennifer's remarriage to Jackson. Particularly if the children live with their mother and

Figure 1.3   Conjugal Unit

Δ = O

Figure 1.4   Extended Families

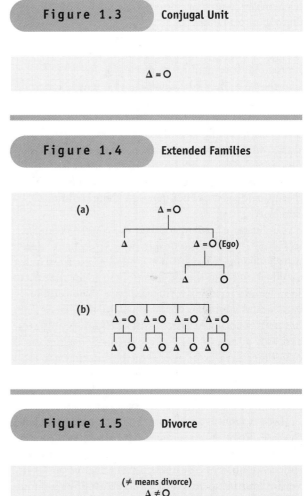

Figure 1.2   Nuclear Family

Δ = O

Figure 1.5   Divorce

(≠ means divorce)
Δ ≠ O

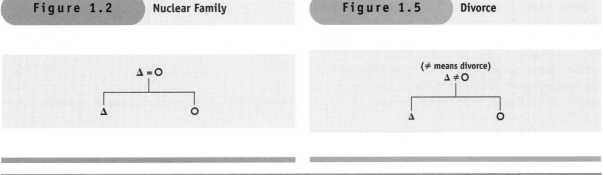

Family of orientation: The family unit that includes one's parents and siblings.   **Family of procreation:** The family unit that includes one's spouse and, at least potentially, one's children.

her new husband, they would be members of a **stepfamily**. This unit is also called a **blended family** or a **reconstituted family**.

Figure 1.7 provides a somewhat different case. Although it cannot be determined from the diagram, we can assume for purposes of illustration that Jennifer and her children are living in the same household. In this case the mother formed an intimate cohabiting relationship with Jackson, but there was no legally recognized wedding ceremony. Jackson has not entered into a formal relationship with Jennifer and her children. Because no marriage is present, some people might not call this entire group a family.

Even more controversy is likely about the group represented in Figure 1.8, where Judy moves into the household. It is identical to that in Figure 1.7 except that the new adult in the household is female rather than male. While intimacy and long-term commitment exist between Jennifer and Judy, the same-sex couple is less likely to be thought of as being part of a family than would Jennifer and Jackson. Some same-sex couples, of course, have children without either having been previously married. Such couples and their children provide yet another question about defining families.

To illustrate further, consider the childless couples in Figure 1.9. The relationship between John and Jennifer in Figure 1.9(a) has previously been defined as a conjugal unit, but this might not be true for the case of Jennifer and Jackson (1.9b). The only obvious difference would be that in the first instance the marriage has been officially registered with the state. Jennifer and Judy in case (c) might have the same feelings for each other as those in case (a) or (b), but they are not allowed to enter into legally defined marriages. Americans are divided about whether this could still be called a family.

Today's families are diverse, but such has always been the case. Single-parent families have always existed, although in the past such families more commonly resulted from parental death than from divorce or out-of-wedlock birth. There have always been couples without children, either because no child has yet been born or because those born have died or left the home. Also,

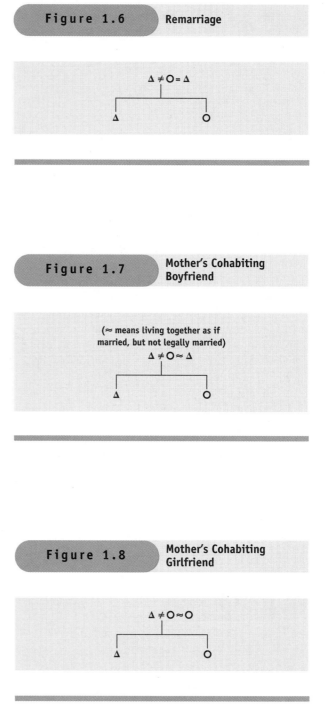

Figure 1.6 **Remarriage**

$$\triangle \neq O = \triangle$$

Figure 1.7 **Mother's Cohabiting Boyfriend**

(≈ means living together as if married, but not legally married)
$$\triangle \neq O \approx \triangle$$

Figure 1.8 **Mother's Cohabiting Girlfriend**

$$\triangle \neq O \approx O$$

Stepfamily: Family unit consisting of a married man and woman, plus children from a previous relationship. A *simple stepfamily* includes children of one parent; a *complex stepfamily* includes children from both adults. Also called a *blended family* or a *reconstituted family*.

Figure 1.9	Couple Families?

(a) Δ = O

(b) Δ ≈ O

(c) O ≈ O

many individuals spend at least part of their lives belonging to both a family of orientation and a family of procreation, and some spend part of their lives living alone.

One way to compare the way individuals live at any given time is to divide them into **households.** Although the majority of households in the United States contain families, the percentage of people living in families is declining. Table 1.1 reveals the percentage of households of various types. The percent of households containing married couples, both with children (nuclear families) and without children (conjugal units) continues to decrease. In 1970, 40.3 percent of households

consisted of married coupled with children. By 2010, that figure is expected to drop to half of the 1970 rate.

Criteria for Judgments

Agreeing on a definition of the family is difficult for several reasons. The purpose of constructing the definition is one factor. In everyday conversation we can usually figure out what definition is implied by the context of the conversation. For legal purposes, however, a more precise definition is required so that legal distinctions between family groups and other types of groups are clearer. These definitions affect inheritance rights, hospital visitation rights, the right to live together in certain parts of town, the right to be included in a "family health plan," and a number of other legal issues. Quite often, the values held by the persons doing the defining will affect the definition and the legal consequences for family and nonfamily groups.

Values are more or less shared by members of a particular society. Especially in today's complicated and diverse societies, however, significant disagreement about values exists. The last few years have witnessed considerable discussion in the United States about what the values ought to be with respect to the family. The phrase "family values" itself has become controversial because it seems to be used primarily by those who support more traditional ideas about what families ought to be.

Table 1.1	Household Composition in the United States, 1970–2010, in Percent of Total Households				
Type	**1970**	**1980**	**1990**	**2000†**	**2010†**
Married Couples with Children*	40.3	30.9	26.3	23.9	20.1
Married Couples without Children*	30.3	29.9	29.8	29.8	31.5
Other Families with Children*	5.0	7.5	8.3	8.2	7.9
Other Families without Children*	5.6	5.4	6.5	7.5	8.3
Men Living Alone	5.6	8.6	9.7	10.8	11.7
Women Living Alone	11.5	14.0	14.9	14.6	15.1
Other Nonfamily Households	1.7	3.6	4.6	5.2	5.4

†Projections calculated from U.S. Bureau of Census, *Statistical Abstract of the United States: 1998,* Table 70.
*Own children, under age 18

Sources: U.S. Bureau of Census, *Statistical Abstract of the United States: 1994* and *Statistical Abstract of the United States: 1996,* Table 68.

Household: A living unit; a group of persons sharing living quarters.   **Values:** Shared ideas about what is good, right, or proper.

Father Knows Best was typical of television shows of the 1950s, with an intact nuclear family and a stay-at-home mom.

By the 1990s, television shows such as *Fresh Prince of Bel-Air* depicted a wide variety of family and living arrangements.

Values, including those related to families, are often based on religious traditions. Support for the traditional image of the family is often based on an interpretation of the Judeo-Christian ethic, as defined by a literal reading of the Bible. This perspective places a high value on the type of nuclear family unit in which the father is the provider, protector, and spiritual leader, while the mother works in the home as a caregiver and nurturer to the children. Nontraditionalists, on the other hand, sometimes refer to values such as fairness, equality, and individualism. To these people, the nuclear family is only one kind of family that is, perhaps, no better than alternative types. The nontraditional interpretation is more likely to be portrayed in today's television shows (see Highlight 1.1).

Norms are another important element in defining a family. While values are general ideas about what is good, right, or proper, norms are more specific guidelines about behavior and are enforced by rewards or punishments of varying degrees of seriousness.

HIGHLIGHT 1.1 | **Television Families in the 1990s**

Leave It to Beaver, Father Knows Best, and other television shows of the 1950s portrayed "wholesome" families with hard-working fathers, kind and nurturing housewife-mothers, and cautious, courteous children. Even at the time not all families were of this type, but television modeled the values of what was considered a "good" family.

To find out if television shows of the 1990s are different, an analysis of television situation comedies of the 1994–1995 season was conducted. Consideration was given to all half-hour, prime-time shows with live actors (not cartoons) and laugh tracks, on the four major networks: ABC, CBS, NBC, and Fox.

Unlike the 1950s, intact nuclear families are rarely portrayed today. Only three of the 30 shows had such a household; in two of these the adult woman was a housewife. Only one of these, *Boy Meets World,* could be considered a "model family" in the *Leave It to*

Norms: Widespread expectations governing behavior. *Prescriptive norms* determine what *should* be done; *proscriptive norms* determine what *should not* be done.

Beaver mold. The other, *Married with Children,* was more a model of a dysfunctional family. The third intact nuclear family unit was depicted in *Home Improvement,* in which the wife was sometimes a full-time nurturing housewife and the husband a well-meaning but bumbling father.

Four shows depicted a family form that could be considered augmented-nuclear, in which there was a nuclear unit but also others in the household, or attenuated-nuclear, in which the nuclear unit was not an original intact group. *Fresh Prince of Bel-Air* was in this category; the Prince lived with his aunt, uncle, cousins, and butler. *Roseanne* was also put in this category; it had a somewhat fluid household, with one daughter's boyfriend in occasional residence.

The single-parent family, with seven shows, was most commonly depicted. This category included *Murphy Brown,* the show that got so much publicity in the flap with former Vice President Dan Quayle because of the out-of-wedlock birth of a child. Five of the seven single-parent families, however, contained another adult person in the form of a nanny, friend, or grandparent. Two of the single parents were fathers, the remaining five mothers.

Childless conjugal households were portrayed in three shows. Simple stepfamilies were shown in two shows. Other families portrayed included a complicated extended family group and a group of orphaned siblings. Nonfamily households, or nonhousehold groups, were depicted in the remaining seven shows.

Shows in the '90s are more racially diverse than those of the '50s. Eight of the 30 (27%) starred a predominantly African American cast, considerably more than the 12% of the general population that is black. One show starred a Korean woman and the rest were apparently European descendents of some kind.

In their portrayal of traditional family values, the television shows of the 1950s were not representative of America's family diversity. In their extensive diversity, shows in the 1990s may not be representative of America's traditional family values.

Source: *Information was gathered expressly for this analysis by Andrea McRobbie.*

Formal norms are written down and enforced by some socially regulated mechanism. In the United States the formal norms are called laws and are enforced by police officers and courts. The most serious violations, such as murder, can sometimes be punishable by death. Less serious crimes can be punished by a prison sentence or fine. Formal family norms regulate violent behaviors among family members and the responsibility of parents to support their minor children.

Informal norms, on the other hand, are not enforced by agencies like the police, but they guide behavior nonetheless. There are uncounted numbers of unwritten rules, violation of which might bring a dirty look, gossip, a rude comment, or other informal sanction. For example, we all know that the norm is to get in the back of the line at the grocery store. Cutting in line will not bring the police, but it is likely to bring stares and grumbling from others in the line. Informal norms affect the way family members interact in public. Parents might scream at their children at home, but they try to resist doing so in the grocery store. In most American groups, children are expected to call their parents "Mom" and "Dad," or perhaps "Mother" and "Father." They do not typically call their biological parents by the parent's first name.

One informal norm is that, when a young couple gets married, they should have children. This is referred to as **pronatalism**. There are no "fertility police" to lock up couples without children, but there are many informal pressures upon them. Friends and relatives might ask them when they are going to have children, or even whose "fault" it is that they do not. Generally, persons who follow the norms are not asked to explain their behavior, but those who deviate from expectations are. In this case, couples who never have children are called upon to explain themselves. In today's society, people who have "too many" children—probably more than three—are sometimes called upon for an explanation.

As both the values and norms change, images of families change. In a diverse society like the United States, not everyone holds the same values and norms. Different ethnic groups, social classes, religious groups, occupational groups, and other categories of people have somewhat different values and norms.

Roles and Scripts. Individuals play parts in the family in ways similar to the parts played by actors on

---

Formal norms: Behavioral expectations that are written and enforced by specialized social mechanisms; laws.   **Informal norms:** Behavioral expectations that lack codified, enforceable sanctions.   **Pronatalism:** A belief system that encourages childbearing.

the stage. In the theater, a **role** is a part played by an actor. The **script** prescribes how various roles are expected to interact. Actors are told what to say, what costumes are appropriate, when to enter and exit the stage, and what emotions to portray.

Role-playing is not limited to actors on the stage. In everyday life, too, persons play roles. During the course of any day, John and Jennifer are likely to play several roles. They might, at different times, behave in ways appropriate to being a student, a son or daughter, a worker, a friend, and a husband or wife.

It is important to note that real-life roles are not as detailed as those found in a movie script. In real-life roles there is usually considerable room in the script for individual variations. At most universities, the student role has only a loosely defined set of expectations regarding the proper costume to wear. Imagine the reaction to a student who wears a bikini or tuxedo to class. Sanctions, in the form of gestures, expressions, and comments, are brought to bear on persons who depart too widely from the expectations of their group.

In a family group, the name that two related individuals call each other provides a tremendous amount of information about how they should treat each other. When Jennifer meets an old friend and wants to introduce the man to whom she is married, she can use the family term "husband" as a way of defining the kind of relationship the two of them have: "Margaret, this is my husband, John." Several other terms define family or kinship relationships, including niece, nephew, cousin, father, mother, brother, sister, grandfather, grandmother, aunt, and uncle.

Some of the groups of persons depicted in the diagrams above have family terms available to describe the role relationship; others do not. Consider again the possibilities that are listed in Figure 1.9. John and Jennifer ($\triangle = \bigcirc$) have the recognizable family terms of husband and wife. Jackson and Jennifer ($\triangle \approx \bigcirc$) might have the emotional and sexual ties of husband and wife, but they lack a widely accepted name for the social relationship and role. How does the woman in this relationship introduce the man? She might simply say "Margaret, this is my friend," but that term does not quite fully capture the nature of the relationship. Nor, quite, do "significant other," "boyfriend," or "lover." The term "partner" is increasingly popular; it can apply to same-sex or opposite-sex couples, married or cohabiting. The term "partner" is a bit ambiguous, however, since it can also be applied to a business relationship. The U.S. Census Bureau suggested the term POSSLQ (pronounced "posselque"), an acronym for "person of the opposite sex sharing living quarters." One implication is that, although cohabitation ("Mother, this is my cohabitant"?) is becoming increasingly acceptable, the cohabiting union might not be considered a family because the kinship terms have not yet been established. This is even truer for the other possibilities in Figure 1.9: John and Jackson ($\triangle \approx \triangle$) or Jennifer and Judy ($\bigcirc \approx \bigcirc$).

If a child calls an adult "mother" or "father," there is a fairly clear understanding of the responsibilities and prohibitions the adult has with regard to the child. Some of those role expectations have become formal norms, written into the law. The parent has the legal responsibility to feed, clothe, and provide medical care; failure to do so can result in punishments for child neglect. These formal expectations are supplemented with such informal ones as providing affection and positive regard. Informal norms change constantly; a new one seems to be developing that mothers and fathers should not smoke in their homes where children might be exposed to second-hand smoke.

A stepparent, too, has role responsibilities toward the stepchild, but they are not as clearly defined as that for a parent (more on this in Chapter 15). The matter is less clear in the POSSLQ relationship between Jennifer and Jackson as represented in Figure 1.7. The role relationship is ambiguous between Jennifer and Jackson, but it is even less clear between Jackson and the children. He might behave as if he is a father, but Kyle and Kayla already have someone in that role. The relationship is more like that of stepfather to stepchild, but since no legal marriage exists with Jennifer, it is not formally a step relationship.

Types of Definitions

We know that a family is a group of individuals who interact in a close, personal way, but emphasis on different elements of these groups can result in different types of definitions. Some definitions focus on what the family does (a **functional definition**) and others on what

---

Role: Expectations associated with a particular position in the social system.   **Script:** Expectations governing the interaction of two or more roles.   **Functional definition:** Definition based on how the family serves the participating individuals (**microfunctional**) or how it serves society (**macrofunctional**).

components a family must have (a **structural definition**). Both types can refer to the interaction among family members.

Functional Definitions. A **microfunctional** definition focuses on how the family serves its individual members. Steinmetz's example (see Highlight 1.2.a) refers to mutual sharing of various kinds. By this definition, the John and Jackson depicted in Figure 1.8(c) could be a family. All of the illustrations, in fact, could be families because of the functions each group serves for the individuals involved.

Microfunctional definitions can include a wide variety of forms under the "family" umbrella. For example, sorority "sisters" live together and share some values, goals, commitment, and resources. They even have a house "mother." Similarly, an urban juvenile gang shares values and commitment while providing a sense of belonging to interacting members. These two groups, however, are not what most people have in mind when they use the term "family."

A **macrofunctional** definition (see Highlight 1.2.b) deals with the functions the family serves for society as a whole. Rather than focus on how the family serves individuals, a macrofunctional definition treats the family as a social **institution** that contributes to society by performing such functions as reproduction, socialization of children, and economic cooperation. The homosexual couples in Figure 1.8 might not be considered families using a macrofunctional definition because such couples do not, by themselves, serve the social function of reproduction. They do, however, sometimes participate in socialization of the young and cooperate economically.

| HIGHLIGHT 1.2 | **Definitions of Family** |

(a) Microfunctional definition:
   A unit of intimate, transacting, and interdependent persons who share some values, goals, resources, and responsibility for decisions, as well as a commitment to one another over time (Steinmetz et al., 1990:12).

(b) Macrofunctional definition:
   The intimate group in which reproduction, socialization of the young, economic cooperation, and social status placement occur.

Definition stressing dysfunctions of the family for some participants:
"The major institution for perpetuating patriarchy and women's oppression" (Tuttle, 1986:100).

(c) A structural definition of family:
   Two or more individuals who share a housing unit and are related by blood, marriage, or adoption (U.S. Census Bureau, 1983).

(d) Definitions with a combination of elements:
   "A group of persons united by ties of marriage, blood, or adoption; constituting a single household; interacting and communicating with each other in their respective social roles (husband and wife, mother and father, sons and daughter, brother and sister); and creating and maintaining a common culture" (Burgess & Locke, 1953).

   "A set of persons related to each other by blood, marriage, or adoptions and whose basic societal function is replacement" (Winch, 1971).

   "The basic social institution. One or more men living with one or more women in a socially-sanctioned and more or less enduring sex relationship, with socially recognized rights and obligations, together with their offspring" (Fairchild, 1970).

   "A social group in society typically consisting of a man and woman and their offspring. B. Two or more people who share goals and values, have long-term commitments to one another, and reside usually in the same dwelling place. 2. All the members of a household under one roof. 3. A group of persons sharing common ancestry" *(American Heritage Dictionary).*

   "Particular societal arrangement whereby persons related by ancestry, marriage, or adoption live together, form an economic unit, and raise children" (Zinn & Eitzen, 1993:460).

Structural Definitions. While other definitions have their uses, they are not very precise. The Census Bureau, faced with the responsibility of counting the actual number of families in the United States, needs a definition that clearly distinguishes what a family is. The Census Bureau definition (see Highlight 1.2c) refers to the parts of a family and how they are held together, rather than what the parts do. It is much easier to decide whether a particular group is a family with this definition than with

---

Structural definition: Definition describing the components and makeup of a family.   **Microfunctional:** Focusing on consequences for individuals or small groups.   **Macrofunction:** Focusing on consequences for institutions or societies.
Institution: 1. a system of norms, values, statuses, and roles that develop around a basic social goal; 2. a regular and traditional way of meeting a society's needs.

others. By this definition neither juvenile gangs nor college fraternities would qualify as families.

By the Census Bureau definition, a family must share a common residence; that is, they must form a household. Extended families would not count as a family unless they all lived in the same domicile. The Census Bureau definition also recognizes **kin groups**. Kin can be uncles, aunts, grandparents and others, but they do not need to live in the same housing unit. This definition would not include the couple represented by either Figure 1.9.b (POSSLQs) or Figure 1.9.c (homosexual couple) because they are not related by blood, marriage, or adoption.

Sometimes persons with no "real" kinship ties end up with kin-like roles. The children might call an elderly neighbor who takes care of young children "Grandma Martha," even though she has no blood relationship to them. These are referred to as fictional or **fictive kin**. In some cases the fact that the kinship is fictional is all but forgotten; in other cases, such as that of godparents, the relationship has its own set of rules and is kept separate from the "real" kin relationships (Vandekerckhove, 1981; Kutsche, 1983). Fictive kin might be counted as family members by a functional definition but not by a structural one.

Because they require kinship relationships, structural definitions are more limiting than functional ones. It is quite possible that the male in Figure 1.6 (a mother's POSSLQ) is the "functional equivalent" of a husband and father, making that unit a family by a functional definition but not by a structural one. The mother/child unit would be a family by either definition. A divorced woman, her two children, and her cohabiting boyfriend might functionally be a family. To the Census Bureau, however, such a household would be categorized as a family with an unrelated individual. The same would be true if it involved the mother and her live-in girlfriend.

Defining Marriage

Some structural approaches identify **marriage** as an essential element of the family; others do not. We have

been reserving the symbol (=) only for those relationships that fit the legal definition of marriage and have used (≈) for relationships that are marriage-like but are not legal marriages. This would follow the legalistic definition of marriage, which requires formal recognition of the relationship.

Other definitions are more commonly used in anthropology and sociology. Societies without a written language have no formal records, but they do have forms of relationships that could be considered marriage. In yet other societies, religious rather than political authorities formally record marriages.

The beginning of a marriage is nearly always accompanied by a **rite of passage** called a wedding. When an individual's **status** changes from "single person" to "married person," role expectations change. Once John and Jennifer are married, they see themselves, and are seen by others, to have new rights, privileges, immunities, responsibilities, and duties.

As is true with the term "family," definitions of marriage are affected by formal and informal norms. Virtually all societies have norms about who can marry whom. An incest **taboo** is universal, although societies differ about which relatives are included. Some societies allow exceptions in certain cases; brother-sister marriages among the rulers in ancient Egypt and Hawaii are examples (Vivelo, 1978).

Other normative expectations are less seriously sanctioned, so they are more openly violated. These include **pronuptialism**, the informal norm that people should get married. Although this norm is not as strong as it was in the past, the vast majority of young adults still follow expectations.

Based on values of chastity, a traditional norm was that young persons should not have sexual intercourse until they were married. Unmarried couples who lived together were considered to be "living in sin," and by this formal norm they could not form the legal basis for a marriage. Laws forbidding premarital sex and adultery began to change in the 1960s but remain on the books in some states. As a practical matter, these laws were not

---

Kin group: Network of persons related by blood, marriage, or adoption.   **Fictive kin:** Persons treated as if they are related.
Marriage: (a) (legalistic definition): The legal union of a man and woman as husband and wife. (b) A socially sanctioned sexual and economic union between two (or more) members of opposite sexes (occasionally between members of the same sex) (from Howard, Michael C., 1989:454) (c) A socially approved sexual union of some permanence between two or more individuals (Robertson, Ian, 1981:630)   **Rite of passage:** A public ceremony in recognition of a change in status.   **Status:** A position in the social system.
Incest taboo: A rule forbidding marriage or sexual activity among closely related persons.   **Pronuptialism:** A belief system that encourages marriage.

often enforced, but they were a symbolic barrier to nonmarital sexual activity. The sexual component of marriage is also recognized in the provision that a marriage is not technically legal until it is consummated by the first complete act of sexual intercourse.

While societies vary in their norms about nonmarital sex, sexual access is universally a privilege of marriage. The sexual distinction between married and unmarried persons in the last few decades has blurred, but other role expectations remain. Economic cooperation and the merging of assets acquired during the marriage still form part of the legal expectations of marriage.

One difference between the legally wed couple and the functionally wed one is that the legally wed are entitled to certain privileges when the relationship ends either by death or by divorce. The exact laws vary from one jurisdiction to another, but all recognize the married couple as a distinct legal unit. One consequence of this is that the state must be asked for permission, in the form of a divorce petition, to end the legal relationship. Couples who are only functionally wed do not have to do this. Legal spouses also have certain assumed rights to inheritance that cohabitants do not.

Married persons are entitled to certain other legal privileges, such as coverage under family medical plans and other job benefits. Here too, however, the line between those who are legally married and those who are not has blurred. In some cases, legal protection has been granted to those who are functionally but not legally married. Homosexual couples might go through a wedding in their church and are sometimes granted some privileges of legally married couples. In 1989, San Francisco enacted a "domestic partners" law; many other jurisdictions have followed suit. Such laws extended marriage-like rights, dealing with such things as health benefits and bereavement leave, to both homosexual and heterosexual cohabitants.

In 2000, Vermont legalized "civil unions" for same-sex couples. Although a civil union is not exactly the same as marriage, registered couples are entitled to the same rights as married couples in such matters as health benefits and inheritance rights. These unions, unlike marriages, are valid only in Vermont, and other states to which the couple might move are not required to extend the same benefits. In spite of this, as many as two-thirds of couples who took advantage of the new law in the first few weeks were from out of state. Some participants anticipate court battles to extend the benefit of their civil union to their home states (Goldgerg, 2000).

Thirteen states (Alabama, Colorado, Georgia, Idaho, Iowa, Kansas, Montana, Ohio, Oklahoma, Pennsylvania, Rhode Island, South Carolina, and Texas) and the District of Columbia recognize what is called a **common-law marriage** (Skoloff, Skoloff, & Wolfe, 1997). Such a relationship has all the rights and responsibilities of a legal marriage, but it lacks the legal registration of a wedding ceremony. In some states the requirement includes a certain length of time that the couple must be together; in others it is a matter of "intent" to live as husband and wife. The intent might be demonstrated in several ways, including the filing of a joint income tax return. The state is still involved, however, because a judge's approval is required before legal status is fully granted, and a legal divorce is required if the common-law marriage breaks up.

Alternative Families Elsewhere

Determining whether a particular relationship is a legal marriage or not is relatively simple in the United States. That decision is more complicated in other societies. In fact, some cultures have arrangements that are difficult for Americans to classify at all. The Nayar and the Israeli Kibbutz provide two examples.

The Nayar. In the 18th century, the Malabar region of southern India was home to the Nayar. In this society women, who owned the property, worked the land. The men made their livings as soldiers (Gough, 1960; Reiss, 1980). At a young age, usually before puberty, a girl was "married." After the ceremony, the man had no further rights or responsibilities to his "wife." Her only responsibility to him was to observe a ceremony at his death.

The woman could then have a series of "husbands" who would spend nights with her, indicating their presence by leaving a spear outside her door so that other men would know she was occupied for the night. To maintain their rights as husbands, the men needed only to provide their wives with gifts at certain ritual times of the year. Men lived not with their wives but with their mother and sisters.

When pregnancy resulted, any of her husbands could claim paternity by paying the midwife for the delivery expenses. After that, the "father" had no further

---

Common-law marriage: A union legally recognized as a marriage in spite of not having been solemnized by the state.

responsibility to the mother or child. The adult male authority figure in the child's life was the mother's brother, rather than the legitimating father.

The Nayar family system operated in a particular social, economic, and religious context. While the women produced most of the food, the men were mercenary soldiers who fought for noblemen who could afford to raise an army. The dangerous nature of their occupation made fulfillment of family responsibilities and obligations uncertain. Alternative family structures developed to fit the economic and social realities of the group. When the Nayar system is seen in its social context, the behaviors, norms, and scripts become more understandable. Understanding families in such context is an important principle of family sociology and of this book.

The Nayar system is usually mentioned when the question arises about whether the nuclear family has universally been found in all societies. There has even been some question about whether it represents a family at all. Since kinship terms were used, and the role of mother is fairly clearly defined, some elements of a family were present. Other role relationships were less clear. The Nayar system shows that the role "father" can mean at least four things: husband of mother; biological progenitor; legitimator who makes the child legal; and adult male with the responsibility to socialize the child.

Although this system seems loosely defined, it was accompanied by severe sanctions for violation of certain expectations. For example, if no man claimed paternity, it might be thought that the woman had been consorting with a person of the inappropriate Hindu caste, or, worse yet, a Muslim or Christian. In such a case the woman could be put to death.

Given their life circumstances, the Nayar developed a system that worked for them at the time. Although the Nayar still exist, their marriage and family customs were significantly altered during the British occupation of India.

The Israeli Kibbutz. History has recorded numerous attempts to form Utopias, or perfect cooperative arrangements, that could perform the functions of the family while avoiding its drawbacks. The kibbutz movement in Israel is a 20th-century example (Spiro, 1956, 1958). These rural communes were founded on the values of equality and shared commitment to the community.

Property was owned in common; work was rotated so that no one was permanently assigned the worst jobs. Children were raised in nurseries with other children of the same age. In the earliest kibbutzim (plural of kibbutz), parents were not allowed to treat their biologi-

Although kibbutzim have changed, they remain important in contemporary Israel.

cal children any differently from the way they treated other children. Expectations associated elsewhere with kin and family groups were the responsibility of the community as a whole.

No one had the advantage, at birth, of inheriting wealth, power, or privilege. Without inherited status, it was easier to ensure that individuals would be treated equally. Few tasks were assigned solely on the basis of sex, so men and women could be treated more equally. Founded partly on ideological and religious grounds, the original kibbutzim also were efficient in developing agricultural production. They were effective quasi-military outposts too, establishing territory for the emerging nation of modern Israel.

The kibbutz system has changed over the years. Individuals have been allowed to own more personal property. Married couples now have more privacy, and there is greater attachment between parents and their biological children. Central control of adolescents is being replaced by parental control (Yuval, 1998). These changes have led some observers to conclude that there are no effective substitutes for the basic functions provided by the family institution (Rabin, 1982; Ishwaran, 1992).

Because they are so different from the typical North American systems, the cases of the kibbutzim and the Nayar further complicate our attempt to arrive at a definition of the family. Perhaps no universal definition exists.

Ideal Types, Dichotomies, and Continua

While some groups of persons clearly fit everyone's definition of family, the inclusion of other groups is less clear. To clarify such situations, German sociologist Max Weber (1949) developed the concept of the **ideal type**. This is a set of hypothetical characteristics that apply to some social phenomenon.

An ideal-typical family might have a list of 10 characteristics. A few actual families might have all 10 characteristics; some groups have 9, others have 8, and so on. A group that had only 1of the characteristics would probably not be considered a family.

An ideal type is not meant to be "ideal" in the sense of being something that is necessarily more desirable than other things. One can imagine, for example, a list of characteristics of an ideal-type mass murderer. The concept means *ideal* type, as in an *idea* about something; that is what makes it hypothetical rather than real. The idea about the thing can be compared to the real thing.

What characteristics the ideal-type "family" has would depend on the purpose for which the defining was being done. If we wanted to count the number of families in America, we would use a clear-cut definition like the one used by the Census Bureau. When Straus and Gelles

(1990) surveyed the country to learn more about family violence, they needed a definition of family. They decided to count the amount of violence by including both married and cohabiting couples. This resulted in a slightly higher count of couple violence than if they had asked only married couples, because the rate of violence among cohabitants is higher than among married couples. When Coleman and Ganong (1997) studied stepfamilies, they obviously needed a definition of family in which stepchildren and stepparents would be included.

Some purposes of family study call for ideal types that appear to be opposites. An ideal-typical family, for example, could have opposite characteristics of the ideal-typical nonfamily. If all human groups were divided into one of the two types, they would form a **dichotomy**; all groups would fall into either the family or nonfamily category. Unfortunate as it may be for our attempts to understand, the world is seldom so easily categorized. Some groups might have nearly all the characteristics of the ideal-typical family or of the ideal-typical nonfamily, but most cases will be some mix of the two types. Construction of a **continuum** would help to more accurately categorize real-world cases.

Such a continuum, as illustrated in Figure 1.10, could help categorize human groups. A woman living with her

---

| **Figure 1.10** | **Continuum of Human Groups** |

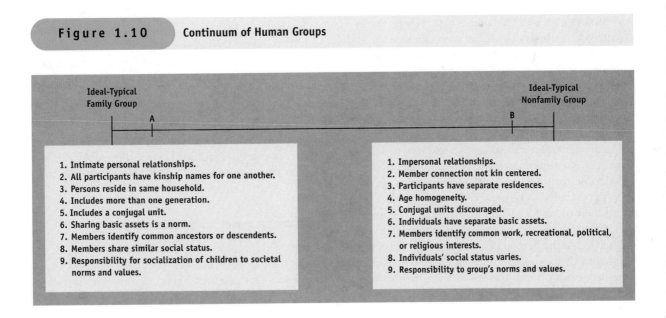

Ideal type: A hypothetical construct used for comparisons.   **Dichotomy:** 1. Divided into two parts. 2. The division of a continuum into two mutually exclusive parts.   **Continuum:** Unbroken degrees of measurement between two extremes.

children and her POSSLQ would have most characteristics of a family group (numbers 1, 3, 4, 5?, 6, 8, 9). That group would be at about point A on the continuum. A juvenile gang would probably have only three characteristics of the ideal-typical family (numbers 1, 3, 8), so it would be at about point B on the continuum.

While continua are usually more accurate ways of depicting real-world phenomena, it is simpler to dichotomize them. It is easier, for example, to put people in the category of either "good" or "bad" than to realize that everyone is a mix of good and bad characteristics. Dichotomizing things that are actually continua is a common way to simplify the world, both in everyday life and in social science. We think in terms of rich or poor, masculine or feminine, tall or short, smart or dumb, and powerful or powerless. The careful student will realize that, even if concepts are dichotomized for purposes of simplifying and discussing them, the real world is more likely to exist in continua. In later chapters, we will look at families as they existed at different times and in different cultures. The diversity of family forms will be compared using several continua as tools for analysis.

Gender

A central characteristic of families is that they are constructed on the basis of gender. Power relationships, calculation of descent and inheritance, residential patterns, and the assignment of tasks are all related to gender. Furthermore, it is in the family that children begin to learn their gender identification and expectations. This distinction is often referred to as **sex** differences, but that term can be misleading because sex is a biological distinction that is usually dichotomized into male and female. We are more interested here in the social distinction, so the term **gender** will be more appropriate.

A new family can be organized in several ways. Either John or Jennifer might have more power than the other; Kyle and Kayla might consider themselves primarily related to their father's or mother's ancestors; and our happy couple has to live with either his parents, her parents, or in a place of their own. Such are the questions of authority, descent and inheritance, and residence. The descriptive terms will borrow word roots from Latin: *patri*, from "pater," which means "father," and *matri*, from "mater," which means "mother."

Authority

One cultural option for family organization is whether the men or women will have the **authority**. To define these options, we can combine our "ma and pa" words with the root *archy*, which means "power," as in mon*archy*, hier*archy*, and an*archy*. The result is **patriarchy** and **matriarchy**. These two terms generally refer to authority held by men or by women, respectively, but they have taken on several meanings. Sometimes the words refer only to authority within the family; at other times they refer to the authority structure in society. In some feminist writing, the term "the Patriarchy" defines a system of male dominance found both in the family and in the larger society (Kramarae, 1992).

Authority has a slightly different meaning than does **power**. Authority is the socially approved arrangement, but power is the actual ability to influence or control others. It is possible to have a patriarchal society in which women exercise considerable influence and control in many families.

No well-documented cases of matriarchal societies exist, but simply to suggest that all societies are patriarchal provides us no way to distinguish among societies' authority and power arrangements. A continuum allows us to compare societies, as well as to talk about changes within a society over time (see Figure 1.11). For example, we can demonstrate that the United States is less patriarchal, or more egalitarian, than it was 50 years ago because more of the persons in positions of power are women. A rapid increase in the number of single-mother families has increased the portion of American families that is matriarchal, even if the preferred form is still more patriarchal.

Descent and Inheritance

Descent and inheritance are closely related to the issue of power in the family. The transmission of property from one generation to the next has been, whenever there is

---

Sex: The biological fact of being female or male.   **Gender:** The social fact of being feminine or masculine.   **Authority:** The socially granted right to control and influence others.   **Patriarchy:** A system in which men have the authority.   **Matriarchy:** A system in which women have the authority.   **Power:** The actual ability to exercise one's will over others.

Figure 1.11   **Gender Authority Continuum**

|—————————————|—————————————|—————————————|

Patriarchal Family
All men have power over all women
Men own all property
Women treated as property
Women have no decision-making
authority in family or society.

Egalitarian Family
Power equally shared
Proper ownership evenly shared
Property treated as property
Equal decision making

Matriarchal Family
All women have power over all men
Women own all property
Men treated as property
Men have no decision-making
authority in family or society.

---

private ownership of property, a major function of the family institution. Whether family property is passed on to men, to women, or to both makes a big difference in opportunities for men and women to acquire wealth. Likewise, when authority is passed from one generation to the next, as in monarchies, it is important to know whether the family connection is traced through male, female, or both lines of ancestry. Since we are dealing with lines of descent, the root *lineal* can be combined with the "pa and ma" terms to produce **patrilineal** and **matrilineal**. These mean, respectively, that descent and inheritance are traced through male or female lines.

The Bellelli Family by Edgar Degas captures an image of patriarchal Victorian-era families.

Patrilineal systems can be identified by the custom that the woman takes her husband's name when they marry. When Jennifer Jones marries John Johnson, she becomes Jennifer Johnson. Symbolically, she becomes part of his family, rather than he part of hers. The children are Kyle and Kayla Johnson. This informal norm is most common in the United States.

In the traditional Spanish system, descent and inheritance are traced through both sides of the family (Stodder, 1998). The term **bilateral** (two sides) is used to describe such systems. While traditionally patrilineal, American marriages are increasingly bilateral. Although brides in the United States are still more likely to change their names than are grooms, couples usually consider themselves connected to both families.

In practice, some preference for male inheritance might remain, especially with respect to agricultural property. State laws, however, require that if a parent dies without a will, the inheritance will be divided among the children without regard to sex. Inheritance of property, then, is now formally bilateral, in spite of the practice of female name changing.

Residence Patterns

In addition to questions of power and descent, societies influence where newly married couples are likely to live. There are three basic options: newlyweds can live with or near his family; they can live with or near her family; or they can find a new place of their own. As the issue here is location or locale, it makes sense to use

---

Patrilineal: Tracing descent and inheritance through male lines.   **Matrilineal:** Tracing descent and inheritance through female lines.   **Bilateral:** Tracing descent and inheritance through both male and female lines.

Figure 1.12	Summary of Gender-Related Family Organization Terms

	Authority (archy)	Descent (-lineage)	Residence (local)
Male (patri)	Patriarchal	Patrilineal	Patrilocal
Female (matri)	Matriarchal	Matrilineal	Matrilocal
Both/neither	Egalitarian	Bilateral	Neolocal

---

the root *local* to describe the alternatives. In a **patrilocal** system John and Jennifer would live with his family of orientation, while in a **matrilocal** one they would reside with hers. The third option is that they would be expected to find a new residence, so *neo* (new, as in *neo*nate, *neo*phyte, and *Neo*lithic) helps form the term **neolocal**.

The United States is clearly neolocal. Although John and Jennifer are expected to keep in contact with their families of orientation, they are also expected to become an independent unit. They might live with one set of parents for a time, but this is nearly always considered to be a temporary situation that will be remedied as soon as they can afford a place of their own.

Figure 1.12 summarizes the terms that deal with authority, descent, and residence. While the three variables are related, they are not interchangeable. The Nayar were matrilineal and matrilocal, but not matriarchal (Gough, 1960). Property was passed down through the women's lineage. Authority, however, was vested in the oldest male sibling. A woman's maternal uncle, rather than her father, was her male authority figure. Although it is also logically possible to have a system in which the women have the authority but the property is passed down through male lines, no such society has been found.

Gender Role Continuum

In addition to authority, descent and inheritance, and residential expectations, all societies assign at least some tasks on the bases of gender. Considerable variation, however, exists in how the roles are determined. Figure 1.13 is a continuum illustrating the gender-role decision-making process.

At point A of this continuum, tradition would assign virtually all tasks by gender. Norms would specify that women do some tasks while men do others. Neither John nor Jennifer would have much choice in the

---

Figure 1.13	Gender Role Continuum

A		C
Total Differentiation; Authoritarian; Determined by Tradition		Androgyny; Roles Blurred; Determined by Choice and Negotiation

Source: Adapted from: Adams, Bert N. 1955. *The Family: A Sociological Interpretation*. Fort Worth: Harcourt Brace. Page 108.

Patrilocal residence: A custom that newlyweds are expected to live with the groom's relatives. **Matrilocal residence:** A custom that newlyweds are expected to live with the bride's relatives. **Neolocal residence:** A custom that newlyweds are expected to live separately from either's family.

Families in the NEWS

A World's First Marriage

On April 1 (no fooling), 2001, Anne-Marie Thus and Helene Faasen became the first same-sex couple in modern history to solemnize a marriage that has the exact same legal standing as heterosexual ones. A new Dutch law took effect at midnight March 31, and they were ready to take advantage of it.

Several other countries register same-sex unions, but the Dutch legislation went further by eliminating all references to gender in the marriage and adoption laws. The change grants gay and lesbian couples equal marriage and adoption rights.

Faasen and Thus have been living together for two years. Last year, with the help of an anonymous semen donor, Thus gave birth to a boy. When she legally adopts the child, Faasen will be registered as Parent Number 2.

Three gay couples joined Thus and Faasen in the exchange of vows at Amsterdam's city hall. A gay newspaper, which helped lead the fight for legal changes, also helped to arrange the mass wedding.

To the disappointment of gay and lesbian couples in other countries, Amsterdam is not going to become the world Las Vegas for same-sex marriages. Only Dutch nationals are eligible.

Source: Associated Press. **www.nytimes.com,** April 1, 2001

---

matter. Individuals who violated the gender expectations would face severe punishments from the family as well as from religious or political authorities. In very traditional societies, violation of the gender roles would be rare because the expectations would be so strongly socialized into the individuals.

At point C of the continuum is a condition of **androgyny**, from the root words *andro* (male) and *gyny* (female). In an androgynous society, no tasks would be assigned by gender. Occupation, recreational preferences, clothing and hairstyles, and all other cultural traits might vary from one individual to another, but not because of gender. John and Jennifer would negotiate the household division of labor themselves. The roles they negotiate for their own relationship might differ from the roles developed by other couples.

Types of Gender Roles

John Money (1980) developed a typology of gender roles. He noted that some gender differences are virtually inevitable, some are likely, and some are totally arbitrary. Money denied that sex, with its biological base in "nature," and gender, with its environmental base in "nurture," are completely separate variables.

It is often assumed that biological traits are innate and unchangeable, while environmentally determined traits are learned and can therefore be fairly easily unlearned, relearned, or changed. Money, however, argued that once an individual learns something, that concept is stored in the brain and becomes part of the individual's biological being. It can be just as powerful an influence as the things thought to be instinctual. On the other hand, biological factors can be altered by environment via drugs, diet, surgery, hormone injections, and other interventions. Such changes can occur even before an infant is born, depending on the influences to which the mother is exposed. Biology and the environment, therefore, are not mutually exclusive, but overlapping and intertwined.

Money combined the notion of biological sex and cultural gender in the discussion of roles. A simplification of his typology yields a continuum with three possible types of sex/gender roles: sex-irreducible roles, sex-influenced roles, and sex-arbitrary roles.

Sex-irreducible Gender Roles. As the term *sex-irreducible gender roles* implies, these are the most basic sex differences between men and women. Men impregnate; women menstruate, gestate, and lactate. The notion of male and female, or masculine and feminine, cannot be reduced more than that. Not

---

Androgyny: A social condition in which there is no gender role differentiation. **Sex-irreducible gender roles:** Basic differences in expectations that define the differences between men and women.

all men, of course, must impregnate to be men; nor must all women gestate in order to be women. If anyone in society is to impregnate, however, it will be a man; if anyone is to gestate and lactate, it will be a woman.

Short of significant technological innovations, the sex-irreducible differences are a given of the human condition. They are not the result of social learning, of oppression by the social structure, or of negotiation between men and women. Societies influence the frequency with which men impregnate or women lactate, and the conditions under which that occurs, but not the option as to who does which. This fact makes complete androgyny impossible.

Sex-influenced Gender Roles. Sex-influenced gender roles are less strictly determined than sex-derivative and sex-irreducible roles, but secondary sex characteristics and other biological differences between males and females can still affect the division of labor. Among other things, Jennifer will always be present for the birth of her children. John might not be, depend-

ing on the birthing practices of his society. This might affect their perceptions of children and their role as parents.

In societies that rely both on large-game hunting and gathering of plant foods for subsistence, it is important that both tasks be done efficiently. It makes sense to have the men do more hunting while the women gather food and supervise children. Biology does not prevent women from hunting, but men are generally bigger, faster, and stronger than women, so they tend to be better big-game hunters. Only women can breast-feed, so it is essential that they be near their infant offspring. They can thus care for the children and simultaneously gather the berries, roots, and other foods that typically supply the majority of nutrition for hunter-gather groups.

In societies with more modern economic systems, such as 21st-century North America, the division of labor is not as directly associated with sex-influenced gender roles. Most jobs today require brainwork, communication, and services that women and men can perform equally well. By the same token, men can bottle-feed children as well as can women. Depending

Sex-arbitrary gender roles are typified in school band instrument choices.

Sex-influenced gender roles: Expectations influenced, but not fully determined, by secondary sex characteristics and other biological differences of men and women.

on the economic system and other factors, then, cultures might have considerable options in dealing with sex-adjunctive roles—or they might have no gender-based assumptions at all for most tasks.

Sex-arbitrary Gender Roles. Men and women could switch sex-arbitrary gender roles with little social impact. They include such things as hair and clothing styles. Women in American society have the acceptable option to wear skirts and use makeup, while men generally do not. There is no inherent reason, however, that it could not be the other way around. In American high school bands, nearly all the flute players are female, while the trumpet players are more likely to be male. The reverse could just as easily be true.

Money's distinctions provide a flexible way of talking about gender roles, but it is not always clear into which type specific differences fit. Researchers have generally found that women score higher than do men on tests of verbal ability, while men do better on tests of math and visual-spatial ability. The differences are small but consistent across cultures. Some researchers argue than the differences are sex-influenced, while others argue that the differences are sex-arbitrary (see Basow, 1992).

Money's typology has several implications for the study of gender roles, a topic that will arise several more times in this text. For now, it is important to recognize that gender roles form an important part of the lives of all the Johns and Jennifers, as well as the marriage and family institution in all societies. It is important, too, to remember that gender distinctions go beyond behavioral expectations; gender is also a social construction that affects the distribution of privilege and resources in society (Fox & Murray, 2000). Families contribute to the perpetuation of gender from one generation to the next.

The "Family Decline" Debate

Family scholars reach very different conclusions about the future of the family, depending on how they interpret the past and present. Pessimists argue that the family is in decline, with far-reaching negative consequences, and that the decline is likely to continue unless corrective action is taken. Some optimists, framing the issue as one of "family change" rather than "family decline," contend that the change has, on balance, been a good thing. Others claim that little basic change has actually occurred.

The Pessimistic Position

Pessimistic observers report that the American family, as a social institution, is in serious decline or breakdown. Such concern is not new in social thought. Fear of family decline was expressed by August Comte, the "father of sociology," in the early 1800s. Comte argued that the French revolution would create anarchy, and he called for a strengthening of the monogamous, patriarchal family (Clayton, 1979.)

Other sociologists argued that the family became less socially influential as many of its functions were either lost or taken over by other institutions (Ogburn, 1933; Davis, 1971). In 1928, the behavioral psychologist John Watson predicted that the family institution would disappear by 1977. The philosopher Bertrand Russell (1929) and social theorist Pitirim Sorokin (1937) also saw the end of marriage and the family; Sorokin complained that marriage was becoming simply an overnight parking lot for sexual encounters.

The end of the Great Depression and World War II ushered in what is sometimes called the golden age of the American nuclear family, but even then there were pessimistic observers. Barrington Moore, Jr. (1958) believed that social and technological forces were consuming too much time and energy of individuals and that the family would be torn apart. Two decades later, Urie Bronfenbrenner (1977) noted that the growing number of single and working mothers was leaving too many children without a close personal bond. Without this essential child-adult bond, he asserted, the children's development was stunted. This contributed, according to Bronfenbrenner, to a number of social ills including drug problems, childhood depression, crime, and problems in school. This problem would only grow worse, because children who received no attachment and bonding when they were young would be ill-equipped to provide the emotional care needed when their own children were born.

Also in the 1970s, sociologist Amitai Etzioni (1977) and historian Christopher Lasch (1977) expressed

Sex-arbitrary gender roles: Expectations that could as easily be the opposite.

concern about family breakdown. Lasch did not think the family could necessarily reach the romantic Victorian ideal of a "haven in a heartless world," but he did believe that the family had been in decline for a century. His evidence was increased divorce rates, decreasing birth and marriage rates, the changing status of women, and a decline in morality.

David Popenoe (1988, 1994, 1996) has more recently championed the family-decline perspective. As is typical of pessimistic scholars, Popenoe uses a macrofunctional definition of family. He concludes that the extended family has been in decline for centuries, but he is concerned that there is now "end of the line" decline in that the nuclear family itself is seriously eroded.

Popenoe and others typically focus on the family decline, which leaves too many children without two parents. In their view, a strong system of enduring marriage is central to a strong family institution (Popenoe, Elshtain, & Blankenhorn, 1996; Glenn, 1996). Popenoe argues that the United States and Sweden lead the world in family decline, but that other postindustrial nations are close behind. Today's "postnuclear family" is characterized by "overindividualism." Adults begin and end relationships for their own reasons, leaving children without proper socialization. There has been a "defathering" of the family institution. A **matrifocal** family structure is increasingly seen as the basic family form (Blankenhorn, 1995).

Family decline, Popenoe (1993) argues, can be found in changing values in contemporary American culture. Adults once were quite willing to sacrifice their personal interests for the sake of their children and for the family unit as a whole. This traditional value of **familism** has weakened, along with related values of pronuptialism and pronatalism. Evidence of the decline is found in declining overall birthrates, high divorce rates, high rates of unwed births, high rates of cohabitation, and declining rates of marriage. The pessimists are especially concerned about the effect of family decline on children.

In the 1990s, a number of politicians discovered that it is good strategy to incorporate rhetoric about family values into their speeches Their concerns are shared by many religious figures. The message of the Million Man March was partly one of a return to male responsibility in a traditional family context. A similar message is promoted by Promise Keepers, Focus on the Family, and other groups. Such advocates urge a return to what they see as traditional family values.

The Optimistic Position

Optimists about the family contend that the family is not in trouble. They fall into two related positions: the "glad it changed" view and the "it did not really change" view. Many scholars with feminist perspectives agree that the family has changed, but they add that what declined was the traditional patriarchal and oppressive family. From this perspective, the breakdown of the family is good news, not bad.

This perspective also has a long history. Karl Marx and Friedrich Engels (1848; Engels, 1884) believed that monogamous marriage was always oppressive to women and that such marriage forms kept private property in the hands of the privileged class and out of the hands of the working class. Marx and Engels looked forward to the time when a communist revolution would destroy the "bourgeois" family form and replace it with communal forms of association and child rearing.

The perspective was repopularized by the feminist movement of the 1960s and 1970s, some advocates of which engaged in antinatalist and antifamily rhetoric (Stacey, 1996). At least one group called for the destruction of marriage and the family (*The Feminists*, 1974). According to this view, marriage was debilitating to women (Bernard, 1972) and an institution that enslaved wives (Aulette, 1994).

Supporters of the "glad it changed" perspective prefer microfunctional definitions of the family that focus on how the family serves the persons within it. Stacey (1993, 1996) contended that the family is not an institution at all, but an ideological, symbolic, political construct that has historically been used to deny the rights of women, homosexuals, and those who do not conform to narrowly defined family expectations. "Glad it changed" optimists, criticizing or dismissing studies that find significant negative impacts of divorce and single parenthood on children (Silverstein & Auerbach, 1999),

---

Matrifocal family: "A family in which the mother-child bond takes precedence over the husband-wife bond and in which the day-to-day problems of family living (especially child care and socialization) are managed by women" (LaRossa, 1984:142). **Familism:** "The belief in a strong sense of family identification and loyalty, mutual assistance among family members, a concern for the perpetuation of the family unit, and the subordination of the interests and personality of individual family members to the interests and welfare of the family group" (Popenoe, 1993:538).

focus instead on negative aspects of marriage such as unequal household division of labor, unequal workforce reward, family violence, and marital rape (Stacey, 1993, 1996). This view maintains that the family's demise increases freedom for individuals to construct their relationships without the constraints of social rules and expectations. Opportunity to develop their individuality and find greater fulfillment in the occupational sphere is increased. The patriarchal marriage form should, they argue, continue to decline and be replaced by egalitarian, androgynous relationships that offer a positive alternative to the traditional nuclear family.

Another group of optimists concluded that the family has not in fact changed very much and that the idea of family decline is a myth. Mary Jo Bane (1976) acknowledged the high divorce rate, but she pointed out that declining death rates meant that more children than ever live to adulthood with at least one parent. Increased interest in proper child rearing, and laws protecting children from abuse, are actually improving the typical parent-child bond. Further, the high remarriage rate indicates concern with specific marital partners, but not disillusionment with the institution of marriage itself.

Rossi (1978) and Kain (1990) contended that what might appear to be a decline in the family is more a matter of perception and bad comparisons. The contemporary family is sometimes compared to what Goode (1963) called the "traditional family of Western nostalgia," a romantic image of the three-generation, agrarian, peaceful family that might never actually have been the most common family form (Coontz, 1992, 1998). Other times, comparisons are made to a romanticized image of the family of the 1950s that was historically unusual in many respects. It is only by comparison to these images that today's family looks to be in decline.

The family-decline debate has important implications for public policy and for all families and the individuals who participate in them. The final chapter of this text will revisit the question.

Summary and Conclusion

We have attempted to figure out what a family is. There are several basic types that everyone would agree upon, including nuclear, conjugal, and extended families. Whether other intimate groups, such as cohabiting opposite- or same-sex couples, are families depends on whether macrofunctional, microfunctional, or structural definitions are used. The U.S. Bureau of Census uses a limited structural definition because that makes its task of counting families much easier.

Several criteria are used by individuals in deciding what a family is, including their perception of values and norms. Whether or not there are existing roles and scripts for the members of a group would also be a factor in deciding whether a particular group is a family.

If marriage is a necessary part of forming a family, then we have to figure out what a marriage is. Systems like the Nayar and kibbutz need to be dealt with in our definition. It turns out that the term "family" might be a good case for applying ideal types, and a definition will depend on the particular purpose that the definition will serve. Use of ideal types and continua makes categorizations more accurate.

Gender variables are important components of diverse family types. Authority patterns, descent and inheritance, and new-family residence norms affect families as well as the men and women in those families. At least some tasks are divided by gender in every society; some distinctions are influenced by biological sex differences and others by socially constructed gender differences.

The family-decline debate still rages among family scholars. Pessimists, who typically prefer macrofunctional definitions of family, are concerned that the family institution is decreasingly serving the needs of society. They also worry that a focus on adult individualism leaves the needs of children unmet. Optimists agree that families have changed, but they applaud the diversity of today's family forms that better serve the interests of individuals, especially women.

In conclusion, this chapter lays the foundation for later discussions of families. It is one thing to say that family can take a number of forms. By naming some of the variations, this chapter makes the diversity more real. This helps shape the discussion in later chapters of families in hunting-gathering, agrarian, industrial, and postindustrial families. Finally, the discussion of the family-decline debate was presented in such a way as to be as fair as possible to both optimists and pessimists. The student can keep this debate in mind while reading the rest of this text and let the evidence presented speak to the issue.

> **Rethinking in Context** Reconsider your initial definition of the family. Did it include all groups you had in mind? Did it exclude groups you do not think of as families? What values and norms are reflected in your definition? Was your definition more functional or more structural?
>
> Ask five acquaintances to tell you about their families. What roles do they identify as part of their families? What kind of families did they describe?
>
> Where do you stand on the family-decline debate? Why? What additional information would you need to be sure you are right?

Additional Resources

Trends in marriage and the family and the future

Booth, Alan, ed. 1991. *Contemporary Families: Looking Forward, Looking Back.* Minneapolis, MN: National Council on Family Relations.

Coontz, Stephanie. 1992. *The Way We Never Were: American Families and the Nostalgia Trap.* New York: Basic Books.

Coontz, Stephanie. 1998. *The Way We Really Are: Coming to Terms with America's Changing Families.* New York: Basic Books.

Kagan, Sharon L., & Bernice Weissbourd, eds. 1994. *Putting Families First: America's Support Movement and the Challenge of Change.* San Francisco: Jossey-Bass.

Popenoe, David, Jean Bethke Elshtain, & David Blankenhorn. 1996. *Promises to Keep: Decline and Renewal of Marriage in America.* Lanham, MD: Rowman and Littlefield.

Settles, Barbara H., Roma S. Hanks, & Marvin B. Sussman, eds. 1993. *American Families and the Future: Analyses of Possible Destinies.* New York: Haworth Press.

Teachman, Jay D., Lucky M. Tedrow, & Kyle D. Crowder. 2000. "The Changing Demography of America's Families." *Journal of Marriage and the Family* 62:1234–46.

Waite, Linda J., & Maggie Gallagher. 2000. *The Case for Marriage.* New York: Doubleday.

Family diversity

Acock, Alan, & David H. Demo. 1994. *Family Diversity and Well-Being.* Thousand Oaks, CA: Sage.

Aylette, Jenness. 1990. *Families: A Celebration of Diversity, Commitment, and Love.* Boston: Houghton Mifflin.

Demo, David H., Katherine R. Allen, & Mark A. Fine. 2000. *Handbook of Family Diversity.* New York: Oxford University Press.

Foster, Lawrence. 1991. *Women, Family and Utopia: Communal Experiments of the Shakers, The Oneida Community, and the Mormons.* Syracuse, NY: Syracuse University Press

Hutter, Mark. 1999. *The Family Experience: A Reader in Cultural Diversity*, 3rd ed. Boston: Allyn and Bacon.

Reigal, Betty Polisar, & Rita K. Spina. 1996. *Beyond the Traditional Family: Voices of Diversity.* New York: Springer Publishing.

The family-decline debate

See the August 1993 issue of *Journal of Marriage and the Family* for the following articles:

Popenoe, David. "American Family Decline, 1960–1990: A Review and Appraisal." Pp. 527–41.

Glenn, Norval D. "A Plea for Objective Assessment of the Notion of Family Decline." Pp. 542–44.

Stacey, Judith. "Good Riddance to 'The Family': A Response to David Popenoe." Pp. 545–47.

Cowan, Philip A. "The Sky IS Falling, But Popenoe's Analysis Won't Help Us Do Anything About It." Pp. 548–52.

Popenoe, David. "The National Family Wars." Pp. 553–56.

Also see:

Berger, Brigitte, & Peter L. Berger. 1984. *The War over the Family: Capturing the Middle Ground.* New York: Doubleday.

Blankenhorn, David. 1995. *Fatherless America: Confronting Our Most Urgent Social Problems.* New York: Basic Books.

Popenoe, David. 1996. *Life Without Father: Compelling New Evidence that Fatherhood and Marriage are Indispensable for the Good of Children and Society.* New York: Free Press.

Popenoe, David, Jean Bethke Elshtain, & David Blankenhorn. 1996. *Promises to Keep: Decline and Renewal of Marriage in America.* Lanham, MD: Rowman and Littlefield.

Stacey, Judith. 1996. *In the Name of the Family: Rethinking Family Values in the Postmodern Age.* Boston: Beacon Press.

Skolnick, Arlene. 1991. *Embattled Paradise: The American Family in an Age of Uncertainty.* New York: Basic Books.

Internet Sites

The Family Science Home Page

http://www.uky.edu/HumanEnvironmentalSciences/ FamilyNetwork/fam.html

A conservative organization with a "family is declining" position, the Institute for American Values

http://www.cyfc.umn.edu/

Links to dozens of family-related sites

http://www.wwwebit.com/familyscholar/ familyscholar/html/professional_organizations.html

Links to feminist sites

http://csf.colorado.edu/gimenez/feminist.html

For links to these sites and additional resources, visit the *Families in Context* Web site at:

http://sociology.wadsworth.com

Chapter 2

Studying the Family

Prelude

We have been learning about family relationships since the day we were born. Our parents and other relatives taught us a lot, but that was only the beginning. Movies, music, novels, magazines, and everyday conversation continue to provide information.

"Oprah" and other television shows add yet more information. Jerry Springer's guests often teach by negative example. Dr. Laura, among others, is happy to give us advice over the radio. Bookstores are brimming with volumes of advice about relationships, marriage, and families. We are told how to raise happy and successful children, how to have happy marriages, and how to get along better with siblings and parents.

This book deals with many of the same topics all these other sources have covered, but the approach is very different. The questions are different, and the answers sometimes uncertain. Ways of organizing and gathering information are different. Rather than simply state the opinion of someone, information is gathered in a rigorous way, and theories guide the process.

Wouldn't you trust this more than the information from television talk shows?

The information in chapter 1 hinted that all of us are strongly influenced, perhaps even controlled, by social forces such as roles, values, norms, and institutions. And so we are, yet we each like to believe that we are individuals, in charge of our own destiny. It is disconcerting to discover that we are not as individualistic as we might have thought. At the same time, it is interesting to discover the larger forces that influence us.

C. Wright Mills (1959) suggested that the best approach to self-understanding was to locate ourselves within our society and our historical period. He referred to this way of understanding ourselves through our social positions and through influential social forces as the **sociological imagination**. A study of sociology can help us develop a sense of identity and self-awareness. As we each locate ourselves in families, social systems, and historical processes, we become better able to understand and control those forces that act upon us.

This book is about our place in families and the place of families is larger contexts, but it is more than that. It is not just a study of families, but a study of the study of families. In this chapter we will begin to explore the methods and theories used by sociologists and others who study families. This is a difficult but essential step in developing our sociological imaginations.

> *Thinking Ahead* Based on what you have learned from this book or elsewhere, make up a definition of "sociology." What do sociologists study? What methods do they use to gather their information? How do you expect a college-level social science course about the family to be different from more popular sources of information such as television talk shows?

What Is Sociology?

The word **sociology** is derived from terms that would be translated literally as "a study of companionship or fellowship." This gives us a general idea of the meaning of the word; specific definitions are found in the box "Definitions of Sociology" (See Highlight 2.1). These and other definitions of sociology have three common threads: sociology is a [scientific] study that uses specific research methods; it deals with humans; and it deals with groups.

As they conduct their analyses, many sociologists treat the field as a science, while others perceive it as a humanistic study. We will consider each of those perspectives in turn.

HIGHLIGHT 2.1	**Definitions of Sociology** The
As**soci**ate	term *sociology* has two stems — the
Social	Latin *socius* (companion) and the Greek
Socialize	*ology* (study of) — and literally means
Society	the study of the processes of compan-
Socio**logy**	ionship. In these terms, sociology may
Psycho**logy**	be defined as the study of the bases of
Geo**logy**	social membership. More technically, so-
Bio**logy**	ciology is the analysis of the structure of

social relationships as constituted by social interaction, but no definition is entirely satisfactory because of the diversity of perspectives that is characteristic of the modern discipline (Abercrombie, Nicholas et al., 1984:202).

Sociological imagination: A way of understanding ourselves through locating our positions in society, and the social forces that affect us (Popenoe, 1986:584).

The science of human societies, groups, organizations and institutions (Wolman, Benjamin B., 1973:352).

The study of the groups and societies humans build and how these affect our behavior (Bassis, Michael et al., 1991:582).

The study of human society and social behavior (Eshleman, 1994).

The scientific study of social structure (Shephard, 1993).

Sociology as Science

Science is characterized not so much by a list of findings as by the method used to make those discoveries. Whether in geology or sociology, the scientific approach is based on four related attributes: objectivity, replication, testability, and precision of measurement and definition.

Philosophically, **objectivity** means that truth is found in the object being studied. This is the opposite of **subjectivity**, which assumes that truth resides in the subject, or the person doing the study. To say "beauty is in the eye of the beholder" is to say that beauty is subjective, not objective. Natural sciences such as geology, physics, and biology are based on objectivity because they assume that the truth of what they study is in the things they study, not in the persons who study them. The scientific method is used to reveal the objective truth.

If truth is in the things being studied, rather than the person doing the study, then everyone who performs the same study should get the same result. This leads to the second characteristic of the scientific method, **replication,** which means to repeat or copy something. If you drop this book, it will fall toward the center of the earth until something stops it. The same thing will happen if your best friend drops the book, or if your worst enemy does. It does not matter who drops it or who observes it being dropped. The truth is in the attraction the book and the earth have for each other, or gravity, regardless of who might be watching. Nor does it

matter how the book might feel about being dropped. The process of falling is not affected by the feelings of the objects involved. The characteristic of replication guards against mistakes in scientific research. If you do not believe what one scientist reports to have found, you can replicate the study and see if you get the same results.

The third criterion of a scientific statement is that it must be **testable;** there must be some way for other scientists to decide for themselves if it is true. If I say, "Very few children living prior to 10,000 BC loved their parents," there is no way for you to test my statement. This does not necessarily mean the statement is false, but it is not scientific. On the other hand, I might say, "The United States today has a higher divorce rate than Mexico," or "Children raised in single-parent homes have higher rates of juvenile delinquency than those raised with both biological parents." These are testable statements.

A statement in testable form is called a **hypothesis.** You might, for example, have the hypothesis that "Women who begin their first marriage after age 20 have lower rates of divorce than those who marry when younger." You could then test your hypothesis by comparing the divorce rates for women in the two age groups. As it turns out, that hypothesis has been tested and has been found to be true, at least for North America (London & Wilson, 1988). The statement about comparative divorce rates is a scientific one; it is objective, can be replicated, and is testable.

Finally, the scientific approach is characterized by *precision of definition and measurement.* Chapter 1 indicated that "family" can be defined in a number of ways and that the way it is defined affects our study of it. Precise definition and measurement are important for other studies as well. Suppose your hypothesis is "Women are more emotional than men." You might reach different conclusions if you define and measure "emotional" in different ways. If you measure "emotional" by how often persons report being sad, you might well find the hypothesis to be true. The General Social Survey finds that women report being sad more often than do men (Davis & Smith, 1998). If you measure "emotional" by the likelihood of being excited, you will get the opposite

---

Objectivity: The assumption that truth resides in the object or phenomenon being studied; the object is something perceptible by one or more of the senses and the objective is based on observable phenomena.   **Subjectivity:** The assumption that truth resides in the subject, or person doing the observing.   **Replication:** A copy or reproduction; repetition of an experiment or procedure using the same process.   **Testable:** Able to be tested (some meanings are just obvious).   **Hypothesis:** A testable educated guess, usually about the relationship among two or more variables.

Use self example

result; by that measure men are more emotional because they report being excited more often than do women (Davis & Smith, 1998).

Neither being sad nor being excited is a complete indication of "emotional," but valid studies have been done measuring those characteristics. You could probably imagine several other ways "emotional" could be defined and measured, not all of which would reach the same conclusion. Students and readers of sociological research must note the way things are defined and measured, or they could be misled by research that is poorly done or inaccurately reported.

It is partly because of the scientific characteristics of objectivity, replication, testability, and precision that references are cited in textbooks and other scholarly works. It allows readers to check the original source of the study. You might, for example, doubt the research that found gender differences in emotion. You could look up the study yourself and see how it was done. You might try to replicate the study, you might form a new hypothesis to test, or you might decide to define and measure the terms differently.

Once the terms are precisely defined, measurement of **variables** can occur. Anything that can take on different attributes can be a variable. In the preceding example, "frequency of crying" and "frequency of public displays of anger" are variables. Marital status is a variable with the attributes "never married," "married," "divorced or separated," and "widowed." Gender is a variable with the attributes "masculine" and "feminine." Other variables commonly used by sociologists include income, race, educational level, marriage rates, divorce rates, family size, and crime rates.

The **positivist** approach to science summarized in this text contends that science should be value-neutral, if not **value-free** (Klein & White, 1996). This means not that all scientists must be completely without values, but that researchers should not let their values influence their results and conclusions. More important, however, is the assumption that the objective truth will ultimately be discovered regardless of the preconceptions of the researchers. The scientific process, not individual scientists, is the ultimate source of value-free methods (Popper, 1959).

For this reason, social scientists are wary of what is called **anecdotal** data. An anecdote is a short story about a particular incident, usually told for its entertainment value. Sometimes the anecdote is used as data, but the truth of the anecdote might be difficult to test. Further, it is usually told from one person's point of view. Even if we rely on anecdotes told by several friends, they still will not be representative of the experiences of other people in the city, state, or country.

Anecdotal data can be powerful. A personal story dramatically told by a woman who was abused by her husband can elicit sympathy, support, and movement to political action that statistical data alone cannot arouse. A positivist, however, can ask several questions about the story: How do we know the anecdote is true? How often does such abuse occur? Is her story typical of other cases of domestic violence? What are the actual consequences of a particular political action likely to be?

Anecdotes may have limited value for sociological discussion, but they are not useless. A person's own experiences might serve as a starting point for broader research. For example, a young man who was abused by his parents might want to find out how many others had the same experience and how they dealt with it. Other social scientists might then attempt to replicate the research. What began as one person's experience, about which there were subjective feelings, has now entered the domain of objective social research; the anecdote has served as a starting point.

Anecdotes have another use in social science. Although the stories cannot properly be used as proof of a larger point, they can be used to illustrate points. For example, a young woman might feel that her boyfriend took unfair advantage of her on a date. She might tell the story as a way of illustrating the kinds of things that can go wrong in early relationships. The anecdote itself, however, would not be sufficient evidence to conclude anything about relationships or boyfriends in general.

Anecdotes can be helpful to social scientists if treated carefully, which makes social science different from natural science. Geologists do not have the advantage of listening to the rock's own story, but neither can they be mislead by such stories. Social and natural scientists,

---

Variable: A concept that has more than one attribute.   **Positivism:** Doctrine emphasizing use of the senses, measurement, and science as a basis for knowledge.   **Value-free:** Unaffected by preconceived ideas about what is good, right, and proper.
Anecdote: A short account of an interesting or humorous event; the **anecdotal method** is the attempt to prove a point by telling a story.

consequently, have different ways of approaching their subject matter.

While science provides an approach sociology uses to find things out, the subject matter is human groups. This emphasis on human variables makes sociology different from what are sometimes called the "natural sciences" (as if sociology is *un*natural!) such as physics, chemistry and geology. Sociology is part of the "social sciences" as are history, anthropology, economics, and political science.

Sociology as Humanistic Studies

Not all scholars accept the social science model for sociological study. While the social sciences have a good deal in common with the natural sciences, there is an important difference: social scientists are part of what they study in a way that natural scientists are not. A sociologist is a member of a society; a political scientist is a member of a nation-state; an economist has to find a way to acquire his or her food and clothing. By contrast, a geologist is not a rock. This difference provides both an advantage and a disadvantage for the social scientist.

Because sociologists are part of what they are studying, they learn about their society from their personal experiences. Geologists have no personal, inside experience about the nature of "rockness." All knowledge they gain must be as outsiders to rocks, while sociologists do have inside knowledge about society. Scholars gain much of their insight by discovering family processes from personal experience (Sprey, 2000).

Some sociologists suggest that they should use the personal knowledge gained from living in a certain segment of society to help them understand society and to help other persons learn. While positivists argue that the scientific method should be the way to search for truth, other scholars, including "postpositivists," argue that different methods need to guide the search for understanding.

Postpositivists argue that, all too often, a statement that poses as objective truth is actually a subjective truth that has become socially acceptable (Haraway, 1990; Silverstein & Auerbach, 1999, 2000; Allen, 2000). They contend that it is virtually impossible for social scientists to be value-free because social scientists cannot divorce themselves from their human condition.

Instead of attempting to be value-free, **humanistic studies** scholars suggest that social scientists should attempt to be value-aware. They then can use their subjective experiences to help others understand. Women might see the world differently from men, Blacks differently from Whites or Hispanics, and divorced persons differently from married ones. If the potential **biases** are recognized, the perspective of each observer, in interaction with the subject, can produce valuable understanding (Gouldner, 1970; Reinharz, 1984; Halfpenny, 1994; Michrina & Richards, 1996).

A disadvantage of subjective approaches is that the knowledge gained by the social scientist's personal experience is individual and unique, while social scientists attempt to understand groups and societies. Each person's experience is different, even compared to others of the same gender, race, or marital status, so replication of findings is difficult. In addition, not everyone has the same idea about what would constitute an improvement in the human condition. Positivists argue that the facts should be uncovered before social scientists attempt to improve society. If the situation is not fully understood, changes might end up being for the worse rather than for the better.

Other Fields in Family Studies

Sociologists are not, of course, the only scholars who study families. Many psychologists specialize in the study of families. Unlike sociologists, who study larger forces that affect families, psychologists generally focus on individuals as they interact and develop from infants to adults in a family setting. Some psychologists focus on therapy and counseling designed to improve the lives of individuals in families.

Anthropologists have contributed a significant amount of knowledge about families, particularly those in non-Western, pre-industrial settings. Such studies provide interesting contrasts to the way contemporary American families are structured. Much of the material in chapters 1, 3, and 4 came from the work of anthropologists. Recent work by anthropologists has taken the methods used to understand tribal societies and used them to study today's families.

In many American institutions of higher education, especially those founded as land-grant universities, there

---

Humanistic studies: Finding ways of improving the human condition.   **Bias:** A perception or process that results in systematic misrepresentation of reality.

are schools of human development, or human ecology, or similar name. These are the descendents of the old schools of home economics; families provide the topic for much of the research of these scholars.

Political scientists, social workers, communications experts, human biologists, and others are interested in learning more about families. As scholars, much of their approach to finding out is similar to that used by sociologists. It is to those methods that we now turn.

Methods of Family Research

The basic goal of research is to gather information about a particular subject. Such information, or data, can be analyzed in one of two basic ways. Information summarized in the form of numbers (quantities) is called **quantitative** data. Complex statistical analysis is often done with such data. By contrast, information summarized in nonnumerical ways is **qualitative** data. These studies often take the form of written summaries by the researchers and selected quotes from the research subjects. Research methods vary in the extent to which they might produce quantitative or qualitative data. Producing data of either type requires the use of a research method of some kind. Babbie (2001) suggested five major options: controlled experiments, survey research, field research, unobtrusive research, and program evaluation. These, along with methods from psychology and other fields, are the ways family researchers find things out.

Controlled Experiments

The advantage of experiments, which are usually done in a laboratory or similar setting, is that the variables can be controlled. An experiment is often designed to test the influence of one variable on another. A medical researcher might want to find out whether a certain food causes cancer in laboratory rats. One group of rats would get that food, while another group would not. Other variables, such as the amount of light, the number of rats per cage, the amount of exercise and water the rats get, and the other food they eat would be the same for both groups of rats. A major difference in cancer rates between the two groups, then, could be attributed to the food being tested.

Controlled observations can reveal a great deal about couple interaction.

While the experimental method is important in some sciences, its use is limited in studies of human families. Social scientists can seldom control all the variables, even if they wanted to. Humans would resist living in a lab so researchers could observe them or test various child-rearing practices on them. It would be unethical to do some of the kinds of experiments on humans that are done on animals, vegetables, or minerals. Further, humans simply do not behave the same way in a lab as they do when living unobserved. It would be difficult to find out how men and women act on real first dates by observing them in a laboratory as they meet partners assigned to them at random.

Controlled observations in laboratory settings have provided a wealth of information about marital conflict (Gottman & Notarius, 2000). Gottman et al. (1998) introduced newlyweds to potentially disruptive topics of conversation. He measured the heart rates of the couples during the discussions to determine whether certain behaviors were self-soothing or soothing to the spouse. The couples were tracked for six years to determine whether the heart-rate data could predict how the marriages turned out. The researchers found, as predicted, that only soothing of the husband predicted positive marital outcomes. Such studies are not technically experiments because the researcher did not expose the subjects to

---

Quantitative analysis: Numerical representation and manipulation of observations (Babbie, 1995:G6). **Qualitative analysis:** Nonnumerical examination and interpretation of observations (Babbie, 1995:G6). **Controlled experiment:** A form of data gathering in which variables are controlled and manipulated by the researcher.

2.1 | Finding Out

The General Social Survey

The National Opinion Research Center (NORC) is affiliated with the University of Chicago. Using the best available scientific methods, the center conducts survey research of many kinds, the most important of which is the General Social Survey (GSS).

The GSS was first conducted in 1972 and was done almost every year until 1994, when it became a biennial project. About 1,500 households were selected for each of the first several studies; now the sample size is nearly 3,000 each time. The database consists of responses from more than 37,000 households (NORC: http://www.norc.uchicago.edu).

Researchers carefully select households so that the sample is representative of the entire population of the United States. The sampling process has several stages. First, the country is divided into counties, some of which are randomly selected. Those counties are then divided into segments composed of census blocks. Some of these are randomly selected for the next stage. Finally, households are randomly chosen from the census blocks (Stark & Roberts, 1998).

Once the household has been selected, trained researchers go to the homes for a personal interview based on predetermined questions. The respondents are asked demographic questions such as their age, income, marital status, number of children, and race/ethnicity. They are also asked their opinions on child raising, national spending policies, marijuana use, race relations, abortion, quality of life, and a host of other issues. The 1998 survey used 858 variables that can be compared with each other in a number of ways. Because many of the same questions have been asked every year, trend studies can be produced. Among the findings is a dramatic increase in support for racial equality and civil liberties over the years (NORC).

The GSS is the largest sociological project funded by the National Science Foundation. Results are made available to researchers in a number of formats; this allows both for creative use of the data and replication of other studies. Queens College has made each year's data available on the internet for free downloading onto personal computers (Queens College: http://www.soc.qc.edu/QC_Software/GSS.html). Other companies such as MicroCase (http://www.microcase.com) provide GSS data in more readily usable form. More than 4,500 scholarly articles have been based on GSS data (NORC).

Because of the objective approach, the scientific sampling, and the continued attention to improving their methodology, the NORC produces widely accepted results. This textbook will use GSS data on topics such as a comparison of life satisfaction of married and single adults, a comparison of marital happiness of men and women, and a comparison of the views about child rearing held by persons of different income levels.

---

different conditions, but they are quite imaginative observational techniques. As is the case for most controlled observations of this type, quantitative data are produced.

Survey Research

Rather than conduct lab experiments, sociologists are more likely to conduct surveys (See Finding Out 2.1).

The researcher must first identify a **population** about which information is desired. If the population of the study includes a large number of persons, such as all married people in the United State, a sample is chosen from the larger group. It is important that the sample is selected in such a way that it is representative of the population about which the researcher wishes to get information. Choosing a true **random sample** increases

---

Survey research: A way of finding things out by asking a sample of persons a set of questions.   **Population:** A specified set of study units, such as all students attending a certain college.   **Random sample:** Sample in which all units in the population have an equal chance of being selected.

the probability that results can properly be generalized from a sample to a population.

Random, in this context, does not mean haphazard. Handing out a questionnaire to every third person on the sidewalk, or tabulating responses from all readers of a particular magazine, does not result in a random sample. Individuals who do not use that sidewalk, or read that magazine, have no chance to be selected for the study. Results from these studies cannot properly be used to generalize findings to other populations.

Once a sample of possible respondents is identified they can be asked to answer the researcher's prepared questions. Sometimes questionnaires, including the Census Bureau forms many people completed in the spring of 2000, are mailed to the respondents, filled out, and returned. In other cases, respondents are questioned over the telephone while the researcher keeps track of the responses. In still other cases (see Finding Out 2.1) a researcher asks questions in person, usually at the respondent's home.

Many surveys, called **cross-sectional studies,** collect data in only one period of time. They take a "snapshot" of some social phenomenon. It is sometimes difficult to demonstrate the effect of one variable on another when both are measured at the same time. Because they gather data at different points in time, **longitudinal studies** are better at detecting causal changes; the cause occurs before the effect, and that can better be detected when measurements are at different times. A special type of longitudinal study, in which the exact same people are studied at different points in time, is called a **panel study.**

The GSS (General Social Survey) could be considered a cross-sectional study if only one year's collection is considered. Because the same questions are often asked from year to year, however, the combined studies are longitudinal. Trends in such variables as divorce rates, marriage rates, and attitudes about same-sex marriage can be measured over time. The GSS is not a panel study, however, because it does not use the same sample of respondents every year.

A number of good panel studies are now available. Alan Booth and others initiated the study of Marital Instability Over the Life Course in 1980. Paul Amato

later joined the team. Follow-up studies on the same respondents were done in 1983, 1988, 1992, and 1997. Children of the original panel were interviewed in 1992 and 1997. This continuing study has yielded extremely valuable knowledge on what factors are associated with divorce, and how divorce impacts children. A recent study (Amato, 2001) found that children of divorced parents have marriages significantly less stable than the marriages of families with intact parents.

Surveys lend themselves to studies involving large numbers of subjects and to quantitative, statistical analysis. A limitation to this approach is the fact that persons do not always tell the truth to researchers, especially about things they believe or have done that are considered very private or socially unacceptable. Also, when making comparisons between groups, it is not always certain that individuals in the different groups interpret the questions in the same way. For example, on questionnaires about domestic violence, men and women may have different definitions of "violence" or "hit" (Fox & Murray, 2000). Surveys are also criticized for being unable to uncover the richness and depth of human interactions as well as can other methods such as field research.

Field Research

When conducting **field research,** the researcher actually observes phenomena in "real life" settings. If the researcher engages in the action being studied, the approach is sometimes called "participant observation." A sociologist interested in family interaction of persons in a particular religion, for example, might conduct field research by attending and participating in the religious services, talking to participants, and recording observations.

Ethnography, a type of field research, is a major tool of anthropologists. An ethnographer usually lives with the people being studied for some period of time. This typically entails learning the language and following the norms of the group. Chapter 3 includes a discussion of the ethnographic work done by Margaret Mead and others.

Field research has yielded fascinating studies on topics such as sociology of religion, crowds, and

---

Cross-sectional studies: Studies bases on observations representing a single point in time.   **Longitudinal study:** A study involving the collection of data at different points in time.   **Panel study:** A type of longitudinal study in which the same people or other cases are observed at different points in time.   **Field research:** Gathering data by direct observation in the natural setting. **Ethnography:** A type of field research on a specific culture or subculture.

Public settings provide an opportunity for field observations of families.

criminal groups. Ethnographers have provided a wealth of information about mate selection, social organization, and other aspects of families in a variety of cultures. Field research is difficult to apply to modern family studies, however, because of the private nature of the family. A researcher could live with a family and make observations, but the family interactions might be different when the researcher was there. The investigator might not, therefore, get a true picture of the way family members acted when they were by themselves.

Supplementing field observations with extensive interviews can provide additional understanding. Norton (1999) studied the interaction between terminally ill patients, their families, and health care providers. She conducted in-depth, face-to-face interviews, but she also observed the interaction of the people involved. She was interested in the understandings about terminal illness that were developed by the persons involved. She concluded that all participants negotiate meanings that are consistent with the patient's and family's wishes. Field studies can provide knowledge about a small number of families, but it is often difficult to know how well these

in-depth studies of a few families can generalize to larger groups. Finally, most fieldwork produces qualitative results. These are more difficult to summarize than the more quantitative results that are usually produced by survey research.

Unobtrusive Research

With controlled experiments, survey research, and most field research, the researcher risks, in one way or another, changing the thing being studied by the fact of studying it. When people know they are being observed, they might behave differently. Even wording a survey question in a certain way can change the way a respondent might think about the subject.

The various types of **unobtrusive research** avoid the risk of having the researcher affect the thing being studied. One unobtrusive approach is **analysis of existing statistics.** William Goode (1993) wanted to compare the divorce rates in several countries that had differing degrees of economic development. Doing original calculations of the divorce rates in all countries

---

Unobtrusive research: Gathering data without influencing the thing being studied.   **Analysis of existing statistics:** Use of previously completed analysis as the raw data in an original study. This differs from secondary analysis of data, in which someone else's raw data are used for a new analysis.

Convenience sample

Finding Out | 2.2

Rubin's *Worlds of Pain*

In preparing to write her classic book *Worlds of Pain* (1976), Lillian Rubin spent nearly 1,000 hours interviewing a convenience sample of working-class couples in the San Francisco Bay area. Rather than to randomly select a large sample of the population and have them answer a prepared questionnaire, she conducted in-depth interviews with 50 couples, talking to the husbands and wives separately.

Rubin did not attempt to maintain the objectivity and detachment usually demanded in scientific studies. Instead, she cited personal experiences that informed her analysis: a working-class childhood, radical feminist politics, and being a marriage and family therapist.

Rather than gather statistics, Rubin attempted to elaborate upon the "flesh-and-blood women and men who make up the numbers" (p. 14). She stressed the importance to social science of "qualitative studies that can capture the fullness of experience, the richness of living" (p. 14).

Rubin's book includes numerous quotes from the interviews, with her analysis and comments. The result is difficult to summarize briefly, except to mention that the lives of her working-class respondents reflect a good deal of pain and struggle, and very little joy and happiness. We do not know the extent to which *Worlds of Pain* belonged to the respondents and how much to Rubin herself. Nor, as Rubin (p. 11) pointed out, can we be sure that these couples' lives are similar to working-class couples elsewhere in the country. She was also aware that she would be criticized for her anecdotal presentation.

Rubin suggested that the quality of the work speaks for itself—"in its ability to persuade by appealing to a level of 'knowing' that exists in all of us but is not very often tapped; in its ability . . . to generate an 'aha experience'" (p. 13). The result is a believable work that is as readable as a good novel and one that allows a glimpse into working-class lives that a scientific survey could not have provided.

---

would have been practically impossible, so he used rates of divorce and measures of economic development that had been gathered by other researchers. His conclusion was that divorce rates generally were higher in countries that were the most industrialized. Since the divorces had occurred before he conducted the study, there is no way the rates could be affected by Goode's analysis.

Content analysis is another form of unobtrusive research. Analysis has been done on paintings and other artwork, books, Web sites, and other recorded human communication. The Cultural Indicators Research Project (http://nimbus.temple.edu/~ggerbner/ci.html) has been analyzing American television programs since 1967. Among other things, project members count the number of violent acts that are portrayed. They have found that network prime-time shows average 5 violent scenes per hour and 5 murders per night (Stossel, 1997). Counting violence in shows that are broadcast anyway does not change the amount of violence portrayed, so this research is unobtrusive.

Program Evaluation

The fifth type of research mentioned by Babbie (2001), program evaluation, is typically used to determine the effectiveness of some kind of social intervention. Such research has been done to determine the effectiveness of such programs as mandatory arrest in domestic violence cases (Sherman & Berk, 1984; Buzawa & Buzawa, 1993) and sex education in the schools (Christopher & Roosa, 1990; Kirby, Waszak, & Ziegler, 1991).

The DARE (Drug Abuse Resistance Education) program is quite popular among schools, parents, and law enforcement officers who want to reduce the use of drugs by young people. Lynam, Milich, and Zimmerman (1999) wanted to find out if the program was actually successful. They identified 1,002 individuals,

---

Content analysis: The study of recorded human communications, such as books, Web sites, paintings, and laws (Babbie, 2001).

some of whom had gone through the DARE program in the sixth grade and others who had not. They compared the two groups 10 years after the program had been administered. They found that the DARE group did no better than the non-DARE group on actual drug use, attitudes toward drugs, or on self-esteem. In short, according to this study, DARE was not found to be effective in meeting its goals. As a result of this and other studies, in February 2001 DARE officials admitted that their program had not been as effective as they had hoped and announced that they were significantly changing their approach (Zernike, 2001).

In addition to the four common research approaches used by social scientists in general, family researchers sometimes make use of other approaches such as clinical case studies, which are commonly used in psychology. The experiences of families or individuals who come to marriage counselors might be compiled to discover what goes wrong with American marriages. While this approach can yield interesting information, it has to be used carefully to avoid the problems associated with anecdotal data. Persons who go to counseling are not necessarily representative of the population as a whole, nor do they necessarily have an objective understanding of their own situations.

Searching for Regularities

Whatever their method, social scientists look for **regularities**—those things that happen over and over in more or less the same way. Regularities vary tremendously in terms of their complexity. At the least complex extreme are **culture traits.** For example, it is a culture trait in the United States that strangers will shake hands when introduced by a third party. Other cultures have similar practices that indicate the persons are unarmed and do not meet as enemies. Norms, as discussed in chapter 1, are regularities. So too are roles.

Institutions are the most complex, large-scale regularities studied by sociologists. All societies, like all individuals, have basic needs that must be met for survival. An individual, for example, must have food and water. A society must have some way to acquire and distribute food and water to its members.

The most basic social institution is the family. Although its form varies considerably, the family is so regular that some form of it is found in all cultures. It is so regular in our society that virtually everyone will par-

ticipate in some form of family at some time in their lives.

Marriage, too, is an institutionalized regularity. It is estimated that 90 to 95% of adult Americans will marry at some time, many of them more than once (Cherlin, 1992). Other social institutions include the economic one that produces and distributes goods and services; the political one that determines the acquisition and wielding of power; and the religious one that, among other things, defines what is sacred. All of these institutions are interrelated regularities in a particular society, as we will see in later chapters.

Finding regularities helps to predict, which is one goal of science. Sociologists have found that, in many ways, people in groups are quite predictable. Though I do not know the names of the students reading this paragraph, nor much else about them, I can predict that approximately 85–95% of them are currently married, have been married, or will get married someday. To put it another way, there is a 9 in 10 probability that each student will get married.

It can also be predicted that, when the students next attend the class for which they are reading this book, they will sit in or near the same seat that they sat in the last time they were in that class. This will be true even if the professor did not assign seats. Predictably, the students have participated in creating a predictable social structure.

Social scientists are able to make predictions because of the regularities produced by society. It is fundamental to sociological inquiry that social structure determines rates of events (Beeghley, 2000). In some societies, the marriage rate will be lower than in the United States because the social structure is different. The divorce rate will be higher in California next year than in New Jersey. The social structure affects many other variables, such as the number of poor persons at a particular time and place, the number of crimes that are committed, the marriage rate, and whether more men or women will attend a religious service this week. It is, of course, individuals who are involved in these actions, and the social structure does not irrevocably determine which individuals will do what, but it does determine the rates at which these things are likely to occur.

It is the rates and probabilities, not individual characteristics, that are predictable. In most American couples, the man is taller than the woman is. An in-depth study could reveal the rate at which this was

---

Regular: Customary, usual, or normal.   **Culture traits:** the simplest functional units into which a culture is divided for purposes of analysis (Fairchild, 1970:83).

true. Finding a couple in which the woman is taller than the man does not disprove the general statement. To say that the divorce rate is higher in California than in New Jersey is not to say that all California marriages end in divorce or that none in New Jersey do. The important thing to remember is that there are exceptions to sociological generalizations because we are dealing with rates and probabilities, not certainties.

Once regularities are discovered in a social system, events that do not follow the predicted pattern stand out. These irregularities can then be studied. Finding regularities or irregularities, however, does not explain them. Explanation is part of the task of **theories,** which both help to explain data and to guide researchers in gathering data. Some theoretical perspectives point to large-scale institutional systems (macrosociology), while others lead to analysis of daily personal interactions (microsociology). We will look first at "big picture" kinds of theories.

Macrosociological Analysis

Some sociology concerns itself with large-scale social processes and structures, not individuals. Rather than study why a particular married couple got divorced, for example, a **macrosociological** analyst might try to understand why divorce rates vary from one time or place to another.

Emile Durkheim (1897), the early French sociologist, said that sociologists could study society as it exists *sui generis,* or "self-generating." By this he meant that social facts could be understood without reference to individual motivations. To demonstrate his point, Durkheim studied suicide rates in different parts of Europe. While suicide is an intensely personal event, with as many specific causes as there are persons who attempt it, those personal reasons need not be considered when studying suicide at the macrosocial level. Durkheim found, for example, that Protestant areas in Europe had higher rates of suicide than Catholic areas. This is an interesting social fact, even though none of the persons involved would be likely to say that they were contemplating suicide solely because they were Protestant.

Macrosociological perspectives consider society at the level of institutions, values, systems, and norms. They tend to be deterministic; that is, since individuals do not choose the society into which they are born, they have no initial choice as to the language they will learn

Macro-level perspectives look at the big picture.

Theory: A systematic explanation for the observations about related phenomena. **Macrosociology:** The study of the large-scale structures and processes of society.

or the social, economic, political, religious, and familial institutions that will influence them. The roles they will play are largely scripted for them. Macrosociologists do not necessarily believe that individuals lack free will, but that group behavior is somewhat predictable.

The most common macrosociological perspectives have been functionalism and conflict theory. An approach called sociocultural evolutionary theory will complete our survey of big-picture perspectives.

Functionalism

The functionalist paradigm analyzes the relationship between the various parts of society and the society as a whole. A basic functional analysis of society would start by finding a regularity of some kind; it might be a trait or an institution. The analysis would then try to find out what **function** that regularity had. The question would be, "How does that trait contribute to the goals and operation of society or of the persons in the society?"

For example, the handshake mentioned earlier served the function of establishing that the two persons who are meeting for the first time intend to behave as friends. This helps their interaction go more smoothly, so the handshaking is functional.

Rites of passage are functional ceremonies because they announce to society that the roles of the participants have changed. Graduation, puberty rituals, baptisms, and funerals change the way the participants are perceived. Weddings, too, are important rites of passage; they announce the joining together of previously unrelated persons into the roles of husband and wife. This changes the role relationship of the newlyweds, their friends, and their relatives.

Although the functional approach assumes that regularities exist because they serve some function, the functions of some traits are not immediately apparent. In American weddings, the custom is for the groom to stand to the right of the bride. What function might this serve? Sometimes it is not as important how the matter is decided as it is that the matter is resolved somehow. Whether we drive on the right side of the road, as in America, or on the left side of the road, as in England, does not really matter. What is functional is that there is agreement among members of the group so that everyone knows the norms. Having a tradition,

then, in which the groom stands to the right resolves that minor issue; it is one less thing to worry about. When students establish a seating chart the first few class meetings, the same function is served: subsequent meetings can proceed more smoothly.

The wedding custom, however, might once have been functional. In some earlier societies, a groom got his bride by bride capture, and sometimes he had to be at least symbolically ready to draw a weapon to defend himself and his bride from other suitors or from her family. Since most men are righthanded, having the bride to his left freed his weapon hand. The custom no longer serves the original function; it is rare these days that a groom has to draw his sword during the wedding ceremony, but he still stands to the right of the bride. This is an example of a **cultural survival,** a culture trait that has survived after its original function has disappeared.

Cultural traditions are functional because they help meet the needs of society. Institutions, too, are functional because they enable society to establish regular, predictable ways of meeting individual and social needs. Since some form of the family is virtually universal it must, the functionalist paradigm would assume, serve important functions.

Various theorists have proposed different sets of family functions. Ogburn, in 1933, identified seven functions of traditional families that he thought were being lost in the modern family. Murdock (1949) identified four functions that contributed to the universality of the family: sexual, economic, reproductive, and educational. Parsons and Bales reduced the number of basic functions to two: socialization and "stabilization of the adult personalities of the population of the society" (1956:17).

The work of these and other theorists can be synthesized to produce a list of four basic functions that are served by the family wherever the family is found. First, individuals die, but societies continue because the members can be replaced. This can happen by recruitment, conquering, or migration, but the most common way is by biological procreation. Regulation and legitimization of reproduction are family functions.

Second, children are not born knowing the language, norms, values, and roles of the society of which they will become a part. Socialization is an important

---

Functionalism: A paradigm that focuses on the way various parts of society have consequences that maintain the stability of the whole.   **Function:** Consequence of an action or trait.   **Cultural survival:** a culture trait that has survived after its original function has disappeared.

Families in the NEWS

Newspapers — or Census Bureau — Not Quite Right

In April 13, 2001, a press release from the U.S. Census Bureau opened with this statement: "The proportion of children living in a traditional nuclear family with their biological mother and father increased from 51 percent in 1991, to 56 percent in 1996 . . . " Newspapers often get their material from government press releases, and several trumpeted what appeared to be good news.

Under the headline, "Exploding the Myth of the Nuclear Family's Demise," the *Los Angeles Times* reported: "The nuclear family of yesteryear — mom and dad living with each other and their biological children — may not be as endangered as it sometimes seems. The percentage of children living in these traditional families rose during the early 1990s." Similar headlines and stories appeared around the country.

Problem is, they didn't quite get the story right. The report referred to in the press release was "Living Arrangements of Children: Fall 1996," by Jason Fields. He didn't write the press release or the news articles.

Whether the press release was accurate or not depends on a definition. In the original report, a *traditional nuclear family* is defined as "a family in which a child lives with two married biological parents and with only full siblings, if siblings are present. No other people are present in the household under this definition, not even close relatives of the family."

In other words, a *traditional nuclear family* cannot in any way be extended. Grandma or grandpa can't live there, nor cousins, aunts, uncles, or anyone else. The reason the number of children living in such households went up in the 1990s was because grandmas, grandpas, and other extended family members moved out. The good economy probably contributed. But the same report also found that the actual percent of children who live with both natural parents has gone virtually unchanged during the same period.

Among other people, David Blankenhorn, president of the Institute for American Values, was upset about the misleading news stories. He said he wished the reports were true, but didn't like people being led to believe that there has been a major turnaround in the decline of the American family.

Mr. Fields, author of the original study, was also concerned. He thought the Census Bureau press release could have been worded a little more carefully.

Sources: Associated Press. www.latimes.com, April 13, 2001
Tamar Lewin. www.nytimes.com, April 21, 2001
http://www.census.gov/Press-Release/www/2001/cb01−69.html

function of the family because, especially early in a child's life, the learning occurs in a family setting.

Third, the family provides status and sense of belonging to individuals. In some societies, the family identification will be the major one throughout a person's life; in others it will serve more as a starting point from which the individual will go on to develop his or her independent status. Either way, both the individuals and society benefit by having a place for each person to belong.

Fourth, economic cooperation occurs within the family. In some societies, families both produce and consume as cooperative units; in others, the cooperation is primarily in consuming. Either way, some economic cooperation is more efficient than having each individual be totally self-sufficient. It is a more efficient use of scarce resources to have several persons share a living unit and cooking space, for example, than to have separate ones for each person.

The family is not necessarily the only institution to be involved in these functions in every society. Indeed, alternatives to the family can be found or, at least, imagined. Nonetheless, the functionalist's sense of what a family is as an institution includes performing these functions.

One way to understand the functionalist view of society is to use the **organismic analogy** that compares a modern society to a human body. The survival of the body as a whole requires the cooperation of many specialized organs. The heart pumps the blood, which is its function; the lungs exchange bad air for good, the kidneys filter the system, and the brain tells everything else what to do. None of the organs can survive on its own; all are mutually interdependent. Each contributes to the survival of the whole.

If a society is like an organism in this way, then all parts of the system have a common interest in the survival of the system as a whole. The heart, lungs, liver,

---

Organismic analogy: The view that society is like an individual life form, with parts that work together to carry on the various processes of life.

and brain — and all cells within each of these — have a common interest in seeing that the body as a whole survives. The social institutions are to society what the organs are to the body. In society, the familial, religious, political, educational, and economic systems — and all individuals within these institutions — have the common interest of survival of the society.

The organismic analogy can be extended further. The theory of evolution holds that species evolved over millions of years from one-celled animals to highly specialized and complex animals such as humans. In the one-celled animals, that one relatively simple cell performs all necessary functions. Gradually, organisms evolved by becoming more complicated and by developing specialized groups of cells. This process is similar to the way human societies have changed over thousands of years. The first societies were simple ones in which one social institution, the family or kin group, performed all necessary functions. Gradually, other social institutions evolved. Religion, politics, economics, and education are major institutions that developed specialized functions, in the same way as the heart, liver, kidneys, and brain of the human organism.

This process of developing specialized institutions in society is known as **social differentiation.** Parsons and other functionalists argued that as other institutions have developed they have taken over some of the functions previously performed by the family (Parsons & Bales, 1955; Ogburn, 1950). The educational institution, for example, now does a good deal of the socialization of young persons, which used to be done more completely in the family. This "loss of functions" perspective leads many functionalists to adopt the pessimistic position in the family decline debate.

Critique of Functionalism

The functionalist paradigm has been criticized for having what appears to be a built-in bias in favor of the *status quo* (the way things are now). Consider again the organismic analogy. If an organ exists, it exists for a reason and operates as it does for a reason. The heart, lungs, liver, and brain are all properly serving their functions for the survival of the organism as a whole, and it would be dangerous to attempt to rearrange the organs. We would not, on the assumption that it is unfair that the heart has to work all the time and the stomach

works only when digesting food, try to route some of the blood from the heart to the stomach to lighten the heart's unfair burden. The entire organism would die, as would the stomach and heart.

If society were like the organism, then, the functionalist would assume that all traits exist for a reason; they are helping the society as a whole to survive. Significant change in one of the parts could be dangerous to the entire society. If the family were significantly changed or destroyed so that its functions were no longer served, society could be destroyed. Seen in this way, functionalism does seem to have a conservative (to *conserve* things as they are) bias.

Critics of functionalism also point out that, although society might be like an organism in some ways, this is just an analogy. In fact, society is not an organism. Parts of it might be able to change without destroying the whole. The United States has changed so much since 1800 that there is some question it is even the same society. It has even added parts, most recently Alaska and Hawaii, that are not physically attached to the larger body. It is difficult to imagine how an organism could do that. A related criticism of functionalism is that it seems to focus primarily on the positive functions, or **eufunctions,** of various institutions. Functionalist analyses of the family seem to focus primarily on the good things about family life and ignore the bad. Part of the problem is that, in looking at the functions of the family for the society as a whole, the possibility of damage to some individuals is ignored. Although the family institution in general may be functional for society, there are persons in destructive, abusive families. The family is not functional for those specific individuals.

Partly to avoid the conclusion that all existing traits are always functional in all societies, functionalists have developed the concept of **dysfunctions,** which are ultimately harmful to society. Slavery might exist in a society, but be dysfunctional. The concept also allows the functionalist to argue that a trait might be functional for society but dysfunctional for some individuals in society, or functional at one time but not another. The functionalist would always assume, however, that all individuals benefit from the fact that there is a society of some kind that regulates the interaction of its members. Without it there would be chaos.

Social differentiation: The division and specialization of social and cultural units such as groups, organizations, and institutions. **Eufunction:** A positive impact on society of a trait or institution. **Dysfunction:** Those observed consequences that lessen the adaptation or adjustment of the system (Merton 1957:51).

Finally, functionalism has been criticized for its apparent false **teleology.** To say that a cultural trait exists because of its consequences is to confuse cause and effect. For example, it might be true that family systems regulate reproduction, but that does not mean the family system exists because it regulates reproduction. More simply, it is true that eyeglasses rest on the nose and ears, but that does not mean that noses and ears were designed so that people could see better.

The Conflict Paradigm

The conflict paradigm provides the second major way macrosociologists organize their views. Recall that the functionalist paradigm assumes that all institutions and individuals within the system have an overriding common interest: the survival of society. The conflict paradigm recognizes that different groups in society do share some interests. More important, however, is the fact that different segments sometimes have conflicting interests.

In its simplest form, theories based on the conflict paradigm assume that society is divided into two groups: the "haves" and the "have-nots," or the rich and the poor. Who the "haves" and "have-nots" are will vary from one society to another, but there will always be some conflict between them. Where these two groups have interests in common, the society will tend to serve those common interests. Where the interests of the groups differ, however, society will tend to be organized in ways that benefit the "haves" at the expense of the "have-nots." Conflict theorists claim that all social institutions, including the family, will be organized as part of a system that primarily benefits the "haves."

The conflict paradigm is more complicated than this brief description and includes many different approaches. Karl Marx made the most influential contribution. His theories were characterized by **economic determinism,** the view that the economic institution is the most important. It determines the class structure; the owners of production, whether that be plantations or factories, will be the "haves." They influence the laws and political system more than do the "have-nots," so the political system will therefore benefit the "haves." The religious institution, in the view of Marx, socializes the "have-nots" to accept their lowly economic position

in exchange for hopes of a better spiritual outcome. If poor people believe that enduring a life of hardship will lead to eternal bliss in Heaven, they are less likely to resist their oppression. This, Marx argued, leaves the wealth and power in the hands of the "haves."

The task of social scientists is partly to bring conflict and oppression to light, but the conflict paradigm argues that social scientists should go beyond uncovering conflict. They should also attempt to improve society by intervening on behalf of oppressed people. This Marxist idea of combining social research and theory with the practice of improving society is referred to as **praxis.** Since the Marxist believes conflict will end only when there is a classless society, praxis would require the use of social science to help end class systems such as capitalism and change the family and other institutions that accompany the oppressive economic systems.

From a conflict perspective, the family in a capitalist system serves the interest of the "haves" in various ways. For one thing, it socializes the young into a set of values that benefit the "haves." In the United States today, conflict theorists contend, the capitalist economic system is controlled by the wealthy, who own the means of production. The economic system survives partly because the values that sustain it are deeply ingrained even into the "have-nots." For example, most Americans believe strongly that it is a right of parents to leave their money and other assets to their children. This belief results in inheritance laws that allow extreme wealth to remain concentrated as it is handed down from generation to generation. This practice has the effect of keeping wealth and power out of the hands of the poor and concentrated in the families of the rich. In the United States, this also keeps more wealth and power in White families than in Black or other families that historically have had less wealth to pass on to their children.

Marx's collaborator, Engels (1884), also argued that the family serves the interests of men at the expense of women. According to Engels, the family was a system that allowed men access to power and wealth while keeping women and children powerless and at men's mercy.

Feminist Thought

At its most basic level, feminism is the belief in the social, political, and economic equality of men and

---

Teleology: The study of final causes; the belief that events are determined by some ultimate design or purpose. **Economic determinism:** The theory that the economic base of society determines the general character of social structure and culture.
Praxis: Combining social research and theory with the active attempt to improve society.

women, but it goes much deeper than that. Many types of feminist thought exist, and feminist analysis can apply at both macro and micro levels (Karmarae & Spender, 1992; Fox & Murray, 2000). The emphasis here will be on those schools of feminist thought that are found in academic scholarship and that have a primarily macro-level focus. Throughout the remainder of this text, the use of the term *feminist* will refer to feminist thought with these five characteristics.

First, feminists make gender the central concern of their analysis. Feminism replaces the economic determinism of Marx with gender determinism. In Marxist theory, individuals are assigned to different social classes, with the ownership classes dominating the working classes. In feminism, classes are replaced by genders as the primary social distinction.

Second, feminist analysis has a decidedly **gynocentric** focus. Analysis centers on the status of women in society and history. This focus is grounded on the assumption that virtually all previous analysis, including analysis of families, was done with an **androcentric** bias. Feminists believe that the record should be corrected.

Third, not only is the focus on women but usually on a particular aspect of women: their social vulnerabilities and oppression. Although men and women share some interests, when their interests conflict, the social structure will tend to benefit men. Heterosexuality, dating, mate selection, and marriage, along with the job market and access to political power, all reflect gender oppression (Kramarae, 1992; Walby, 1990).

Fourth, feminist thought emphasizes praxis (Fox & Murry, 2000). To the Marxist, praxis implies active efforts to destroy class-based systems and usher in a classless communist system. Although feminists see women as victims of gender oppression, they also see women as potential agents of social change (Ferree & Martin, 1995; Catlett & McKenry, 1996). To the feminist, praxis implies active efforts to abolish those institutions, traits, values, and other elements of society that are believed to perpetuate the patriarchy. Targets include the traditional family, which perpetuates gender oppression by assigning women to less valued and powerful roles. Feminists therefore gravitate toward the "glad it changed" position in the family decline debate.

Finally, feminists tend to have a distrust of the traditional model of objective science (Fox & Murry, 2000). Some theorists assume that social science, like other ele-

ments of society, will tend to be constructed in such a way as to benefit the "haves" rather than the "have-nots." Such "science" contributes to the oppression of people. The traditional scientific approach, especially in social science, is therefore seen as part of the problem (Smith, 1994, 1998). Other feminists view the positivist study of society as a male-constructed approach that disguises bias with a cloak of objectivity. Feminists generally prefer to treat sociology as a humanist study rather than a science, and typically prefer qualitative research as a method that is more likely to give a voice to the oppressed.

Because of the concern about traditional science, feminist thought tends to blur the lines between social science, on the one hand, and literature on the other. Most feminist study programs at colleges and universities are interdisciplinary. What feminist scholars have in common is not a traditional discipline but the five characteristics mentioned here.

Feminist influences have significantly altered the landscape of family studies in the past 30 years. One change has been in the topics that family scholars investigate. Until Jessie Bernard proclaimed in 1972 that "there are two marriage, his and hers," there was little recognition that families could affect men and women in different ways. Feminist scholars were instrumental in bringing domestic violence to the attention of family scholars. Concerns about potential conflicts between work and family, the problematic nature of the household division of labor, gendered raising of children, and a number of other areas of interest have also been heavily influenced by feminist thought. On some of these topics, the feminist view may well be the dominant view in social science.

Critique of the Conflict Paradigm and Feminist Thought

It is generally assumed that theories based on the conflict paradigm give a better account of social change than do those based on functionalism. While functionalism may have a bias in favor of the status quo and might paint too rosy a picture of the past, conflict and feminist theories may have a bias in favor of social change and might paint too grim a picture of the present.

Since the conflict perspective assumes that there are conflicting interests among groups, it may "find" conflict where such might not actually exist, while

---

Gynocentric: With women at the center of interest.   **Androcentric:** With men at the center of interest.

Table 2.1	Criteria for Classifying Primary Types of Societies					
Type of Society (Origin Date)	Plant Cultivation	Metallurgy	Plow	Iron	Inanimate Energy	Electronic Information
Hunting and gathering (1 million – 40,000 BPE)	−	−	−	−	−	−
Simple horticultural (7000 BC)	+	−	−	−	−	−
Advanced horticultural (4000 BC)	+	+	−	−	−	−
Simple agrarian (3000 BC)	+	+	+	−	−	−
Advanced agrarian (1000 BC)	+	+	+	+	−	−
Industrial (AD 1800)	+	+	+	+	+	−
Postindustrial (1970 –)	+	+	+	+	+	+

The symbol + means that the trait is widespread; the symbol − means it is not.

Source: Adapted from Lenski, Gerhard, & Jean Lenski. 1987. *Human Societies: An Introduction to Macrosociology,* 5th ed. New York: McGraw-Hill. Pages 80 and 83. Postindustrial stage added.

minimizing those aspects of social life that are built on consensus and cooperation. Also, because of the emphasis on praxis, conflict and feminist approaches are sometimes accused of being based more on political ideology than on verifiable research.

Like conflict theory, feminist analysis is accused of starting with the assumption that there is oppression and thus may "see" conflict and oppression even where it does not exist. It tends to see all differences between men and women as sex-arbitrary and oppressive, while minimizing the influence of sex-irreducible roles as a source of social or psychological differences between men and women.

Conflict and feminist theories focus on the negative aspects of social systems and attribute those to a particular form of oppression. For example, unemployment is attributed to capitalism and gendered unequal pay to the patriarchy, but it is not clear what causes the positive elements in society. For example, the advances in scientific medicine have significantly increased life expectancy in this country, and more for women than for men, but conflict and feminist theorists tend not to mention "capitalist medical care" or "patriarchal medicine" except in negative terms.

Finally, some conflict and feminist theorists, like some functionalists, suffer from false teleology. For example, it is true that women make less money than do men when the women have primary child-care responsibilities. This does not mean, however, that women are primary family workers for the purpose of increasing men's relative earnings.

Sociocultural Evolutionary Framework

The next two chapters of this text will draw heavily from the sociocultural evolutionary framework. A central concept in this perspective is **modes of production,** which are different ways in which societies have organized the basic forms of economic production. Marx pioneered this approach, but others have refined it. Gerhard Lenski and others (Lenski & Lenski, 1987; Lenski, Lenski, & Nolan, 1991; Lenski & Nolan, 1984; Lenski, Nolan, & Lenski, 1995) applied a **sociocultural evolutionary** approach. It treats modes of production as stages of development in societies, from the first human groups to the complex kinds of societies now found in such areas as North America, Japan, and Europe. Not all societies have gone through these stages, and the experiences are different in each society, but Lenski provides a useful framework for analysis. His approach defines six major stages, and one can be added (see Table 2.1).

Modes of production: The method by which the majority of a society's members produce or develop the goods needed by the society. **Sociocultural evolution:** The process of social and cultural change in response to the environment, made possible by the accumulation of technical knowledge.

Table 2.2	Comparison of Macro-Level Perspectives			
	Functionalism	**Conflict Theory**	**Feminist Thought**	**Sociocultural Evolutionary**
Nature of society	System or organism with interdependent parts.	Groups with conflicting interests.	Gendered system, with men privileged.	Response to knowledge base and environment.
View of social change	Gradual disorganization/ reorganization.	Continuous, necessary, inevitable.	Continuous, necessary, inevitable.	Cumulative and gradual growth in technological base.
Key element of society	Integration of system parts.	Class conflict over scarce resources; power and exploitation.	Gender conflict over scarce resources; power and oppression.	Technological base.
Basic analytic question	How do traits affect parts and the whole?	How do traits affect class oppression? How can that be changed?	How do traits affect gender oppression? How can that be changed?	How does techno-logical base affect social institutions?
View of the traditional family	Essential to well-functioning society.	Propagates class oppression.	Propagates gender oppression.	Appropriate in certain modes of production.

The mode of production of a particular society is closely associated with the available **technology**. It is important to remember that technology is not the ax, wheel, automobile, or computer; technology is the accumulated knowledge required to build and use these material objects. Each type of society can add its discoveries to the knowledge base of earlier societies.

For the vast majority of their history, humans and their ancestors were of the hunting and gathering type, surviving by **foraging**. Very few such groups exist today. Hunting and gathering are now done mainly for recreation, rather than for survival.

Groups that planted and grew their food gradually replaced hunting-gathering societies in some parts of the world. The practice of plant cultivation produced simple horticultural groups in the Middle East around 7000 BC and independently in other parts of the world somewhat later. The ability to produce tools and weapons from metal, especially copper, ushered in the advanced horticultural systems around 4000 BC.

The development and general use of the plow, which occurred by 3000 BC in Mesopotamia and Egypt, defined the arrival of the simple agrarian system. The advanced agrarian system, characterized by the widespread use of iron for tools and weapons, occurred for the first time around 1000 BC.

Advanced agrarian systems changed over time, eventually resulting in the next major revolution in modes of production. The industrial revolution, occurring first in Britain around 1800, used inanimate energy sources such as coal and oil. This kind of production has spread to most of the world and has altered even remote societies where other modes of production are still dominant.

Finally, the world might now be in the next revolution in modes of production, referred to as the postmodern or postindustrial era. The major icon of the era is the computer, which has far-reaching effects on the family and all other aspects of society.

The sociocultural evolutionary approach joins functionalism, conflict theory, and feminism as major macrosociological approaches. The three are compared in Table 2.2.

Technology: The body of knowledge available to a society that is of use in fashioning implements, practicing arts and skills, and extracting or collecting materials.   **Foraging:** Collecting plants and animals for subsistence.

Microsociological Perspectives

Functionalism, conflict theory, and sociocultural evolutionary theory are each macrosociological perspectives. In contrast to these "big picture" views, **microsociological** perspectives analyze society at the level of face-to-face interaction among individuals. The emphasis is on the creation of meaning in day-to-day life.

Symbolic Interactionism

The term **symbolic interactionism,** coined by Herbert Blumer (1969) to describe the work of George Herbert Mead, is sometimes used to include a variety of theoretical viewpoints. Roles can be studied at the macrosociological level, but symbolic interactionists are more interested in how those roles are played out, constructed, and revised in the interaction of particular men and women.

This paradigm assumes that humans are actors, in two senses of the word. First, individuals are actors in that they play a role in a script that society provides for them. George and Martha, individuals, interact in the roles of husband and wife. They are able to do so partly because they have been socialized into the married-couple script. Because George and Martha each have had experiences different from those of Salvador and Maria, they will play their roles somewhat differently than Salvador and Maria will.

Persons are actors in another sense. Humans, unlike other animals, can *take action,* not just behave. Humans can decide how they would like to play their role and then make some conscious effort to create the desired impression. This is what Erving Goffman (1959, 1963, 1967) referred to as **impression management.** Goffman developed a branch of microsociology known as the **dramaturgic** approach. Everyday life is seen as a series of performances individuals put on, as actors, for other persons, who are their audience. Anticipating the reaction of the audience is not always a conscious process; in everyday life actors do not always realize they are acting. Sometimes they think they are being themselves. When you are "just being yourself," however, you are playing a role designed to get certain reactions from your audience and from yourself, in a certain social context. You would not "just be yourself" the same way

Micro-level analysis is concerned with personal interaction.

in church with your grandmother as you would with an intimate friend at his or her home.

Symbolic interactionists suggest that individuals do not respond to the world as it "really is" but as they interpret it to be. This is the meaning of the statement by W. I. Thomas (1920), now referred to as the Thomas Theorem: "If men define situations as real, they are real in their consequences." If a couple defines an event as a marriage-threatening crisis rather than as a challenge to be overcome together, for example, the marriage is more likely to end. This is an important consideration in models of family crisis, as will be discussed in chapter 14.

Meanings about social interaction are constantly being created and revised. This interpretation of meaning is a subject of study and description used by symbolic interactionists. Because of the emphasis on socially constructed and changing meanings, the pure scientific method is not usually appropriate for studies

---

Microsociology: The study of small-scale social processes like face-to-face interaction.   **Symbolic interactionism:** Study of the interaction between persons that takes place through symbols, such as signs, gestures, and language.   **Impression management:** Process in which a person manipulates others' perceptions of himself or herself to achieve a desired outcome.
Dramaturgy: The study of interaction as impression management by an actor for an audience.

using the dramaturgic or other symbolic interactionist approaches.

Since symbolic interactionism stresses the importance of symbols and meanings, it is quite useful in the study of the socialization process. Individuals, although unique, must have common meanings in order to communicate; these must be learned and constantly refined. This idea will be applied to the concept of "love" in chapter 8.

Critique of Symbolic Interactionism

The symbolic interactionist approach is generally credited with capturing the richness and depth of meaning of human group behavior that is missed by conflict theorists or by functionalists. At the same time, however, it is criticized for not putting enough importance on broad social forces. People bring meanings and influences from social institutions when they interact with each other. They know the gender, social status, and other socially defined characteristics of the actors, and the norms of the action. They do not have free rein to invent themselves; or, if they do, they will discover the power of such social forces such as the police, jails, and mental institutions.

Symbolic interactionists usually study specific small groups, commonly using field research methods. The descriptions that result from such studies can be fascinating, but it is sometimes difficult to know the extent to which knowledge about one group can generalize to others or to society as a whole.

Other Family Study Perspectives

Functionalism, conflict theory, and symbolic interactionism are the major paradigms in the field of sociology. Other approaches, however, are quite useful in the study of marriage and the family. These include social exchange theory, developmental theory, and systems theory.

Social Exchange Theory

The **social exchange** perspective looks at personal interactions as if they are analogous to economic exchanges. Human beings are assumed to be rational, and their behavior is directed to the maximization of pleasures (getting rewards) and minimization of pains (reducing costs). When a person is considering divorce, for example, it is as if he or she compares the benefits and costs of staying in the marriage with the benefits and costs of divorcing, and then acts accordingly. Individuals are assumed to have resources that they use in the social market place to exchange for profit. The profit is not solely in terms of money, as economic analysis would have it, but can include a number of other things, including social approval (Klein & White, 1996).

Social exchange views of the family were pioneered by Gary Becker (1981) and, in a variation known as "rational choice theory," by James Coleman (1990). Later in the book, we will apply this perspective to the mate-selection process as well as other aspects of marriage and the family. Other approaches using terms and methods borrowed from economics, such as rational choice, human capital and social capital perspectives, will also be applied.

The Developmental Perspective

The **developmental** approach was pioneered by Reuben Hill (1949; Hill & Rogers, 1964) and has more recently been refined by Joan Aldous (1996). A key concept is that families have a **life course** in much the same way that individuals do. For individuals, the stages in the life course might be infancy, childhood, adolescence, young adulthood, middle age, and old age. For families the stages might be identified by such events as early marriage, birth of a child, departure of the last child from home, or retirement of the husband or wife. Each of these stages poses its own developmental tasks, challenges, and adjustments.

The lifespan of a family is referred to as a **family career,** but defining the exact stages is somewhat arbitrary. Rubin (1976) proposed four stages. Duvall's (1967) eight-stage model is widely used, as is Rodgers's (1962) 10-stage approach. In other work, however, Rodgers identified as many as 24 categories.

A problem with applying the developmental model to today's families is that most families do not go through all the stages as posed. About half of today's marriages are now remarriages for one or both partners (Goode, 1993), and many of these include children. They have no "early marriage" childless stage. Still other couples never have children, and many divorce before they reach a "retirement" stage.

In spite of its limitations, considerable research on the family has been done using this framework, including

---

Social exchange paradigm: Explanations of social behavior based on calculation of resources, costs, and benefits of alternative actions. **Developmental paradigm:** Explanations of social behavior emphasizing stages of life cycles. **Life course:** A developmental perspective that focuses on individuals' lives, in their entirety, in historical and social context. **Family career:** The entirety of events and stages traversed by a family.

some very interesting work on the levels of marital satisfaction throughout the life cycle of a marriage.

Family Systems Theory

Another way of looking at the family is to compare it to a **system.** This perspective grew from the work of such sociologists as Parsons and Bales (1955) and is consistent with functionalist theory. Rosenblatt (1994) referred to the family systems approach as a metaphor that provides a useful way of looking at the family. Systems theory has been widely applied as a model to help guide family therapy, as chapter 14 will discuss.

Five important assumptions underlie the family systems metaphor. First, the family is made up of interdependent individuals, comparable to a home heating system that has different parts such as a thermostat, a fan, a burner, and heat ducts. The whole of the family is more than the sum of its parts; the system allows family members to interact in certain ways that would be impossible if they were not part of a family system.

Secondly, a family system has boundaries. Some persons belong in the family as members, while others do not. As we saw in chapter 1, there are a variety of ways of determining family boundaries. Family systems theory assumes that the boundaries, however they are drawn, provide relatively clear guidelines about who belongs in a particular family unit.

A third assumption is that a family system is part of a larger system of community and society. Just as the home heating system requires power and maintenance from outside, families can survive only within a larger network of systems. A family system interacts with educational, economic, legal, and religious systems.

Fourth, family systems contain subsystems. Members of the family can form alliances that result in conflict between subsystems. The family depicted in Figure 2.1 has a number of subsystems. One is the parental subsystem; in traditional families this would be the dominant subsystem. Another could be a sibling subsystem, consisting of all the children. There could also be a male subsystem, consisting of the father and son, and a female subsystem consisting of the mother and daughter. The two oldest children could form a subsystem that excluded the youngest child. A number of other possibilities exist in just this five-member family. The family system as a whole can operate smoothly only as long as the subsystems mesh.

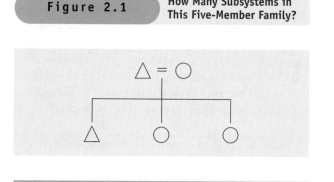

Figure 2.1 How Many Subsystems in This Five-Member Family?

Fifth, systems theorists look at families as if they were **homeostatic** mechanisms. Families have a system goal, and strive to maintain a constant condition in achieving that goal. When something gets out of balance, the system attempts to return to its former condition. The home heating system is a homeostatic mechanism. When the temperature drops below a certain point, the furnace operates until the temperature returns to its previous level. A person will eat when hungry, returning the body system to its nonhungry state. After a family argument, attempts are usually made, through apologies and other mechanisms, to return to a nonargumentative condition.

Macro-Micro Synthesis: The Scripting Model

Although not a theoretical perspective in the same sense as conflict theory, functionalism, or symbolic interactionism, the *scripting model* provides a way of organizing what the other theories teach us about the family. This approach is based on the work by Simon and Gagnon (1986, 1987) on the topic of human sexuality, but is expanded in this text to cover other aspects of marriage and the family.

This model organizes social life as scripts that can be studied at four levels: societal scripts, personal scripts, scenes, and mutual scripts. This perspective helps integrate the macrosocial and microsocial levels of analysis.

Societal Scripts

The broadest, most abstract level at which scripts can be studied is called the **societal script.** At this level,

---

System: A functionally related group of interacting parts that form a complex whole. **Homeostasis:** The tendency of an organism to maintain internal equilibrium by making adjustments to changing conditions. **Societal script:** Societywide, macrosocial expectations.

Both theater productions and everyday life are scripted. Here, the actors know their roles—but members of the audience know theirs, too.

macrosociological variables and rates of behavior, not individuals, interact. Durkheim's comment about *sui generis* studies applies. The institutions, values, roles, and norms are studied here. Both functionalism and the conflict paradigm can be used to understand societal scripts.

Personal Scripts

Through the process of socialization, individuals learn the values, norms, language, and other elements of the societal script. Since individuals each have somewhat different experiences, however, their understandings of the world will be slightly different from those of everyone else. These learned and shaped expectations form the **personal script**, which the individual carries around and acts upon.

In homogeneous societies, each individual's personal script will be a relatively undistorted reflection of the societal script. If, for example, the societal script portrays the proper marriage as monogamous, egalitarian,

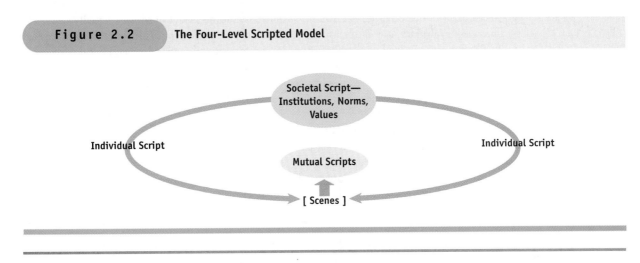

Figure 2.2   **The Four-Level Scripted Model**

Societal Script—
Institutions, Norms,
Values

Individual Script

Individual Script

Mutual Scripts

[Scenes]

Personal script: Expectations learned by socialization and shaped by an individual's unique experiences.

and bilateral, then virtually all members of society will personally believe that is the kind of marriage they should have. In more heterogeneous societies, where identification is problematic, there will be a wide variety of personal scripts.

Scenes

When two or more individuals interact, each actor begins with the assumptions in his or her personal script. This face-to-face interaction, called a **scene**, is the third level at which scripting occurs. The participants construct the scene themselves and they interact; old meanings are confirmed or challenged, and new meanings are formed. If the personal scripts of the actors are compatible, the scene will go smoothly. If not, one or both partners will have to

change their definitions of the situation or conflict might ensue; the interaction might even be terminated.

Mutual Scripts

If two or more persons meet, get along well, and continue their relationship, they will begin to develop expectations and understandings that apply only to their particular relationship. They will develop memories and meanings that others do not share, private jokes, and the ability to read each other in ways that less familiar persons cannot do. These couple-specific traits form the couple's unique **mutual script.** Symbolic interactionist paradigms, as well as theories developed in social psychology and psychology, are fruitfully applied to an understanding of personal scripts, scenes, and mutual scripts.

Summary and Conclusion

One view of sociology is as a science that assumes objectivity, replication of findings, testable statements, and precision of definition and measurement. Sociology can also be pictured as a humanistic study that prefers to focus on creating a humane society.

Sociology studies human groups, as do other social sciences such as history, anthropology, political science, and economics. Social sciences differ from natural sciences in that the social scientist is part of what is studied. An advantage of this difference is that social scientists have knowledge of their subject matter in ways that natural sciences cannot. This also has disadvantages, including use of anecdotal data and threatened objectivity.

Social scientists use a variety of methods in their work. Laboratory experiments have limited use in studying families, but they provide a model of controlled observations. Surveys can gather information from large representative groups. Field research allows for study in natural circumstances, and can be combined with in-depth interviews for richer information. Unobtrusive research occurs in such a way that it does not affect or alter the subject being studied. Program evaluation finds out whether attempts to improve some aspect of society actually work.

Theories are abstract ways of organizing information and guiding research. The two most historically common macrosociological perspectives are structure-functionalism and conflict theory. Feminist theory, with similarities to conflict theory, is a more recent large-scale perspective that can also be applied at the microsociological level. Sociocultural evolutionary theory includes elements of both functionalism and conflict theory; it will provide the framework for the next three chapters.

Symbolic interactionism incorporates a number of approaches at the microsociological level. Intermediate level perspectives include social-exchange theory, the developmental perspective, and systems theory. The scripting approach provides a framework for integrating macro- and micro-level theories.

In conclusion, the use of rigorous methods of investigation and the application of theories set social science apart from popular and everyday considerations of the family. Knowledge of

Scene: Interpersonal interaction among more than one individual.   **Mutual script:** Expectations developed from interaction between specific actors.

methods and theories helps evaluate information. The reader might want to refer back to this chapter when the concepts are applied later in the book.

> ***Rethinking in Context*** Consider your Thinking Forward answers. Would you change any of them now that you have read this chapter? Why or why not? Of conflict theory, functionalism, and symbolic interactionism, which provides a better explanation for gender-role differences?

Additional Resources

An overview of sociological theory

Collins, Randall. 1985. *Three Sociological Traditions.* New York: Oxford University Press.

An overview of theories in family study

Winton, Chester. 1995. *Frameworks for Studying Families.* Guilford, CT: Dushkin Publishing. Klein, David M., & James M. White. 1996. *Family Theories: An Introduction.* Thousand Oaks, CA: Sage.

A popular textbook with an overview of research methods

Babbie, Earl. 2001. *The Practice of Social Research,* 9th ed. Belmont, CA: Wadsworth.

Research methods from a feminist perspective

Reinharz, Shulamit. 1992. *Feminist Methods in Social Science Research.* New York: Oxford University Press.

Research methods from a qualitative, hermeneutic perspective

Michrina, Barry, & Cheryl Anne Richards. 1996. *Person to Person: Fieldwork, Dialogue, and the Hermeneutic Method.* Albany, NY: State University of New York Press.

Internet Sites

Family science
http://www.uky.edu/HumanEnvironmentalSciences/FamilyNetwork/fam.html

Feminist theory
http://csf.colorado.edu/gimenez/feminist.html

Marxist/conflict perspectives
http://www.tryoung.com/

E-texts in macrosociology and history
http://www.nsu.ru/filf/pha/arch/

Structure-functionalism (Merton)
http://www.thepoint.net/~usul/text/merton.html

Symbolic interactionism (Blumer)
http://www.thepoint.net/~usul/text/blumer.html

National Survey of Families and Households
http://www.ssc.wisc.edu/nsfh/home.htm

National Opinion Research Council (General Social Survey)
http://www.norc.uchicago.edu

"Dead Sociologists" Society (Major Theories)
http://raven.jmu.edu/~ridenelr/DSS/DEADSOC.HTML

For links to these sites and additional resources, visit the *Families in Context* Web site at:
http://sociology.wadsworth.com

Chapter 3

Families in Preindustrial Context

Prelude

One way of exercising your sociological imagination is to imagine what your life might be like in a different cultural context. Today, your extensive occupational choices include computer-related careers that would not have been options 50 years ago.

In China or Europe 500 years ago, you would probably have been working on land you did not own—with almost no chance of any other kind of life. In most of the world 5,000 years ago, you would have primarily been a hunter if you were male and a gatherer if you were female.

Your family life would have been as different as your occupational choices. Your chances of getting married, the number of spouses you might have, how many children you would probably have, and your chances of living long enough to see your grandchildren—these and other life experiences reflect the time and place in which you live.

Can your "freedom of choice" extend beyond the possibilities provided by your society?

The "how things used to be" material in this chapter illustrates the variety of family contexts that have existed through the course of human history. The "how today got to be the way it is" considers some of the roots of modern American families. The sociocultural evolutionary approach, introduced in chapter 2, provides the framework of the discussion. We see here how the economic, political, religious, and educational context affects families and therefore the intimate lives of people.

Thinking Ahead If you lived in a hunting-gathering society 15,000 years ago, what do you think your family would be like? How about the colonial North American family? What would your marital role structure be? How would the mate-selection process work? Would you prefer that life, or the one you have today? Why?

Overview of Preindustrial Societies

Written records provide information about many societies. Societies that existed without a written language, however, are more difficult to study. Much of what we know about hunting-gathering and early horticultural groups comes from ethnographies done by anthropologists on such groups that still existed in the 19th and 20th centuries. Hundreds of such studies were done by anthropologists such as Margaret Mead (See Finding Out 3.1). George Murdock (1949, 1957, 1967, 1969) and others compiled these studies, allowing for comparative analysis of different types of early societies. Results of the combined analysis provide much of the information for this chapter.

Life as a Hunter-Gatherer

The earliest human groups used hunting and gathering as their mode of production. A few such groups survived throughout much of the 20th century. By far the longest era for humans, then, has been hunting and gathering. If there are genetically inherited human characteristics, they developed primarily as adaptations to this period.

Reliance on foraging resulted in certain characteristics that were common to hunter-gatherers, including small group size, frequent migrations, and a relatively simple technological base. The median size of such groups was about 40 persons (Murdock, 1957). Seldom did the group include more than 50 persons. Most foragers lived and traveled in **nomadic** hunting-gathering groups. Murdock found that only 10% of these groups had a permanent settlement. The few groups with permanent or semipermanent settlements either supplemented their foraging with horticulture or relied heavily on fish and other aquatic life.

Forager technology resulted in relatively simple tools and other aspects of material culture. General-purpose tools, or those that could quickly be made from materials at hand, were preferable to having several specialized tools.

Small group size, nomadism, and simple technology are all related. The larger the group, the more quickly they would exhaust the food resources in a particular area, so the group would have to move more often. The group would have to be large enough, on the other hand, to provide cooperation and mutual protection. Simple technology is also compatible with nomadism. Everything these groups owned had to be carried with them. The all-purpose tool was much easier to carry than a host of specialized tools.

Another characteristic of hunting-gathering societies is the lack of division of labor compared to today's complex societies. They did not have one person who specialized in making arrowheads, another who specialized in building fires, and another who specialized in gathering a certain type of berry. About the only division of labor was by age and gender. All the men knew how to

---

Nomadic: Moving as a group from place to place in search of food, water, or grazing land.

3.1 | Finding Out

Margaret Mead, Ethnography, and Samoa

In 1925, as a 23-year-old graduate student, Margaret Mead undertook a study that launched her career as one of the most well-known anthropologists of all time. One controversy of her day was whether human behavior is more determined by biological, innate factors (nature) or by learned factors (nurture). To address that question, Mead resolved to study adolescence on the island of Samoa.

Mead and her mentor, Franz Boas, reasoned that if sufficient variation in certain cultural traits can be found, the importance of nurture, or cultural determinism, would be established. The specific issue Mead chose to study was female adolescence. In Western societies, adolescence was assumed to be an inherently difficult and stressful time in the developmental process. Reports from various South Pacific islands indicated that adolescence was not at all stressful in those cultures. Mead, using typical anthropological methods, wanted to find out.

Mead first spent about three months in a town that had both English and Samoan speakers, learning as much as she could about the language. She then moved to a more isolated area composed of three related villages with a population of about 600 Samoans. She accumulated background data such as who lived in each household, their approximate age, relationships within and between households, and relative status of each family. She diagramed kinship patterns and conducted various kinds of psychological inquiries.

The households she studied in depth contained 68 girls between the approximate ages of 6 and 20. These girls were studied extensively for the 6 months that Mead remained in the community. Nearly all discussions with the girls were conducted in Samoan, without use of an interpreter. Extensive field notes were taken; these notes were preserved so that other scholars could review them.

Mead published her results in 1928 in the book *Coming of Age in Samoa: A Psychological Study of Primitive Youth for Western Civilisation*. Mead concluded that the stress and strain of adolescence were culturally determined, since there was little sign of it on Samoa. Part of the reason, Mead concluded, was the freedom of sexual expression allowed Samoan adolescents. By her accounts, Samoan youth lived an idyllic life, free to play, talk, and have sex as their inclinations prompted. They assumed their adult roles after passing through adolescence with relative ease. For decades, Mead's portrayal of Samoa served as a major argument for the cultural determinist position.

In the 1980s, sociobiologist Derek Freeman (1983, 1989) challenged Mead's findings. Based on his own studies of Samoa, which spanned about 40 years and included interviews with some of the same women Mead had talked with, Freeman questioned both Mead's methods and her conclusions. Among the specific points raised by Freeman was the low incidence of premarital pregnancy among Samoan women, a factor not compatible with the sexual freedom claimed by Mead.

The nature-nurture argument is far from resolved in social science, and the Mead-Freeman debate continues to flare up from time to time. Grant (1995) recently attempted to resolve some of the difference of opinion. She pointed out that in the Samoan language, the most common word for engaging in sexual activity is the word literally translated "to play" (Scheper-Hughes, 1984; Ortner, 1981). Grant suggested that, while "having sex" to Westerners usually means sexual intercourse, to the Samoans the phrase applied to all kinds of sexual activity, including manual and oral stimulation and not necessarily including coitus. Thus, Samoans could "have sex" frequently, without penile-vaginal intercourse. This could explain the low rates of premarital pregnancy.

The debate between this supporter of Mead (Côté, 1998; Shankman, 1998) and Freeman (1999) continues, but Margaret Mead's studies set the agenda for decades of ethnographic research. They remain classics in the field of anthropology.

---

perform all tasks assigned to men; all the women knew how to do all tasks assigned to women.

Although there was not much division of labor within a gender, the division of labor between genders was usually fairly clearly defined. Figure 3.1 illustrates the male monopoly on hunting. The Agta people of the Philippines seem to be the rare exception of a group in which the women hunted in rough equality with men (Estioko-Griffin & Griffin, 1981), but this group was not included in Murdock's sample.

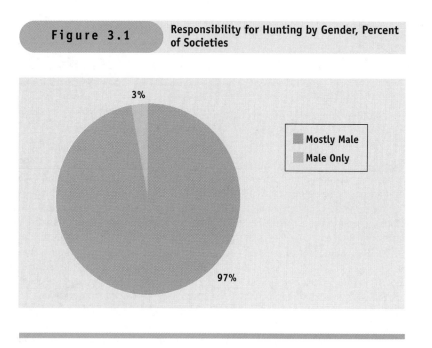

Figure 3.1 **Responsibility for Hunting by Gender, Percent of Societies**

3%

97%

Mostly Male
Male Only

Source: Data from Murdock's compilation, as summarized in Lenski, Gerhard, Patrick Nolan, and Jean Lenski. 1991. *Human Societies: An Introduction to Macrosociology*. New York: McGraw Hill.

Where fishing occurred, it was solely or predominately male work in 93% of societies. (Murdock, 1967). Gathering of fruits, nuts, and wild plants, as Figure 3.2 shows, was largely female labor.

The division of labor might not always be as clear-cut as Murdock's data appear. Men certainly did some gathering to support themselves on long hunts; women often provided small animals that were found in the process of gathering. Except in arctic regions, where hunting provided virtually all the food, gathering provided 60% to 80% of the food bulk (Lenski & Lenski, 1987).

In addition to their gathering responsibilities, women were the primary child-tenders. Both tasks were typically done communally, rather than in isolated households. Since more than a third of the population was 10 years of age or younger because of high death rates, child care was a time-consuming and important job (Quale, 1992).

In addition, women usually tended the shelter and did most of the cooking, processing, and food storage. Men manufactured the tools for hunting and warfare, while it was primarily women who produced the early crafts such as basketry, leatherwork and, where it existed, pottery. All of this occurred in the family or kinship unit and was a cooperative endeavor (Gough, 1992).

Children played at tasks considered appropriate to their gender. Older children were expected to assume considerable responsibility for young ones until, at a relatively young age, those who survived assumed adult status. Many, however, did not reach adulthood. In some foraging societies, the life expectancy at birth probably was less than 20 years (Quale, 1992). Many deaths were in infancy and youth; only about half the children born would reach age 15. Foragers in more hospitable regions of the world had life expectancies at birth as high, perhaps, as 35 years. At this rate, half the children born could reach age 20 (Quale, 1992:4).

Hunting-gathering groups lived at subsistence level. Because of the difficulty of preserving foods, they did not have long-range food supplies available. Meat, particularly, can rot quickly, especially in hot climates. Hunter-gatherers would get just enough food for a day or two. This could take several hours or be accomplished quickly. McCarthy and McArthur (1960) studied the amount of time spent gathering food in two groups of Australian aboriginals. Although time spent on food-related tasks varied considerably from day to day, the average was from just under 4 to a little over 5 hours daily for men and women. While hunter-gatherers did not exactly live in

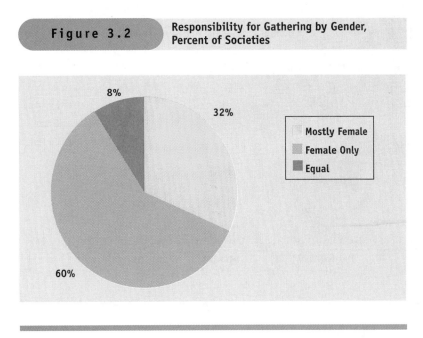

Figure 3.2

Responsibility for Gathering by Gender, Percent of Societies

Legend:
- Mostly Female
- Female Only
- Equal

8%
32%
60%

Source: Data from Murdock's compilation, as summarized in Lenski, Gerhard, Patrick Nolan, and Jean Lenski. 1991. *Human Societies: An Introduction to Macrosociology*. New York: McGraw Hill.

the lap of luxury, most were not constantly working to get enough to eat.

Transition to Agrarian Societies

Simple horticultural societies emerged in various parts of the world in about 7000 BC. At first they probably got most of their food from hunting and gathering, but growing their own food became an increasingly important source of nutrition. They generally raised crops that were like potatoes, using a pointed stick to create holes into which the seeds or cuttings would be planted. Often they would burn down a new section of land for their crops, allowing the old field to return to its original state.

Advanced horticultural groups arose about 4000 BC, adding metallurgy to the technological base. The ability to work with metals made production more efficient, but was particularly useful in decoration and in making weapons.

About 3000 BC, simple agrarian societies appeared. These groups introduced plow agriculture, and most used animals to pull the plow. Advanced agrarian societies, about 1000 BC in parts of the world, added the use of iron. This produced much superior plows, weapons, and other tools.

A number of social changes occurred when people began to grow their own food. These changes were made possible by the increased productivity of horticulture and agriculture. Rather than being nomadic, horticulturists became **sedentary**, developing permanent settlements. Communities grew larger than the 40 or so members of hunter-gatherer groups. Simple horticultural societies had a median size of 95. Advanced horticultural societies averaged 5,850 members, and agrarian ones grew to over 100,000 (Murdock, 1957, in Lenski & Lenski, 1987).

Work patterns changed as societies became increasingly agricultural. Rather than the few hours per day, work took many more hours, especially during planting and harvesting seasons. This contributed to a surplus of food, which had to be stored and preserved for use between harvests. The surplus of food made it possible for some persons to develop occupational specialties that were not directly related to food production.

Sedentary: Remaining in one place; not migratory.

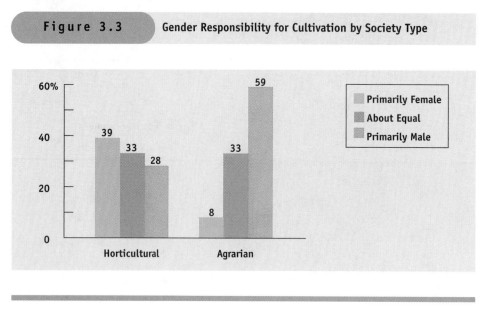

Figure 3.3 Gender Responsibility for Cultivation by Society Type

Source: Lenski, Nolan, and Lenski (1995:149)

Craftspersons specialized in producing tools, pottery, clothes, and other goods. Others specialized in teaching, religion, and the arts.

In early horticultural societies, men were involved in the heavier work of clearing the land, but women did most of the planting, child care, and harvesting. Men's role in cultivation increased in advanced horticultural groups and again in agrarian ones. Use of heavier equipment and draft animals, which men were better able to handle, contributed to this change (see Figure 3.3).

Preindustrial Institutions

In hunting-gathering societies, all important activities were related to the nuclear family, kin group, or larger group of relatives called a **clan.** As societies became more complex, specialized institutions developed to perform the major social functions. Increasingly the religious functions move from the family to specialists; the social power rests outside most families; and eventually the education institution developed socialization. Functionalists see this process of increasing institutional specialization as resulting in a long-term decrease in the social importance of the family.

The Political Institution

The small foraging groups were usually independent and autonomous. There was no level of government above the kin group. Even within the kin group, there was not usually a strong central leader. Decisions tended to be made by the elders, usually men, who would discuss an issue until they arrived at a consensus.

Murdock's sample (in Lenski & Lenski, 1988:116) found that 88% of hunting-gathering groups did have a headman, and in about half the cases it was a hereditary position. In fewer than 10% of the cases, however, did the headman have substantial power. The headman often had only ceremonial power; he might determine whose turn it was to talk by passing around a "talking stick." Even a headman had authority only as long as he could persuade others that he was right.

In advanced horticultural societies, larger villages and groups of villages were united under leaders who were able to appropriate enough of the surplus food and other wealth. They were able to hire advisers, accountants, and warriors who were not related to them, expanding their power beyond their own clan (Mair, 1962). Leadership typically became hereditary; arranged marriages among members of neighboring ruling families were used to form alliances and stabilize governments.

Clan: A group of kin who believe themselves related to a common, sometimes mythological, ancestor.

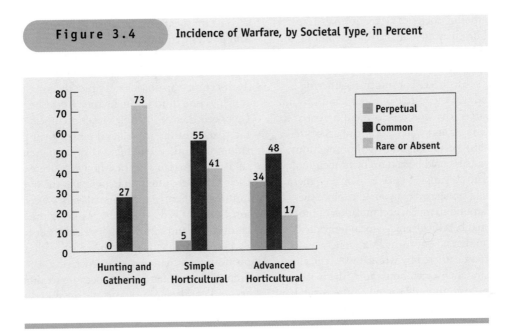

Figure 3.4 Incidence of Warfare, by Societal Type, in Percent

Source: Lenski, Nolan, and Lenski, 1995:152

The plow and other technology greatly increased productivity of the society and along with it the power of the rulers. Some societies became productive enough that they could have a year-around, standing army. Maintaining such an army, and keeping it under control, required a powerful central government that could raise taxes and keep the support of the citizenry, either by force or ideology.

Warfare consists of hostility between different organized coups. Such organization is found in the political institution. Although religion is often involved, warfare can be seen primarily as an extension of the political institution.

Warfare was not as common in hunting-gathering as in later horticultural and agrarian societies. Sparsely populated nomadic groups had less reason to fight than did groups with developed land and homes. Leavitt (1977) found no hunting-gathering societies in which warfare was perpetual, but 34% of advanced horticultural societies experienced constant warfare (see Figure 3.4). Warfare among hunting-gathering groups usually consisted of raiding or feuding, rather than wars of conquest.

Even when warfare is a remote possibility, however, societies take it into account, sometimes by honoring warlike characteristics of potential soldiers. Men were always the warriors. Women fought to protect themselves and their children, but legends of the Amazons aside, there is no good evidence of a society that relied upon women as a first line of defense (Blumberg, 1984). Where warfare was common, role expectations of men and women have traditionally been quite different. Family socialization, at least of boys, is directed toward the goal of preparing soldiers. In agrarian societies, that often resulted in a parental regime of strict discipline of the type required in military operations.

The Social Stratification System

All modern societies are characterized by some degree of **social stratification,** which provides the unequal distribution of whatever is valuable. The stratification system is reflected in the family, religious, political, and economic institutions. Individuals at different levels of the stratification system have different **life chances.** Persons at the bottom of the hierarchy have less chance of getting the desirable food, clothing, housing, and respect that those higher in the system get.

Social stratification: The hierarchical ranking of individuals on the basis of wealth, power, or prestige.   **Life chances:** The probability a person has of sharing in the economic and cultural goods of a society.

Hunting-gathering societies lacked formal stratification systems. Life chances were distributed among the members in roughly equal fashion. One reason for this is that particular individuals or groups did not own the source of their subsistence. For hunting-gathering groups, the land was the source of food. Land was not divided into parcels that could be owned; it existed for everyone, like the air and water. All members of the group had equal access to the means of production.

While individuals could be said to "own" their tools, the devices were relatively simple to make, so owning them gave no one an advantage over anyone else. Since the groups moved around so much, accumulation of property of any kind would be a disadvantage to an individual. People were equal in that no one owned very much.

While the food gathered by women was typically consumed separately by each household, the meat from hunting was more commonly shared by the entire band. There was cooperation in the process of hunting, so the results were shared. No single hunter could kill the necessary game every day. Successful hunters shared the kill in a reciprocal arrangement whereby the other hunters shared their game when they were successful. All individuals were therefore more likely to survive, and all were roughly equal in their access to food (McCarthy & McArthur, 1960).

The custom of sharing might have had long-term influence on humans. Even in today's societies, members of small groups such as families are more likely to share with one another, even at some sacrifice to themselves, than they are to share with strangers. There are limits to the size of a group within which members will extend this special care and concern. The maximum size of these "sympathy groups" is roughly the same as the average size of hunting-gathering groups. This has lead some social-psychologists to the conclusion that sympathy group size is genetically limited in the human species, a result of the tens of thousands of years that humans and their ancestors were organized in foraging groups (Buys, 1992).

Over time, the concept of shared group territory gave way to group ownership and then to family or individual ownership. In general, the more developed the agrarian system, the more rigid was the concept of land ownership, and the more rigid was the system of stratification (Lenski & Lenski, 1987).

The most extreme differences between the wealthiest and poorest families probably occurred in the advanced agrarian societies just prior to industrialization. The ruling family of a large state was in a class by itself. In early 16th-century Spain, for example, the king received as much as one third of the income of the entire country (Lenski & Lenski, 1987). Other members of the aristocracy were wealthy as well and passed their privileged positions on to their children. Most families in horticultural and agrarian societies, however, were quite poor; their lives were often no better than the lives of their hunting-gathering ancestors. Slavery was common; most others lived as peasants, working the land for the landowners and receiving a bare subsistence in return.

Horticultural and agrarian societies allowed little opportunity for change in one's social-class position. Children of wealthy landowners became wealthy landowners, and children of peasants nearly always ended up as peasants themselves. Peasant family life was often quite different from family life among the nobility.

Religion

Religion in some form is found in virtually all societies. Because of their capacity to communicate and think using symbols, humans can ask questions about the world around them and about the meaning of life and death. A major function of religion has always been to answer such questions.

At least as long ago as 100,000 years, some hominid groups buried their dead with a stock of food and other supplies. This implies belief in an afterlife, which is a nearly universal characteristic of religion (Parrinder, 1984).

Animism was a common belief among foragers; rocks, trees, waterfalls, flowers, lightning, and other phenomena were believed to have a spirit. **Totemism,** another common feature of foraging religions, held that some object became sacred because it represented a relationship that was revered. Ancestral totems provided a link between an individual and his or her clan because the totem represented the common ancestor from which the group believed itself to have originated. Totemic religious practices were functional because they emphasized the sense of "we-ness" or shared meaning of the clan. Again, the religious practice is closely related to the family institution because it gives a religious explanation for the origin of the clan (Parrinder, 1984).

Animism: The belief that spirits can reside in all aspects of nature (Latin *anima,* soul). **Totem:** Symbolic representation that links individuals or groups with human ancestors, plants, animals, or other natural phenomena.

Religious leaders were historically among the first to develop nonfamily roles. This more modern Ndebele shaman divines the setting sun. He also "throws the bones" to determine the future.

Stories that explain the origin of the clan are a kind of **myth** common to all religions. Creation myths are told about the origin of plants and animals, the origin of humans, and the origin of the cosmos. These myths, which have thousands of variations in human groups, provide explanations for physical events and a common set of meanings for the group that holds to a certain myth.

A particular group's spirits were often so numerous that not all could be named. Some spirits got special names, however, because they represented animals, weather conditions, or other phenomena that were important to a group.

Important spirits sometimes were promoted to god or goddess. Foraging societies that had such beliefs tended to name many spirits rather than just one, which made them **polytheistic.** Most languages have proper names that are gender-specific, so naming a spirit would also give it a gender. Whether a spirit became a god or a goddess depended on how it reflected the division of labor in the society. Those that represented the hunt, war, and the sun usually became gods; those that represented fertility, birth and growth, love, and sexuality tended to become goddesses (Campbell, 1949).

Animism, totemism, polytheism, and other religious practices reflect the political, stratification, and family systems of hunting-gathering societies. Animism and polytheism are relatively egalitarian practices. Power was dispersed throughout the family and clan, as it was throughout the spirit world. There was a division of labor among gods and goddesses just as among the people. Totemism reflected the importance given to nature and to the clan and kin group.

In most groups, anyone could interact with the spirits through dreams, drug-induced hallucinations, or visions. Some groups developed a specialist, called a **shaman,** for this purpose. The shaman in foraging societies, usually a man, was not typically a full-time specialist, but was still part of the family group and was not excused from economically productive activities. As the shaman increasingly relied on others to provide food and sustenance, the first social differentiation occurred. The religious institution was separating from the family group (Lenski & Lenski, 1987).

Both the political and religious institutions demanded part of the surplus agricultural products. The religious institution relied on the political one for grants of land and other privileges; the political institution relied on the religious one for justification of its authority. Religious beliefs either treated the ruler as a god or assumed the god chose the ruler.

Religious belief systems, as well as religious structures, changed as modes of production changed. In

---

Myth: A sacred tale expressing the unobservable realities of religious belief in terms of observable phenomena. **Polytheism:** The belief in many gods. **Shaman:** A person who acts as a medium between the visible world and the invisible world of the spirits.

simple horticultural groups, as in hunting-gathering ones, animism, totemism, and polytheism were common. Since kin groups often included the dead, ancestor worship reached its peak in horticultural societies. The majority of hunting-gathering and simple horticultural religions lacked a notion of a supreme creator; only 2% of each believed in a supreme creator who was active and supported human morality. In agrarian societies, however, such a supreme creator was worshiped in 67% of societies (Lenski & Lenski, 1987).

Advanced agrarian times saw the growth of three major religions that claimed to be a **universal faith:** Buddhism, Christianity, and Islam. These religions spread to many parts of the world. As believers conquered nonbelievers, the political conquests were seen as religious conquests as well, and the spread of religion was often used as a justification for conquest. Missionaries and warriors carried both religion and culture with them. Normative family structures of Native Americans, among others, changed under Christian influences.

Another important change was the development of **monotheism** in such major religions as Judaism, Christianity, and Islam. Just as societies came to be ruled by monarchs (rule by one), their religions became monotheistic. All major monotheistic gods are referred to as males, which reflected the increased power of men in the societies in which the religions developed. Goddesses disappeared, as women had few positions of formal authority in the religious organization. God was referred to as "king," which reflected the male political authority, or as "father," which reflected the authority of the man in the family (Parrinder, 1984).

Since pronatalist attitudes were functional to the society, they were incorporated into religious beliefs. All successful world religions include such instructions as "Be fruitful and multiply," which is found in the Jews' Torah, the Christians' Bible, and Muslim's Quran. This command was functional for the religion as well, since high birthrates meant more followers in the next generation (Parrinder, 1984). Only with the development of industrial nations such as the United States did pronatalist values weaken.

Education and Socialization

While the mothers and fathers were the primary socializers of children, responsibility was widely spread among the adults. Hunters and gatherers had no formal educational institution. Children learned "job skills" by observation and playing games. In postindustrial societies, assuming adult roles is a slow and often painful process. For hunter-gatherers, the line between childhood and adulthood was often marked by one or more rites of passage that occurred around the time of puberty.

Socialization was family-kin controlled; children rarely came into contact with anyone other than kin. Children would identify, then, with adult kin. Among peoples whose religion included ancestor worship, identification would sometimes be with idealized kin who existed in mythological form.

In horticultural and early agrarian societies, most persons continued to learn what they needed to know from their kin groups. A few, however, began to be apprenticed for purposes of learning occupational skills, and a few even had something like a formal education. This process was accelerated by the development of writing.

For centuries in Europe, writing was kept alive primarily by scribes loyal to the kings, by religious orders, and by a few literate members of nobility. For these few, teachers were generally hired by the wealthy to teach children in their own homes, but in some areas separate locations were established for schools. Although some industrialization was occurring when schools were established in the United States, the educational system had its roots in an advanced agricultural system. The 9-month school year is a remnant of that; the labor of children was needed on most farms during the summer, when labor was most in demand.

Whether taught in schools or by parents, the values taught to children changed. Agrarian societies stressed greater compliance, as discipline became more important to society as a whole (Barry, Child, & Bacon, 1959). The military required that soldiers obey their leaders; increased social stratification required that those lower in the system obey those who were more privileged; increasingly patriarchal families required that wives defer more often to their husbands; religious obedience to an all-powerful single god was required; and it was expected that children obey their parents.

Horticultural and agrarian societies were not as child-centered as today's industrial societies, partly because of the high mortality rate. Emotional and material investment in infants who were likely to die

---

was dysfunctional psychologically and socially. On the other hand, children were valuable for their labor at relatively young ages. Adult children provided support for their elderly relatives. Given the high death rates, it was functional to have, and try to care for, large numbers of children.

Sexuality

As is true in all societies, sexuality serves several purposes in hunting-gathering groups. In all ongoing societies, sexual activity serves the purposes of reproduction and pleasure. In some, sexual activities also take on religious, political, or economic functions.

Reproduction. Understanding the reproductive function of sexuality is a major concern of **demography.** For thousands of years, human populations grew slowly and unevenly. Human populations on earth did not reach 1 million persons until less than 10,000 years ago (Hassan, 1973). Many groups died out because of disease, starvation, and war. Others probably died out because they overpopulated and used up their food supplies. Groups that survived did so because they reached balanced population levels; this occurred in several ways.

Forms of birth control, usually employed by women, existed in virtually all societies (Tannahill, 1980; Freed & Freed, 1993). Although information about abortion is difficult to find in the anthropological literature, all indications are that it was widespread. Whiting (1964) found its use in 13 of the 15 cultures he studied, although the frequency with which it occurred in those societies is not known.

Infanticide was also widespread. Davale (1972) found at least occasional use of infanticide in 80 of the 86 societies studied. Daly and Wilson (1984) found infanticide in 39 out of 60 randomly selected societies. In the eyes of the adult members of society, however, these were not necessarily horrible crimes. Sometimes infants were not considered humans until they were named a year or more after birth.

Nonreproductive Sexual Functions. While reproduction is the primary or sole purpose of sexuality in

other animals, such is not the case for humans. As Reiss (1986:31) put it, "sexuality would be universally viewed as important even if storks brought babies." Pleasure is associated with sexuality in all societies, although all societies place normative limitations on the pursuit of sexual pleasure.

Marriage is a universally approved sexual union. Societies that limit sexual expression solely to marriage, however, are relatively rare. Murdock's 1949 sample of societies included 115 in which sufficient sexual information was available; of these, only 3 enforced taboos on all nonmarital sex. While acceptance of premarital sexual intercourse is common, most societies condemn extramarital sex, or adultery. Of Murdock's sample, only 3 had a generalized acceptance of adultery. In addition, several others allowed it under certain conditions. Among the traditional North Alaskan Eskimo, for example, a form of institutionalized "wife swapping" existed (Burch, 1982).

Among some other groups, the normal rules against adultery are relaxed for special occasions such as weddings, funerals, festivals, or religious ceremonies. Kehoe (1993) found such a practice among the Mandan-Hidatsa, Algonkians, Arapaho and other northern North American plains tribes. An older, more powerful man would have ritual sexual intercourse with the wife of a younger man; the woman was the symbolic conduit of power from the older man to her husband.

The sexual mores and behaviors of some groups make little sense until they are put into the context of the family, kin, religious, and other systems of the society in which they occur. Herdt (1993) reported one such case. The Sambian Melanesian society invested bodily fluids, including blood and mother's milk, with symbolic importance. Semen was especially exalted. Sambian boys moved from their family of orientation into bachelor houses prior to puberty. It was believed that they could reach puberty only if they ingested the semen of older adolescents by performing oral sex. All Sambian boys went through this stage. As they got older and more developed, they became the ones upon whom the oral sex was performed. Thus the power was passed down from one age group to another.

When they got married, usually to relatively young girls, the men would pass on their power to their

---

Demography: The study of the characteristics of populations, including birthrates, death rates, growth, and vital statistics. **Demographics** are characteristics of human populations. **Infanticide:** The killing of infants, usually as a population control mechanism.

wives, who performed oral sex on their husbands. This helped the girls, Sambians believed, develop their fullness of breast and prepare for motherhood. After menarche, penile-vaginal sexual intercourse was substituted for fellatio.

While all Sambian males went through a homosexual phase, many other societies either allowed homosexual practices or institutionalized them in some way. Although it is more properly understood as a cross-gender phenomenon than as a sexual one, Callender and Kochems (1993) found the **berdache** in 113 separate North American cultures.

A berdache was often respected and even revered. Some cultures also had female berdaches, who dressed as men, hunted, and did the other tasks associated with men. While berdaches did engage in homosexual activity, it was never with other berdaches but with partners who otherwise led heterosexual lives. Male berdaches assumed the "passive" role in sexual activity, performing oral sex and being penetrated in anal sex.

In some societies, male and female berdaches were allowed to have long-term relations and even to marry, although they were not allowed to assume primary social mother or father roles. There is some evidence that their marriages were typically to partners who already had other spouses or to spouses who had not otherwise been successful with marriage. While the berdaches do not usually suffer negative sanctions, their marital partners often were victims of scorn (Callender & Kochems, 1993).

Contrary to the Western idea that there are only two genders, the berdache has been interpreted as representing a third and fourth gender. Since berdaches could not perform the sex-irreducible roles of the opposite sex, Callender and Kochems (1993) referred to them as mixed gender, rather than cross-gender, individuals.

Kinship Systems and Families

In hunting-gathering societies, the kin group performed all economic, political, and religious functions. Kin groups could include dozens of relatives; individuals were likely to be able to define their kinship relationship to almost every person with whom they ever interacted (Radcliff-Brown, 1930). In fact, they would be suspicious of someone with whom a kinship term could not be applied.

The kinship name by which persons call each other determines their role relationship and helps define how they should behave toward each other. You behave differently with someone you call "grandma" than with someone you call "brother" because the kinship relations are different.

Not all societies define kinship in the same way. Each has its own **kinship system** that determines the kinship names persons call each other. The traditional Oglala Sioux system illustrates the point that kinship systems of hunting-gathering groups can vary widely compared with modern European ones. Figure 3.5 illustrates the Oglala system from the point of view of a female. All relationship names are given in reference to a female Ego, which means "self." You can put yourself in the place occupied by Ego and determine what you would call each of your relatives. Oglala Sioux words are used rather than English ones because there are no exact translations. These terms illustrate a different kinship system than most of today's Americans are familiar with.

Several things are notable about the Oglala kinship system. One characteristic is the blending of what English-speaking peoples would call mothers and aunts, or fathers and uncles. Whether Ego is male or female, the term Ina applies to both his or her mother and his or her mother's sisters. Symmetrically, Ego's father and his brothers are all called Ate.

The Oglala system reflects the fact that both age and gender are important, constituting the two ways by which division of labor is assigned. One's brothers and sisters have different terms depending on whether they are older or younger. For example, female Ego's older sister is Chuwe, while her younger sister is Tanke.

The sister and brother terms are not limited to what English speakers call siblings. They also apply to mother's sister's children and, although it is not reflected on the diagram, to father's brother's children. One type of what we would consider cousins, then, would be brothers and sisters to the Oglala. These are what are called **parallel cousins.** Their parent and Ego's parent, who are siblings, are the same sex.

Berdache: "A person, usually male, who was anatomically normal but assumed the dress, occupations, and behavior of the other sex to effect a change in gender status" (Callender & Kochems, 1993:367).   **Kinship system:** The way in which a society defines the relationships of those who are inter-related by blood, marriage, or adoption.   **Parallel cousins:** One's mother's sister's or father's brother's children.

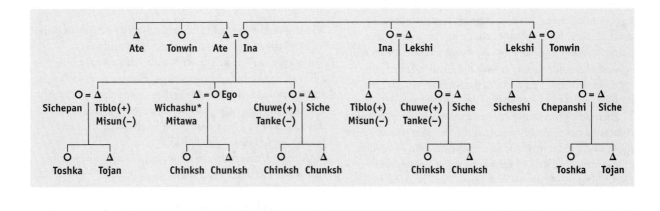

| Figure 3.5 | Traditional Oglala Kinship Terminology—Female Ego |

EGO is the person to whom all other relationships refer. The (+) symbol refers to the older brother or sister of Ego; the (−) refers to Ego's younger sibling.

*There is no generic word for "husband," without reference to whose husband. This word means "my husband."

Source: Maynard, Eileen, and Gayla Twiss. 1969 *Hechel Lena Oyate Kin Nipi Kte—That These People May Live*. Indian Health Service, U.S. Public Health Service. Pine Ridge, South Dakota

If a cousin's parent and Ego's parent are of opposite sex, that cousin is Ego's **cross cousin**. For a female Oglala, these are called Sicheshi and Siche. For the male, they are Hankashi and Tanhan. The English term "cousin" lumps together all these possible relationships: Tiblo, Misun, Chuwe, Tanke (female's younger female parallel cousin), Sicheshi, Chepanshi, Chiye, Misun, Tanke (male's older female cross cousin), Tankshi, Tahanshi, and Hankashi.

Matters are a bit simpler in the generation younger than Ego. Sons and daughters are Chinksh and Chunksh, respectively, for either male or female Ego. Those terms are not limited, however, to Ego's own biological children. Sons and daughters of parallel cousins are also Chinksh and Chunksh, as are sons and daughters of Ego's same-sex sibling. Sons and daughters both of Ego's opposite-sex sibling and of cross cousins, however, are Toshka and Tohan. In English these would be niece and nephew or second cousins, respectively.

One consequence of varied kinship systems is that the incest taboo does not mean the same thing in all societies. The Oglala incest taboo forbids marriage among parallel cousins; after all, they are referred to as brothers

and sisters. Marriage between cross cousins, however, is encouraged.

As a general rule, the closer the kinship relationship is, the more cooperation, sharing, and mutual assistance is expected. Having several close relationships like mother, father, brother, and sister increases an individual's chances of getting help when it is necessary, as when a parent dies. Most kinship systems of foragers provided this "social security" network in which virtually all adults shared responsibility for all children.

The kin group remained important in the long change from horticultural to advanced agrarian societies. It remained the major socializing agent, and production and consumption of material goods were still centered in the family. The economic importance of the family unit is reflected in the rates of economic transfers that occurred at marriage. Whether the transaction included bride wealth, dowry, or some other form, there was an economic transfer in 49% of hunting-gathering marriages. This figure went to 61% in simple horticultural and 97% in advanced horticultural societies (Murdock, 1967).

While the majority of horticultural societies were either bilateral or patrilineal, more were matrilineal than was the

Cross cousins: One's mother's brother's or father's sister's children.

case for any other mode of production. Locality follows the same trends as lineality. In most cases, matrilineal descent was accompanied by matrilocal residence (Martin & Voorhies, 1975). Where women stayed in an area to work the land and traced descent through female lines, they brought their husbands into the group upon marriage. The Navajo were such a group, where a household might consist of an older women with her husband, their unmarried children, and a married daughter with her husband (Queen & Habenstein, 1967; in Nielson, 1990). Higher rates of matrilineality and matrilocality in horticultural societies probably reflected the fact that women were more likely to be involved in cultivation than were men.

Although agrarian families were still concerned about alliances with other groups, they became increasing concerned with inheritance of property and position, primarily along male lines. Nearly all agrarian societies, then, were both patrilineal and patrilocal (Quale, 1988). Newly married couples moved in with the groom's family, making patrilocal residence much more common than either matrilocal or neolocal patterns. Because of high mortality rates and other factors, however, the extended family household was less common in practice than in ideal (Laslett, 1972).

In agrarian families, parents had considerable control over their children. The child's future depended almost entirely on the status of the parents, who controlled inheritance, occupation, and mate selection. Individuals had little place to go in the society if they had no family base.

In hunting-gathering and early horticultural societies, marriage and family life was regulated by informal norms. With writing and the development of more formal government and religion, family life gradually became regulated. Marriages were registered and legitimated by the government, the church, or both. Although the regulations limited what people could do, they also provided protection from other people and made large-scale society possible.

Family Formation

A wide variety of marriage forms can be found in preindustrial societies. Diversity is found both in numbers of partners in a marital unit and in the process of mate selection.

Number of Partners

Monogamy is the sole allowable marriage form in only 12% of the societies summarized by Murdock. **Polygamy,** any marriage with more than two spouses, is allowed in the remaining groups. **Polygyny** is by far the most common preferred marriage form. Even when the social preference is polygyny, however, the majority of marriages at any given time are likely to be monogamous (Welch & Glick, 1981).

Almost universally, in all types of marriage systems, husbands are older than their wives (Quale, 1988:22). Perhaps this is because it takes men longer to acquire the skills and material goods necessary to perform their expected provider/protector role than it takes women to prepare to perform their child-bearing/child-care/provider role.

Given a relatively high death rate among both men and women, and the expectation that older men marry younger women, there will be fewer males of eligible marriage age than there will be of females at eligible marriage age. This makes polygyny more demographically workable. Further, a man will generally marry just one woman at first. Only later will he add second or subsequent wives. For some period of time, then, his will be a monogamous marriage before it becomes polygynous.

It sometimes turns out that, even in a society that prescribes polygyny, the women will have more husbands over a lifetime than men will have wives. Since women marry at a younger age, especially if they are the second or third wives, they will in all likelihood outlive their husbands. They then remarry and might do so several times (Quale, 1988).

Polyandry is quite rare. While Murdock found polygyny in 77% of his 415 societies, he found polyandry in only four. The Nayar system, which Murdock counted as polyandrous, might as easily be called group marriage or polygyny (Gough, 1960; see chapter 1). The other logically possible type of polygamy, **group marriage,** is not found except as a subculture within a larger society.

Monogamy: Marriage with one husband and one wife. Gr. *mono* (one) and *gamy* (marriage).   **Polygamy:** Any marriage with more than two partners. Gr. *poly* (many) and *gamy* (marriage).   **Polygyny:** A marriage with one husband and more than one wife. Gr. *poly* (many) and *gyny* (woman).   **Polyandry:** A marriage involving one wife and more than one husband   **Group marriage:** A marriage involving more than one husband and more than one wife.

Polygyny, practiced in many earlier societies, remains common in much of the world. This contemporary Islamic man has four wives.

Mate Selection

All societies have norms that regulate marriage choice. Some, such as the incest taboo, are **proscriptive norms,** which specify whom one cannot marry. Others, such as preference for marriage to a cross cousin, are called **prescriptive norms.**

In hunting-gathering societies, mate selection is regulated both by individuals in the kin group and by proscriptive and prescriptive norms. There is, however, some measure of individual choice, especially in cases of remarriage.

Family/kin control of mate selection increased in horticultural and agrarian societies. Property-owning families used marriage to form alliances and maintain extended family ownership. Because the family controlled the economic positions of offspring, it could control mate selection of its children. Rules that govern mate selection often serve a purpose for the society. Exogamy, for example, is functional at both the genetic and cultural levels. Requiring marriage from outside a small, interrelated group provides diversity in the genetic pool. The cultural advantage is more likely to have

been understood by hunting-gathering groups. Exogamy creates connections and alliances among various kinship groups, which increases the probability of cooperation and decreases the probability of war.

The European Family

Characteristics of modern American families had many historical roots. One of the most important, ancient Rome (around 500 BC to AD 500), influenced European and English language, customs, and traditions. The influence of Christianity, as it spread throught Europe and the Americas, remains clearly in evidence.

The Roman Family

Rather than referring to kinship, the Latin term **familia** originally referred to the groups of servants and slaves in a household and came to mean everyone in the household whether related or not. There was no Latin term for the unit that included only the husband, wife, and their children who lived together. In fact, no such terms

---

Proscriptive norms: Expectations about what *should not* be done.   **Prescriptive norms:** Expectations about what *should* be done.   **Familia:** Latin word for the group of slaves and servants in the household; came to refer to the household as a whole.

This Roman funerary relief with a scene of a funeral banquet dates from the 2nd century BC in Plovdiv.

existed in any European language before the 18th century (Gies & Gies, 1987).

The term *family* as applied to Rome is best thought of as a "house" or "household" rather than a group of specifically related persons. A *familia* could include various levels in the stratification system. The **patricians** were the landowners and were considered the truest members of the **gens;** it was their ancestors who were worshiped. Freed persons might also be included in the familia, most commonly serving as craftspersons or other skilled assistants. Slaves comprised the lowest stratification level in the *familia.*

The *familia* was the basic unit of production. Essentially all persons on a farm or plantation would be members of a single *familia.* In the cities, the *familia* might include a merchant or skilled craftsman, his wife and children, servants, and slaves all living and working under one roof.

High mortality rates prevented the widespread establishment of multiple-generation extended families. Of those Romans who lived to age 20, only 41% were likely still to have a living father. At birth, only 10% had a living grandfather on their father's side; only 1 in 50 teenagers had a living paternal grandfather (Saller, 1987).

Divorce rates, like death rates, were fairly high in Rome, and in both cases remarriage rates approached 100% (Bradley, 1991). Considerable numbers of familial units would therefore include stepchildren, stepbrothers and sisters, second and third wives or husbands, and men and women of various classes. The oldest male of the patrician class would serve as the ***pater familias,*** who had considerable power. He decided who could become and remain a member of the *familia;* this included life or death power over infants of all classes in the *familia.* He had 10 days after the birth to determine whether the infant should be kept. If not, it would be set outdoors to die of exposure.

In terms of life chances, women had more in common with men of the same social class than they did with women of a different class. Patrician women could not hold office as could their fathers, husbands, and sons, but they had considerable influence over others in their *familias.* Women were especially active in such matters as arranging marriages and apprenticeships. They were also entitled to equal inheritance with their brothers; the difference was that women took their share of the inheritance into their marriages in the form of dowries (Dixon, 1992).

In the earliest days of the republic, marriage was accompanied by bridewealth, paid by the groom's *familia* to the bride's *familia.* This later dwindled to a mere token payment and was replaced by a dowry, the portion of wealth a bride kept from her family of origin. A different form of payment developed by the third century of the empire. Called the **donatio,** this payment to the bride from the groom's *familia* grew so large that it constituted a major barrier to marriage for some young men whose families could not afford it. (Gies & Gies, 1987).

There was a sexual double standard in Rome, as in most agrarian societies. Virginity at marriage was not a particularly strong value, but adultery was punished more severely for wives than for husbands. Male patricians were relatively free to take sexual advantage of both male and female slaves, but female patricians faced severe punishments for doing so (Gies & Gies, 1987).

Men were allowed to have **concubines,** who were informal wives. They could not, as in some cultures, have both a wife and concubines. Roman marriages were generally for the purpose of having children, for

---

Patrician: member of the Roman aristocracy; the ruling class from which Senators came.   **Gens:** Roman clan; group of persons of both *gen*ders who believe themselves to share a common *gen*esis for many *gen*erations, and who treat each other *gen*tly.
Paterfamilias: The male head of household.   **Donatio:** A payment at marriage from the groom's *familia* to the bride.
Concubine: A women who cohabits with a man; a live-in mistress.

consolidating alliances between the groom's *gens* and the bride's *gens,* and for other practical reasons. Although they required agreement by the couple, marriages were arranged to serve the best interests of each *familia*. Negotiations about marriage partners were extremely important business operations.

Romantic love was not typically a feature of Roman marriages. A good relationship did strive, however, for *concordia*. This refers more to a state of tranquility than passionate love; it meant that the couple got along without major disagreements or arguments (Bradley, 1991).

Christian Influence

What was later to become the Christian religion took root in Jewish colonies that had spread throughout the Mediterranean area. First treated by the Romans as just another bothersome cult, its influence was significantly increased when, in 380, it became the official religion of the Roman Empire. Even though the empire was disintegrating, it still helped Christianity establish a foothold throughout Europe and the Mediterranean.

In many cases, Christian doctrines coincided with Roman ones. Gradually, Christianity had five major effects on the European and American family systems: marriage became a sacrament; monogamy became prescriptive; divorce was banned; repressive sexual scripts evolved; and contraception, abortion, and infanticide were banned.

Marriage as Sacrament. The Catholic Church gained considerable control over the marriage and family institution when it declared marriage to be a sacrament. Marriage became a sacred event, defined by rituals prescribed by the church. This gave the church tremendous power over what had previously been the business only of the families of the bride and groom. While the Roman Empire saw some control over family matters by the central government, there was little control by religious authorities. Now the church had authority to decide who was and was not qualified to participate in the sacrament of marriage. Even church officials did not immediately accept the idea that the church should have authority over marriages. The first church weddings were not performed until the fourth century (Herlihy, 1985). In the 14th century, as many as four fifths of weddings were still "informal" or "clandestine" in that they were not performed by the church (Sheehan, 1978).

It was not until the Council of Trent in 1563 that the church required all weddings to be sanctioned by the church. Even then, many marriages continued to be of the "informal" variety in both Catholic and Protestant countries (Gies & Gies, 1987). As late as 1750, between one fifth and one half of weddings in Britain were informal. "Broomstick weddings" occurred in Wales and other areas; couples got married by stepping across a broomstick (Parker, 1990).

Early church weddings took place at the door of the church. A tradition required people who wished to be married "at the doors of the church" to publish **banns** announcing their intended marriage a certain period ahead of time. This was to make sure that neither party was promised to another and that their marriage would not violate church laws. By the 14th century, the vows exchanged by a couple during the wedding were established in their modern form.

Monogamous Marriage Only. The second Christian influence was on the acceptable number of marriage partners. The Old Testament of the Bible records numerous instances of polygyny and concubines, including Solomon's record-setting 700 wives and 300 concubines (Cole, 1959). Although there is no encompassing monogamous requirement in the New Testament, the Hebrew tradition became monogamous by the time of Christ, and Christianity reinforced the monogamous tradition (Shaffern, 1994). In parts of Europe, however, concubines were tolerated, even among the clergy, at least through the 12th century (Broke, 1991).

No Divorce. The third influence was a change in **divorce** norms. Getting a divorce was relatively easy in the Roman Empire. Christianity, however, disallowed or significantly reduced divorce. **Annulments**, originally the same thing as divorces, became a different matter. A divorce would have meant that a legal marriage, considered a sacrament before God and therefore unchangeable, had been changed. An annulment, on the other hand, meant that for some reason the purported marriage had never been legal in the first place. This made a big theological difference, if not much difference in the lives of the participants.

Sex Limiting. A fourth major departure from either the Roman or Germanic traditions was the early Christian

---

Concordia: A state of harmony and lack of disagreement between Roman husband and wife.   **Banns:** A proclamation that a marriage was agreed to and would occur.   **Divorce:** An official end of a marriage.   **Annulment:** Official declaration that a supposed marriage was never valid.

view on human sexuality. Several religious sects existing at the time of early Christianity, including the Gnostics, believed that participation in bodily pleasures interfered with the development of the soul. These views influenced the early Christian church (Starbuck, 1980).

Considerable theological debate ensued about the role of sexuality in the life of a good Christian. Any sexual activity among persons who were not married to each other was considered sinful almost from the beginning. The controversy was more about the role of sexuality in marriage. Couples could have sexual intercourse, Saint Augustine decided, if it resulted, or could possibly result, in childbirth. Since "original sin" was equated with sexual lust, however, children still required infant baptism to symbolically wash off the sin under which they were conceived (Augustine, c. 425, quoted in Bullough, 1976). Since procreation was the only forgivable reason for engaging in sexual activity, all other forms of sexual behavior were considered sinful.

Oppose Contraception, Abortion, and Infanticide. The fifth Christian influence was the Catholic Church's opposition to contraception. Use of contraception would mean that a couple was having sexual activity for some purpose other than that which could result in conception; the sin of lust had thus overcome the duty to procreate. Abortion was opposed partly because it would cause, in the eyes of the church, the death of an infant who had not undergone infant baptism and whose soul would thus be condemned (Katchadourian & Lunde, 1975).

For these and humanitarian reasons, the church also opposed infanticide. Penalties for these sins were assessed on the basis of increasing seriousness. Contraception was the least sinful, followed by an abortion that occurred before the fetus showed signs of life. After "animation" or "quickening," at which time it was assumed the soul had entered the fetus, the act was more serious; infanticide was more serious still (Gies & Gies, 1987:61).

Although Christianity may not have been its major influence, one of the most significant changes in the Middle Ages was the gradual movement away from arranged marriages and toward choice. As individuals gradually came to have more voice in their own mate selection, new institutions arose that allowed youth the opportunity to meet and court each other. Shorter

(1975) described a practice known in Northern Europe as "nightcourting" that came to be called **bundling** in America. The practice, especially common in the cold climates of Sweden and Finland, usually began on a Saturday evening when a group of young men would walk by the homes of young women.

The young women would be waiting, usually in a loft, storeroom, or other dwelling somewhat apart from the main room of the house. One boy would stop at the first house. The boys continued on their walk until all had found a place for the evening or ran out of girls. This provided an opportunity for the young couples to get to know each other, but no sexual activity was allowed. To stay warm, the couple would often bundle up in bed together, separated by a "bundling board." The next Saturday night, different partners were together. Gradually, the young persons would begin to pair off in couples. Only when a couple became engaged was sexual intercourse allowed. These couples nearly always married once pregnancy or childbirth occurred.

Other European regions developed different **courtship** practices. These formed part of what was becoming a commonly recognizable script. Demographic and other changes were in motion, creating a distinctive western European pattern, different from that found in eastern Europe and elsewhere. Quale (1988:182) found five characteristics of this Western European marital script.

1. Men and women both married in their mid-20s, which was relatively late compared to other systems.
2. Many did not marry at all. In 1700, as many as half of the women never married (Parker, 1990:15).
3. Age difference between the partners was relatively small.
4. Because of the widespread practice of apprenticeship, the boarding out of children as servants, and other factors, most men and women had lived outside their parents' home for some period before marriage. This made them more independent and provided them with alternative models for setting up their own households.
5. Childbearing began relatively late for women. This slowed population growth at a time when life expectancy was increasing.

These five characteristics contributed to a family script that prepared Europe for the coming industrial revolution.

Bundling: A courting custom by which a couple would spend an evening together in bed, but fully clothed, separated by a "bundling board" or other material.   **Courtship:** Socially scripted process by which potentially sexual pairs interact to form relationships that can result in marriage.

Changes in Inheritance

In the 12th century, small farms were giving way to large estates, often surrounding a castle or monastery. Slavery had essentially disappeared in Europe, but the life of serfs was similar to that of slaves. They worked the land for their masters, owning very little of their own. Rather than being bought and sold as slaves were, serfs belonged with the land when the land was passed down in the families of the nobility.

Development of the large estates was accompanied by the increasing popularity of **primogeniture**. The earlier practice of dividing estates equally among the children, sometimes including the girls, resulted in smaller and smaller parcels of land upon which it was difficult to support a family. Primogeniture, on the other hand, was accompanied by the assumption that estates could not be divided up. The eldest son inherited the entire parcel and then tried to add to that by accumulating other holdings. The result was increasingly larger estates, owned by a smaller and smaller group of nobility. In most of late medieval Europe, the owner of the land and castle was essentially the government of the area.

Extremely powerful members of nobility, who consolidated their holdings by war and marriage, granted landholding privileges to lesser nobility. The former became the kings and queens of Europe. Having legitimate heirs became extremely important to this small group of landowners, some of whom objected to the church's telling them who they should and should not marry.

This change in the economic and political base of society clearly affected the family institution. For one thing, since only one offspring could inherit, daughters and other sons were often left without a means of support. There was pressure on parents to get their daughters married to husbands who could support them, but there were fewer potential husbands with the means to support them. Fewer persons married, and the value of a bride went down relative to the value of a groom.

HIGHLIGHT 3.1 **The Origin of European Surnames**

In the early Middle Ages, most children were simply given a single name, selected from a relatively short list approved by the *familia*. As long as people stayed in small villages, one name was all that was necessary.

In the latter part of the 11th century, however, the use of surnames became common in Venice and the practice gradually spread throughout Europe (Gies & Gies, 1987). Since these were patrilineal societies, the surnames became hereditary through male lines. Elsdon Smith (1956) found that nearly all European surnames could be derived from one of four sources: place of residence, occupation, father's name, or descriptive nickname.

From the man's place of residence. A word describing the place a man lived often became the surname for his descendents. Rivers, forests, and other landforms identified many families. Persons living near a hill or mountain might become *Maki* in Finland, *Dumont* or *Depew* in France, *Zola* or *Coletti* in Italy, *Jurek* in Poland, *Kopecky* in Czechoslovakia, *Montaña* in Spain, or *Hill* in England.

Another kind of place name occurred when a village or large estate became a family name, used mostly when a person left that place. This device is indicated by the *de* prefix in French, the *von* in German, and the *van* in Dutch.

From the man's occupation. Since an occupation tended to be passed from father to son, it became a common source of surname. The common *Smith* or *Smyth* in England might have been a blacksmith, silversmith, goldmith, or other forger of metals. Its counterpart is *Schmidt* in Germany, *Smit* in Holland, *Herrero* in Spain, *Kovac* in Bulgaria, *Smed* in Denmark, *Kovars* in Hungary, *Lefevre* or *Faure* in France, *Ferraro* in Italy, *Kuznetzov* in Russia, and *Kowal* in Poland. Other common English occupational names with counterparts in most other languages are Carter, Cooper, Baker, Thatcher, Wainwright, Wright, Tylor (Tiler), Taylor (Tailor), Farmer, Fowler, Miller (Mills), Tanner, Teller, Brewer, and Carpenter.

From the father's name. **Patronymics**, or names derived from one's father or paternal ancestor, are common in many languages. These can be recognized by the use of a suffix or prefix that means "son of." The obvious English version is *-son.* Equivalent suffixes are *-sen* in Danish and Norwegian, *-ian* in Armenian, *-nen* in Finnish, *-pulos* in Greek, *-wiecz* in Polish and *-ez* in Spanish. The prefix *Ap-* means "son of" in Welsh, as does the Scotch and Irish *Mac-* and the Norman *Fitz-*. The Irish prefix *O'-* means "grandson of."

Many of the original names were from the Bible. The name John resulted in the patronymic *Johnson* and *Jackson* in England and Ireland, *Johns* and *Jones* in Wales,

---

Primogeniture: The right of the eldest child, especially the eldest son, to inherit all property of the parents.

Jensen, Jansen, and *Hansen* in Denmark, *Johanson* in Sweden, *Janowicz* in Poland, *Ivanov* in Russia and Bulgaria, *Ianson* in Scotland, *Janosfi* in Hungary, *Jantzen* in Holland, and *MacEoin* in Ireland. Similar derivations are found for the Biblical names Peter, Paul, James, Simon, Michael, and Thomas, among others.

From a descriptive nickname. Sometimes a nickname taken after a person's physical characteristics, character, or abilities would be passed on and became a surname. Even today, a red-faced or redheaded person is likely to be nicknamed "Red." This was the source of the English names *Reid, Reed, Read, Ruff, Russ, Russel,* and *Ruddy.* The same person might be *Rousseau, Rouse,* or *Larouse* in France, *Purpura* or *Rossi* in Italy, *Voros* in Hungary, *Roth* in Germany, *Pelirrojo* in Spain, *Cokinos* or *Pyrrhos* in Greece, or *Flynn* in Ireland.

Households

The household was the major residential and productive unit in preindustrial Europe. For most persons, home was a one-room dwelling that served for sleeping, eating, making love, and all else. There was no privacy. If there were servants, they ate and slept in the same room as their masters.

This arrangement held for all but the very wealthiest of the nobility. The home of a minor noble might be larger than that of a peasant, but privacy was still lack-

ing. Even for those wealthy enough to have more than one room, the rooms were lined up so that one would have to pass through one room to get to the next. The innovative central hallway, which significantly increased the privacy of separate rooms, was not widespread in Europe until the 18th century (Quale, 1988).

Although the household lacked privacy, it did not typically contain large numbers of persons. Laslett (1977) found that the average household size was much lower than most sociologists would have expected for preindustrial communities. From 1699 to 1881, the average household size in western Europe varied from 4.3 to 5.77 persons and may have contained extended members at one time or another.

Although only a small percentage of households contained extended families at a given point in time, it remains possible that the extended family was the ideal. That was seldom achieved, however, because of high mortality and relatively late marriages. Stone (1986) pointed out that, in one English community, 80% of the persons who were over age 65 lived with one of their children. Only 9% of households, however, contained grandparents. Stone and others concluded that the extended family was the ideal. Even if extended families did not live in the same household, they probably lived nearby and participated in daily interaction and mutual support.

Laslett (1977), on the other hand, maintained that the isolated nuclear family was the preferred residential unit throughout late preindustrial Europe, especially

This medieval family is having supper at Wakehurst Place, England. Like most who could afford portraits, this was a much wealthier family than others of the time.

in England. Dependence upon kin groups appears to have decreased in England before it did elsewhere. The government was, to some extent, willing to assume responsibility for the welfare of its citizens. The first recognition that a central government had some legal responsibility for the poor was the Elizabethan Poor Law of 1601 (Trattner, 1979). Only one's parents, spouse, and children were required to provide support in the case of poverty; extended kin probably helped if they could, but they were not legally required to do so.

Gender

At least for the "ladies" of the medieval privileged classes, the ideal of **chivalry** established a kind of respect for women. This was demonstrated by knightly protection and gallantry. The image of a brave knight fending off the dragon to protect the lady became part of folklore. When in danger, women and children should be saved first, while men fended off the danger, to the death if necessary.

Day-to-day reality was perhaps not quite so romantic. The Christian view of marriage held that the husband and wife became one flesh. The legal manifestation of this was that property was also merged into one holding, under control of the husband. Under this concept of **coverture,** the wife was not allowed to exercise property rights on her own; her authority was covered by her husband, who had the responsibility of providing financial support for her and for their children. He assumed any debts she brought into the union, in addition to those she accumulated during marriage. He became responsible not only for her property but for her behavior as well, sometimes being punished for her misdeeds (Liss, 1987).

Children

Raising children was a woman's responsibility, although not always that of the mother. The practice of hiring a wetnurse was common. The wealthy would sometimes hire a wetnurse to live in, but would often send the infant to the home of a peasant woman for a few years. By one estimate, in the Paris region in 1777, one sixth of all infants were boarded out in this fashion. Mortality rates were much higher for infants who were boarded

out. Shorter (1975) used this as evidence that parents cared little about their young children.

Children were apprenticed at young ages, usually by their parents. In England, the Henrician Poor Law of 1536 allowed parish authorities to apprentice children as young as 5 years of age if they had no means of support (Trattner, 1979). These practices might have been the result of harsh conditions rather than lack of caring by parents, but it is clear that childhood was not an easy time for many western Europeans in the late agrarian era.

The North American Family

When Europeans began arriving on the shores of North America, they met natives who had modes of production ranging from simple hunting-gathering to relatively sophisticated horticulture. As Europeans and their descendents spread, native peoples and their customs were largely pushed aside. European languages could not accommodate the complex kinship systems of many Native Americans. The Christian norm of monogamy, and other expectations, was contrary to the norms of many Native Americans. Ideas of having a single powerful ruler, private ownership of property, plowing the ground, and many other taken-for-granted European assumptions did not fit the traditions of Native Americans. The Spanish first brought the European family system to North America. To the north, the English influence was predominant, with areas of influence by the French, Dutch, and others. Eventually, emigrants from all of Europe brought their versions of European institutions to North America. Different patterns emerged, which we might divide into the New England, southern White, and African American slave family systems.

Puritan New England Families

In 1600, England was undergoing major changes. Towns were growing, and merchants were challenging landowners for power. Protestantism, in the form of the Church of England, had already replaced Catholicism as the official religion. Formally constituted as a business

Chivalry: Medieval norms of knighthood, including bravery, courtesy, honor, and gallantry toward women.   **Coverture:** The doctrine that a man and woman became one flesh at marriage, with the consequence that a wife's property rights are controlled by her husband.

The First Thanksgiving by Jerome Brownscombe re-creates an image of early American life.

corporation, a small group left England aboard the Mayflower for the "New World."

This group of Puritans objected to both Catholicism and the Church of England. Puritans settled New England with the idea of being a "city on a hill," an example to the world of how a proper Christian society would operate; in a sense, it was a "back to basics" movement, an attempt to return to God's word (Erikson, 1966).

Although there were strong influences by the clergy and the small community, the *familia,* or household, was the basic social unit. This domestic unit was somewhat larger than that found in western Europe, but fewer of them had extended family members. Many New England households included fluctuating numbers of servants, apprentices, and boarders who interacted much like family members (Laslett, 1977).

Mortality rates were very high at first. Within a year after their arrival, half the original passengers on the Mayflower had died. Life improved as the settlement became more established, and mortality dropped to rates lower than those found in England at the time. Even so, infant mortality rates were much higher than are found today. The portion of infants who died in their first year ranged from 1 in 10 in healthier areas to as many as 1 in 3 in less healthy districts (Mintz & Kellogg, 1988).

Parents in New England felt love and affection toward their children, but they expressed it partly through an emphasis on strong discipline, including physical punishment. The Christian view at the time was that children

were inherently sinful and that this tendency to sin had to be forcefully combated. The Massachusetts colony even passed a law, based on the Bible, that allowed for the death penalty for children who flagrantly disobeyed their parents. There is no evidence that this law was widely applied, but it was used, along with fear of everlasting Hell, as a form of social control (Pfohl, 1994).

Adults were also controlled by fear and punishment. The dunking stool, being tarred and feathered, public whippings, and burning at the stake were common punishments. Adultery was subject to a wide range of punishment, including the death penalty (Erikson, 1966).

Mothers handled most of the child rearing, although the practice of wet-nursing, in the home or out, was brought from Europe. Women were responsible for the household management and some agricultural duties. Men cleared the land, handled the livestock, dealt with the natives, and participated in the political and official religious life of the community. In whaling and trading communities, men would be at sea for many months at a time, sometimes for years, leaving their wives to handle the household business in their absence (Starbuck, 1924).

When they were present, men were clearly the heads of household. The tradition of coverture applied in the New World, limiting the technical legal rights of women, especially the married ones (Liss, 1987). In spite of legal limitations, widows, never-married women, and wives whose husbands were away for long periods managed farms, businesses, and crafts

separation of work & home

operations. These were all included as part of the household, so economic production was not as clearly separated from domestic life as it is today.

Compared to earlier societies, young persons had considerable choice in marriage partners. Parents still had influence, especially when inheritance was involved, but the young were not forced to marry against their will. Romantic love was not yet a significant factor in mate selection. Strength of character and compatible personality were important for both men and women. Men looked for women who could raise children and contribute their economic share; women looked for men who could work hard and be good providers.

Given the sparse population, spouses in the earlier years of New England were often "chosen" primarily because they lived nearby. As communities grew, other mechanisms came into play. Gatherings at church and in homes gave the very young a chance to interact. The practice of bundling was common. Many Protestant groups, including the Puritans, rejected the doctrine that marriage should be a sacrament. New England marriages, therefore, were initially civil, not religious, ceremonies. Posting of the banns occurred in the village square or other prominent location. As the colony grew, many marriages were informal, being unrecorded by a church or secular authority. Most colonies accepted such "common law" marriages as valid, especially after a child was born (Nass & McDonald, 1982).

Bundling common

common law marr.

Although life was difficult, most married partners developed respectful and even affectionate relationships. While Puritans believed that sexual activity outside of marriage was sinful, they were not as antisexual as were some of the early leaders of the Catholic Church. Puritans recognized sex as a human need and, in marriage, were apparently highly sexual. Marital intercourse was forbidden only when it would interfere with specific religious duties, such as on the Sabbath (Nass & McDonald, 1982). While the Puritans agreed with the pronatalist "go forth and multiply" and appear to have practiced the belief, they were not as theologically opposed to birth control as were Catholics.

African American Slave Families

While slavery existed in many parts of the world, what made the institution unique in 16th-century America was the coupling of slave status with race. Roman slaves,

for example, had come from a wide variety of conquered groups, most of which were Caucasian like their masters. Native Americans enslaved Native Americans from other tribes, as did native Africans.

The first Africans arrived in Virginia in 1619. They were indentured servants, as were many European immigrants at the time (Luhman & Gilman, 1980). In this status, the individual agreed to work for a period of years in exchange for the cost of passage to the New World. Many early African Americans earned their freedom, and a few of them or their descendents owned slaves. Just before the Civil War, a total of nearly 4,000 Blacks, or about 1 out of every 1,000 Blacks in the slave states, owned slaves (U.S. Census, 1830, 1860; Burnham, 1993).

Within 50 years of the arrival of the first Africans, the institution of chattel slavery was established; race became the marker of American slave status. Africans recognized tribal, not racial, differences, and tribal animosities were exploited by slave traders. Europeans did not usually capture slaves in Africa themselves. Instead, they acquired slaves by trading with native African groups. The exchange was typically in such material as hardware, tools, cloth, liquor, and guns. The slave trade seriously disrupted the social structures of West Africans, many of whom became either traders or captives (Chambers et al., 1979).

Most African survivors of the trans-Atlantic voyage were taken to Brazil, the Spanish Americas, and the Caribbean islands, but many found themselves in the British colonies of North America. The first United States census, in 1790, found 750,000 Blacks, 90% of whom were slaves. In 1860, in the last census before slavery ended, there were nearly 4 million slaves (U.S. Census, 1860; in Mintz & Kellogg, 1988). The first slaves to arrive in the Americas suffered severe cultural disruption. Most had been uprooted from individuals they had known previously. Slaves were sold without regard to origin, language, or custom. Most slave owners had only a few slaves, and it was unlikely that they had come from the same African culture.

slave culture rework

The cultures of origin were typically hunting gathering or horticultural. They had their own religious customs, modes of production, languages, occupational skills, and family scripts. Most of this was stripped from the slaves, who had to learn a version of English and Christianity in order to communicate and worship with one another. Family customs, too, had to change. The part of West Africa from which most slaves came had high rates of polygyny; there is no record of polygyny among American slaves. Forms of weddings and other rites of passage were also largely lost.

What came to be the African American slave family was a combination of a few traditional customs, reflections of the English culture, and adjustments to the demands of slavery. What that institution was like, however, has been the topic of controversy in sociology. Early sociologists like W. E. B. DuBois (1899), Frazier (1957), and Elkins (1959) influenced the image of the slave family for decades. They emphasized the instability of family ties, disruption of kin networks, and the extent of matrilocal, matrifocal units.

Some sociologists, such as Gutman (1976) and Anderson (1991) have more recently challenged this "family disorganization" perspective. They find that 70 to 90% of African American slave families had a husband or father present, plus two or more members of a nuclear family. This view points out that matrilocal and mother-headed families were actually relatively rare; when single mothers did exist they usually lived with extended kin. This view concludes that the slave family was stronger, more durable, and more intact than had been thought.

Differences of opinion hinge partly on whether formal or informal marriages are counted. Slaves could not legally marry at all. All children born of slaves were technically illegitimate. Slaves themselves, however, did recognize their relationships as marriages. Some preachers performed church weddings; other marriages were celebrated by less formal ceremonies like jumping over a broomstick together. The slave owners sometimes recognized the marriage by providing a wedding gift (Mintz & Kellogg, 1988).

The marriages had no legal authority, however, and could be broken up by the sale of one or the other partner. This happened to somewhere between 1 in every 6 (Mintz & Kellogg, 1988) and 1 every in 10 (Laslett, 1977) "marriages." Although children could be separated from their parents, Fogel and Engerman (in Laslett, 1977) found that, when this did occur, it happened at about the same age that White children were separating from their own parents.

The extent of matrifocal families was partly dependent upon the size of the landholding upon which the slaves worked. Using records for several large plantations, Laslett (1977) found that the rate of two-parent households was about the same as was found in England at the time. The households differed, however, in who these parental figures were. Laslett's data suggested a pattern he called "serial polyandry." Many of the father figures in the home were not the biological fathers of all the women's children, suggesting that more than one father had lived there.

Serial polyandry could have resulted from the slaves' high death rates. Also, since marriages were informal, "divorces" were also informal and easily accomplished. Finally, the slavemaster or his children fathered some of

Slaves, like cattle, were bought and sold at auctions. A family could be sold as a group or separated and sold individually.

the children; this was more likely for the slaves who worked in homes rather than in the fields. The extent of this is unknown, but 4.5% of former slaves who were interviewed in the 1930s reported having a White father (Mintz & Kellogg, 1988). In spite of all this, slaves on large plantations managed to have a relatively stable family life (Laslett, 1977).

Large plantations were not the only place where slaves could be found. Most owners had fewer than 20 slaves (Gutman, 1976). These were located mainly on small farms, but a few served as house slaves of merchants and in other nonagricultural locations. Some large property owners housed slaves at widely scattered locations or on separate pieces of property. Family life in these situations was more difficult than on the large plantation. Mates were difficult to find; when they were found, they were likely to be on another farm to which the slave was not allowed to travel except, perhaps, on Sunday. Both birthrates and marriage rates were lower for slaves in this situation (Laslett, 1977; Stevenson, 1996).

It was difficult for slaves in any condition to have much authority over their children. Although many tried, parents could not usually protect their children from the abuses of slavery. They could only informally influence their children's choice of mates, and parents had no control over their children's occupations. Strong feelings of kinship were evidenced by the common practice of naming children after grandparents and other ancestors. Surnames were passed down from an owner, in a manner similar to that found among serfs and servants in medieval Europe.

Kin groups formed an important support network for slaves, although many of the kin ties were fictive rather than consanguinal or conjugal. Gutman (1976) reported that in at least some areas, children were taught to call all adult slaves "aunt" and "uncle" and all younger slaves "brother" and "sister." This emphasized the feeling that all slaves had mutual obligations and responsibilities. Whether they recognized these fictive kin for purposes of defining incest and mate selection is not known. If so, family formation would be all the more difficult.

Debate continues about the composition of the slave family, but all scholars agree that it influenced the condition of the Black family today. We will take up this topic again in chapter 8.

Southern White Families

Only a small percentage of southern Whites were wealthy plantation owners. In 1860 just over 8 million Whites lived in the 15 slave states. Of these, only 4.8% of the individuals owned slaves, but nearly one fourth

---

Families in the NEWS

Dani Caught between Stone Age and Computer Age

Western explorers did not come to Indonesia's most remote province until the late 1930s. There they encountered the Dani, a group that lived the way their ancestors had for thousands of years.

Now, Christian missionaries, anthropologists, and government officials have introduced modern life to the Dani — with mixed results. According to Mice Rumbiak, an anthropologist at the University of Cenderawasih in Jayapura, many Dani shun the old ways once they are educated or converted. The tribal traditions and animist religious beliefs are endangered, but not gone.

The mix of eras is often striking. Some Dani men still wear only their penile sheaths, while their children play in Pokémon outfits. Some Christian Dani wear only their penile sheaths to church, while others wear suits and ties.

While some women wear Western clothes, others prefer to remain bare-breasted and wear grass skirts. Both men and women still, sometimes, coat their bodies with pig fat to help stay warm, in preference over coats or jackets.

Dani still refrain from sexual intercourse for as much as five years after the birth of a child, while the mother is breastfeeding. Occasionally a mother will breast-feed piglets if the sow is lost. The old practice of women amputating finger joints when a relative dies has been outlawed by the government, but it continues.

In some areas, the government built concrete-block houses for the Dani, but the Dani preferred their thatched-roof huts. The block houses got too hot in the daytime and too cold at night, while the huts were properly ventilated. The block houses are now used to shelter their pigs.

Source: Calvin Sims. www.nytimes.com, March 11, 2001.

of Whites lived in a family in which someone owned one or more slaves (U.S. Census, 1860). From 70 to 85% of 17th-century immigrants to Maryland and Virginia arrived as indentured servants (Morgan, 1975:159). The vast majority of indentured servants and other immigrants were male. New England arrivals, too, were predominantly male; indeed, it is nearly universal that initial migrant groups are predominantly male. In New England, however, two fifths of immigrants were women, usually immigrating with husband or father. In the south, two thirds of immigrants were male as late as 1704 (Morgan, 1975). This resulted in relatively low marriage rates for the early settlers of the south.

Although the climate of New England was harsh, it harbored fewer diseases than the warmer southern areas. While the New Englanders were reaching mortality rates the same or lower than that in England at the time, settlers in the Chesapeake region had death rates almost twice as high (Smith & Daniel, 1978). Malnutrition was more common in Virginia and the Carolinas, where many Whites and slaves alike died from beriberi, infant cholera, pellagra, rickets, scurvy, and other diseases (Morgan, 1975).

Mintz and Kellogg (1988) concluded that demographic factors made the establishment of a stable family difficult for early European settlers of the south. Marriages occurred at older ages than in New England; in half, one or both partners died before their seventh

wedding anniversary. Two thirds of all children lost at least one parent before their 18th birthday; one third lost both parents. Infant mortality rates ran at 25%. These problems, plus the fact that the population was more widely dispersed than in the north, resulted in less social control in spite of strong religious beliefs. Even in the face of punishments ranging from fines to whippings, one fifth of White female servants in one Maryland county had a child out of wedlock (Mintz & Kellogg, 1988).

Even against these obstacles, many constructed strong family and kinship bonds. Death rates dropped by the end of the 17th century, and the imbalance of women and men improved as increasing numbers of residents were born.

The southern family stabilized, especially on the larger plantations. These gentry families developed lifestyles that were reminiscent of English country houses. Emotional displays were discouraged; the hunt, entertaining, and political service occupied the men. The actual farming was often left to hired managers and the slaves. Women ran the household and raised the children, often with the help of servants and slaves.

The influence of northern and southern Whites of all classes, slaves, and to some extent indigenous Americans, helped form the diverse family scripts that characterized the United States toward the end of the advanced agrarian era.

Summary and Conclusion

The sociocultural evolutionary perspective of modes of production provides a valuable macrosociological framework. The family institution, along with religion, politics, education, and sexuality, changed significantly as societies went through changes in modes of production.

Politics and land ownership became increasingly hierarchical as hunting-gathering societies became horticultural and then agrarian. Social and gender inequalities likewise increased, and religions reflected those changes.

Reliance on kinship groups declined somewhat as political and religious authorities gained power and specialization of labor increased. Kin groups and nuclear families, however, retained considerable authority over the mate selection process.

The Roman *familia,* which was an important influence on the European family system, was altered in several respects by the Christian tradition. The European system, in turn, influenced the North American family system.

The colonial American family differed depending on whether it was the New England, African American slave, or southern White system.

Table 3.1 summarizes much of the information from this and following chapters.

Table 3.1		Summary of Modes of Production and Social Institutions						
			Social Institutions					
Society Type	**Basic Characteristics**	**Additive Technology**	**Economic (Productive Labor on)**	**Political (Power Group)**	**Stratification (Inequality)**	**Religious**	**Familial**	**Educational**
Hunting-Gathering	Small groups; migratory; little division of labor except by gender and age		Nature	Diffuse power systems	Little inequality	Nature and ancestor worship; animism; totems; polytheism	Clan/kin group central	No formal system
Horticultural (Simple/Advanced)	More sedentary; larger groups; some division of labor	Plant cultivation/ metallurgy	Nature/ land	Some concentration of power in hereditary land ownership	Increasing inequality	Continued from above; development of priesthood, active gods	Clan/kin group central; some familia	Some specialty training
Agrarian (Simple/Advanced)	Sedentary; larger groups/ nations; increased division of labor	Plow/iron	Land	Extreme concentration of power in hereditary land ownership	Extreme inequality	Universal religions; monotheism with male god	Familia; extended family	Apprentice-ships; formal education for elites
Industrial	Urbanization; highly specialized division of labor	Inanimate energy	Machines	Concentration of power by by capitalists	Extreme inequality to decreased inequality	Secularization; competitive religions	More nuclear; separation of home (women) and work (men)	Universal mass education
Post-industrial	Suburbani-zation; extreme division of labor	Electronic information	Informa-tion	Technocrats??	Decreased in-equality??	Continued seculari-zation? Return to older forms	Less stable nuclear; mother-child unit central?	Increased educational necessity

Source: Most information from Lenski, 1994; Lenski and Lenski, 1987; Lenski, Lenski, and Nolan, 1991; Lenski, Nolan, and Lenski, 1995; chapters 2, 3, and 4 this volume.

Rethinking in Context Now that you have read the chapter, have you changed your mind about living in a hunting-gathering society? In colonial America? Specifically, what traits would you like? What traits would you dislike? On what values are you basing your choices?

Additional Resources

Anthropological works

Freeman, Derek. 1983. *Margaret Mead and Samoa: The Making and Unmaking of an Anthropological Myth.* Cambridge, MA: Harvard University Press.

Lizot, Jacques. 1985. *Tales of the Yanomami: Daily Life in the Venezuelan Forest.* New York: Cambridge University Press.

Mead, Margaret. 1928. *Coming of Age in Samoa: A Psychological Study of Primitive Youth for Western Civilisation.* New York: Blue Ribbon Books.

Segalen, Martine. 1986. *Historical Anthropology of the Family.* New York: Cambridge University Press.

Shostak, Marjorie. 1981. *Nisa: The Life and Words of a !Kung Woman.* New York: Random House.

Tapper, Nancy. 1991. *Bartered Brides: Politics, Gender, and Marriage in an Afghan Tribal Society.* New York: Cambridge University Press.

Turnbull, Colin. 1961. *The Forest People.* New York: Simon & Schuster.

European-based histories of the family

Engels, Friedrick. [1884] 1972. *The Origin of the Family, Private Property and the State.* New York: International Publishers.

Gies, Frances, and Joseph Gies. 1987. *Marriage and the Family in the Middle Ages.* New York: Harper & Row.

Shorter, Edward. 1975. *The Making of the Modern Family.* New York: Basic Books.

American histories

Coontz, Stephanie. 1988. *The Social Origins of Private Live: A History of American Families, 1600–1900.* New York: Verso.

Demos, John. 1986. *Past, Present, and Personal: The Family and the Life Course in American History.* New York: Oxford University Press.

Gutman, Herbert G. 1976. *The Black Family in Slavery and Freedom, 1750–1925.* New York: Pantheon.

Mintz, Steven, & Susan Kellogg. 1988. *Domestic Revolutions: A Social History of American Family Life.* New York: Free Press.

Moynihan, Ruth B., Susan Armitage, & Christine Fischer Dichamp, eds. 1990. *So Much to Be Done: Women Settlers on the Mining and Ranching Farms.* Lincoln: University of Nebraska Press.

Smith, Daniel Blake. 1978. "Mortality and the Family in the Colonial Chesapeake." *Journal of Interdisciplinary History* 8:403–27.

Stevenson, Brenda. 1996. *Life in Black and White: Family and Community in the Slave South.* New York: Oxford University Press.

Internet Sites

Family and kinship among the Yanomamo natives

http://www.umanitoba.ca/anthropology/tutor/
case_studies/yanomamo/

History of the European family

http://www.familydiscussions.com/books/goody.htm

Genealogy of colonial Americans

http://www.linkline.com/personal/xymox/

PBS Web site for "Africans in America"; history of slavery

http://www.pbs.org/wgbh/aia/

American Indian resources

http://jupiter.lang.osaka-u.ac.jp/~krkvls/naindex.html

For links to these sites and additional resources, visit the *Families in Context* Web site at:

http://sociology.wadsworth.com

Chapter 4

Industrialization and Families

Prelude

Martha Starbuck (nee Boggs) was born in 1880 and saw incredible social change before she died in 1975. At the dawn of the 20th century she married and moved from Missouri to Colorado in a covered wagon. She and her husband started a dairy farm and a family.

Martha bore 10 children, 3 of whom died before reaching adulthood. The boys all helped milk the cows and bottle and deliver the milk in the morning. Then they walked to school; after classes they milked the cows again. The only surviving daughter helped Martha cook the meals from scratch, wash the clothes, tend the garden, and clean the house.

The farm was not big enough to support everyone, so all but one boy left for greener pastures. Four finished college, supporting themselves with jobs and athletic scholarships.

In Colorado, Martha could vote as soon as she turned 21. But she was 41 before all women in the United States were guaranteed the right to vote.

Martha saw the first automobiles and electric lights along the dirt streets of Salida, Colorado. She eventually owned an automobile, a Victrola, an automatic clothes washer, and a radio. She was 89 when she sat in her living room and watched the live broadcast of the first man walking on the moon.

Such were the changes powered by the industrial revolution.

Will such momentous changes occur during your lifetime?

We have now seen what life was like in hunting-gathering, horticultural, and agrarian societies. With industrialization there was once again a major change in the way societies and families were organized. The patterns of life with which you are more familiar developed. In a relatively short time, the technological base was revolutionized. This chapter has more "how today's American family got to be the way its is" material, but it takes a few visits to non-American systems.

> *Thinking Ahead* Imagine that you are responsible for explaining your life and society to a hunter-gatherer and an agrarian who have both been transported into their future, which is your present. How would you explain what you do every day? How would you explain your family and other relationships? Are there some things that might be very difficult for your visitors to understand?

Industrial Institutions

The industrial revolution was accompanied by changes in all aspects of people's lives and in all social institutions. We will look first at the economic institution and related technological innovations. We will then turn to the religious, political, and educational institutions. Demographic forces, associated with institutional changes, will also be considered as both a cause and result of family change.

The Economic Institution

The industrial revolution occurred first in western Europe, especially England, and a handful of English-speaking countries: the United States, Canada, Australia, and New Zealand. Japan and a few other areas industrialized as well. In each of these cases, industrialization occurred under a **capitalist** form of market economy. In this system, means of production such as farms, factories, and mines were owned by private individuals, families, or groups rather than by the government. Decisions about what and how to produce were made by private entities, largely based on what would return the greatest profit to the owners. Workers, lacking ownership of machines and factories, sold their labor for wages.

Lenski and Lenski (1987) divided the industrial revolution into four phases, based on the technological innovations that appeared (see Figure 4.1). The years are approximate because none of the changes happened overnight. Nor is there anything that requires other countries, now developing, to go through the process in the same order. The four phases do provide guidelines about the order in which industrialization occurred in Western societies.

Phase 1 (1760–1850). This phase began in England with major developments in the textile, iron, and coal industries. The invention of the first true steam engine was the most significant development.

Phase 2 (1850–1900). The industrial revolution spread throughout most of Europe and North America. The steam engine was adapted for transportation by steamships and railroads. Demand for iron, steel, and coal expanded. New kinds of equipment, machines, and chemical fertilizers were developed that significantly increased agricultural production.

The organizational structure of production also changed. In some industries, hundreds and even thousands of workers were required in a single enterprise.

Capitalism: An economic system in which production and distribution are controlled by private individuals or groups and guided by the profit motive.

| **Figure 4.1** | Phases of Industrial Revolution and Major Historical Events |

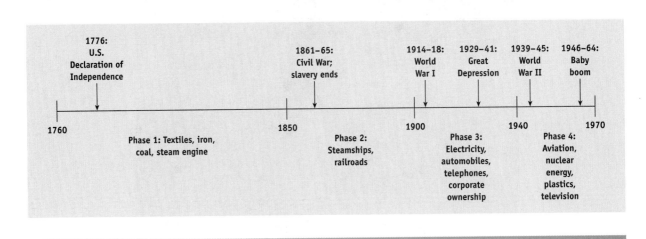

Family ownership of companies began to give way to the corporation, with its hierarchy of professional managers.

Phase 3 (1900–1940). Major advances in energy technology characterized this phase. Electricity and the internal combustion engine had already been invented, but large-scale application of those developments occurred in this stage. Automobiles changed the face of America and many other countries. The petroleum industry boomed. All factories and most homes were electrified and connected to each other by telephones.

The media and entertainment were increasingly designed for a mass audience, with the development of motion pictures, the Victrola (record player), and radio. The influence of industrialization continued to spread around the world.

Phase 4 (1940–1970). Spurred by World War II, this phase saw major changes in the aviation industry, in aluminum production and use, electronics, and nuclear power. Plastics were taking increasing numbers of forms, and television sets appeared in most American homes.

An entirely new development, however, was beginning. Previous phases of the industrial revolution saw new machines, materials, and forms of energy. What now happened were innovations, based on electronic computers, which expanded upon or replaced the human brain. The nature of labor changed. Machines could now be automated or designed to replace both the heavy labor and much of the decision making originally done by humans.

Lenski and Lenski (1987) assume that today's most developed societies are still in phase 4 of the industrial revolution. Because of the significance of some recent technological innovations, however, we follow the lead of Daniel Bell (1973, 1979) and others by assuming that, beginning in about 1970, society began to undergo a postindustrial revolution. This revolution's influence on the family of the present and future will be the topic of chapter 5.

The Industrial Workforce. Women and children worked in the earliest factories. White immigrants to Europe and Black immigrants not from the southern states provided cheap labor for factories in the industrializing northern states.

The urban middle class expanded in phase 2 of the industrial revolution. Increasing numbers of male workers made enough money that the labor of their wives was no longer required to support the household. It was considered a sign of high status that a wife's income was not required. Most industrial work of the time was dangerous, difficult, dirty, and generally undesirable. Protecting his wife from such conditions was a source of pride for many husbands, and there is no indication that many middle-class women preferred factory work to their homemaker role.

The industrial labor force became highly sex-segregated. This is the screw-cutting department in an early 20th-century automobile factory.

Women in working-class families, in addition to child-care and home maintenance, frequently contributed monetary income as well. Some worked in the factories, others as servants for wealthier families. Those who did not work outside the home often took in washing and ironing or did home production work for factories. Many families took in boarders, which added to the cooking and housekeeping chores (Mintz & Kellogg, 1988).

Data about the percentage of women in the labor force have been biased because much of women's economic contribution has not been counted. Available data indicate, however, that even entry of women into the official

Figure 4.2   Women in Paid Labor, 1900–2006

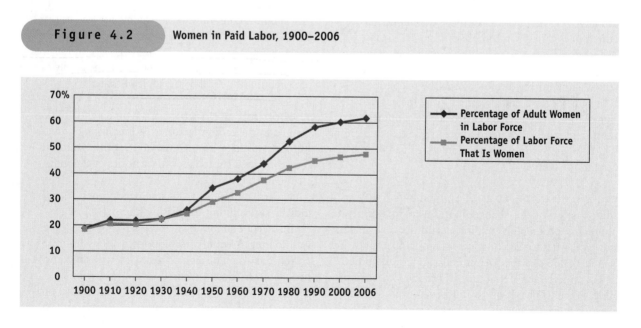

Sources: Department of Commerce, Bureau of the Census, Department of Labor, and Bureau of Labor Statistics: in Johnson, 1992:56. U.S. Census Bureau, *Statistical Abstract,* 1999, Tables 650 and 652 (2006 figures are estimates).

Martin Luther (1483–1546) was a major leader of the Protestant Reformation. Here, along with Phillip Melanchthon, he is offering a written scroll to a king at the Diet of Augsburg.

paid labor force is not a recent phenomenon. Women's participation in the paid labor force doubled between 1880 and 1900 (Mintz & Kellogg, 1988). The development of the telephone and typewriter opened entirely new fields of employment that were largely filled by women.

Figure 4.2 shows a general increase each decade of the 20th century in the paid labor force. The portion of adult women, defined as those 16 and older, in the paid labor force went from 18.8% in 1900 to 59.7 in 2000. Women constituted 18.3% of the adult labor force in 1900, compared with 46.8% in 2000.

The increase of women into the paid labor force was gradual in phase 3 of industrialization. Prior to World War II, many women worked in the paid labor force only until they married. In some occupations, such as school teaching, women were not allowed to continue working after they married. During World War II, with millions of men in the military and a need for increased production, there was a significant increase of women in paid labor.

After the war, surviving men returned to the labor force. Some women got married and left the labor force, or returned home as their husbands took jobs, but many continued in paid employment. The numbers of women working has increased rapidly since then. This

has had a significant impact on gender roles and other aspects of the family, as we will see.

The Religious Institution

Two major religious developments are relevant to the industrial revolution in the Western world. The first, the Protestant Reformation, preceded industrialization. Secularization, the second phenomenon, accompanied industrialization.

The Protestant Reformation. In 1517, a German cleric named Martin Luther publicized several objections to Catholicism. Although he did not know it at the time, his actions precipitated what later was called the Protestant Reformation. Max Weber's classic book *The Protestant Ethic and the Spirit of Capitalism*, published in English in 1930, argued that four major beliefs resulting from the Protestant Reformation were an essential ingredient in the development of capitalism.

First, **Protestants** took a different view of work than had medieval Catholics. The traditional view was that work was a punishment for sin or, at best, a necessary evil. Protestants came to believe that any occupation, not just the priesthood, could be used to glorify God. A person

---

Protestants: Christians who are the theological descendents of Martin Luther, John Calvin, or Ulrich Zwingli. For practical purposes, a member of any Christian denomination that is not Catholic.

could be "**called**" to a career; success in the career could be a sign that one was in the grace of God. It was no longer assumed that children would automatically take up the occupation of their parents. This made workers available for the new jobs required of industrialization.

Second, Protestants rejected control by a hierarchy such as that found in the Catholic Church. Instead, they espoused a "priesthood of all believers." Each person established a compact between himself or herself and God. Most importantly, Protestantism strongly emphasized individuality. Although it took many years, the notion of individuality spread from religious matters and influenced democracy, individual choice of mate selection, and other social changes.

Third, Protestantism encouraged rationality instead of superstition and fatalism. People began to believe that, if they organized their lives in certain rational ways, they could improve their lot in this life as well as the afterlife. Methodists, for example, were so named because they believed in living by a certain rational method.

Fourth, Protestants emphasized frugality and denial of pleasure. They believed in hard work and achieving success in their calling, but monetary gains from such success should not be spent on foolish pleasures. Instead, it was used as capital to be invested back in the business to hire new workers or buy new machines. The belief was that frugal, hard-working persons could improve their lot in life, while demonstrating their good standing in the eyes of God, by becoming good capitalists.

Secularization. The second major religious change associated with industrialization is the process of **secularization**. People increasingly saw the world through secular, rather than sacred, lenses. Protestantism no longer demanded a religious ceremony for a valid marriage; the state, rather than a religious body, became the arbiter of marriage. Scientists developed rational explanations of such natural phenomena as lightning and thunder, the movement of the planets, and human illness. Consequently, daily events lost their religious significance.

This does not mean, however, that persons necessarily became "less religious" as a result of secularization. Images of God and other religious concepts were and remain extremely powerful in politics and society in general. Only about 10% of North Americans were members of a church in 1776 (Stark & Finke, 1988). By 1850 membership rolls counted 16% of North Ameri-

cans; this compares to almost 60% in 1988 (Jacquet, 1989). In the United States today, 92% of people say they believe in God (Kosmin & Lachman, 1994).

Political Institutions

In 1600, Europe was ruled by a handful of hereditary monarchs. In 1776, a group of Americans began to institute the radical notion of **democracy** for the first time in advanced agrarian societies. The notion that individuals were capable of governing themselves echoed concepts of individualism also found in Protestantism and the supporters of capitalism.

Those who developed the new form of government were predominantly land-owning men of English descent. Political participation was initially limited to members of that group. Gradually, the right to vote and other civil rights were expanded to include non-property owners, former slaves, women, and 18-year-olds. It is not clear that industrialization causes, requires, or is caused by democracy, but there does seem to be a relationship.

The size and importance of government in people's lives increased significantly since the industrial revolution began. Part of that growth was required for the enforcement of increasingly formalized norms. Many things that were once handled by families or individuals became regulated by complex systems of laws. The belief that the government had a responsibility to help solve problems such as unemployment, poverty, and family violence contributed to the growth of government. Governmental influence is also seen in the growth of public education.

The Educational Institution

In preindustrial America, children learned primarily in a family context. Occupational skills were learned by watching and doing, either under parental supervision or as an apprentice. Even before industrialization, however, schooling was considered important on the grounds that a democracy needed well-educated citizens.

Initially, schools were for those who were qualified to vote and participate in politics. Girls from wealthy families were educated on the grounds that it would help make them better homemakers and mothers. Increasingly, children of all classes received at least some schooling. By 1850, literacy rates for women and men were equal (Coontz, 1988).

Calling: In Protestant theology, an occupation to which one could be "called" by God.   **Secularization:** The process by which religious control over social institutions and individual behavior declines.   **Democracy:** Government by the people.

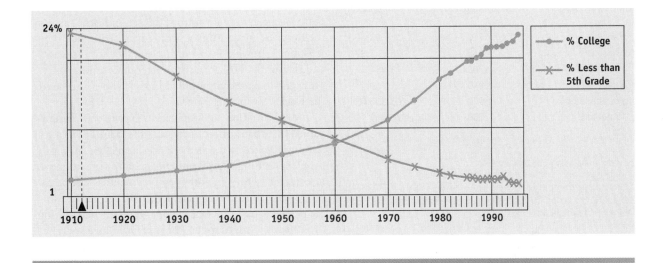

| **Figure 4.3** | **Percent of Persons over 24 with 4 or More Years of College and with Less than 5 Years of Elementary School, 1910–1998** |

Source: *Digest of Educational Statistics,* 1999. U.S. Department of Education. Accessed through USTrends Dataset, MicroCase, Seattle, Washington. Analysis by Gene H. Starbuck.

In 1900, 60% of those who graduated from high school were women. College, however, was still predominately reserved for the sons of the wealthy. Only 19% of college graduates were women in 1900. It was not until 1982 that there were more female college graduates than there were male (Johnson, 1993:862).

The idea that everyone should be educated, at public expense if necessary, was well established in the United States by the end of the Civil War. By World War I, all states had compulsory education for primary school; by World War II, all states required secondary education (Bassis, Gelles, & Levine, 1991).

Figure 4.3 reveals the tremendous explosion of education in the 20th century. From 1910 to 1998, the percentage of adults with 4 or more years of college soared from 2.7% to 23.0%. By contrast, adults with less than a fifth-grade education dropped from 23.8% to only 1.8%.

Several factors contributed to the growth in the educational institution. For one thing, industrial jobs increasingly required at least the ability to read, write, and do basic arithmetic. Somewhat later, the increased demand for managers and other professionals required advanced education.

Education was believed to be important in teaching the "American way" to waves of immigrants. An "Americanizing" curriculum was designed to foster a collective awareness that there was a common American experience. This curriculum included an emphasis on time sense and discipline necessary for factory and other industrial work, along with the "Protestant ethic" of hard work and frugality. It also taught the English language, sometimes accompanied by punishments for children who spoke other tongues.

It was taught that individuals could, by their own efforts, improve their lives. A formal education was a part of the prescribed ladder of success; millions of American parents sacrificed so that their children might have a better education and better life chances than they themselves had. This investment in children's lives was partly the result of demographic changes that encouraged parents to make a larger investment of resources in fewer children.

Demographic Changes

The population distribution in the United States changed significantly during the industrial revolution. Three major trends occurred: significant overall growth in population; migration to cities and the western frontier; and increased life expectancy.

Population Growth. Table 4.1 documents the tremendous population growth that occurred in the United States during the industrial period. When the first phase of industrialization began, there were about 1.5

Table 4.1	Population Growth in Industrial United States	
Industrial Stage	**Beginning Year**	**Population**
Phase 1	1760	1,593,600*
Phase 2	1850	23,191,876
Phase 3	1900	75,994,575
Phase 4	1940	131,669,275
Postindustrial	1970	203,302,031
Projected	2000	270,259,000

*Estimate including official colonies.

Source: Department of Commerce, Bureau of the Census, in Johnson, 1992:821. Projection from U.S. Bureau of the Census, *Statistical Abstract*, 1994:Table 2.

million persons in colonial America. Today, there are 270 million. Most of this growth resulted from immigration, first predominately from Europe and more recently from other countries in the Americas and from Asia.

Migration. Growth has occurred not only in numbers of persons but also in the amount of area being

occupied. For the first three phases of industrialization, the western frontier was inhabited by indigenous Americans but untouched for industrial purposes.

Americans continue to be migratory. Since the 1970s there has been migration from the old industrial areas of the midwest and northeast, sometimes now called the "rust belt", to what is called the "sun belt" of the west and the south. While nearly all regions continue to grow, the most recent population shift appears to be to the Rocky Mountain region.

Industrialization and population growth were accompanied by **urbanization**. Increasing mechanization of farming resulted in less demand for farm labor. Young people increasingly left farms and small towns and moved to cities for factory and other employment, as well as educational opportunity. Figure 4.4 shows the increase in the percentage of Americans living in urban areas during the 200-year period from 1790 to 1990. There was a steady and consistent increase from 5.1% to 75.2%.

Life Expectancy. As industrialization proceeded, better nutrition and living conditions began to improve life expectancy. The biggest gains, however, resulted from the germ theory of disease. Large city sanitation improved after people realized that trash and sewage carried disease.

Figure 4.4	Percent of Americans Living in Urban Areas, 1790–1990

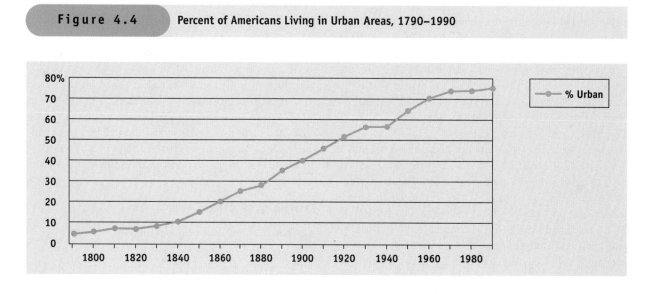

Source: U.S. Census. Accessed through USTrends Dataset, MicroCase, Seattle, Washington.

Urbanization: An increase in the percentage of a population living in cities.

Figure 4.5 — Twentieth-Century Life Expectancy

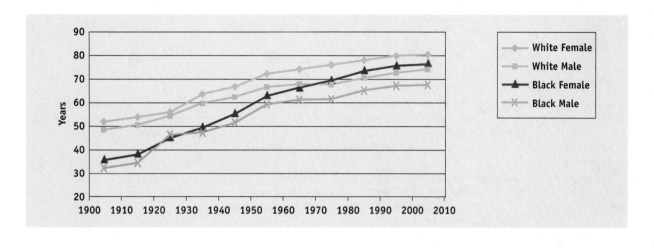

Sources: 1900, 1910, National Center for Health Statistics, in Johnson, 1993:842. 1920–1990, National Center for Health Statistics, in Famighetti, 1993:972. Estimates for 2000 from *Statistical Abstract,* 1999, Table 127. In some years figure for Blacks included other non-White groups.

Inoculation against such diseases as smallpox saved the lives of millions. These factors, along with safer working and living conditions, resulted in a major increase in life expectancy. Improvements in life expectancy have continued in the 20th century, as Figure 4.5 demonstrates.

Overall life expectancy for all races and both sexes increased significantly in the 20th century. Life expectancy for White females increased from 51.1 to 80.5 years. White males can now expect to live to 74.2, compared to 48.2 a century ago. Life expectancy for Blacks more than doubled. In 1900, black male expectancy was 32.5 years; it is now 67.4. Black females could expect 35 years at century beginning; they can now expect to live longer than White males, at 76.7 years.

These figures have clear implications for families, including anticipated lengths of expected marriage and widowhood, and the probability that aging adults will have to care for even older parents. A much smaller portion of parents' lives is spent caring for dependent children. Although people have fewer children today, they are more likely to know their grandparents and grandchildren. These and other demographic changes associated with industrialization have had a profound influence on the American family script.

Industrialization and Families

The preindustrial family, Frederic Le Play (1897) asserted, consisted of a three-generation **stem family** system. Compatible with primogeniture, this extended family type consisted of a patriarch and his wife, along with their oldest son, wife, and children. Younger siblings left home to live and work elsewhere. Industrialization, Le Play argued, was breaking down this traditional three-generation family system. Well into the 20th century, the idea persisted that industrialization destroyed the multigeneration family.

Goode's Family Analysis

William J. Goode (1963, 1970) studied the effects of industrialization and the family in several parts of the world (see Finding Out 4.1). In 1993, Goode confirmed many of his earlier findings and extended his analysis to the topic of divorce.

Goode recognized that forces other than industrialization were at work in producing the conjugal family, and that the changes were complex and sometimes only a matter of degree. Four major points can summarize

Stem family: A type of extended family composed of the parents plus only one child, who might marry and have children.

Finding Out | 4.1

Goode's Family Revolutions

William J. Goode's best-known work was his 1963 *World Revolution and Family Patterns*. The reference in the title was to the industrial revolution, which Goode found was associated with predictable changes in family patterns.

Goode used analysis of existing data from sources from all over the world in his macrosociological analysis of the family. His unobtrusive research uncovered a vast amount of data, much of it quantitative. He used government data where such existed, along with other sources. *World Revolution* contained an in-depth analysis of industrialized Western nations, along with thorough chapters on Arabic Islamic societies, sub-Saharan Africa, India, China, and Japan.

Goode found that the Western family was never quite the ideal extended, self-sufficient, harmonious unit that some earlier scholars had described. Goode (1963:3) referred to this as "the classical family of Western nostalgia." He did, however, find that individuals had become less dependent on extended family groups during

the industrial revolution in the west, and predicted that other societies would go through the same process as they, too, went through the industrialization and urbanization processes.

Goode saw the rise of the conjugal family unit. The nuclear family was becoming less embedded in the extended family, bringing a host of specific changes. These changes were compatible with industrial production, wherever that occurred. In 1993, Goode published a follow-up volume, focusing on the topic of divorce (see chapter 15). In the intervening 30 years, Goode concluded, his findings had generally been confirmed.

Goode's work set the agenda for decades of macrosociological and historical research, and it remains influential. Most scholars agree with his central theses (Cherlin, 1996). By formulating specific, testable hypotheses, Goode contributed significantly to the scientific nature of family studies. He widened the scope of family studies and increased the respectability of the field of study (Aldous, 2000).

Goode's argument: geographic mobility, social mobility, "achieved" occupational status, and increased specialization and functional differentiation of the social structure.

Industrial Economies Require Geographic Mobility. Industrialization was characterized by a rapid change in geographical location of jobs. When factories opened or expanded, new workers, including managers and professionals who were free to relocate, were required. Getting appropriate education or training itself often required relocation. A conjugal family, with only one major earner, was in a better position to relocate than was an entire extended family.

Industrialization Produces, and Requires, Social Mobility. The kinds of workers needed, not just their location, changed as industrialization proceeded. Factory workers were needed where none ex-

isted before. Phase 2 required a new group of salaried managers, and phase 4 required computer experts; neither group of workers previously existed. Parents could not, by themselves, provide the necessary training, skills, or jobs. Individuals had to be socially mobile enough to move into the new occupational niches, which often led to lifestyles different from those of their parents.

Industrialization Is Associated with "Achieved" Occupational Status. In preindustrial societies, one's occupational role was determined almost entirely by one's family. Sons of peasant farmers become peasant farmers, daughters of patricians become patrician mothers, and so on. Those who did not end up in the same occupational role as their parents typically had their occupation assigned to them when they were apprenticed; in either case the occupational position was **ascribed status**.

Ascribed status: A social position that is assigned to the individual at birth or other life stage, based on criteria over which the individual has no control.

In industrial systems, families and kin groups had less control over occupational entry. Some families had more resources than did others to find jobs and pay for college or other occupational expenses, but individuals were more able to pursue their own interests and undergo the training provided by extrafamilial agencies. Their position in the social system was still heavily influenced by their parents' position, but it was increasingly the result of **achieved status.** Since persons were increasingly on their own in terms of finding an occupation in the industrial economy, their individualism was increased and reliance on family and kin was decreased.

Industrialization Increases Specialization and Functional Differentiation. Underlying the influences of industrialization was the fact that the household was no longer the center of economic production. Although the family still cooperated as a unit of economic consumption, social differentiation separated the family from its economic production function. Whether it was in a factory, mine, office, or classroom, most activity for which workers got paid was done outside the home.

Work was not alone in being separated from family. Recreation, health care, religion, and problem solving increasingly became extrafamilial activities, especially when families were geographically and socially separated. Until the 20th century, most women gave birth in their homes, assisted by female midwives or kin. Increasingly, as medical professionals took over, birth took place in hospitals. For the first half of the 20th century, doctors worked in patients' homes, but later they required all patients to come to them.

The Conjugal Family Form

Goode generally concluded that industrialization was associated with movement to the conjugal family form. In its ideal-typical form the conjugal family had five characteristics: a nuclear household, bilateral kinship, mate selection by choice, few economic transfers at marriage, and egalitarian interactions.

The Family Became More Nuclear and Less Extended. One way in which the family became more nuclear is that the parent-child unit was less

likely to live with nonrelatives. We have seen that the *familia* once often included persons not related by blood. In one town in Massachusetts in 1880, more than one third of all households had nonrelated boarders (Morgan & Golden, 1979). Significant numbers of urban families continued to take in boarders through the first third of the 20th century (Hareven, 1997).

Unlike the family with unrelated members, the extended family was never common in the United States. One colonial Rhode Island sample studied by Laslett (1977) found that only 3% of households contained extended family members. This is a considerably lower figure even than that for England of the time, where about 11% of households were extended. Immigration to America from Europe, then from coastal to inland settlements, probably decreased the extent to which adult children lived with their parents, even before industrialization. Although the actual number of extended family households was quite small, several researchers (see Lee, 1987) have argued that the extended family might well have been the preferred or normative form, but high mortality and other factors limited its practice.

Families have, however, gotten smaller. In the New England colonies, families averaged eight or nine children (Demos, 1970). At any one time, household size was about six persons (Laslett, B., 1977). By contrast, in 1990 the average family size was 3.17 and the average household size was 2.63. Although women are healthier, reach menarche at a younger age, and live longer, they now have fewer children during their lifetimes.

Several factors account for the decline in childbearing in industrial societies. For one thing, children become economic liabilities in urban societies; they cannot be economically productive until they receive many years of education, after which time they move out of the home. Also, as increasing numbers of women enter the paid labor force, they postpone the birth of their first child and have fewer children.

Not only did families get smaller, but they also became more socially isolated. By the early 19th century, the idea of the private family had begun to emerge. The term "family" itself increasingly came to mean the conjugal or nuclear unit. Rather than being integrated into the community or the kin network, the family was increasingly seen as a retreat from work and other aspects

---

Achieved status: A social position that results from a person's own life events.

of community life. Family matters were less accessible to the inquisitive eyes of the community. In the first part of the 20th century, architecture reflected the desire for privacy. City homes were less likely to have porches, which had been the meeting place between family and community. The middle classes set aside one room in the house, the parlor, for formal visits. Only family members and close friends were allowed access to the remainder of the house.

Although kin groups became less important during industrialization, their influence was still important. Immigrants often relied on kin who had preceded them for support upon arrival to America. Those who arrived first sent money to those who had been left behind (Bodnar, 1985). The same kinds of dynamics operate with many of today's immigrants (see chapter 7).

Many recent family scholars have concluded that the family did not become as small and isolated during the industrial revolution as previous researchers believed. Households were smaller, but significant numbers of persons still interacted with extended family and kin on a regular basis. The nuclear household with extended family ties has been called a **modified-extended** family (Litwak, 1965; Litwak & Kulis, 1987). This might best describe the American family just prior to the postindustrial revolution.

Kinship More Bilateral. Goode found that unilateral forms of descent and inheritance, whether patrilineal or matrilineal, declined when societies underwent industrialization. This has clearly been the case in the United States. The idea of keeping an estate in a family for centuries was not as applicable to the early American experience as it had been in Europe. For those who wished to farm, land was relatively cheap in terms of capital; the expense came in terms of hard work in often-dangerous conditions. The emerging democratic ideal was antithetical to primogeniture.

In both the working and professional classes, it was labor and knowledge that provided a living, not inheritable property. What family property there was got divided equally among children (Leslie & Korman, 1989). Although persons can will their property to anyone they wish, most states now provide that if a parent dies without a will, the surviving spouse gets a certain share, with the remainder to be divided equally among the children. Bilateral kinship is also evidenced in the declining number of women who change their last name when they marry.

Mate Selection Based on Choice. Goode found that as societies industrialized, young adults were freer to pick their own mates. Even prior to industrialization, the European family was allowing more choice in mate selection. This was the result of many of the same factors that allowed individuals to pick their own careers. Parents had less control, since occupational entry did not depend so much on parental authority. The spreading sense of individualism and democracy also influenced movement toward the "choice" position on the mate selection continuum.

In a later chapter we will deal more extensively with the mate selection process, but it is appropriate here to point out the impact industrialization had on the development of using "romantic love" as a criterion for mate selection. As parental control waned, some mechanism had to replace arranged marriage. Prolonged adolescence in the form of more years of schooling and later age at marriage gave young persons more opportunity to interact with members of the opposite sex in less supervised settings. Romantic love, then, replaced rational self-choice or parental choice in the mate selection process.

Economic Exchanges at Marriage Disappear. Neither young couples nor their parents talk today about bride wealth, dowry, *donatio*, or *morgengeld*. The only property transfers at weddings today typically come in the form of wedding presents from families and close friends. The gifts serve a similar function as some older forms of economic transfer — helping the newlyweds establish their own household.

Families Become More Egalitarian. Goode found that relationships between spouses, as well as those between parents and children, became more egalitarian under industrialization. Increasing democratization and individualism, along with the decline of patrilineal inheritance, accompanied increasing equality of married couples.

In 1831 and 1832, Alexis de Tocqueville visited the United States from France. He expressed surprise at how egalitarian American marriages were compared to those found in Europe. In the mid-19th century, a series of laws called the Married Women's Property Acts

---

Modified-extended family: Nuclear family that retains considerable autonomy but maintains emotional and economic ties to other related groups.

Families in the NEWS

Daughters-in-Law in Japan Becoming More Assertive

Japan's practice of two- and three-generation households is all but gone in urban areas, and is now declining in the countryside as well. Part of that change is due to the increasing desire for independence by the daughters-in-law, or oyome-san.

It was once assumed that a bride would move into her husband's home, where she would be required to demonstrate obedience to her mother-in-law. Part of her responsibility would be to care for her parents-in-law as they got older. The oyome-sans sometimes felt that their opinions were not listened to and that they were treated like unpaid servants in their own homes. Their only relief from the burden was to live long enough to see their sons marry, when they could have their own oyome-san.

Now increasing numbers of daughter-in-law are insisting on living in their own homes. Under 30% of Japanese now live in three-generation homes, compared with 56% in 1972.

The change has left increasing numbers of the elderly living alone. In 1999, 46% of those over 65 lived alone or only with their spouse. This is up from less than 20% in 1972. The government has become increasingly involved in caring for the elderly.

Ironically, though, it may have been the government that encouraged the three-generation family in the first place. According to family sociologist Emiko Ochiai of Kyoto, most Japanese couples lived apart from their parents prior to the Meiji era, 1868 to 1912.

The Meiji government wanted the family to become the basic element of welfare, so they made it a legal obligation for younger family members to care for older ones. Most of the responsibility for this care fell to the oyome-san.

Now, in a pattern found in other industrial societies, Japan is moving away from the extended family household.

Source: Stephanie Strom. www.nytimes.com, April 22, 2001.

repealed the old coverture laws. The right of married women to keep and acquire their own property was thereby recognized. Although there are still echoes of the old laws, most states now treat property rights of husbands and wives the same (Collins & Coltrane, 1995).

Marital expectations were not always in favor of the wives, however. Men were traditionally expected to financially support their wives, but wives had no such responsibility toward their husbands. It was not until 1979 that the Supreme Court, acting on a case from Alabama, granted men and women the same right to expect support from each other (Orr v. Orr, 440 U.S.268).

Equality in inheritance law and ownership laws did not translate into identical gender roles. Industrialization created different spheres of influence for husbands and wives. This was reflected in the "cult of domesticity" which glorified the role of the homemaker and mother. The image, probably reaching its peak in the 1950s, was that the father went off to work every day while the mother maintained the home and nurtured the children. This was, at the time, considered a "companionate" marriage (Mintz & Kellogg, 1988).

Consistent with the "cult of domesticity," women began to be awarded custody of children in the still rare divorce cases. In agrarian societies, patrilineal norms awarded custody of minor children to the father and his kin group. Early in phase 2 of industrialization, however, many states adopted the **tender years** rule. By this doctrine, custody of children younger than puberty would automatically be awarded to their mothers unless the mother was proved unfit (Grossberg, 1983). In the United States today, custody is still awarded to the mother in about 90% of the cases, but increasing numbers of courts are considering joint or paternal custody (see chapter 15).

Treatment of Children

The question of how children were perceived and treated in preindustrial societies is part of a larger question that Dixon (1992) referred to as "the indifference debate." On one side of the issue is the mistreatment hypothesis, which states that the history of handling children is one of abuse, neglect, mistreatment, killing,

---

Tender years rule: The norm that, in divorce, a mother should automatically get custody of minor children unless proven unfit.

selling, or simply ignoring. In this view, such mistreatment of children is still commonplace in many parts of the world, and it was only recently in Western history that proper treatment of children has occurred.

Shorter (1975) concluded that indifference was characteristic of all traditional societies, and that good mothering is an invention of industrialization. Shorter also proposed a class difference, arguing that indifference characterized the lower classes until well into the 19th century. DeMause (1974), a psychologist, painted perhaps the bleakest picture of treatment of children, arguing that treatment of children worsens the further one goes back in history.

On the other side of the debate are those like Gies and Gies (1987), who wonder how the human race survived if treatment of children was as bad as the mistreatment school argues. Pollock (1983) reviewed the literature on historical treatment of children and reached two important conclusions. First, she found that researchers reported an improvement in child care toward the end of whatever historical period they studied. Second, she found that whenever researchers did an in-depth study of a narrow time period, using only original sources from that period, they concluded that children were generally valued and treated well. This perspective suggested that the mistreatment hypothesis was partly a product of flaws in the research.

We do know that the way children were perceived and treated changed with industrialization (Ariàs, 1962). Early factories often employed children, but that changed. The "family wage" movement in England and North America in the late 19th and early 20th centuries pushed for industrial wages high enough that one male earner could support a family. Child labor laws, controlling the hours children could work and eventually making it illegal to hire children at all, were passed, as were compulsory school attendance laws.

Infant and childhood mortality rates went down, as did the number of children per family. The 17th-century couple who wanted to have three or four children to support them in old age would need seven or eight live births to increase the odds that enough children would survive. That was no longer true in the 20th century. In addition, retirement programs such as social security were introduced in most industrialized nations. These programs decreased the need to rely on children for economic support.

All of these factors cast children in a different light. Child-rearing techniques, especially in the middle classes, changed focus from harsh discipline to developing creativity and spontaneity. Families became more child centered. Smaller family size and generally increasing prosperity contributed to child-centered views. In a 19th-century family with 10 children and little but cabbage and potatoes to eat, a child's preference about what to have for dinner was neither sought nor, probably, appreciated. In a late 20th-century family with one or two children and an entire supermarket from which to choose groceries, children's preferences are solicited and acted upon. The notion of democracy has been extended to children with the "children's rights" movement (Hareven, 1987).

The Industrialization Backlash in North America

Periods of rapid social change disturb patterns of behavior, including societal family scripts. During industrialization several groups, usually with strong religious convictions, clung tenaciously to preindustrial lifestyles. The Mennonites, Old Order Amish, and Hutterites, even today, reject various aspects of industrialization and maintain rural lifestyles. They have traditional sex roles. Their marriages are endogamous within their religion and result in large families and little divorce. These are all groups with successful and expanding farming operations.

The Hasidim, a group of relatively recent Jewish immigrants, maintain in New York City lifestyles much as they were in their villages in eastern and central Europe 200 years ago (Kephart & Zellner, 1994). Other groups emerged in the 19th century as intentional groups determined to carve out for themselves a perfect religious society in the face of social turmoil.

Both the Oneida community and the Mormons demonstrate the diversity of family forms that developed in industrializing America. Both protested the impersonal lifestyle and disruption of tradition they saw going on around them in a rapidly industrializing society. Both also demonstrate the importance religion can have on family life. To some extent, we can hear similar concerns being expressed today as the uncertainty of a postindustrial revolution results in demand for a return to traditional family forms.

The Oneida Community

The Oneida experiment in family, economy, religion, and community was produced by a combination of social disruption in the 1830s and the charisma of its founder. John Humphrey Noyes graduated from Dartmouth College in New Hampshire as a Phi Beta Kappa. Inspired by a 4-day revival in Putney, Vermont, in 1831, he entered theology seminary at Yale University in Connecticut. He lost his preaching license in 1833, however, because he refused to recant his statement that he was without sin. His doctrine of Perfectionism formed a basis for the sermons he continued to deliver.

During the years he spent preaching, Noyes married Harriet Holton, granddaughter of the lieutenant governor of Vermont, in 1838. Over the next 6 years he fathered five children, four of which were stillborn. The suffering this caused his wife had a lasting effect on Noyes and his theology.

Noyes gradually attracted a following of both believers and detractors. In 1844 his "Putney Perfectionists" adopted the ideal of economic communism. They lived together, sharing property and means of production. This was not a totally uncommon practice at the time, but some of his other innovations were. In 1844, the group began to share not only their property but their spouses as well (Leslie & Korman, 1989).

Commune members lived in a large house where, when possible, each adult would have a private room for sleeping. Almost everything else, however, occurred communally. Meals were prepared and eaten in the central kitchen and dining room. There was an attempt to rotate tasks so that some workers would not gain higher status than others. While the division of labor was largely traditional, women did perform some jobs in the commune that they would not typically have done on the outside.

That outside world, although agreeing that Oneidans were hard-working folks, did not always agree with Oneidan practices. The practice that got them into the most hot water was a form of group marriage that Noyes called complex marriage. He believed that monogamy and romantic love were selfish and overly individualist. In a true family there would be no paired marriage. This was based in part on Noyes's interpretation of the Bible verses that say that there is no marriage in Heaven (Matthew 22:23–30). Rather, the intimate union is not reserved to pairs but extends to the whole body of believers (John 17:21).

While the believers were expected to do without monogamy, the same was not true for sexual expression. Noyes remembered his wife's terrible experiences with miscarriages. He allowed his followers to have sexual intercourse, but they were expected to practice what Noyes called "coitus reservatus." This was different from the practice of "coitus interruptus," where men were expected to withdraw the penis before ejaculation. In Noyes's system, men were expected not to ejaculate at all. Women

This 1855 depiction of children dancing in the Oneida community was originally titled *The Children's Hour in the Upper Sitting Room.*

were allowed to have orgasms because theirs, Noyes pointed out, were not directly related to conception.

The Oneida conception of "ascending fellowship" contributed to the maintenance of the sexual script. According to this concept, older members had achieved greater "perfection" in religious, moral, and sexual matters. Consequently, Noyes believed that adolescent girls should have their first sexual experiences with older men who had mastered coitus reservatus and were therefore closer to perfection. Since postmenopausal women could not get pregnant and were also closer to perfection, men were allowed to ejaculate with them. Young men, who had not yet learned to control themselves, were expected to choose these women as partners, from whom they could learn.

After the first 20 years, Noyes finally allowed childbirth, but not in the uncontrolled manner of nearly constant pregnancy that was common on the outside. Although the word **eugenics** was not yet coined, the program Noyes called "stirpiculture" was designed for biological improvement of the Oneida community. Fifty-three women and 38 men were initially chosen to reproduce; a few others were added later. Sixty-two births eventually resulted from the project, several of whom were offspring of Noyes. In what would have to be considered a success for the time, no women died in childbirth and, although there were four stillbirths, no children were born who were considered defective by the standards of the time (Kephart & Zellner, 1994).

Oneida children were raised communally. They recognized their birth parents, but came to think of all adults as parents and all children as brother and sister. These children went on to produce a quite successful record of achievement in the outside world after the commune dissolved.

Although most members of the community were happy with their way of life, there was dissent. Some who were not chosen to reproduce were upset, and there was grumbling among the young at the limited choice of partners. Forces from outside were even stronger. Noyes was himself a regular participant in the sex life of the community, often reserving the right of "first husband" for himself. Since this involved being the first lover of a recently menarcheal adolescent girl, he was susceptible to charges of statutory rape.

In 1877 John Humphrey Noyes resigned, but he did not provide for solid leadership to replace himself. In 1879, he migrated to Canada. In 1886, at the age of 74, Noyes died and was buried in the Oneida cemetery. Although most members continued to live in the vicinity, and such economic ventures as the production of tableware became well known, the Oneida community really ended with the death of Noyes.

Mormons

Another group arose at about the same time as the Oneida community, with very different results (Kephart & Zellner, 1994). Joseph Smith, born in 1805 in Sharon, Vermont, moved frequently with his family. Joseph was not well educated and had no precocious tendencies.

After one of his treks into the woods, the young Smith reported being visited by God, Jesus, and the angel Moroni, who told him where to find plates on which the "true gospel" was written. By age 23, Smith had translated the plates and returned them to Moroni. The result was the Book of Mormon, which, along with the Bible, constitutes the holy word for Mormons, more formally referred to as followers of the Church of Jesus Christ of Latter Day Saints, or LDS.

Smith began to spread the word, attracting considerable attention in the process. As with many who espouse religious views that are contrary to what is accepted at the time, Smith and his followers became quite unpopular in his hometown. In an unsuccessful attempt to avoid persecution, Smith and his followers headed toward the western frontier. Smith, his brother, and four others were jailed in Carthage, Illinois. A mob stormed the jail, killing Smith and his brother on June 27, 1844.

Under the leadership of Brigham Young, the group struggled on. On July 24, 1847, Young and a small advance party arrived in the Salt Lake Valley and decided that it was the right place to settle. Thousands of believers, most from English or Scandinavian ancestry, followed. In the next 30 years of his leadership, Young participated in the settlement of a vast area the Mormons called the State of Deseret (see Figure 4.6). The name came from the Book of Mormon and translates as "land of the honey bee." A considerably reduced area was recognized by Congress in 1850 as the territory of Utah. An even more limited, but still large, area became an official state in 1896, with the beehive as an official state symbol. Statehood did not come easily, however, because of a distinct practice of the Mormons.

Eugenics: The study of hereditary improvement of the human species by controlled selective breeding.

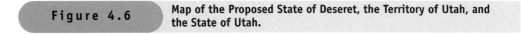

Figure 4.6 — Map of the Proposed State of Deseret, the Territory of Utah, and the State of Utah.

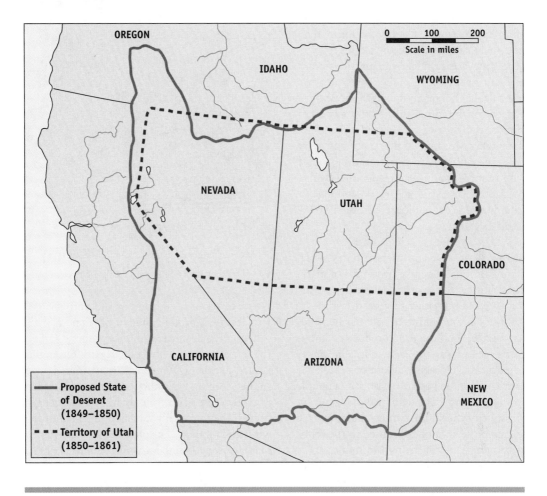

Polygyny. In 1852, church leaders publicly announced that, before his death, Joseph Smith had received a revelation from God endorsing polygyny. Several leaders, including Brigham Young, had taken up the practice. The number of Mormon males who actually married plural wives was relatively small, probably around 10 to 15% (Kephart & Zellner, 1994).

Most who participated had only two wives. A few church leaders had considerably more. John D. Lee had 18 wives and 65 children; Brigham Young himself had 27 wives and 56 children (Kephart & Zellner, 1994).

In the Mormon style of polygyny, a present wife or wives had to give permission before an additional wife could be taken. As is true in many cultures with plural wives, sororal polygyny (marriage of sisters to the same husband) was common. Joseph Smith reportedly married three sets of sisters. John D. Lee married one set of three sisters as well as their mother. All wives were supposed to be treated equally, although that was difficult. Children knew their biological mothers, who were their primary caretakers, and referred to the other wives as "aunt."

Since polygyny had not been practiced in European societies for centuries, it caused quite a stir in the rest of the country. In 1862, President Lincoln signed a bill outlawing polygamy of any kind in U.S. territories. After the Civil War, federal judges and troops were dispatched to Utah to enforce the law. The Edmunds-Tucker Act, which provided for dissolution of the Mormon Church and confiscation of church property, was passed in 1887. In 1890, that act was upheld by the U.S. Supreme Court in a 5 to 4 decision. Had one of the five voted the other way, the history of marriage in the United States might have been different (Ellsworth, 1985).

Shortly thereafter, the church president, Wilford Woodruff, proclaimed an end to polygyny. It took 6 more years for Utah to achieve statehood. During the entire episode, there had been 573 convictions for polygamy. A few rebels maintained the practice simply by not officially marrying the second or subsequent wife. To counteract this, Utah remains one of the few states in which unmarried cohabitation is against the law.

A small number of persons who consider themselves to be fundamentalist Mormons still practice polygyny, although doing so results in excommunication from the church. Such instances are now largely ignored by the state. Although polygyny is a dead practice among Mormons, another unusual but less controversial one remains.

Celestial Marriage. One of Joseph Smith's revelations was that Mormons recognize two forms of marriage. "Marriage for time" is like a secular marriage in that it ends at the death of either spouse. "Marriage for eternity" continues in Heaven, after both partners die, as "celestial marriage," and can even produce children. Higher levels of Heaven can be reached by achieving this type of marriage. Marriage for eternity is "sealed" by private rites that can be performed only in a temple. Both bride and groom must be demonstrably good Mormons. In spite of the strong family emphasis, even close family members cannot be admitted to the ceremony if they are not good practicing Mormons.

Usually marriage for eternity is also marriage for time, but that does not have to be the case. A woman who died without ever being married could be married for eternity to an LDS man, even after her death. The fact that the man might already have a wife was no problem when the practice was combined with polygyny.

On the other hand, marriage for eternity does not necessarily preclude another marriage for time when one's spouse dies. After his death, some women who had been married to Joseph Smith for time and eternity married Brigham Young for time only (Kephart & Zellner, 1994).

Dealing with sealed marriages after secular divorce remains a problem in the Mormon Church. The tradition has been that a divorced man could remarry in the temple; polygyny was still acceptable in celestial marriage. A woman who got divorced after having been sealed in marriage required permission from her former husband and a "cancellation of sealing" from the First President of the Church. In February 1994, the church rules were changed so that the man, too, would have to have church permission to be resealed (Scarlet, 1994).

Some early Mormons, like these, practiced polygyny.

Gender Roles. In addition to favoring large, strong families, the Mormon Church still supports traditional gender roles. As is true with many other religious bodies in the world, only men hold official positions in the Mormon Church hierarchy. Women are active in their aide society. In the Mormon view, however, the gender distinctions exist not because women are second-class citizens, but because they are highly valued for their contributions as wives and mothers. The preferred role for women remains that of wife and mother (Associated Press, 1996).

Noncapitalist Industrialization and Families: The Soviet Union

In Europe and North America, industrialization occurred in a capitalist and democratic framework. The process evolved largely without direction by a strong central government or other powerful agency. Although the Oneida community and many other experiments were communal, they were subcultures within a larger capitalist, democratic society. Mormons, while having a strong sense of community, were proudly capitalist in their economic enterprises and patriotically supported democracy.

We turn our attention now to countries where industrialization ensued in a different political and economic environment. Our major interest is the Chinese experience, but a short description of the Soviet Union case will precede that discussion.

In 1917, the time of the Bolshevik Revolution, Russia was still largely a peasant country. Although

Marxist precepts formed the foundation of the new government, they had to be altered by Lenin and others to fit the Russian experience.

A major goal of communism was to replace private property with communal or state-owned property. Private ownership of means of production had to be destroyed, communists argued, partly because it deprived women of equal rights. Under the old system, according to Engels (1884), marriage was like slavery for women. They sold their lives and bodies to their husbands, who used their wives solely for their own lust and as mere instruments for the production of children, whom the men also owned (Marx & Engels, 1848). To the Russian communists, that description applied to the feudal family as well as the capitalist industrial one, and change was needed.

In the second month of the new Soviet regime, decrees regulating marriage and the family were issued. Divorce was made available at the request of either party. Religious marriages were replaced with secular ones. This was designed to reduce the control of the Russian Orthodox Church, which was seen as an enemy of communism.

By 1926, several laws led in the direction of eliminating the traditional patriarchal marriage and family institution: marriages no longer had to be registered with the state; the concept of "illegitimacy" was eliminated; divorce could be obtained by either partner, on demand; and legal obligations between parents and children and family inheritance of property were minimized. Laws related to sexuality were also changed. Abortion was legalized. Adultery, bigamy, homosexuality, and incest were eliminated as punishable offenses (Leslie & Korman, 1989).

Additional laws were designed to liberate women. Previous custom and law had required a wife to assume her husband's surname. New laws allowed both to take her surname or each to keep his or her own. Laws requiring mutual agreement about where they would live challenged the custom of patrilocal residence. Discrimination in employment was formally ended.

Equality for women was always an ideal of the Soviet Union. Article 122 of the 1936 Soviet constitution reads: "Women in the USSR are accorded all equal rights on a footing with men in all spheres of economic, government, political and other social and cultural activity" (in Field, 1968:11).

These values and laws did elevate the status of women and bring more of them into the work place. They did, however, have other consequences that caused concern among the nation's leaders. By the early 1930s the divorce rate was about 50% higher than at the time of the revolution. The birthrate fell significantly, largely due to availability of abortion. In Moscow in 1935

Konstantin Rodko's oil painting of a traditional Russian village.

there were 155,000 abortions and 70,000 live births (Leslie & Korman, 1988).

Providing universal primary education was a goal that was largely achieved. Schools, teaching strict obedience to the communist party, encouraged children to report suspicious political behavior of their parents. Juvenile delinquency, or what the Soviets called "hooliganism," increased sharply.

Part of the problem was that, while many elements of the traditional family had been destroyed as intended, functional substitutes for the family were not provided as promised. There was not enough money for the public day care nurseries that were originally planned. Very young children and juveniles were increasingly left unattended. The great depression that hit the United States in the 1930s hit the Soviet Union even harder, limiting the ability of the government to provide services.

From the mid-1930s into the 1950s, family law in the Soviet Union took back some of the earlier changes. Abortion and homosexuality once again became illegal, and parents were held responsible for the hooliganism of their children. After 1944, registration of marriages was made mandatory and divorce became more difficult to get than in the United States. After the death of Joseph Stalin in 1953, laws once again loosened.

Women's participation in the labor force continued to rise throughout Soviet history, partly because of egalitarian ideology, which did not extend to military service, and partly because of needs of the economy. World War II killed 6,115,000 Soviet soldiers and left another 14,000,000 soldiers wounded, in addition to millions of civilian casualties of both sexes (Johnson, 1992:329). This expanded opportunities for women.

Russia now has one of the highest rates of women in the paid labor force in the world.

The Soviet Union no longer exists; it is splintered into Russia and other nations, and further into ethnic enclaves. It will be quite interesting to see how each of these deals with marriage and family matters, but the information is not yet available. We turn now to developments in China, for which more information is at hand.

Noncapitalist Industrialization and Families: China

China, with a geographical area just slightly larger than the United States, has a population 4.5 times larger. There are nearly 1.3 billion persons in China, more than one fifth of the world's population (Population Reference Bureau, 2000). It has a long and complex history, which for our purposes will be simplistically divided into two periods. Traditional China and communist China are separated by the 1949 revolution led by Mao Zedong.

Traditional China

There was some industrialization in China toward the end of the traditional period, but for most of the time it was essentially a feudal society (Watson & Ebrey, 1991). The most powerful social institution was the clan or **tsu**. The power of these patriarchal systems was largely unfettered by central governments.

The Tsu. The *tsu*, like the Roman *gens*, included both the large peasant class and the gentry, who were landowners constituting less than 20% of the population (Levy, 1949). The few artisans and craftspersons who existed were also included. The *tsu* lent money to members, collected taxes, exercised judicial control, maintained the important graves of the ancestors, and assumed responsibility for religious observances (Chao, 1977).

Religion. Ancient Chinese religions stressed nature worship and ancestor worship. These elements were also important to the major indigenous religions of Taoism and Confucianism.

Taoism is based on the sixth-century teachings of Lao-tzu. "Tao" means the natural "way," which Taoists

Figure 4.7　　**Yin-yang Symbol**

seek to find and follow. Central to Taoism is the *yin-yang* principle. All things are composed of a certain integrated balance of the two opposites. The Chinese word *yin* refers to the moon, shade, and femininity. It is associated with moistness, passivity, fertility, and weakness. *Yang* is a Chinese word for sun, light, and the masculine principle associated with strength. Both are considered essential elements of all life.

For Confucius, the "way" was less importantly a natural phenomenon and more a system of behavioral patterns among individuals. These patterns are exemplified by the concept of **filial piety**, which originally referred to reverence to dead parents and ancestors, and the sacrifice and sustenance due to them (Parrinder, 1984). Role relationships between fathers and sons were clearly defined in Confucianism.

Age, like gender, was an important determinant of how a person was supposed to be treated. A person's chronological age was often not as important as the point in the life cycle relative to someone else. Like the Sioux kinship system (see chapter 3), for example, the Chinese system had a different term for "older brother" than for "younger brother." In fact, these kinship terms themselves were often used in place of a given name. The "older brother" term was also used as a form of address to someone deserving of great respect.

The Traditional Family

The ideal Chinese family was extended, patriarchal, patrilineal, patrilocal, and polygynous. Although most Chinese marriages were monogamous, wealthy men took additional wives. Concubines were also available for wealthy men and were especially common when the

---

Tsu: The Chinese version of the *gens* or clan.　**Yin-yang principle:** Taoist unity of opposites: female-male; dark-light; passive-active; moon-sun.　**Filial piety:** Central Confucian ideal involving devotion and reverence of a son to his father; extended to other dominant-subordinate relationships.

patriarch's wife had not given birth to a son. In addition to their amorous and reproductive responsibilities, concubines were given routine household tasks under the authority of the primary wife (Goode, 1963).

There were several types of family formation, but the preferred form was by arrangement. Often, a go-between would be employed by the children's mother in the name of their father (Ziaziang, Xinlian, & Zhahua, 1987). Among the gentry, at least, men married at comparatively late ages. Goode (1963) found that, in years from 1150 to 1800, men averaged 32 years of age—just a few years short of male life expectancy—when their first child was born. This is because of the many years of training and because they often had to await their inheritance before they could afford marriage. Given this and the short life expectancy, as was the case in Rome, few children would know their grandfathers in person.

Women got married at considerably younger ages, typically as soon after puberty as the marriage could be arranged. Because of higher rates of female infanticide and other factors, brides were in relatively high demand. The groom's family traditionally provided bride wealth to the family of the bride. In more modern times, this would frequently be passed on to the bride as part of her dowry. It was, in effect, a gift from the groom's family to the bride, like the Roman *donatio*. Occasionally, however, a poorer couple would have to keep part of the groom's family's gift so that they could afford bride wealth when their son got married (Leslie & Korman, 1989).

Children born of the marriage faced different life experiences depending on whether they were boys or girls and whether they were gentry or peasants. Assuming they survived the infant mortality rate, which was probably higher for peasants, they could have a relatively enjoyable first few years. Discipline was less emphasized than parental affection. Children learned obedience and filial piety from stories and by example, rather than harsh discipline (Leslie & Korman, 1989).

Not much is known about the childhood of peasant children. Among the gentry, at least, gender separation became evident at about age 4. Girls continued to receive the affection and attention of their parents, but they were gradually separated from the males of the family and became aware that they would leave the family when they got married. Boys moved to the men's quarters, where they began a period of severe discipline along with intense physical and intellectual training. Wealthier gentry hired authoritarian teachers, who prepared the sons for their exams.

At age 16 or 17, gentry girls and peasants of both sexes entered full adulthood. Gentry boys entered a period of more relaxed discipline. They moved out into the world, traveling and not infrequently getting involved with drinking, gambling, and sexual intercourse with servants or prostitutes. They then reached adulthood, when they married and assumed family responsibilities.

If the period of rigorous childhood training was the most difficult time in the life of a male, the early marriage period was extremely difficult for the female. The wedding ceremony, similar to the Roman ceremony, involved her moving from the *tsu* of her parents to that of her husband. His ancestors became hers. Husband and wife got a night together; the next morning the bride was expected to get up early and serve tea to her mother-in-law. She was thereafter expected, as part of her role obligation, to show deference to her mother-in-law as well as her husband. Just as the husband had to await the death of his father before he could become the dominant male, the bride had to await the death of her mother-in-law before she gained any authority in the home. The status of the peasant husband and wife is not clear. He was certainly the head of the household, but they might have been more equal in the sense that neither had much control over their lives, and work was hard for both.

Status of some gentry women was illustrated by the practice of foot binding. The girl's feet were tightly and permanently wrapped at childhood, so that as an adult her feet might measure only 3 to 6 inches long. She could be permanently crippled. This was both a sign of beauty and a status symbol of the very wealthy. Less well-off families needed the labor of everyone, including women; foot binding was a way of saying that the *tsu* was wealthy enough not to need the women's labor. The practice, which was probably never very widespread, began in the 10th century and lasted until the 20th (Leslie & Korman, 1989).

The Family in the People's Republic of China

In many respects, the early Chinese communist experience paralleled that of the Soviet Union. The ideas of Marx and Engels were central to both, and the two countries were at roughly the same point in industrial development when the revolution occurred.

Institutional Context. The Chinese Communist Party (CCP) was not as threatened by religion as was the case in the Soviet Union. To hold any position of authority in China one had to be a member in good standing of the CCP. One did not do that and remain a devout Confucian.

Most of the economy was put in government hands with the goal of selective modernization. The CCP set out to provide mass education and universal literacy to a huge population that was largely illiterate. They have been largely successful in doing so. Nine years of schooling are now compulsory; an estimated 93% of children enroll in the first grade, and literacy rates now stand at 81.5% (*Microsoft Encarta Encyclopedia,* 1999). China has a university system that, at least in technical fields, is of high quality.

Family Changes.   The Chinese were not as keen on destruction of the nuclear family as were the Soviets. The bigger enemy of communism was the *tsu* structure, especially its ownership and control of the land. Most large estates were broken up and distributed to peasants, who formed first into cooperatives and then into large communes. The communes now performed many of the functions originally performed by the *tsu*. Especially in the rural areas, where 80% of the people lived, allegiances of individual and family moved from kin group to commune. Urban areas were never as controlled by *tsu* and provided a more difficult milieu for formation of communes.

Gender equality was, from the beginning, a goal of the CCP. In 1922, years before the communists took power, a party conference called for voting rights for all persons and the abolishment of legislation restricting women. The old notions of filial piety and low status of women were branded enemies of the people (Chao, 1977).

To help achieve their goal of gender equality, the CCP instituted "speak bitterness sessions" for women. These served as models for feminist "consciousness raising" sessions in North America in the late 1960s and the 1970s. Depending on one's perspective, the speak bitterness sessions either allowed women to speak out about the oppression they had felt for centuries or served as propaganda media for the CCP, which needed women's support and labor.

Only a year after the revolution, major changes in China's formal norms resulted from the Marriage Law of 1950. This law abolished the feudal system of patriarchy, arranged marriage, concubinage, child betrothal, and economic marriage exchanges. Individuals were to choose their own mates, and spouses were to have equal status in the home as well as free choice of occupation and participation in social activities (Chao, 1977).

Family law was further changed with the Marriage Law of 1980. Divorces became easier to get. Expected relationships among family members were clarified, with special concern for the rights of women, children, and the elderly. Efforts to lower the birthrate made contraception a responsibility of both men and women (Zhangling, 1990).

Some goals of these laws are being achieved; others are not. While extended families or *tsu* no longer have full control of marriage partners for their children, free choice does not yet exist. Part of the problem is that, unlike the situation in the United States, China never had an institutionalized system of choice by romantic love. There is still no well-established custom of dating or courtship, although the practice is developing in the cities. While China is moving toward using love for mate selection, it is not the kind of romantic love common in the United States. In Chinese, the applicable translation of the word *love* implies companionship, mutual understanding, and respect (Pimentel, 2000). Both custom and lack of housing prevent large numbers of singles from living alone, or even having a private place to go out together. Consequently, couples are perhaps no more personally compatible than they had been under the system of arranged marriage (Wolf, 1988).

A major goal of the communist revolution was to create a more egalitarian society by ending the power of wealthy families. One way to do that was to end the practice of arranged marriages whereby the sons and daughters of privileged families would marry each other. Even today, however, children from families with high educational, occupational, or political status tend to marry each other (Xu et al., 2000). The result is a new group of privileged families.

There is, however, change in the direction desired by policy. In 1946, 83% of marriages were arranged and none were reported to be freely chosen. In 1986, only 2% were said to be arranged, and 22% were freely chosen. The remainder are mostly some combination of parental involvement and individual choice (Kejing, 1991).

Women are in the paid labor force in large numbers but, as in Russia and other countries, also remain the major child tenders and homemakers. Grandparents, especially grandmothers, do a considerable amount of childcare, and some state-funded day care centers exist. Many people eat their meals in communal dining halls, relieving some of the housework burden (Zhangling, 1990). Women still face some job discrimination and are seriously underrepresented in executive positions, political offices, and the more dangerous occupations.

Most marriages, up to 80% in rural areas but fewer in the cities, are still patrilocal (Watson & Ebrey, 1991:350). Other rural-urban differences exist as well. Rural marriages occur at younger ages, and rural divorce settlements tend to favor men, while those in urban areas might be biased in favor of women (Eshleman, 1994).

Family size has declined in both rural and urban areas, but is still larger in the countryside. In 1955, the average rural family had 6.39 children, compared to 5.67 in urban areas (Chen, 1985). By 1985, average number of children had dropped to 2.45 in rural areas and to 1.38 in urban ones (Feeney et al., 1989).

There were 341,000 divorces in 1980 and 800,000 in 1990, representing a 135% increase (WuDunn, 1991). Although the Chinese are concerned about the increase, the divorce rate in the United States is about five times higher.

The increase in the divorce rate and the increased marriage age have contributed to the decline in the birthrate in China. Falling birthrates accompanied urbanization and industrialization in the west, and the same thing happened in China. In addition, China has made a concerted effort to control population growth, resulting in perhaps the most controversial of China's family policies.

The One-Child Policy. In 1971, realizing that overpopulation was a serious problem, Chinese officials instituted a major campaign to lower the birthrate. Initially, the focus was on later marriage, longer intervals between births, and a limit of two children for urban couples and three for rural couples. By 1979, officials recognized that even two children per couple would result in population growth when life expectancy was increasing. The one-child-per-couple campaign was subsequently launched (Ching, 1982).

A massive advertising campaign glorified the virtues of the one-child family. Free birth-control counseling, devices, and prescriptions were made available, and their use was strongly encouraged. Abortion, too, is widely available. Some coercion has been reported, but a series of voluntary compliance procedures has been instituted.

A special "one-child glory certificate" has been made available for couples who pledge to so limit their childbearing. Couples who signed were entitled to lower-cost health care, increased income, larger pensions, and preferential treatment for their child in schooling and employment. Failure to carry out their pledge could result in the loss of these privileges as well as loss of face for breaking their word. For the first 5 years, signing the pledges was quite popular, after which signing rates dropped sharply (Cooney, Wei, & Powers, 1991). The one-child policy did help lower the birthrate, but many couples continued to have more than one child.

A major concern about the one-child family is related to the traditional Chinese preference for male children. If a couple could only have one child, the overwhelming preference would be to have a boy. Observers noted that there were fewer girls on the birth records than would be expected. Natural birth and mortality rates would predict a **sex ratio** at birth of 105 or 106, meaning a few more boys born than girls. Instead, in the mid-1980s, some areas had infant sex ratios of 111 to 112 for registered births (Johansson & Nygren, 1991). Concern arose over the "missing girls," the difference between the expected 105 boys per 100 girls

This Chinese couple is apparently happy with the one-child policy.

Sex ratio: A demographic calculation of the number of males per 100 females in a given population.

and the actual 112 boys per 100 girls. This could have amounted to as many as 500,000 missing girls per year.

Researchers set out to find out what was going on, strongly suspecting a resurgence of female infanticide. One study that investigated several possibilities concluded that adoption accounted for about half of the missing girls. Many more girls than boys were being adopted out and were not being recorded on the birth records. An unknown number of girls were probably kept by their parents, who never officially recorded their births. Another possibility, selective abortion, was not a major contributor because the medical technology required to determine the gender of the fetus had not been widely available in China (Johansson & Nygren, 1991). The remainder of the gap was probably the result of intentional female infanticide or early neglect of baby girls.

Some regions of China have modified their one-child policy in recognition of the preference for boys; if the first child is a girl, the couple may have another child and retain their one-child privileges. Laws have changed to increase the value of girls; daughters have been made responsible for their parents' welfare and support in old age to the same extent as sons have always been.

Other exceptions to the policy are also occasionally granted. Parents of children with extreme physical handicap or mental retardation are sometimes allowed to have another child. In the name of eugenics and efficient use of scarce food and other resources, however, some provinces require persons with such handicaps to be sterilized before they get married (Eshleman, 1994).

Overall, China's efforts to industrialize have been characterized by considerably more government control than was exercised in the west. This control has extended to significant regulation of the family.

Summary and Conclusion

The four phases of the industrial revolution had a major impact on all social institutions in Europe and North America.

The religious institution saw the Protestant Reformation, which preceded and provided a foundation for capitalist industrialization. Individualism and the ethic of "getting ahead" were important developments. Secularization accompanied urbanization and industrialization.

The Western political experience included a gradually spreading application of democracy and individual rights. At the same time, informal norms became increasingly formalized through governmental rules and regulation. Public schools arose to socialize immigrants to the "American way" and to provide the education necessary for an effective democratic citizenry and productive workforce.

Better health care and other factors increased life expectancy, contributing to a growing and geographically expanding population. The contrast between traditional and modern societies provided a fertile ground for sociological theorizing about society in general and the family in particular.

William Goode produced a classical analysis of the family and industrialization, finding that industrialization was associated with an increasingly nuclear and egalitarian family. Also, there was movement of some functions from the family to other institutions.

Not all Americans were pleased with industrialization. Several religious groups established communities with their own family values. The Oneida community was one such group, establishing a form of group marriage and a eugenics program. The Mormons were much more successful from a survival standpoint. Espousing polygamy initially, Mormons were subject to considerable persecution until they changed that policy. They thrive today with a belief in strong family values and celestial marriage.

Industrialization and its associated family changes do not always occur in capitalist frameworks. Both the Soviet Union and China have attempted communist industrialization while changing the traditional family structures by legislation. Recent events have proved the Soviet experiment to be a failure, at least from an economic standpoint, but they did have success in some family areas. The Chinese experiment continues, but might have internal conflicts between the

what affected sex ratio in China?

freedoms required with industrialization, on the one hand, and their strong central government, on the other.

> *Rethinking in Context* How is a "successful" life defined in an industrial society? A hunting-gathering society? An agrarian society? What characteristics are necessary to achieve that success in each society? How does the family into which one is born affect one's chances of having the characteristics that lead to success in each society?

Additional Resources

General sociological perspectives

Goode, William J. 1963. *World Revolution and Family Patterns.* New York: Free Press.

Chafetz, Janet S. 1984. *Sex and Advantage: A Comparative, Macro-Structural Theory of Sex Stratification.* Totowa, NJ: Rowman and Allanheld.

Parsons, Talcott, & Robert Bales. 1955. *Family Socialization and Interaction Process.* Glencoe, IL: Free Press.

Zaretsky, Eli. 1976. *Capitalism, the Family, and Personal Life.* New York: Harper & Row.

Industrialization in Japan

Smith, Thomas C. 1988. *Native Sources of Japanese Industrialization, 1750–1920.* Berkeley: University of California Press.

Third-world industrialization, feminist view

Wolf, Diane. 1992. *Factory Daughters: Gender, Household Dynamics, and Rural Industrialization in Java.* Berkeley: University of California Press.

The United States, feminist view

Coontz, Stephanie. 1992. *The Way We Never Were: American Families and the Nostalgia Trap.* New York: Basic Books.

History—government and marriage

Cott, Nancy. 2000. *Public Vows: A History of Marriage in the U.S. as a Public Institution.* Cambridge: Harvard University Press.

Internet Sites

Modernization and the family
http://www.familydiscussions.com/books/gillis.htm#1

American family history
http://www.familydiscussions.com/books/mintz.htm
http://www.familydiscussions.com/books/stacey.htm

The economy, industrialization, and the family
http://www.familydiscussions.com/headings/economy.htm

For links to these sites and additional resources, visit the *Families in Context* Web site at:

http://sociology.wadsworth.com

Chapter 5

Gender, Work, and

Postindustrial Families

Prelude

Victor's father was a western Pennsylvania coal miner, his mother a homemaker. When the mine closed in 1978, their family moved to Johnstown to look for work. His father was a proud man and wanted to support his family; he would consider himself a failure if his wife had to work. He managed, although he sometimes had to work two jobs in order to make ends meet. When Victor graduated from high school, he took a job in a local outlet of a national furniture store to help pay his family's expenses and save for a place of his own.

Mira's father deserted the family when she was 7. Her mother, who had been a homemaker for 10 years, had difficulty finding a job. They struggled on the brink of poverty. Mira vowed that she would never be in the position her mother was. After high school, she got a job as a nurses' aide while going to night school. In 3 years she received an Associate of Arts degree in nursing and her Registered Nurse certification. Her pay went up significantly.

By the time Mira met Victor, he had worked himself up to the assistant manager position at his store. After a year of seeing each other, they married. They wanted to have an egalitarian marriage. His salary was bigger than hers, but not by much. Victor was a good cook, but his dishes lacked variety. Besides, Mira was a better cook, and she didn't like the way he stored the spices and rearranged the kitchen every time he cooked. Gradually, she ended up doing all the cooking—except, of course, for outdoor barbeques.

Mira had higher cleanliness standards than did Victor. They would work together cleaning house until it was clean enough for Victor, then he would move on to something else. She finished the rest of the cleaning by herself. Gradually, she began to do all the cleaning.

Two months after they found out Mira was pregnant, Victor got an offer to become the manager of a much larger store. He would make a much larger income, but would be working 60 hours per week or more. Taking the promotion would require moving to Pittsburgh. If he didn't take the promotion, he might not get another chance. If he did, he had a good chance of becoming regional manager in a few years. That would significantly increase his income once again.

Mira and Victor had a decision to make. They could stay put, with her working full time, after the baby was born. They could move to Pittsburgh where his income, if they were frugal, could support them all. If they did that, she could stay home with their baby for a few years, then look for part-time nursing work when their children were in school.

What did they do?

Daniel Bell's 1973 book, *The Coming of Post-Industrial Society,* claimed that the United States, along with a handful of other countries, was becoming a society with modes of production very different from those of the industrial era. The kinds of jobs and careers available to individuals have changed, as have major social institutions such as education. These, as well as demographic changes, have affected the family institution by changing the gender division of labor and marital role structure.

Thinking Ahead Considering the long-term trends that have occurred in the family in the past, what would the family be like in the future if the trends continued? Could any recent changes in technology affect those trends?
What do you think is the best way for married couples to divide up the work and family roles? Should both plan lifelong careers? If the couple has children, should one parent quit work for a while? Which one? Why? How should the household tasks be divided up?

The Postindustrial Revolution

The defining characteristic of the postindustrial revolution is found in technological and economic modes of production that are increasingly based on information and services. This economic change is associated with changes in religion and education. These, in turn, are related to changes in families.

The Economic Institution

Broadly defined, the growing information and services sector of the economy includes jobs that do not directly produce food or a tangible manufactured product. Some information occupations, such as lawyers, investment counselors, and accountants, are paid well, but many services positions such as retail clerks, fast-food workers, and custodial workers, are usually not.

In contrast to service work, skilled and semiskilled manufacturing jobs in such areas as steel, automobile production, and mining have declined. Only about 10% of new manufacturing jobs require high degrees of skill and training. The remaining 90% are routine, easily learned, and require few skills. This "deskilling" of the American workforce makes jobs susceptible to replacement by automation, lower-wage workers, foreign competitors (*Oxford Analytica,* 1986)

While the economy generally did well in the late 1990s, the gap between the rich and the poor seems to be growing. In the 1950s and 1960s, wages, even counting for inflation, went steadily upward. Since 1970, however, only families in two-earner households saw a real gain in income (*Statistical Abstract 1998:* T750). The poorest 60% of families lost a share of family income to those in the upper 20%, who now receive nearly half of all income (*Statistical Abstract 1998:* T747; Greenstein, Jaffe, & Kayatin, 1999). Between 1997 and 1999, the poorest one fifth of households lost 9% of income share, while the wealthiest 1% increased their share by 115% (Shapiro & Greenstein, 1999). Increasingly, maintaining a reasonable family standard of living requires two wage earners.

If present trends continue, young persons of working-class and lower middle-class backgrounds face the possibility of being worse off financially than their parents (Gannett News, 1994). Prospects are generally brighter for those who gain the skills necessary to fill high-tech, high-skill positions.

The Religious Institution

The postindustrial revolution has not only influenced the economy and the types of jobs and careers available, it has also affected the religious institution. Although religion remains as important to individuals in the 1990s as it was in the 1920s (Bahr & Chadwick, 1985), the differences between various religions have been declining.

Historically, families with different religions had different family scripts. In the 1950s Protestants had higher divorce rates than did Catholics. Catholics, however, had more children than either Protestants or Jews, but the latter two groups were more likely than Catholics to stress personal autonomy in child rearing and were more mobile (Lenski, 1961).

Since the 1960s, studies have been finding that the differences between Catholics and Protestants have been disappearing, largely due to changes among Catholics (Alwin, 1986). Although denominational differences are growing smaller, differences remain between those who

Postindustrial American religious groups have to advertise and compete like businesses do.

regularly attend religious services and those who do not. Churchgoers are more likely to be married, to have more children, and to take more conservative positions on several social-familial issues. Churchgoers are also more likely to oppose abortion, homosexuality, and premarital sex and to support traditional gender roles (Davis & Smith, 1999).

The finding of a convergence between Catholics and Protestants but a divergence between frequent churchgoers and nonchurchgoers is due partly to a resurgence of fundamentalism since 1970. Membership in fundamentalist segments of all religions has been growing, while many mainstream groups have lost members (Roberts, 1995). The increase in fundamentalism is associated with support for traditional families and the pessimistic family decline position.

The Educational Institution

The public educational system developed to prepare the young to live in a democratic, industrializing nation. Both skills and industrial work habits, like punctuality and discipline, were stressed. In the 1960s, as postindustrial production loomed, objections arose to the "factory model" of public education.

During the 1960s and 1970s, educational focus shifted from rigid academic requirements and discipline to individual development. Attention was increasingly turned to the development of independent thinking, exploration, and understanding one's self and the world. The 1980s and 1990s brought another shift in educational focus. Cultural pluralism, mainstreaming handicapped students, equity, ethics, and understanding diversity became important, along with a renewed emphasis on math and science (Ryan & Cooper, 1988).

The increased need for more years of formal education affects families in a number of ways. Higher occupational levels require more education and more financial responsibility for parents who send their children to college. Many young adults are postponing marriage and childbearing in order to complete the increased years of education necessary and to establish careers. This, in turn, contributes to a declining birthrate and smaller family size among the highly educated population.

Formal education is becoming a lifelong necessity as the job-market shifts and workers are required to acquire new skills. The average age of college students has been driven up by returning workers and women who are making the transition from housewife to the labor force.

Day care might also be considered part of the society's educational institution. Public education now begins for children at age 5 or 6, while children younger than that are usually cared for by the family or the family's privately arranged provider. Increasing pressure is put on educational institutions to extend their traditional child-care function not only earlier in the life of the child but for more hours each day.

Demographics

In 1946, immediately after World War II, the rate of childbearing increased dramatically, then leveled out about 1964. The first wave of "boomers" graduated from high school around 1965; many of them served in the Vietnam War or graduated from college around 1970.

The significant increase in both the divorce rate and the crime rate, which occurred in the 1970s, is partly a result of the baby boom; there were millions more teenagers and young adults, the age groups most likely to divorce and to commit crimes. Both the crime rate and the divorce rate leveled off around 1980, when the oldest of the baby boomers were in their mid 30s and the youngest were outgrowing their teenage years.

We saw in the last chapter that life expectancy increased significantly during the industrial revolution. That trend is likely to continue in the postindustrial era. If death rates continue to fall as they have since 1968, life expectancy at birth in the year 2050 will be almost 100 years (Seigel & Taeuber, 1986).

In 1900, a woman could expect to spend 19 years caring for a dependent child and only 9 years with an elderly parent. A woman today can expect to spend 17 years with a dependent child and 18 years assisting an elderly parent (U.S. House Select Committee on Aging, 1987). As a consequence, perhaps as many as 20% of caregivers of the elderly also have children under 18 (Family Caregiver Alliance, 1998). These people, called the **sandwich generation,** are faced with providing care both to their children and to their aging parents (*Congressional Quarterly,* 1988). This is not generally seen as a burden, however; the increased family responsibilities have little or no effect on the caregivers' well-being (Loomis & Booth, 1995).

Partly because they are marrying later and partly because of economic conditions, young adults are

---

Sandwich generation: An age group with care-taking responsibilities both to their aging parents and their own offspring.

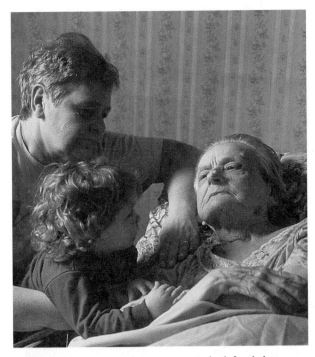

Middle-aged adults sometimes have to care both for their own children and for their aging parents.

living with their parents longer. The proportion of 20–24-year-olds living with parents increased from 43% to 55% between 1960 and 1988 (Glick, 1990).

Although marriage rates have declined slightly, the vast majority of adults will get married. While 95 to 98% of those who came of age in the 1950s got married, about 90% of those born in the '50s ultimately marry (Rodgers & Thornton, 1985). Lifetime probability of marriage remains close to 90%, slightly higher for men and slightly lower for women.

Fertility rates, like marriage rates, have gone down. It is impossible to know for sure whether the declining fertility rate will continue or if it is a temporary phenomenon, but most experts agree that fertility will remain low (Cooney, 1993). Today, women age 65 have an average of 3.08 children. By one prediction, the figure will drop to 2.00 between 2011 and 2015 and dip below 2.00 by 2016 (Zedleswki et al., 1990).

Part of the reason for later age of marriage and declining fertility rates is the increase in numbers of women in the paid workforce. There is no indication that the trend is likely to reverse itself, and it is extremely important to the family and to gender roles and marital role structures. It is to this and related topics that we now turn our attention.

Men and Women in the Paid Labor Force

In all societies with a paid labor force, men have done the bulk of paid labor while women have done most of the unpaid household labor. Although this gender role division of labor has changed significantly, it remains a major influence in the postindustrial era. Women's experience in the labor force has a different history from that of men in terms of opportunity, conflict with family, commitment, and reward.

Labor Force Participation

We saw in the last chapter that there was an influx of women into the paid labor force throughout the industrial revolution. Between 1890 and 1940, the official participation of married women in the labor force varied from 5% to 15% (Wandersee, 1981:68). Since then, however, married women have become a rapidly increasing part of the paid labor force (see Figure 5.1). In the 35–44 year age group, 76.0% of married women now work, compared to 95.7% of their male peers.

Perhaps the most important change of the post-industrial era is the rapid increase in the numbers of working mothers. As Figure 5.2 indicates, labor force participation did not change much from 1980 to 1994 for single mothers, but significant change occurred for married women with children. Participation for those with preschool age children went from 18.6% in 1960 to 63.6% in 1997. When their children were all of school age, 39.0% of married women worked in 1960; that rate went to 77.6% in 1997. This is an extraordinary change in one generation. It has affected families, schools, and the workplace.

The Earnings Gap

When married women first entered the labor force in large numbers, most saw their contribution as a supplement to their husband's income. Because family work was seen as their primary role, many took part-time or temporary jobs in the lower-paid information and services occupations that the postindustrial revolution was creating. As the divorce rate increased, however, more and more women were forced to support themselves, and often their children, on their own income.

Other women, realizing that they might have to support themselves eventually, began to see their participation in the labor force in a different light (Harris, 1987). Participation in career-oriented and

| Figure 5.1 | Labor Force Participation, by Sex and Marital Status, in Percent |

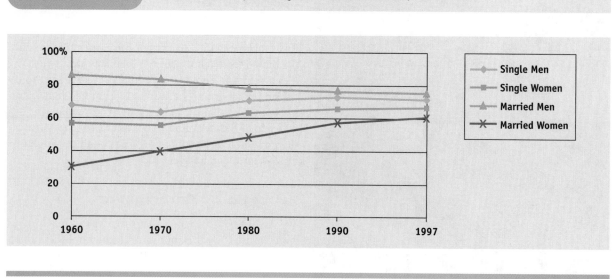

Source: U.S. Bureau of the Census, 1999: *Statistical Abstract of the United States*. Washington, DC: U.S. Government Printing Office. Table 652.

professional occupations increased. As a result of this and other factors, the ratio of women's wages to men's wages increased. In the early 1970s, a woman employed full time (35 hours per week or more) made around 60% of wages made by a full-time employed man. By 1998 that figure had risen to 76.3%. Although Blacks and Hispanics made less money, their gender gap was less. The wage gap narrows for younger workers. For workers under 25, the female percentage of men's income was 91.3. Income of women and men in the workforce is detailed in Table 5.1.

Two basic approaches have emerged to explain the gendered wage gap that is reflected in Table 5.1. Both

| Figure 5.2 | Mothers in the Work Force, by Marital Status, in Percent |

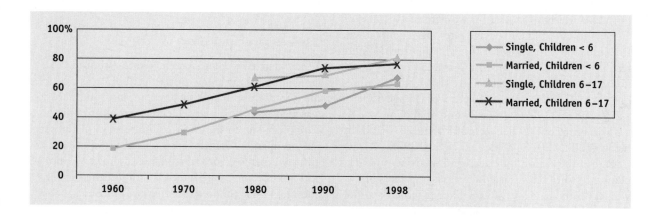

Source: U.S. Bureau of the Census, 1999: *Statistical Abstract of the United States*. Washington, DC: U.S. Government Printing Office. Table 659.

| Table 5.1 | Full-Time Wage and Salary Workers, Earnings by Sex, 1998 | | |

	Median Weekly Earnings		
Category	Men	Women	Women's as % of Men's
Managerial and Professional	905	655	72.4%
Exec., admin, managerial	915	626	68.4%
Professional Speciality	895	682	76.2%
Technical, Sales, Admin. Support	606	419	69.1%
Technical and related support	701	511	72.9%
Sales	622	372	59.8%
Admin support, including clerical	518	418	80.7%
Service	389	296	76.1%
Private household	N/A	220	N/A
Protective	613	481	78.5%
Other service	325	295	90.8%
Precision Production	587	408	69.5%
Operators, Fabricators, Laborers	456	327	71.7%
Farmining, Forestry, Fishing	307	272	88.6%
All Workers	598	456	76.3%
16–24 Years old	334	305	91.3%
25 years and older	639	485	75.9%
White	615	468	76.1%
Black	426	400	93.9%
Hispanic	390	337	86.4%

Source: *Statistical Abstract of the United States,* 1999. Table 702.

the discrimination perspective and the **human capital** perspective explain part of the difference.

The Discrimination Perspective. The discrimination perspective suggests that discrimination remains a major, if not primary, reason for the difference. This view tends to be supported by research conducted by sociologists, especially those with a feminist or conflict-theory perspective. Prior to the Civil Rights Act of 1964, blatant discrimination of the type illustrated in Figure 5.3 was completely legal. Employers could legally choose to hire only men, or only women, for certain jobs. Employers also could legally pay men more, often on the grounds that men "had a family to support" while women did not.

Although several laws now make gender discrimination in employment illegal, it still exists and accounts for a part of the gender wage gap (Fox & Murray, 2000; Blau et al., 1998). Illegal gender discrimination can take a number of forms (Graham et al., 2000). One gender might get preferential treatment in hiring or in initial pay for the same job. Discrimination can also hold down pay raises or promotion, resulting in what some call a **glass ceiling.** Sexual harassment is also a form of gender discrimination.

The Equal Opportunities Employment Commission (EEOC) is responsible for enforcing federal discrimination laws. In 1999 the office resolved 30,643 sex discrimination suits. Of those, 82% were dismissed either because the EEOC found no reasonable cause that discrimination occurred or for administrative reasons. The remaining 18% resulted in some benefit to the person filing the charge. This amounts to 5,515 successful cases, or about 1 successful case for every 11,800

Human capital: Potential means of production held by an individual that was acquired through formal training, education, or experience.   **Glass ceiling:** An alleged invisible barrier to women's advancement in the workforce.

Figure 5.3	Letter from an Accounting Firm in Response to a High School Senior's Query about Career Possibilities, 1962

ARTHUR ANDERSEN & CO.
1700 BROADWAY
DENVER 2

February 7, 1962

Miss Paula Starbuck
Box 702
Meeker, Colorado

Dear Miss Starbuck:

Thank you very much for your letter of January 29.

You asked for my frank opinion concerning women in the public accounting profession, and I am sorry to tell you that our Firm does not hire women. While we have no prejudice against women in business, we have not found it practical to make use of women accountants in our public accounting activities. I believe if you will write to Haskins & Sells, American National Bank Building, Denver 2, Colorado, or Price, Waterhouse & Co., First National Bank Building, Denver 2, Colorado, there might be a possibility for you to work out something with these firms since it is my understanding that they do occasionally hire women for their staff.

I am sorry that this is the policy of our Firm, but I should like to wish you great success in your career.

Very truly yours,

ARTHUR ANDERSEN & CO.

By *A. Bruce Matthews*
A. Bruce Matthews

(Reprinted by Permission of Recipient)

women in the labor force (EEOC, 2000; *Statistical Abstract,* 1999). Some additional sex discrimination cases are handled in civil courts, and many (perhaps most) are never reported at all. Sex discrimination counts for some of the wage difference, and fear of discrimination perhaps does also.

The Human Capital Perspective. The human capital perspective finds that most of the gender wage difference is explained by the fact that women bring different characteristics to the marketplace in such matters as hours worked, number of years experience, years on the job, and choice of different kinds of careers. This

Table 5.2	Average (Mean) Hours Worked per Week, Full and Part Time, Men and Women, 1998		
	Men	**Women**	**Women as % of Men**
Part Time	26.51	21.99	82.9%
Full Time	47.78	43.98	92.0%
All Workers	45.73	39.09	85.5%

Source: Davis, James Allan, and Smith, Tom W.: General Social Survey(s), 1998. (Machine-readable data file). Principal investigator, James A. Davis; director and co-principal investigator, Tom W. Smith; co-principal investigator, Peter V. Marsden, NORC ed. Chicago: National Opinion Research Center, producer, 1998; Storrs, CT: The Roper Center for Public Opinion Research, University of Connecticut, distributor. Micro-computer format and codebook prepared and distributed by MicroCase Corporation, Bellevue, WA. Analysis by Gene H. Starbuck.

view is generally supported by research done by classical economists, business researchers, and sociological functionalists. This view would suggest that most of the wage gap is based on family-related differences in women's and men's roles.

The postindustrial occupational structure generally rewards workers who have a continuous work record, who work full time and are willing to put in extra hours, and who are willing to be geographically mobile when their career demands it. Women have more family and child-care responsibilities than do men, whether by choice or by necessity. These responsibilities can interfere with bringing to the marketplace the kinds of human capital that are most rewarded.

Sometimes the data in Table 5.1 are summarized to read, "Women working the same amount of time, in the same jobs, only make 76.3% of the money men make." This is not an accurate interpretation of the data. Men are more likely to be in the paid labor force, and are more likely to work full time. Of Americans between the ages of 18 and 65, about 76% of men are employed full time, compared with about 56% of women. Another 14.7% of women work part time, compared to 7.2% of men. Put differently, just under 9% of all employed men work part time, compared to 21% of working women (Davis & Smith, 1998). In the 25–44 age group, when people are likely to have minor children at home, two out of three working women put in fewer than 40 hours per week (Williams, 1999).

While Table 5.1 counts only full-time workers. The Department of Labor considers 35 hours per week or more to be full time for these purposes. According to the GSS (Davis & Smith, 1998), among full-time workers, men work about 3.8 hours more each week. Among part-time workers, men work 4.52 more weekly hours. For all workers in the labor force, men work 6.64 more hours (see Table 5.2).

Women also worked fewer weeks per year. Schor (1993) found that women put in 45.4 weeks per year, compared with men's 48.5. The average male full-time worker would put in 2,124.3 hours of paid labor per year, compared with 1,679.8 annual hours for the average female worker, or 79% of the male's hours (Schor, 1993). This figure is close to the percentage of men's pay that women get.

Although Table 5.1 used broad job categories, there are considerable differences in both pay and gender distribution between the specific jobs included in each category. In the broad category "professional speciality," each woman earned 76.2 cents for every dollar made by a man. This category includes nurses, elementary school teachers, physicians, and computer engineers. The first two examples are paid considerably less than the second two; they are also much more likely to employ women. So averaging the salaries of all workers in that group would result in a large gender gap, even if male and female nurses might make the same salary and if male and female computer engineers might make nearly the same amount.

Differences exist even within specific occupations. Among physicians, for example, women are more likely to be in lower-paid specialties such as pediatrics, gynecology, and family practice, which are more closely associated with traditional female roles (Lorber, 1984). According to the American Medical Association (in Famighetti, 1994:967), 41% of all pediatricians are female, but only 3% of neurological surgeons, who are paid more, are women.

Women Probably Majority Entering Law Schools in Fall 2001

In 1970, only about 10% of students entering law schools were women. In the fall of 2000, 49.4% were women. The American Bar Association expects women to top 50% for the first time in the fall of 2001.

Other professions have seen similar change. Last fall, 46% of entering students in medical schools were women. They continue to dominate in veterinary medicine, social science and psychology, and schools of education. In 1998, women received 38% of the nation's M.B.A. degrees.

Entry of more women is changing both law schools and the practice of law. According to Lani Guinier, once nominated as U.S. attorney general and now a professor at Harvard Law School, law classrooms need to change to be more female-friendly. Professors need to encourage more participation and tone down the adversarial nature of some classrooms, she said.

Some law firms are also changing because women are more likely to raise concerns about the balance of work and family. Judith Thoyer became a partner in a large law firm in 1974. At that time, the firm had neither flex-time nor part-time schedules. Now they have both.

According to sociologist Cynthia Fuch-Epstein, women still do not have proportionate representation in top-level legal positions. There remains some prejudice against women, she says, but some women also do not "go for broke" because of their greater share of family obligations.

Source: Jonathan D. Glater. **www.nytimes.com,** March 26, 2001.

In the legal field, women are more likely to be in the specialties of family law and real estate law. They are also more likely to be employed by corporations and the government, rather than in the more traditional fee-for-service professional firms or independent practice (Hodson & Sullivan, 1990).

The differences result primarily from the traditional gender-role expectations that assign to husbands the primary earner role and to wives the primary family role. For family purposes, women move in and out of the labor force more than do men. While men may change jobs or be unemployed for periods of time, they are generally in the labor force for virtually their entire adult lives. Very few women have this experience (Moen, 1985). Job turnover is higher for women, who are more likely to leave a job to follow their husbands (Women's Bureau, 1992; McElrath, 1992).

Studies of lifetime work experiences find that men spent only 1.6% of all potential work-years away from work while for women workers, 14.7% of all potential work-years were spent away from paid work. Ten years of job seniority raises the wage of the typical worker by over 25% (Women's Bureau, 1992).

Women who make lifetime career commitments to paid labor approach their work differently from women who do not, and they generally get more promotions and make more money (Lopata, 1993). The fact that

there are fewer such women than men has resulted in pay differences. However, the fact that the numbers of such women are increasing also can result in apparent gender differences.

In the early 1980s, Seiling (1984) compared salaries of men and women in large accounting and legal firms. Overall, a women in accounting made only 83% of a man's earnings. However, further analysis revealed that, at the entry level, a woman made 99% of a man's earnings. At the highest seniority level, a woman got 90% of a man's pay. The reason the overall gap was so low is that 46% of the entry-level employees were women, while only 5% of the senior level accountants were women. At first this appears to be an example of a glass ceiling, where women were not promoted to senior positions. Instead, Seiling concluded, it represented the fact that only recently were women entering the field; at the time the current senior workers were originally hired, only about 5% of accounting graduates were women.

Seiling's study supports both the discrimination and the human capital explanations of the gender pay gap. Prior to the 1964 Civil Rights Act, women were discriminated against by not being hired into many accounting firms, so few women became accountants (see Figure 5.3). After 1964, it took awhile for large numbers of women to choose that profession and get the training for it. By 1980, however, nearly half of accounting graduates were women. They were employed at nearly the same pay as their male counterparts, but did not have as much experience, on the average, as male accountants who had generally been in the field longer.

Because of changing gender norms and antidiscrimination legislation, women are increasingly entering other jobs previously dominated by men. As increasing numbers of young and relatively inexperienced women enter any particular labor force category, they will hold down the average wage for women relative to men, even though they might make as much in a lifetime as men their same age and with the same experience. If they drop out of the labor force for some period of time for family purposes, they will generally have less job experience than men in the same occupation and will probably make less money. McElrath (1992) found that male faculty members in higher education, for example, average about 50% more years of service (10.6 to 15.12 years), partly accounting for women's lower average rank and salary.

Although jobs traditionally considered "women's jobs" continue to be paid less than those considered "men's jobs," there is increasing evidence that, when women make the same occupational and career choices as men, they stand to be paid very nearly the same as men. Gerhart (1990) studied a large firm in which the overall proportion of female to male income was 88%. Most of the difference was because women had different college degrees and majors, had fewer years of job experience, and worked in different kinds of jobs.

Gerhart (1990) found that the biggest difference between women and men was in initial salary; whether this was because they had less experience when hired or for other reasons was not determined. Women made about 98% of the salary made by men with the same years of experience in the firm, the same educational level, and the same job description.

Wright and Baxter (1995) found, in the United States and other postindustrial workforces, that barriers existed to women in initial placement in an occupational structure, but they found little evidence of a "glass ceiling." In a similar study, Nadeau, Walsh, and Wetton (1993) compared male and female wages at a large Canadian public sector employer. While men made more money overall, it was largely because more of them were in higher-paying job categories. Women in those same categories made virtually the same amount of money as did the men. When occupation, experience, and other characteristics of the workers were considered, the wage difference between women and men became statistically insignificant.

Morgan (1998, 2000) found that in engineering, overall, men made more than did women. These differences, however, were found primarily among older men and women in the field. Some of these women had interrupted their careers for family purposes. Morgan found, however, that gender pay difference among younger cohorts of engineers was essentially zero.

Both the discrimination perspective and the human capital approach have empirical support. The degree to which each contributes to the gender earnings gap is unsettled. Blau et al., using a broad definition of discrimination, concluded that discrimination accounts for at least half of the difference in wages for men and women. Graham et al. (2000), using a legal definition, found that workplace discrimination could account for no more than 3% of the gap. Gerhart (1990) contended it is only 2%.

The human capital approach would suggest that, as long as the occupational structure continues to reward what it currently rewards, and as long as family responsibilities are gendered, there will continue to be a gendered pay gap. This is not, however, necessarily due to employment discrimination. If today's young women treat careers in exactly the same way men do, in terms of career choice, work hours, career focus, and other factors, they stand to make virtually the same amount of money as their male counterparts (Taniguchi, 1999). Not all women want to treat their career that way, however, and women's family role makes it difficult. As long as some women put family work ahead of paid labor, while few men do the same, the overall average wage difference will persist.

Family-related variables clearly influence the experiences men and women have with paid labor. Family and gender differences also affect other aspects of individuals' life chances, as we will see next.

The Danger Gap

Partly because of the influence of feminist researchers, hundreds of studies have been devoted to the gender pay gap. Very few social scientists have examined the danger gap. In a review of feminist literature, Fox and Murry (2000) mention the "family security" issue. They suggest that women actually do more of the family security work by doing community networking, supervising children, and other family-related tasks. They further suggest that men may be counterproductive in the "family protector" role; men might cause more family danger by such actions as bringing guns into the home and by physically abusing other family members.

Table 5.3	Deaths in Recent American Wars, by Gender			
	Number of Deaths			
War or Action	**Total**	**Female**	**Male**	**Male Ratio**
Vietnam	58,191	8	58,183	.0001
Panama	23	0	23	.000
Persian Gulf	390	15	375	.04

Source: Farrell, Warren. 1993. *The Myth of Male Power*. New York: Simon & Schuster. Pp. 129, 187.

Family protection goes far beyond the bounds of the home, however. In spite of recent changes in occupational roles, the division of risk still is based on traditional gender expectations. The risks for women include the possibility of economic insecurity in the event of divorce and the difficulties of combining a successful career with family life. With the exception of dangers associated with the sex-irreducible role of childbearing, physical dangers are more likely to be part of the male gender role. Danger has an impact on pay differences, but it also impacts literal life chances.

"Major provider" and "protector" have long been part of the male role. The most obvious case is the warrior role, which has historically been almost universally male. Nearly all American battle casualties have been to men, including those in more recent wars (see Table 5.3).

Traditional exclusion of women from military combat has saved women's lives, but it has also precluded many military career opportunities. This has only recently changed. While women are now allowed in almost all military positions, only men are required to register for the draft.

The male provider role has assigned to men the role of working longer hours in order to be the primary economic support of the family. The male protector role has assigned men to the most dangerous occupations. The industry group with the highest fatality rate is agricultural work, which is 91% male; second most dangerous is mining and quarrying, which is 98% male (U.S. Bureau of the Census, 1993:433). High fatality rates are also found in fire fighting, logging, heavy trucking, and construction, all of which are at least 98% male. Secretary and receptionist jobs, which are about 97% female, are lower paying but among the safest of jobs (Farrell, 1993:106). As a result, men are significantly overrepresented in the risk of employment-related fatalities. Men make up about 54% of the workforce but constitute 92% of job-related deaths (see Figure 5.4).

In addition to job-related dangers, men are more likely to be victims of homicide, suicide, and accidents (see Table 5.4). For both Blacks and Whites, death rates are higher for men than for women. Differences are especially pronounced in the homicide category; White men are 3.2 times more likely to die by homicide than White women; Black men are 5.1 times more likely to be homicide victims than Black women. The extraordinarily high rate for Black men is 7.7 times that of White men and 24.7 times that of White women.

Table 5.4	Death Rates from Accidents and Violence, by Race and Gender, per 100,000 Population, in 1990			
	White		**Black**	
Type of Death	**Male**	**Female**	**Male**	**Female**
Motor vehicle accidents	26.7	11.6	28.1	9.4
All other accidents	23.6	12.4	32.7	13.4
Suicide	22.0	5.3	12.0	2.3
Homicide	9.0	2.8	69.2	13.5

Source: U.S. Bureau of the Census, 1993. *Statistical Abstract of the United States: 1993* (113th ed.). Washington, DC: U.S. Government Printing Office. P. 98.

| Figure 5.4 | Gender Composition of U.S. Workforce and Employment-Related Deaths |

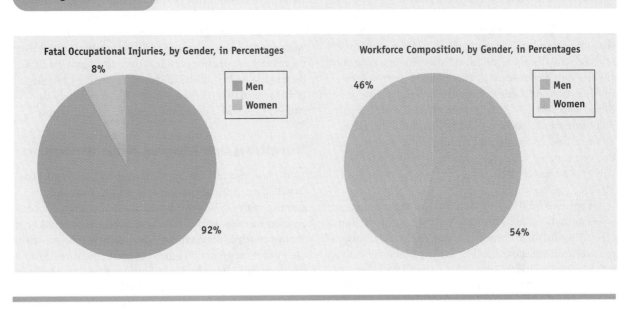

Source: U.S. Department of Labor, Bureau of Labor Statistics, 1997. National Census of Fatal Occupational Injuries, 1997. Table 4. Accessed on-line December 17, 1999, at **http://www.osha.gov/oshstats/bls/cftb0100.pdf**

Women and Men in the Family Workforce

Although scripts are changing in the postindustrial era, women are still responsible for most of the child care, housework, and kinkeeping in American families. Women have generally increased their participation in the paid labor force more rapidly than men have increased participation in the unpaid family workforce.

History of Housework

We saw in previous chapters that women have always worked, but did not generally participate in paid labor. In preindustrial societies, most men did not work for wages either, but grew or made most of what they needed and traded for the rest. While the men were more likely to do the heavy work in the fields, women did the spinning, weaving, sewing, candle and soap making, often the butchering and beer brewing, food preparation and storage, and other tasks closer to home (Schor, 1993).

Until well into the industrial era, many chores associated with today's housewife took little time. Most meals consisted of relatively simple one-pot dishes like soups and stews. Very little time was spent cleaning house

(Margolis, 1984). Houses were much smaller, and many had dirt floors, open hearth fires, and other conditions that made cleaning difficult. In addition, standards of cleanliness and child care were considerably different than today (Schor, 1993).

Washing clothes was an arduous task, but it was done infrequently. Many individuals had only one change of clothes, and those might not be washed for several days. The shortage of closets in older homes, even those with several children, attests to how few clothes were owned (Schor, 1993).

The term "housework" did not appear in the English language until 1841, signaling recognition of a separation of family work, which occurred in the home, and economic production, which occurred elsewhere (Cowan, 1983). Along with the development of the "cult of domesticity," which defined a new role for women, came the "cult of cleanliness." Beginning in the late 19th century, increasing numbers of upper- and middle-class women began to be full-time housewives in the more modern sense. Industrial processes could do some tasks, like preserving foods and weaving cloth, more efficiently. Throughout the 20th century, technological developments made specific chores easier; these developments were, however, offset by changing expectations. Automatic washing machines made clothes washing considerably easier, but families bought more clothes and expected to keep them cleaner.

The "family wage" movement sought to give married men a high enough wage to support a family. As that movement gained strength, so did the "domestic science" and "home economics" movements. A host of experts taught housewives how to keep their homes spotless, how to prepare more lavish and nutritious meals, and how properly to raise children. One result was more sterile homes, lower infant mortality rates, more nutritious meals, and a more child-centered society, but another result was that housewives had to devote more time to these tasks (Ehrenreich & English, 1978).

In spite of laborsaving devices, full-time housewives actually saved no time. A classic study by Vanek (1974) found that housewives put in about 52 hours per week on their duties. The same number of hours was worked in 1929, 1936, 1943, and 1953. In 1967–68, housework hours actually went up to 56 per week.

Although workweek hours remained relatively constant, the tasks changed somewhat. Between the 1920s and the 1960s, food preparation time decreased almost 10 hours per week, largely because of the availability of packaged foods, but this was offset by an increase in shopping, managing, transporting, and child-care tasks. The only new home appliance that actually reduced overall housework time was the microwave oven (Vanek, 1974; Cowan, 1983).

The woman's role in the traditional family script goes beyond housework; **kinkeeper** tasks are usually assigned to women also. Kinkeepers are the extended family communicators, providing links between and within generations. They write, call, and visit family members and friends. They organize family gatherings for holidays and special family events like birthdays and anniversaries. They are also likely to act as the family helper, problem solver, or mediator (Rosenthal, 1985). Women are also more likely to be the caregivers of elderly or disabled relatives (Abel, 1991).

Most of the duties listed as part of the kinkeeper role are instrumental tasks, but women are also involved in expressive activities. In what Hochschild (1983) referred to as **emotion work,** women help hold relationships together by analyzing and discussing feelings more than do men. This process actually manages, shapes, and defines feelings, and is not just part of a set of tasks for women but is also a source of power within the home.

Mederer (1993) divided household work into management and task components. The wives reported that they did most of the tasks, but they also reported that they made nearly all the decisions regarding how the tasks were managed. The women did not simply do chores; they made decisions that affected the family.

Scripting the Marital Role Structure

To explain the process by which a married couple constructs their mutual marital role script, West and Zimmerman (1987) combined symbolic interactionism and feminist analysis. They developed the concept of "doing gender." In everyday life, partners interact with each other in such a way as to construct and reaffirm their notions about being feminine or masculine. Behaving in stereotypical gender fashion, by cooking dinner or mowing the lawn, for example, is a way a wife and husband reaffirm their gender identities (Berk, 1985). To depart from expected behaviors is somewhat risky in terms of self-identity and social acceptance, and it requires negotiation both with the partner and oneself.

"Doing gender" is not a single event that a couple does once and is done with; it is a continuing process that lasts throughout the life span of the relationship. Each partner brings his or her own notions of gender, part of his or her individual scripts, into the relationship. If the two images are compatible, the couple is likely to construct their mutual script without much discussion or negotiation. If the husband and wife have different ideas, or if circumstances like his loss of job require that the script change, new meanings will need to be negotiated.

The "myth of separate worlds" has sometimes led to seeing work and family as completely separate entities (Kantor, 1977), but many scholars have pointed out that there is a connection between the two institutions (Piotrkowski et al., 1987). Like "doing gender," the relationship between family and work is an ongoing and interrelated process (Voydanoff, 1987).

Couples have a range of options when negotiating their work-family scripts. Some prefer to develop

---

Kinkeeper: A role that holds family and relationships together by communication and organization. **Emotion work:** "Efforts to shape and control one's emotions by socially defining them, through conversations or personal reflections on one's feelings" (Collins & Coltrane, A-3).

Table 5.5		Median Annual Income by Type of Family, 1997	
Married Couple Families		**Single-Headed Families**	
Both Work	**Husband Only Works**	**Male-Headed**	**Female-Headed**
$58,381	$33,748	$31,600	$19,911

Source: *Statistical Abstract of the United States: 1998.* (118th ed.). Washington, DC: U.S. Government Printing Office. Table 750.

"Soccer moms" contribute hours of service to their families and have become an important political constituency.

complementary scripts, in which all responsibilities are fulfilled because each person specializes in certain tasks. In the most common and traditional of this type, the wife is the primary family worker while the husband is the primary paid worker. Others couples like **parallel scripts,** in which the husband and wife are essentially interchangeable; both are co-family workers and both are co-paid workers.

Complementary Scripts.   Complementary scripts have both advantages and disadvantages for some couples. Family income difference can be a major drawback. Dual-earner couples generally have more income and are cushioned more from the possible loss of the husband's job. Table 5.5 compares the income of one-earner and two-earner families.

The traditional single-earner script can be disadvantageous to a wife in the event of divorce or death of her husband. She becomes a "displaced homemaker," often without marketable job skills or recent educational experience, and she faces the real prospect of poverty. Divorced husbands who were sole breadwinners have a higher proportion of child support obligations than their peers who had working wives.

Not all traditional single-income families are poor. Some couples fall in the category of the "two-person one-career" script. Traditionally, professions such as physicians and college professors, as well as many corporate executives, were arranged such that the husband held the paid position but the wife was part of the culture of the profession. Wives who could entertain clients or colleagues and participate in charity events were considered essential to a successful career. Such wives might also provide career support services such as typing, bookkeeping, researching, and writing (Papanek, 1973).

Some working-class occupations have characteristics of the "two-person, one-career" script. Highway construction workers, for example, must move frequently. Their workweeks are long and arduous. Many such workers are men who rely on their wives to set up and organize their homes, enroll their children in schools, buy work clothes, and tend to other tasks that keep the workers on the job and providing income.

While full-time homemakers are not directly paid for their work, they are materially compensated at roughly the same level as their husbands. They live in the same home, eat the same food, and take the same vacations. Their compensation is based on their husband's earning power, rather than being directly related to their own

Complementary scripts: A role relationship in which actors assume different roles, but those roles mesh with and support one another.   **Parallel scripts:** A role relationship in which actors assume the same, identical, interchangeable roles.

labor. For doing roughly the same tasks, the housewife of a physician is compensated considerably more than the housewife of a construction worker.

In the modified complementary script, the wife is a full-time family worker as long as young children are in the home. During this period the couple's marital role structure resembles that of couples who adopt the traditional one-earner approach. Before children are born, or after they have grown older, the couple more closely resembles a modified parallel or even a complete parallel script.

Women at all educational levels prefer some form of modified complementary script. Only 1% of a sample of 821 college undergraduates said they would prefer remaining single and working full time. The lifestyle sequence "graduation, full-time work, marriage, children, stop working at least until youngest child is in school, then pursue a full-time job" was preferred by 53% of the women. Only 6% of 535 undergraduate men picked this option for themselves (Schroeder et al., 1993:243).

Many couples see a trade-off between the advantages of the single-earner home and that of the two-earner home. One study found that one-earner families were more satisfied with family life but less satisfied with finances. Two-earner families, on the other hand, reported more satisfaction with finances but less with married life (Hilton et al., in Knox & Schacht, 1994). Roxburgh (1999) found that, although women work fewer hours, mothers are more satisfied with their jobs than are either fathers or female nonmothers.

In some cases, adding a second worker adds considerably more expense as well as additional income. If a woman returns to work after a period of homemaking, work-related expenses take from 25 to 50% of her take-home pay, with child-care expenses consuming the biggest part (Israelsen, 1991). Additional expenses include housecleaning services, use of more packaged and restaurant meals, and transportation (Oropesa, 1993).

Part-Time or Shift Work. Part-time or shift work are options for some couples. While men who work part time rather than full time report lower levels of well-being, studies are mixed about well-being of women with part-time employment. Moen (1992) found that women with part-time employment had higher levels of well-being. Baker (1995a), however, found that married women with children who worked part time were less satisfied with their gender roles than were either full-time employed women or full-time homemakers. Perhaps this is because women's part-time

work does little to change the home expectations; only full-time employment develops significantly more household equality (Stier & Lewin-Epstein, 2000).

Because of the growth in the services sector of the economy, increasing numbers of people are working weekends. In as many as one quarter of two-earner couples, at least one partner is involved in **shift work.** The husband is the sole shift worker in about 15% of dual-earner couples; in 6% only the wife works shifts; and both do in 3% of dual earners (Presser, 1987).

Some couples prefer shift work because wage differentials often pay more or because it helps with the child-care problem. Child care by fathers increases significantly for shift workers (Brayfield, 1995). When fathers work days and mothers work shifts, 37% of preschoolers have fathers as primary care providers (O'Connell, 1993).

Most workers participate in shift work because it is a requirement of their job rather than because it is their first choice. Shift work limits a couple's leisure time together and makes scheduling of rituals such as family meals difficult. Hertz and Charlton (1989) found that male shift workers are more frustrated by their inability to protect their family and provide companionship to their spouses. Female shift workers are also less satisfied with their family time than day workers.

In a nationwide survey, White and Keith (1990) found that couples with a shift worker were less satisfied with their sexual relationship and were more likely to get a divorce. Shift work seems particularly difficult for parents early in marriages. Father with less than 5 years of marriage are six time more likely to separate or divorce if they worked nights rather than days. Working nights increases the odds of divorce for mothers by a factor of three (Presser, 2000).

As a strategy to reduce work-family conflict, some working couples reduce their commitment to paid work in a process that Becker and Moen (1999) called "scaling back." Although either or both of the partners may scale back, it is most often the wife who does so, especially during the childrearing years.

Parallel Scripts. Parallel scripts are increasingly common. In a modified parallel script, the husband remains the full-time primary provider while being a secondary family worker. The wife is the primary family worker and secondary provider. For these couples, although both have permanent and full-time income-producing positions, the husband's career is considered most important. If relocation is required for the

---

Shift work: Any work schedule in which more than half of an employee's hours are before 8 AM or after 4 PM (Bureau of Labor Statistics).

With parallel scripts, parents are essentially androgynous and interchangeable.

husband's career, the wife becomes the **trailing spouse,** who moves with him and then finds employment for herself. Although increasing numbers of husbands have been the trailing spouse, wives still assume that role in 70% to 90% of dual-earner couples (Shihadeh, 1991).

Lifetime earnings and advancement will be limited for the trailing spouse compared with the primary breadwinner; this factor helps account for the overall lower incomes of women compared with men. Advancement and higher pay for the wife are sacrificed so that the husband's career can advance. This is sometimes done because the husband is already making more money, and the net income gain to the couple will be greater if his career is advanced. This can become a cycle, however, in which the gap in earnings of husband and wife continually grows (Shihadeh, 1991).

The relationship between husband-wife wage gaps and trailing spouses is part of "doing gender" that can become a **self-fulfilling prophecy.** If a couple believes that the hus-

band's career will earn more money in the long run anyway, they will behave in ways that maximize his earnings; consequently, his career ends up making more money.

Some couples arrange their parallel script in such a way that they do nearly equal amounts of home/family work, as well as devoting equal time to their paid labor. These have been called two-housekeeper couples (Ferree, 1991) and co-provider couples (Hood, 1986). In many cases, both husband and wife have a **career** that requires extensive training and commitment; these are called dual-career couples.

Regardless of how this type of script is defined, it is relatively rare. Ferree (1991) defined a two-housekeeper couple as one in which the wife did less than 60% of the housework. Only 10% of the two-earner families in her sample met this criterion. Potuchek (1992) estimated that in only about 15% of two-earner couples was the wife considered equally responsible for providing.

Some researchers have argued that true dual-career couples have been so statistically rare that the concept itself is flawed and should not be used (Benenson, 1984). Married women in high-status professional positions are more likely to be single or divorced than men in similar positions, and the married professional women are more likely to be without children than their male co-workers (Hiller & Dyehouse, 1987; McElrath, 1992). Also, professional women tend to marry men in even higher, better paid, more prestigious professions. All of these factors make true egalitarian dual-career marriages rare.

An even more rare script is the **commuter marriage,** in which the husband and wife have separate residences, usually in separate cities, for extended periods of time. There is nothing new about marriages in which husband and wife have to be separated for long periods. Navy couples have had this arrangement, as have politicians, professional athletes, salespersons, and long-haul truckers. The idea that each partner will have at least a semipermanent residence, however, is relatively new.

As is true for shift work, commuter marriages generally arise from work demands rather than being a planned first choice. Often one person's career advancement requires residence in a different city than the other's career calls for. As increasing numbers of women are focusing on careers, they are less willing to be the trailing spouse; men have not traditionally been expected to

---

Trailing spouse: Husband or wife of an income-producer who relocates for employment purposes. **Self-fulfilling prophecy:** A prediction that comes true because of the effect of the prediction itself. **Career:** A long-term professional or occupational path with commitment and opportunities for promotion, advancement, and change. **Commuter marriages:** Dual-career marriages in which husband and wife live separately.

Finding Out | 5.1

Measuring Workweeks

There are differences of opinion among researchers about just how much the "second shift" expands women's work compared with men. Three studies of paid and home labor done by men and women are labeled A, B, and C in Table 5.6. The studies measure the variable in somewhat different ways.

Study A in Table 5.6 compares labor-force hours and housework hours for men and women in 1969 and 1987. Schor's (1993) original data were given in total annual hours and have been converted to weekly hours for this table. Between 1969 and 1987, both labor-force hours and homework hours increased for men. While average housework hours decreased for women, paid labor hours increased more. The ratio of total hours for women and men remained almost unchanged.

When data for all U. S. adults were considered in study A, Schor found women doing more hours of homework while men did more hours of paid labor. In 1987, men worked a total of 103.2 hours for every 100 hours women worked. When only men and women in paid labor were considered, their total hours worked per week were almost identical: 54.5 hours for men and 54.4 for women in 1987.

Study B looked at work hours in several industrial countries, of which three are reported here. Unlike most studies, this one found that men averaged significantly more total hours than did women. This results partly from the fact that commuting hours are included in the paid labor hours; most studies do not include that as work time.

Men in the United States commuted 1.5 hours more per week than did women. Also, this study included all men and women, not just those in the paid labor force. The inclusion of housewives, with no paid labor time, brought down the average total work time for all women.

As work was defined in this study, men had 108.7% of women's hours, or 4.9 more hours each week. The ratios were similar in Japan and Sweden, although the mix was different. Japanese men worked longer hours in the paid labor force but did considerably less housework than men in the United States (Juster & Stafford, 1991).

Calculations for Study C were made by Shelton (1992) from data collected by the National Survey of Families and Households (Sweet et al., 1988). Full-time homemakers were excluded from the calculations. Based on their definitions of homework and paid work, married men totaled only 86.8% the total hours worked by women, or 9.4 fewer hours per week. For workers with no children, the ratio was more nearly equal, but for workers with two or more children, women did considerably more home labor that was not matched by an equivalent decrease in paid labor. The data for those with children, however, include both single and married parents with children in the household. A number of very busy single mothers bring up the average for mothers as a group. There are considerably fewer single fathers with caretaking responsibilities to bring up the average for men.

---

sacrifice their careers for those of their wives. Ultimately, a divorce or commuter marriage is likely in this situation.

Partners in commuter marriages report less stress from role overload than single-residence couples and are more satisfied with their work lives. They are considerably less satisfied with their marriage and family life, however, and report less satisfaction with life as a whole (Bunker et al., 1992). Couples who have lived together for a considerable period before commuting probably handle it more successfully than do partners who are recently married (Gross, 1980). There is no evidence, however, that more than a small handful of couples can make a commuter marriage work for extended periods.

A Second Shift?

Cases in which both husband and wife work can result in what Hochschild (1989) called the "second shift" for some women with paid employment. They keep their traditional role as homemaker but add the role of worker. Most of the time, their husbands do not increase their homemaking work as much as the wives increase their income-producing work. Wives can end up with a longer overall workweek than do their husbands. While men's relative contribution has increased, women still do about twice as much routine housework than do men (Coltrane, 2000).

The "second shift" is not just about hours. According to Hochschild, women's family work is underrepresented, underappreciated, and more tedious than men's. The ef-

Table 5.6			Studies Comparing Men's and Women's Work, in Hours per Week Paid and Home Labor				

	Men			Women			Men as % of Women
Study and Sample Percent	Paid	Home	Total	Paid	Home	Total	
A All U.S. adults 1969	33.7	13.1	46.8	13.9	32.4	46.3	101.1
A All U.S. adults 1987	32.2	16.0	48.2	19.1	27.7	46.7	103.2
A U.S. labor force 1969	39.4	11.9	51.3	32.8	21.5	51.3	100.0
A U.S. labor force 1987	41.3	13.2	54.5	32.8	21.5	54.4	100.2
B All U.S. 1981	47.5	13.8	61.3	25.9	30.5	56.4	108.7
B All Japan 1985	56.5	3.5	60.0	25.8	31.0	56.8	105.6
B All Sweden 1984	43.6	18.1	61.7	25.8	31.8	57.6	107.1
C U.S. full-time employed, married, 1987	48.1	21.9	70.0	38.9	41.7	80.6	86.8
C U.S. employed, no children	46.6	18.5	65.1	39.8	28.2	68.0	95.7
C U.S. employed, 1 child	49.5	26.1	75.6	38.8	43.8	82.6	91.5
C U.S. employed, 2 or more children	49.8	23.8	73.6	37.6	51.2	88.8	82.9

Adapted from: A: Schor, Juliet B. 1993. Pp. 35, 36. *The Overworked American: The Unexpected Decline of Leisure.* New York: Basic Books.
B: Juster, F. Thomas, and Frank P. Stafford. 1991. "The Allocation of Time: Empirical Findings, Behavioral Models, and Problems of Measurement." *Journal of Economic Literature* 29:471–522.
C: Shelton, Beth Anne. 1992. Pp. 39, 67, 68. *Women, Men and Time: Gender Differences in Paid Work, Housework, and Leisure.* New York: Greenwood Press.

fect of the "second shift" might not always be felt more by employed wives than employed husbands in terms strictly of hours spent, but women are more likely to experience **role conflict** between their worker and wife/mother roles. Women are generally expected to be responsible for arranging child care, to deal with sick children, and generally to organize their work around child-care responsibilities (Presser & Cain, 1983.) Plumbing repairs, appliance installations, and other tasks performed by professional service persons generally require that someone be in the home while the repairs are made; this more often becomes the woman's responsibility (Hochschild, 1989).

Estimates about time spent doing home and family work are particularly difficult to make. Devault (1991) pointed out that homemaker work is organized differently from labor market work. Most wage and salaried jobs have a fairly clearly defined beginning and end, so that total hours can be counted. While some household tasks have a time allotment, others do not.

Caring, whether for children, one's spouse, or one's parent, is not a timed event. Much family work is spread out over time and mixed with other activities. If a mother takes her children for a walk, for example, should that be counted as child care or as leisure time? Baking homemade cookies or neatly trimming a hedge can increase the quality of life, but neither is really essential to family survival. Should such activities be counted as home and family work or as hobbies? It is no wonder that estimates about the amount of time men and women spend on paid and family labor are so mixed (see Finding Out 5.1).

Negotiating Gendered Housework

Recall from the gender role continuum (chapter 1, Figure 1.13) that, in very traditional societies, the household division of labor was clearly established and authoritarian. At the other end of the continuum,

Role conflict: Incompatibility between two or more roles that an individual is expected to play.

the division of labor was unclear and had to be negotiated by each couple. America is moving closer to that condition. The negotiating in today's couples often includes constructing reasons why they continue to have a more-or-less traditional household division of labor.

Although both spouses in working couples recognize the disparity that typically exists in the household division of labor, they do not generally consider it unfair (Coltrane, 2000; Biernat & Wortman, 1991; Major, 1993). John, Shelton, and Luschen (1995) found that a little less than 32% of Black, 30% of White, and 22% of Hispanic women considered their household division of labor to be unfair to them. Among husbands, 27% of White men thought their role structure was unfair to their wives, compared with 19% of Hispanic men and 13% of Black men. Survey respondents were not asked whether they thought the division of paid labor was unfair to the men.

Using GSS data, Milkie and Peltola (1999) found that husbands and wives report almost identical success in dealing with work-family trade-offs; 84.7% of men and 85.7% of women felt at least some degree of success. When dissatisfaction does occur, however, it is associated with negative family characteristics. Perceptions of unfairness with the division of labor are related to psychological distress for the mother and lower marital quality for the mother and father (Voydanoff & Donnelly, 1999).

Theories about why women do more housework generally start with the assumption that housework is always burdensome, and anyone with the resources or power to avoid it will do so. Feminist analysis of housework has typically pointed out its low status and other undesirable aspects, comparing that work negatively to what are considered the more desirable aspects of middle-class, professional work (Ferree, 1976; Oakley, 1985; Ahlander & Bahr, 1995). The theories also assume that, since men have more resources and power, they avoid housework, leaving it for their wives. Reviews of research, however, have concluded that there is limited support for this model (Thompson & Walker, 1989; Major, 1993).

Gender ideology does make a difference in how couples divide the housework. Greenstein (1996) found that husbands are not likely to do a major share of the housework unless both the husband and wife have egalitarian beliefs about gender and marital roles. Other approaches study the ways couples negotiate understandings about their division of labor. Knudson-Martin, Carmen, and Mahoney (1998) suggest that newlyweds often use a "language of equality" to create a "myth of equality" even though they are not identical in the division of work.

Major (1993) found that, when couples consider their own situations, they do not compare themselves to some ideal parallel script in which the husband and wife do exactly the same amount of the exact same things. Instead, couples make comparisons with models that make their own look acceptable and fair. Major (1993) also found that both women and men generally accept the norm that husbands should be more responsible for breadwinning, while wives are more responsible for home and family care. Deviating too far from this internalized norm can produce discomfort and guilt. Biernat and Wortman (1991) found that the greater the wife's income relative to her husband's, the worse each felt about their performance as spouse. The more the husband earned, and the more child care the wife did, the better both felt about their respective role performances. Overall, husbands rated their wife's role performances more highly than did the wives themselves, suggesting more internalized role conflict on the part of the wives.

Couples also make comparisons to other feasible arrangements (Major, 1993). Wives who enjoy their employment compare their current employment to the prospect of having no job, rather than to the possibility of being identical with their husbands in terms of job and housework (Spitze, 1988). Couples are less likely to make cross-gender comparisons than within-gender ones (Thompson, 1991). Women make comparisons with other women, many of whom do not work outside the home or seem to do more housework than they themselves do. Women also compare their own husbands, who are usually doing at least some housework, to other husbands rather than to their own amount of work. Both the husband and wife compare the husband's performance with the work done by their own fathers, who probably did less housework; they compare the wife's housework with that done by their own mothers, who probably did more. By these comparisons, their own division of labor seems fair (Thompson, 1991).

Hawkins, Marshall, and Meiners (1995) confirmed Thompson's conclusions and further found that the best predictor of wives' sense of fairness was whether they felt their husbands appreciated their work. Making mutual decisions about family labor also increased wives' sense of fairness.

Another part of the reason that women do not generally consider the division of household labor to be unfair is that it is generally they who set the standards, and they often have higher standards of household cleanliness than do their husbands. South and Spitze (1994) found that never-married, divorced, and widowed men do less housework in their own homes than do their single female counterparts. Wives might believe that an unkempt house is a greater negative

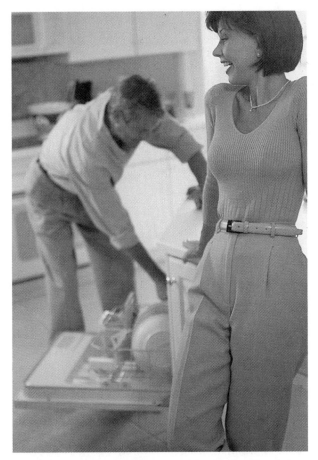

This scene is more common than it once was but is still noticeable for its "role reversal."

reflection on them than it would be on their husbands. Since wives have higher standards, a couple might believe it is fair that the wives do more of the work to reach those standards. Different types of employment, however, can affect this negotiated sense of fairness.

Other Family-Work Scripts

The scripts we have mentioned so far are not the only ways couples can organize their family and work lives. One variation is to reverse the genders in the complementary script. In rare cases, men become "househusbands" who earn no income but do housework and child care while their partners are "breadwinner wives." This is rare. The Census Bureau (CPS, 1998: t. 15) estimated that there were 741,000 married-couple households in which the wife but not the husband was employed. This represents 1.3% of all households. For married couples with children under 18, 1.6% were wife-earner-only

households. In only a few of these cases is such an arrangement the couple's first choice. This script generally results from the husband's unemployment or earlier retirement and is not seen as a permanent lifestyle.

Breadwinner wives do more housework than would be expected by a strict male/female role reversal. Greenstein (2000) suggested that this might result from an attempt to normalize what might otherwise be seen as a deviant role relationship.

Little is known about the work-family scripts of homosexual couples, but the portion of couples with parallel, dual-career scripts is probably much higher than among heterosexual couples. This would be true both because of the more egalitarian nature of same-sex relationships and the fact that fewer homosexual couples have children to care for (Blumstein & Schwartz, 1983).

Some wage earners, of course, remain single throughout their lives; many others are faced with renegotiating their work and family roles after divorce or the death of the partner. Finally, there are a few very wealthy or very poor couples in which neither has a work role.

Work-Family Impacts on Children

Much more will be said later in this text about socialization of children. Here, though, it is worth mentioning that children are socialized into the society's work-family expectations. Boys and girls are treated differently in the process.

Blair (1992) found that school-aged children average just under 6 hours of routine housework each week. Younger children's work is less gendered than that for teenagers or adults, and boys and girls do roughly equal amounts (Coltrane, 2000; Hilton & Haldeman, 1991). Teenage girls, however, do about twice the amount of housework than do boys; the girls concentrate on routine indoor chores while the boys focus on the outdoor work (Coltrane, 2000; Antill et al., 1996).

In single-parent families, girls perform more household tasks, for longer periods of time, than do girls in two-parent families. Boys in such homes, on the other hand, do less than do boys in two-parent families. The more hours of employment mothers have, the more housework children, especially girls, do. Boys do a larger share of housework in homes with stepparents and parents with gender-egalitarian values (Benin & Edwards, 1990; Coltrane, 2000; Hilton & Haldeman, 1991).

For housework purposes, adult children who live with their parents continue the teenage pattern. Adult sons create more housework than they perform, while

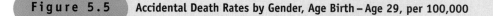

| Figure 5.5 | Accidental Death Rates by Gender, Age Birth – Age 29, per 100,000 |

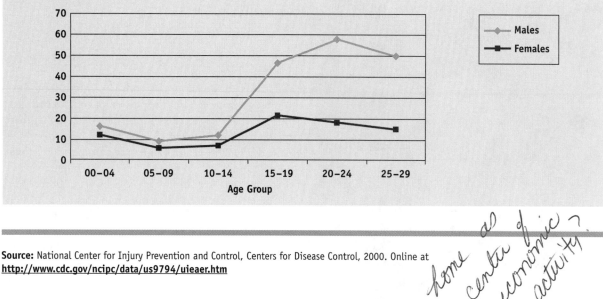

Source: National Center for Injury Prevention and Control, Centers for Disease Control, 2000. Online at
http://www.cdc.gov/ncipc/data/us9794/uieaer.htm

home as center of economic activity?

adult daughters perform more than they create (South & Spitze, 1994).

Generally, parents are recreating, in their children, the same household division of labor that they themselves have. Social scientists have done a number of studies on that phenomenon. Very few, however, have studied the socialization of the gendered danger gap. Only the general raw data were available. Figure 5.5 provides the rate of unintentional deaths, by gender, for different ages. These figures include work accidents, home accidents, recreational accidents, and other forms of unintentional but not disease-related deaths.

Males at all ages have significantly higher accidental death rates. The difference begins at birth and becomes extreme beginning in the teen years. It is possible that the difference results from some genetic influence that results in males' being more prone to taking physical risks, but at least some of the difference is learned. Just as girls learn the housework and kin-keeping roles, boys are apparently learning that they are expected to perform the dangerous tasks in society.

The Future of Work and the Family

Technological changes will certainly continue to affect the relationship between families and work, but exactly how is difficult to say. One possibility involves telecommunication; increasing numbers of workers can

now perform their jobs from home. Almost anyone who uses a computer in his or her work could do at least part of that work at home. As many as 8.4 million American workers are "teleworkers" at least 8 hours each week (Hill, Hawkins, & Miller, 1996).

Professors could deliver their lectures in front of a video camera in their living rooms; students could access the lecture at any time from anywhere. Many colleges, in fact, already deliver programs this way. Accountants, bookkeepers, typists, engineers, and many others could work more frequently from their homes. If this became a common practice, the home would once again become the center of economic production, as it was before the industrial revolution. Families could live anywhere, and each family member could do work or schoolwork via computer.

The few studies of the effects of teleworking on families have gotten mixed results. Teleworking provides considerably more work flexibility. Some workers found this to bring significant improvements in their family life. Others, however, reported having problems because the line between home and work life was no longer clear (Hill, Hawkins, & Miller, 1996).

For those who leave home to go to work, there will probably be increasing numbers of shift workers. Although the United States lags behind most other postindustrial nations in development of family-friendly work policies (see chapter 16), some family-supportive employers have provided benefits such as paid **family leave.** Federal law now requires most employers to allow at least some unpaid leave. Employer-sponsored child care, on or near the work site, is another possible benefit. Some schools are extending their hours to accommodate working parents, so that the schools expand their child-care function.

A variety of flexible schedules is possible. Job sharing allows two persons to fill one position and possibly provides benefits to both. Flextime gives employees some choice about the starting and ending times of their jobs.

In recognition of the fact that many parents, especially mothers, are reluctant to devote full time to careers at the expense of time with their children, Felice Schwartz (1989) proposed a work option that was labeled the **mommy track.** On this career path, workers would put in fewer work hours, especially while their children are young, so that more time could be spent with the family. This would allow the worker to maintain a career with less family conflict, but it would probably result in less advancement and lifetime earnings for women or men who were on a traditional career path.

Although she herself did not apply the term "mommy track," Schwartz's proposal was criticized by some who argued that it perpetuates the stereotype that women should still play the primary child support role and consequently receive second-class employment status. It also does not appear to give fathers an option for a "daddy track." Schwartz (1992) responded that she was only proposing another option for women, not imposing a requirement. She argued that modern corporations were going to have to develop a range of profamily policies to take advantage of the increasing pool of highly talented women who wanted to spend more time with their families.

The number of employers who take the advice of Schwartz and others who propose more "family friendly" work situations remains to be seen. As long as even a few more women than men opt out of the workforce for family purposes, however, the average earnings and career advancement will be less for women than those for men. It is reasonable to expect that those who work the longest hours for the longest time will generally get the greatest reward from employment, whether they be men or women. These same persons will continue to pay the personal cost of decreased time with their families.

Economy and Family in Global Perspective

The postindustrial system described so far in this chapter applies mostly to the United States and a handful of other nations. The situation is different in most of the world, much of which remains in agrarian or industrial modes of production.

Selected International Comparison

Table 5.7 compares selected countries in terms of certain economic and demographic characteristics, all of which are related to the family. The countries have a range in terms of the extent to which they have developed industrial or postindustrial modes of production. The United States, Canada, Japan, and Sweden are among the most developed nations. Ethiopia and Sudan, two African nations, are among the world's poorest in economic terms. Mexico and China fall between the most and least developed.

Table 5.7 illustrates several points that would be even clearer if more countries were included. Postindustrial societies have more literate, wealthier persons who give birth to fewer children, live longer, and lose fewer children to death. Women outlive men in every region of the world, although the gap varies. Poorer countries devote considerably more of their limited educational resources to men than to women. These factors clearly affect family life in the respective countries.

Today's Nonindustrialized Patterns: Sub-Saharan Africa

Societies that are postindustrial got there through a gradual evolutionary process. Institutions, norms, and values changed to adapt to one another. Images of time, work, and family remained compatible with the economic, religious, and educational systems.

In parts of the world that have not become heavily industrialized, work and family are seen differently than in industrial or postindustrial societies. Agrarian work patterns are based on doing the job that needs done at the moment. Some days or seasons will be much busier than others. Work is not something from which a person expects to get personal fulfillment, but something that one

---

Family leave: A leave from employment for family matters, especially the birth of a child.   **Mommy track:** Career path that would allow more time for families.

Table 5.7	Economic and Demographic Characteristics of Selected Countries							
Characteristic	United States	Canada	Sweden	Japan	Mexico	China	Sudan	Ethiopia
Percent Urban	75	77	84	79	74	30	27	14
GNP per Capita, 1997*	$29,080	$19,640	$26,210	$38,160	$3,700	$860	$290	$110
Literacy Rate, Overall	99.5	96.6	99.0	99.0	89.6	81.5	46.1	35.5
Male	N/A	N/A	N/A	N/A	91.8	89.9	57.7	45.5
Female	N/A	N/A	N/A	N/A	97.4	72.7	34.6	25.3
Male Life Expectancy	74	76	77	77	69	69	50	41
Female Life Expectancy	79	82	82	84	75	73	52	42
Total Fertility Rate**	2.0	1.5	1.5	1.4	3.0	1.8	4.6	7.0
Births per 1,000	15	11	10	10	27	16	33	46
% of Children Who Die Before Age 5	1	1	<1	<1	4	4	11	18

*GNP per capita is the average dollar value of all spending for goods and services each year per person.

**Total fertility rate is the expected lifetime number of children born to each adult woman.

Sources: Literacy rates from *Microsoft Encarta Encyclopedia* 1999. Redmond, WA. Other information from Haub, Carl, and Diana Cornelius, 1999. *World Population Data Sheet*. Population Reference Bureau: Washington, DC.

simply does. There are no time clocks to establish starting and quitting times, as is the case in industrial societies.

There is also no rigid separation of "work" from "leisure" time, nor of "work" from "family" time. When preindustrial tasks are completed, the person moves to the next event that might be a nap or an arduous chore, but there is no established schedule by which the tasks are accomplished. The work habits required of industrial production, like 8-hour days and 5-day workweeks, are alien to the patterns of life of much of the world's population, including most of Africa (Salz, 1984).

Sub-Saharan Africa is a vast area with several distinct cultures. Because national boundaries were drawn by European colonists, they do not always coincide with tribal and ethnic boundaries. This, along with a historical lack of experience with European-style state governments, extreme poverty, low literacy, rapid population growth, and other factors, makes political systems unstable.

Sub-Saharan Africa is the poorest region in the world, with a per-capita GNP of $520 (Haub & Cornelius, 1999). The population has been expanding more rapidly than have food supplies, most of which are produced on household farms (Hynen, 1986).

The gender division of labor is clearly defined within each family, but varies somewhat by region and social class. Men have greater access to formal education and tend to have the power and authority, but women do much of the agricultural work. When crops are grown for cash, rather than subsistence, the position of women

whose husbands have high standing in the community tends to improve, while it can get worse for others. In either case, women are dependent upon their husbands and are expected to have large families (Savane, 1986).

Families and extended kin groups are still very important in Africa, although they are becoming less so as urbanization and industrialization continue. A study of eastern Africa found that 63% of households contained extended families. A little over 10% of households contained polygamous marriages. Mate selection is increasingly by choice, but most couples at least follow the ritual forms of extended kin negotiation and payment. Marriages between persons from different ethnic groups are generally taboo (Kilbride & Kilbride, 1990).

Traditional African religions exist alongside Islam and Christianity in many parts of Africa (Nsamenang, 1992). Some Muslim clans still practice female genital mutilation, believing that it is called for in the Quran, Islam's holy book. The extent of the practice is unknown, but it continues in spite of pressure by international feminist groups and others (Walker & Parmar, 1993). As with other religious and cultural traditions, this one changes only slowly.

Swedish Family Scripts

In contrast to sub-Saharan Africa, Sweden is a highly developed country and is held by some to be the best model for the future of the American family. Table

In parts of sub-Saharan Africa, living conditions remain traditional.

5.7 reveals Sweden's high income and life expectancy, along with its low child death rate and number of children born to each woman. The marriage rate in Sweden is the lowest in the industrialized world and is accompanied by a very high average age at first marriage: about 27 for women and 30 for men (Hoem & Hoem, 1988).

The low marriage and divorce rates are largely the result of the high cohabitation rate. At any one time, about one in four couples that are living together is unmarried, living in "marriage-like relationships." Nearly all Swedes live together for at least some period prior to marriage. Unlike the case in the United States, Swedish partners have a specific relationship name, *sambo,* that institutionalized the cohabiting relationship. This is partly the result of the old Germanic tradition of waiting until pregnancy before a couple married and partly the result of significant changes in the postindustrial era (Popenoe, 1987, 1988).

In spite of high cohabitation rates, illegitimacy is not considered a problem in Sweden, for several reasons. For one thing, contraception is widely used, so there are considerably fewer unwanted pregnancies than in the United States. Also, fewer cohabiting couples now marry when pregnancy occurs, so many children are

technically born to single parents but actually have both a mother and father in the home. The term "illegitimacy" has not officially been used in Sweden since 1917; any distinction of a child born "out of wedlock" was removed from Swedish legislation in the early 1970s (Popenoe, 1987). There are, however, children in single-parent homes. Over 15% of families are headed by a lone mother and 3% by a lone father (Sandqvist, 1987).

A strong work ethic and extensive social-welfare system have contributed to the virtual elimination of poverty in Sweden. As is true for all postindustrial societies except the United States, health care has been considered every citizen's right for several decades. Single parents receive a standard subsidy for children, regardless of other income (Kindlund, 1988).

Sweden is usually understood to be the most gender-egalitarian country in the world. It committed itself to gender equality before women in the United States were even guaranteed the right to vote. It has the highest percentage of women in the labor force, and the lowest rate of full-time homemakers, in the world (Haas, 1992).

Swedish family leave policy is extensive. A father or mother is entitled to a year of family leave at 90 to 100% of regular pay; government provides the income (Haas, 1992). In spite of the efforts, husbands and wives still have somewhat different relationships to work and family. Wives are more likely to take family leave than husbands are. The majority of young mothers work less than full time, while the majority of fathers continue with a full-time work schedule. Men are more likely to have jobs that require physical labor and supervise subordinates; monotonous tasks are more likely to be part of the jobs women have (Moen, 1989).

Modified parallel scripts seem to be the norm in Sweden, with greater frequency of complete parallel scripts than would be found in the United States. Women who work full time in Sweden make 91% of the income of working men. Policies designed to eliminate the remaining differences in gender roles continue (Sandqvist, 1992).

The experience in Sweden provides one model for the future of the family in America. The two countries, while similar in many ways, are also different; what works in one might not be appropriate for the other. Sweden has less inequality between the rich and the poor than in the United States, has considerably lower crime rates, and lacks the racial and ethnic diversity found in America. These factors, which will influence the future of the family, will be the topic of the next two chapters. A more complete discussion of the family's future will be found in the final chapter.

Summary and Conclusion

The postindustrial revolution has been primarily characterized by a growth in the information and services sector of the economy, especially one resulting from computer and telecommunications applications. The labor force now undergoes continual transformation as the industrial base declines and other jobs open up.

Religion remains important to most North Americans. The differences among various denominations seem to be declining, while those between religious and non-religious persons are growing larger. Opposing trends of secularization and fundamentalism vie for supremacy.

Government has been an expanding influence in the lives of individuals and families. Some programs, such as social security and Temporary Assistance to Needy Families (TANF), have decreased the economic responsibility that extended families have for each other.

Education has changed along with every other institution. Increasingly complex, lifelong training and retraining bring increasing numbers of persons under the influence of the educational institution for increasing portions of their lives.

Demographic changes are part of the story of the postindustrial revolution. The baby boom has had a complex influence on society, as have the longer-term trends of smaller families, later marriages, and longer lives.

A major change in society has been the rapid increase of married women in the paid labor force. This has been accompanied by adjustments in both the workforce and in family life. In spite of the changes, however, the traditional gender role expectations remain powerful. Men are still expected to be the primary breadwinners and perform the most dangerous jobs. While most mothers now work for money, they are still expected to be primarily responsible for unpaid family work.

While gender discrimination still exists, human capital factors also affect the gendered wage gap. Partly because of their family responsibilities, women average fewer hours of paid labor per week, fewer weeks per year, and fewer years in a working lifetime. Women also select, subject to social expectations, careers that are paid less than are predominantly male careers. Men continue to have more dangerous jobs and lifestyles.

Couples work out the work/family gender roles in various ways. Common scripts range from traditional complementary, in which the husband and wife have separate roles, to completely parallel, in which the husband and wife are androgynous and essentially interchangeable.

Much of the world remains predominantly agrarian. The pressure to move to industrial and postindustrial systems is influencing families in sub-Saharan Africa, which remains poor.

Sweden, by contrast, is a model of postindustrial social and familial systems, with a strong emphasis on gender equality and extensive social welfare systems. It might indicate the direction in which the United State will travel.

In conclusion, we once again see in this chapter how changes in the economy and the nature of the work world affect families. One of the most significant changes is the rapid entry of women, especially mothers, into the workforce. This has probably made the economy more efficient and productive; it has also been associated with profound changes in family life and male-female role relationships in America.

Rethinking in Context Given the current workforce structure, if a mother takes time and energy away from work to devote time to her children, she is likely to suffer long-term lower earnings than would a man or woman who devotes full-time energies to her career. Is it worth the sacrifice? Why are men less likely to make the same sacrifice? How are the children affected by this? Should changes be made to change this situation? If so, what?

Additional Resources

General works on the postindustrial society

Bell, Daniel. 1973. *The Coming of Post-Industrial Society.* New York: Basic Books.
Kennedy, Paul. M. 1993. *Preparing for the Twenty-first Century.* New York: Random House.
Garbarino, James. 1992. *Future as if It Really Mattered.* Chicago: Noble Press.

The postindustrial family

Popenoe, David. 1988. *Disturbing the Nest: Family Change and Decline in Modern Societies.* New York: Adline de Gruyter.
Wheelock, Jane. 1990. *Husbands at Home: the Domestic Economy in a Post-Industrial Society.* New York: Routledge.

Readers and books on work and the family

Bowen, Gary L. and Joe F. Pittman, eds. 1995. *The Work and Family Interface: Toward a Contextual Effects Perspective.* Minneapolis: National Council on Family Relations.
Hood, Jane C. 1993. *Men, Work, and Family.* Thousand Oaks, CA: Sage.
Hochschild, Arlie. 1989. *The Second Shift: Working Parents and the Revolution at Home.* New York: Viking/Penguin.
Hochschild, Arlie. 1998. *The Time Bind: When Work Becomes Home and Home Becomes Work.* New York: Owl.
Phizacklea, Annie, and Carol Wolkowitz. 1995. *Homeworking Women: Gender, Racism, and Class at Work.* Thousand Oaks, CA: Sage.
Plath, David W., ed. 1983. *Work and Lifecourse in Japan.* Albany: State University of New York Press.
Robinson, John P., and Geoffrey Godbey. 1997. *Time for Life: The Surprising Ways Americans Use Their Time.* University Park, PA: Pennsylvania State University Press.
Williams, Joan. 1999. *Unbending Gender: Why Family and Work Conflict and What to Do About It.* New York: Oxford University Press.

Internet Sites

The Families and Work Institute
http://www.familiesandworkinst.org/

Feminist views
http://csf.colorado.edu/gimenez/feminist.html

National Child Care Network
http://www.nncc.org/

Clearinghouse for federal government statistics
http://www.fedstats.gov/

The Time Bind (Hochschild)
http://www.familydiscussions.com/books/ hochschild.htm

For links to these sites and additional resources, visit the *Families in Context* Web site at:

http://sociology.wadsworth.com

Chapter 6

Social Class and Families

Prelude

Jollia, 15, was born to a poor single mother and lives, like her mother always has, in a housing project in inner-city Chicago. She has a brother and sister, both of whom have different fathers than does she. Her mother dropped out of high school when she got pregnant at 15, and about all Jollia knows about her father was that he spends most of his time in jail. Few of the adults Jollia knows well have graduated from high school, and few have steady jobs. Nearly all the adult women she knows are single mothers and nearly all the adult men have spotty work records at best; most have been in trouble with the law at some point. Several of Jollia's girlfriends already have children. Every day on the way to school Jollia walks past dirty, boarded-up buildings and witnesses drug deals. Gang members have shot three of her male friends.

Janette, 15, was born in a wealthy suburb of Chicago. She lives with her architect mother and her attorney father. Her brother is away at prep school and has been accepted to Harvard next year. Nearly all the adults Janette knows have advanced college degrees and prestigious jobs. None of Janette's girlfriends has had a child, although a few have had abortions. Janette met most of her close friends at her parents' country club, where she takes tennis lessons, swims, and plays golf. Several of her friends have experimented with drugs, but none has ever been caught.

What are the comparative life chances of Jollia and Janette?

We have now discussed the family of the past, and we even had a glimpse of what the future might be like. We have seen the wide variety of family forms that human groups have constructed around different modes of production and other variables. We have seen, too, that not all persons in a particular society at a particular time have the same kind of lives.

The fact that you are reading this book means that, in all probability, your family was not among the poorest in the country; the poorest do not usually go to college. This is only one of the ways peoples' lives are affected by the amount of wealth, power, and prestige they have. Status-related differences are intricately woven into the fabric of family life as well. This chapter will look more closely at the relationship between the family and the distribution of privilege in society.

> **Thinking Ahead** In what ways might your values, norms, and family life have been different had you been born among the very poorest of Americans? How about the very richest? What life advantages and disadvantages came to you from your family of orientation?

Accident of birth determines an individual's sex, race, and beginning social class. These three variables affect almost everything about a person's life. This chapter focuses on the relationship between social class and the family.

Race, class, and gender are important influences on a person's life chances, but they operate differently. We have seen that sex-irreducible gender roles have an underlying biological/anatomical basis. While persons are assigned racial categories on the basis of genetically inherited characteristics, these differences are not directly responsible for different status and role assignments, which are entirely social constructions. There are no "race-irreducible" roles. Social class, even less rooted in biology, relies almost entirely on social dynamics.

Theoretical considerations will provide background for a discussion of social class in the United States. The relationship between poverty and families, as part of North American class structure, will be explored. We will then look at the family among those in the middle class and upper class.

Why Social Inequality?

All societies more complex than those with hunting-gathering modes of production have a more or less rigid system of social stratification. Individuals are located in the stratification system in terms of how much of socially desired resources such as money, prestige, or power they have access to, relative to others in the society. Geologists know that layers of rock are stratified, one on top of the other. Boundaries between the layers are clearly defined. In social systems, the boundaries are not usually so clearly defined, and there is some movement between the strata. The extent of stratification and movement between layers depends on the type of society.

Types of Stratification Systems

The family system of a society is intertwined with the system of stratification and inequality in that society. At one end of an ideal-type social mobility continuum (see Figure 6.1) is a system in which it is impossible for an individual to change his or her class position; everyone lives and dies in the same social class as the family into which they are born. This type of society, where there is no social mobility at all, is called a **closed mobility system**. Each individual's social status position is totally determined by **ascription**.

At the other extreme end of the social mobility continuum, the social class into which one is born has no influence on where one ends up. All positions in the

---

Closed mobility system: An ideal-typical system of social stratification in which there is no mobility; all status is by ascription.
Ascription: Assignment to a position because of characteristics, such as race, sex, or family ancestry, over which the individual has no control.

Thousands of Zabaleen, or garbage collectors, survive in Cairo by living off of the garbage of others.

George Bush?
v.s. Clinton
Bill Clinton

social system are arrived at by achievement. This would be an **open mobility system,** in which the status of one's parents would have no influence on one's own ultimate status. Although there could be inequality in this type of system because of individual differences in ability and contribution, there is no intergenerational stratification. Individuals move up and down because no boundaries separate layers of inequality. This kind of ideal-type system is sometimes called a **meritocracy,** especially in the context of political leadership or occupational advancement. No actual such society has existed.

The United States is more open than many societies, but inheritance of family wealth, values, and opportunity remain important factors in influencing an individual's ultimate class position. In the postindustrial society, one's class placement depends increasingly on his or her knowledge base, which can be acquired, and decreasingly on ascribed factors. It must be remembered, however, that access to formal education is unequally distributed by class, so complete elimination of class as a variable in people's lives is unlikely, even in a relatively open system.

Figure 6.1	Inequality and Mobility Continuum

Completely Closed	Completely Open
Status by Ascription	Status by Achievement

Open mobility system: An ideal-typical system of social stratification in which there is total mobility; all status is by achievement.
Meritocracy: Government by persons found to be most capable.

Explanations of Inequality

Most Americans can provide an explanation about why some people are rich while others are poor, about why some are powerful and others powerless, and about why some people are looked up to while others are looked down upon. Like everyday explanations, sociological answers to these questions can be divided into three levels (Rank, 1994).

Structural explanations such as conflict theory and functionalism look at such macrolevel causes as economic systems. Cultural explanations focus on the lifestyles and values of families and other groups of people that produce similar class outcomes. Personal-level explanations are concerned with individual abilities and differences on life chances.

Structural Explanations: Conflict Theory. To Karl Marx, hunting-gathering societies were characterized by "primitive communism"; they did not have a class system. Other modes of production produced class systems in which some persons owned the means of production and others worked and were exploited. In agrarian systems, the "haves" were the nobility who owned the land and the "have-nots" were the serfs and peasants who worked the land.

While Marx recognized that there were other classes, such as artisans and merchants, he thought that industrial capitalism would increasingly divide society into the capitalist owners, or **bourgeoisie,** versus the workers, or **proletariat.** Ultimately, the workers would take over the means of production, which became very efficient under capitalism. At this point, the owners and workers would be the same persons. There would no longer be a basis for a class system or conflict between classes, and advanced communism would result.

To Marx, the class system was perpetuated by the family system through the inheritance of private property. Wealth, power, and prestige are passed from generation to generation. Such inheritance is supported by both the informal and formal normative systems, which primarily serve the interests of the "haves."

Modern conflict theorists still agree with Marx on certain points. First, conflict theorists assume that stratification systems are unfair because they lock persons

into positions that they are largely powerless to change. Second, conflict theorists assume that stratification systems are associated with considerable exploitation of the "have-nots" by the "haves." Third, stratification systems are destructive not only to individuals and families but also, because of the conflict the systems produce, to society as a whole. Fourth, they believe that eliminating the stratification system should be a top priority of social change.

Analysis done by conflict theorists emphasizes the negative aspects of inequality: exploitation, prejudice, and conflict. They find the cause of most social problems to be related to the stratification system in one way or another. Functionalist theorists take a much more benign view of social stratification.

Structural Explanations: Functionalism. Kingsley Davis and Wilbert Moore (1945) wrote the classical statement of the functionalist perspective on social stratification. They agreed with conflict theorists that stratification systems were universally found in post–hunting-gathering societies. In typical functionalist fashion, they argued that if a trait is universal, it must be functional to the society. Unlike the conflict theorists, Davis and Moore concluded that stratification was necessary to society.

Davis and Moore maintained that some tasks in society are either more functionally important or more difficult to do, so societies need to have a way to make sure those tasks get done in the most effective way possible. The stratification system encourages the most able persons to do the important or difficult jobs by rewarding them with wealth, prestige, or other desirables. For example, physicians make life-and-death decisions, and becoming a physician takes years of hard work, study, and postponement of gratification. Few highly qualified persons would do the job, functionalists argue, if society did not reward it highly with money and prestige.

Functionalists would agree that wealth and other privileges are passed on to subsequent generations via family inheritance, but note that this can, within reason, also be functional in two ways. First, it provides a smooth and well-ordered transition from one generation to the next. Wealth does not have to be constantly

---

Bourgeoisie: The social class that, in Marxist theory, controls the means of production and uses capital, natural resources, and exploited labor to make profits.   **Proletariat:** The social class that, in Marxist theory, labors as the instrument of production for the bourgeoisie.

redistributed by a government, church, or other institution. Also, when a younger generation inherits capital, they also usually have been taught how to make the capital productive. Children who inherit their parents' farms, for example, usually grow up working on them, care about them, and know how to run them.

Responding to concerns that stratification is unfair, Davis and Moore pointed out that they were not referring to what was fair or unfair, or to what might conceivably be. They were referring to what has always been and is likely to be.

Neither the conflict nor functionalist theories can be completely proved nor disproved. Each perspective provides sets of assumptions that guide research and interpretation, but are too general in themselves to allow definitive proof. Both can provide a framework for comparing different types of stratification systems.

Cultural Explanations.   Neither individual differences nor poverty is randomly distributed in the population. Some groups consistently have more poverty than do others and some have less formal education than do others. One reason might be the "culture of poverty" concept that stemmed from the work of Oscar Lewis, who did in-depth studies of a small number of families in Mexico (1975) and of Puerto Rican families in New York (1966). Lewis found a particular lifestyle and worldview among people living in poverty. When people live in poverty for generations, they develop values and norms that help them survive but that also help trap them in poverty.

One characteristic attributed to persons in a culture of poverty is an inability to defer gratification. Middle-class individuals postpone pleasure while saving money or going to college in order to have more money and pleasure later on. Those adapted to poverty, in contrast, seek immediate gratification instead.

Critics of the culture of poverty argument point out that the poor have insufficient money in the first place, which is why they do not save much. They cannot afford the luxury of looking too far ahead because their present position is so precarious. Ryan (1976) referred to the culture of poverty argument as "blaming the victim." In his view the poor are victims of an unjust,

unequal, oppressive social system and should not be blamed for faults in the social system.

Setting aside the question of blame, it is quite clear that, even in a relatively open system such as the contemporary United States, children generally grow up to hold the same class position as their parents. Children who grow up in working-class families tend to be working class themselves. Children who grow up in upper-middle-class homes tend to become upper middle class also. This process of **social reproduction** is influenced by all social institutions, including the schools.

Bowles and Gintis (1976) found that schools are an integral part of social reproduction in capitalist societies. Schools teach an achievement ideology, stressing that individuals can achieve any class position if they are good enough, work hard enough, and do the right thing. But schools subtly teach their students to assume a particular position in the class system. Schools in working-class neighborhoods, often at the request of their parents, emphasize teaching discipline and control. These are characteristics necessary in most working-class jobs. Middle-class parents, on the other hand, want their children exposed to more creative, flexible education that fosters independence. These qualities are important in middle-class occupations. Even within schools, tracking and guidance often sort students by social class. Pierre Bourdieu (1977, 1990) found the schools, family and neighborhood to be heavily involved in social reproduction of the class system. It is not simply money that determines one's class position, but also one's **cultural capital.** Children learn styles of dress, grammar and other verbal characteristics, recreational preferences, and other characteristics from their parents, other relatives, their community, and their school. Many of these traits are specific to a particular social class and become part of a person's worldview.

Schools and employers tend to reward the cultural capital of the middle and upper classes over that of the working class and the poor. A middle-class familiarity with standard English, classical music and books, styles of dress, art museums, and travel experiences increases chances of success in school and in the job market. Even if a poor child develops a strong achievement ideology, a lack of middle-class cultural capital can significantly

cultural capital

Social reproduction: The process whereby a society reproduces its system of inequality from one generation to the next.
Cultural capital: The general cultural background, knowledge, disposition, and skills that are passed from one generation to the next.

lower his or her chances of mobility in the class system (MacLeod, 1995).

Individual Explanations. Explanations that attribute poverty to attitudinal or motivational characteristics are most common among the general public. Kluegel and Smith (1986) found that most Americans attributed poverty to individual characteristics of persons who are poor. These included lack of thrift or effort, lack of talent or ability, or failures such as loose morals or drunkenness. The common belief is that poor persons lack the motivation to work hard and pull themselves out of poverty.

Sociologists tend to disagree with such explanations, for several reasons. First, some things are difficult to measure. There is no good measure of "laziness," for example; many persons burn up considerable numbers of calories, which is a measure of work, and are still poor. Also, surveys of values and attitudes have found few general differences between persons who are poor and those who are not (Rank, 1994). Finally, sociologists realize that even differences that do exist between the poor and the not poor came originally from outside the individual. Persons are not born with attitudes and values, but develop them from their culture and society.

One kind of individual-based explanation that has received support from some social scientists, especially economists, is based on the idea of human capital (Dolan & Lindsey, 1991). We saw that applied in chapter 5 to the gender wage gap. It can also be applied to general individual differences in labor-force rewards. The labor force is a competitive place, and those with the appropriate skills, education, and training will bring those forms of personal capital to the competition. Individuals who lack the skills will lose out and become poor. Plans to reduce poverty by providing skills and training are based on the human capital model.

By itself, however, the human capital model is incomplete because it does not explain why the capital is unequally distributed in the first place. With regard to social class, the human capital of one's parents is a strong determinant of one's own human capital. The cultural capital ascribed to an individual affects the human capital that individual develops.

Social Class in the United States

In the first decades of the 20th century, Max Weber took issue with Marx's analysis of stratification. While Marx focused on the unidimensional variable of ownership of production as the key to one's class position, Weber proposed a multidimensional classification based on three variables: wealth, prestige, and power. It was possible, Weber demonstrated, for a person to be at different levels on each dimension of inequality. A college professor, for example, might be high in prestige but relatively low in wealth and power. A drug dealer, on the other hand, might be high in wealth but low in social power. The dealer's prestige could vary considerably depending on the subculture doing the evaluating. A drug-dealing college professor would have a confusing status profile indeed.

Weber's more complicated system has generally been accepted as a better description of the industrial European and North American systems of stratification. Some theorists have gone further, arguing that there is no class structure at all in the United States, but rather a number of dimensions of inequality (Wrong, 1987). A continuum from very low to very high exists for each dimension. Figure 6.2 illustrates a multidimensional system of social inequality that would apply to

In a working-class environment, middle-class professionals are easy to pick out.

| Figure 6.2 | A Multi–Dimensional System of Social Inequality |

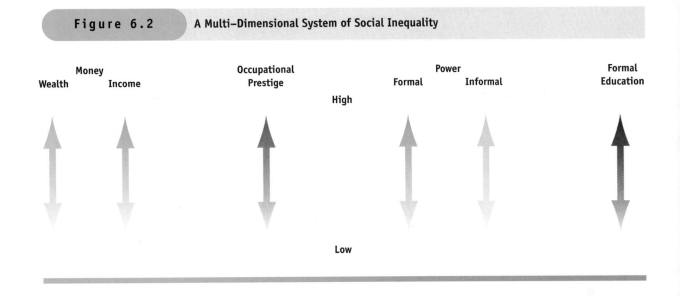

---

postindustrial systems. All variables are family related. The institution of inheritance provides individuals from privileged families with numerous advantages in income, wealth, and power (Miller & McNamee, 1998).

Money

Perhaps the most obvious form of social inequality is in the distribution of income, although two families with the same income are not necessarily in the same social class. A couple whose sole source of income is from the husband's position as college professor might make $50,000, as might a couple whose husband is a plumber, as might a waitress who combined her income with that of her laborer husband. Most observers would probably consider these three couples to have different social class positions because, while their income is the same, other factors are different.

Life chances of individuals and families vary considerably by income. The wealthy live longer than do the poor; they are much less likely to suffer from heart disease, obesity, and other ailments; they are less likely to be victims of crime; they are more likely to have children who attend college; they are more likely to describe themselves as "very happy"; they are less likely to be victims of child and spouse abuse; and they are less likely to get divorced (Gilbert & Kahl, 1993; Beeghley, 2000).

Table 6.1 indicates that, of those who were in the bottom third of family income when they were 16, 37.2% ended up in the lower third as adults while only 25.5% ended up in the top third of family income. By

contrast, of those with top-third family incomes as teenagers, 20.3% ended up in the bottom third while 44.6% ended up in the top third.

If the United States had a completely closed mobility system, Table 6.1 would look very different. In that case, 100% of those with bottom-third childhoods would have bottom-third adulthoods, while 100% of those with top-third childhoods would have top-third adulthoods. If the United States had a completely open system the table would look different yet. In this case, all columns in the table would look the same. The same percent of bottom-third children as top-third children would end up in top third, and vice versa. This is only a rough measure, but it shows that the United States is somewhere between a completely closed and a complete open system where family income is concerned.

The distribution of wealth is a different matter. No information such as Table 6.1 is available for wealth, but it would look different. Wealth is considerably more unequal than the distribution of income, and is more likely to be passed down in families. Inequality in wealth appears to be increasing. In the mid-1960s, the wealthiest 1% held just over 20% of the wealth. By the mid-1990s, the share of the nation's wealth owned by the richest 1% had increased to 37% (Beeghley, 2000). Inheritance and other family-related dynamics account for most of the reproduction of the wealth distribution (Hurst, 1998).

Family systems are clearly related to wealth. Estimates are that about one third of extremely wealthy individuals inherited virtually all their wealth. Most of the rest inherited a small fortune that they parlayed into

Table 6.1	Association Between Family of Orientation Income at 16 and Family Income at Age 30 and Over		
	Family Income at Age 16		
Family Income after Age 30	**Low**	**Medium**	**High**
Low	37.2%	28.3%	20.3%
Medium	37.8%	39.6%	35.1%
High	25.0%	32.1%	44.6%

Source: Davis, James Allan, and Tom W. Smith: General Social Survey(s), year(s). (Machine-readable data file). Principal investigator, James A. Davis; director and co-principal investigator, Tom W. Smith; co-principal investigator, Peter V. Marsden, NORC ed. Chicago: National Opinion Research Center, producer, 1998; Storrs, CT: The Roper Center for Public Opinion Research, University of Connecticut, distributor. Microcomputer format and codebook prepared and distributed by MicroCase Corporation, Bellevue, WA. Analysis by Gene H. Starbuck.

a huge fortune. Only a minority acquired their largess almost entirely on their own via real estate or financial speculation, successful inventions or innovations, discovery of oil, or other avenues (Gilbert & Kahl, 1993).

Occupation and Social Class

Wealth is not the only class variable passed on in families; so is one's general occupation standing. One of the dimensions of social class studied by Weber was **prestige,** especially as it is associated with the occupation one holds. Sociologists, expanding on Weber, have devised several ways to measure occupational prestige, one of which was developed for use with National Opinion Research Center (NORC) surveys (Miller, 1991:335). A sample of occupational prestige scores is given in Table 6.2. The higher the score, the more prestige is generally associated with the occupation.

Occupational prestige is remarkably consistent. Studies have been done in the United States since the 1940s, revealing very little change over time. Similar studies have been conducted in at least 52 countries, not just in highly developed ones like Canada, Japan, Sweden, and Switzerland but also in Zaire, Pakistan, Namibia, and Russia. These studies find a very similar ranking of occupations in all countries (Treiman, 1977).

Income and occupational prestige operate similarly; parents' prestige had an influence on one's own ultimate prestige, but the association is far from perfect. It would appear from GSS data that the mother's occupational prestige is more strongly associated with her children's adult prestige than is the father's prestige. The same holds true for both sons and daughters (Davis & Smith, 1972–98).

Early research on occupational prestige was done with the assumption that it was primarily men who had occupations. Later, more traditional women's occupations were added to the list. Bakker (1993) found that occupations with high concentrations of women had somewhat lower prestige, on average, than occupations with high concentrations of men. In terms of family social class, however, there has been considerable debate about the social class of wives. The conventional approach has been the "status borrowing model," which finds that women consider themselves, and are considered by others, to have their status determined by their husband's occupation (Goldthorpe, 1983, 1984).

While the status-borrowing model does appear to apply to homemakers, there is a question about its applicability to wives with occupations of their own. For most couples, the occupations of husbands and wives have similar levels of prestige (Collins & Coltrane, 1991), but this is not always true. Jackman and Jackman (1983) found that the status-borrowing model did seem to apply to couples except that women's judgments of their status were more affected by their own education than that of their

status borrowing

Prestige: Respect or favorable regard attached to a person because of his or her position in the social system.

Table 6.2	Sample of NORC Occupational Prestige Scores, by U.S. Bureau of Census Occupational Classification

Occupational Category	Occupational Prestige Score	Occupational Category	Occupational Prestige Score
Professional, technical, and kindred		**Craftsmen and kindred workers**	
Physicians	81.2	Electricians	49.2
Teachers, college and university	78.3	Carpenters	39.7
Lawyers	75.1	Automobile mechanics	36.7
Engineers	67.0	Roofers	31.5
Registered nurses	60.1	**Operatives, except transport**	
Teachers, public secondary school	59.8	Drill press operatives	31.7
Accountants	55.9	Meat cutters	23.6
Social workers	52.4	Clothing ironers and pressers	21.9
Computer systems analysts	50.6	**Laborers, except farm**	
Managers and administrators		Gardeners	22.1
Bank officers and financial	66.1	Laborers, not specified type	17.5
School administrators, elementary and sec.	61.7	Garbage collectors	17.3
Buyers, wholesale and retail trade	50.0	**Farm work**	
Restaurant, cafeterias, and bar managers	38.7	Farm managers	43.7
Sales workers		Farm laborers, wage workers	18.9
Stock and bond sales persons	51.2	**Service workers, except private household**	
Insurance agents, brokers, underwriters	46.8	Police and detectives	47.7
Real estate agents and brokers	44.0	Practical nurses	36.8
Sales clerks, retail	28.7	Child-care workers	24.0
Clerical and kindred workers		Janitors	19.5
Bank tellers	49.5	Chambermaids	16.6
Bookkeepers	47.3	Welfare service aides	14.4
Secretaries	46.5	Shoeshiners	9.3
File clerks	31.4	**Private household workers**	
		Child-care workers	22.6
		Maids and servants	18.0

Source: Adapted from Miller, Delbert C. 1991. Pp. 341–350, *Handbook of Research Design and Social Measurement,* 5th ed. Newbury Park, CA: Sage. Department of Labor occupational classifications. Scores taken originally from tabulation in Hauser, Robert M., and David L. Featherman. 1977. *The Process of Stratification: Trends and Analysis.* Pp. 286–302. New York: Academic Press.

husband's. Husbands' own class identifications were not affected by any status characteristics of their wives.

Baxter (1991) found that women who worked part time were more likely to derive their class location from their husband's class position than were women who worked full time. Davis and Robinson (1988) suggested a version of the borrowing model referred to as a "status maximization strategy." This means that a couple will identify with whichever of them has the higher status. Since that is usually the husband, the conventional model would usually apply, but when the wife had the higher status, the husband would "borrow" hers.

Davis and Robinson (1988) also proposed that there is increasing independence in the way husbands and wives defined their class, with men becoming even more independent and women moving to a perspective of "sharing" rather than "borrowing" their status (see also Wright, 1989). Baxter (1994) found the husband's position still to be the main determinant of both the husband's and wife's perceptions in the United States, Sweden, Norway, and Australia. This provides support for the traditional "status borrowing" model. She also found no significant differences in the patterns of the four countries.

Power and Social Class

Power is a more difficult thing to measure even than prestige, but it is clearly related to social class. It was one of the three major determinants of social class in Weber's multidimensional approach. There are many types of power, including the ability to control one's own actions or those of one's family. We will address those in later chapters. In the present context, we are referring to **social power,** which refers to control over others in the broader social system.

Formal Education and Social Class

We have seen that education is correlated with occupational prestige. Every study done on the matter has found that the more years of formal education a person has the

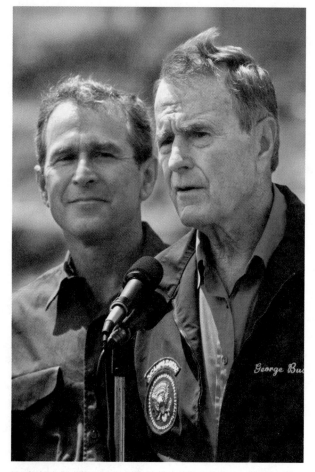

Maybe any American can achieve a position of power, but family connections sure do help.

higher his or her income is likely to be, and persons with power are usually highly educated as well. Even for persons with the same income, the one with more education is likely to have more power and prestige.

Technically speaking, families do not have an education, but the family members do. The exact relationship between education, social class, and families has been the subject of considerable research. The perspectives tend to fall into one of two camps. The conventional view of formal education in America is that it provides a route by which those from lower social classes can earn social mobility into higher classes. This assumes a relatively open mobility system.

Opposing the conventional view is the perspective that the formal educational system generally tends to reproduce social class, rather than reduce inequality. This view would assume a relatively open mobility system.

The social class of one's parents, especially their educational level, is a strong predictor of one's success in school. Table 6.3 divides college attainment into three categories: those who did not finish high school; those who graduated from high school and had no more education; and those who had at least some college, although they might not have graduated. Sons and daughters of parents who had some college education were much more likely to have some too.

It would appear that the mother's education has more effect on a child's college chances than does the father's education, for both boys and girls. When the mother had some college, 78.4% of the sons and 74.0% of the daughters had some college. When the father had some college, 71.1% of the sons and 63.1% of the daughters had some college. This might be because more children grow up with mothers as major role models than with dads. It is not in the table that when both mothers and fathers had some college, 78.7% of the sons and 77.7% of the daughters got to college.

The data on education again suggest that the United States has a mobility system somewhere between completely closed and completely open. Even though the parents' education is a strong predictor of a child's education, many children exceed their parents' educational level and some fall below it. As Table 6.3 indicates, even of the children whose mother did not finish high school, 38.2% of sons and 28.9% of daughters had at least some college. Although it is not indicated in the table, the same source found that, even when neither parent had

---

Social power: The probability of controlling or influencing the behavior of other persons, even against resistance.

Table 6.3	Relationship Between Mother's Education and Father's Education on Education of Adult Men and Women					
Adult Child's Education (Ages 30–49)	**Mother's Education**			**Father's Education**		
	Not HS Grad	**HS Grad**	**Some College**	**Not HS Grad**	**HS Grad**	**Some College**
Son's Education						
Not HS Grad	28.5%	7.5%	7.6%	24.9%	5.8%	11.1%
HS Grad	33.3%	32.6%	14.0%	35.5%	32.0%	17.8%
Some College	38.2%	59.8%	78.4%	39.6%	62.2%	71.1%
Daughter's Education						
Not HS Grad	26.7%	6.5%	7.0%	21.4%	6.4%	13.4%
HS Grad	44.3%	38.8%	19.0%	45.7%	39.4%	23.5%
Some College	28.9%	54.7%	74.0%	32.9%	54.2%	63.1%

Source: Davis, James Allan, and Tom W. Smith: General Social Survey(s), year(s). (Machine-readable data file). Principal investigator, James A. Davis; director and co-principal investigator, Tom W. Smith; co-principal investigator, Peter V. Marsden, NORC ed. Chicago: National Opinion Research Center, producer, 1998; Storrs, CT: The Roper Center for Public Opinion Research, University of Connecticut, distributor. Microcomputer format and codebook prepared and distributed by MicroCase Corporation, Bellevue, WA. Analysis by Gene H. Starbuck.

finished high school, 28.6% of sons and 24.8% of daughters got some college. On the other hand, even when both parents had some college, 8.6% of sons and 8.8% of daughters failed to finish high school.

The influence of SES (socioeconomic status) on school success is not explained simply by the fact that wealthier parents can buy more things for their children. Children with higher class backgrounds are more likely to have a two-parent home, to be encouraged to do well in school, to have role models of successful college graduates, and to have more school-approved patterns of behavior, including grammar and vocabulary. These facts have led many researchers to conclude that the schools themselves have little overall effect on the system of inequality in America, although they can provide avenues of social mobility for individuals in all classes (Jencks, 1972, 1979; Gilbert & Kahl, 1993).

Poverty and Families

It is quite clear that some families are poorer than others. But exactly who is poor and who is not is a matter of debatable definition. This raises the issue of exactly what poverty is and how it is measured. The definition preferred by the U.S. government is explained in Finding Out 6.1. That definition is generally used by the federal government to collect data on poverty.

Who Are the Poor?

Some persons appear to be locked into long-term or permanent poverty; these have been called the "underclass" (Auletta, 1982) and occupy a position only slightly better than persons in Third World countries. In the United States, poverty is a temporary condition for most. Only about 12% of the poor remain in poverty for 5 or more consecutive years (O'Hare, 1996). A somewhat larger number move in and out of poverty as employment and family conditions change.

Census data (*Statistical Abstract*, 1999: t. 769) reveal who the poor families are. There are more poor families with White householders. However, higher percents of Black families (23.6%) and Hispanic families (24.7%) are poor than are Whites (10.3%). Education also makes a difference. Of families headed by a person without a high school diploma, 24.1% are poor. Of those headed by a person with a bachelors' degree or more, 2.0% are poor.

Work experience, too, matters. Even when the householder works full time, year-round, a few families (3.3%) are poor. A single parent with two children would need a $13,133 income to get to the poverty threshold (see Table 6.4). A minimum-wage, 40-hour-a-week, year-round job paid only about $10,500 in 1998, well below the poverty line. Even two such jobs would leave a married couple with three children below the poverty level, and minimum-wage jobs do not usually include benefits such as health insurance (*Statistical Abstract*, 1999: t. 769).

Finding Out | 6.1

Defining and Measuring Poverty in the United States

Poverty can be defined in several ways, one of which is used by the United States government to determine poverty rates. The government annually establishes a **poverty threshold,** which is a dollar amount of income. Persons with incomes below the threshold are considered poor, and those above it are not.

The poverty index is based on a U.S. Department of Agriculture survey, done in 1955, that found that families of three or more persons spent approximately one third of their income on food. The Department of Agriculture also developed an Economy Food Plan, which was essentially the lowest cost of purchasing the minimum daily requirements of nutritional food.

The cost of the food plan was multiplied by three to determine the actual poverty level. Each year, as food costs changed, the cost of the Economy Food Plan was recalculated, and the poverty threshold adjusted accordingly. Beginning in 1969, changes in the poverty threshold were based on the overall change in cost of living as measured by the government Consumer Price Index (CPI), rather than just the cost of food. The threshold is adjusted for family size, age, and other factors.

Table 6.4 provides the 1998 poverty thresholds. The threshold for a family of four with two adults and two children was $16,530. Divided by four, this comes to $4,132.50 for each family member. Of this, one third, or $1,377.50 is assumed to be the annual food cost. Divided by 365 days, the daily food cost per person comes to $3.77. Per capita daily costs are lower for larger families, higher for smaller ones. The table also reveals that the poverty threshold for elderly persons is slightly lower than for others.

For purposes of determining the poverty threshold, only before-tax cash income is included. Capital gains are excluded, as is any noncash resource such as food stamps, employer-provided benefits, Medicaid, and rent reductions or subsidized public housing. Poverty thresholds are the basis for calculations used by other federal agencies to determine eligibility for government support of both cash and noncash varieties that are designed to help lift recipients to the poverty threshold.

Once the poverty thresholds are determined, the Census Bureau can estimate the number and percentage of

---

Children are particularly at risk of poverty (see Figure 6.3). Nearly 20% of children are poor. This includes 15.4% of White children, but 36.8% of Black and 36.4% of Hispanic youngsters. While this is the percentage of poor children at any one time, the risk of being poor at some time during their childhood is even higher. Before their 18th birthday, 30% of White children and 69% of Black children will experience a period of poverty. Of children in unmarried households, 81% will be poor at some time; 63% of children whose head of household did not finish high school will be poor (Rank & Hirshl, 1999).

Recent Trends in Poverty

America's "war on poverty" made progress in the 1960s and 1970s; the poverty rate for families dropped from 18.1% in 1960 to 9.1% in 1978. Not much progress

has been made in reduction of childhood poverty since then; the rate actually went up during the late 1970s and the 1980s. The rate for Black children went down substantially in the 1990s (see Figure 6.3).

Poverty rates follow employment patterns. The 1980s saw a high loss of jobs and realignment of the occupational structure. Of job positions lost, a disproportionate number were the type that paid relatively well but did not require college degrees or other extensive training. Although many jobs were created during that period, they were predominantly in the low-paid service occupations. The result was downward mobility for millions of American workers, many of whom slipped into poverty (Newman, 1988:12).

The 1980s also saw a realignment of government programs that were designed to help the poor. After

---

Poverty threshold: An annual income amount that separates the poor from the nonpoor.

American households and individuals who fall below the poverty threshold. This is done by using the Current Population Survey, a sample of about 30,000 households nationwide. This survey, updated monthly, is the source of government estimates about income and poverty in the United States.

Table 6.4	Poverty Thresholds by Size of Family

Size of Family Unit	Related Children Under 18 Years						
	None	One	Two	Three	Four	Five	...
One person (average)	$8,316						
Under 65 years	8,480						
65 years and over	7,818						
Two persons							
Householder under 65		10,915	11,235				
Householder 65 plus		9,853	11,193				
Three persons	12,750	13,120	13,133				
Four persons	16,813	17,088	16,530	16,588			
Five persons	20,275	20,570	19,940	19,453	21,780		
Six persons	23,320	23,413	22,930	22,468	21,780	21,373	
Seven persons	26,833	27,000	26,423	26,020	25,270	24,395	
Eight persons	28,166	30,275	29,730	29,253	28,575	27,715	
Nine persons or more	36,100	36,275	35,793	35,388	34,723	33,808	

Source: U.S. Bureau of the Census. 1999. "Poverty Thresholds in 1998 by Size of Family and Number of Related Children Under 18 Years." http://www.census.gov/hhes/poverty/threshld/thresh98.html

1975, the dollar value of cash benefits to the poor began to decline and continued to do so throughout the 1980s. At the same time, however, the dollar value of noncash benefits increased. By the mid-1980s, these in-kind transfers such as Medicaid, food stamps, and housing assistance had become more than two thirds the value of all transfers to the poor. The result was that more persons were officially poor but were eligible for more noncash benefits (Tregarthen, 1988). Significant changes in the welfare system were made in 1996, but the effect of these changes is not yet fully known.

Welfare benefits help the poor, but generally are given for a relatively short time. Rank (1994) looked at female heads of household who were receiving Aid to Families with Dependent Children (AFDC). He found that the median length of time his sample of women received the benefits was 33.6 months. Of those who got off welfare, 23.8% returned within 6 months and 41.8% were back on the rolls within 30 months.

Changes in employment are one route to dropping into poverty, or to rising out of it. Duncan et al. (1984) found that the most important factor associated with changes in economic well-being was a change in family structure. These included divorce, death, marriage, birth of a child, or having a child leave home.

The Poverty Gender Gap

The term **feminization of poverty** has led to the impression that an increasing percentage of poor

---

Feminization of poverty: The impression that women are increasingly likely to be poor because of the increasing concentration of poverty in female-headed families.

| Figure 6.3 | Percentage of Children in Poverty, 1960–1999, by Race/Ethnicity |

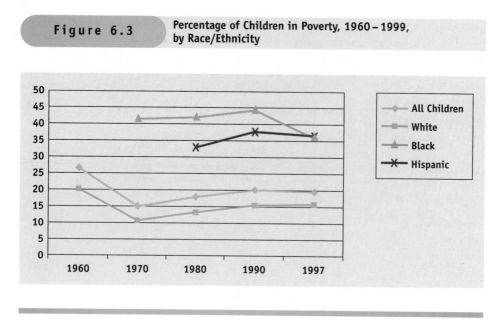

Source: *Statistical Abstract,* 1999; Table 761.

individuals are women. In fact, since data were first available in 1966, women have made up about 57% of the poor. Since 1973, poverty rates have actually increased more among men, slightly narrowing the gender gap (O'Hare, 1996).

What has happened is a dramatic increase in female-headed families, a family form that has always been at high risk of poverty. In 1960, 10% of families were headed by women. By 1998, that figure had almost doubled, to 18% Consequently, female-headed families became a rapidly increasing portion of poor families, from 23.7% in 1960 to 53.3% in 1998 (see Figure 6.4). The percent of nonpoor families headed by women has increased also, and is now 13.9% of the nonpoor group.

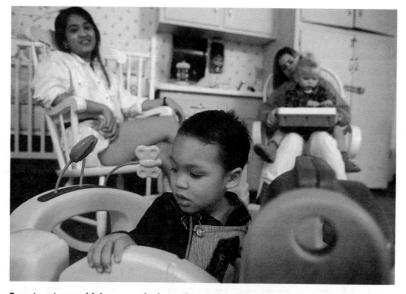

Poverty rates are high among single mothers, who often depend on the government's assistance.

Even though the portion of female-headed families in poverty is still large (29.9%), it is considerably smaller than in 1960 (42.4%). We could conclude from Figure 6.4 that the major reason poverty rates remain as high as they are is that the number of female-headed households has rapidly increased, and those families are more likely to be poor. Without the increase in families headed by a woman, the poverty rate for children would be substantially lower.

Single female householders are more likely to be poor than are single male householders. A large part of this difference is due to the differential treatment of women in the workforce that we discussed earlier, but other forces may be operating also. Not much is known about the relatively small population of families headed by single men, but they probably differ from single-female households in various ways. Single-father heads of household become such almost entirely as the result of a marriage that ended by death or divorce, rather than unplanned single parenthood. They are older as a group than single mothers, and there is a strong connection between low parental age and low family income. Also, single fathers are more likely to have a job, and job experience, at the time they become single parents than are single mothers.

Rates of unwed births have gone up for all groups, but they vary considerably by race and ethnicity (see Figure 6.5). More than one fourth of White children are born out of wedlock, and over two thirds of Black children are. These are about five times the 1965 rate for Whites and about three times the 1965 rate for Blacks. Asian Americans have the lowest rate, at under 16%.

In one sense, the increase in births to unmarried mothers is deceiving. About one fourth of technically out-of-wedlock births now occur in cohabiting couples (Bumpass & Raley, 1995), and an additional number occur to couples who maintain a close relationship in spite of not living together. Although not married, these couples provide a two-parent family for their children. Such couples, however, have a high rate of breakup, so the majority of their children end up living in single parent, nearly always single mother, families (Thompson & Amato, 1999).

Not only the number but also the composition of female-headed families has changed. It has been the case historically that the most common way to become a single mother was by widowhood, with divorce, separation, or desertion also being major factors. For unwed or divorced women, part of the reason for

---

Figure 6.4   **Poverty and Families, 1960–1998**

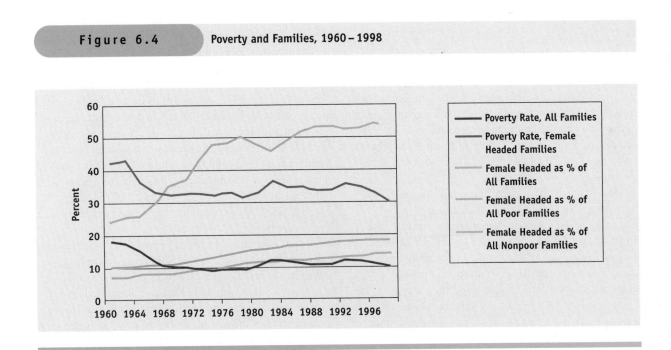

Legend:
- Poverty Rate, All Families
- Poverty Rate, Female Headed Families
- Female Headed as % of All Families
- Female Headed as % of All Poor Families
- Female Headed as % of All Nonpoor Families

Source: U.S. Census Bureau, Historical Poverty Tables, Table 13. http://www.census.gov/ftp/pub/hhes/poverty/histpov/hstpov13.html

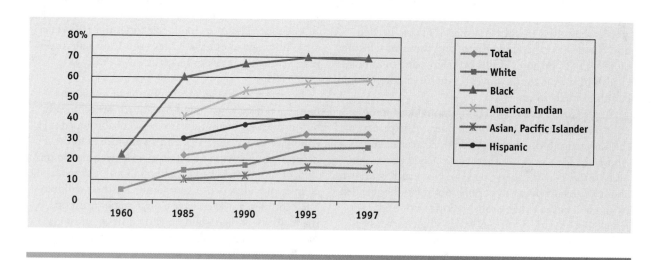

Figure 6.5 **Percentage of Births to Unmarried Mothers, by Race/Ethnicity, 1965–1997**

Source: Data for 1965 from Moynihan, 1970. All others from *Statistical Abstract,* 1998; Table 100; Centers for Disease Control, National Center for Health Statistics, **www.cdc.gov/nchswww/data/hus99.pdf**

poverty is failure to receive child support payments. For custodial women whose partners were absent, 61% were awarded child support by a court. Of those who were supposed to receive support, 40% received full payment and 30% got partial payment (*Statistical Abstract 1999:* t. 637).

Among poor women, only 51% of single or divorced custodial mothers were awarded child support; full or partial payment was received in 62% of cases (*Statistical Abstract 1999:* t. 637). Women who become mothers while unwed have a low probability of receiving support payments from the child's father. In fact, the U.S. Office of Child Support Enforcement found that fathers are not even legally identified in 65% of unwed births (Worthington, 1994).

Unwed births have risen in most industrial countries since 1980 (see Table 6.5). Although unwed parenthood is closely associated with poverty in the United States, the same is not necessarily true elsewhere. For example, Sweden now has an unwed pregnancy rate of about 50% but almost no poverty. Because cohabitation is so accepted there, most of the unwed children have a father in the home, and for those who do not there is an extensive welfare system. Also, unwed pregnancies are much more likely to be planned in Sweden (Popenoe, 1994). In addition,

Swedish companies have more family-friendly policies than in the United States. Finally, women have greater earning power relative to men.

American women who become mothers as teenagers, especially when unwed, are less likely to finish high school, more likely to have difficulties getting and keeping well-paying jobs, and more likely to be in poverty for significant periods. If they do get married, they are more likely to divorce than are brides without children (Zabin et al., 1992). Several health hazards to mothers and their babies have been associated with teenage pregnancy, including more difficult and dangerous childbirth, low-birth-weight babies, and more stillbirths and infant death (Luker, 1992). Children born of unwed mothers are more likely themselves to become unwed parents, and at younger ages (Hayes, 1987; Hofferth & Hayes, 1987). This contributes to social reproduction of the class system.

A factor in rates of unwed pregnancy is that fewer young women who get pregnant are marrying the father of their child. The traditional informal sanctions against unmarried motherhood have given way to social acceptance; in some subcultures unwed motherhood is the norm. The ideal of socially responsible fatherhood is being replaced, in some central cities and other poverty areas, by matrifocal, or

Table 6.5	Percentage of Births to Unmarried Women, Selected Countries, 1980–1995			
Country	**1980**	**1990**	**1994**	**1995**
United States	18	28	33	32
Canada	13	24	25	26
Denmark	33	46	47	46
France	11	30	36	37
Germany	8	11	15	16
Italy	4	6	8	8
Japan	1	1	1	1
Netherlands	4	11	14	16
Sweden	40	47	52	53
United Kingdom	12	28	32	34

Source: *Statistical Abstract,* 1998; Table 1347.

women centered, families supported at least partially by welfare. The father role is increasingly being treated as an unnecessary part of family relationships (Popenoe, 1996).

Welfare and Families

The first major commitment of the federal government to help the poor came with the passage of the 1935 Social Security Act. Part of the act included a program that came to be called AFDC. Poor families were thenceforth entitled to certain benefits; that is, the benefits could not be taken away as long as the family remained poor and met other requirements.

In 1950, Congress increased the benefits. This was seen as a profamily act, since the hope was that widowed and divorced mothers would be able to stay home and take care of their children. But AFDC and other welfare programs remained controversial. One charge was that the program simply encouraged women to remain single and have children.

Ellwood and Bane (in Eschleman, 1994:404) compared states with high AFDC payments with those that had low AFDC payments. They found that level of payment had little impact on fertility rates, but it did influence the mothers' familial arrangements. Women in states with higher levels of payment were less likely to marry when they got pregnant and more likely to move out of their parents' home into a place of their own. Also, in those states, young mar-

ried mothers were more likely to become divorced or separated. In an extensive Wisconsin study, Rank (1994) found that women receiving welfare actually had lower fertility rates than women of the same age and socioeconomic circumstances who were not receiving welfare. Studies such as this, however, were generally ignored as the debate about welfare heated up.

Finally, in the summer of 1996, a sweeping change was enacted. AFDC was abolished and replaced with Temporary Assistance to Needy Families (TANF). Welfare was no longer an entitlement, and recipients had to take job training or get a job within a certain amount of time—typically 2 years or less. Further, a 5-year lifetime limit was placed on the amount of time a person could receive benefits, and states could enforce even a shorter limit if they chose.

Millions of former or potential "welfare mothers" have gotten jobs since the act was passed; some observers claim that the 1996 act accomplished its goal. During this time, however, the economy has had record low unemployment rates; there have been more jobs available. No one knows what will happen when jobs become more scarce and thousands of families have used their lifetime limits of government help.

TANF and other forms of welfare seldom pay enough to provide a comfortable, or even marginal, standard of living for poor families. Welfare mothers adopt a variety of strategies to survive, as Edin and Lein (1997) found in their pioneering study of welfare mothers. The researchers talked in depth with welfare recipients in four major American cities. They found that many (from 2% to 19%) had survival strategies that broke the law, the rules of public assistance, or both; these included prostitution, dealing in stolen property, or selling drugs. Some worked "off the books" for income they did not report. From 27% to 41% received support payments from their children's fathers; sometimes this was not reported because it might make the women ineligible for more public support. Nearly all the successful mothers had a wide support network of friends and family. Ironically, the mothers who did not work had an easier time of it than mothers who worked at the low-paid jobs that did not have benefits (Edin & Lein, 1997).

HIGHLIGHT 6.1 **Economics, Government, and Transfer Payments**   There are two basic views in economics about the proper role of the government in helping the poor. One, sometimes called **trickle-down economics,** argues that leaving money in the hands of wealthy individuals, through tax breaks and other means, will result in investments in the economy. These, in turn, will result in jobs that will help the poor. The Republican Party, wealthy persons, and political conservatives have traditionally supported this view. It was the prevailing view of the Reagan administration. Arguing that most money runs off rather than trickling all the way down to the poor, others support **trickle-up** or percolate up economics. This view advocates providing money or services directly to those who need them. The poor, receiving a direct benefit, will purchase food, housing, and other goods. Their spending, in turn, provides a demand for food and other services, and provides jobs and profits to retail grocers, landlords, and others. The Democratic Party, poor persons, and political liberals have traditionally supported this perspective.

Neither approach affects the overall system of stratification that is based on wealth; the poor do not accumulate wealth, but spend their money, providing wealth to the producers.

AFDC, food stamps, and other welfare programs are one type of what economists call **transfer payments,** which re-

distribute things of value within the stratification system. While private charities institutionalize voluntary forms of transfer payments, the largest and most controversial are administered by federal, state, and local governments.

It has generally been found that transfer payments have the overall impact of transferring from the wealthy to the poor, reducing the system of inequality by operating in trickle-up fashion (Danziger, Haveman, & Plotnick, 1981). Beeghley (2000) concluded, however, that traditional measures are biased because they typically include only social insurance and public assistance payments, which do tend to redistribute to the poor. Beeghley argued that many "welfare" or transfer payments benefit the middle class and wealthy, rather than the poor. These include government expenditures such as farm price supports, and tax considerations such as deductions for home interest payments, untaxed employment benefits such as health insurance, and deferral of capital gains on home sales. If these kinds of transfers are included, Beeghley found, total transfer payments have no net redistribution effect.

The debate about the overall impact of transfer payments to the poor, or welfare, is bound to continue in America. Much of the concern comes from working-class Americans who themselves feel squeezed by changes in the economy. Many of these are taxpayers who are not poor enough to receive the transfers for which the poor qualify but are not well off enough to benefit from transfers of other types.

Working-Class Families

The term "working class" is misleading, since most persons in other classes work also. This category is sometimes called the "blue-collar" class, in honor of the traditional blue work shirts, but this is also misleading since many blue-collar workers now wear white collars. In terms of occupational categories, working-class families consist of workers in the census categories of precision production, craft, and repair; machine operating, assembling, and inspecting; transportation and material moving, and handling, equipment cleaning, helping,

---

Trickle-down economics: The view that increased wealth in the hands of the rich will result in an improved economy that will help the poor.   **Trickle-up economics:** The view that directly helping the poor will create a demand for goods and services that will improve the economy.   **Transfer payments:** Redistribution of something of value from one person or group to another person or group, not based on work the receiver is performing.

and laboring. Usually, lower-income service jobs are classified as working class, although many persons holding them are below the poverty line. We have pointed out earlier that the higher paid of these jobs are those most likely to have been lost in the postindustrial era.

Collins (1988) argued that many occupations held by women that are thought to be middle-class work are more appropriately classified as "white collar working class." In this category he included nurses who, although highly educated, have working conditions more like blue-collar workers. They, like secretaries, are "order takers" and have little control over the conditions of their own employment.

In general, blue-collar workers are less economically stable than are middle-class professionals. Rather than being salaried, as is typical among white-collar workers, blue-collar workers are more likely to be paid by piece-work or by the hour, day or week. This makes them more susceptible to swings in the country's economic health. Some, like operators of large construction equipment, receive high hourly wages but are subject to seasonal and between-contract layoffs.

Working-class men perform most of the dangerous jobs mentioned in chapter 5. Also, many of the jobs require considerable strength and physical stamina. In these cases, men often hit their peak earning years considerably younger than do middle-class men and have little to look forward to by way of career advancement. Women in this class, too, have limited advancement opportunities and are more likely to be victims of sexual harassment and other on-the job dangers than are middle-class women (Gruber & Bjorn, 1986).

As there is more economic uncertainty, there is more familial instability in the working class. Although not as frequent as among the chronic poor, divorce is more common in the working class than in wealthier classes.

Persons raised in working-class homes marry at younger ages than do those with middle-class backgrounds (Davis & Smith, 1990–98). This is partly because they considered their formal education to be completed upon high school graduation, and partly because marriage is a way to get out of their own parents' home. The idea of marriage and a home of their own carries at least the illusion of freedom (Rubin, 1976).

Working-class couples tend to have their first child at a relatively young age, which adds to the economic pressures. Working-class couples whose marriages survive often rely on kin for emotional and financial support. They are less mobile than middle-class couples and are more likely to live near their parents and siblings, so "pooling resources" is easier (Rubin, 1976; Rosen, 1987).

The marital role structure is more likely to be traditional in the working class than in any other segment of the population. The majority of marriages are of the complementary or modified complementary type, with the husband as the sole or primary breadwinner and the wife primarily responsible for home and children. The kin-keeper role is extremely important for working-class women. Many of the wives need to work for financial reasons, however, and this can result in a conflict between the couple's ideal and real role situations, making script construction problematic (Komarovsky, 1962; Rubin, 1976; Halle, 1984). If the women have employment while they are raising small children, working-class couples are more likely to use relatives for day care than are middle-class ones.

Working-class men and women are likely to have gender-segregated leisure activities. Men form companionship groups that often focus on sports, both participatory and spectator. Although working-class persons probably drink no more, or have more alcoholism, than other classes, there is at least a subculture whose social life centers in a bar (Calahan & Room, 1974; Le Masters, 1975). If they are not participating in leisure pursuits with their husbands, working-class wives are often interacting with their families, in person or by telephone. Much of their activity centers around children and, for many, church activities.

Different patterns of speech and interaction, and different ways of looking at the world, help distinguish working-class from middle-class families. Collins and Coltrane (1991) brought together several studies that provide a framework for looking at cultural differences between working-class and middle-class persons. Since the differences are a matter of degree and probability, we can illustrate them with use of a continuum. At one end of the continuum is what Bernstein (1971–75) referred to as the "restricted code" of the working class. At the other end is the "elaborated code" of the middle class (see Figure 6.6). These distinctions draw on the classical analysis of groups by Durkheim (1893/1947; 1912/1954) as well as Collins and Coltrane (1991).

The elaborated code is more typical of persons who come into contact, through their jobs, travel, or education, with others who have a diversity of experiences. Linguistic patterns must be more elaborate in order to communicate with other persons who lack local knowledge and background of the small group. When telling a story, the speaker would refer not just to a person's name but would place him or her in a larger context, such as his or her relationship to the speaker.

<table>
<tr><td>

Figure 6.6
</td><td>

Cultural Continuum, From Restricted to Elaborated Code
</td></tr>
</table>

Restricted Code	**Elaborated Code**
Localistic, group conformist	Cosmopolitan
Interact with small group of similar persons	Interact with large number of different persons
Distrust of differences and outsiders; lack power to insulate themselves	Tolerance of differences; have power to insulate themselves
Jobs require conformity to external authority; obedience	Jobs require initiative, self-control, creativity
Socialization of children stresses behavior, obedience, being strong	Socialization stresses intent, feelings, politeness, self-direction
Moral code has clear distinction between right and wrong; strong punishment for deviation	Moral relativism, situational ethics; understanding and help for deviation
Strong bonds with kin and friend	Flexible relationships with allies

The restricted code is associated with relatively small groups who do not have a good deal of voluntary interaction with larger society. Within this small group, there is considerable pressure to conform to the group's norms; strangers or outsiders, who do not conform, are looked upon with suspicion or even hatred.

One point not stressed by Bernstein is that strangers often do mean danger to the working class. From bill collectors to school principals, strangers make working-class life more difficult. Working-class people do not have the resources to insulate themselves from undesirable strangers. They often live in high-crime areas. Working-class Whites sometimes see themselves as victims of affirmative action; working-class minorities are often the first to lose their jobs in bad economic times. Working-class persons of all racial and ethnic groups are competing against each other for shrinking job opportunities.

The middle classes might interact with a wider variety of persons, but they have the resources to insulate themselves from the diversity they consider most dangerous. They live in safer environments, and when they do interact with strangers they are more likely to be in a position of authority, an insider dealing with an outsider.

The elaborated code of the middle class is more likely to be a part of cultural capital that becomes useful in children's educations and searches for professional employment. According to Kohn (1977), working-class and middle-class socialization patterns tend to reflect the job requirements of the two groups. Working-class workers are required to work under close supervision

and are often expected to follow orders without question and to deal with whatever their boss deals out. What counts is their productive behavior. Their children are socialized accordingly.

More middle-class professionals are required to interact, in polite ways, with other persons. They are less closely supervised, so personal self-direction and responsibility are required. Creativity is valued, at least within certain bounds. Their children are treated in similar terms. The child's intent and feelings are emphasized, not just their behavior. Blue-collar workers are somewhat more likely to approve of the use of spanking as a form of discipline than are white-collar workers (Davis & Smith, 1998).

The restricted moral code of the working class is more likely to have clear distinctions between right and wrong; strong punishments are more likely to be called for in cases of deviation from the norm. For example, there is less tolerance for homosexuality and for such forms of political dissent as flag burning, and more calls for religious conformity. The working-class person is more likely to belong to fundamentalist and other conservative churches. Churches that wealthier segments of society belong to are more likely to emphasize pluralism and tolerance of differences (Roof & McKinney, 1987).

Interactions between families and the outside world are different in working- compared to middle-class couples, and so are interactions within families. Krakoff, Gottman, and Roy (1988) found that blue-collar husbands expressed more negative feeling to their wives.

Families in the NEWS

Debutante Balls and Mardi Gras Queens

Throughout the United States, especially in the south, debutante balls introduce daughters of the wealthy and well connected to society. In New Orleans, the debutante tradition got incorporated into that city's complex system of Mardi Gras queens, parades, and pageants.

Queen Elizabeth I of England is often credited with beginning the debutante custom nearly 400 years ago. Daughters of the nobility were celebrated as they were formally introduced into elite society and, not so coincidentally, to the princes, dukes, and other male nobility.

Queen Victoria opened the celebration to daughters of the wealthiest industrialists in addition to the gentry. Queen Elizabeth II ended the practice in 1958, long after it had become rooted in the United States.

In 1874 in New Orleans, one of the elite original Mardi Gras men's clubs took a debutante as queen of the club. Since then, the debutante balls and the Mardi Gras celebration have become intertwined.

One of the debutante-queens this year was Blayne Yves Laborde. She was queen of one of the men's clubs, attendant of three others, and debuted at one of New Orlean's two debutante societies. She is also an architecture major at the University of Virginia.

Participants must have both family connections and family wealth. A queen can expect to spend between $6,000 and $12,000 for her queen's dress alone. Attendant's gowns are also expensive.

Blayne needed four gowns. Her queen's dress was encrusted with pearls and rhinestones, and had an 80-pound train. She also needed a jeweled crown, a scepter that she designed herself, and lots of other clothes and royal paraphernalia. She said that the queenly duties were more fun than she thought they would be. She "honestly felt like a queen."

Source: Julia Reed. www.nytimes.com, March 25, 2001.

Blue-collar wives, however, expressed fewer marital grievances than their middle-class counterparts.

Working-class persons identify closely with their small groups of like-minded compatriots. They form especially close ties with family and friends. Middle-class persons treat friendship in a more flexible manner, perhaps more like allies than friends. As they change jobs, social positions or geographic locations, they develop new sets of allies (Higman, 1970).

Recent years have seen changes in working-class families. They remain different from the middle classes in certain ways, but their home division of labor has become increasingly egalitarian. Rubin, in a 1992 introduction to her classic 1976 study, noted that working-class women were increasingly likely to view working outside the home as proper and as a source of satisfaction and self-esteem.

The Middle and Upper Classes

We have already made several comparisons between the working class and the middle class in general. We will focus here on the group sometimes referred to as the professional class or the upper middle class, and then on wealthy families.

Upper Middle Class

Upper-middle-class workers see themselves as having careers, not jobs, in fields that typically require at least a bachelor's degree. Their occupations are in the census classifications of professional, technical, and kindred workers; managers, officials, and proprietors; and some sales positions. They work longer hours than do the working class, but their work is more likely to be seen as intrinsically rewarding. It is more likely to be a central concern in their lives, and the distinction between work time and other activities is less clear.

Many upper-middle-class couples have parallel or modified parallel marital scripts, with each holding relatively high-paying jobs. Part of the reason for the increasing gap in the stratification system between financially well-off families and poor families is the increasing number of couples in which both have lucrative careers.

This class also has a number of "two-person one-career" couples (Papanek, 1973). Kanter (1977) analyzed the lifestyles of corporate career families in the 1970s. Corporations were concerned about the family lives of their executives and expected their wives and children to reflect well on the company and to give the male executive support and time to work. Part of the difficulty female executives have had advancing in the corporate world is that they have no one playing the "corporate wife" role with them. They tend either to be unmarried, or married to an even wealthier, higher level professional. The extent to which corporate culture has changed to accommodate upper-middle-class women executives, or the men married to such women, since Kanter's study has not been fully researched.

Partly because they can afford to, upper-middle-class families value delayed gratification. They get married later than their working-class counterparts and delay having children longer. When children are born, they are more likely to have been carefully planned, and the couple's financial position is more likely to be such that the wife can opt out of the labor force for a period of time if that is what they want. If not, they have the resources to provide high-quality day care or nannies for their children.

For children of the upper middle class, the choice after high school is not whether to go to college, but where. It is likely that the vast majority of their extended family has attended college, as have the families of their closest friends. The possibility of not going to college might never even be considered. In accord with reasonable expectations about their opportunities, they might have worked very hard in school so that they could be admitted to the most prestigious colleges.

The upper middle class is not plagued by basic financial concerns as are the working class and the poor. Their security allows them to take the broader view; they are more concerned about abstract ideas than are other classes. They are more likely to be informed on a variety of social issues and more likely to have an opinion. They are the most likely to be politically and socially active, to vote, run for office, and be involved in political campaigns (Collins & Coltrane, 1995). Both conservative and liberal causes draw their most active supporters from the upper middle class. Health fads and such activities as jogging are almost exclusively upper-middle-class phenomena.

The upper middle class would tend to be at the extreme end of the elaborated code continuum, with cosmopolitan attitudes. They are likely to claim many more "friends" than the working class, but their relationships do not have the depth and closeness found in other classes.

The Upper Class

This section of text is the shortest discussion of all the class groups. Not a lot is known about the family lives of upper classes; they are generally able to insulate themselves from social science research. Wealth is a better indicator of upper-class status, but income can pro-

Table 6.6	Money Income of Households: Percent in Upper 5% of Incomes for Selected Characteristics

Characteristic	Percent of Group in Top 5%
All Households	5.0
White	5.4
Black	1.7
Hispanic	1.8
Family Households	6.4
Married-Couple Families	7.8
Male Householder	3.1
Female Householder	0.9
Nonfamily Households	1.8
Male Householder	2.6
Living Alone	1.8
Female Householder	1.0
Living Alone	0.5
Age of Householder	
15–24	0.5
25–34	2.8
35–44	6.4
45–54	9.9
55–64	6.4
65 and Older	1.9
Worked	6.6
Worked Full-Time Job	7.1
Worked Part-Time Job	2.8
Did Not Work	1.1

Source: *Statistical Abstract, 1995.*

vide some information. Table 6.6 indicates some characteristics associated with being in the top 5% of family income.

Non-Hispanic Whites are more likely to be in the highest income group of the three listed here. Those in married-couple families are more likely to be in the top 5% than other types of households. As the head of household gets older, the family incomes increase until the 55-to-64 age group, when the process is reversed. Those in the top 5% of income, however, may not be in the upper classes as measured by wealth.

Warner and Lunt (1941) divided the American upper class into two subcategories: the upper-upper class and the lower-upper class. The distinction is not one of money; both are extremely wealthy, and the lower-upper group might even be wealthier. The distinction is one between the old wealth of the upper-upper group and the new wealth of the lower-upper group.

Entrance into the elite circle of the upper-upper group is almost entirely by ascription. These families can trace their wealth back several generations. Their children are channeled in marriage within their own class. Parents isolate their children from other classes by sending them to elite private schools and camps. Their leisure time often revolves around private clubs or in doing things, like sailing, that few others can afford. This group has a certain disdain for the ostentatious displays of wealth in which the class just below them sometimes engages.

Susan Ostrander (1984) found that upper-class women were heavily involved in maintaining the elite status of their families. Such women tend not to have careers of their own, but participate in their husband's powerful and lucrative career. The wives perform charity work and oversee the supervision of children who attend elite schools and are guided away from interaction with youths considered "beneath" them.

There is some movement in and out of the upper class. The wealthier of the upper-middle class cross into the lower-upper group, and the lower-upper aspire, over time, to be part of the highest group. Occasionally, a family fortune is lost and downward mobility results.

In many American cities, especially in the South, young women are introduced to "society" at a debutante ball.

Summary and Conclusion

Social class has long been of interest in sociology, which has developed two classic perspectives on the issue. Conflict theory, originating with Marx, sees social stratification as destructive and unfair. Functionalism sees it as universal and necessary. Both recognize that families are inextricably linked to the class structure.

Societies have evidenced different kinds of stratification systems. In terms of social mobility, societies range from completely closed, where status is ascribed, to completely open, where status is achieved.

It is difficult to find clear-cut lines between social classes in the United States. Using a multidimensional approach, at least four major dimensions of inequality can be found: money, occupational prestige, power, and education. They overlap but do not exactly coincide.

For the past 20 years, somewhere between 10 and 12% of Americans have been poor; these families include nearly 20% of the country's children. The rate of poverty fell in the 1960s but began rising again in the late 1970s. An increasing portion of the poor is single mothers and their children, while children in two-income homes are much less likely to be poor.

Working-class families are likely to be characterized by a restricted code, rather than the elaborated code of the middle class. They have a smaller circle of friends and are more suspicious of persons who are different. Their jobs require discipline and obedience, and these qualities are instilled through the socialization process. They have a clear sense of what is right and wrong.

The middle class, especially the upper middle class, is more cosmopolitan. They are politically active, and nearly all their children attend college.

The upper-upper class is the most closed of American classes. The lower-upper class may have as much wealth, but it is new wealth rather than the old family wealth of the upper-upper group.

In conclusion, this chapter puts individual life chances in the context of class-related variables that operate through families. In all societies, family of orientation provides initial placement of individuals on a system of social inequality. More mobility exists in the United States than in most contemporary societies, but we are far from an equal-opportunity society. In the next chapter, race and ethnicity are woven into the tapestry of family, individual, and life chances.

Rethinking in Context How much social mobility has occurred in your family in the last three generations? In what ways did the social structure and economic system contribute to the mobility or lack thereof? Is upward mobility more difficult now or in the time of your great-grandparents? Why? Do you know any married couples whose social-class backgrounds were quite different from each other? Was this a problem in their marriages?

Additional Resources

General works on stratification and family

Beeghley, Leonard. 2000. *The Structure of Social Stratification in the United States.* Boston: Allyn and Bacon.

Kohn, Melvin & Carmi Schooler. 1983. *Work and Personality: An Inquiry Into the Impact of Social Stratification.* Norwood, NJ: Ablex.

Kulis, Stephen Stanley. 1991. *Why Honor Thy Father and Mother? Class, Mobility, Family Ties in Later Life.* New York: Garland Publishing.

Langman, Lauren. 1987. "Social Stratification," pp. 211–49 in *Handbook of Marriage and the Family*, edited by Suzanne K. Steinmetz and Marvin B. Sussman. NY: Plenum

Poverty and families

Goldberg, Gertrude Schaffner & Eleanor Kremen. 1990. *The Feminization of Poverty: Only in America?* New York: Praeger.

Harvey, David L. 1993. *Potter Addition: Poverty, Family, and Kinship in a Heartland Community.* New York: Aldine de Gruyter.

Kotlowitz, Alex. 1991. *There Are No Children Here: The Story of Two Boys Growing Up in the Other America.* New York: Anchor.

Lewis, Oscar. 1966. *La Vida: A Puerto Rican Family in the Culture of Poverty—San Juan and New York.* New York: Random House.

MacLeod, Jay. 1995. *Ain't No Makin' It: Aspirations and Attainment in a Low Income Neighborhood.* Boulder: Westview Press.

Wilson, William Julius. 1996. *When Work Disappears: The World of the New Urban Poor.* New York: Alfred A. Knopf.

Working-class families

Komarovsky, Mirra. 1962. *Blue Collar Marriage.* New York: Vintage.

Rubin, Lillian B. 1992. *Worlds of Pain: Life in the Working Class Family.* New York: Basic Books.

Rubin, Lillian B. 1995. *Families on the Fault Line.* New York: Basic Books.

Middle-class families

Katz, Donald. 1992. *Home Fires: An Intimate Portrait of One Middle-Class Family in Postwar America.* New York: Aaron Asher Books.

Newman, Katherine S. 1988. *Falling from Grace: The Experience of Downward Mobility in the American Middle Class.* New York: Free Press.

Upper-class families

Ostrander, Susan A. 1984. *Women of the Upper Class.* Philadelphia: Temple University Press.

Internet Sites

Social class and families, links to sources
http://www.familydiscussions.com/headings/class.htm

Government data
http://fedstats.gov

http://www.census.gov/

Conflict perspective of social class
http://www.tryoung.com/

For links to these sites and additional resources, visit the *Families in Context* Web site at:

http://sociology.wadsworth.com

Chapter **7**

Race/Ethnicity and Families

Prelude

Jorge was born in 1980 in a small village near Hidalgo del Parral, Chihuahua, Mexico. His dad, whom Jorge saw infrequently, was in Southern California, working for a landscaping company. Jorge, his mom, and two sisters lived mostly off the money his dad sent home.

When Jorge was 10, his dad got permanent resident status in the United States, and a few years later the family joined him. They moved in with Jorge's uncle, who had not yet gotten legal status, and his wife. Soon Jorge's brother was born. A year later, Jorge's mother's sister, on a temporary work permit, joined them. She married a U.S. citizen and had a baby.

All the adults in the familia worked at various shifts, so there was usually an adult at home to watch the children. Jorge's mom usually worked part time for a janitorial service. All the children who were old enough went to school and worked hard to improve their English skills. The family wanted them all to finish high school; they would be the first in the family to do so. Sometimes, though, Jorge's sister had to stay home from school to take care of the little ones if the adults' schedules didn't work out.

Their family had a variety of residence statuses. Jorge's brother and cousin were U.S. citizens. Jorge was technically in the country illegally, as were his mom and two sisters; they would probably get legal residency soon. His mother's sister was a permanent resident, as was his father. Jorge's uncle and his wife were undocumented workers. From time to time, other family and friends would stay with them while between jobs or on their way to or from Mexico.

How would the Census Bureau characterize this family?

We have seen how family experiences vary by social class. Race and ethnicity are also intertwined with family issues and are further mixed with social class. Power, wealth, and poverty are unequally distributed to America's racial and ethnic groups. Experiences with prejudice and discrimination have influenced family structures, as have the conditions under which various groups became Americans. This chapter explores the contexts of family racial and ethnic diversity.

> **Thinking Ahead** Are you more likely to be good friends with someone who is the same race as yourself but of a very different class, or someone who is the same class but a different race? Which are you most likely to live next door to? To marry? Why? What advantages or disadvantages, if any, have you experienced because of your race or ethnicity?

What Are Race and Ethnicity?

Peoples have been divided by religion, by "kin" versus "nonkin," by nationality, by tribe, and by language group. Two common distinctions today are race and ethnicity. These groupings provide ways of identifying ourselves and others, and affect the life chances of families and individuals.

The Concepts of "Race" and "Ethnicity"

As a way of sorting persons into categories, **race** has a relatively short history. The word did not appear in Europe in its modern sense until the end of the 16th century; its increasing use coincided with the developing institution of slavery in the Americas (Hannaford, 1994). In the 19th century, the emerging science of genetics and the theory of evolution gave apparent credence to the belief that groups of persons carried different genetic characteristics and that these groups represented different points in the evolutionary process. This led to some extreme forms of racism such as Hitler's notion of Aryan supremacy and various eugenic movements designed to eliminate "inferior" races. Matters of race continue to be among the most emotional and important issues in America today.

The term **ethnicity** is closer in meaning to the idea of "a people," a concept that has a much longer history than does the idea of race. Since the concept does not assign group membership primarily on the basis of physical characteristics, "ethnicity" refers to some perceived historical or cultural commonalities.

Race: A group defined by socially selected physical characteristics.   **Ethnicity:** Group distinction based on national origin or distinctive cultural patterns such as religion, language, or region.

Gans (1979) applied the idea of "symbolic ethnicity" to ethnic groups in the United States. From this perspective, one's ethnicity is not simply a historically continuous culture, but a continuous cultural construction. Identification is more or less voluntary, and is often as much a matter of reinventing a cultural trait as passing one from generation to generation (Morawska, 1994). African American heritage today takes on this sense of symbolic ethnicity with a "rediscovery" of names, styles, and other aspects of ethnic identity associated with Africa. Many Americans with Native American ancestors, and some without, are also "rediscovering" their Native heritage by adopting religious practices and other identifications that may or may not be authentic to their particular nation.

One's ethnicity is determined not only by one's origin, but also by one's current location. In Italy, for example, Italians see considerable difference between northern Italians, southern Italians, and Sicilians. In the United States, that distinction tends to get blurred and the identification becomes "Italian" or "Italian American." The term "African American" lumps together persons whose ancestors in Africa were bitter enemies and who would in no way have considered themselves similar.

Categorizing "Race" and "Ethnicity"

For a variety of reasons, government agencies and academic researchers study race and ethnicity, but defining the terms is difficult. Among others, the U.S. Bureau of the Census has historically kept track of American diversity (see Finding Out 7.1).

The purpose of an identification scheme is to fit each person into one, and only one, category. This has created problems for the millions of Americans who can identify with more than one ethnic/racial category. Many "Blacks" have at least one "White" ancestor, and this might be even more true for Native Americans. Many "Whites" have a "Black," "Indian," "Hispanic" or other ancestor. Although most marriages in a particular generation are same-race matches, there is considerable mixing of some groups. In 1991, about 7% of all marriages involving an African American were interracial. A little over one fourth of all married Hispanics had a non-Hispanic spouse in 1991, and Asians had a similar rate of out-group marriage (O'Hare, 1992; Lott, 1993). If all persons with European ancestry named their heritage, the portion of "mixed ancestry" would probably include most Americans, with mixes such as "part

English, part Welsh, part German, with a little French and Irish."

In 1989, partly because of the mixed-race issue, the National Center for Health Statistics changed the way it classifies the race of newborns. Rather than taking both the mother's and father's race into account, as had been done, only the mother's race is now used. This matrilineal approach slightly reduced the number of minority births, because the majority of mixed births are to minority fathers and White mothers (O'Hare, 1992).

On the census and for other purposes, persons volunteer their category. A variety of factors influence the ethnicity individuals, especially those with mixed backgrounds, might select. These include the perceived advantages and disadvantages of identification, and changing political consciousness. This could partly account for some changes in America's ethnic composition, such as the 30.7% increase in the number of Native Americans between 1980 and 1992. Their birthrate is not high enough to account for that much growth, and there is very little increase by immigration (O'Hare, 1992). If the official census term was changed from American Indian to Native American, the count would go even higher, since many Americans consider themselves to be "Native" Americans if they were born in the United States, regardless of their race (Knapp & Cunningham, 1991).

In addition to race and ethnicity, religion sometimes provides a key variable by which persons categorize themselves and others. In the United States and other countries, Jews represent a kind of minority group that, for some purposes, is different from other kinds. Jews have suffered discrimination and prejudice, but "Jewish" is not a race, nor, precisely, an ethnicity. Sometimes it is called a "religio-ethnic" group, but most Jews are counted as "White" for census purposes. Mennonites and Hutterites are other religio-ethnic groups. Hispanics are overwhelmingly Catholic, which accounts for part of their commonality. Religious distinctions sometimes separate what might otherwise be ethnic groups; Irish Protestants and Irish Catholics are sometimes considered distinct groups.

Race/Ethnicity in America's Past and Future

The United States is often referred to as the world's most diverse nation, a nation of immigrants. All Americans, even Native Americans, have ancestors who came from somewhere else. The mixing of groups has

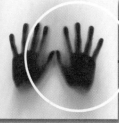

Finding Out | 7.1

Defining and Measuring Race and Ethnicity in the United States Census

Classifications used by the Census Bureau, which is the federal agency with the primary responsibility of measuring demographic trends, change regularly. These categories are reflections of the way Americans have perceived the divisions by race and affect the way social scientists study the subject. The divisions imply that race is a "socially constructed" phenomenon, since it can be categorized in many ways.

In 1860, only the racial categories of White, Black, and Mulatto (mixed White and Black) were used (see Table 7.1). In 1890 the categories Quadroon (one quarter Black) and Octoroon (one eighth Black) were added, along with Chinese, Japanese, and Indian. All degrees of Black ancestry were combined in the 1900 census; this effectively created the "one drop of blood" definition that included anyone with any degree of "Negro descent."

Another major change occurred in 1970. As the number and percentage of persons with Spanish-speaking ancestors grew, debate ensued about how these persons should be counted. The problem was that "Spanish-Surname" or "Hispanic" or "Latino" are categories of ethnicity rather than race, so overlap occurred. Until a separate category for Hispanic was included in the census, most were included under the racial heading of "White." Others fell into the "Black" category, while a few were counted as "Asian" or "American Indian" (O'Hare, 1992). Hispanic ancestry was recognized in 1970 for the first time and was divided into several categories that included "None of these" or non-Hispanic descent. Individuals self-identified with one racial category and one ethnicity category.

In the 2000 census, the Asian category was significantly expanded and a variety of terms were allowed for Hispanic ethnicity. A person can be Mexican, Mexican American, or Chicano, for example. More importantly, individuals for the first time could select more than one racial category. This recognition of multiracial ancestry will have major implications for the counting of various groups, since many Americans are of mixed ancestry and no longer have to choose one of their ancestries to the exclusion of others.

been both one of the strengths of the United States and one of its biggest concerns.

Immigration and Changing Diversity

The movement of people from all over the globe has been influenced by economic, political and moral considerations. Generally, when the American economy is good and labor is needed, **immigration** increases. When many Americans are out of work, immigration is reduced. This has resulted in significant changes in the numbers of immigrants allowed under U.S. policy (see Figure 7.1).

Because of changes in immigration law, the early 1990s saw the largest wave of immigration of the previous century. The law changed so that reuniting families became a high priority. There was also an amnesty

---

Immigration: Movement *into* a non-native country or region; compare with **Emigration:** Movement *out of* a native country or region.

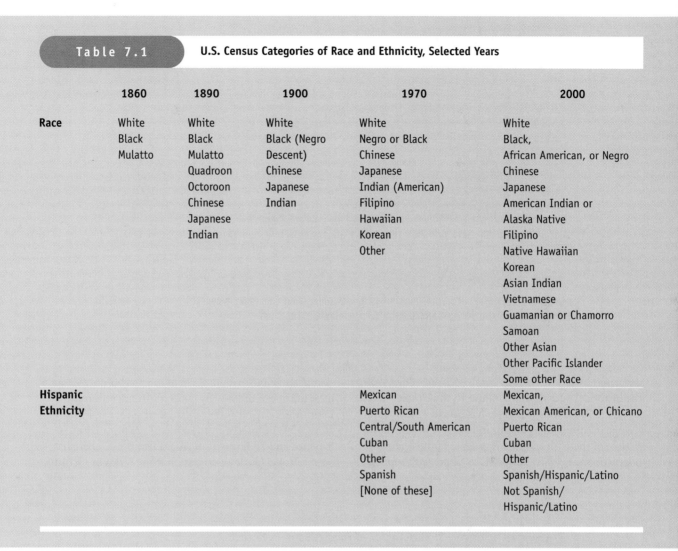

Table 7.1	U.S. Census Categories of Race and Ethnicity, Selected Years				
	1860	**1890**	**1900**	**1970**	**2000**
Race	White	White	White	White	White
	Black	Black	Black (Negro	Negro or Black	Black,
	Mulatto	Mulatto	Descent)	Chinese	African American, or Negro
		Quadroon	Chinese	Japanese	Chinese
		Octoroon	Japanese	Indian (American)	Japanese
		Chinese	Indian	Filipino	American Indian or
		Japanese		Hawaiian	Alaska Native
		Indian		Korean	Filipino
				Other	Native Hawaiian
					Korean
					Asian Indian
					Vietnamese
					Guamanian or Chamorro
					Samoan
					Other Asian
					Other Pacific Islander
					Some other Race
Hispanic Ethnicity				Mexican	Mexican,
				Puerto Rican	Mexican American, or Chicano
				Central/South American	Puerto Rican
				Cuban	Cuban
				Other	Other
				Spanish	Spanish/Hispanic/Latino
				[None of these]	Not Spanish/ Hispanic/Latino

for illegal immigrants who could prove that they had been contributors to the economy for a certain period of time. Many single or partial-family groups became legal residents; they could more easily bring family members into the country legally. Immigrants from Mexico were the primary beneficiaries of the changing laws.

The circumstances under which people migrate greatly affect to agree how well the group has fared in America. Voluntary immigrants have fared much better than those who were forced, like African Americans, or who were "immigrated upon" like Native Americans and some Hispanics. Of voluntary immigrants, those groups whose members have been in America the longest are generally better off than recent immigrants. Some groups, like German immigrants during Hitler's reign and Cubans who escaped during Castro's takeover, were relatively well educated and well off in their homeland. Others, such as the Irish who escaped the 19th-century potato famine, were poor in their country of origin and started poor in America. Groups from countries with continued high rates of poor immigrants, such as Mexicans, tend to have higher average poverty rates in the United States. American standards of living increase with time, but the average income of the entire group is

Figure 7.1   **20th-Century Immigration Numbers**

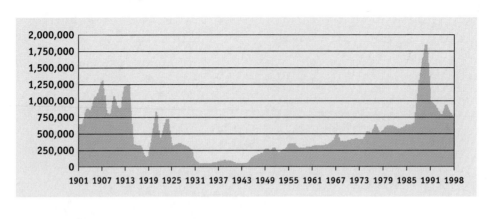

Source: U.S. Department of Justice. 1999. "Legal Immigration, Fiscal Year 1998". Online at
http://www.ins.usdoj.gov/graphics/publicaffairs/newsrels/98Legal.pdf

decreased by recent arrivals. Figure 7.2 provides a look at the historical rates of immigration to the United States.

Figure 7.2 reveals that there has been considerable change in immigrant patterns in recent years. Until the middle of the 20th century, over 80% of the foreign-born population was from Europe. That figure has dropped significantly. Now about 23% of foreign-born residents have European origins. By contrast, immigration from Latin America and Asia has exploded since the 1960s. Now, 45% of foreign-born residents are from Latin America and 27% are from Asia. Historically, there has been relatively little immigration from Africa or Oceania.

Figure 7.2   **Birth Region of Foreign-Born, in Percent**

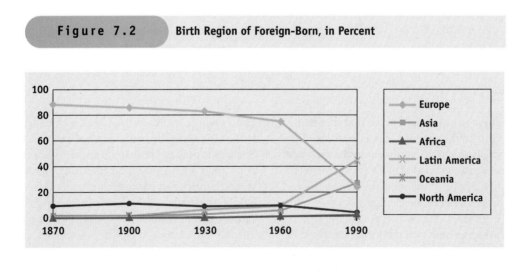

Source: U.S. Census Bureau. 1999. "Region of Birth of the Foreign-Born Population." Online at
http://www.census.gov/population/www/documentation/twps0029/tab02.html

Although the United States is a country of immigrants and is becoming increasingly diverse, most citizens are misinformed about the composition of the population. A Gallup Poll taken in 1990 asked adults what percentage of the population they thought was made up of certain minority groups. The average guess for African Americans was 32% and for Hispanics 21% Actually, African Americans were 12.3% and Hispanics were 9%.

The Gallup Poll (1990) found that guesses were even further off about the Jewish population; the average guess was 18%, but their actual numbers are between 2 and 3% (Gallup & Newport, 1990). Similar results were found in a 1995 poll conducted by the *Washing Post,* Kaiser Family Foundation, and Harvard University (in Gladwell, 1995). When respondents were asked what percentage of the population they thought was White, the average of the estimates by Whites was 49.9%. Blacks guessed 45.5%, Asians guessed 54.8%, and Hispanic guesses averaged 46.7%. In fact, non-Hispanic Whites constituted about 74% of the population.

Because of different birthrates and immigration, the population in the United States is becoming increasingly diverse. All categories of minority groups have higher **fertility rates** than do non-Hispanic Whites. Hispanic Americans have by far the highest fertility rates; rates for Asians are similar to Whites (see Figure 7.3). Americans with Asian or Pacific Islander heritage have the longest life expectancy at 83 years, while African Americans have the lowest at 70.2 years (Day, 1993).

These factors, along with immigration rates, make it possible to make guesses about the mix of race/ethnicity in the United States in the future. Figure 7.3 projects an overall growth of the U.S. population from 249 million to 392 million by the middle of the 21st century. This is an increase of 57% in 60 years. The growth is not evenly distributed among the major groups.

As Figure 7.4 indicates, the number of Whites will continue to grow slowly until 2030, when their numbers will begin to shrink. Their percentage of the population is expected to drop from 72% in 2000 to 53% in 2050. Shortly after the middle of this century, non-Hispanic Whites will become a minority in the United States, although they will still number twice as many as Hispanics, who at 24% will be the next largest minority.

These projections are, of course, made under certain assumptions about continued birth and immigration rates. Hispanics especially, followed by Asians, will be heavily affected by immigration regulations. If the Mexican border is opened more, the number of Hispanics could grow much more rapidly than the projections indicate. A tightening of immigration would result in slower proportionate growth.

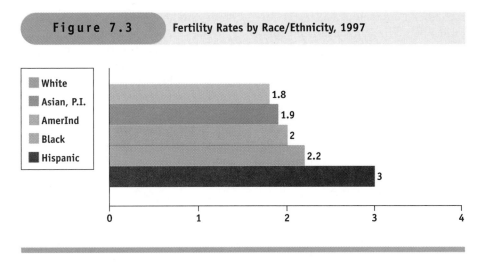

| Figure 7.3 | Fertility Rates by Race/Ethnicity, 1997 |

White — 1.8
Asian, P.I. — 1.9
AmerInd — 2
Black — 2.2
Hispanic — 3

Source: Population Reference Bureau. 1999. *Population Bulletin* Vol. 54, No. 3.

Fertility rate: The total number of children each woman is expected to have over a lifetime.

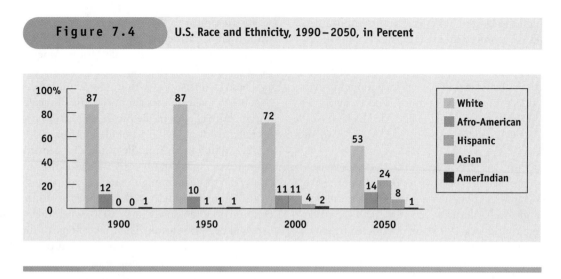

Figure 7.4 **U.S. Race and Ethnicity, 1990–2050, in Percent**

Source: Population Reference Bureau. 1999. *Population Bulletin* Vol. 54, No. 3.

Immigrants bring their own values, language, and practices. Once in their new homes, they undergo at least some degree of **acculturation.** Different generations in a family, however, often do not acculturate at the same rate. Children born in the United States, or who were young when their family immigrated, acculturate at a faster rate than their older relatives. They might grow up speaking English more than they do their parents' native language and adopt American tastes in music, dress, and other characteristics. This can distance immigrant children from their parents as the cultural gulf grows wider between them (Silverstein, 2000).

Many of the regions from which immigrants come have different family values than they find in their new country. Americans of recent Hispanic origin have significantly more traditional profamily, pronatalist, and pronuptial values than do mainstream Whites who have been in the country for several generations. Asians, too, tend to have traditional family values. Recent emigrants from Europe are more similar to, but still more traditional than, native-born Americans. Among Hispanics and Europeans particularly, longer exposure to mainstream values tends to weaken the traditional family values (Oropesa & Gorman, 2000).

Korean and Vietnamese families have traditionally expressed love largely in instrumental ways. When young immigrants see the images on television and elsewhere of American families who emphasize expressive love, the immigrants can feel like there is something abnormal with their own families (Pyke, 2000). As the children learn English, cohesion between Mexican American children and their grandparents is weakened (Silverstein, 2000). Younger family members often feel less sense of family togetherness than their parents, and although parents want their children to "make it" in America, it is difficult for the children to do so without alienating themselves from their families.

Values do not always translate directly into behavioral patterns; various constraints might prevent some people from achieving what they value. Among urban Americans, Blacks, Hispanics, and Whites value the marriage institution in roughly equal proportions. Although marriage rates have declined for all groups in spite of these expressed values, they have dropped fastest among Blacks. This trend has been influenced by economic disparity and other social factors (Tucker, 2000).

Race/Ethnicity, Social Class, and Family

We have seen that Blacks and Hispanics have higher rates of poverty than do Whites. Not only do they

---

Acculturation: Process by which immigrant groups assimilate into a dominant or host culture and change their values, language and practices (Silverstein, 2000).

have lower incomes, but they also have less wealth. Household net worth, or the difference between what is owned and what is owed, is provided in Table 7.2. White households have a median net worth about seven times higher than that of Blacks and Hispanics. Part of the difference in net worth reflects the lower rate of home ownership. Whites are also more likely to have assets such as individual retirement accounts and savings bonds that will help them after retirement.

Many whites immigrated with capital or have had several generations to accumulate it. Blacks certainly did not immigrate with capital, and persistent prejudice and discrimination have hindered the ability to accumulate family wealth. Many Hispanics are recent immigrants who brought little capital with them. Also, on average, Hispanic households have a younger householder than do Whites, and younger householders tend to have fewer assets.

The inequality of wealth reveals a general social class difference among the three largest groups in America. As Table 7.3 indicates, the relationship between social class and race/ethnicity is also found in the labor force. Whites (62%) and Asians (61%) have about the same percentage of their populations in the labor force, and both have low rates of unemployment. Native Americans (53%) and African Americans (54%) have lower percentages in the labor force, with Hispanics (59%) in the middle.

Asian Americans have the highest proportion in the more prestigious occupations (66%), followed by Whites (60%). Hispanics have a higher percentage (37%) in the blue-collar occupations than do other groups. African Americans have comparatively more of their numbers (23%) in the services sector of the economy.

Perhaps the most telling relationship between race/ethnicity and social class is the difference in median family income. Asians have the highest household income, at $45,400, nearly twice as high as for African Americans, at $25,100. Whites are the second highest group, with $40,600 per household, and Hispanics were closer to Blacks with $26,600 (see Figure 7.5).

With lower incomes, Blacks and Hispanics have a greater chance of falling into poverty. In 1997, 26% of all Blacks, 27% of Hispanics, and 23% of Native Americans were below the poverty threshold. About 12% of each of these groups had incomes at less than half of the poverty level, dropping them into what is termed the "extreme poverty" level. Consequently, over half of families in these groups received some kind of welfare (see Table 7.4).

A big part of the income difference is accounted for by race/ethnicity-related family and household characteristics. Table 7.5 indicates that Hispanics (80%), Asians (77%), and American Indians (75%) are most likely to live in households that contain families. Whites (70%) and African Americans (70%) have somewhat lower rates of family living.

Fewer Hispanic (15%), Asian (17%), and American Indian (20%) households consist of persons living

Table 7.2	Net Household Worth and Percentage Owning Certain Assets, by Race/Ethnicity, 1995			
Assets	**All Groups**	**Whites**	**Blacks**	**Hispanics**
Median Net Worth	$40,200	$49,030	$7,073	$7,255
Percentage Owning . . .				
Own home	64.3%	67.4%	45.3%	41.4%
Interest-earning assets at financial institutions	69.1%	72.4%	46.4%	49.0%
Regular checking accounts	46.7%	48.9%	31.9%	38.1%
IRA or Keogh Accounts	24.1%	26.5%	7.9%	8.5%
U. S. Savings Bonds	24.1%	26.5%	7.9%	8.5%

Source: Economics and Statistics Administration, U.S. Census Bureau. 2001. "Household Net Worth and Asset Ownership." *Current Population Reports: The Survey of Income and Program Participation.* Online February 23, 2001, at **http://www.census.gov/prod/2001pubs/p70-71.pdf**.

Table 7.3		Labor Force Participation, Occupational Distribution, Poverty Status, and Income by Race/Ethnicity			

Working Status, 1992	White	African American	Asian/Pacific Islander	Native American	Hispanic
Working (%)	62	54	61	53	59
Unemployed (%)	4	8	3	7	7
Not in labor force (%)	34	39	36	40	34
Category of Employed, 1990					
White collar[1] (%)	60	46	66	43	39
Blue collar[2]	25	30	20	34	37
Services[3] (%)	12	23	15	19	19
Farming, fishing, and forestry (%)	2	2	1	4	5

[1]Includes managers, administrators, professionals, teachers, technicians and related support staff, administrative and clerical support and sales.

[2]Includes precision production, craft, repair workers, machine operators, assemblers, inspectors, transportation workers, handlers, equipment cleaners, helpers, and laborers.

[3]Includes private household workers, protective service, and other service workers.

Sources: Bodovitz, K., and B. Edmondson. 1991. "Asian America." *American Demographics Desk Reference.* July:16–18. Others adapted from O'Hare, William P. 1992. "America's Minorities—The Demographics of Diversity." *Population Bulletin 47,* No. 4. Washington, DC: Population Reference Bureau. Figure 10, Table 8, and Table 11.

alone. In these three groups, young single persons are more likely to live with their parents until marriage or cohabitation, and the elderly are more likely to live with their adult children. About one fourth of White and Black households contain persons living alone.

Table 7.5 also reveals that only 48% of White households have members under 18 years old. About two

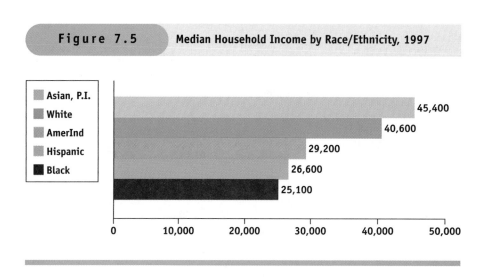

Figure 7.5	Median Household Income by Race/Ethnicity, 1997

Source: Population Reference Bureau. 1999. *Population Bulletin* Vol. 54, No. 3.

Table 7.4	Poverty and Welfare Receipt by Race and Ethnicity, United States, 1997				
	White	**Black**	**Asian**	**American Indian**	**Hispanic**
Total Population (1,000s)	191,859	33,631	10,317	2,035	30,637
Percentage in poverty	9	26	14	23	27
% in extreme poverty	3	12	6	13	11
% receiving welfare	33	56	31	50	54
% of poor receiving welfare	69	87	67	88	83

Extreme poverty is below 50% of the poverty threshold.

Source: *Population Bulletin* Vol. 54, No. 3, September 1999. Population Reference Bureau. Table 8.

thirds of family households in all other groups have children. Family households that do contain children are headed by a married couple in 84% of Asian households. Only 44% of Black households with children are headed by a married couple.

The portion of family households with children that are headed by an unmarried man is low in all groups. Half of all African American households with children are headed by a single female. The lowest rate of female-headed households is found among Asians, followed by Whites.

Perhaps the most encouraging news for American minority groups is in the field of education. Asian American youth are now more likely to attend college than Whites. There has been a rapid percentage increase in the numbers of minority students attending institutions of higher education in the last quarter century (see Table 7.6). The increase for Asians and Hispanics is partly accounted for by the rapid increase in the American population of those two groups, but all groups have made significant progress.

Table 7.5	Household and Family Structure by Race/Ethnicity, Percentages, 1990				
Household Type	**White**	**African American**	**Asian**	**American Indian**	**Hispanic**
Families	70	70	77	75	80
Nonfamilies					
One person	25	26	17	20	15
Other nonfamily	5	4	6	5	5
Family Households with Children, Total %	48	66	63	68	69
Married couple	79	44	84	60	68
Male head	4	6	5	9	7
Female head	17	50	11	31	25

Source: Adapted from U.S. Bureau of Census data in O'Hare, William P. 1992. "America's Minorities—The Demographics of Diversity." *Population Bulletin* 47, No. 4. Washington, DC: Population Reference Bureau. Table 5.

Table 7.6	Enrollments in Higher Education, by Race/Ethnicity, 1976–1997		
	Total Enrollments, in Thousands		
Race/Ethnicity of Students	1976	1997	Percentage Increase
White	9,076.1	10,160.9	11.95
Black	1,033.0	1,532.8	48.38
Hispanic	383.8	1200.1	212.69
Asian, Pacific Islander	197.9	851.5	330.27
American Indian	76.1	138.8	82.39

Source: National Council for Educational Statistics, 1999. *Digest of Education Statistics,* Table 209. (**http://nces.ed.gov/pubs2000/digest99/d99t209.html**)

Native American Families

Of all the groups lumped together by Census Bureau categories, Native Americans are undoubtedly the most diverse. The pre-European Americas were home to tribal groups ranging from the most simple of hunting-gathering technology to extremely sophisticated horti-culturalist groups. A variety of languages were spoken, and too many family forms to describe existed. Kinship systems were generally quite different from European ones, as the illustration of the Oglala Sioux system in chapter 3 demonstrated. Polygyny was relatively common, as it was in many preindustrial societies.

Many of those diverse cultural patterns and languages have now disappeared, but many Native Americans are far from fully assimilated into American culture. Family systems can no longer exist as they once did. Polygyny is illegal; most Native Americans are now Christian anyway and would not want to practice polygyny. The tradition mode of production, such as roaming widely to hunt buffalo as the plains Indians did, is no longer possible. With it went a way of life.

Herring (1978) found three groups that differed with respect to retention of Native American values. One group remains traditional. The members of this group tend to live in remote parts of reservations; the older ones still speak their native language, and a few continue to practice their ancient religions. This group is rapidly disappearing. A second group might be bicultural; they have adopted most of the non–American Native styles. They listen to country-western or rap music and often live in cities for at least part of their lives. Many of these have mixed Native American–

European ancestry. Finally, there is the pan-traditional group. These people are attempting to redefine and reconfirm—some would say invent—cultural styles

The Pine Ridge Indian Reservation in South Dakota, by many measures the poorest area in the United States, was visited by President Clinton in 1999.

that have been lost. Many of these Native Americans are active in political groups such as the American Indian Movement.

Some reservations are characterized by problems of unemployment, alcoholism, violent crime, and family breakdown that may be the most serious in the United States. These problems stem from the decimation of family, economic, religious, and political systems, which have not been replaced by viable alternatives. The cultural destruction resulted from "the taking of land, forced relocation, an institutionally racist educational system, removal of Indian children from their homes, U.S. government paternalism obstacles to self-governance, stripping of tribal recognition, and denial of religious freedom [that] continue to place great stress on Indian families" (Harjo, 1999:71). In spite of these problems families, often quite extended, provide a source of strength and belonging to many Native Americans.

The Family among African Americans

Over the years, attempts to reduce negative stereotypes have resulted in changes in the names by which various groups are called, and by which they call themselves. After addressing this issue, we will bring the history of the group up to date, then look at various interpretations about how that history affects Black families today. It is important to remember that, while a dominant image of the Black family is often one of poverty, two thirds of Blacks live above the poverty level. Their families are discussed in the final segment.

Changing Terminology

The polite term for the group under discussion was, at one time, "colored." Although that is now considered inappropriate, the term "persons of color" is sometimes used to refer to all persons with non-White, non-European ancestry. Use of the term "colored" was not always considered derogatory; one of the most powerful civil rights groups in the country called itself the National Association for the Advancement of Colored People (NAACP) and still proudly does so.

For a time, the term "Negro," which is Latin for "Black," was preferred. During this period, the important organization United Negro College Fund originated. In the 1960s, "Negro" was replaced by

"Black" as the appropriate term, although it too had been used negatively at one time. The U.S. government still uses the term "Black" in many of its reports, and that term is most often preferred by those who belong to the category. Younger persons and scholars who themselves belong to the group increasingly prefer "African American" (Edmondson, 1993). Like all terms that are used to categorize persons, neither "Black" nor "African American" is completely satisfactory. To dichotomize between "Black" versus "White" ignores the impact of variability of complexions. Lighter-skinned Blacks have higher occupational status, educational attainment, and incomes than darker-skinned ones. The Black community itself often discriminates against its darkest-skinned members (Keith & Herring, 1991).

The term "African American" has the advantage of avoiding the issue of color, which is associated with the concept of race, in favor of geographical origin, which is more commonly associated with ethnicity. One problem is that most African Americans have very little cultural connection with Africa, except that which has been revived in the last generation or so (Willie, 1991). Some Blacks more closely identify with the Carribean or other areas than with Africa (Edmonsdon, 1993). Also, it was only from sub-Saharan Africa that those identified as today's African Americans came. The term would, if applied literally, also include Americans from Libya, Egypt, and other countries of northern Africa, most of whom are not Black and who have very different histories and cultures.

The reader might have noted that "Black" and "African American" have been used interchangeably in the text. That will remain the practice as we bring our discussion of African American history up to date from the discussion of slavery in chapter 4.

African Americans since Slavery

Until recently, most scholars accepted the "historical instability" hypothesis that the current Black family is characterized by instability, a feature that is rooted in conditions of slavery. Gutman (1976) challenged that view, finding that the slave family was surprisingly strong and nuclear. He found that sons were often named after their fathers, and extended kin relationships were recognized in other naming practices. Slaves preferred maintaining separate family households, as is evidenced by the fact that they rejected communal kitchens in preference for their own, even though it meant more work (Hynmowitz & Weissman, 1978). After the Civil War, large numbers of former slaves officially registered their marriages, something they had previously been unable legally to do.

The nuclear family was the predominant form in the system of sharecropping that developed after the Civil War. Jones (1985:62) found that, in Black households of the Cotton Belt in 1870, 80% included a husband and wife. Husband, wife, and children all worked on the land, as they had done in slavery. Men most often dealt with the outside world by negotiating with owners, selling crops and engaging in other activities. Women were responsible for their own households and, often, performed wage labor as well. In 1870, over 40% of Black women performed at least some work for wages, usually as field laborers (Jones, 1985).

The major change in the Black family, many scholars now argue, resulted from the "Great Migration" from the rural south. Even until World War II the south was predominately agricultural. The industrial revolution was occurring mostly in the north, but production of tractors and other machines was altering agriculture everywhere. Replaced by machines and attracted by relatively high-paid manufacturing jobs, many Blacks left the rural south.

The migration was massive. An estimated 1 million Blacks migrated north between 1910 and 1930, and even more went to large southern cities (Marks, 1985). Between 1930 and 1990, the portion of Blacks living in the south dropped from 80% to 55% (U.S. Bureau of the Census, 1992b:33). The migration did not involve all segments of the Black population in the same way. It was predominately young men who first moved to the cities. This left a higher proportion of women, both married and unmarried, in the rural south and perhaps contributed to the inclination toward matrifocal families.

The women who did migrate were more likely to find employment in domestic work than in manufacturing. In 1950, 60% of Black working women were in institutional and private household service jobs; this compares to 16% of employed White women who held such jobs (Jones, 1985:235).

In spite of racial discrimination and the separations caused by migration, Black families were taking advantage of the education and job opportunities in the cities to improve their position. Rates of Black poverty were falling in the 1950s, even before the civil rights legislation of the 1960s.

Ruggles (1994) found that, as far back as 1880, Blacks had higher rates of both single parenthood and extended households than did Whites, but the difference was small. In 1880, 11.7% of Black households had single parents, compared to 8.2% of White households. The rate for Blacks remained roughly stable until recently; it jumped from 9.9% in 1960 to 20.5% in 1980. The percentage of White households with single parents remained nearly constant, increasing from 5.1% to 7.1% between 1960 and 1980 (Ruggles, 1994:138).

Black families have developed a number of ways of coping with slavery and more recent difficult times. In the 1970s, a number of qualitative studies were conducted that demonstrated the amount of sharing that occurred among Black families, kin, and friendship networks (Allen, 1979; McAdoo, 1980; Stack, 1974). The sharing included not only economic assistance but also advice and emotional support, baby-sitting and child-care services, and help around the house. Although these studies did not directly compare Black and White families, they left the impression that Blacks did more sharing of resources than did Whites (Jayakody, 1998).

Several later studies directly compared Black and White families and generally found that, in fact, White families did considerably more sharing, especially in economic assistance, than did Black families (Cooney & Uhlenberg, 1992; Goldscheider & Goldscheider, 1991; Hogan, Eggebeen, & Clogg, 1993). Jayakody (1998) attempted a more thorough study of the assistance question (Walker, 2000). She considered different family structures, the resources and needs of both parents and children, and other factors. She found that, when these factors were considered, only among the very poor was there more sharing by Whites. In families with incomes of $15,000 or more, there was no difference in the amount of sharing by Blacks and Whites.

A consideration implied by Jayakody's (1998) work is that the term "family" might have a different meaning among Blacks than among other groups. Taylor (2000:233) supplied a definition of family that more closely fits the Black experience than do other definitions considered so far in this text. His definition views the family as "an intimate association of two or more persons related to each other by blood, marriage, formal or informal adoption, or appropriation." This definition recognizes the prevalence of fictive kin and alludes to the fact that Black families, particularly among the poor, have more fluid households than do White, middle-class families. People move in and out of such households frequently, and some of those people share family-like roles without actually being related. It might well be that this is also a characteristic of poorer families of groups other than Blacks.

Slavery and the great migration clearly impacted African American families. More recent changes have, perhaps, been even more influential. In some respects, there is more instability now in Black families than in previous times.

Family Instability, Poverty, and Society

Most research about the Black family has focused on its association with poverty and other social problems. The discussion was brought into focus in 1965 when Daniel Patrick Moynihan released a study that became known as the *Moynihan Report.* Accepting the "historical instability" model of the Black family, Moynihan saw slavery as an extremely destructive force on the family.

Moynihan accepted Frazier's (1957) argument that emancipation further eroded the Black family as starvation and unemployment forced men to wander the country in search of work. This, along with the great migration, left the family in tatters. Moynihan referred to high rates of delinquency, school failure, and illegitimacy as evidence that the Black family was a "tangle of pathology."

The Moynihan Report received considerable criticism because of the perception that he was saying the Black family was a cause of poverty, crime, and other social problems. Billingsley (1968) concluded that the Black family was not the cause of problems, but was an adaptive and resilient response to prejudice, discrimina-

tion, unemployment, and other elements of a predominantly White, racist society.

Changes in the conditions of African American families since Moynihan and Billingsley wrote have been mixed. The good news is that overall rates of poverty are lower, and Blacks have made considerable headway in educational achievement. Unfortunately, Black unemployment remains, as it has for several decades, at about twice the rate for Whites (U.S. Bureau of the Census, 1995:628). While Moynihan worried about the fact that one fourth of Black babies were born out of wedlock, that number is now two thirds, while rates for Whites went from 5% to 22% in the same time period (O'Hare, 1992).

Partly because of the reception accorded the Moynihan Report, studies of the Black family increasingly stressed positive aspects, or produced analyses that indicated that the Black family was not as different from the White family as was originally thought. William Julius Wilson's books—*The Declining Significance of Race* (1978), *The Truly Disadvantaged: The Inner City, the Underclass, and Public Policy* (1987), and *When Work Disappears: The World of the New Urban Poor* (1996)—argued that more attention needed to be paid to the impact of social class in explaining the Black family.

Although a higher percentage of Blacks than Whites are below the poverty level, poor Blacks and poor Whites

The inner-city environment in poor areas sends different messages than those that are found in upper-class communities.

have many similar family characteristics. Both have higher rates of out-of-wedlock births, higher unemployment, higher rates of family violence, and more children who get in trouble with the law than their middle-class counterparts. Wilson was not arguing that prejudice and discrimination had disappeared, but that it was becoming a less important part of Black life in America, while social class was becoming more important.

Inner cities contain areas of what are sometimes called the "underclass" (Auletta, 1982). Wilson (1987) referred to this group as the "truly disadvantaged," a segment of the African American poor among whom fatherless families were the norm. A major reason for this, Wilson argued, is the scarcity of stable, employed young men. This, in turn, has several causes.

We have seen that young male Blacks have a higher death rate than other groups, resulting in a lower sex ratio (fewer males per 100 females) in the 15- to 25-year-old group than is the case for Whites. Although the proportion is relatively small, more Black men than women marry Whites, further reducing the available number of potential Black mates for Black women (Usdansky, 1992).

As is true for other inner-city groups, young male Blacks are more likely than young female Blacks to be in trouble with the law. Nearly one out of three Black men in the 20–29 age group is, at any given time, either in prison, awaiting trial, or on probation or parole (Sentencing Project, 1995). Since middle- and upper-class Blacks have law troubles at much lower rates, in neighborhoods populated by the underclass nearly all men are at risk of running afoul of the law. These factors all make it difficult for young Black women to find stable husbands (Wilson, 1987).

Wilson (1987, 1996) focused on the lack of jobs for men in the inner city. In the postindustrial era, most lost jobs have been of the relatively unskilled type in the center cities. Most of the new jobs, especially the high paying ones, have been in the suburbs and require high levels of education. The new jobs increasingly were being filled by more highly educated White women, who were entering the job market in large numbers at the time (Harris, 1987). The shifts in the job market have disproportionately impacted inner-city neighborhoods, where poor Blacks are concentrated.

All of these factors have contributed to a long-term decline in what Wilson (1987) referred to as the "male marriageable pool index" (MMPI). Because of the gender role structure, women look for husbands who can fill the provider role, and few unemployed men can do that. Men are not eligible for most welfare programs, and

marriage can disqualify mothers from receiving some benefits. Relying on welfare payments that are small but regular might be a more sure means of support than relying on a man with uncertain employment prospects.

Wilson therefore calculated the MMPI based on the number of employed men per 100 women of various ages. The rate was calculated for each year beginning in 1954. Although the figures varied by age group, the MMPI was consistently lower for non-Whites than for Whites. Especially for younger groups, the difference for Whites and non-Whites began to widen significantly around 1970, the beginning of the postindustrial era. For the 20–24 group in the early 1980s, there were more than 70 employed White men for each 100 White women, but only about 45 employed Black men for each 100 Black women (Wilson, 1987:86).

At other times in history, there have been shortages of marriageable men that did not result in high rates of unmarried pregnancies and single-mother families. The system of primogeniture in late medieval England did not result in a high rate of illegitimacy but in a low rate of marriage and high rate of persons who neither married nor had children. The major loss of young men in World War II did not result in an explosion of out-of-wedlock births in the Soviet Union. In both of these cases, traditional moral views and repressive sexual standards suppressed single motherhood. Couples were less likely to engage in nonmarital sexual intercourse than is the case today, and if pregnancy did result from such an act the couple was more likely to marry.

Unprotected sexual activity, not poverty, is the most direct cause of unwed pregnancy, but poverty is associated with unwed pregnancy in all racial and ethnic groups. Higher rates of poverty among Blacks therefore result in higher rates of unwed pregnancy. Blacks engage in sexual activity at younger ages than do Whites, and are less likely to use contraception. Black women are less likely to get abortions if they do get pregnant, are less likely to marry the father of their child if they choose to keep it, and are more likely to divorce if they do get married (Eshleman, 1994). Wilson's argument addresses only the last two points.

Although the rates have historically been low by today's standards, Blacks have probably always had somewhat higher rates of single mothers than have Whites. While the ideal was a family with husband and wife, the ideal was not always possible because of high mortality rates, the search for work, and other factors. Fictive and real kin shared resources in order to survive, with or without the father in the home (Willie, 1991). A multigeneration household, often matrifocal, was one adaptation that was functional in aiding survival. Unmarried pregnancy was not historically normative but was probably less censured and more accepted in the Black community than in the White.

Community solidarity was disrupted in the postindustrial era just as some conditions began to improve. Wilson argued that, ironically, desegregation made matters worse for the lowest class of Blacks. When Blacks were segregated from Whites, the poor and middle classes lived in nearby neighborhoods. Black professionals and stable working-class families interacted with the poor. Black shop owners, lawyers, barbers, teachers, preachers, and others helped form a stable infrastructure in Black communities. Along with low income but stable working-class families, the professionals supported the schools and churches, and kept more of the economic base in the community. They and their children provided role models of successful adult achievement and behavior. They got married at later ages, did well in school, maintained steady employment, and were less likely to have unwanted pregnancies.

In the late 1960s, desegregation allowed Blacks who could afford to do so to move out of all-Black sections of small town and central city areas; many took advantage of the opportunities. As conditions began to worsen in core city areas, even more of the families who could afford to move out did so, leaving an increasingly impoverished group behind. The remaining underclass was more likely to be poor, young, and unemployed. The culture of the inner city changed as it lost its stable core. Those families that remained had increasing problems maintaining stability.

Children who tried to use education, part-time work, and other traditional routes to success were often put down by other youngsters for their efforts. At the least, they were exposed to increasing numbers of young persons who used drugs, dropped out of school, committed crimes, resorted to violence, and got pregnant. These lifestyles, perpetuated in part by continued discrimination, do not help to build human or cultural capital (MacLeod, 1995).

Cultural instability can result if the youngest generation gets enough power to redefine culture. James Q. Wilson (1983) looked at the impact of a rapid increase in the number of young persons in a population. Although he was referring more generally to the effect of the baby boom on the increase in crime rates in the late 1960s, his argument was that the number of teenagers in a population can reach a "critical mass" at which the youth culture sets off an explosion of crime, addiction,

and welfare dependency. This critical mass was reached in many core city areas, especially when massive low-income housing projects were built there. The result was a culture in which welfare, crime, unwed births, and joblessness are accepted aspects of daily life. An underclass developed, William Julius Wilson argued, and its influence went beyond the boundaries of the core city where it originated.

Wilson's analysis has been labeled a "culture of poverty" argument by some, and has been accused of "blaming the victims" of oppression. Wilson argued, however, that the culture will exist only as long as the conditions that cause it, particularly joblessness among young Black men, continue to exist.

Other researchers point out that not all single mothers depend on welfare. Educational attainment and income opportunities have improved for Black women, making many of them less dependent on either a husband or welfare. Such women are more likely to delay marriage and to end unsatisfactory relationships because of their financial independence (Farley & Bianchi, 1991; Taylor, 1994). Teen births are a problem, but two thirds of unwed births are to women 20 years old or older. The majority of unwed births are not to never-married women, but to women who are divorced or separated (McAdoo, 2000).

Other studies have found that unemployment of Black men accounts for part, but not all of the drop in Black marriage rates (Mare & Winship, 1991; Loury, 1996). Black women are more likely to marry if they live in areas of high employment for Black men, but even in areas where employment and other factors are similar for Blacks and Whites, Black marriage rates are lower (Lichter et al, 1992; Smith & Lloyd, 1992). Wilson (2000) continued to assert that highlighting racial differences continues to block the kind of multiracial support that is necessary to combat the rising inequality between the very rich and the very poor.

The 1990s provided something of a test of Wilson's analysis. Black unemployment rates fell to the lowest level in a generation. At the same time, the crime rate went down, the teen pregnancy rate went down, and the unwed birthrate declined slightly, reversing a long-term climb. Causal relationships among all these variables is unclear, but Wilson's suggestion that increased number of jobs will help Black families is apparently sound (Adelman & Jaret, 1999; Cherry, 1999; Parker & Pruitt, 2000).

Some scholars have taken issue with Wilson's assumption that race has become a less important factor.

Willie (1991) pointed out that Blacks have lower incomes and higher unemployment than Whites with similar educations. Willie also disagreed with the implication that middle-class Blacks have benefited at the expense of lower-class Blacks, finding that conditions have improved for both groups. Massey (Massey & Denton 1989; 1993; Masy & Kumiko, 1995) disagrees with Wilson that race is no longer a significant part of the problem. They both agree that neighborhood characteristics are part of the problem, but argue that segregation, born of discrimination, continues to contribute a major share of the problem.

Working-Class and Affluent Black Families

The majority of Blacks are not poor. There are stable working-class families, professional middle-class families, and a small but influential upper-class elite group of Black families.

Working-class Black families are, in most ways, similar to working-class White ones. They are hit hard by economic changes, and their struggle to stay out of poverty usually requires more than one income. Wives generally work, often in cleaning and other low-wage jobs, and the income of older children is important to survival. Although the nuclear family is the ideal, it is often not the reality. The jobs held by the family do not generally require much more than a high-school diploma; parents hope their children will finish high school, but they do not generally harbor expectations for college educations (Willie, 1991).

Households tend to be large and fluid, with relatives and lodgers moving in and out, and several children belonging to the primary household. Grandparents, especially grandmothers, are often used for child care; some of these grandmothers are less than 40 years old and have young children of their own in addition to grandchildren.

Working-class Blacks generally have traditional role expectations about housework when there is a man in the house, although their mutual dependence results in egalitarian relationships between husband and wife, and they have learned that flexibility is sometimes required. Working more than one job sometimes requires a sacrifice of family time for economic survival. Shift work, different schedules, and crowded living conditions can make it difficult for a couple to have private time together.

Working-class Blacks share American values of hard work and of raising families of which they can be proud. In the face of considerable difficulty, and without much help from nonkin social institutions, they survive. Willie (1991:55) said that working-class Blacks "probably are the best manifestation of self-reliance in American society."

In spite of historical oppression, a class of relatively well-off Blacks has emerged. Willie (1991:48) refers to these as the affluent Blacks, one out of every three or four Blacks. As Table 7.4 indicates, 46% of employed Blacks are in the white-collar segment of the economy. Willie found that many are in public sector occupations such as teaching, social work, and postal workers.

Because of the relatively rapid growth of the Black middle class, many have working-class or poor backgrounds. The lack of inherited family wealth means that they have fewer assets than their White counterparts with the same income, and they might be only one paycheck away from slipping back into poverty (McAdoo, 1988). They are also likely to have poor and working-class relatives who call upon them for assistance from time to time. Blacks who achieve middle-class status have more difficulty passing their advantages on to their children than do middle-class Whites (Featherman & Hauser, 1978).

Like middle-class Whites, middle-class Blacks marry later and have fewer children than their working-class counterparts. At least one spouse usually has education beyond high school, and often both do. They are more likely than White graduates to have gotten their degrees at one of the publicly supported urban campuses, and they are likely to have worked part time or full time while attending college. They strongly encourage their children to go to college and struggle to provide a middle-class life for their family. Willie suggested that middle-class Blacks have the most egalitarian marriages of any group. Haynes (2000), however, found that husbands and wives agree that the man should be the primary provider and the women the primary nurturer.

The past 30 years have seen a rapid increase of Black families into corporate America. Blacks who succeeded in this arena often feel that they had to produce more than their White counterparts to achieve the same recognition, but they also credit affirmative action for giving them an opportunity they might not otherwise have had. They are also quite likely to have grown up in intact families (Toliver, 1998).

There is in the United States a Black upper class. The new rich of this group are often highly publicized stars in

Lives of wealthy Blacks are similar to lives of wealthy Whites; both are different from the lives of poor Blacks or Whites.

professional athletics and other entertainment fields. Less in the public eye is a group with what has been called the "patriarchal affluent" family pattern. Many of these families have inherited wealth. A study of the origins of highly successful Blacks found that they were likely to come from stable two-parent families. They were more likely than others to be descended from Blacks who had attained freedom before the Civil War. They were also likely to be lighter skinned than other Blacks. This might be because they had White ancestors and were treated better by their slave owners, perhaps being taught to read or receiving other treatment not afforded most slaves. The highly successful Blacks had also achieved high educational levels (Mullins & Sites, 1984).

An elite group of these Black families was described by Graham's (1999) book, *Our Kind of People*. Like the White elite, these families have their own clubs for both children and adults. They generally attend one of the elite Black private colleges and belong to certain fraternities and sororities. Increasing numbers are sending their children to integrated prep schools and Ivy League colleges.

Socialization of children is more strict in this group than among other Black classes; children are encouraged to marry within their own elite group. Private school attendance and membership in elite clubs make that more likely. As with the White elite, young children often learn that they have special responsibilities as a result of the fact that they are "different than other people."

One study found that the husband-led family pattern, typical of upper-class Blacks, was correlated with greater marital satisfaction than was either the egalitarian or the women-led script. It is possible that African Americans consider the husband-led pattern to be ideal and that the couple's happiness is reduced when economic factors make that ideal less attainable (Gray-Little, 1982).

Hispanic Families in the United States

As was the case with African Americans, terminology is problematic for Hispanic Americans also. A few families migrated directly from Spain; some were settled before the United States expanded to include them. Most arrived in the United States via Mexico, Cuba, Puerto Rico, or Central or South America. The term "Hispanic" has only recently been applied to all peoples with historical ties to Spain and the Spanish language. Many scholars of the groups themselves prefer the term "Latino," while others say the groups are too diverse to fit in one category.

Hispanic Diversity

We have seen that Hispanics generally fall between non-Hispanic Whites and non-Hispanic Blacks in

Table 7.7	Characteristics of Various Hispanic Groups in the United States and Country of Origin					
	In the United States				**In Country of Origin*****	
	Percentage of Hispanic Population*	Percentage of Families Below Poverty Level*	Median Family Income*	Infant Deaths Per 1,000 Births**	Infant Deaths Per 1,000 Births	Per Capita G.N.P.
Cuban	4.9%	13.8%	$31,400	9.20	10.2	N.A.
Mexican	62.6%	25.0%	$23,200	12.46	35.0	$3,470
Puerto Rican	11.1%	37.5%	$18,000	13.46	13.0	$6,610
Cen/South Amer.	13.8%	22.2%	N.A.	N.A.	49.0	$2,710
Other Hispanic	7.6%	19.4%	N.A.	8.07	N.A.	N.A.
Spain		7.9%	$14,020			
United States	11.5%	8.3%	$36,300	8.30	23,120	

Sources: *U.S. Bureau of the Census. 1991. "The Hispanic Population in the United States: March 1991." *Current Population Reports* Series P-20, no. 455, pp. 2, 7, 18–19. Washington, DC: U.S. Government Printing Office.

**Hummer, Robert A., Isaac W. Eberstein, and Charles B. Nam. 1992. "Infant Mortality Differentials Among Hispanic Groups in Florida." *Social Forces* 70: 1055–1075.

***Haub, Carl, and Machiko Yanagishita. 1994. *1994 World Population Data Sheet*. Washington, DC: Population Reference Bureau.

social indicators such as unemployment and rates of poverty. Largely because of rapid immigration of Hispanics with little formal education, only a little over half (51.3%) of Hispanics 25 and older have finished high school, compared to about four fifths of Whites and two thirds of Blacks (U.S. Census Bureau, 1991c). Segments of the Hispanic population exhibit differing standings on economic and social characteristics (see Table 7.7).

Cuban Americans, who constitute 4.9% of the Hispanic population in the United States, have the highest median family incomes, lowest rates of poverty, and lowest infant mortality rates of all Hispanic groups. Large numbers of Cuban Americans fled the communist revolution of 1959; many were from the Cuban middle and upper classes and were highly educated professionals fearing the confiscation of their property. They were welcomed by the U.S. government as political refugees. They established an "immigrant enclave" in Miami, where they have been relatively successful while retaining much of their language and culture (Suarez, 1993; Wilson & Portes, 1980).

Puerto Ricans, 11.1% of all Hispanics, are the worst off in these categories. Their rate of poverty (37.5%) is higher than the rate for Blacks (33%). The infant mortality rate for Puerto Ricans in the United States (13.46)

is slightly higher than the infant mortality rate in Puerto Rico itself (13.0).

Several reasons have been given for the high poverty rates of Puerto Ricans in the United States. One factor is the heavy concentration of Puerto Ricans in New York City, where they originally found jobs that did not require extensive formal education. Many of these manufacturing jobs have left the city, leaving high rates of unemployment. Those who are employed are most often in the low-wage end of the services sector. Another factor is the high proportion of Puerto Rican families headed by single women; 64.4% of these were below the poverty level in 1990 (U.S. Bureau of the Census, 1991c).

In spite of the economic conditions, or perhaps partly because of them, Puerto Ricans have a strong family focus typical of other Hispanics. Strongly pronatalist, partly because of their overwhelming Catholic religious affiliations, Hispanics have the highest fertility rates of major groups in the United States (review Table 7.2). They are the most likely to live in family households, and they have the highest percentage of households that contain children. Compared with Black families with children, half as many Puerto Rican families with children are headed by a single woman, although nearly the same percentage rely on welfare (review Tables 7.5 and 7.6).

Mexican American Families

The Mexican American or **Chicano** family has received the most attention from family scholars because it includes 64% of all Hispanics in the United States. More than 1 million of the 15 million Mexican Americans have at least one ancestor who lived in the region of the United States that was part of Mexico until 1848. Most are immigrants, or descendents of immigrants, who came to the United States for work on farms, railroads, mines, and other employment that was strenuous but did not require extensive formal education. More recently, Chicanos have taken urban service jobs. Such workers are valued by employers because they are willing to work hard for wages that are high by Mexican standards but low by U.S. standards. These workers are sometimes exploited because they have little legal protection.

In addition to Mexican Americans, there is also a large number of Mexican nationals in the United States. They are in the country either illegally or as legal temporary workers originally known as **braceros** or as exchange students, diplomats, businesspersons, or other legal aliens. Whether here legally or illegally, many of these persons, or their children, remain and claim U.S. citizenship. Rapid immigration and the presence of large numbers of Mexican nationals result in a difference in family structures of recent arrivals compared with Mexican Americans who were born in the United States (Zinn, 1994). Patterns of those born in the United States, especially those in the middle class with more than one generation of U.S. citizenship, are less traditional than of those born in Mexico.

The strong family ties characteristic of Chicanos are part of *familism,* in which the interests of individual family members are subordinated to the interests of the family system. The term **La Casa** refers to the immediate or nuclear family, but the term also refers to "house" in both the sense of physical dwelling and the old Latin sense of "household." The phrase "Mi casa es su casa," literally "My house is your house," is effectively an offer of fictive kinship. This honor is extended only to friends who are worthy of being family.

Familism goes beyond *la casa.* Extended kinship networks provide linkages between recent and more settled immigrants, providing assistance in housing, employment, finding food, and making connections to U.S. institutions (Alvarez, 1987; Zinn & Eitzen, 1993). Even after considerable time in the United States, Chicano kin continue to rely on one another for financial assistance (Moore, 1971).

A comparison between Chicanos, Anglos, and African Americans found that Chicanos were most likely to use extended kin for support; Anglos had the lowest levels of extended familialism (Mindel, 1980). Wagner and Shaffer (1980) found that there were patterns of specialization within the kinship network that reflect gender and age roles. Men did car repairs for their female relatives; parents lent their children money; daughters moved into their parents' homes during times of illness; siblings and others of the same generation were turned to for advice.

Exchanges of services and sharing living quarters are mechanisms by which Mexican American families adapt to limited financial resources, but sometimes the focus on familism makes long-term individual advancement more difficult. A teenager might drop out of school to get a job, which would help the family in the short run but decrease long-term financial security. Chicano youths who go to college or take jobs that distance them from their families sometimes face censure from their peers and family.

Additional ties among Mexican Americans were traditionally created as a result of the Roman Catholic custom of godparents, or **compadrazgo.** The fictive kinship sanctioned by the church baptismal ceremony established a set of responsibilities of the godparents of a child, such as providing spiritual, emotional, and financial support when needed. The godparents were expected to become *compadres,* or close friends, of the natural parents and thus be co-parents of the child. Although the *compadrazgo* pattern still exists, various elements have changed or even disappeared among today's urban Mexican Americans (Williams, 1990).

Gender expectations in traditional Chicano culture clearly distinguished between male and female roles. The male role was referred to as **machismo** and included authority in the home, an emphasis on sexual

---

Chicanos: Alternative name for Mexican-Americans. A contraction of *Mexicanos,* pronounced "meschicanos" in Nahuatl, an ancient language of Mexico (Eshleman, 1994). **Braceros:** Workers who are expected to return to Mexico after a temporary period of employment. **La Casa:** House, immediate family, household. **Compadrazgo:** A traditional Mexican custom of co-parenthood that developed from God-parenthood. **Machismo:** Ideal-typical characteristics of manliness in a highly differentiated Mexican or Mexican American gender role structure.

Extended families can become quite large.

prowess, and the responsibility for protection of women, children, and family honor. The proper role for women was to marry and assume homemaking, child-care, and kin-keeping responsibilities.

This role division has been reinforced by the belief structure of the Catholic Church. Williams (1990) found that, while contemporary Mexican Americans still express traditional gender-role values, their behaviors reveal an increasingly egalitarian marital role structure. This is especially true among couples with wives employed outside the home. Even in these couples, Mexican American couples probably retain more traditional gender and family scripts than is the case among non-Hispanic Whites.

Asian American Families

Asian immigrants have, in spite of considerable prejudice and discrimination, had remarkable success in America. We have seen that Asian Americans have the longest life expectancy of major groups, the highest percentage of its workforce in white-collar positions, and the highest family income. This success is associated with family variables such as the highest percentage of families with children that are headed by a married couple (see Table 7.6). Asian Americans are a diverse group,

however, and the success is not equally distributed among those from different countries.

Asian American Diversity

Although median income is considerably higher for Asians than for Whites, rates of poverty and use of welfare are also higher. While immigrants and their descendents from Japan, China, South Korea, and India have done well, Southeast Asians are struggling. Research by Paul Ong (in Brooks, 1994) found that Vietnamese, Cambodians, and Laotians have the highest welfare dependency rate of any groups in America. Southeast Asians constitute only 13% of all Asian Americans but make up 87% of Asians on welfare.

High rates of poverty among Southeast Asians and many Pacific Islanders, which bring down average income and occupational success rates for Asians as a whole, make the success of other Asian groups even more remarkable. Peterson (1966), commenting particularly on the amazing success of Japanese Americans just 20 years after their disgraceful treatment during World War II, called Asian Americans the "model minority." Although this characterization is resented by some Asians, there is enough truth in it to warrant an attempt at an explanation.

A strong family and economic success are clearly related, and both have many causes. One important factor is the long tradition of emphasis on learning and study as a means of achieving a better life. As we saw in chapter 4, the study of Confucianism was crucial to advancement in China's traditional society. Confucian tradition also influenced other Asian societies; the emphasis on filial piety was particularly important in holding the family together. Although this tradition has been challenged in the United States, with its value on individualism rather than familism, filial piety remains an influence in many Asian families (Lin & Liu, 1993).

Part of filial piety is the belief that an individual's actions, both good and bad, are attributed to the entire family. Divorce is rare, partly because it would bring disgrace not only on the couple but on the extended family as well (Wong, 1988). Such things as juvenile delinquency and unmarried pregnancy are more likely to be avoided than in American society as a whole. On the other hand, success in school or at other pursuits brings honor to everyone in the family, so study is encouraged and help is widely given by parents and other adults. This is true even among the poorer Vietnamese and Laotian families, who see making sacrifices for the education of their children, along with hard work, as the route to success in America (Kaplan, Whitmore, & Choy, 1989).

Although parents provide considerable assistance, their children are expected to learn maturity at early ages. Aggressive behavior is not tolerated; politeness, as stressed by Confucianism, is extremely important. It is considered poor taste to display affection in the company of others. Like the reserve typical of aristocratic British, Chinese children are unlikely to see their parents hug and kiss each other, although there is no evidence that the children feel any less loved than is the case in more demonstrative cultures (Wong, 1988).

Familism and sharing with the larger ethnic community are typical of Asian immigrants, just as they are with many other groups including Native Americans, African Americans, and Hispanics. For Asians, however, the pooling of resources has resulted in more upward mobility than has been true for other groups. For Asians, family, kin, and ethnic sharing have built capital, while the other groups have shared primarily at the survival level.

An Asian family that pools its labor to run a restaurant or grocery store is not only cooperating for survival, but building capital for the future. When resources are pooled to send a child to college, the degree can become human capital to raise the position of the family line. This kind of familism encourages individual achievement, which is more compatible with American individualism, but it also encourages individuals who have achieved to share the fruits of their success with the family. While young persons might feel considerable pressure to achieve, the stress has paid off in terms of academic and professional success.

At an extrafamilial level, Koreans and other immigrant groups have maintained self-help societies that lend money and provide other services to in-group members. In most cases the services are provided at less cost than would be paid in the commercial market; other times the self-help society is the only available source of financial aid because commercial firms would consider the loan too risky. Once a family achieves success, it is expected to make money available for others who need help.

A major factor in accounting for success of Asians, as well as the differences among Asian groups, is the difference in immigration experiences. Takaki (1989) studied Asian immigration since 1965, finding that newcomers from China, Japan, South Korea, and India generally were from more privileged classes in their countries of origin. They brought not only strong educational values but educational achievement as well, and many had capital to invest in their new homeland. Daniels (1990) found that 66% of recent Filipino immigrants were professionals, most commonly nurses or other medical personnel. About 70% of Korean householders in New York and Los Angeles came with college degrees (Takaki, 1989). Recent emigrants from Vietnam, Laos, and Cambodia, on the other hand, were more likely to be from rural and illiterate backgrounds, had fewer employment skills, had less capital, and were younger (Daniels, 1990).

Different patterns of immigration are now several generations old in Chinese American and Japanese American groups. The first wave of Chinese immigrants arrived just after the California gold rush began in 1849. These were mostly young men who worked in mines, on railroads, and at other physically demanding tasks. They sent much of their earnings to their wives and children, who remained in China with their extended families (Nee & Wong, 1985). Anti-Chinese sentiment in the United States resulted in the Chinese Exclusion Act of 1882; this isolated many who were already here from their families, who were not allowed to immigrate.

Japanese Americans

Succeeding generations of Japanese Americans have had very different experiences in America (Takaki, 1994). Not long after the stream of Chinese immigrants dried up, the first large group of Japanese began to arrive. They were faced with a transfer of the resentment still smoldering toward the Chinese, but the Japanese were more likely to be of the middle class or to possess agricultural skills that they immediately put to work. They were fairly quickly joined by their wives and began families. By 1910, mostly in California, there were 30,000 Japanese working on farms, about 6,000 of whom were landowners (Portes & Manning, 1986). Dominant groups saw their success as a threat, and legislation in California severely limited the right of Japanese immigrants to own land or become citizens. Federal legislation in 1921 and 1924 cut off emigration from Japan. In 1940, there were 127,000 persons of Japanese ancestry in the United States proper and 157,000 in Hawaii, which was not then a state (Kitano, 1976:10–29).

Many of the Japanese had opened businesses in cities, often aided by the informal banking services of the Japanese American community. This was part of an "enclave economy" whereby the Japanese were sufficiently established that they could provide goods and services to one another when discrimination reduced support from other groups.

After the Japanese attack on Pearl Harbor, mass arrests of Japanese citizens in America, along with Japanese Americans, took place. As many as 120,000 were moved from the west coast to relocation camps inland. More than two thirds of the internees were American citizens. Their property confiscated, many families were financially ruined. This, along with the migration of thousands of younger Japanese Americans to the midwestern and eastern United States, severely weakened the traditionally strong family structure. After the war was over, Japanese Americans rebuilt and quickly outpaced other groups once again (Kitano, 1976).

Conflict between American and Japanese institutions and values has occurred with each successive generation. **Issei** brought with them the traditional image of the Japanese family. Like the American family of the time, it was patriarchal and relied more heavily on extended family than did the European family of the time. Filial duty, especially involving patrilineal relations, was emphasized. Marriages were arranged with the help of a matchmaker or go-between. If not married when they immigrated, most Issei men had wives selected for them from their home region of Japan. Marriage was seen as a responsibility to the lineage and economic unit. Emphasis was on the parent-child unit, rather than the husband-wife dyad. While instilling traditional values in their children, Issei had left their own parents. It might have been more difficult for them to model the traditional family for their own children than was the case for persons who remained in Japan. Issei did, nonetheless, model self-sacrifice and educational values.

In the 1940s, Japanese American families were forcibly moved into "relocation camps."

Issei: First-generation Japanese immigrants to the United States, mostly between 1890 and 1920.

Nisei, the second generation, underwent considerable assimilation into American culture but retained many traditional characteristics. Although generally affluent and successful, their social contacts are mostly with other Japanese Americans. They are somewhat more likely to marry non-Japanese and to live in integrated suburban areas than was the case with their parents (Fugita & O'Brien, 1985).

Third-generation Japanese Americans, or **Sansei,** are fairly typical of successful American baby boomers. Adopting the American pattern of choice in mate selection, more than half married non-Japanese partners. They have very high rates of educational attainment, low fertility rates, and small households that reflect a strong preference for neolocal and nuclear family residence (Gardner, Robey, & Smith, 1985).

Between 1892 and 1930, nearly 20 million new Americans passed through Ellis Island.

White Americans and the Family

The tendency to treat the 75% of Americans who are not African American, Asian, Hispanic, or Native American as if they are a monolithic and homogeneous majority has obscured the differences that exist in this group. We will explore these differences, then have a closer look at Irish American and Italian American families.

European American Diversity

As is true with other categories, there is disagreement about an appropriate term for this group of Americans. The concept of "Whiteness" has evolved slowly in American history. Irish immigrants were originally classified as a non-White race, but they became "White" in the 19th century. Italians and Greeks were not classified as "White" until early in the 20th century (Coontz, 2000).

The label "White," often contrasted with the term "people of color," disguises a wide range of skin tones that varies considerably by season and by national origin. The terms "Euro American" or "European American" would include Hispanics, who derive at least their basic language from Europe. The term "Anglo" technically refers only to persons of English ancestry, who are a minority among Whites. Acronyms like WASP (White Anglo-Saxon Protestant) are even more limiting. The Census Bureau uses the term "White," which for some purposes includes many Hispanics. In

this text, the labels "White" and "European American" will not include Hispanics unless otherwise indicated.

In the 1970s, sociological research on family diversity began to focus more on Blacks, Asians and Hispanics rather than on Italians, Irish, Polish, and other White groups. Much of the research on White ethnicity is, consequently, somewhat dated. Perhaps the most complete study of its time on ethnicity was Andrew Greeley's *Ethnicity in the United States* (1974). Greeley took a positive view of ethnicity, referring to it as "an island of Gemeinschaft in a sea of Gesellschaft." Put differently, ethnic ties provided a sense of community for a network of families, in the midst of an impersonal and sometimes hostile larger society.

Greeley found significant differences among European American ethnic groups in terms of income, educational level, occupational level, and political participation and ideology. Family differences were found in family size, gender roles, the importance of the mother compared with the father in the home, and the self-esteem of daughters.

Various groups differ in terms of the extent to which they have assimilated into American culture. In most parts of the country, Americans with German-speaking ancestors are now virtually indistinguishable as an ethnic group (Roeber, 1993). Others maintain more distinctive cultural differences.

Most American Jews came to the United States from eastern Europe, although others came here from Germany and elsewhere. They have been very successful in America, for some of the same reasons as Asians. Jews

---

Nisei: Second-generation Japanese Americans, mostly born between 1910 and 1940. **Sansei:** Third-generation Japanese Americans, mostly born after World War II.

have a long tradition recognizing the importance of study and learning; Greeley (1974) found them to have by far the highest educational levels in the United States, along with very high rates of both men and women in professional occupations.

A strong sense of family and religious solidarity has encouraged community and sharing among Jews, which has helped them survive the centuries of oppression at the hand of Christians and Muslims. Perhaps ironically, when oppression is reduced, as it is in the United States, the sense of solidarity declines also. The percentage of the American population that identifies itself as Jewish has declined from 3.7% of the population in 1937, to about 2.5% today. This is partly because of lower than average fertility rates, a characteristic of nearly all highly educated groups, but it is also partly the result of marriage to non-Jewish partners. In the 1980s, 32% of all marriages involving Jews were to non-Jews. Rates are lower in cities like New York, with large Jewish populations, but are much higher in other cities like Denver, where rates of outmarriage have been as high as 50% (Tenenbaum, 1993). Divorce rates, while still not as high as among Christians, are rising among Jews.

Jews, of course, do retain their own religious institutions, but they are highly integrated into other institutions in the United States. Two other groups that are highly assimilated but retain some distinctiveness are the Irish and the Italians, both of whom represent large numbers of Catholic Americans.

Irish Americans

Except in the north of the island, Ireland is predominantly Catholic and sees itself as a victim of centuries of oppression by nearby Protestant England. Like the late medieval English, however, rural Ireland has historically had a stem family form, in which only one child inherited the family property rights.

Ancestors of most Irish American immigrants were peasants who practiced a form of sharecropping on land technically owned by others, usually Protestant and often English. Farming rights were handed down, but in the stem family form only one of the children could inherit the farm or farming rights. No system of primogeniture developed, so the owner was free to bequeath the property to any child. The inheritor was usually a son, but it could have been a daughter (Biddle, 1981).

As we saw in chapter 4, an advantage of the stem system is nonpartible inheritance, which keeps the farms from being split into smaller and smaller parcels each generation. A consequence is that many persons are unable to

accumulate enough land to support a family; many non-inheriting offspring never marry. No stigma was attached to those who remained single for life, as long as they also remained childless. This system is workable in a society, such as Ireland, that is sexually repressive enough that the unmarried persons do not have offspring.

Often, even the person who was to inherit had to wait a long time, often being 40 or even 50 years old before getting the inheritance and being in a position to marry. Wives were often considerably younger than their husbands, but they too were older at marriage than was the case in other systems.

Noninheriting children had less security but more freedom. They became landless laborers on other farms or moved to cities looking for work. In spite of the geographical mobility, most remained in close contact with their families of orientation, developing close relationships with nieces and nephews who remained on the home farm. Among men, noninheritors often joined their nephews in what Stivers (1976) called an "avunculate," which engaged in social activities, many of which revolved around alcohol consumption. Roman Catholicism remained very important in the lives of Irish, partly because it became associated with their nationality as against the Protestantism of the British.

Irish farming in the 19th century depended heavily on the potato, which was relatively easy to grow in the depleted soil, but which was subject to periodic blights that increased poverty and starvation. The most serious of these was the "Great Famine" of 1845–1848 (Kennedy, 1973). Although more than one-half million Irish had already immigrated, mostly Protestants from the North, the Great Famine significantly increased rates of emigration (Adams, 1932). In 1845 and 1846 about 120,000 Irish immigrated, and from 1847 to 1854 about 1.25 million Irish arrived in America, mostly in New York. All told, 3 million Irish immigrated to the United States in the second half of the 19th century (Schrier, 1958).

These immigrants were overwhelmingly Catholic, mostly peasants from western and southern Ireland. Most were young, single adults; about two thirds were between the ages of 15 and 35 (Schrier, 1958). In addition, the sex ratio of this group was unusual among immigrants. By one count, 52.9% of Irish immigrants were women (Kane, 1993).

Most immigrants probably came from the ranks of noninheriting children, so they were mostly poor, illiterate, and unskilled except at potato farming. Because of this, and the fact that their numbers flooded the unskilled labor market and drove down wages, Irish immigrants were subject to considerable prejudice and discrimination from more established Americans. They found work in factories, mines, and railroad building.

Available for any manual labor, Irish were the bulk of construction workers on every northern canal built before the Civil War (Adams, 1932). Unmarried Irish women worked in factories and as domestics for wealthier families. After marriage, those who could afford to do so remained in their homes but contributed to family labor by providing room and board, often for more recent Irish immigrants. Thanks to hard work, mutual aid societies, political machines, and the growth of the American economy, many Irish Americans rose to powerful position in labor unions and found employment on police forces and in other civil service positions.

Through all this, the Irish maintained strong family and religious ties by forming ethnic enclaves in such cities as Boston and New York. Biddle (1981) referred to these as "Parish districts" with the church as the center of social and family life. The church often had its own parish school. All necessary shopping was located near the church, as was the neighborhood tavern, which was often the center of social life for unmarried men.

As with all small communities, most persons in the parish district knew each other on sight, and children who got out of hand were admonished by any available adult. Child rearing was designed to produce children who were "subordinate, obedient, and respectful" (Biddle, 1981:101). Socialization was primarily done by women, using shame, ridicule, and community pressure as means of social control.

As was true in Ireland, many individuals remained unmarried. More women of Irish descent remained unmarried throughout their lives than was the case for any other group in 19th-century America (Kane, 1993). Irish Americans of the time also had a relatively high rate of female-headed households, about 16% in 1875 in Buffalo, New York (Mattis, 1975; in Biddle, 1981). These were headed by widows produced by a combination of late marriages, large age differences between husbands and wives, and high fatality rates from the dangerous work done by the men. Households containing extended family members and boarders were common, especially among households headed by women (Mattis, 1975).

Kinship, traced bilaterally, was important to Irish Americans. This provided a large network of cooperation that was further strengthened by the addition of godparents. These, too, were usually bilateral, one being chosen from the groom's side of the family and one from the bride's side (Biddle, 1981). A close-knit parish community further expanded the availability of resources available to the Irish American family.

Today, many Irish Americans, especially the middle class, have moved to the suburbs, although they often maintain close ties to the "urban villages." Many others remain in their cultural enclaves, near extended families, friends, and the parish community. In the 1970s, in cities like Boston, busing was imposed to racially integrate public schools. Many Irish Americans were strongly opposed, a few violently. In their view, they were fighting for a way of life that included strong family and neighborhood ties. In the eyes of much of the national media, they were racists.

Italian Americans

Americans with Italian ancestry share several characteristics with the Irish Americans. Both come from a tradition of strong Catholic families and suffered prejudice in the United States. Both came generally from peasant classes in their countries of origin, and they survived in America by forming strong families and ethnic enclaves. There are differences between the two groups, however.

Most Americans of Italian descent derive from southern Italy and Sicily. Although they were peasants, their ties to landowners were tenuous so they relied heavily on strong, extended families for security. They endured considerable political instability at the state level, which also increased reliance on the family. They developed a significant distrust for strangers with whom they shared no familial, kin, or community ties (Quadagno, 1981).

Southern Italian and Sicilian cultures were patriarchal, but the man's power often stopped at the kitchen door because women exercised considerable power in the household (Greeley, 1974). According to Gabaccia (1993:789), the family was "father dominated but mother centered." An extended family council, usually headed by the elderly father, made decisions about the amount of dowries, how much to spend on funerals, and whether to extend credit to a family member (Covello, 1967).

In spite of the power accorded to men, women had their own sources of authority and respect. Women could own property and dispose of it without their husband's consent. Peasant women often worked in the fields, giving them further economic value. In addition, a wife, not her husband or father-in-law, maintained control of the dowry supplied by her family. Upon her death it would go to her children or, if she were childless, would revert to her family of orientation. Finally, the role of mother earned considerable respect because it was the center of the family in a culture in which the family was the primary institution (Covello, 1967).

Families in the NEWS

Response to Multiracial Census Option Varies

Millions of Americans have a multiracial heritage, but not all indicated that fact on their 2000 census forms. Many such respondents chose to identify with only one race.

Nationally, of those who identified as Black, 5% also selected another racial category. Significant regional differences, however, were found in the census results. Mississippi had one of the lowest multiracial counts in the country, while Oklahoma had one of the highest.

In Mississippi, the heritage has been to identify people with one, and only one, racial category. Strict segregation laws, including laws forbidding Blacks or Asians from marrying Whites, forced individuals into one race or another. That tradition is still strong, even among many who know that their parents were of mixed race.

Once referred to as Indian Territory, Oklahoma has a long history of racial mixing. Native Americans often married Whites. Freed slaves founded all-Black towns after the Civil War, but they, too, often married Native Americans. The continued presence of large military bases has also contributed to racial mixing.

Whether they so indicated on their census forms or not, many Oklahomans are of mixed ancestry. Representative J. C. Watt of Oklahoma is usually identified as the only black Republican in Congress. But he is also part Choctaw.

Source: Eric Schmitt. **www.nytimes.com**, March 31, 2001.

For the Italian peasant, the value of work was in the tangible fact of making an adult contribution to the family, not in an abstract concept of self-fulfillment, glorifying God, or finding signs of one's own salvation. The disregard for intangibles was also reflected in attitudes toward education. Although there was strong value placed on raising offspring who were *bon educato* (well educated), such a child was not necessarily schooled by formal educational systems but by a knowledge of the practical world and the importance of the family. The "well educated" traditional Italian child knew that without a family one had no identity.

Given that the family was so important, it might appear somewhat surprising that so many Italians left their families to immigrate to the United States, but poverty provided a major incentive. Economic conditions for peasants were difficult; the soil was worn out from centuries of cultivation using ancient techniques. Workers often lived in dugouts, caves, or small huts, which they shared with cattle if they were lucky enough to own any. There were too many persons for the land to support comfortably (Chapman, 1971; Quadagno, 1981).

Under these conditions, for a person to emigrate was not seen as an act of individualism but as an act of personal sacrifice for the family. The emigrant either planned to send money back to the family, to save money and return to Italy, or to finance later emigration of other family members (Quadagno, 1981).

The dawn of the 20th century saw a major wave of immigration to the United States. Between 1899 and 1910, 2.3 million Italians made the journey (Lalli, 1969). Unlike the Irish immigration, 74.5% of Italians were male, mostly single or married men who left their wives in Italy. The rate of return to Italy was 45.6% higher than for most immigrant groups (Archdeacon, 1983).

As with other groups, Italian immigrants faced considerable discrimination in the United States. They were poor, did not speak English, were largely unskilled, and provided more competition for the manufacturing jobs being created by industrialization. Also like other groups, they carved out ethnic enclaves, called "Little Italy" in many cities.

Italians had more difficulty assimilating than did some other European groups, facing particular hostility from recently arrived Irish. Although nearly all Italians were Roman Catholic, the church had been largely controlled in America by the Irish. Even though Italians came from the birthplace and center of worldwide Roman Catholicism, southern Italians and Irish Catholicism differed in certain respects, and Italians did not always feel welcome in Irish American Catholic churches. In addition, Italians were competing with many recently arrived Irish for jobs, and those Irish Americans who had worked their way into the middle class saw little reason to befriend the newer Italian arrivals (Quadagno, 1981).

Some cultural characteristics of the arrival from southern Italy also hindered their assimilation into American culture. While many other immigrant groups saw education as a way for their children, if not themselves, to succeed in their adopted country, Italian immigrants were more likely to see it as a threat to their familism. For one thing, schools were run by strangers, of whom the immigrants were suspicious. "Good education" was provided by the family, not outsiders. Compulsory attendance laws also conflicted with Italian customs of work and economics. Young persons were expected to work, not go to school, and to turn their earnings over to the family. Finally, schools taught abstractions that interfered with the tangible lessons learned from work (Gambino, 1974). As a result of the discrimination they faced and their parents' concerns about formal schooling, Italian youths frequently dropped out of school. Many young persons developed a youth-focused culture that today would probably be called gangs (Gans, 1962).

Even those who finished high school and went on to further training exhibited a materialist orientation. They generally focused on vocational and technical skills rather than the broader educations typically required for higher status professions. Consequently, most ended up in blue-collar occupations that better fit their cultural and educational values (Alba, 1985). Although it has not been widely studied, there seem to be parallels between early Italian American work and education experiences and the experiences of contemporary Mexican Americans.

Italian immigrants also faced discrimination because their family values appeared to be out of the mainstream. Their family structure was perceived to be much more patriarchal than was the Anglo pattern, although we have seen that even in Italy there were considerable checks on the power of the patriarch. In America, the first-generation family was found to be "fictitiously patriarchal" (Campisi, 1948). The formal structure and symbols were patriarchal, but the actual behavior was, while sex-segregated, more egalitarian.

Although Italian Americans have become economically and socially successful they, perhaps more than any other group that came directly from Europe, are likely to retain some ethnic identity. Italian neighborhoods remain strong, with more middle-class couples remaining there than is the case for many groups. They often rebuild old neighborhoods, rather than leaving for the suburbs. Greeley (1971:77) found that Italian Americans were more likely to live in the same neighborhood as members of their family of orientation, and were more likely to visit them regularly, than any other ethnic group of the time. Although this pattern was true for all social classes, it was especially strong in the working class.

Italian Americans retain, after several generations, low divorce rates, high incidence of caring for the elderly in their own homes, and other evidence of familism. Quadagno (1981) concluded that Italian Americans were likely to continue to retain some cultural identity and that there may be an increase in ethnic identification.

We have focused on the large groups of Italian Americans and Irish Americans, but there are many other groups of European origin that also retain vestiges of ethnicity. Whether assimilation or cultural pluralism will prevail for these groups remains to be seen. Rubin (1994) found evidence, especially among the working classes, of a resurgence of interest in White ethnicity. Seeing the increasing social emphasis on "multiculturalism" and "diversity," many Whites believe that rewards are going to Blacks, Latinos, and Asians. Some Whites believe that the only way they can be noticed is to emphasize their own ancestry, which was often accompanied by discrimination, prejudice, and other difficulties.

A reawakening of ethnicity directly implies an increased emphasis on family, since it is through families that ethnicity is traced, defined, and perpetuated. At the same time, increased focus on diversity has the potential to increase prejudice and hostility among groups. There is a fine line between in-group pride and out-group hatred.

Summary and Conclusion

Both the newer concept of "race" and the older one of "ethnicity" have been applied to differences among groups.

The United States has always been a diverse nation because it has been a country of immigrants. The first immigrants were voluntary ones, mostly from Europe, and involuntary ones from Africa. Immigrants today are more likely to be Hispanic or Asian. Families from all areas vary and have had varying degrees of success in their adopted country.

The African American family has typically been described in terms of its instability. Explanations range from those that attribute Black family characteristics to the legacy of slavery to those that find the cause in conditions in today's central cities. Most Black families are not poor, however. Black families tend to resemble White families of the same social class.

Hispanics will soon become the largest minority in the United States, if they are not already. Coming from many places, they share a belief in Catholicism and familism. Those who have been in the United States for some time are generally better off than average African Americans but not as well off as non-Hispanic Whites or Asians.

Asian Americans have been called the "model minority," although there are wide differences in various Asian groups. Partly because of their strong family system, Japanese Americans have thrived in spite of tremendous discrimination.

White ethnic groups such as Irish Americans and Italian Americans also have strong family systems and appear to retain some ethnic identification in spite of being largely assimilated.

In conclusion, race remains one of the most challenging issues in America today, although many characteristics once thought to be racial are more related to social class. Families perpetuate racial and ethnic differences, both in the selection of mates and in the inheritance of privilege. Racial and ethnic differences, however, are largely socially constructed, and racial divisions will continue to change as the demography of the country changes.

This chapter concludes the section of text primarily devoted to macrolevel analysis. Students should keep this background in mind as they read the remainder of the text.

> *Rethinking in Context* Are class-related or race-related variables better predictors of family life? If interracial marriages become more common, how would that affect the concept of race and ethnicity? Have you changed your view of the advantages and disadvantages of your race/ethnicity? Which groups have been most advantaged? Least advantaged? How have families affected these differences?

Additional Resources

Edited readers on race, ethnicity, diversity, and families

Demo, David H., Katherine R. Allen, & Mark A. Fine, eds. 2000. *Handbook of Family Diversity.* New York: Oxford University Press.

Ingoldsby, Bron B., & Suzanna Smith, eds. 1995. *Families in Multicultural Perspective.* New York: The Guilford Press.

McAdoo, Harriette Pipes, ed. 1999. *Family Ethnicity: Strength in Diversity*, 2nd ed. Thousand Oaks, CA: Sage.

Taylor, Ronald L., ed. 1994. *Minority Families in the United States: A Multicultural Perspective.* Englewood Cliffs, NJ: Prentice Hall.

Race, racism, and families

Farley, Reynolds, & Walter R. Allen. 1987. *The Color Line and the Quality of Life in America.* New York: Russell Sage Foundation.

Massey, Douglas S., & Nancy A. Denton. 1993. *American Apartheid: Segregation and the Making of the Underclass.* Boston: Harvard University Press.

Black families

Billingsley, Andrew. 1992. *Climbing Jacob's Ladder: The Enduring Legacy of African-American Families.* New York: Simon & Schuster.

Edmondson, Brad. 1993. "What Do You Call a Dark-Skinned Person?" *American Demographics* 15(10):9.

Stack, Carol B. 1974. *All Our Kin: Strategies for Survival in a Black Community*. New York: Harper & Row.

Wilson, William Julius. 1987. *The Truly Disadvantaged: The Inner City, the Underclass, and Public Policy*. Chicago: University of Chicago Press.

Wilson, William Julius. 1996. *When Work Disappears: The World of the New Urban Poor*. New York: Alfred A. Knopf.

Hispanic families

Bean, Frank D., & Marta Tienda. 1987. *The Hispanic Population of the United States*. New York: Russell Sage Foundation.

Lomnitz, Larissa Adler. 1987. *A Mexican Elite Family, 1820–1980: Kinship, Class, and Culture*. Princeton, NJ: Princeton University Press.

Zambrana, Ruth E. 1995. *Understanding Latino Families: Scholarship, Policy, and Practice*. Thousand Oaks, CA: Sage.

Multiracial families

Dalmage, Heather M. 2000. *Tripping on the Color Line: Black-White Multiracial Families in a Racially Divided World*. New Brunswick: Rutgers University Press.

Root, Maria P. P., ed. 1995. *The Multiracial Experience: Racial Borders as the New Frontier*. Thousand Oaks, CA: Sage.

Rosenblatt, Paul, Terri Karis, & Richard Powell. 1995. *Multiracial Couples: Black and White Voices*. Thousand Oaks, CA: Sage.

Immigrant experience

Chin, Ko-Lin, & Douglas S. Massey. 1999. *Smuggled Chinese: Clandestine Immigration to the United States*. Philadelphia: Temple University Press.

Pedraza, Silvia, & Ruben Rumbault. 1995. *Origins and Destinies: Immigration, Race and Ethnicity in America*. Belmont, CA: Wadsworth.

Portes, Alehandro, & Ruben G. Rumbault. 1996. *Immigrant America: A Portrait*. Berkeley, CA: University of California Press.

Portes, Alehandro, & Ruben G. Rumbaut. 2001. *Legacies: The Story of the Immigrant Second Generation*. Berkeley, CA: University of California Press.

Internet Sites

Links to several sources about race and ethnicity

http://www.georgetown.edu/crossroads/asw/race.html

The Ethnic Minority Section of the National Council on Family Relations

http://www.asn.csus.edu/em-ncfr/

Links to Web sites relevant to the study of ethnic minority families

http://web.missouri.edu/~c539613/ncfr.html

From the book *Without Sanctuary,* very disturbing photos and discussion about lynchings of Blacks in America

http://www.journale.com/withoutsanctuary/main.html

For links to these sites and additional resources, visit the *Families in Context* Web site at:

http://sociology.wadsworth.com

Chapter 8

Forming Intimate Relationships

Prelude

Janeen and Armando each had three or four romances, each seeming more serious than the last, before they met each other their last year in high school. There was initial mutual attraction and rapport. They gradually came to talk to each other about their hopes, fears, and dreams. They began to depend on each other for companionship and going places together.

The couple began to develop their own shared private jokes and views of the world, based on their experiences together. They didn't talk much about the future, though; they weren't sure they would have a future together. Once in a while they talked about living together, but the question of marriage never came up.

Janeen and Armando became sociology majors. They learned both from their classes and from their professors' lives. Sociologists often pride themselves on their objective and rational view of society. But sociologists, too, are human products of that society.

Sociologists also fall in love, sometimes with the wrong person. We have good and bad relationships. We do heroic and silly things for the sake of those relationships.

Professional objectivity does not always lead to personal rationality, because romantic love has inherently irrational properties. Falling in love is gloriously risky business.

But who would want to give up on the possibilities?

The process of forming close personal relationships is complicated. Love is a major reason for two persons to form a relationship that is considered special to both partners. Only some of these relationships result in marriage. This chapter focuses on the development of close personal relationships, particularly those that have the potential to include sexual activity or a romantic commitment as part of the relationship. The following chapter looks at intimate relationships in the context of selecting marriage partners.

> **Thinking Ahead** Make a list of the characteristics that would attract you to a member of the opposite sex; make another list of those characteristics that you would find desirable in a close same-sex friendship. How do the lists compare? How do you think your lists would compare with the lists made by someone of the opposite sex?

This chapter is about that intimate phenomenon we call love, especially the type now associated with romance and marriage. It is only recently in history that romantic love has become the preferred mechanism for selecting mates, but that does not necessarily mean love was unknown in earlier times.

Historical Images of Love

Perceptions of love vary from one culture to another. Love has also changed over time and therefore has a history (Swidler, 1980, 1986; Barich & Bielby, 1996). This section will first present different viewpoints on the question, "Is love universal?" Then we will look at love in ancient Greece and Rome. Courtly love in Europe will be our next historical era, followed by the intertwined developments of romanticism and industrialization. This history contrasts with today's views of love, but also helps us understand how today's views developed.

Is Love Universal?

Strong feelings of attachment have probably always been characteristic of human groups. The relationships between mothers and their children, between brothers and sisters, and between adult men and women who have known each other for a long time, had characteristics that today could be defined as love. There is debate, however, about the universality of the type of love referred to as "romantic" or "passionate" love.

Hatfield and Rapson (1987) argued that passionate love could be found throughout all human eras. They found that children as young as 4 years of age have intense experiences of falling in love. Hatfield and Rapson (1987) also found no differences in the incidence of love for men and women or for different ethnic groups. This evidence would indicate that romantic love is indeed universal.

Jankowiak and Fisher (1992) undertook a cross-cultural study of romantic love, which they defined as "The idealization of the other, within an erotic context, with the expectation of enduring for some time into the future" (p. 150). Using the standard cross-cultural sample compiled by Murdock and White (1969), Jankowiak and Fisher found enough information about 166 cultures to determine whether romantic love, by their definition, existed or not. The concept of romantic love was known in 88.5% of cultures. Not all persons in these cultures experienced romantic love; in some, evidence of romantic love was found only in myths and in stories. Even where many individuals in the culture experienced romantic love, it was not necessarily associated with marriage. One's spouse and one's romantic lover were often different persons. Although it is not quite universal, Jankowiak and Fisher wrote, they believed romantic love to be characteristic of human groups even in early hunting-gathering societies.

Other researchers maintain that passionate love is a more recent arrival on the human scene. Solomon

(1981) argued that romantic love can only exist in a society, such as the modern United States, that has a high emphasis on individuality, self-identity, independence, and social mobility. Perhaps the safest conclusion is that something like romantic love probably existed for at least some persons throughout history, but that the meanings and uses of this form of intimacy have varied considerably. A short historical comparison, beginning with the ancient Greeks and Romans, illustrates this diversity of love in western societies.

Love in Ancient Greece and Rome

Along with other Greek philosophers, Plato spent a good deal of time discussing love. The purest kind of love, in his view, had little to do with interpersonal intimacy, but involved a spiritual quest for truth and beauty. Less lofty love, involving sexual attraction and fulfillment was also recognized, but even this form of love had little to do with marriage. Instead, it often involved a homosexual relationship, usually between an older man who served as political mentor and his younger apprentice. In his book *Symposium,* Plato had the character Aristophanes reserve passionate heterosexual love for the class of adulterers and promiscuous women. Passion between a husband and wife was not mentioned.

Female homosexual love was also recognized in ancient Greece, best exemplified by the teacher and poet named Sappho who wrote about her affection toward one of her students. Because she lived on the Greek island of Lesbos, female homosexuals came to be called lesbians.

Ancient religions and myths recognized the existence of passionate sexual love. In Greece, the goddess of love was Aphrodite, from which comes our word *aphrodisiac.* Her son was named Eros, the root of our word *erotic.* The Roman counterparts of this pair were Venus and her son Cupid, whose fateful arrows could transform men and women into helpless lovers.

Passionate love, however, was not expected to be part of marriage and family life. A couple could best hope to achieve the state of harmony and lack of disagreement known as *concordia* (see chapter 3).

Even though Christianity began as a religion of love, its form of love was spiritual, not physical. Any kind of bodily manifestation of love, especially sexual activity, was believed to contaminate Godly love and was to be avoided if at all possible. Even marital love was not emphasized; the ideal person was one who denied all desires of the flesh. Some early Christian theologians said that intense love of one's spouse, because it conflicted with true love of God, was adultery (Hendrick & Hendrick, 1992).

Most early Christians, of course, continued to marry and have children; some had affairs, and some, presumably, were occasionally smitten by Cupid's arrows. Such occasions, however, were more often seen as tragedies than as models of appropriate behavior. Marriages continued to be arranged because they were seen as too important to be left to the glands of impetuous young lovers. The story of Romeo and Juliet was told in the Middle Ages as a reminder of what can happen when young lovers ignore their parents' wishes and marry for love. The story does indicate, in the telling, that marriage for love was possible and did occasionally occur. By about 1595, when Shakespeare told the tale, more sympathy was with the young lovers and less with their warring families (Benet, 1987).

Courtly Love in Europe

In the 12th century, in the context of feudal Europe, a new form of love arose. Pagan stories of passionate heterosexual love probably were still told, but the major form of human love referred to a relationship between an aristocratic lord and his follower. Kissing was a symbol of loyalty, as when a new knight knelt and kissed his master's ring. After a heroic action by a knight, his master might kiss him on both cheeks. Remnants of that custom remain in parts of Europe, in rituals that seem awkward to some Americans (Collins & Coltrane, 1995).

The new **courtly love** had elements of the three older forms: spiritual love for God, passionate heterosexual attraction, and loyalty of a servant to his master. Rather than a code of loyalty to a male master, however, the knight or other noble figure expressed love toward an exalted lady. She might recognize his attention by granting him a scarf or other garment as he went into battle. In most stories of courtly love, actual sexual contact occurred, if at all, only after a long period of trials and temptation during which each of the lovers would carry on their more mundane relationships with spouses and children. The essence of courtly love was a spiritual attraction that kept the woman on a pedestal, but there was enough hint of sexual temptation to keep the story interesting.

Courtly love: A code of romantic behavior idealized among the aristocracy of medieval Europe.

Medieval knights, the stories go, lived for the attention of their ladies.

Embellished by traveling storytellers and poets known as troubadours, tales of courtly love spread. The stories were told in the courts of the aristocracy, and it was assumed that only in such courts could this noble type of love occur; hence the label "courtly love." Such stories are still told today. They are found in Arthurian legends about King Arthur and the Knights of the Round Table and in such accounts as "Tristan and Iseult" and "Brunhild and Siegfried."

Stories of adultery were probably based on some amount of fact, since marriages were not based on love and men were frequently away from their wives fighting wars. Ample opportunity existed for behavior that was not quite as spiritual as stories of courtly love might imply. Among commoners, however, the Church often harshly punished adultery and other nonmarital sex. Marriage remained an economic, not romantic, relationship, and those who could not afford a marriage were expected to remain chaste. Gradually, however, images of love changed throughout European societies.

One outgrowth of courtly love was an idealized form of etiquette that prescribed how a "lady" was to behave and be treated. The term "lady," originally a title of nobility, came to mean any woman of high standard who deserved to be treated in a certain way by a "gentleman." Such expectations later spread beyond the nobility and influenced behaviors of all women and men, especially in formal situations.

Romanticism and Industrialization

A different form of love evolved in Europe in the late 1700s along with a broader movement known as **romanticism.** This movement in the artistic and intellectual life of Europe and North America was pervasive but difficult to categorize. Benet (1987:840) suggested several characteristics of romanticism:

> a belief in the innate goodness of man in his natural state; individualism; reverence for nature; primitivism; philosophic idealism; a paradoxical tendency toward both free thought and religious mysticism; revolt against political authority and social convention; exaltation of physical passion; the cultivation of emotion and sensation for their own sakes; and a persistent attraction to the supernatural, the morbid, the melancholy, and the cruel.

Although there are apparent contradictions in this list of characteristics, some of them were quite compatible with what came to be known as "romantic love." Individualism, revolt against authority, and cultivation of emotion all justify rebelling against one's family of orientation to cling to the new lover; exaltation of physical

---

Romanticism: An artistic and intellectual movement originating in Europe in the late 18th century.

passion and sensation for its own sake justify unleashing the power of sexuality, whether fulfilled or not; and interest in mysticism and the supernatural justifies the irrational nature of romantic love.

By the 19th century, the phenomenon of romantic love was well established, but its connection with mate selection was not firmly made. Although not all elements of romanticism are compatible with industrialization, individualism is. The power of extended families to choose mates for young persons waned as industrialization progressed. The power of romantic love increasingly became acceptable as a mechanism by which individuals could choose their own mates. In the United States, 20th-century leader of the industrial revolution, the triumph of romantic love over parental choice reached its peak. Today, a parent's suggestion that he or she might have a voice in his or her child's mate selection is treated as an unwarranted threat to the young person's "right" to choose to marry the partner chosen by love.

Defining Love

Trying to define and describe love has long been an interest of poets; only recently have social scientists attempted to do so. Before love can be studied, it must be defined in a way that makes measurement possible. The first approach to clarifying the concept "love" is to compare several different definitions in use in American culture. Next, we will consider the word "love" as a symbol with consequences when used in certain contexts. This section ends with a mention of what three different sociological perspectives have to say about love.

Descriptive Variation in Defining Love

Some linguists argue that the importance of a concept to a particular culture can be determined by the number of words in the language that express shades of variation in that concept. Given the importance of love in American society, then, it is surprising that the English language lacks an extensive vocabulary for naming various types of love (Hendrick & Hendrick, 1992). Consider the many kinds of phenomena that can be referred to in the context of "love," as a fill-in-the-blank exercise can illustrate:

I love _____

> my parents.
> my lover.
> my spouse.
> my children.
> my grandparents.
> my dog.
> my shirt.
> my job.
> my sociology class.
> my car.
> colorful sunsets.
> God.
> rare prime rib.
> summer vacation.
> the Denver Broncos.
> a good laugh.
> a parade.
> rock music.

The list could go on extensively.

Although the word "love" can be appropriately used to describe one's orientation toward each of these persons or things, that orientation is different in each case. One does not, hopefully, love one's spouse in the same way as loving one's shirt. Different emotions and different behavioral expectations are involved.

One way to clarify the meaning of a vague concept is to compare it to other concepts through the use of simile and metaphor. Kovecses (1991) found several metaphors used in our culture to make sense of love. Among these are love as unity, as in "we are one"; love as insanity, as in "I'm crazy about you"; and love as food, as in "I'm hungry for your love."

The western world's intellectuals have differed on their images of love. Some of their insights are given in Highlight 8.1. The quotes reflect both negative and positive images of love, and both serious and whimsical ones.

Love as a Symbol

Symbolic interactionist theory can provide one way of looking at love. Like every other word, "love" is a **symbol.** Understanding the characteristics of symbols

---

Symbol: A thing that stands for something else.

HIGHLIGHT 8.1　　**Selected Images of Love**

When a couple of young people strongly devoted to each other commence to eat onions. James M. Bailey.

To endure for others. Henry Ward Beecher.

When another person's needs are as important as your own. Abe Burrows.

The word used to label the sexual excitement of the young, the habituation of the middle-aged, and the mutual dependence of the old. John Ciardi.

The drug which makes sexuality palatable in popular mythology. Germaine Greer.

The wisdom of the fool and the folly of the wise. Samuel Johnson.

To place our happiness in the happiness of another. Gottfried von Leibnitz.

A mutual admiration society consisting but of two members . . . the one whose love is less intense will become president. Joseph Mayer.

Quicksilver in the hand. Leave the fingers open and it stays in the palm; clutch it and it darts away. Dorothy Parker.

When a person's . . . own boundary expands to include the other, that was previously outside himself. Frederick S. Perls.

A little haven of refuge from the world. Bertrand A. Russell.

A little foolishness and a lot of curiosity. George Bernard Shaw.

A mutual self-giving which ends in self-recovery. Fulton J. Sheen.

Friendship set on fire. Jeremy Taylor.

A mutual misunderstanding. Oscar Wilde.

Just another four-letter word. Tennessee Williams.

Source: Compact Disk Computer Search of the Software Toolworks Reference Library. 1990. Novato, CA: Software Toolworks.

To say that symbols are arbitrary means that any symbol can stand for any referent. With rare exceptions, there is no inherent connection between a spoken or written symbol and its referent. Whatever arbitrary symbol is used for a particular referent, people must learn to make the connection. Unless the group shares these meanings, communication will be impossible. A major part of the socialization process is learning the arbitrary symbols by which a group shares meanings.

A baby might first hear the word "love" when its mother is softly cuddling it. If that process is repeated, a connection begins to be made between the word "love" and a feeling of safety, warmth, and softness with another person. If a dad bounces his baby on his knee and says, "I love you," a sense of playfulness is added to the feeling of love. As the baby grows older, other family members, the religious institution, the media, friends, and others add more information to the concept of "love."

Our experiences associated with the symbol "love" are sufficiently similar that we can use the word in everyday language and believe that we share its meaning with others. We each learned the word in our own unique experiences, however, so no two persons have exactly the same referents for the symbol "love." There is room for honest disagreement between two lovers about exactly what their love means to each other.

The symbol "love" refers to a set of emotions and feelings, but we can never be sure that two people are referring to the same internal state when they use any "emotion" word. The feelings are subjective and nonempirical. The actions associated with feeling words, however, are more empirical. Although we might occasionally engage in the action of hugging someone we hate, it is a behavioral expectation more often associated with love.

The symbol "love" is associated with many behavioral expectations. When the word "love" is first used in a relationship, when one person first says, "I love you," the nature of the relationship changes. It is as if the person using the word is offering the other person a contract agreeing to certain expectations between the parties. If the other person accepts the offer, perhaps by saying "I love you too," the new relationship contract is in force. Exactly what the new expectations are is not usually clear, but generally a more committed and exclusive relationship now characterizes their mutual script.

Once two persons agree to a **love-appropriate relationship,** the word "love" occurs in certain predictable

---

can help in our search for what love means. Symbols have two major characteristics. First, symbols are arbitrary and learned and second, symbols stand for types of **referents**.

Referent: The something else for which a symbol stands　　**Love-appropriate relationship:** An affiliation in which the partners mutually accept the use of the word "love."

We cannot see love itself, but we can identify behaviors that are associated with love.

ways. It is likely to be used in almost ritual fashion on some occasions especially when the two lovers are going to be apart from each other for a time. Use of the word in that context might refer to an emotional state, but it also is a reminder of the committed and exclusive nature of the relationship. It is like saying, "While we are apart, I will behave myself and I expect you to do likewise."

Another common expectation in a love-appropriate relationship is that the expression be reciprocal. In such a relationship, an effective way for one partner to get the other to use the word "love" is to first say, "I love you." The partner is expected to reply, "I love you too." Once this script has been established, the failure of the partner to respond properly is sometimes an indication that something is wrong with the relationship.

While a particular couple might agree on most of the expectations about love, there are frequently differences of opinion that do not arise until one person's expectations have been violated. One partner, for example, might expect to receive flowers on his or her first common Valentine's Day because "that's what people in love do." If the other partner has not learned about that particular expectation of the **love contract,** hurt feelings and relationship disruption are possible. The exact meanings of the love contract, like many other aspects of a relationship, have to be negotiated over time. That negotiation process is more difficult in a society in which love contract expectations are not clearly defined.

The idea that there is a set of expectations associated with the use of the symbol "love" can help social scientists figure out what persons mean when they use the word. Once these expectations are isolated, they can be used as a measure of how much love exists in a particular relationship. Finding Out 8.1 illustrates an example of such an approach. Although the meaning of love is difficult to pin down, Rubin found that it could be measured.

Although Rubin's scales provide both a definition and a measurement device, they do not cover the entire range of variation in the meanings associated with the symbol "love." There are several types of love, to which we now turn our attention.

Typologies of Love

The descriptions of love in Highlight 8.1 indicate that there are many different types of love, including some that might have negative consequences. Several researchers have attempted to organize this variation by developing **typologies** of love.

Lee's Love Styles

Perhaps the most widely known typology of love was developed by Canadian researcher John Lee (1973, 1988).

Love contract: Expectations partners in a love-appropriate relationship have for each other and themselves. **Typology:** A systematic classification of related phenomena based on defined characteristics or traits.

Finding Out 8.1

Rubin's Measures of Liking and Loving

Zick Rubin (1970, 1973) was one of the first researchers to develop a quantitative measurement of romantic love. He began by constructing several statements that might be indicative of either loving or liking. He asked more than 200 undergraduate students whether they thought they would agree with each of the statements if applied to someone they loved and someone they liked. By process of elimination, he ended up with 13 statements associated with liking and 13 associated with loving. After further research, he narrowed it to 9 statements for each category, including:

Sample Love Scale items:

I feel that I can confide in _____ about virtually everything.

If I were lonely, my first thought would be to seek _____ out.

I would forgive _____ for practically anything.

I feel responsible for _____'s well-being.

Sample Liking Scale items:

I have great confidence in _____'s good judgment.

_____ is one of the most likable people I know.

_____ is the sort of person whom I myself would like to be.

It seems to me that it is very easy for _____ to gain admiration.

Once Rubin's scale was developed, he administered it to experimental subjects by having them indicate how strongly they agreed with each statement when different persons' names were used in the blank statement. These degrees of agreement were then converted into numerical scores.

As Rubin predicted, when the person whose name was in the blank was identified as a friend, "liking scores" were considerably higher than "loving scores." When the other person was a dating partner, both scores were very high, with "loving scores" being somewhat higher.

Rubin tested his measuring scale in other ways also. By observing as couples interacted, in addition to administering the scale to them, he discovered that couples who scored high on the "loving scale" spent more time looking into each other's eyes when they engaged in conversation; mutual eye contact is another behavioral measure of love.

In addition, couples who scored high on the "loving scale" were more likely to say that there was a high probability they would get married. Follow-up studies found that couples with high love scores were more likely still to be dating each other 6 months later than were those who scored lower on the "loving scale." All of these tests indicate that Rubin's scales provide valid measurements of what most North Americans mean by the words "loving" and "liking."

He visualized "colors of love" that were different styles adopted by individuals in their love relationships. We might think of them as components of a person's individual script that apply to love relationships with other persons.

Lee emphasized that these should not be seen as right or wrong kinds of love, but as individual variations. He also pointed out that the types were not mutually exclusive; most persons have styles that combine two or more major types. Lee sometimes portrayed the major types as being like colors on a wheel that, when spun, would combine to produce a distinctive style for each person. Lee's six "colors of love" are not associated with specific colors like red or green, but rather constitute basic love styles.

Eros is intensely passionate. Physical and sexual attraction are important components of Eros, but the physical image is based on a sense of beauty rather than lust. The erotic lover is eager to get deeply involved quickly and is quite willing to self-disclose. Although intense, Eros is self-confident and not characterized by possessiveness or jealousy.

Eros (AIR-ohs): Love style with intense emotional and sexual attachment, but without possessiveness.

The Couple by Graham Dean illustrates that eros is sexual but not blatantly so.

get the best deal they can in terms of the characteristics they define as important.

Mania is obsessive and compulsive love. It has the sexual attraction and emotional intensity of Eros, but it lacks confidence and is possessive and jealous. The manic lover has extreme emotional highs and lows, feeling especially anxious when his or her partner is not present. Manic lovers might be more prone to extreme jealousy and to violence to themselves and their partners when the relationship is threatened.

Agape is altruistic love, giving and nourishing without expecting anything in return. "Agape" is a Greek word meaning "love feast." In some Christian theologies, it is the kind of love God has for humankind and is celebrated as such in the Eucharist. Among human lovers, Agape is the rarest of Lee's types. Partners are chosen by agapic lovers because of what can be done for the chosen, not what can be done for the chooser. While sexuality might be a part of the relationship, Agape operates on a more spiritual plane.

Storge develops much more slowly than does Eros and is less intense. It is the kind of friendship an adult might have for a favorite brother or sister. Storgic lovers typically have common attitudes, values, and interests. If sexual intimacy occurs, it grows out of a developing understanding of each other, rather than the intense passion that is characteristic of Eros.

Ludus is love for mutual fun. The Ludic lover often has several partners at the same time in order to avoid too serious a relationship with any one. Although approaching love as a game and entertainment, the Ludic lover does not intend to deceive or hurt other persons; the "love contract" is often spelled out early in the game when the lover tells a partner that a long-term commitment is not wanted. Sexual activity is seen as good fun, rather than an outgrowth of a deep relationship or as an intensely passionate involvement.

Pragma forms the root of the word "pragmatic." It is practical love, based on a rational assessment of the partner's assets and liabilities. The pragmatic lover would choose a mate in somewhat the same way parents chose mates for their children when marriages were arranged. In looking for a mate, pragmatic lovers try to

Research with Lee's Typology

In a process similar to that used by Rubin in developing his Loving and Liking Scales, Hendrick and Hendrick (1992) used Lee's typology to develop their Love Attitudes Scale. This scale has been used to compare the love styles of different categories of persons.

Religiosity, a variable measuring how religious a person is, is related to love styles. The most religious persons most strongly endorsed *Storge, Pragma,* and *Agape.* They were least likely to endorse *Ludus* and *Mania* (Hendrick & Hendrick, 1987).

Ethnic differences in love styles have also been found. Contreras (in Hendrick & Hendrick, 1992) compared Mexican American couples with Anglo couples. The Mexican Americans were divided into a high-acculturation group, whose language and values were more like the dominant Anglo culture, and a low-acculturation group. No group differences were found on endorsement of Eros, Storge, or Agape. The Anglo group was less endorsing of Ludus than either Mexican American group. The high-acculturation group was most manic, followed by the low-acculturation group, with

---

Storge (STOR-gay): Affectionate, companionate style of loving.   **Ludus** (LEWD-us): Love as play and recreation.   **Pragma** (PRAG-mah): Love style emphasizing practical elements in relationships and rationality in partner selection.   **Mania** (MAY-nee-ah): Love style with strong emotional intensity, sexual attraction, jealousy, and moodiness.   **Agape** (ah-GAH-pay): Love style characterized by nurturing concern and self-sacrifice.

Anglos scoring the lowest. The low-acculturation group was higher in Pragma than either of the other groups.

Research using the Love Attitudes Scale has also been done on dating couples (Hendrick, Hendrick, & Adler, 1988). Partners in relationships tended to have love styles similar to each other. It is not known whether the similarity was negotiated as the relationship developed, or if persons with similar styles are attracted to each other. Couples who were still together a few months later were compared with those who had broken up. The major difference was that couples who scored high on Eros were likely to stay together, while those high on Ludus were more likely to break up. The latter finding is not surprising, since staying together is not necessarily a goal of the Ludic lover.

It should be noted that most of the studies utilizing the Love Attitudes Scale have been done on relatively small samples of college students. While interesting, it is not certain that the results would also apply to other groups of persons.

Passion, Companionship, and Commitment

While Lee's typology had six types of love, Hatfield and Walster (1978; Hatfield, 1988) proposed a two-type system composed of passionate and companionate love.

Passionate love, in Hatfield and Walster's system, is quite similar to Lee's Mania. If there is "love at first sight," it is probably passionate love. This type has a powerful physical component that might be associated with other forms of physical arousal. Dutton and Aron (1974) compared men who had just made a dangerous and frightening crossing of a wobbly suspension bridge with men who walked across a much safer, solid bridge. A female researcher handed all the men a questionnaire after they had crossed their bridge. The high-danger group of men exhibited more emotional and sexual arousal, and more attraction to the researcher, than did the low-danger group. Dutton and Aron concluded that the fear and anxiety were translated, in the minds of the men, into romantic interest.

Another study found that men who had just finished jogging found a woman to be more sexy and exciting than did men who had been sitting still (White, 1981). These studies suggest that, at least among men, a strong initial attraction to someone results partly from a coincidence of the presence of a socially approved love object combined with a generalized state of physical arousal. Whether that initial attraction results in "falling in love" depends on other factors such as perceived reciprocal interest (Aron et al., 1989).

Peele and Brodsky (1975) saw an analogy between romantic love and drug addiction. The person possessed by romantic love, like the drug addict, has tremendous emotional highs and lows; withdrawal symptoms; high dependency; inability to concentrate on anything else; and sometimes a difficulty performing other role responsibilities to family, work, and school.

Romantic love is nearly always short lived, and sometimes destructive. John Money (1980) explained this characteristic of passionate romantic love by comparing it to a "love blot." He noted that clinical psychologists, in studying a patient, sometimes use a Rorschach inkblot test. Patients, shown a series of essentially random ink patterns, are asked what the patterns remind them of. The answers given are purported to reveal hidden aspects about the patient. The image seen is not found in the inkblot itself, but is projected onto the inkblot by the observer. The pattern itself merely triggers what is in the mind of the observer, who then reveals a part of himself or herself.

Money (1980) concluded that individuals sometimes have images they carry around as part of their individual script. These images are triggered by, and projected onto, another person. The person doing the projecting falls in love not with the other person but with the "love blot" projected onto the other person. The other person cannot possibly live up to the idealized image thrust upon him. The initial lover becomes disillusioned, takes back the "love blot," and goes in search of a person who fits the ideal image. Whether Money's theory accurately describes what happens or not, it does provide an explanation of why romantic love rarely lasts long in the face of reality. The other type of love studied by Hatfield and Walster (1978), however, can last throughout a person's life.

Companionate love is most similar to Lee's Storge. Hatfield and Walster (1978:9) define it as "affection we feel for those with whom our lives are deeply entwined." Companionate love develops more slowly than does passionate love; it requires a sense of shared history that can develop only over time. While companionate lovers are first and foremost friends, they can also be sexual partners and have fun together, as erotic and ludic lovers might. Because the element of strong passionate attraction is absent, however, companionate love requires a greater level of intentional commitment.

Sternberg's triangle of love is an image of love made up of three components: passion, intimacy, and commitment. To Sternberg (1986, 1988), passion consists of psychological and physical arousal. Intimacy provides a sense of connectedness and closeness. As a cognitive rather than emotional component,

commitment involves a decision to maintain the relationship over time.

Sternberg proposed a typology in which types of love were determined by varying degrees of the three major components. A love with large amounts of passion, intimacy, and commitment is called "consummate love." All other types would be low in at least one of the three components. If none of the components were present, there would be no love at all (see Table 8.1).

The more similar the love triangle for each partner, the higher the probability of each feeling happiness in the relationship (Sternberg, 1986; Hendrick & Hendrick, 1992). If both Mark and Mary are very high in passion and intimacy but only moderately high in commitment, they will have a compatible relationship. On the other hand, if Mark is very high in passion and intimacy and low in commitment, while Mary is very high in commitment but only moderate in passion and intimacy, they are mismatched.

Typologies by Rubin, Lee, Hatfield and Walster, and Sternberg derive from psychology and social psychology. The major sociological perspectives also have viewpoints about love, most of which look at its mate selection aspects.

Sociological Viewpoints on Love

We mentioned in chapter 2 that the three most important theoretical perspectives in sociology are symbolic interactionism, functionalism, and conflict theory. Each of these is applied throughout the text, but can briefly be reviewed as they might look at love.

Symbolic Interactionism. Symbolic interactionism has already been applied in this chapter to the discussion about how persons learn the meaning of the symbol "love." Even if love is associated with particular brain chemicals, persons must still learn what to label the feelings they associate with the presence of the chemicals. They must learn what actions are considered appropriate for persons with such feelings.

In some societies, the feeling of passionate romantic love might be seen as something that, like stomach gas, is uncomfortable but will go away. In other societies it might be seen as a tragedy. In still others, it might form the basis of marriage. If a person enters a relationship with a loved one, the love contract and other elements of the involvement must be negotiated to form a mutual script for that couple. How persons learn, label, negotiate, and act with others in a particular society is the business of symbolic interactionism.

Conflict Theory. Conflict theory in general has not been extensively involved in the study of love, although feminism puts love in the context of other forms of exploitation of women (Collins & Coltrane, 1995). From this perspective, love is a social institution that tends to primarily benefit the "haves" of the society.

In the "battle of the sexes," Safilios-Rothschild (1977:3) argued, men are the "haves." Since men have more power, they are able to define love in such a way that women sacrifice their own best economic and emotional interests when they "love" their husbands and children. The assignment of women to the home and

	Component of Love		
Table 8.1 Sternberg's Typology of Love			
	Intimacy	**Passion**	**Commitment**
Nonlove	−	−	−
Liking	+	−	−
Infatuated Love	−	+	−
Empty Love	−	−	+
Romantic Love	+	+	−
Companionate Love	+	−	+
Fatuous Love	−	+	+
Consummate Love	+	+	+

Source: After Sternberg, R. J. 1986. "A Triangular theory of love." *Psychological Review* 93:119–35.

family "love" roles is used to encourage economic and social dependence (Kramarae & Treichler, 1985).

When analyzing love in this way, feminists are generally referring to the more passionate forms of heterosexual love. Safilios-Rothschild (1977:10–11) called for more "mature love" that would be an equal, genuine caring for the welfare and individualism of both partners. Similarly, Cancian (1987) called for an androgynous form of love in which there would be no difference in the way men and women feel and act. Dworkin (1976) argued that, in contemporary society, lesbianism is the only way for women to avoid sexist love.

Structure-functionalism. Structure-functionalism sees love as part of the glue that holds families and communities together. This approach generally refers to companionate and other kinds of love that help form attachments between brothers and sisters, aunts and uncles, close friends, and spouses. Even when mate selection is arranged, companionate love often develops as a foundation upon which couples build their lives together.

There are disagreements about whether passionate, romantic love is functional. It has the capacity, as cautionary tales such as Romeo and Juliet indicate, to be the enemy of the extended family and social stability (Jankowiak & Fisher, 1992). For reasons we have discussed above, it can be a temporary and unrealistic basis for a life-long partnership. For both of these reasons, romantic love could be seen as dysfunctional.

On the other hand, in a society where mate selection is by choice, romantic love serves as a cohesive force to help a couple through the difficult process of negotiating meanings in a new relationship. By the time romantic love wears off, companionate love has had time to develop. In this sense, romantic love can serve as a functional bridge between single status and stable marriage.

We will return to sociological theories of the mate selection process in the next chapter. Although we have by now looked at several different perspectives on what love is and how it operates, we have not addressed the question of how love develops between two persons.

Processes of Love

Of all the persons one is likely to meet in a lifetime, only a few are potential romantic lovers. Questions about how persons fall in love, and with whom, have three basic kinds of theoretical answers: individualistic compatibility, value and role compatibility, and sequential stage models.

Individualistic Compatibility Theories

This category of theories focuses on psychological or personality characteristics of individuals, and how these characteristics might incline two individuals to be attracted to each other. The two types of individualistic compatibility theories most commonly discussed are parental image and complementary needs.

Parental Image Theories. [*Selecting people like parents*] Parental image theories suggest that individuals, usually unconsciously, tend to select mates who are similar to their opposite-sex parent. Most variations on this theme stem from the psychoanalytic theories of Sigmund Freud. In his view, part of the developmental process involved boys and girls learning that love and sexual attachments are supposed to be toward members of the opposite sex. In the process, boys learn to identify with their father and desire their mother—or women like her. Girls learn to identify with their mother and see their father, or men like them, as proper love objects. Less Freudian versions of the theory more simply assume that parents are role models whose characteristics children come to see as desirable.

It is true that persons' mates tend to have at least some characteristics in common with their parents (Jedlicka, 1984). Part of the problem with researching theories of this type is determining what similar characteristic between parents and love-objects to look for. Defined broadly enough, some common characteristics could be found between any two randomly selected persons on earth. It is not surprising, then, that one's spouse has some characteristics in common with one's opposite-sex parent, but that is not proof that the similarities were the cause of the attraction. Most characteristics that one's intimate partner and one's opposite-sex parent have in common are due to the fact that individuals tend to partner with those of the same social-class background, race, and religion. Both one's mate and one's parents are likely to share those characteristics.

Complementary Needs. Complementary needs theories were first developed by Robert F. Winch (1958) to explain mate selection in societies, like the United States, where romantic love was the basis of choice. The theory assumes that individuals vary in the kind of psychological needs they have, and that they will be attracted to others who help meet those needs. If the other also has a need that the first person can meet, the two individuals have complementary needs and are likely to develop a mutual love.

Opp. att. doesn't work

This view finds popular support in the folk saying, "opposites attract," but it lacks empirical support from several studies that have attempted to test it (Booth, Carver, & Granger, 2000). It is difficult enough in research clearly to define "needs"; it is even more troublesome to define complementary ones. Most of the complementary needs that have been studied are variations of dominance and submission. Finding that one partner is generally dominant in a relationship, however, does not mean that the couple got together for that reason. The dominance might have developed after the couple fell in love. Also, the fact that one is dominant does not prove that he or she has an inherent need to be that way, or that the partner has a need to be submissive. Like other theories relying on the measurement of needs or personality traits, complementary needs approaches lack empirical support and have been severely criticized (Cate & Lloyd, 1992; Eshleman, 1994).

Value and Role Compatibility

These theories also have support from folk wisdom, this time in the sayings "birds of a feather flock together" and "water seeks its own level." Some of these perspectives focus on the importance of similarity in values, while others emphasize the compatibility of roles.

Value Theories.   Value theories suggest that individuals will be attracted to others who have similar ideas about what is good, right, and proper. Early studies using this approach found empirical evidence that premarital and marital partners do tend to have similar attitudes and values (Burgess & Wallin, 1953; Schellenberg, 1960). Value similarity can reduce the potential for conflict in relationships. Two lovers who both value either premarital chastity or premarital promiscuity, for example, are less likely to have problems about that issue than partners without such shared values. Conversations are freer among persons with shared values, as are decisions about mutual activities. When two persons share values, they are each reciprocally validated.

Although values similarity theories have commonsense support they, too, have been criticized. Kerckhoff (1974) found that couples tend to have similar values, but argued that the similarity resulted from homogamous variables and the fact that similar individuals are more likely to meet each other. Stephen (1985) also found that married couples held similar values, but he concluded that the similarities were more likely to have evolved along with the relationship rather than having been a cause of initial attraction.

Role Consensus.   Role consensus theories are similar to the value theories, except that roles are more specific behavioral expectations while values are more general. Role consensus theories propose that couples who have similar role expectations are more likely to become intimately involved (Berman & Miller, 1967; Lewis, 1973).

We have seen that persons have their own individual scripts, which provide expectations about the roles they and their partners should play. As a relationship develops, the partners need to negotiate a mutual script that will guide their interaction as a couple. If the young man and young woman both expect that the man will pay for the meals when they go out to eat, there is role compatibility in individual scripts, which will easily become their mutual dating script. If he expects to buy her meal, while she wants to buy her own, their individual scripts conflict and the mutual script must be negotiated. If the negotiation is successful, they have achieved script and role consensus even though it was lacking to begin with.

This example implies that becoming intimate is actually a process, rather than something that happens all at once. The next category of theories follows this assumption.

Sequential Stage Theories

Perhaps the most promising theories of developing intimacy are those that combine several of the elements discussed above, but assume that different elements are important at different stages in a process. Two of the most widely accepted sequential approaches are Reiss's wheel theory and Murstein's stimulus-value-role model.

The Wheel Theory of Love.   The wheel theory of love, developed by Ira Reiss (1960; Reiss & Lee, 1988), was one of the first to combine several elements into a stage theory (see Figure 8.1). Reiss imagined love as a wheel with four spokes. While all four spokes are necessary for fully developed love, they turn in a particular order, creating a four-stage process. The wheel always turns in the context of cultural and value systems.

The first stage is the development of *rapport,* which encompasses a feeling of being at ease and able to communicate with each other. Similarity of social and cultural background increases the probability that two persons will develop rapport, as do value agreement and role consensus. If a couple develops rapport, the relationship is more likely to move to the next stage.

The second stage is *self-revelation,* or what is now generally referred to as self-disclosure. As partners trust

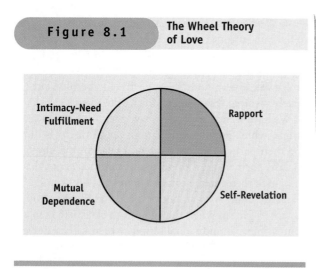

Figure 8.1   **The Wheel Theory of Love**

Intimacy-Need Fulfillment

Rapport

Mutual Dependence

Self-Revelation

Source: Adapted from Reiss, Ira L. 1960. "Toward a Sociology of the Heterosexual Love Relationship." *Marriage and Family Living* 22:139–45.

each other more, they will each reveal more information about themselves. There is sharing of dreams for the future, sins of the past, political and religious beliefs, and other value orientations. The amount of self-revelation varies by gender and social class. Women are likely to reveal their feelings more than are men (Rubin et al., 1980), and middle-class persons tend to self-disclose more quickly than do those in the working class (Rubin, 1976).

Sharing interests aids in the development of rapport.

As rapport and self-revelation increase, a couple builds up "interdependent habit systems" (Reiss & Lee, 1988:101). They each get used to doing things that require the other person. This *mutual dependence* is the third process in the development of love. Once the partners begin to work out ways of coordinating their time, money, and activities, they are much closer to a long-term commitment to each other (King & Christensen, 1983).

Couples who navigate the first three stages will then assess whether the relationship provides *intimacy-need fulfillment*. Reiss referred not to the notion of complementary needs, but to the meeting of more universal human needs such as the need for someone to love, someone to confide in, and someone to provide sympathetic understanding. These are related to the need for intimacy. Again, needs vary depending on cultural and social conditions and definitions.

The Stimulus-Value-Role (SVR) Model. The stimulus-value-role (SVR) model was developed by Bernard Murstein (1970, 1976, 1987). He found that the process of developing an intimate relationship worked somewhat differently depending on whether it took place in a "closed" or "open" field situation (Cate & Lloyd, 1992). In the "closed" setting, persons are operating in relatively well-defined role situations such as boss-employee, worker–co-worker, or professor-student. "Open" field situations, on the other hand, allow either individual the choice to initiate interaction or not. They might be in the same college class together, meet at a party or other social event, or simply come across one another in the process of day-to-day living. The SVR theory was generally fashioned to explain the development of relationships in more "open" field situations.

The *stimulus* stage involves personal characteristics that might provoke an initial response in other individuals. Since little actual interaction is involved at this point, physical attractiveness is an important component of the stimulus stage. Social exchange theory, which would look at physical attractiveness as a resource, would predict that the best-looking persons would be the most desirable potential partners. Considerable research bears out the preference for attractive partners (Walster et al., 1966; Cate & Lloyd, 1992). Persons' attractiveness can even affect evaluations of aspects of their personality. Both men and women perceive attractive persons to have more socially desirable personality traits than less attractive ones are thought to have (Saks & Krupat, 1988).

Although individuals express a preference for more attractive partners, the choices of partners might better be predicted by the "matching hypothesis." Perhaps because of fear of rejection, individuals seem to initiate relationship interaction more with others who are more nearly like themselves in levels of attractiveness. A person of average physical attractiveness is more likely to attempt a relationship with someone who is also average in looks than with one who is much more attractive (Berscheid & Walster, 1974).

Although physical attractiveness is very important at the stimulus stage, it is not the only factor. A person's reputation, behavior, sense of humor, apparent wealth and friendliness, and a number of other factors might also be considered. If both persons are stimulated enough by the potential rewards of a relationship, they will move to the second stage.

Interaction leads to the *value comparison* stage. Increasing self-disclosure leads to an appraisal of the value compatibility of the couple. Views on such matters as politics, religion, gender roles, and leisure activities are revealed and evaluated. Self-disclosure of more personal matters will probably proceed more slowly as trust develops. If this stage is negotiated, the couple will move to the third stage.

The *role* stage involves an evaluation of each person's perception of how he or she and his or her partner would be likely to play various roles in his or her relationship. Compatibility is sought in such roles as companion, lover, housekeeper, breadwinner, and parent. If behavior or conversation reveals a potential role fit, the two are likely to be married or establish some other form of relationship that involves a long-term commitment.

Although Murstein portrayed the three stages as distinct processes that occurred in sequence, more recent formulations of SVR theory hold that all three processes can operate throughout the relationship (Murstein, 1987). Some processes will dominate, however, at different stages of the relationship. Physical attractiveness is very important at the stimulus stage, but continues to operate throughout. At later stages, new forms of stimulus arise to maintain interest in continuing the relationship.

The process of establishing role and value agreement does not stop after the couple develops a relationship that they want to be permanent. They continue to communicate and negotiate meaning for the duration of their time together (Duck, 1994).

Both Reiss and Murstein developed their sequential theories to explain the process by which two persons progress from being strangers to being married. In this mate-selection context, the theories have received criticism. For one thing, many couples marry without ever establishing intimacy or role compatibility (Cuber & Harroff, 1968). On the other hand, some couples go through all the stages but never get married. Because of these criticisms, the sequential models have been presented in this chapter to explain the process of developing intimacy in relationships.

Gender Differences in Love

Interest in studying gender differences has, in recent years, produced considerable discussion about the difference in love styles of men and women. We will first review one perspective on these differences, and then summarize specific research findings.

Feminization of Love

Francesca Cancian (1986, 1987, 1989) wrote that there has been a "feminization of love" in American history. For purposes of her study, Cancian (1989:219) defined love as:

> a relatively enduring bond where a small number of people are affectionate and emotionally committed to each other, define their collective well-being as a major goal, and feel obliged to provide care and practical assistance for each other. People who love each other also usually share physical contact; they talk to each other frequently and cooperate in some routine tasks of daily life.

In Cancian's view, both men and women demonstrated this kind of love in families prior to the development of capitalism. As industrialization and capitalism proceeded, family life and work life were separated. This resulted in the public life of work and the private life of family; men were assigned roles in the public sphere while women were assigned roles in the private one (Ryan, 1979).

Cancian used the distinction, made earlier by Parsons and Bales (1956), between instrumental and expressive roles. As the "cult of domesticity" emerged, women were increasingly associated with the emotional work of expressive roles, while the men took care of instrumental tasks. Love became part of the emotional work assigned to women, so the definition of love was historically altered. The instrumental tasks of "doing things" for a loved one became separated from the former meaning of love.

Traits associated with emotion and feeling were assigned to the "feminine" role: warmth, expressiveness, revealing tender feelings, being gentle, and being aware of the feelings of others. Men were seen as independent and unemotional, with only their interest in sex having a connection to love (Rosencrantz et al., 1968; Cancian, 1986). Although working-class Americans are more likely than the middle class to see instrumental things such as giving money or washing someone's car as a possible sign of love, the general public still associates love primarily with emotion.

The belief developed that men are inherently less capable of love and intimacy than women. This view was supported by the psychoanalytic views of such writers as Chodorow (1978). Psychologists and others in the "helping professions," especially those who write for the popular press, still refer to the alleged inability of men to "share their feeling," to "commit to intimacy," and to truly love (Phillips, 1994).

Cancian argued that, if men appear not to love as much as women, it is because measurements of love are made with a feminine-biased ruler; they have tended to measure the expressive components of love, but not the instrumental and sexual ones. Even on the measures that show that women love more, Cancian maintains, the difference is generally very small. It is even possible that the stereotype that women love more than men is not borne out by available research.

Male and Female Loving Styles

Some studies do find that women are more loving than men, especially when companionate types of love are involved. Women may invest themselves more deeply in intimate relationships (Sacher & Fine, 1996). Throughout their lives, women have more close friends than do men. Interactions among women are more likely to involve expressive discussions of family and relationships, while men are more likely to gather for an instrumental purpose such as playing or watching a sport (Dickens & Perlman, 1981).

Both men and women report closer relationships to their mothers than to their fathers (Komarovsky, 1976). If a father has to spend long hours away from his family to provide financial support, this is more commonly seen as an avoidance of love rather than as an instrumental expression of love.

Some research finds gender differences, but smaller ones than might first be guessed. Adams (1968:169) found that 58% of adult urban women said that their parents and relatives were very important to them,

compared to 37% of men. Comparisons of actual contact, however, yielded different results. Of those who lived in the same city as their parents, 88% of women saw their parents weekly while 81% of men did so.

When Rubin (1973) compared scores of men and women on his "loving scale" and "liking scale" (review Finding Out 8.1), he found only small differences between men and women. When "love for partner" was measured, women scored 90.57 while men scored 90.44. In the category "liking for partner," women scored 89.10 while men scored 85.30. Only in the category of "love for friend" was there a significant difference; women scored 64.79, while men scored 54.47. Finally, in the category "liking for friend," women scored 80.21 compared to the men's 78.38.

Various studies about gender differences and Lee's "love styles" consistently find men to be more ludic (more playful) than women, and perhaps more erotic as well. Women usually score higher for Storge, Pragma, and Mania (Hendrick & Hendrick, 1992). One's gender-role orientation appears to make more difference than one's actual sex. To study this issue, Baily, Hendrick, and Hendrick (1987) used the Sex Role Inventory developed by Bem (1974). Significant differences were found on all love scales except Storge. Subjects who scored high in masculinity also endorsed Ludus the most. Those labeled feminine most endorsed Mania and Agape. The androgynous subjects also endorsed Agape, along with Eros and Pragma.

By some measures, contrary to popular perception, men behave in more romantic ways in relationships than do women. Men are more likely than women to use the word "love" first in a relationship. Kanin et al. (1970) found that men fall in love earlier in the relationship, and report being surer that they are in love. Men average higher scores on the "romanticism scale" than do women (Barich & Bielby, 1996).

These findings are often explained by the supposition that women have more to risk in relationships than do men. The "status-borrowing" model (see chapter 6) implies that women are more dependent for economic support and social status on their husbands than the husbands are on their wives. Because more is riding on their choice of partners, the argument goes, women must move more slowly and carefully in making a choice. Men, with less to lose, can afford to give freer rein to their emotions.

Another explanation is that men are more likely to base their interest on physical attractiveness, which can be determined almost immediately. Women look for other qualities that take longer to assess, so they fall in love more slowly (Collins & Coltrane, 1991). Not only do men fall in love sooner, they also stay in love longer, and are more likely to resist the breakup of a relationship (Hill, Rubin, & Peplau, 1976). Greater love by men appears to continue into marriage, after the marital choice has been made. As perceived by both partners, there are twice as many marriages in which the man loves more than ones in which the woman loves more (Safilios-Rothschild, 1977:72).

Male-female differences in love are still not fully understood, but they can be exaggerated. An emphasis on the differences can obscure the significant similarities. Both women and men believe that love is very important in their lives and are capable of strong love of both the expressive and instrumental types (Cancian, 1989; Barich & Bielby, 1996).

Biological-Evolutionary Theories

As with every other major topic in this text, there are competing theories about human intimacy. Most of the theories we examine focus on social variables, but some approaches look at the development of human intimacy as a matter of biological strategies. Attempts to explain human and social behavior by referring to biological variables have been around a long time, but a specialized modern science with that goal began to be referred to as **sociobiology** in the 1970s, especially with the work of Edward O. Wilson (1975). The goal of this approach was to "expand the Darwinian . . . model of evolutionary dynamics to explain animal behavior as well as animal morphology" (Boulding, 1978:260).

The human behaviors of interest here are those related to selection of intimates that might have resulted from human evolution. Both genetics similarity theory and sexual strategies theory offer explanations about human selection of intimates. Such theories assume that individual behaviors that increase the chances of successfully passing on one's genes will be more likely than other behaviors to appear in the next generation. As long as the environment remains similar, then, humans will generally come to exhibit behaviors best adapted to that environment (Booth, Carver, & Granger, 2000).

These behavior patterns need not be consciously thought out, but they can take the form of predispositions to behave in a certain way. As a simple example, persons who hate sexual intercourse and avoid coitus are less likely to reproduce than those who enjoy sexual intercourse. If disliking or liking sexual intercourse is an inherited trait, then the species is likely to produce individuals who tend to like sexual intercourse.

Genetic Attraction Theories

Genetic similarity theory has been advanced by Rushton, Russell, and Wells (1984). This is an extension of older theories proposing that choice of love partners was an instinctual process of some kind. In all animal species, the theory goes, individuals have a tendency to form groups with others who are genetically similar to themselves. Genetic similarities thus have a more supportive environment and, if mating results, are more likely to be perpetuated.

A genetic version of compatibility theory suggested that feelings of love toward family members have evolved as a mechanism to strengthen family and clan relationships (Williams, 1997; Davis & Daly, 1997). Since family and kin are typically like ourselves biologically, we would thus tend to be attracted to others who share those characteristics.

This might help explain why humans do not generally have romantic involvements with other species, and it is true that similar-looking persons tend to be attracted to each other. However, the most genetically similar individuals are those, like brothers and sisters, between whom romantic love does not generally occur.

Some biological theories are highly speculative, but interesting and promising. Human immunological theory, for example, has an explanation for why individuals do not want to form sexual relationships with others who are most like themselves. Every person's immune system can recognize that some molecules are not part of self and so should be destroyed. The more such dangerous molecules that can be recognized, the better the chances of the person surviving. People might seek mates who have different immunities (Booth, Carver, & Granger, 2000).

Each person has a unique "immunological fingerprint" that can be detected in body odors from sweat

Sociobiology: A scientific approach that attempts to use biological and evolutionary principles to explain the behavior of all social animals, including human beings.

(Wedekind et al., 1995). The odors from close family members become familiar over time and, since they are more likely to be similar to one's own, are avoided when searching for an intimate partner. Instead, according to this theory, people are attracted to those with immune systems different from their own. This increases the survivability of their offspring and passes that behavior along to the next generation. Perhaps the phrase that lovers have to have "chemistry" has some truth to it.

This theory does explain some interesting phenomena. Shepher (1971) studied mate selection in Israeli kibbutzim, where all children of the same age grew up together as if they were brothers and sisters. Shepher found that these children never married partners from the same kibbutz communal age group. Presumably, they were looking for partners with unfamiliar immunological fingerprints.

Additional support for the theory comes from a study of Chinese arranged marriages (Wolf, 1995). Often the marriages were arranged when the children were very young. In one form of marriage, the bride-to-be moved into the potential groom's home and the two virtually grew up together. In another form of marriage, the female continued to live with her birth parents until she was mature enough to be married. Wolf found that those who lived together as children had less successful marriages. Fewer couples had children; some marriages were never even consummated. The men were much more likely to be unfaithful. Again the familiarity prevented a good intimate relationship.

These theories are intriguing, but need much more research before they can be fully accepted. Other biologically based theories, such as evolutionary psychology, have been more fully researched.

Sexual Strategies Theory

One group of biologically based theories is called have been called "evolutionary psychology" (Wright, 1994). When applied specifically to human intimacy and attraction, the theories have been called "sexual strategies theory" (Buss & Schmitt, 1993). This view attempts to explain both male and female selection of intimates, and why the two might differ.

Adult human intimacy is explained in terms of "sexual strategies" that increase the probability of reproducing one's own genetic material. In a sense, human beings are the sperm's and egg's way of producing more sperm and eggs, and the successful human being is one who best does the job in a particular environment. Sexual strategies, however, vary for men and women

because their reproductive systems are different. The sex-irreducible difference (Money, 1980; see chapter 1) limits reproductive possibilities for women to about one child per year during a relatively short reproductive life, while the reproductive possibilities for men are much less limited. Given the opportunity, a man conceivably could father thousands of children.

Buss and Schmitt (1993) contend that gender differences in intimate human behavior can best be explained in terms of male and female sexual strategies. Although the strategies are directed toward successful mating, not all are guided by the kind of long-term mating that is implied by life-long monogamy. There are short-term mating strategies, too, that can result in the possibility of reproduction. Whether they last one night, a few weeks, or a few months, they call for somewhat different approaches than long-term strategies. For both men and women, long-term and short-term strategies have both advantages and disadvantages. Under certain social conditions, long-term strategies benefit both men and women, but short-term strategies generally have more payoffs for men, who can maximize their reproductive potential by having a great many short-term sexual relationships (Buss & Schmitt, 1993).

Generally, sexual strategies theory concludes, women get greater payoffs from long-term mating. Since they can have only a limited number of genetic offspring during their lifetimes, they are best served by finding a mate who will provide long-term, quality material support and protection for themselves and their offspring. The mating strategies of women generally reflect these requirements.

Several studies support the contention that "short-term mating will represent a larger component of men's sexual strategies than of women's sexual strategies" (Buss & Schmitt, 1993:210). Surveys find that, while men and women are equally likely to be seeking a long-term mate, men are more likely to also be seeking a short-term mate. Men report desiring more sexual partners during any given time period, from 6 months to a lifetime, and are willing to have sexual intercourse after knowing the potential partner for a shorter period of time.

One study on a college campus had attractive men and women ask strangers whether they would be willing to go on a date, go back to their apartment, or go to bed with them that evening. Of the women who were asked for a date, 50% accepted; only 6% agreed to go back to the man's apartment; and none agreed to have sex that night. Fifty percent of men who were asked to go on a date agreed, the same proportion as the women; 69% agreed to go back to her apartment, and 75% agreed to go to bed with her that night (Clark & Hatfield, 1989; see Table 8.2

Festive settings such as bars are probably more conducive to short-term than long-term mating strategies.

Short-term mating does have some payoffs for women. Immediate material support, as in prostitution and dating, is one reward. Perhaps most importantly, short-term mating can provide criteria by which long-term mates can be selected. Only by knowing a man for a period of time can she judge his ability to meet her standards. Women see promiscuity on the part of a man, or the fact that the man is in a relationship with another person, as highly undesirable characteristics for short-term relationships. While men see these characteristics as undesirable in long-term mates, they do not see them as being particularly undesirable for short-term mating (Buss & Schmitt, 1993).

That women are less likely to lower their standards for short-term mating implies they are judging all relationships on the basis of long-term standards. Men who are stingy early in a relationship are major turn-offs for women, while spending money and giving presents are highly valued. These are indicators that he has the capability and desire to support her later on.

While men and women both report high standards for long-term mates, men are more likely than women to apply less stringent standards for short-term mates (Kendrick et al., 1990). Men also have fewer criteria by which they would refuse a partner as a short-term mate; only in the case of physical attractiveness did men maintain high standards (Buss & Schmitt, 1993).

While short-term mating has considerable reproductive advantage for men, according to sexual strategies theory, so does long-term mating. Under certain conditions, at least, long-term mating can provide a better quality mate and offspring, and provide mutual cooperation and division of labor. If women demand long-term mating patterns, it will be to men's advantage to go along (Buss & Schmitt, 1993).

Sociobiologists find that the interest women have in the potential of mates to support them is the result of evolutionary programming, not just the result of a social structure that prevents women from having access to material goods. In the United States, occupationally successful women still look for mates with superior supportive capacity, even though they could support a man who has fewer resources (Townsend, 1989). Cross-cultural studies have found that economic parity of men and women in society has no statistical association with the different stress women and men place on the material resources of prospective mates (Buss, 1989).

Today's college students still have somewhat traditional expectations with respect to their potential mates. Women generally expect their partners to be more

Table 8.2	Agreement with Various Relationship Propositions, by Gender, in Percentage Accepted	
	Percentage Who Accepted	
The Proposition	**Males**	**Females**
Go on a date?	50%	50%
Go back to questioner's apartment?	69%	6%
Have sex that night?	75%	0%

Source: Clark, Roger D., and Elaine Hatfield. 1989. "Gender Differences in Receptivity to Sexual Offers." *Journal of Psychology and Human Sexuality* 2:39–55.

intelligent, to be better able to solve problems, and to make more money than they themselves do; this fulfills the provider-protector role. Men expect their wives to do more of the parenting, a fulfillment of the nurturing role (Ganong et al., 1996). These findings applied to both Black and White students.

Studies of personal want ads in newspapers provide additional support for sexual strategies theory. Baize and Schroeder (1995) did a content analysis of want ads to find out what qualities men and women used to describe themselves, and which kinds of ads got the most responses. Younger women got more responses, while older men were better received. The woman's income and education had no influence on the number of responses, but better educated and wealthier men did get more. Descriptions of personality characteristics increased the number of responses for men's ads but not for women's. Finally, mention of physical attractiveness increased responses to both men's and women's ads, but significantly more so for women's. A similar study by Goode (1998) looked at ads that included photographs, as well as written information, of the men and women placing ads. Results confirmed that men were more influenced by physical attributes and women more by financial and occupational success.

Questionnaire data of students in junior high and senior high confirmed the well documented finding that women prefer men older than themselves (Kenrick et al., 1996). The researchers also found, however, that the young men also preferred slightly older partners. They concluded that women in their 20s, the prime reproductive years, were most desirable for all ages of men, while women of all ages tend to prefer men somewhat older than themselves.

Keenan et al. (1997) surveyed college undergraduates to find out how men and women would behave on dating situations. The research was particularly interested in how much deception would be expected in the students' dates. Results showed that women expected deception in their dates, particularly with respect to the sexual interest of the men. Men, on the other hand, expected very little deception from their female dates. The researchers concluded that women are more cautious than men in dating situations because they bear the brunt of reproduction. This supports predictions made by sexual strategies theory. The basic difference between men and women, and the sexual strategies those differences imply, can help explain some emotional differences between men and women. Members of both sexes get jealous, but do so in response to somewhat different things. A woman is always secure

in the knowledge that her birth children carry her genetic material; she is not always secure in knowing that her mate will continue to provide material and emotional security. Men can never be absolutely certain that the child of their mate is actually carrying their genes. The kinds of things men and women become jealous about tend to reflect the areas of their greater insecurity.

To test this hypothesis, Buss et al. (1992) conducted a study of jealous responses to two different conditions. Men and women were asked how they would feel if the person with whom they were seriously involved was enjoying sexual intercourse with another person (sexual infidelity). They were also asked how they would feel if their current partner was developing a deep emotional attachment to another person (emotional infidelity). The result was that 60% of men said sexual infidelity was more distressing, while 85% of women thought emotional infidelity was worse.

If sexual strategies theory is accurate, men and women with the highest "mate value" should best be able to put their strategy into effect. The highest mate value for men is provided by the ability to provide material and physical security to women and their children, while the highest mate value among women is determined by their physical attractiveness and greater reproductive potential. Men and women who have high mate value should best be able to maximize their strategies (Buss & Schmitt, 1993).

Young and attractive women have a clear advantage in finding mates who can provide material support; their high mate value allows them to actualize their sexual strategies. High-value men also are able to act on their strategies. We have seen that polygyny is found in most cultures, but that within those cultures only the wealthy and powerful have more than one wife. It is these men who maximize their reproductive potential. Moulay Ismail, an emperor of Morocco who died in 1727, holds the record. He reportedly fathered more than 1,000 children (Wright, 1994).

In modern societies, however, polygyny is generally limited or banned outright, and contraception limits reproduction. Richer and more powerful men might no longer have significantly greater reproductive success. According to sociobiologists, however, human behavior is still influenced by reproductive strategies that evolved long ago. If this is true, dominant men should still get more sexual opportunities, whether they reproduce more or not. Mazur, Halpern, and Udry (1994) tested this hypothesis for teenage American males. The men were divided into categories based on how dominant they looked in pictures and asked about their sexual experiences. As was predicted, the dominant-looking men reported that they had been offered more sexual opportunities, although they had not had more offspring.

Sexual strategies theory would also predict that use of various sexual strategies would be influenced by the availability of potential mates. Barber (1999) conducted an historical analysis of women's dress styles and related them to the sex ratio, which indicates how many men are available for every 100 women. When sex ratios were low, there were fewer men available and marital opportunities were limited for women. In these periods, short skirts, which the researchers say signaled sexual availability perhaps even for short-term mating, were popular. When there were more men than there were women, the women had a better chance at long-term mating; the styles then featured narrow waists and low necklines, which signals reproductive value.

Factors other than a male's potential to provide and protect a woman and her offspring are important in women's selection of partners. One study found that such prosocial behavior as altruism in a man was more attractive than was dominance (Jensen-Campbell, Graziano, & West, 1995). This might imply that women are attracted to men who are dominant over others but altruistic to them.

Sociobiology and other gene-related theories have been controversial in the social sciences. Such theories do provide explanations for several findings about human intimacy, but the data do not necessarily prove the theory. A key theoretical assumption is that a wide variety of behaviors is passed on genetically from one generation to another. There is no definitive proof that such things as sexual interest and preferences are inherited characteristics.

Unconscious, genetically determined sexual strategies are only one possible explanation for such phenomena as age preferences in mate selection (Davis, 1998). It is quite likely, for example, that women have traditionally been interested in marrying older, more economically secure men because the opportunities for women to gain economic security on their own have been limited. As occupational opportunities for women have changed in the 20th century, the marital age gap between men and women has significantly declined (see chapter 9).

Sexual strategies theory, like many gender-based perspectives, tends to exaggerate gender differences. Doosje et al. (1999) found some differences between men and women in mate preferences, but they also found that such differences account for only a small fraction of the variation in partner desirability. Mostly, men and women are looking for similar characteristics in mates.

Personality types, compatible interests in hobbies, political views, religious views, and several other factors are of equal importance to men and women but vary significantly from one individual to another.

Sociobiology, like structural-functionalism, has also been criticized on the grounds that it is a conservative justification for the status quo. It appears to justify less sexual responsibility on the part of the man, for example. Sociobiologists and evolutionary psychologists respond that the sexual strategies and genetic predispositions are not imperatives; cultures and individuals can, through institutions and values, organize themselves so that such things as long-term commitment and responsible parenthood become the best individual reproductive strategies. Because that would become the environment in which humans operated, evolutionists would argue, the strategies would adapt accordingly. Because human beings have evolved the capacity to communicate symbolically in large groups, any behaviors resulting from biological predispositions are highly flexible and subject to social forces.

Breakdowns and Breakups

In the mate selection process, an individual typically has a series of relationships of various degrees of intensity. Before they marry, most persons face the end of at least one serious relationship. We will look at the major factors that result in premarital relationship breakup, briefly address the issue of jealousy, then address dating violence.

Relationship Risks and Strengths

One of the first studies of relationship breakups was done by Burgess and Wallin (1953). They followed 1,000 engaged couples to see which broke up and which did not. Those that broke up were more likely to have exhibited "parental disapproval of the engagement, differences in leisure-time preferences, differences in religious faith, lower levels of affectional expression and less confidence in the happiness of the future marriage" (Cate & Lloyd, 1992:84).

Twenty years later, a study of 231 college-aged premarital couples reached similar conclusions (Hill, Rubin, & Peplau, 1976). At the beginning of their relationships, couples that eventually broke up were more characterized by "lower level of love, unequal level of involvement between the partners, discrepant age and educational aspirations, differences in intelligence and physical attractiveness, a tendency to date less exclusively and shorter length of relationship" (in Cate & Lloyd, 1992:84).

Hill and colleagues (1976) also looked at gender differences in breakups. They reported that women initiated 51% of breakups, 42% were initiated by men, and 7% were by mutual agreement. Hill also found that two former partners were more likely to remain friends if the man initiated their breakup.

Hill (1976) conjectured that women end relationships more commonly because marriage is more important to them; they are more dependent on men for their money and status. Women, therefore, have to be more practical while the men can afford to be more romantic. It has also been suggested that relationships are more important to women, who are more attuned to relationship quality and are therefore more likely to end a relationship they see as low quality (Schwartz & Scott, 1994).

Relationships operate on what Waller (1951) referred to as the **principle of least interest.** The partner who demonstrates the least affection or love in the relationship is in a position of power because the end of the relationship would be less painful to her or him than to the partner.

More recent research on relationship breakup has generally confirmed the findings of Burgess and Wallin (1953) and Hill et al. (1976), but has found other factors as well. When interpersonal communication became a popular research topic in the 1980s, it was generally found that poor communication put a relationship at risk of breaking up.

Good communication does not always mean complete self-disclosure, however. Baxter and Wilmot (1985) found several "taboo topics" that dating couples avoided or were very careful about. Generally, couples avoided extensive talk about the relationship itself, about prior and other current relationships, about the norms they were developing for their own relationship, and negative things about themselves. While avoiding some of these can threaten a relationship, dwelling on them or discussing them too soon in a relationship can also be risky.

After a thorough review of studies about relationship termination, Cate and Lloyd (1992) classified relationship risks into three categories. The first is social incompatibility, which involves discrepancy in educational aspirations, social class and other social characteristics. The second category is low relationship quality, including low levels of love and poor communication. The third category is social network influence. A supportive social network, including parental approval and a set of other people who approve and treat the pair as "a couple," is important to the success of a relationship. Sprecher and Femlee (1991) found that such support from the female partner's network was an especially important predictor of relationship stability.

Jealousy

While some jealousy might be inevitable in contemporary American relationships, and in small amounts might actually benefit partnerships, it can also be very destructive. That might not be the case, however, in all societies. Hupka (1991) reviewed anthropological studies and found that cultures ranged from very rare to very common. The Todas of southern India discouraged possessiveness of either material goods or of people. There were few restrictions on sexual gratification. The American Apache, by contrast, highly prized virginity and paternity; jealousy there was common. This supports the conflict-theory position that jealousy occurs when relationships are treated like property ownership (Collins & Coltrane, 1995).

Even in property-owning societies, however, the reasons for jealousy, and the typical strength of that jealousy, varies considerably. Buunk et al. (1987) compared jealousy in seven countries. Jealousy over a partner's sexual relationship was high in all countries, including the United States, but was much higher in the Soviet Union than in Mexico. In fact, in Mexico, flirting caused as much jealousy as a sexual relationship for both men an women. Kissing caused considerable jealousy in Hungary, but it did not cause nearly as much concern in the Netherlands.

It is reasonable to conclude that jealousy occurs in all modern societies, but its origins vary. The behavioral reaction to jealousy, too, can vary. Relationship jealousy is a major cause of dating violence.

Dating Violence

Concern about family violence, which will be addressed more fully in chapter 14, has led to the discovery that there is a considerable amount of violence among dating couples. Exactly how much there is depends on how violence is defined and measured. A national survey of high school students (Centers for Disease Control and Prevention, 2000) asked, "Have you during the past twelve months been physically hurt by a boyfriend or girlfriend on purpose?" Nearly 9% said yes, including 9.3% of the females and 8.3% of the males. In

---

Principle of least interest: Idea that the partner who cares the least about the relationship has the most power.

Families in the NEWS

Traditional Swaziland Now Has Modern Dating Service

Swaziland has one of Africa's few remaining monarchies. It has a very traditional culture. It has a king, referred to as "The Mouth That Tells No Lies," who has seven wives. Swaziland has much talk of witches and magic. But it also has Internet cafes, and now it has a dating agency.

Badeli Mamba, 26, says the Swazi language has no word for "romance." There is no custom of giving roses and chocolates, of reading poetry, or of sharing candlelit dinners. Mamba could hardly believe it when she saw a newspaper ad promising to help find husbands or wives.

Pholile Hlatshwayo, a man who embroiders clothes for a living, placed the ad after helping a friend find a husband. Hlatshwayo was surprised when he was deluged with calls and decided he had a good business going. Although the police investigated, they could find nothing illegal about the operation.

His customers are about evenly divided between men and women. One man wanted help finding a second wife, but most are only looking for monogamous relationships. Some men want a new professional woman, while others use the service to find a more traditional wife.

Mamba was not impressed with the first man she was arranged to meet. She dumped the second when he confessed that he was HIV-positive. She was smitten, though, with the third. He even agreed to pay her family the traditional bride price of 17 cows. But when he failed to return from a business trip to Johannesburg, she was heartbroken.

Within a few weeks she had sufficiently recovered to call Hlatshwayo's dating service again. She still believes she can find love there.

Source: Rachel L. Swarns. **www.nytimes.com**, April 14, 2001.

addition, 12.5% of the females and 5.2% of the males reported being "forced to have sexual intercourse."

Sugarman and Hotaling (1989) looked at 20 studies and calculated the average percentage of persons involved in dating violence over their lifetimes. They estimated that 33% of males and 39% of females would be perpetrators of violence at some time during dating, while 33% of males and 36% of females would be victims. Today's figures might be lower than that. Billingham et al. (1999) found declining rates of dating aggression and violence from 1976 to 1996.

Exposure to violence in one's family of orientation appears to increase the probability of being involved in courtship violence. Most studies find that either witnessing parents engaged in abuse or being a victim of child abuse increased the chances for both men and women of being victims and perpetrators of courtship abuse (Cate & Lloyd, 1992; Foshee, Bauman, & Linder, 1999). Of course, not all young people who witness or are victims of abuse in their families of orientation will become abusive in their own relationships. If they have little exposure to violence in their schools and communities, and if they believe that dating violence is unacceptable, young men and women will be less likely to become abusers (O'Keefe, 1998).

Evidence suggests that some peer groups are more prone to violence than are others. Victims of abuse are more likely to report having peers who were also abused than do nonabused persons; perpetrators report having more friends who were also aggressive in dating (Gwartney-Gibbs, Stockard, & Bohmer, 1987).

One study asked about the respondents' exposure to parental violence, exposure to peers who had been involved in violence, and their own experiences with violence. The best predictor as to whether individuals had been victims of violence was whether they had inflicted violence, and the best predictor of whether they had inflicted violence was whether they had been a victim. This "reciprocal influence" of aggression and victimization applied to both men and women (Gwartney-Gibbs, Stockard, & Bohmer, 1987).

The research indicates that, in violent courtships, partners tend to be both aggressors and victims. The forms and consequences of violence are different for men and women, however. Men are more likely to use the more severe forms of violence, and women are more likely to be injured (Sugarman & Hotaling, 1989). For both men and women, those who are verbally abusive and threatening are more likely to be physically aggressive, and those who are physically aggressive are more likely to also be sexually aggressive (Ryan, 1998).

Most observers would see violence as a sign of serious problems in a relationship, but partners involved in courtship violence do not report that its impact is as negative as might be expected. Cate and Lloyd (1992) found that in only a few cases did an act of violence cause a relationship to break up. One fourth to one third of partners in their sample reported that violence made the relationship worse, at least for a time. In the remainder of cases, either the violence had no effect or was even reported to have resulted in improvements in the relationship. Partners who are in relationships in which abuse has occurred report no less love for each other than do those in nonabusive ones, nor do they report high dissatisfaction with their relationship (Gryl, Stith, & Bird, 1991; O'Leary et al., 1989). This finding results partly from the fact that most of the courtship violence was of a relatively minor type like pushing, grabbing, or shoving (Schwartz et al., 1997).

Rape is a form of violence that has historically been thought to occur primarily among strangers. In recent years, however, "date rape" has received considerable attention in both the popular press and research journals. This issue will be more fully addressed in chapter 10.

Summary and Conclusion

Love of some kind has probably always been part of human interaction, but it has taken many forms. In ancient Greece and Rome, love for the truth, homosexual love, and romantic love were all recognized, but they were not necessarily related to mate selection or married life.

A form of distant but interpersonal intimacy, called courtly love, developed in the late medieval times. Romanticism as a literary, artistic, and philosophical movement made romantic love acceptable. As industrialization made mate selection an individual matter, romantic love became the mechanism of choice.

Many definitions of love are available. One way to investigate the meaning of love is to see how it operates as a symbol. Such an approach has resulted in the development of ways to measure love.

The typology of love developed by Lee includes six types of love: Eros, Storge, Ludus, Pragma, Mania, and Agape. Other approaches distinguish between passionate love, companionate love, and commitment. Sternberg includes passion, intimacy and commitment in his three components of love.

The major sociological perspectives each have a different way of looking at love. Symbolic interactionism looks at the way love is learned and how it operates in the lives of individuals and families. Functionalism generally finds that love provides a mechanism to hold human groups together, although it recognizes that some forms of love might be dysfunctional. Conflict-feminism sees love as another mechanism that helps keep wealth and power out of the hands of women.

Various theories look at the way love between two persons develops. Some views are that two persons are inherently compatible because of genetic similarity, similarity to parents, or because they possess complementary needs. Another perspective looks at similarity of values and role consensus. Several variables are combined in the sequential stage theories of Reiss and Murstein.

Our society's images of love might have been "feminized" by capitalism and other forces. Research finds that women might demonstrate more companionate love, but men might be more romantic. Such differences, however, are small.

Sociobiology and related approaches explain attraction in terms of its reproductive consequences. Sexual strategies theory suggests that men benefit more than do women from short-term mating strategies, while both men and women can benefit from long-term strategies.

Most people go through more than one close, intimate relationship before they make a long-term commitment. The end of those relationships can cause great pain and unusual behavior. Dating violence can be a cause of breakup, or a response to a threatened breakup.

In conclusion, this chapter has drawn from historical, psychological and sociological sources to discuss love and the formation of intimate relationships. Not all love relationships end in marriage, so this and the next chapter have been separated. Chapter 9 looks at the process of mate selection, which today involves intimate relationships but has not always done so.

Rethinking in Context Reconsider the list of attractive characteristics you made before reading the chapter. Did your list correspond with the gender expectation suggested in the chapter? Were the characteristics you desired more compatible with short-term or long-term mating selection? What process of developing intimacy does your list imply?

Additional Resources

History of love and intimacy

Ackerman, Diane. 1994. *A Natural History of Love*. New York: Random House.
Fisher, Helen. 1992. *Anatomy of Love: The Natural History of Monogamy, Adultery, and Divorce*. New York: Norton.
Kern, Stephen. 1992. *The Culture of Love: Victorians to Moderns*. Cambridge, MA: Harvard University Press.

Studying love

Buss, David M. 1994. *The Evolution of Desire: Strategies of Human Mating*. New York: Basic Books.
Cate, Rodney, & Sally A. Lloyd. 1992. *Courtship*. Newbury Park, CA: Sage.
Hendrick, Susan, & Clyde Hendrick. 1992. *Romantic Love*. Newbury Park, CA: Sage.
Tavris, Carol. 1992. *The Mismeasure of Woman*. New York: Simon & Schuster.
Tzeng, Oliver. 1993. *Measurement of Love and Intimate Relations: Theories, Scales, and Applications for Love Development, Maintenance, and Dissolution*. Westport, CT: Praeger.
Walsh, Anthony. 1996. *The Science of Love: Understanding Love and Its Effects on Mind and Body*. Buffalo, NY: Prometheus Books.

Dating violence

Lloyd, Sally A., & Beth C. Emery. 1999. *The Dark Side of Courtship: Physical and Sexual Aggression*. Newbury Park, CA: Sage.

Internet Sites

Types of love, a love test, courtship strategies
http://world.topchoice.com/~psyche/love/

Online matchmaking
http://www.matchmaker.com/http://www.match.com/

A somewhat unusual history of love
http://www.neo-tech.com/pleasures/history.html

Dating violence
http://www.cdc.gov/ncipc/dvp/yvpt/datviol.htm

For links to these sites and additional resources, visit the *Families in Context* Web site at:

http://sociology.wadsworth.com

Chapter 9

Mate Selection

Prelude

There is probably no more important process in our lives than the selection of someone we hope will be a life partner. The outcome of that process affects our personal happiness, our economic potential, our standing in the community, and what we pass along to the next generation. Yet how much do we really think about our partner choices?

When Janeen was in high school she spent several months actively thinking about where she would go to college. She discussed the matter often with her parents, her friends, and her school guidance counselor. She got catalogs from several of her top choices, comparing costs, size and location of the school, and the school's reputation for good scholarship and social life. She talked to several adults about how they liked the colleges that they had attended. She made lists of advantages and disadvantages for each college. She applied to her top five choices, then compared the kinds of scholarships she qualified for at each one.

Once she got to college, it took her 2 years of investigation before deciding on a major. When her parents said they would help her buy a car, she checked out *Consumer Reports* and other car-rating sources. It often took her several hours of comparison shopping before buying a pair of shoes or a new blouse. She nearly always checked the reviews before she would spend money going to a movie.

In September of her senior year in college, Janeen broke up with her long-term boyfriend, Armando, when she found out he was cheating on her. In November she met Jarrad and they hit it off right away. In March he asked her to marry him, and she immediately said yes. There were no consultations with friends or family, no background checks, and no minutes spent thinking about it before making the decision. They were married in June.

Is this the most effective way to find a life's partner?

The selection of mates is always a combination of individual choice and social forces. In postindustrial America, individual forces such as those discussed in the last chapter are a much bigger part of mate selection than has been the case historically. Social forces, however, are still at work. Love may help determine whom one marries now, but a whole host of variables seem to influence with whom one is likely to fall in love. It is to those variables that we now turn our attention.

We saw in the last chapter that love has a history; we will find in this chapter that forms of courtship, too, can be looked at in historical perspective. Preindustrial mate selection will be reviewed, and then courtship patterns in the four phases of the industrial revolution will be outlined. Class and race differences will be covered as part of the discussion of courtship in the postindustrial era.

Many theories of intimacy (see chapter 8) noted that individuals are attracted to persons who are similar to themselves. In this chapter, we will look more closely at homogamous variables, especially race, religion, and social class, which affect the mate-selection process. Other factors affecting mate selection will also be mentioned, including nonmarital relationships that end before marriage, premarital cohabitation, and relationships among gays and lesbians. Homosexual couples raise numerous legal issues, a brief discussion of which will end the chapter.

> *Thinking Ahead* Suppose you ran an agency whose task it was to select mates for customers. You get paid when a couple you arrange gets married, plus an annual fee for each year the marriage lasts. What kinds of characteristics are you going to look for in matching your couples? How will you decide which individuals to introduce to each other?

History of Mate Selection

Some form of marriage is virtually a universal characteristic of human groups, but the way people choose—or are chosen—to be married to a particular partner has varied considerably. We will first discuss a continuum that helps understand the diversity of mate-selection processes. Then we will see how the processes are affected by particular modes of production.

The Mate-Selection Continuum

Adams (1995) developed a continuum describing mate-selection options (see Figure 9.1). At Point A on the continuum, individuals have no choice in their own mate-selection process. One way this can happen is through **arranged marriage,** where the potential couple's marriage is determined by someone else, usually their fathers. This system is used in many parts of the world today, including India. A similar approach makes use of some third party, or matchmaker, who is employed by the families of the marriageable men and women. This method is still common in Japan, although customs in that country are moving toward choice on the continuum because, increasingly, the matchmaker is hired by the individual mate-seekers and many youth are selecting their own mates (Quale, 1988).

In some societies, mate selection is controlled, not by relatives or matchmakers, but by restrictions that are a normative part of the social structure. Such systems, sometimes called **prescriptive mating systems,** require or prohibit marriage of certain persons based on kin relationship or other social category. Some can become quite complex, as is this example of the Iatmül of New Guinea:

The Iatmül say that they use sister-exchange, cross-cousin marriage at first-cousin level between a man and his father's mother's brother's son's daughter (or a woman and her father's father's sister's son's son). . . . [They also say that they do not allow a man to marry his wife's brother's daughter or his mother's brother's daughter, even though women do in fact occasionally marry their father's sisters' husbands or their father's sisters' sons (Quale, 1988:54).

The researcher goes on to say that it is not altogether clear that the Iatmül follow their own rules all that closely, but if they did it would seriously limit the number of one's possible mates. However it is accomplished, societies at the "completely controlled" end of the continuum allow the marriage partners no choice in the mate-selection process.

Point B on the mate-selection continuum represents the position labeled "restricted choice." Mate selection in colonial America would fall roughly at this point. Because there were so few potential partners of the appropriate age and social desirability, individuals actually had only a few possible partners from which to choose. Even today, some parents so control the lives of their children that the potential number of mates is limited because the number and kind of persons they meet are controlled. This can be done by sending children to private schools, summer camps, certain religious activities, or selected colleges.

Point C on the continuum represents "open choice." At this point, each individual has complete freedom to decide who his or her mate will be. Farber, writing in

Prescriptive mating

Figure 9.1   **The Mate Selection Continuum**

Completely Controlled By Arrangement or Normative Structure	Restricted Choice	Open Choice; Universal, Permanent Availability	Total Choice; Random Liaisons, No Marriage System
A	B	C	D

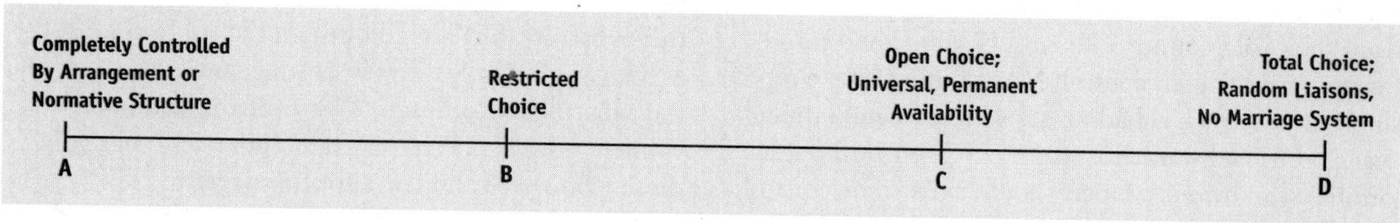

Source: Adapted from Adams, Bert N. 1995. *The Family: A Sociological Interpretation,* p. 108. Fort Worth: Harcourt Brace.

Arranged marriage: Mate selection by someone other than the potential mates.   **Prescriptive mating system:** A set of norms that specify whom a person should marry.

1964, asserted that the United States was moving rapidly to this position, which he called **universal permanent availability.** Everyone is a potential mate, even if he or she is already married. They can, if they choose, get a divorce and marry someone else, so they are always available for mate selection.

At point D on the continuum there is no marriage system and no pretense of permanent relationships. Adams (1995) refers to relationships at this point as random liaisons. The extreme end of the mate-selection continuum is, therefore, the point at which there is actually no selection of marriage partners at all.

Preindustrial Mate Selection

Nearly all agrarian societies were toward the extreme left end of the continuum (see Figure 9.1). Marriages served the purposes of political alliances and property consolidation for wealthy families, and lineage continuity for all families. Families and kin groups, therefore, had a significant interest in marriages, and were heavily involved in arranging them.

Hunting-gathering societies, too, tended to be at the "controlled" end of the continuum, but property exchange was less important to these groups who owned little property. Instead, endogamous restrictions were involved in determining mates.

In few societies were the potential mates completely without choice. Both the Roman and medieval Christian practices specified that marriage could not occur without the consent of the mates, although the marriages were formally arranged and normative constraints made refusing consent rare.

In preindustrial America, parental control of mate selection was probably weaker than was the case in Europe at the time. New immigrants were separated from their "old country" kin groups who could no longer have as much control. Many immigrants were single and older, and had no access to parental input even if they had wanted it (Coontz, 1988). Although families who owned property could exert some control over the mate selection of their offspring by regulating the transfer of ownership, acquisition of agricultural resources was easier in North America than in Europe, where all available land was already claimed (Glenn & Coleman, 1988).

Because there was a labor shortage in the "new" world, men and women were encouraged both to marry and to procreate. In some communities, bachelors were harassed, fined, or run out of town if they refused to marry. Remaining single was considered slothful and rebellious (Murstein, 1974).

Even though the society was moving to the "restricted choice" point on the mate-selection continuum, the choice was based on Pragma, not Mania (see chapter 8). The family was still seen as both an economic producing and a consuming unit, and these factors dictated mate selection.

Other forms of love, however, were recognized. Bundling (see chapter 3) and other courtship practices allowed for the development of some amount of passionate attachment. Both the Puritans and the Quakers recognized the importance of affection to the success of the marital unit. Intimacy and affection were connected to the courtship process relatively early in American history (Rothman, 1984).

Courtship in Industrial America

The process of mate selection became increasingly choice-oriented as the industrial revolution unfolded. The four phases of industrialization can be used to trace the historical development of courtship (Lenski & Lenski, 1987; see chapter 4).

Phase 1 (1760–1850). When the industrial revolution dawned, most Americans lived in rural areas where the potential number of mates was quite small. First marriages occurred at a later average age than is the case today. Informal interaction among the young took place at churches, schools, and social gatherings. Unwed persons, especially women, were expected to maintain their virginity, but not all of them did so. In the 1770s, as many as 30% of brides were pregnant at the time of their marriage (Rothman, 1984). Births to unmarried women, however, were very rare, indicating that only those who were candidates for marriage were likely to have sexual intercourse. If pregnancy resulted, marriage quickly followed.

The split between work and home caused by industrialization also divided the lives of men and women. Interaction between the two became increasingly formalized,

---

Universal permanent availability: A social condition wherein any individual is always a potential mate for anyone else.

especially among those considered to be of courting age. At least in the middle and upper classes of established cities, young men and women could not speak to each other until they had been formally introduced. The first stage in the courtship process was typically an invitation issued to the young man by a young woman's mother. He could then visit the prospective bride's home. After the first visit, the young woman herself could, if she wished, invite him to return (Bailey, 1988). If a couple thought of marriage, the young man would formally ask his intended bride's father for her hand in marriage.

Phase 2 (1850–1900).   In the second half of the 19th century, premarital sexual norms became even more restrictive than had been the case in earlier eras. The attitudes of this era were known as **Victorianism,** after Queen Victoria of England, who reigned from 1837 to 1901. The increased formality of courtship and sexual norms came as romantic love was increasingly considered acceptable as a form of mate selection.

Working-class families lacked the formal control over their children that was enjoyed by middle-class parents, and they also lacked privacy in their homes. Rather than see each other in their homes, working-class youth did their courting in public places. The couple would agree, almost always in response to the man's initial query, to do something together on a certain date and time. He would go to her house, meet her parents, and then take her to the agreed-upon event. The time at which she was to be returned home was typically set in advance, often by the girl's father. Thus was born the custom of "dating," which eventually spread to the middle and upper classes (Bailey, 1988).

The expanding American frontier influenced 19th-century mate selection. There were typically many more men than women in the earliest wave of settlement. Some men married before leaving for the frontier and sent for their wives after they were settled. Others married Native American wives, and still others remained single. Some selected mates from a distance, using intermediaries or selecting "mail-order brides" (Steinfirst & Moran, 1989).

Phase 3 (1900–1940).   Urbanization continued in the early 20th century, and the courtship practice of dating became well established. This occurred along

Hooking up, Victorian style. Her mother is probably in the next room, listening to every word.

with an increasing emphasis on romantic love and the emergence of adolescence as a distinct period in the life cycle (Bailey, 1988). Increasing numbers of young persons stayed in school longer. Male-female interaction, uncontrolled by parents, occurred in schools as well as factories and other workplaces. Many other forces were at work in the development of the dating custom, including the development of mass culture and "the shift from rural to urban society, the emancipation of women, the emphasis on companionate marriage, widespread ownership of cars, the emergence of motion pictures, and the resulting decrease in community control" (Cate & Lloyd, 1992:22).

The more formal interactions of earlier times had taken place in the fairly conscious context of a mate-selection process. While dating began that way, it evolved into an activity valued for its own sake. As the "major recreational pastime of youth" (Waller, 1951), dating changed the interaction between young men and women. Since courting had previously occurred in the young woman's home, she and her parents had

---

Victorianism: A value system emphasizing a strong sense of duty and strict sexual morality; after Queen Victoria of England.

considerable control. This was partly because it was assumed that women needed protection from young men's voracious sexual appetites.

The dating process allowed more opportunity for sexual experimentation. One study done in the 1930s found that, while 87% of women born before 1890 were virgins at marriage, only 30% of those born after 1910 were (Terman, 1938). While Terman's study resulted in higher figures for sexual activity than did other studies of the time (Caplow et al., 1982), it is generally agreed that major changes occurred in that time period.

Another result of the dating custom was reported in Willard Waller's (1937) classic study, "The Rating and Dating Complex." By that time, dating was not so much about love and mate selection as about competition and status attainment (Bailey, 1988). Although money and wealth were always important in courtship, they became a more obvious factor in the dating competition. Men rated highest if they could afford an automobile, flowers, fancy dinners, and expensive entertainment. Women were valued for their physical attractiveness and their ability to have a number of dates with different men while remaining sexually "pure" (Waller, 1937).

Phase 4 (1940–1970). Increasing use of the telephone gave adolescents and young adults more opportunity for private, unsupervised conversation. Automobiles gave them the opportunity to be with each other in unsupervised settings. Increasingly, young people moved out from under their parents' influence and took over their own courtship.

By midcentury, courtship in America was centered almost entirely on a well-defined process. Dating began in junior and senior high school. School dances, movies, and other activities provided the stated reason for making the date. At first, most young persons "dated around" with more than one partner, but relationships got more serious and exclusive over time. At some point, the couple might agree to "go steady," a step made public by the exchange of a ring, article of clothing, or other symbol (Bailey, 1988).

Most individuals went steady and broke up with others before getting engaged. Engagements implied more commitment, and were less often broken than were "going steady" agreements. A number of young men and women, especially those not intending to go to college, married the person with whom they were going steady when they graduated or dropped out of high school.

Relationships of those who were leaving for college, the military, or out-of-town work were more likely to end, and the dating process began anew with other partners (Gordon, 1981; Modell, 1983; Rothman, 1984).

Although the dating scene was somewhat disrupted by the Great Depression and World War II, the courtship pattern of dating, going steady, and marrying for romantic love returned in full force in the 1950s (Bailey, 1988). Sprecher and Metts (1989) characterized this romantic ideal as having five basic elements (in Hendrick & Hendrick, 1992:61):

1. Love at first sight.
2. There is only one "true love" for each person.
3. Love conquers all.
4. True love is absolutely perfect.
5. We should choose a partner for "love" rather than for other (more practical) reasons.

The romantic ideal had become institutionalized as the normative basis for mate selection in the United States. It was glorified in popular music, movies, novels, and television shows. Because of the romantic ideal in courtship patterns and other factors, average age at marriage in the 1950s was the youngest of any time in the 20th century (Mintz & Kellogg, 1988).

The dating script of the time contained well-defined gender roles. Men made the initial plans and asked the women to go along. Men arranged transportation and did the driving, if they had access to a car. On formal occasions, at least, he opened doors for her. Women essentially had right of refusal and veto power over his initiatives. As the couple got closer to "going steady," it was assumed they would be together on various occasions.

Males were the sexual initiators at each step of a well-defined, and often drawn-out, series of scenes. Although it might vary by class and ethnicity, the sequence of events known as "petting" was predictable (Gagnon, 1977:174): "experimentation begins with hugging and kissing, moves on to tongue kissing, to his touching her breast, his touching her genitals, perhaps her touching his genitals, and then simulated intercourse (clothed or nude) . . . ." For some couples who were going steady or were engaged, intercourse would follow. The male's role was to attempt to move as rapidly as possible through the steps; the female's role was to control that process. There was a clear double standard, which will be addressed later in this text, but there appears to have been little change in the incidence of premarital intercourse, which was about the same in the 1950s as it had been in the 1920s.

Courtship in Postindustrial America

The American postindustrial era is clearly one of diversity in mate selection. Among some who live in homogeneous ethnic communities, parents have considerable direct influence on the mate selection of their children. For the country as a whole, however, there has been significant change toward the open choice side of the continuum (see Figure 9.1). Various new approaches to getting together have evolved along with technology.

Getting Together

As society moved toward the "total choice" end of the mate-selection continuum, mechanisms of choice changed. Traditional dating norms remain part of courtship, especially among high school students and in the southern and midwestern parts of the United States (Rose & Frieze, 1989). Particularly among urban young adults, however, a pattern known as "getting together" has evolved. This is less formal and appears more spontaneous (Murstein, 1986; Whyte, 1990).

Unattached persons go out or meet in groups in shopping malls, at parties, for recreation or sports, in bars, or other locations. From these groups, pairs sometimes split off. As a couple becomes more serious about their relationship, they are more likely to arrange to meet each other away from the group. Stages in the relationship are less likely to be identified by such tokens as exchanging rings or making announcements of "going steady." The degree to which the partners see themselves, and are seen by others, as an exclusive, committed couple is less clear than in traditional dating.

Gender roles are now less clearly defined than was the case in the traditional dating script. It is more acceptable for the woman to initiate conversation with the man and to suggest activities. Splitting the costs of being together is more common than was previously the case, although it is still rare for the woman to pay the man's expenses. It would appear that, when the couple has access to a car, the male is still primarily responsible for driving. Formal occasions such as proms are more likely to revert to more traditional roles.

Although social movement toward gender equality and androgyny is part of the reason for the change in courtship patterns, change in age-appropriate behaviors is also a factor. Average age at first marriage is higher than at any time in the 20th century and would appear to be increasing (see Figure 9.2). In 1890, the average age at first marriage was 26.1 for men and 22.0 for women. The age then continually declined until 1959, when it was 22.5 for men and 20.2 for women. The average age then began to climb and in 1998 stood at

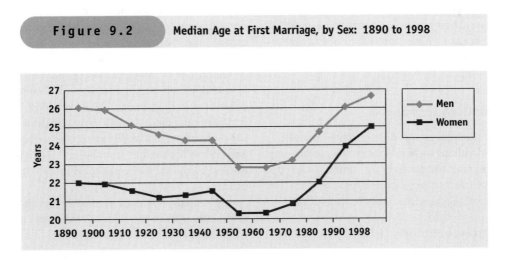

Figure 9.2   **Median Age at First Marriage, by Sex: 1890 to 1998**

Source: U.S. Bureau of Census, 1999. Current Population Survey, Historical Time Series, Table MS2.
http://www.census.gov/population/socdemo/ms-la/tabms-2.txt.

historic highs of 26.7 for men and 25.0 for women. Although there has been a U-shaped curve for average age at first marriage, there has been a continual decrease in the difference between the age of the average groom and that of the average bride. In 1890 the groom was 4.1 years older; in 1998 the groom was only 1.7 years older.

Although Americans now get married at somewhat older ages, dating begins at younger ages. The median age at which dating begins dropped from 16 to 13 between World War I and the early 1980s (Hennessee, 1983), and the average age at which adolescents first go steady dropped from 17 in 1958 to 15.9 in 1978 (Bell & Coughey, 1980).

Because participants start at a younger age and get married at a later age, individuals average a considerably longer period when they are single and potentially available for a mate. A typical courting period is now 10 years, considerably longer than in earlier eras. Dating and getting together have therefore become somewhat more separated from the process of selecting a spouse and have become more a way of life in itself. In addition, first-married partners are much more likely to have had previous intimate partners—and more of them—than at any previous time.

In searching for partners, American adolescents today focus more than do those from more traditional societies on individualistic qualities such as being fun, being sexy, and having money. Guatemalan youngsters, by contrast, focus more on such qualities as liking children and being a good parent; being fun and good looking is unimportant (Gibbons et al., 1996). Americans, then, are likely to carry their adolescent perceptions of the ideal opposite-sex person well into adulthood. These ideals might not be the best criteria for selecting a lifelong partner.

The Selection Process

The choice of the right spouse is extremely important, both to the individuals and to a society that is concerned about the stability of the marriage institution. In spite of that, relatively little attention has been paid to that process by sociologists in recent years (Glenn, 2000).

Social Exchange Theory. Most sociological analyses of the mate-selection process rely on some version of social exchange theory (see chapter 2). Norval Glenn (2000) developed the specific version of social exchange theory discussed here, especially as the theory is used to explain why mate selection might be less successful today than in the past.

According to social exchange theory, the search for a spouse is similar to the search for goods and services in the economic marketplace. Each person has a varying degree of resources, such as intelligence, looks, sense of humor, or money. Using those resources on the **marriage market**, each individual attempts, in a way that appears to be rational, to get the best deal possible in a spouse.

In a particular subculture at a particular time there are shared ideas about what makes a desirable mate, so individuals can be roughly ranked in **general marital desirability**. In the United States today, wealth and earning capability are generally thought to be desirable, especially for men, and physical attractiveness is particularly desirable in women. These and all other agreed-upon resources provide a way to measure the desirability of each potential partner. It is as if each person could be evaluated and assigned a score of 1 to 100, with the highest score being the most desirable. In that case male 100s would marry female 100s, male 40s would marry female 40s, and so on because they would be matched in terms of general marital desirability.

Especially in a diverse society like the United States, however, there is considerable individual variation in desires, so there is also **person-specific marital desirability**. Being a good dancer, or poet, or mountain bike rider, might be very desirable for some persons, but is not necessary for most. Because of these individual preferences, not every man has the same points score for every woman, and vice versa.

Glenn (2000) suggests that a good match is likely to be one in which each spouse is more desirable to each other than to the general marriage market. Individuals in a particular couple might only be 50s in general marital desirability, but be 90s to each other because their person-specific marital desirability is so high. Each one thinks he and she got a great deal in the exchange process.

Individuals, however, are not always the best judges of their own fit in the marriage market, especially when infatuation and other irrational factors interfere. The process works better when the choice is

---

Marriage market: The concept that individuals or their families shop and bargain for mates in a way similar to economic transactions. **General marital desirability:** The desirability of a person as a mate based on socially agreed-upon resources.
Person-specific marital desirability: The desirability of a person as a mate based on another individual's particular preferences.

influenced by one's family and friends, and by a thorough knowledge of one's own and potential partner's desirability. This, according to Glenn, leads to some obstacles to good marital matching in contemporary society. In agricultural societies, the **pool of eligibles** was generally much smaller than it is today because the number of people with whom one interacted was limited. Today, the potential pool of eligibles is much larger, making it more difficult to settle on one choice. Also traditionally, a person's family and friends generally knew a great deal about potential mates and their families and could influence a person's marriage market process.

In the rapidly industrializing 1950s, Glenn suggests, marriage choices were perhaps better than is the case today. There were some problems generated by the young age at which many married, but there is little evidence that even the young marriages then were any more or less happy than today's marriages; they were less likely to end in divorce then. Most individuals selected their mates during high school or college. These institutions provided situations in which most interaction was with potential mates, but in relatively supervised situations. A mate shopper would know a good deal about the resources of potential mates, both from a personal perspective and from the perspective of their friends and families.

Today, with later marriage age, selection typically occurs after one's education is complete and the individual is in the workforce. Coworkers are likely to include people who are not in the pool of eligibles because they are the wrong age, are already married or otherwise involved, or are of an inappropriate level of authority in the workplace. Also, early adulthood is a time of both social and geographic movement, thus reducing the influence of family and friends. In short, it is probably more difficult today to find and stay with a compatible mate than in previous times (Glenn, 2000).

Social exchange theory provides a useful model for describing what kinds of people get married to each other, but the more personal kinds of predictions are more difficult. It is true that rich people tend to marry rich people, but that does not tell us who among the rich they will marry. Such characteristics as wealth are easy to measure, and perhaps looks can be quantified, but it is much more difficult to assign resource values to such things as personality or sense of humor. To fully test social exchange theory, such measurements would be necessary.

New Rational Partner Selection. Because of the difficulty in meeting and learning about potential mates and because of the high rate of failure in marriages,

College students have a larger "pool of eligibles" than they will at any other time in their lives.

Pool of eligibles: The group of individuals constituting realistic potential mates.

Americans might be altering their mate-selection procedures to reduce risk and improve odds of success. There is some evidence that the mate-selection process is becoming increasing rationalized, which conflicts somewhat with ideals of romance (Bulcroft et al., 2000).

An indicator of rationalization of the selection process is the increasing use of a number of self-selection methods. Large newspapers now provide the opportunity for singles to place advertisements for himself, and to respond to ads from others. "Voice mail" is available. Private matchmakers have made a comeback, although it is now more commonly the interested single, rather than his or her parents, who avail themselves of the service. Some matchmakers screen applicants, and some produce videocassette recordings to be viewed by prospective dates (Woll & Young, 1989).

For a small minority of men, there are still women who advertise their availability as mail-order brides. By one estimate, there are 2,000 to 3,000 such marriages annually in the United States (Belkin, 1986). Catalogues contain photographs of women who are usually from developing countries such as the Philippines or South Korea, although increasing numbers have been from Russia since the breakup of the Soviet Union (Schillinger, 1994). Men who use the services are often disillusioned with American women, preferring ones who they believe will be more traditional, less promiscuous, and more deferential (Krich, 1989). The men agree to pay for the women's passage to the United States, in addition to a fee. The women, typically 20 years younger than the men, hope to have a more prosperous life and better opportunities than they anticipated having in their homeland (Belkin, 1986).

Women are not the only ones who advertise for spouses. The popular press report several marriages resulting from advertisements by men living in remote locations such as Alaska. Like the 19th-century frontier, but unlike other contemporary states, Alaska has more single adult men than single adult women. Magazines such as *Alaska Men USA* serve as a catalogue of such men (Johnson, 1993). Now online at www.alaskamen-online.com, it is the Alaskan men who advertise for mates, while it is the overseas women who do so. In both cases, however, the woman is expected to move to where the man is, while the man is expected to pay the expenses. While mail-order spouses are not new, some of the technology linking them is. Widely separated couples now communicate by e-mail and leave messages on computer network bulletin boards. Computer-mediated dating might provide a relatively safe and easy way to initially meet people, but the interactive process is different in a number of ways from face-to-face dating (Merkle & Richardson, 2000).

Whether the new rational approaches to partner selection are effective or not is not altogether clear. Such processes have, however, been a boon to researchers who study the qualities that men and women are looking for in a mate. When people write an ad for a paper or are interviewed on videotape, they carefully choose what to say about themselves and the kind of person they are looking for. These descriptions provide raw data for content analysis.

Several researchers have taken advantage of this research opportunity. Generally the research finds that men and women are looking for similar qualities but that definite gender differences exist. Men are more likely to look for younger women who are attractive; women tend to look for older men who are financially secure (Baize et al., 1995; Goode, 1996, 1998; Sakai & Johnson, 1997; Stack, 1996). People also look for partners who are similar to themselves in race, religion, and social class.

Class and Race Differences

There is some variation in the mate-selection process by social class, race, and ethnicity. Upper-class parents exert the most control over their children's dating. In some parts of the country, debutante balls and "coming out" parties are still given to announce the entry of upper-class young women into the pool of eligible mates. Activities are planned for the young at country clubs, private schools, and other places that are inaccessible to adolescents who are not in the upper class. Engagements are typically announced in the newspaper society pages, and weddings are expensive, formal, and elaborate affairs.

Middle-class parents have some control over their children's mate selection, but less so than in the upper class. Dating, going steady, and formal engagements remain common. Formal weddings, which were disparaged by some in the 1960s and 1970s, appear to be making a comeback now in the middle class. For inter-class marriages, wedding styles tend to follow the pattern generally accepted in the social class to which the groom belongs (Whyte, 1990).

Dating is less formal, and less controlled by parents, in the lower classes. It was in this class that "getting together" first appeared as an alternative to dating. Formal engagements are less common, and are less likely to be mentioned in the local newspapers. Large, formal weddings, too, are less common (Schwartz & Scott, 1994).

Mate-selection among African Americans generally follows the same class patterns as are found among Whites. Dating and formal engagements are more common among middle- and upper-class Blacks just as for upper-class Whites. Informal patterns are more common among the poor of both racial groups (Staples, 1991).

Homogamy in Mate Selection

It is impossible for an individual to be completely free from society's influence on selection of his or her husband or wife. Even in 21st-century America, where people pride themselves on their freedom, norms govern and limit their choices. These norms have been identified by social scientists and given descriptive names. The Greek term *gamous,* which means spouse, forms the basis of several words dealing with marriage partners.

One set of terms could be used to describe whether, in a particular society's mate-selection process, the mates were chosen from within the group or from outside the group. The terms *endo-* and *exo-* mean "inside of" and "outside of," respectively. The resulting words **endogamy** and **exogamy** describe whether mates are selected from inside the group or outside the group. Since endogamy and exogamy are words typically employed by anthropologists, the group referred to is usually a small group such as the clan or tribe. The incest taboo is an exogamous rule, since it requires marriage outside some specified family relationship.

In complex societies such as the contemporary United States, individuals do not commonly divide themselves into tribes and clans in the same way as do hunting-gathering groups, so the terms *endogamy* and *exogamy* are not particularly useful. We can, instead, note whether mates are selected from those individuals who are similar or different in terms of social characteristics such as religion, social class, and race. The root *gamous,* combined with "homo-" (same) and "hetero-" (different), describes these options.

The terms **homogamy** and **heterogamy** thus distinguish between those cases in which mates have similar characteristics from those in which mates are different. In the United States, the folk saying "Birds of a feather flock together," which implies homogamy, is truer than "Opposites attract," which implies heterogamy. American marriages tend to be homogamous with regard to religion, social class, race, and other characteristics.

If mates were selected without regard to social classifications, the American marriage system would look different than it does today. Since about 72% of Americans are non-Hispanic Whites (see Figure 7.4), for example, about 72% of Whites would marry other Whites if marriages were racially random. Also, if marriages were racially random, about 72% of Blacks would marry Whites, and 72% of Hispanics would marry Whites, and 72% of Asians would marry Whites. Clearly, this is not the case. Individuals are more likely to marry someone of the same race than these random predictions would indicate. Evidence of this **assortive mating** process is found not only with race but with social class and religion as well. The marriage system is largely homogamous, both in the United States and around the world (Kalmijn, 1998). Intermarriages between individuals of different groups are sometimes called **mixed marriages.**

Typically, only those marriages that are contrary to homogamous expectations are referred to as mixed. A marriage between a man and a woman, even though men and women are clearly different, is certainly not referred to as mixed. Marriage between a left-handed and a right-handed person is also not referred to as mixed because society does not see handedness as a criterion for mate selection and is therefore not covered by homogamous norms.

If marriages were by chance, there would always be more mixed marriages among the smaller group than among the larger group. For example, nearly all left-handed persons have right-handed partners, while relatively few right-handers have a left-handed partner. In the above racial example, Blacks would have a much higher rate of mixed marriages, simply by chance, than would Whites, because there are more Whites. Before we can say that assortive mating is a real social phenomenon, we would have to see that the actual rate of mixed marriage for that group is lower than one would expect

---

Endogamy: Mate selection from within the group.   **Exogamy:** Mate selection from outside the group.   **Homogamy:** Selection of mates from those with similar social characteristics.   **Heterogamy:** Selection of mates from among those with different social characteristics.   **Assortive mating:** The phenomenon that persons marry others like themselves more often than would be expected by chance.   **Mixed marriage:** Marriage between individuals with characteristics that society generally defines as grounds for homogamy.

simply by chance. This criterion holds true with respect to race, religion, and social class.

Racial Homogamy

The strongest homogamous norms in the United States have been based on race, especially where Black/White marriages were concerned. In fact, laws against racially mixed marriages were enacted in several southern states. These **miscegenation laws** were still on the books in 16 states in 1967. Then, in the case of Loving v. Virginia, the Supreme Court struck down a miscegenation law that had been passed in 1924 (Ramu, 1989; Harrison & Gilbert, 1992). Support for such laws still exists, but has decreased rapidly in recent years. The General Social Surveys (Davis & Smith, 1998) found that, in 1972, 39.3% of Americans agreed that laws should exist against Black/White marriages. By 1998, that figure had dropped to 11.2%, including 12.9% of Whites and 4.2% of Blacks.

Although interracial marriages are no longer illegal, such intimate relationships are still informally considered deviant in some segments of the American population. One recent survey found that 66% of Whites would oppose the marriage of a close relative to a Black, and 45% would oppose a relative's marriage to an Asian or Latino (Wilkerson, 1991:A11). These expectations can raise unique issues for mixed-race relationships that require good communication and trust to resolve (Foeman, 1999).

Figure 9.3 reveals that, although the number of interracial couples has increased in the United States since 1960, they remain only a small percent of all couples. Black/White marriages never reached 3% of all marriages, and the total of all interracial marriages involving Blacks and Whites is less than 5% of all marriages. These are racial categories, so Hispanics are listed as Black, White, or other. Marriages involving a Hispanic and non-Hispanic would constitute about another 3% of all marriages (*Statistical Abstract, 1995*).

Women in some groups have had very high rates of out-marriage. Historically, 48% of all Native American women were married to Whites, while only 46.3% were married homogamously. Almost one third of Japanese American women, one fourth of Filipino women, and one eighth of Chinese American women were married to Whites. At the same time, however, less

| **Figure 9.3** | **Black or White Interracial Marriage, as Percent of All Married Couples, 1960 to 1998** |

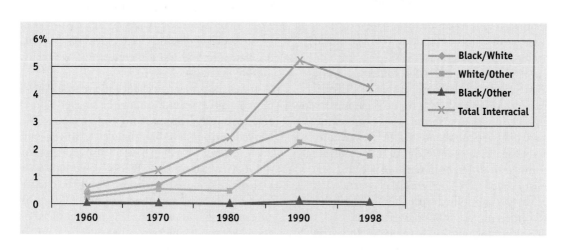

Source: U.S. Bureau of Census, Current Population Reports 1999, Historical Time Series, Table MS3
http://www.census.gov/population/socdemo/ms-la/tabms-3.txt.

Miscegenation laws: Formal norms against marriage of persons of different races.

9.1 | Finding Out

Calculating Mixed Marriage Rates

Researchers in racial homogamy use a variety of ways of calculating mixed marriage rates. The resulting figures can vary significantly.

First, with respect to rates for Blacks, in 1994 there were 3,972,000 couples in which one or both partners were Black. This includes the Black/Black, Black/White, and Black/other categories. There were 374,000 couples in the two mixed groups. This constitutes 9.42% of all marriages involving Blacks. This is the **mixed marriages rate** for marriages involving Blacks.

That figure does not mean, however, that 9.42% of all Blacks married non-Blacks. Each Black/Black marriage, of course, involves two Blacks. Using 1994 data from the Census Bureau, there were 7,196,000 Black persons in Black/Black marriages; 296,000 in Black/White marriages; and 78,000 in Black/other marriages. This is a total of 7,570,000 married Black individuals, of whom 7,196,000 (95%) were in homogamous Black/Black marriages. The remaining 374,000 (4.9%) were in mixed marriages. This is the **mixed marriage rate for individuals** who are Black.

Again using 1994 data, the mixed marriage rate for Whites was 2.47%; the mixed marriage rate for White individuals was 1.01%. The fact that the rates are lower than for Blacks confirms the observation that, generally, the larger the group the smaller the rate of mixed marriage is likely to be. It also confirms the concept of assortive mating. Only a little over 1% of Whites married non-Whites, compared to the figure of more than 12% that would be expected if marriage partners were selected without regard to race.

Even though there are fewer Hispanics than Blacks in the United States (see chapter 8), there are many more mixed marriages involving Hispanics. We can calculate, in 1994, that the Hispanic mixed marriage rate was 25.47. The mixed marriage rate for individuals was 14.59 among Hispanics.

The different ways of calculating rates can sometimes result in very different impressions of what is going on. This is one example of how statistics can be manipulated to make a point. Both figures are correct, but in the examples above the mixed marriages rate yields a number considerably higher than the mixed marriage rate for individuals.

than 1% of Black women were married to White men (Census Bureau, 1980).

Because there are more Black women available for marriage than Black men (see chapter 8), it would be reasonable to expect more out-marriage among the women than the men. Explaining the fact that just the opposite is true has been the subject of considerable speculation but little actual research. It has been found that marriage to a White woman is more likely among more educated Black men. Interracial marriages are most common among Black men who have attended graduate school, but there is no similar trend for Black women (Carter & Glick, 1976).

The gender differences in Black/White marriages are reversed for Japanese-White and Filipino-White marriages; the husband is more likely to be White in these couples. The gender ratio is about even for Native American-White and Chinese-White marriages (U.S. Bureau of the Census, 1980).

Religious Homogamy

Assortive mating also occurs with respect to religion. North American data indicate that between 80 and 90% of Protestants are married to other Protestants, while the expected figure if marriages were random would be 70%. Catholics have an actual homogamous rate of between 64 and 85%, compared to an expected rate of 25%. Jews have an actual rate of 90% but an expected rate of less than 3% (Eshleman, 1994:253).

Mixed marriages rate: The percentage of marriages involving members of a particular group that includes a partner who is not in that group. **Mixed marriage rate for individuals:** The percent of individuals of a particular group who are married to an individual who is not in the group in question.

Religious and racial homogamy are interrelated because persons of similar racial and ethnic backgrounds are likely to have similar religious backgrounds, and vice versa. The vast majority of American Blacks are Protestant, especially Baptist and Methodist (Roberts, 1995). When one Black person marries another, it is quite likely that there is also one Baptist or Methodist marrying another. Hispanics are overwhelmingly Roman Catholic, as are Italian Americans, Irish Americans, and Polish Americans. Again, ethnic homogamy generally entails religious homogamy. The same holds true with those of close English heritage, who are typically Episcopalian, Presbyterian, and Methodist. Scandinavian Americans are predominately Lutheran.

While religious affiliation can often be predicted by race or ethnicity, the latter can sometimes be predicted by religion. American Mormons are overwhelmingly White, with English or Scandinavian heritage (see chapter 6). When an American Mormon marries another Mormon, there is a good chance that there are two non-Hispanic Euro-Americans involved. Shinto believers are overwhelmingly of Japanese ancestry. Muslims in America are most commonly of Middle Eastern origin or are African American converts.

The extent of religious homogamy depends heavily on how churches, denominations, sects, congregations, and other religious groups are aggregated for purposes of study. Most studies have simply used the categories "Protestant," "Catholic," "Jewish," and "other or none." If each of these is further divided, rates of inter-religious marriage increase accordingly. While 80 to 90% of Protestants are married to other Protestants, denominational homogamy is not that high; fewer than 80% of Methodists will marry Methodists, for example, and fewer than 80% of Baptists will marry other Baptists. Since both are Protestants, however, a Methodist and a Baptist are more likely to marry each other than would either be to marry a Roman Catholic. Since they are both Christians, however, the Roman Catholic and Methodist are probably more likely to marry each other than either is to marry a Muslim.

The same can be said for the other major groups. Rates of Jewish homogamy would drop if Orthodox, Conservative, and Reform groups were considered separately. Likewise, Sunni Muslims are more likely to marry each other, but they are more likely to marry Shiah Muslims than to marry Christians. The general rule is that the more similar the religious affiliation and belief two persons have, the more likely marriage is to occur.

A problem with studies of religious homogamy is that they typically ask married couples what their religious views are, without asking what the views were before the marriage. Some amount of apparent marital homogamy is a result of the fact that, either during dating, at the time of marriage, when children were born, or at some other time when the issue became more important, one partner switched to the affiliation of the other partner (Glenn, 1982). Because women tend to be more active in day-to-day religious activities and are generally responsible for the religious instruction of their children, it is probable that more men switch to their wife's denomination than the reverse.

However it is defined, religious homogamy is probably declining as a force in mate selection in North America. Kalmijn (1991b) concluded that educational level is now a more important factor in mate selection than religious homogamy. Glenn (1982) also found that religious intermarriage has become more acceptable in American culture. More partners are willing to consider switching their religious affiliation, and the negative effects of intermarriage are reduced when relatives and friends of the couple express less disapproval.

Social Class Homogamy

At least in societies that have developed since the hunting-gathering era, social class homogamy seems to be a factor in all societies. The closed class system of Hindu India prescribed specifically the caste and subcaste from which a person's spouse should originate. In some cases, couples who dared to violate the endogamous rule by having intercourse with someone of the inappropriate caste could be put to death (Gough, 1960).

In the Soviet Union, which was theoretically ridding itself of social class, 75 to 80% of marriages were within the same social class. Class homogamy actually increased slightly after the communist revolution, and never fell to prerevolution rates (Fisher, 1980).

There is probably more mixed-class marriage in the United States than in most other societies, but virtually every study on the matter still finds assortive mating by social class. Exactly how much class homogamy exists is difficult to determine because of the difficulty of defining and measuring social class.

Parental wealth and income have always been similar for husbands and wives. Systems of bride wealth, dowry, *morgengeld,* and other economic exchanges associated with marriage have historically assured class homogamy. Although the United States is a more open society than

Social class homogamy is most pronounced in the upper classes.

most, lacking clear systems of economic exchange at marriage, persons nonetheless marry within similar wealth and income groups. It is a long-established pattern that persons find mates whose parents have occupations of similar status of the occupation held by their own parents. Educational homogamy is even stronger than occupational, and has increased since the 1930s (Kalmijn, 1991a).

While most marriages involve partners of the same social class, some persons have partners who would be considered somewhat higher in wealth, income, occupational status, or educational level. If the gap in status is large enough to attract comment, the marriage might be an example of **mésalliance,** which literally means "bad alliance."

Since mésalliance involves both upward and downward marriage, in terms of social class, two separate terms have been developed: **hypergamy** (up-marriage) and **hypogamy** (down-marriage). Even with these terms, however, it is unclear whether *hyper* and *hypo* are up and down for the woman or the man. To make this distinction, we can rely on a linguistic convention that, while many terms in our language start from the point of view of the man, those having to do with family matters more often start from the female perspective, as in "bride" and "bridegroom." With this convention, we

conclude that "hypergamy" and "hypogamy" refer to upward or downward marriage from the woman's perspective.

For marriages that are not homogamous by social class, hypergamy is more common than hypogamy. Numerous studies have found this general pattern, which holds regardless of how social class is measured. In educational terms, for example, only about a third of women with 4 or more years of college marry men with less education, while about half of men with 4 or more years marry women with fewer years (Westoff & Goldman, 1988). Now that there are more women each year than men who earn 4-year college degrees, either educational hypergamy will decrease or there will be considerably more college-educated women who remain unmarried.

Since women marry men who are the same or higher in social class, while men marry women who are the same or lower, a **mating gradient** results. There are some women toward the top of the status system in wealth, occupation, and education who have a smaller pool of eligible mates; they are looking for men who are at the same or higher level, and there are fewer such men. The men at the higher levels, on the other hand, can select from a wider pool that includes women who are somewhat lower than themselves. For men toward

---

Mésalliance: Marriage with a person of lower social position.　**Hypergamy:** Marriage in which the woman marries into a higher social level.　**Hypogamy:** Marriage in which the woman marries into a lower social level.　**Mating gradient:** Result of a tendency to have more hypergamy than hypogamy in a mate-selection system.

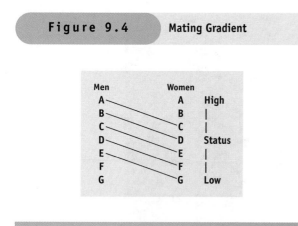

Figure 9.4 **Mating Gradient**

the bottom of the status hierarchy, however, the situation is reversed. They have a smaller pool of potential mates, because the women at their level can marry upward more easily (see Figure 9.4). As a consequence, "unmarried women may be, disproportionately, high-status women, and unmarried men may be, disproportionately, low-status men" (Leslie & Korman, 1989:373).

Theories about Class Homogamy

Various perspectives attempt to explain how it happens that individuals tend to marry others of similar social class standing. Social exchange and equity theory offer somewhat different explanations. Functionalism, conflict theory, and symbolic interactionism can also be applied to the issue.

Social Exchange Theory. As we have seen, social exchange theory predicts that people with more resources are able to bargain for more resources in their spouse. Since social class includes such resources as income, education, and prestige, it is easy to correctly predict that persons with high income, education, and prestige will tend to marry each other.

The reason women are more likely to marry upward in social class, however, is more difficult for the theory to explain. The reason is that women can use physical attractiveness as a resource to get wealth and power in return. This explains why the mating gradient applies to age as well as social class. The more desirable man is one who has money, power, or status, which take time to accumulate. Since our society generally defines young women as more attractive, the bargain is struck between the attractiveness of the younger woman and the wealth and status of the older man.

This can be seen in the dating habits of high school and college students. The older male is more likely to

have a car, an apartment of his own, more respect because of his larger size and strength, and other desirable characteristics. The male high school senior has considerably more dating options than his freshman counterpart; the female senior might have more trouble getting dates unless she dates older nonstudents.

Equity Theory. Equity theory (Walster, Walster, & Berscheid, 1978) is a modification of exchange theory. Rather than assuming that each person is out to maximize his or her own rewards even at the other person's expense, equity theory assumes that persons act on a principle of reciprocity. Rather than assuming that everyone is looking for the wealthiest, most powerful, and most attractive partner possible, this perspective assumes that individuals look for a fair, even match of resources. When each person gives as much as she or he receives, the relationship is equitable.

An equitable match does not mean that the partners are identical in each resource. In individual terms, one person's musical ability might make an equitable exchange for a partner's sense of humor. In terms of gender differences, the man's higher occupational status might be seen as an equitable trade for the woman's attractiveness. In this sense, such a relationship would not really be "marrying up" for the women when both general marital desirability and person-specific desirability are taken into consideration.

Functionalism. Functionalism argues that homogamous matches make for a more smoothly functioning relationship and a more organized society. At the micro-level, persons with the same social class backgrounds have fewer differences to negotiate. Social class is not just a matter of one person having more money than another. Norms in several realms of behavior vary by class. The kinds of foods one eats, how and at what time one eats, how one dresses, the grammar one uses, the entertainment one enjoys, and numerous other expectations vary by class. Persons of the same class are more likely to have compatible patterns and therefore fewer points of contention. Having parents with compatible expectations makes life more consistent for children as well.

At the macrosociological level, the reproduction of culture from one generation to the next is expedited when families have predictable behavioral expectations. Matters of ownership and inheritance, as well as occupational preparation and other factors, are expedited by the fact that most marriages are homogamous. Functionalists would not say that there is anything wrong with occasional mésalliance; this can sometimes help realign the class structure. As a general pattern, however, homogamy appears to be more functional both for individuals and society.

Conflict Theory. Conflict theory concludes that homogamy, like most other social arrangements, benefits the wealthy in the existing class structure. The practice of wealthy individuals marrying each other results in increasing concentration of wealth and power in fewer and fewer families. This prevents the circulation of wealth and power, keeping it out of the hands of some in lower classes who might be better qualified to exercise the power, but are prevented from doing so.

Feminists object to the kind of bargaining that reduces women to sex objects, forcing them to rely more heavily than do men on physical appearance as a resource in the mate-selection process. This is not an objection to exchange theory as an explanatory device, but to the gender difference in the distribution of the kinds of things society has defined as resources. Women are "sex and appearance" objects, while men are "success and power" objects. Both are objectified, but in different ways.

Symbolic Interactionism. Symbolic interactionism, too, can explain social class homogamy. This view emphasizes the creation of shared meanings among individuals, especially in face-to-face interaction. When people tend to see the world in similar ways, they have more shared meanings. This eases communication.

An upper-class girl might be into sailing, while a working-class boy might like off-road motorcycling. If this girl talks a lot about sailing when with the boy, he might conclude that she is "uppity" and holds her privilege over him. When the boy talks about motorcycling, she might think he is boorish. In fact, each one is talking about the worlds they know. Each person might be more comfortable with those who share more meanings, and those people are more likely to be of similar backgrounds. Hence, people with similar class backgrounds are more likely to select each other as long-term intimate partners.

Propinquity

Propinquity is not a theoretical perspective but a factor that increases the extent of racial, religious, and class homogamy. In North America, at least, marriages between persons who have never met each other are very rare. We are more likely to meet individuals who live nearby, so they become the pool of potential mates.

Bossard (1932) conducted the classic study of propinquity in Philadelphia. He got the premarital address of 5,000 couples from marriage licenses. Half of all couples lived within 20 blocks of each other; one third lived within 5 blocks. One in eight couples listed the same address prior to marriage, suggesting the possibility of an unexpectedly high rate of premarital cohabitation. Each of these figures is considerably higher than would be predicted if persons selected their mates at random from the Philadelphia metropolitan area. Considering all the potential mates in the world, the rates of propinquity are even more remarkable.

Several studies have duplicated Bossard's early research (Katz & Hill, 1958; Morgan, 1981). Propinquity is still a major factor in mate selection, although it might have weakened somewhat because of the increased availability of rapid transportation, telecommunication, e-mail, and the increased tendency to commute to work and school.

Because American neighborhoods remain racially segregated, propinquity and racial homogamy reinforce each other. It is difficult to know how much racial homogamy is the result of preference for one's own race and how much is the result of the fact that persons of the same ancestry tend to live near each other. This is true not only for Blacks and Whites generally, but also for such ethnic groups as Greeks, Italians, Poles, Koreans, and Chinese. Larger American cities and especially their suburbs tend to be divided into ethnic enclaves where propinquity reinforces racial homogamy.

Social class residential segregation is perhaps more rigid even than racial and ethnic divisions. Few poor persons live next door to, or even in the same neighborhood as, the very wealthy. Even when they are relatively close in actual distance, they are typically separated by natural barriers such as rivers or hills, or by human-made barriers like fences, highways, or parks.

In American cities, the poor generally live close to city centers and along major transportation corridors, while the wealthiest live out and up from the city center (Hoyt, 1939). Each suburban housing development has typically been designed for homes of a particular price range. Since the houses in such developments have roughly the same market value, they attract buyers of roughly the same social class. Low-income housing projects typically result in high density housing for the poor.

Since persons of each social class live near one another, they are likely to meet in neighborhood schools,

---

Propinquity: Nearness; the tendency to select mates from persons who live nearby.

churches, stores, bars, restaurants, and parks. They are thus more likely to marry someone of the same class than a person of a different class who lives elsewhere.

Although it is not as obvious as with race and social class, America is also somewhat segregated by religion. Ethnic neighborhoods congregate persons of a particular religion as well as a particular race or nationality. Once again, propinquity reinforces homogamy.

Propinquity continues to operate in spite of the high geographical mobility that is characteristic of America. When individuals or families move, they tend to find housing in neighborhoods of similar people. This will not affect the mate selection of a couple who move together, unless they divorce and each marry neighbors, but it will affect the mate-selection prospects of their children.

Going away to college is a form of mobility that results in class propinquity. Sons and daughters of the poor and working classes do not commonly go to residential colleges. Elite private colleges attract students from the highest social class, while middle-class students more commonly attend state universities. Some private colleges are administered by specific religious groups, so students associate with those of common religious background. While there are clearly many exceptions to these generalizations, colleges do tend to bring together young adults of similar social backgrounds who live near one another, date one another, and select mates from their own group.

Age Hypergamy and the Marriage Squeeze

Just as expectations exist about the similarity of mates in terms of race, religion, and social class, there are expectations about the ages of marital partners. In the case of age, the expectation is not that the husband and wife will be of exactly the same age, but that they are close in age with the man being a few years older. By a small margin, age hypergamy is more normative in mate selection than is age homogamy.

Age hypergamy is the norm in every country for which data exist, with a worldwide average of 3 years' difference between husband and wife (Buss, 1989). At any given time, the older the husband is at time of marriage, the greater is the age difference between him and his wife. In the United States, men marry women an average of 5 years younger than themselves in their second marriage and 8 years younger than themselves in their third (Kenrick & Keefe, 1992).

Norms about age differences become most notable when they are broken, as Woody Allen found out.

Age hypergamy, combined with higher death rates for men, can result in a **marriage squeeze** for women. At every age, more men than women die. If women tend to marry older men, there will be a smaller pool of potential mates for women than for men. The older the women are, the greater the squeeze becomes. For women age 25 to 29 there is a sex ratio of 77 eligible men per 100 eligible women. For women age 45 to 49, the eligible sex ratio is only 38 eligible men for every 100 women (Westoff & Goldman, 1988). For Blacks the ratio is even more unbalanced at all age groups (Wilson, 1987; see chapter 7).

Metropolitan areas differ considerably in the extent of the marriage squeeze. Generally, the faster growing cities of the west and south have more available men per 100 women than the cities of the northeast and midwest (Westoff & Goldman, 1988:40). The reason appears to be that men, more than women, are likely to migrate from areas with depressed economies to those with more employment opportunities.

Marriage squeeze: A demographic condition in which there are considerably more eligible mates for one sex than for another.

In large populations, the marriage squeeze is generally greater for women if the population is growing. If there are more children born each year than the year before, there will be more women at each age compared with men a few years older. There would, for example, be more 20-year-old women than 23-year-old men. If a population is getting smaller, however, the marriage squeeze might be in the opposite direction. There would be more 23-year-old men than 20-year-old women. Since there was a declining birthrate in the United States in the 1960s and 1970s, the 1990s should have seen a slight marriage squeeze for young men, or at least a reduction in the marriage squeeze for young women.

The Singles Option

Not all individuals are participating in the mate-selection process. Increasing numbers of Americans are remaining single. We will look at that phenomenon in historical perspective, then find out who the singles are. We will consider the emerging institution of cohabitatio n. We will then discuss relationships between same-sex couples.

Singlehood in Perspective

In feudal Europe, like most advanced agrarian societies, a smaller proportion of persons married than is the case today. The men had to wait for their inheritance, or demonstrate some way to support a family, before they were likely to strike a bargain for a wife (see chapter 3). An unmarried woman was called a **maiden**, of whom virginity was assumed. If she was still unmarried well beyond the typical marriage age at the time, it was assumed she would probably always be single. She was then referred to as a **spinster** because spinning thread was a typical way unmarried women earned their living.

Single men came to be referred to as **bachelors.** The English term referred specifically to a young nobleman who was in service to a knight, but it was earlier the word for a tenant farmer. Since both tenant farmers and knight's squires were usually single, the word *bachelor* came to refer to all single men. No separate term comparable to spinster developed for an older unmarried man, perhaps because it was assumed always to be possible for the tenant farmer or knight's servant to

accumulate enough resources to arrange a marriage, no matter how old they got.

Americans, in comparison to Europeans, have historically been more likely to marry (see chapter 3). Whether by choice or by circumstance, however, Americans today are increasingly likely to spend more of their adult lives as unmarried individuals. Three groups make up the unmarried adult population: those who are widowed and not remarried, those who are divorced and not remarried, and those who have never married. Figure 9.5 provides the percentage of the adult population in each of these single categories, along with the percentage married, from 1950 to 1998.

The percentage of the adult population that is currently married has gone down considerably, from a high of 68% in 1960 to 56% in 1998. Many of these adults are in their second or subsequent marriage. The percentage of persons over 15 who are divorced but not remarried climbed from only 2% in 1950 to over 9% in 1998. The percentage who never married generally declined, and the widowed population dropped slightly.

To explain these changes, some social analysts have pointed to an increasing focus on individuality in American culture; individuals are no longer embedded in nuclear families and kin groups. Bellah et al. (1985), for example, proposed that a cult of individualism and personal fulfillment was eroding the ability of Americans to make a commitment. Similarly, Stein (1976:5) suggested that marriage and family norms conflict with "potentials for individual development and personal growth."

While some of these personal-cultural arguments appear to make sense, data suggest alternative explanations. The increase in singles since 1970 does not seem so extreme when put into historical, demographic, and economic context. The percentage of single 20-year-olds follows the same general trend as age at first marriage. The percentage of 20-somethings who were single was the lowest in the 1950s, and it has now gone back up to a level that is more historically typical.

The increasing number of singles does not necessarily mean a major rejection of marriage. Most young singles plan to be married sometime, a factor consistent with the historical American pattern that sees more than 90% of each age cohort marry at least once (Cherlin, 1992). Relatively prosperous times in the 1950s and 1960s allowed young adults to marry with some

---

Maiden: An unmarried girl or woman, usually assumed to be virgin. **Spinster:** A woman who remains unmarried beyond the typical marriage age. **Bachelor:** An unmarried man.

| Figure 9.5 | Marital Status of Population 15 Years and Older, in Percent, 1950 to 1998 |

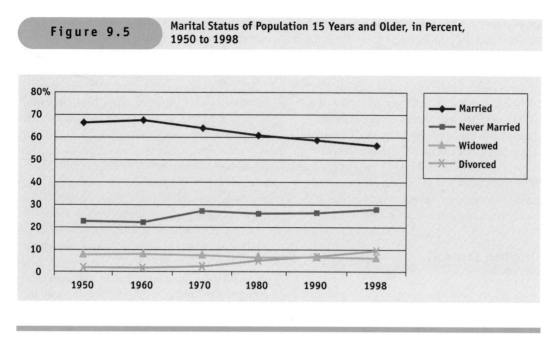

Source: U.S. Bureau of Census, 1999 Current Population Survey, Historical Time Series, Table WS1. http://www.census.gov/population/socdemo/ms-la/tabms-1.txt.

reasonable expectation of financial success. Economic dislocations brought on by the transformation to a postindustrial economy reduced economic stability in the 1970s and 1980s and caused some young adults to postpone marriage (see chapter 6).

Other factors are at work as well. More young adults, especially women, are postponing marriage while they get college degrees, which are increasingly necessarily for economic survival. As important as educational factors are, perhaps a more significant factor in the increased number of single adults is the increasing frequency of cohabitation.

Cohabitation

Many persons who are counted as single are, in the more traditional sense of the term, not single at all but cohabiting or "living together." This has become both more common and more acceptable in the past few decades (Oropesa, 1996; Seltzer, 2000). The number of cohabiting couples has increased from about 1 million in 1977 to nearly 5 million in 1997 (Casper, Cohen, & Simmons, 1999).

Cohabiting and the Unmarried Couple Household. In the present context, the term **cohabiting** couples connotes heterosexual individuals who live together as a couple and are sexually intimate. Prior to 1990, the arrangement that was actually counted by the Census Bureau was called an **unmarried couple household,** which also included persons in such roles as tenant roommate, caretakers of the disabled or handicapped, or opposite-sex roommates who are not a sexually intimate couple. The census term does not include homosexual couples or heterosexual cohabiters who have another adult living with them. In 1990, the Census Bureau began providing the household option "unmarried partner" (Seltzer, 2000).

Demographics of Cohabiting. Each decade, younger adults are more likely to cohabit than were their slightly older counterparts. Nearly 40% of women age 19 to 24 have already cohabited at some time, and more of that group will as they get older. Over half of first unions that occurred in the 1990s began with cohabitation (Bumpass & Lu, 2000). Had these couples married instead of cohabiting, there would have been

---

Cohabiting: Living together, especially as an intimate couple in a marriage-like relationship.   **Unmarried couple household:** Two adults, not related and of opposite sex, but no additional adults; and any children present are under 15 years old (U.S. Bureau of the Census).

Table 9.1	Unmarried Couples by Selected Characteristics, 1970, 1980, 1990, and 1998, in Thousands and Percentages			
Characteristic	1970	1980	1990	1998
Total Number (thousands)	523	1,589	2,856	4,236
No children under 15	62.5%	73.0%	68.9%	64.1%
Some children under 15	37.5	27.1	31.2	35.9
Under 25 years old	10.5	25.9	20.9	18.3
25 to 44 years old	19.7	52.7	62.2	58.4
45 to 64 years old	35.6	13.9	12.5	18.8
65 years and older	34.0	7.3	4.4	4.4

Source: U.S. Bureau of the Census. 1995. *Statistical Abstract of the United States 1995.* 115th ed. Washington, DC: U.S. Government Printing Office. Table 60; 1999, 119th ed., Table 68.

very little change in either age at first marriage or percentage of the population that was single (Bumpass, Sweet, & Cherlin, 1991; Bumpass & Lu, 2000).

As Table 9.1 reveals, cohabitation in 1970 was more common among persons 45 and older; 34% of cohabitants were over 65 years of age. Since then, because of the rapid increase in younger cohabitants, the portion among the elderly has plummeted to 4.4%. Only 18.3% of unmarried partners were under 25 in 1998. The large majority of cohabitants, 58.4%, are in the 25-to-44 age bracket (see Table 9.1).

Religious and political views of cohabitants are somewhat different than noncohabitants. Cohabitants are less likely to be religious than are noncohabiters; they are more politically liberal, and hold more liberal attitudes about sexual and other personal behavior, than couples who do not cohabit. Men and women whose parents divorced are more likely to cohabit than those who grew up in intact homes (Bachrach, Hindin, & Thomson, 2000).

Social-class variables are related to the probability of cohabiting. Young persons who are not attending college are more likely to cohabit than are college students (Bumpass, Sweet, & Cherlin, 1991). Persons whose mothers were young and pregnant at marriage are more likely to cohabit (Thorton, 1991). Likelihood of cohabiting is also increased by a failure to complete high school, by growing up in a family that received welfare, and by growing up in a single-parent family (Bumpass & Sweet, 1989; Seltzer, 2000). When the man's economic future is uncertain, couples are more likely to cohabit; when his future is more secure, they are more likely to marry (Bumpass & Lu, 2000).

Racial differences also exist in cohabitation rates. Although rates are going up fastest among non-Hispanic Whites, African Americans still cohabit at nearly three times the rate of Whites. It is reasonable to conclude that many of the "single" Black mothers actually do have a father figure for their children in the home (Bumpass & Lu, 2000; Seltzer, 2000).

Life among Cohabitants. The past few decades have seen a change in the meaning of cohabitation. In some ways, cohabitation is like a stage in the courtship process, but it is increasingly being seen as formal marriage. To find out how cohabitants themselves now see their situation, Casper and Sayer (2000) had them categorize their relationship in one of four ways. Ten percent said that their relationship was a substitution for marriage. Forty-six percent saw it as precursor for marriage, and 15% called it a trial marriage. The least committed option, coresidential dating, was the choice of 29% of cohabitants. Five to seven years later, about 40% of the cohabitants had gotten married, 21% still lived together, and 39% had separated. Those who were in a "precursor to marriage" were most likely to get married; the trial marriagers (51%) and coresidential daters (46%) were most likely to separate (see Table 9.2).

Cohabiting women have a fertility rate three times higher than noncohabiting single women (Tanfer, 1987). Traditionally, if an unmarried couple got pregnant they were quite likely to get married. If cohabiting were a step in the mate-selection process, they would be likely to marry if pregnancy occurs. If cohabiting were seen as a substitute for marriage, however, marriage would be less likely upon pregnancy. Manning (1993) found that cohabiting White women in their 20s were likely to marry if pregnancy occurred. White teenage cohabitants and Black cohabitants of all ages, however, were no more likely to marry upon pregnancy than were noncohabitants.

Table 9.2		Perception and Outcome of Cohabiting Relationships		
		Outcome of Relationship after 5 to 7 Years		
Type of Relationship, 1987–88	All Couples	Still Live Together	Got Married	Separated
All Unmarried Couples	100%	21%	40%	39%
Substitute for Marriage	10%	39%	25%	35%
Precursor to Marriage	46%	17%	52%	31%
Trial Marriage	15%	21%	28%	51%
Coresidential Dating	29%	21%	33%	46%

Source: Casper, L. M., and L. C. Sayer. 2000; in Bianchi, Suzanne M., and Lynne M. Casper. 2000. "American Families." *Population Bulletin:*55(4) Page 17. Washington, DC: Population Reference Bureau.

Landale and Fennelly (1992) studied 2,033 Puerto Rican women living in metropolitan New York City. They found that women who were cohabiting generally defined their relationship as a form of marriage; their childbearing behavior was more similar to married than to single, noncohabiting women. More importantly, the researchers concluded, "It is too simplistic to regard the non-legal unions of Puerto Rican women as either 'marital' or 'nonmarital'" (Landale & Fennelly, 1992:269). Theirs is probably a good general conclusion about the role of cohabitation. For some partners it is functionally a marriage; for others it is a step in the mate-selection process; and for still other couples it serves as some kind of intermediate relationship.

Many cohabiting couples are happy with their relationship, but living together does have its problems. Cohabiting couples have more domestic violence than do married couples, a difference that is probably related to the fact that cohabiters tend to be more socially isolated (Stets, 1991). Male cohabiters are more likely to be unemployed than married men, which could also contribute to higher violence rates and other problems (Glick & Spanier, 1980).

Gender roles are less traditional among cohabiting couples than among married pairs. Cohabiting college students appear to have more egalitarian attitudes than do couples who are dating, partly because they tend to be less conventional in general (Risman et al., 1981). Cohabiting men do no more housework than do married men, but cohabiting women do considerably less housework than their married counterparts (Shelton & John, 1993).

Although many couples see cohabiting as "practicing for marriage," practice makes far from perfect in this case. Several studies have found less successful marriages among couples who cohabited (Bumpass & Lu, 2000; Seltzer, 2000). The National Survey of Families and Households provided data confirming that couples who cohabited prior to marriage generally had less satisfactory marriages and had less commitment to the institutions of marriage. Cohabiting women, but not men, had more individualistic attitudes toward marriage than their married counterparts (Thompson & Colella, 1992). The couples with premarital cohabitation experience had divorce rates about 46% higher than couples who did not cohabit before their marriage (DeMaris & Rao, 1992).

Compared to their married peers, cohabitants reported lower levels of overall life satisfaction, lower levels of sexual exclusivity and satisfaction, and poorer relationships with their parents (Nock, 1995; Waite & Joyner, 1996; Forste & Tanfer, 1996; Amato & Booth, 1997). Married couples fare better in labor force productivity, physical and mental health, and longevity (Turner & Marino, 1994; Waite, 1995; Akerlof, 1998.)

Entry into a cohabiting relationship is different than entering a marriage. Although couples presumably spend considerable amounts of time being together prior to marriage, the marital arrangement itself is the result of a rite of passage that clearly distinguished the premarital from the marital state. By comparison, becoming cohabitants is typically a gradual process. The couples begin to spend more and more nights together and end up cohabiting almost by default. At some point, they decide to give up one residence and move in together. There is typically no rite of passage to clearly define the change in status, so role differences are less

Immigration Law Causes Increased Marriage Rates

In March and April 2001, several cities saw significant increases in the number of recorded marriages. The increases were accounted for by thousands of immigrants who were rushing to beat an April 30 deadline.

American immigration has generally held that foreigners have to apply from their country of origin if they wished to be considered for legal status. For several years there has been an exemption in the law (Section 234(i)), allowing some illegal immigrants to remain in the United States while applying for legal status. They had to pay a $1,000 fine for illegal entry to the country and a $225 application fee, and they had to be sponsored by a close family member or employer.

The exemption was set to expire at the end of 2000, but it became an election issue. President Clinton wanted a permanent restoration of Section 245(i), while Republican lawmakers wanted the provision to expire. As a compromise, they agreed to a four-month extension, due to expire on April 30, 2001.

One of the easiest ways to qualify for the exemption is to be married to a legal resident. Hence the huge increase in marriages. Even the Immigration and Naturalization Service, whose toll-free hotline was receiving a million calls per month, was advising people to consider "moving up their marriage dates" to take advantage of the law.

In January, Houston reported a 58% increase in the number of marriage licenses issued compared to the same month in 2000. Cook County, Ill., reported a 20% increase, while Los Angeles County had a 59% increase. More recently, some jurisdictions were reporting increases of as much as 300%.

Some couples had been living together for a long time but had not legalized their residency. Other couples planned to marry anyway, but sped up the process to take advantage of the law. Some, probably, got married when they might otherwise not have done so. The Immigration and Naturalization Service, however, issued a warning that anyone who gets married just to get a green card faces a marriage fraud charge and a possible $260,000 fine.

Sources: Lopez, Robert J., Patrick J. McDonnell, and Daniel Yi. **www.latimes.com**, March 15, 2001. Susan Sachs. **www.nytimes.com**, April 28, 2001.

clearly drawn. There is no recognized point at which cohabitants publicly make a commitment to each other.

It might not be the cohabitation itself that results in lower probabilities of successful marriages, but the characteristics of the cohabiters. Some characteristics of cohabiters, such as lower educational levels, welfare backgrounds, interracial relationships, and presence of stepchildren, are associated with higher divorce rates whether the couple cohabits before marriage or not (Booth & Johnson, 1988).

Schoen (1990) found that earlier cohabiters were generally experimental, nonconventional individuals who had to face social disapproval for cohabitation; this pressure might have contributed to the failure of some relationships. This is referred to as the "unconventionality hypothesis." As cohabitation becomes more socially acceptable, increasing numbers of more conventional individuals participate, which might lower the rate of postcohabitation marriage problems.

Other studies (DeMaris & MacDonald, 1993; Lillard, Brian, & Waite, 1995) cast doubt on the "unconventionality hypothesis." Additional doubt comes from research in Sweden, where cohabitation has long been more acceptable than in the United States. A study of almost 5,000 Swedish women found that those who cohabited premaritally had divorce rates nearly 80% higher than noncohabiters. The longer a couple remained married, however, the less effect cohabitation had. For couples married 8 years or more, there was no difference between cohabiters and noncohabiters on the marriage-dissolution rate (Bennett, Blanc, & Bloom, 1988).

Marriage and Single Life Compared

An historical American assumption has been that marriage is superior to remaining single, especially for women. Unmarried women came to be stigmatized, as the epithet "old maid" implies. Even the word "spinster," neutral in Europe, developed a negative connotation in the United States. This view began to change in the 1960s and 1970s, when feminist scholars began to question the assumption that marriage was the primary appropriate role for women.

Jessie Bernard (1972) reported that, while married men were considerably better off than single ones, married women were worse off in some respects than their single sisters. She concluded that for every couple there were two marriages, his and hers, and that hers was much worse than his. Many other studies began to question the happiness of American wives.

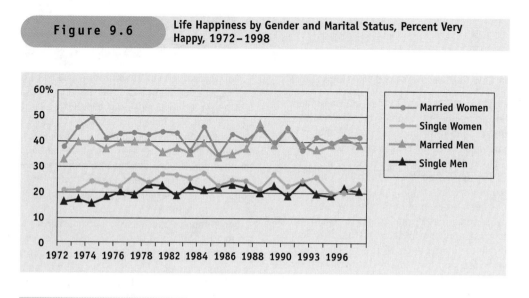

| Figure 9.6 | Life Happiness by Gender and Marital Status, Percent Very Happy, 1972–1998 |

Source: Smith, Tom W., and James Allan Davis: General Social Survey(s), 1972–1998. (Machine-readable data file). Principal investigators, Tom W. Smith and James A. Davis. Produced by the National Opinion Research Center, Chicago. Tape distributed by the Roper Public Opinion Research Center, Storrs, CT. Microcomputer format and codebook prepared and distributed by MicroCase Corporation, Bellevue, WA. Analysis by Gene H. Starbuck.

More recently, results of several studies have conflicted with Bernard's findings (Waite & Gallagher, 2000). Many of these studies ask respondents a question like "How happy are you with your life?" Respondents typically choose among such answers as "Very happy, pretty happy, or somewhat unhappy." Figure 9.6 provides the results of one such study that combines the surveys given for several years (NORC, 1998). This national survey found that, for both men and women, married respondents were considerably happier than their single counterparts.

Stack and Eshleman (1998) conducted a similar study using a sample of people from 17 countries. They found that married respondents reported greater life happiness than all groups of singles, including cohabiting couples. They also found that marriage increases levels of happiness equally for men and women. Mastekaasa (1994) studied life satisfaction of married and single individuals in 19 countries. By almost all measures in all countries, married persons had higher life satisfaction than singles, and the association was equally strong for men and women.

Rather than directly asking persons about how happy or satisfied they are, some studies look at frequency of symptoms of unhappiness such as bouts of depression and suicide. These studies confirm that married men are better off than their single brothers, having lower rates of alcoholism, suicide, schizophrenia, and other psychiatric problems. Cohabiting men have more problems with alcohol than either married or single men; cohabiting women have more alcohol problems than married women (Horwitz & White, 1998).

Married men live longer than single ones (Coombs, 1991). Nock (1998) found that, when men get married, they show improvement in achievement, social participation, and generosity. When men get divorced, they score lower in these traits. Several studies have confirmed what has come to be called the "marriage premium," that married men earn substantially more income than comparable single men (Gray & Vanderhart, 2000).

The assumption is that something about being married, as opposed to being single, provides some protection from unhappiness, from certain mental health problems and from lower economic productivity. It could also be true, however, that unhappy, mentally ill, and unproductive individuals have more trouble getting or staying married. This issue has not been resolved. The mating gradient would predict that conditions that reduce men's ability to earn a living and be good mates would, in turn, reduce their competitive position in the mating and dating game. Single men, then, would tend to be lower in social desirability than those who have gotten married (Bernard, 1972).

On the other hand, Gove, Style, and Hughes (1990) found no evidence for the "social desirability" hypothesis, concluding instead that the married lifestyle has more rewards for men than does the single lifestyle. While men with higher incomes are more likely to get married than their poorer brethren (Nakosteen & Zimmer, 1997), evidence also exists that being married has a positive influence on men's earnings (Gray & Vanderhart, 2000).

Contrary to studies that ask women directly about their happiness, some mental health studies found that single women exhibit fewer symptoms of selected mental illnesses than do their married sisters. A major study in the early 1970s found that married women reported more nervousness, insomnia, nightmares, and headaches than did single women (Knox, 1975).

On the other hand, single women generally appear to suffer more loneliness and sense of meaninglessness (Etaugh & Malstrom, 1981). Waite (2000) compared married and single men and women on several dimensions of well-being. She concluded that married women, like married men, are healthier than their single counterparts. On no dimension she compared did single men and women exhibit greater well-being than their married brothers and sisters.

It would appear that, considering all measures, marriage is associated with greater happiness, life satisfaction, and overall well-being for both men and women. Cohabitants are midway between singles and marrieds on most measures of well-being (Kurdek, 1991; Waite, 2000). Whether men gain more from marriage than do women remains a close call.

Marriage alone, of course, does not guarantee happiness. Ross (1995) found that social attachment (having a close partner, whether married or not), social support, and economic well-being all increase personal well-being. People can be happy without marriage if they have those qualities, and unhappy in marriage if they do not. Being married, however, increases the chances that people will have a close partner, have social support, and have economic well-being. Therefore, being married increases the probability of being happy.

Gay and Lesbian Relationships

Little research has been done on the lives of homosexual adolescents, partly because survey research is difficult to do with such a relatively small population. Less than 1% of adolescents identify themselves as either homosexuals or bisexuals (Savin-Williams, 1994). Some youths who will later adopt a homosexual identity go through the adolescent dating process as heterosexuals. Young persons who do identify as homosexuals generally face a considerable sense of isolation from parents and peers (Savin-Williams, 1994).

Adolescents can be unkind to those they consider different. A 1988 survey of males between 15 and 19 years old found that 89% thought sex with a man was "disgusting." Only 12% thought that they could be friends with someone they knew was gay. This severely limits the opportunity of homosexual adolescents even to have friends, let alone to find lovers (Marsiglio, 1993).

Like heterosexual men and women, most gays and lesbians want a secure, intimate relationship. Perhaps as many as 40 to 60% of gays and 45 to 80% of lesbians are, at any one time, involved in steady romantic relationships. Their self-reported relationship quality seems to be about the same as for heterosexuals (Peplau & Cochran, 1990; Peplau et al., 1996; Patterson, 2000).

In general terms, gay men and lesbians look for the same qualities in relationships as do heterosexual men and women. Persons of all sexual orientations tend to want relationships in which they can reveal intimate feelings, spend time together, hold similar attitudes, have an equal-power relationship, and have sexual exclusivity (Peplau & Gordon, 1991:482).

Same-sex couples have a smaller pool of eligibles than do heterosexuals but are generally looking for the same qualities in long-term relationships.

In spite of a stated desire for sexual exclusivity, however, homosexual relationships, especially those among males, are less likely than heterosexual ones to be exclusive (Bryant & Demian, 1994; Harry, 1983; Peplau, 1981). Rates of relationship breakups appear to be about the same for gay, lesbians, and cohabiting heterosexuals, all of which are considerably higher than for married heterosexuals (Kurdek, 1995; Kurdek, 1998). It is not known whether going through a religious or other kind of ceremony increases the longevity of same-sex relationships.

Like heterosexuals, many homosexuals use personal want ads to help them find partners. Gonzales and Meyers (1993) conducted a content analysis of such ads with an eye to comparing male and female heterosexuals and homosexuals. The characteristics looked for in partners, as well as the self-descriptions, were studied. The four groups were found to vary in several ways:

1. Gay men emphasized physical characteristics most; lesbians did so least;

2. Heterosexual women mentioned attractiveness more than lesbians did;

3. Women (lesbian or heterosexual) solicited more expressive traits and offered more instrumental traits than did men (gay or heterosexual);

4. Gay men mentioned sexuality more than did other advertisers; and

5. Heterosexuals were more likely than homosexuals to pursue long-term relationships and to mention sincerity and financial security (Gonzales & Meyers, 1993:131).

These findings seem to indicate that, in some areas, gender differences tend to be greater among homosexuals than among heterosexuals. Heterosexual men, for example, generally are more attuned to physical appearance and sexuality than heterosexual women; male homosexuals are most likely to express these interests more often, while lesbians express them least often. The emotional/instrumental distinction was expressed in the ads for both homosexuals and heterosexuals.

Summary and Conclusion

Preindustrial mate selection was generally controlled by kin groups and such customary restrictions as endogamy and incest taboos. Industrialization saw movement toward "choice" positions on the mate-selection continuum.

The split between work and home, which increased in the first phase of industrialization, made male-female interaction more formal, while industrialization itself was encouraging independence and individuality. Victorianism governed the formal courtship process that evolved in the upper classes in the second half of the 19th century. The less formal courting pattern of the working class became the "dating" practice of the early 20th century. As mate selection became increasingly the domain of young singles themselves, individualism and love became a more important basis for marriage.

In the postindustrial era, a "permanent availability" model of mate selection has evolved and "getting together" has become a less formal mechanism of mate selection. Age at first marriage has increased to 19th-century levels from the midcentury low. New avenues for getting together have evolved with newer technology.

Social exchange theory underlies most contemporary theorizing about mate selection. Individuals use the resources available to them to get the "best deal" in a mate. Homogamy governs mate selection in the areas of race, religion, and social class. Assortive mating is more common than mixed marriage in all these areas. Various theoretical perspectives have views about homogamy, but propinquity clearly plays a part. Age hypergamy is the norm and contributes to a marriage squeeze for women.

For economic, educational, and personal reasons, more Americans are living as singles for more of their lives. Part of the reason for this is the increasing rate of cohabitation, which stands between dating and marriage as an evolving social institution. Cohabiting appears to be associated with less success in marriage. While being single is much more socially acceptable than it has been in the past, most American men and women still prefer marriage and are generally better off in many ways when married than when single.

Some homosexual relationships become long-term functional equivalents of cohabitation or marriage, although the role structure in such relationships is more problematic. The legal status of homosexual couples varies across the country and around the world.

In conclusion, social forces are constantly at work, even in the extremely important and apparently personal process of mate selection. In spite of high rates of divorce and of cohabitation, America retains its pronuptialist values. Only a generation or two ago, sexual intercourse was reserved primarily for marriage but this, too, has changed. That is the topic of the next chapter.

> *Rethinking in Context* Consider the criteria you used in matching your prospective couples. Based on what you found out in this chapter, would you make any changes? Considering the importance of homogamy in mate selection, did you include matching by social class, race, religion, and age? If you were actually running a matching business, would this be considered a discriminatory practice according to federal civil right laws? Would you request payment if the couple moved in together rather than getting married?

Additional Resources

Historical mate selection

Bailey, B. L. 1988. *From Front Porch to Backseat: Courtship in Twentieth Century America.* Baltimore: The Johns Hopkins University Press.

Coontz, Stephanie. 1988. *The Social Origins of Private Life: A History of American Families, 1600–1900.* New York: Verso.

Rothman, Ellen K. 1984. *Hands and Hearts: A History of Courtship in America.* New York: Basic Books.

Contemporary singlehood and mate selection

Bozett, Frederick W., & Marvin B. Sussman, eds. 1990. *Homosexuality and Family Relations.* New York: Harrington Park Press.

Brehm, Sharon S. 1992. *Intimate Relationships,* 2nd ed. New York: McGraw Hill.

Chapman, Audrey B. 1994. *Entitled to Good Loving: Black Men and Women and the Battle for Love and Power.* New York: Holt.

Gordon, Tuula. 1994. *Single Women: On the Margins?* New York: New York University Press.

Internet Sites

Links to mail-order bride sites

http://www.planet-love.com/

A conservative, "family values" source on courtship, marriage, and family

http://www.frc.org/

A guide to gay, lesbian, bisexual, and transgendered history

http://www.fordham.edu/halsall/pwh/

Find out about life during the Victorian era

http://landow.stg.brown.edu/victorian/victov.html

For links to these sites and additional resources, visit the *Families in Context* Web site at:

http://sociology.wadsworth.com

Chapter 10

Varieties of Sexual Scripts

Prelude

Readers of this book are sexual people, but they have a wide variety of experiences. Most have had sexual intercourse, but some are waiting for the right person. Most, especially of the men, have masturbated and many continue to do so regularly. Virtually everyone has romantic and sexual fantasies. Virtually no one, however, would be willing to stand up in front of the class and talk about all of his or her sexual thoughts and experiences.

Perhaps nothing is more private and personal to each of us than our sex life: with whom we have sex, what we do sexually, and how we feel about it all. And yet social forces intrude even into our most private sexual moments.

Are people's sex lives so private in all cultures?

By virtue of the fact that they are human beings, people have the capacity to become sexual; it is a biological fact. What humans define as appropriate sexual things to do, however, is socially constructed. We have, in earlier chapters, already had a hint about the vastly different ways in which societies can organize sexuality. That topic will be further explored in this chapter, as will the way particular couples become sexual. As it turns out, humans learn to be sexual in much the same way they learn to do other kinds of things.

Thinking Ahead If you could personally design today's sexual folkways, mores, and formal norms, what would they be like? Would premarital sex be acceptable? Would extramarital sex be approved? In what ways would your norms be the same as the ones currently in place? How would they be different? Why?

Theoretical perspectives organize information about human sexuality, like other aspects of interaction. Three major types of sociological perspectives that have been applied elsewhere in the book will also be applied to sexuality: functionalism, conflict theory, and symbolic interactionism.

The remainder of the chapter applies the scripting theory introduced earlier in the book. A variety of social scripts will be covered, with examples of how sexual meanings vary from one time and culture to another. Individual scripts, scenes, and the construction of mutual scripts complete the picture.

Sociological Theories of Human Sexuality

In most species of animals, sexual activity is directly connected to reproduction. Most animals engage in behavior that can connect sperm and egg only when fertilization of the egg is likely. By contrast, there was, until quite recently, no known way that either male or female humans could directly determine the most efficient time to connect sperm and egg. The human female can be receptive to sexual activity at any time; the human male's arousal is triggered by stimuli other than female reproductive receptivity.

Since humans cannot rely directly on inherited biological "instructions" about sexuality, they must rely on socially constructed guidance. Although the sexual potential is biological, it is actualized as the result of social forces. The vast array of different sexualities that can be found historically and cross-culturally indicates the power of social forces to shape sexuality. It is these forces that sociological perspectives attempt to explain. We will focus here on functionalism, conflict theory, and social learning/sexual scripting theory.

Functionalism

Kingsley Davis (1971) developed the first thorough application of functional theory to the topic of sexuality. He believed that the sex drive is a natural biological force but that well-functioning societies direct that force in constructive ways. Davis pointed out that all societies have normative limits regarding sexual behavior; the limits generally guide individuals into behavior that is supportive of the family-kinship system and the economic exchange system of the society. Generally, sexual practices such as prostitution and homosexuality that do not support the family-kinship system are either negatively sanctioned or less valued than married heterosexual activities.

Davis (1971) noted that premarital sex is not universally banned because it does not necessarily affect the marriage and family system as long as there is a mechanism to prevent illegitimate births, which affect both the family-kinship system and the property inheritance system.

Davis noted that in Western European societies that punished premarital sex, women could use the promise of sexual access as a bargaining chip to encourage a man into marriage. This was functional because it provided material support for women, while strengthening the family unit.

Since sexual norms tend to reflect sociological requirements, change in the norms can threaten social structure. The acceptance of premarital sex, for example, removes one of the structural supports for marriage and family. Davis and other functionalists refer to this social disorganization as a possible "breakdown in moral standards." It is possible, however, that changes represent a reorganization of family structure to more closely fit other social institutions.

Conflict Theory

As with their analysis of other topics, conflict theorists add issues of power to the sexual equation. They agree with functionalists that strong moralities will develop around sexual issues. They add, however, that the moralities that develop will tend to reflect power differences among groups.

Feminists, in particular, have pointed out the way in which power differences between men and women are reflected in sexual behaviors, values, and norms. The "double standard" attempts to control the sexuality of women, while leaving men freer to engage in premarital and extramarital sexual activities. The patriarchal system, according to some feminists, limits sexual expression to male-female forms; the result is "compulsory heterosexuality" that discriminates against homosexuals (Rich, 1980).

Symbolic Interactionism/Sexual Scripts

Building on the symbolic interactionist and social learning schools, the scripting approach to sexuality was developed by Simon and Gagnon (1986, 1987). According to this perspective, humans have no powerful, innate sex drive. Instead, humans learn to be sexual in much the same way they learn other kinds of behavior, "in the same mundane ways we have learned how to play tennis or to bowl, to become a doctor or airline pilot, to like pizza or snails" (Gagnon, 1977:2).

Simon and Gagnon proposed three levels of scripting. As chapter 2 described, we are applying four levels: societal scripts, individual scripts, scenes, and mutual scripts (see Figure 10.1). At each of these four levels, scripts designate an appropriate *who, what, where, when,* and *why* of sexuality.

At each level, the script defines "who" is supposed to be sexual, and with whom. Incest taboos are universal

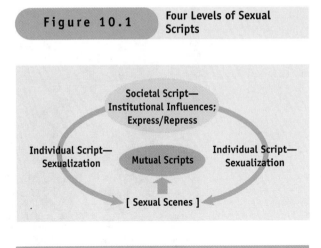

Figure 10.1 Four Levels of Sexual Scripts

prescriptions about the "who" of sex. Issues of nonmarital sex are partly concerns about who are appropriate sexual partners, as are questions about homosexuality.

The "what" of sex is concerned with what is defined as appropriate to do sexually. Sexual activities such as masturbation, oral sex, and anal sex vary in their social acceptability. Individuals within a society develop views about what is appropriate for them. Even deciding what is "sexual activity" and what is not is socially defined. One study found that 60% of college students did not define oral-genital sex as "having sex" (Reinisch & Sanders, 1999). The editor of the *Journal of the American Medical Association* was fired for printing this finding; it had obvious implications during the Clinton-Lewinsky scandal. If President Clinton said he "did not have sexual relations with that woman," when in fact there was oral-genital contact, was he lying?

While persons in the United States generally consider lip kissing to be an erotic activity, it is not considered a sexual "what" if it occurs quickly between a mother and daughter. In many cultures, men kiss each other to seal a bargain, while in still other groups lip kissing never occurs. As any *National Geographic* reader knows, many peoples think nothing about women exposing their breasts (Lutz & Collins, 1993). In many cultures, breasts are considered baby-feeding organs, not objects of erotic desire. In those societies, breasts are not considered to be **erogenous zones**. There is no nongenital part of the body that is genetically programmed to be an erogenous zone; almost any part can, if touched

---

Erogenous zones: Parts of the body that, when stimulated, can lead to sexual arousal.

Eroticism is socially constructed. These dancers on Yap Island only occasionally reveal their bare feet.

in a context that is defined as sexual, become an eroge-nous zone (Gagnon, 1977).

The "where" of sex is also a learned part of a sexual script. Having separate bedrooms for privacy is a rela-tively recent, largely Western contributor to the "where" of sex. In most earlier societies, sexual activity was semi-private only because more people were likely to be in the same living area. Today's couples who do not have children are more varied in the places they choose to have sexual activity; once children are in the home, the "where" becomes more limited.

The "when" of sex does not refer just to time of day or night, but to other periods of time. Whether cou-ples are supposed to have coitus on holy days, or on certain days of the week, or on special occasions like wedding nights, is part of the normative "when." Sex-ual activity can also be prescribed or proscribed de-pending on the phase of the woman's menstrual cycle. The "when" variable can also refer to the time in a per-son's life cycle when sexual activity is considered ap-propriate. Most cultures have rules about sexual activ-ity among prepubescent children, and some have negative perceptions about pregnant, nursing, or post-menopausal women enjoying sexual activities.

The most important element of sexual scripts is the "why" of sex. In this context, "why" does not necessarily refer to the "real" reason a person does sexual things. Rather, the "why" is the accounts persons give themselves or others for their behavior. They might also give different

"whys," depending on their audience. One "why" might be given to a spouse, another to a lover, and yet another to themselves. As Gagnon (1977:8) put it:

> The why of sex is its rhetoric. Sex is for: having children; pleasure; lust; fun; passion; love; variety; intimacy; rebel-lion; degradation; expressing potential/nature/instincts/ needs; exploitation; relaxation; reducing tension; achieve-ment; service.

In some cultures, the "why" of sex is couched in reli-gious terms. Both Hinduism and Buddhism have tantric branches that find in sexual coupling a pathway to Nirvana (Tannahill, 1980; Spellman, 1964). Fertility beliefs have been an integral component of religions in many parts of the world (Parrinder, 1984). These beliefs often provided a religious and procreational "why" of sexual activity.

The "why" is a socially constructed phenomenon, as are other aspects of sexuality. In its purest form, the scripting approach assumes that even the idea that hu-mans have a sex drive is socially constructed. If individ-uals come to believe that they have a strong sex drive, at least some of them will behave in accord with that be-lief. Even though it is learned, it can still become part of brain chemistry and make a powerful determinant of behavior (Money, 1980).

Like hunger and eating, sexuality is universal. Also like eating, sexuality takes different forms in different soci-eties. Sexuality, however, is unlike eating in a major way.

People who do not eat die. There is a direct causal relationship. On the other hand, there is not yet a recorded case in history in which a person has died as a direct result of not having sex. Because of the symbolic power of sex, there might be people who think they might as well be dead, or might even commit suicide over a sexual matter, but that is not a direct causal relationship.

It is not necessary to adopt the pure form of sexual scripting, however, for the scripting approach to be a theoretically useful one. Even if humans do have the guidance of a sex drive, they still construct scripts that include a who, what, where, when, and why. We turn our attention now to the scripting process itself.

Societal Scripts

Some elements of sexual scripts seem arbitrary. Whether or not couples practice lip kissing in a particular culture seems unrelated to the larger social system. In other cases, however, the script is related to larger cultural and institutional forces, including religious moralities.

Modes of production influence sexual scripts. Hunting-gathering societies had quite diverse sexual scripts and did not always reserve sexual activity solely for marital relationships. Agrarian societies were much more limiting about their sexual expression. Since property was passed down in families, it became much more important who "legitimate" heirs were. The best way to ensure this was to reserve sexual expression to marriage. Every child then had a mother and father, making inheritance easier to determine.

Industrial societies generally retained the norms that linked sexual activity to marriage because inheritance of property and capital remained important. Sexual scripts appear to be more open in postindustrial societies, perhaps reflecting the fact that individually achieved characteristics are rivaling family-assigned status, making inheritance less important.

Most cultures treat sexuality as a more or less powerful force, behaving as if humans do have an innate sex drive. The question at the level of social structure and morality then becomes one of what the society should do about the "sex drive."

At one end of a continuum (see Figure 10.2), a society can behave as if the sex drive is not only powerful but evil and destructive as well. In this case, the logical approach would be to repress, punish, and hold down the amount of sexual expression. The other extreme would be to assume that the sex drive itself is good, and to encourage individuals to express their sexuality freely. Societies of this type might assume that it is the repression of sexuality, not its expression, that is a cause of problems. Between these ideal types lies a range of intermediate options.

Control-Repression Scripts

Control-repression scripts assume that the "powerful sex drive" must be controlled by society and by individuals. Without such restrictions, social life as we know it would be impossible because each individual would be attempting to meet his or her own needs, often forcefully or violently, at the expense of others. Some

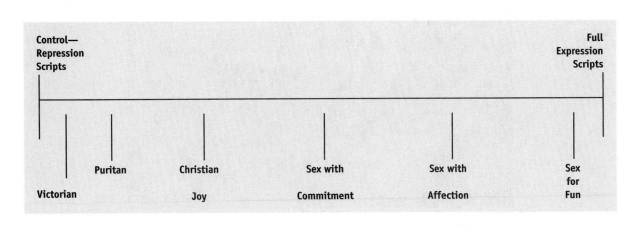

Figure 10.2 The Repression-Expression Continuum

supporters of these scripts have based their views on religious interpretation, while others use secular arguments.

The Traditional Christian Control-Repression Script.

We saw in chapter 3 that one strain of early Christian thought in Europe attempted to institutionalize an antisex morality. This formed the basis for the traditional Christian control-repression script, although it has never been endorsed by all Christians.

The primary "why" of sex, in the traditional Christian control-repression script, is procreation. This "why" determines all other elements of the script. The "who" is spouse only. Adultery and premarital sex, which can result in conception, are deemed wrong because each child has a right "to be born of a father and mother known to him and bound to each other by marriage" (*Catechism of the Catholic Church*, 1994:571). Homosexuality is wrong because it is unmarried sex and because it cannot result in reproduction. Homosexuality has variously been called "an abomination" (Bible, Leviticus 18:22), "grave depravity" and "intrinsically disordered" (*Catechism*, 1994:566). It is homosexual acts, however, not homosexual persons or homosexual orientations, that are considered sinful (*Catechism*, 1994).

The "what" of the control-repression script is also dictated by the procreative "why." Only sexual acts that might result in procreation are allowed: "Each and every marriage act must remain open to the transmission of life" (*Catechism*, 1994:569). All forms of birth control except those that rely on abstinence are "intrinsically evil." The requirement of potential procreation also rules out oral sex, anal sex, and masturbation, which is seen as "an intrinsically and gravely disordered action" (*Catechism*, 1994:564). In the eighth century, church documents further specified that the "what" be the male-superior, or "missionary position," and prescribed penalties for couples who used other coital positions (Harmatz & Novak, 1983).

To extreme control-repressionists, the "what" of sex does not include talking about it. Repressionists tend to oppose explicit portrayals of sexual activities and such things as sex education in the schools; there is a fear that talking about or depicting sex will arouse the "strong sex drive" and incline persons to engage in wanton and destructive sexual activities.

The "where" of sexuality is not dealt with directly by Catholic or fundamentalist Protestant theology, although privacy and decorum are certainly assumed. The "when" is limited to times when procreation is possible. Postmenopausal sex is not specifically forbidden, but American culture has generally considered sexual activity by older women to be inappropriate. Nursing home policies have historically reflected such assumptions.

Secular Control-Repression Approaches.

It is not solely from religion that Western repressive scripts derive. Perhaps echoing the religious view of the times, some early scientists also warned against the evils of unbridled sex. One of the first "scientific" treatments of

The first Methodist sermon in Baltimore almost certainly included warnings about the sins of the flesh.

sexuality was the writing of the Swiss physician Tissot (1728–1797) about masturbation. In keeping with the medical views of his time, Tissot believed that disease was caused by an imbalance of bodily fluids. Since masturbation prematurely released bodily fluids, it could result in imbalances that caused everything from acne to insanity.

Victorian (19th-century) scientists and physicians extended the fear of masturbation to all sexual activity, and economic philosophers even contributed. The favorite 19th-century slang expression referring to orgasm was "to spend," a reference to a waste of valuable resources. Paralleling capitalist ideologies of saving and investing, any kind of sexual activity risked wasting vital bodily fluids. Only such acts as could result in reproduction were considered wise investments (Gagnon, 1977).

Fear of out-of-control sexuality was at the heart of the 19th-century American health-food fad. William Alcott and Sylvester Graham (Graham crackers) warned against spicy and fatty food, white bread, and other diets that were thought to stimulate the "carnal appetites." They advocated dietary products that were bland, unprocessed, and wholesome and that purportedly reduced the sex drive. James Harvey Kellogg, a vegetarian, advertised his products as both healthy and sex-drive-reducing. His "Granula," marketed in 1877, is credited with being the first cold prepared breakfast cereal (Trager, 1992).

During the industrial era, science might have had a greater influence on repressive sexual scripts than did religion (Money, 1985). In the first half of the 20th century, Freud (1913, 1930) developed his own version of a repressive script. He believed that the sex drive had to be redirected in a socially acceptable form or civilization would be impossible.

Inis Beag. An island community off the coast of Ireland, called Inis Beag by Messinger (1971), the anthropologist who studied it, is often used as an example of a society living a control-repression script based on conservative Catholic theology. Ireland itself retains a repressive sexual script, and Inis Beag is even more restricted. Sex is never discussed, even in jokes, and there is no sex education. Girls usually do not know about menarche until it happens to them.

Messinger noted that there was little or no sex play or touching among adolescents, nor was there any indication of premarital coitus. This was the case in spite of the relative late average age at first marriage, 25 years for women and 36 for men.

Intercourse on Inis Beag was seen as a duty, its only justification being procreation. The act occurred in the dark, under the covers, with the participants as fully clothed as possible. The men probably ejaculated as quickly as possible, and orgasm for women either never occurred or was not referred to because it was thought to be abnormal (Messinger, 1971).

Full-Expression Scripts

The relatively rare proponents of full expression in Western society propose a different script than do the repressionists. Like the repression script, the full-expression script assumes that humans have a strong sex drive. In the expressive view, however, the sex drive is a positive and natural phenomenon. Social and personal harm comes from repression of the sex drive, not its expression.

The "why" of sex, in this script, is pleasure, achieving human potential, or other positive construction. The reproduction function is recognized, but separated from the pleasure function of sexuality. Wilhelm Reich (1933, 1942) argued that the pleasure function is at least as natural and important as procreation:

> Biologically speaking, the healthy human organism calls for three to four thousand sexual acts in the course of a genital life of, say, 30 to 40 years. The wish for offspring is satisfied with two to four children. Moralistic and ascetic ideologies condone sexual pleasure even in marriage only for the purpose of procreation; carried to its logical conclusion, that would mean at the most four sexual acts in a lifetime (Reich, 1942:175).

Given the pleasure "why" of sex, the "who, what, where," and "when" are easy to determine. In the expressive script, any sexual act, with anyone, is acceptable as long as it is mutually agreed to by adults and brings pleasure to the participants. Reich believed, however, that sexual activity would be self-limiting. People would discover that the best, most pleasurable sex acts result when they are with partners for whom they have deep feelings, trust, and commitment. Although there will be considerable experimentation, a vast majority of individuals will, when allowed full expression of their sexual drives, develop long-term relationships with loving partners (Reich, 1942).

Reich and others who advocate expressive scripts believe that women and men are equally capable of sexual pleasure, and that anyone's pleasure is enhanced when his or her partner is also experiencing pleasure. Both women and men must be free to express their sexual drives, which would eliminate a double standard.

Since the sex drive itself, and its natural expression, are considered good things, there is no fear of talking about sex. Expressionists advocate various forms of sex education, including those that provide young persons the contraceptive knowledge that allows them to separate the reproductive and the pleasure functions if they wish to do so.

Reich believed that there would be fewer true sexual "perversions" if society allowed full and natural expression of sexuality. Expressionists believe that aggression arises only when human needs are blocked, so the way to create a peaceful, harmonious society is to allow human beings to meet their needs without interference by repressive laws.

Mangaia. Anthropologist Donald Marshall (1971) studied the people on a southern Polynesian island who have come to represent a culture with a full-expression sexual script. Adults have intercourse in the room with all their kin, and there is frequent lingual manipulation of the penis of young boys by female members of the family. By age 7 to 10, boys and girls are shown how to masturbate. After puberty rituals at about age 13, boys are given sexual instruction and practice by older women. The boys are taught how to postpone ejaculation and provide multiple orgasms to their partners. Girls receive a comparable education with older men.

Premarital sex is not only accepted, it is virtually required. Young adults have sex almost every night; girls and boys both average three orgasms each night, not always with the same partner. There is much talk about sex, with the women openly comparing the sexual ability of their partners. They have several words for parts of the genitals, and varieties of genitalia, that most Westerners fail even to notice. While married partners have sex less frequently, the expectation remains that they will please each other (Marshall, 1971).

With Mangaia and similar cultures at one end of the continuum and Inis Beag at the other, the world's cultures have a wide range of scripts from which to choose. While the American pattern has historically been closer to the script on Inis Beag, it is a complex and diverse society. Many competing scripts can be found among American groups and individuals.

Intermediate Scripts

We have presented two extreme sexual scripts. Although both have their advocates in America, the majority of persons adopt a script somewhere between the extremes. Close to the traditional Christian control-repression script is the Puritan one, which reigned in colonial America. The Puritans were strongly opposed to sexual activity outside of marriage, vigorously punishing transgressors with flogging, the stocks, forced public confessions, and other "cruel and unusual" approaches. Their language was lusty, however, and a premarital pregnancy was only mildly treated if it was discrete and quickly followed by marriage. Within marriage, sexual activity was encouraged and seen as healthy (Bullough, 1976).

Somewhat less repressive is a "Christian joy" model. Sexual acts are still limited to marriage, but "spiritual togetherness" and "pleasure among married partners" are added to the "why" of sex. This script is supported by some Catholics and is advocated by some Protestant denominations. It allows for the use of contraceptives for married couples and expands the allowable "what" to include oral sex and other activities beyond missionary-position sex.

Further along the continuum is the "sex with commitment" script. To the "why" is added "sex as mutual expression of love and commitment." In this script, premarital sex would be considered appropriate as long as the couple had plans for marriage or at least a monogamous commitment with the possibility of marriage.

Somewhat more expressive is the "sex with affection" script (Reiss, 1967), to which is added a "why" of "expression of caring and friendship." As long as the partners like each other, premarital sexual activity is considered appropriate. The most expressive contemporary view is "sex for recreation." In this view, sex is for fun, and one-night mating is appropriate as long as both partners are willing. Anything to which they mutually agree is acceptable.

Contemporary American Values

As diverse as the American script is, we can learn something about it by looking at sexual values as expressed by survey results. Beginning in 1972, the General Social Surveys began asking questions about the acceptability of various forms of sexuality. Respondents were asked whether they thought the practice was "always wrong," "almost always wrong," "wrong only sometimes," or "not wrong at all." Figure 10.3 provides the results of those surveys in the form of the percentage of the adult American population who responded "always wrong."

The data show a gradual decrease in objections to premarital sex, although there was an increase from 1996 to 1998. In the latter year, 28.5% thought it was always wrong. Significantly more women (32.5%) than men (23.3%) agreed.

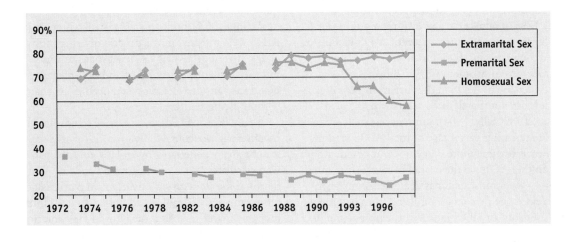

| Figure 10.3 | Percent Saying Types of Sexuality Are "Always Wrong," 1972 to 1998 |

Source: Davis, James Allan, and Tom W. Smith: General Social Survey(s), 1972–1998. (Machine-readable data file). Principal investigator, James A. Davis; director and co-principal investigator, Tom W. Smith; co-principal investigator, Peter V. Marsden, NORC ed. Chicago: National Opinion Research Center, producer, 1998; Storrs, CT: The Roper Center for Public Opinion Research, University of Connecticut, distributor. Microcomputer format and codebook prepared and distributed by MicroCase Corporation, Bellevue, WA. Analysis by Gene H. Starbuck.

In contrast to decreasing objections to premarital sex, a gradual but steady increase in objection to **extramarital sex** has occurred. The change was most noticeable in the 1980s, with little change in the 1990s. In 1998, 79.3% of Americans thought extramarital sex was always wrong. This included 81.6% of women and 76.2% of men.

The views regarding homosexuality have seen the most dramatic change, especially in the 1990s when objections declined rapidly. By 1998, the portion of Americans who thought same-sex activity was always wrong had dropped to 58.0%. A slightly higher fraction of men (59.8%) than women (56.7%) agreed.

Sex in a Time of AIDS

Changes in sexual scripts have contributed to the spread of sexually transmitted diseases, including the most deadly. **AIDS** is tragic to persons who contract the disease, and to their families and friends. More than 430,000 Americans have died of AIDS since it was diagnosed in 1981 (Centers for Disease Control, 2000). Although AIDS has fallen out of the list of 10 most frequent causes of death in the United States, it is reaching catastrophic levels in Africa and other parts of the world.

Adding to the tragedy is the fact that transmission of **HIV** is relatively easy to prevent. While it is reasonable to fear AIDS, it is also easy for the fear to result in unnecessary panic and for various groups to manipulate that fear for their own purposes. AIDS activists argue that not enough is being done to find a cure or vaccination for AIDS. Others point out, however, that considerably more money per death is now spent on AIDS research than on either heart disease or cancer, both of which kill more Americans annually (Stout, 1992).

One fear has been that AIDS will become rampant in the heterosexual population. Although almost as

Extramarital sex: Sexual intercourse between a married person and someone not his or her spouse; adultery.   **AIDS** (acquired immune deficiency syndrome): Fatal condition in which the body loses its natural ability to protect itself from disease.   **HIV** (human immunodeficiency virus): The virus that causes AIDS.

many women as men have AIDS in Africa, that is not the case in the United States; health care conditions and sexual practices are different in Africa than in the United States. As of 1999, women were the victims of just over 17% of all AIDS cases ever reported in the United States. Women's proportion of AIDS victims has increased, however; in 1999, just over 23% of new AIDS cases were in women (CDC, 2000).

Rapid increase of AIDS in the American heterosexual population has not materialized as many had feared (Fumento, 1989; Sills, 1994), but heterosexuals are making up an increasing percentage of total AIDS victims. Homosexuals became more diligent about practicing **safe sex** in the 1980s, so the overall ratio of AIDS cases transmitted by homosexuals has decreased somewhat. This increased the percentage resulting from heterosexual transmission. In 1999, however, the proportion of total AIDS cases that had been contracted by heterosexual activity was still under 11% (see Table 10.1).

The majority of women who got AIDS from heterosexual intercourse were infected by an intravenous drug abuser. Considerably fewer were infected by a bisexual lover (see Table 10.1). Cases of transmission from one non-drug-using heterosexual to another are actually quite rare (Fumento, 1989).

As Table 10.1 indicates, 42% of all women with AIDS were infected in the process of using intravenous drugs. It is not the drug use itself that transmits AIDS, but the accidental injection of an HIV-infected user's blood into another person when needles are shared without being sanitized.

Nearly half of all AIDS cases were transmitted by male homosexual intercourse. The most risky sexual behavior is to be anally penetrated by an HIV-infected partner who ejaculates and is not wearing a condom. Anal penetration sometimes causes small tears in rectal tissue, exposing the bloodstream. In addition, the large intestine probably is able to absorb the virus in HIV-infected semen (Sills, 1994). Some of the heterosexual transmission also results from anal intercourse, although how much is not known. There is much less risk to the man who penetrates than to the partner who is penetrated.

Table 10.1	Cumulative AIDS Cases Reported Through 1999, by Exposure Category, Percentage by Gender, and Percentage of Total Cases					
	Males			**Females**		
Exposure Category	**Number**	**Percent of Male**	**Percent of Total**	**Number**	**Percent of Female**	**Percent of Total**
Homosexual sex	341,597	56	47	—	—	—
Injecting drug use	134,356	22	19	50,073	42	7
Homosexual and drug use	48,582	8	7	—	—	—
Hemophilia	4903	1	1	272	0	<1
Heterosexual contact	26,530	4	4	47,946	40	7
Sex with drug user	8,696	1	1	19,523	16	3
Sex with bisexual male	—	—	—	3,368	3	<1
Sex with other/unspecified	17,834	3	2	25,065	21	3
Receipt of blood transfusion, blood components, or tissue	4,963	1	1	3,668	3	<1
Other/ not identified	46,112	8	6	17,851	15	2
Totals (724,656)	604,843	100	83	119,810	100	17

Source: Adapted from Centers for Disease Control and Prevention, 2000. *Surveillance Report Vol.* 11 # 2, Table 5. http://www.cdc.gov/hiv/stats/hasr1102/table5.htm.

Safe sex: Use of condoms or other practices that significantly reduce the risk of spreading the AIDS-causing virus. Perhaps better thought of as safer sex.

In unprotected penile-vaginal intercourse, transmission from man to woman is more likely than the reverse. Semen is placed into contact with tissue that is more likely to absorb the virus, especially if the tissue is damaged in some way. Entry of fluid into the man's bloodstream through the penis or some other entry point is less likely. It has generally been believed that transmission of HIV by oral sex, heterosexual or homosexual, is extremely unlikely (Fumento, 1989). More recent evidence, however, indicates that unprotected fellatio is far from perfectly safe (Stephensen, 2000).

Use of condoms reduces risk of contracting AIDS. By one estimate, the odds of a person who is not in the high-risk category being infected by HIV in one random sexual encounter is about 1 in 5 million. If a condom is used, the odds are reduced to about 1 in 50 million (Hurst & Hully, 1988). Condom use has the additional advantage of reducing transmission of syphilis, gonorrhea, chlamydia, and other sexually transmitted diseases that are more common than AIDS and can also be quite serious. In addition, condoms serve their original purposes of greatly reducing the probability of conception (Masters, Johnson, & Kolodny, 1992).

Although the probability of contracting AIDS in a random act of heterosexual intercourse is extremely small, the consequence of the disease, once caught, is probable death. Some change in sexual patterns appears to have occurred as a result of concern about AIDS. A nationally representative sample of 8,500 American women found that nearly one third of sexually experienced unmarried women reported a change in sexual behavior as a result of AIDS. The most common change was to reduce the number of sexual relationships to one at a time (McNally & Mosher, 1991). Ironically, their AIDS risk is increased if that one partner happens to carry the AIDS virus.

Although AIDS is distributed throughout the country, incidence is highest in the central areas of New York, San Francisco, Los Angeles, and other large cities. These areas also have a high proportion of African Americans and Hispanics, who have disproportionate rates of AIDS. Whites have a rate of 9.0 AIDS cases per 100,000. The same number of Blacks has 84.2 cases, and Hispanics have 34.6 (CDC, 2000: Table 19). High rates of intravenous drug use and active but unprotected sexual activity in central-city areas also contribute to disproportionate rates of other sexually transmitted diseases among poor minorities. In 1988, Blacks accounted for 78% of all reported cases of gonorrhea and 76% of

all reported cases of syphilis; Hispanics accounted for 12% of syphilis cases (National Commission on AIDS, 1992). This makes the problem of AIDS in the Black and Hispanic communities worse because syphilis and gonorrhea make the spread of HIV more likely, and these diseases are more deadly to persons with AIDS (Sills, 1994).

Gender Differences in Sexual Scripts

The diversity of American society ensures that there will always be competing sexual scripts. Such disagreement can be seen in the continued debates about abortion and about sex education in the schools. Many of the debates center on what is appropriate behavior for men as compared with women, an area that has changed considerably in recent years. Another area affected by social changes in sexual understandings is the issue of what constitutes consent and rape.

The Double Standard

The traditional Christian repression model is, in its doctrinal statements, an egalitarian script (*Catechism,* 1994). As it is practiced, however, this and other repressive scripts have a tendency toward different sexual standards for men and women. The double standard follows from assumptions made about the nature of sexuality.

The traditional control script assumes that men have a more powerful sex drive than women. Men are expected to be the sexual aggressors and initiators. Further, the man's pleasure, in the form of ejaculation, is necessary to the procreative act. Women's orgasm is unrelated to conception. In effect, the man's pleasure is a necessary evil, while women can remain "pure" by not desiring or enjoying the sex act too much.

This results in a "why" of sex that, if not fully acceptable, is at least understandable: the man's strong sex drive gets out of control. The Biblical Eve was the primordial temptress; this image of women sometimes is used to excuse sexual behavior of men who were "tempted" by women. Scripting theory assumes that this is a learned phenomenon, however, and both men and women sometimes learn to play their roles accordingly.

Whether because it is learned or is genetic, as sociobiologists argue, men and women do approach sexuality differently. Although the double standard has weakened in the United States, it still exists. Both men and women

Men and women still differ in their public appraisals of each other. He is probably pondering her intellectual capabilities. Or maybe not.

continue to believe that men are more sexual and should more often be the sexual initiators. Men remain in the "sexual entrepreneur" role while women are more commonly in the "moral gatekeeper" role (Benokraitis, 1993).

Men and women differ somewhat in their orientations to sexuality. The broadest difference is that women have a more "general" sexual orientation, while men have a more "genital" approach (Gagnon, 1977). The "general/genital" difference manifests itself in three major ways. First, men are more likely to separate sex from relationship. As sexual strategies theorists have found, men are more likely to employ short-term mating strategies, which involve sexual activity but not emotional involvement or commitment. Women are more likely to put sexual activity into a relationship context (Buss & Schmitt, 1993).

The general/genital difference is also manifested in the image men and women have of the sex act itself. Women tend to prefer that genital contact be part of more general bodily touching, holding, rubbing; "making love" for women is a much broader category of events, which might not even include genital sexuality. Men are likely to define sex acts in terms of more specific genital activity. The happiest sexual couples appear to be those in which men have a variety of genital stimulation, including frequent oral sex, and women receive tender and considerate arousal (Blumstein & Schwartz, 1983).

Men and women are similar in that both have sexual fantasies of all types. Nearly all men and as many as 94% of adult women at least occasionally combine sexual stimulation with fantasy (Crépault & Couture, 1977; 1980). For both men and women, use of fantasy is more common during masturbation than during intercourse (Crépault & Couture, 1980). Of those who use fantasies, nearly all enjoy them rather than try to repress their thoughts; 89% of women and 92% of men reported enjoying the feelings associated with their fantasies (Ellis & Symons, 1990).

Although some research finds no gender differences in sexual fantasies (Rokach, 1990), differences that have been found reflect the general/genital distinction (Dubois, 1997). Ellis and Symons (1990) found greater sexual variety in male sexual fantasies and greater emotional focus in women's fantasies. When asked whether they had ever fantasized about a variety of 23 sexual acts, more men than women reported fantasizing about all 23 choices. For both men and women, fantasizing about oral sex was the most common; 75% of men and 43% of women reported such thoughts (Patterson & Kim, 1991).

Fantasy differences carry over into the kinds of written and pictorial depictions of erotica in which women and men are interested. Most X-rated books and movies are produced for a male audience; they contain graphic and explicit images of genitals and sexual activity. The romance novel is a form of erotica produced for women. The forms of sexual portrayals designed for men are frequently controlled by laws and attempts at censorship. Women's erotica, considered less threatening, is widely available in grocery stores and elsewhere.

Most of the research on the double standard and male-female differences in images of the sexual script has been done in the United States or other postindustrial societies. While some of the differences might be the result of genetic predispositions, major double standards do not seem to be universal. Less repressive societies tend to have fewer male-female differences.

Defining Consent and Rape

As the double standard is changing, so are other elements of the sexual script, including those related to defining what is consensual intercourse and what is not. In the broader social context, there is a continuum of greater or lesser degrees of consent; the formal norms vary on this continuum from one time and place to another.

At one extreme on the contemporary consent-rape continuum, we have a hypothetical case in which a married couple agrees that they will have intercourse next Saturday. They cooperate in planning a romantic evening. On Saturday, they carry out their romantic plans and, just before they actually begin to have intercourse they both sign a statement saying that they consent to the sex act. Then, at no time during the lovemaking does either partner believe, state, or imply that they have changed their minds. Unless there are some strange circumstances not covered by the scenario, virtually everyone would agree that consent was given in this case, and that the sex act was not rape.

At the other extreme of the consent continuum would be a case in which a women is home alone in her own bed; a stranger breaks into her home and forces himself on her. She fights back, but her attacker is stronger and beats her severely in addition to forcefully penetrating her. This is a scenario that virtually everyone would agree is nonconsenting and therefore rape.

In between these extremes, however, is a wide range of circumstances that make the decision about consent less widely unanimous. First, there is a distinction between "general consent" and "specific consent." While most societies do not reserve approved sexual activity solely to married couples, all societies do approve of sexual activity in the marriage bond. Marriage provides general consent by two persons to be a sexually active couple. This is not the same thing, however, as providing consent to each and every specific sexual advance. Historically, married couples were left to their own devices to work out methods of specific consent. Divorce was generally allowed for a person who either never gave specific consent, or for one who was forced to do sexual things against his or her will. Informal sanctions by church, community, and kin helped enforce norms of specific consent, but few societies' legal systems made it possible to prosecute one spouse for forcing sex on another.

Husband exclusion clauses in the rape laws have recently changed. In only two states are husbands still completely excluded from rape prosecution; in at least 13 states, husbands are treated no differently than strangers in rape cases; and in the remaining states there are at least some different treatments of marital rape compared to other types (Aulette, 1994).

While husbands were historically exempt from rape laws, men have always been punished for some forms of nonmarital intercourse. In cases of **statutory rape,** girls under a certain age are not deemed to have the legal capability to give specific consent to intercourse. The age varies from one state to another, but even if she consents, an older male who has sex with a girl under the stated age can be charged with rape. More recently, statutory rape laws have been made gender-neutral in several states, but prosecution of female perpetrators is quite rare.

Historically, it has been legally impossible to charge a woman with the rape of a man. Several states have changed that aspect of the law. A California statutory rape law that allowed for prosecution only of men and boys was challenged on the grounds that it discriminated on the basis of gender. The U.S. Supreme Court upheld the law in 1981 on the grounds that such statutes provide a necessary tool in the prevention of teenage pregnancy (Michael M. v. Superior Court of Sonoma County; in Inciardi, 1993).

In the past, it was thought that strangers committed most rapes; it is now generally agreed that most rapes are committed by a person known to the victim (Koss, 1987). This has complicated definitions of rape. Some

---

Husband exclusion clause: Part of a rape law that makes it impossible to charge a husband with the rape of his wife.
Statutory rape: Having intercourse, even if consensual, with a person not considered old enough to give consent. In some states only female victims are considered; others are gender-neutral (Inciardi, 1993:82).

marital, **acquaintance** and **date rape** can be as violent and cause as much physical and emotional trauma as stranger rape (Russell, 1990), and it can clearly indicate a lack of consent. The issue of consent in other cases is less clear.

In some cases, general consent has been at least partly established by the fact that the couple has engaged in consensual sex on other occasions. In other cases, the woman has voluntarily gone with the man to the location where the sex act occurred. Americans are somewhat less likely to define the act as rape under these circumstances (Inciardi, 1993).

Some apparent date rapes result from miscommunication derived from the way the sexual script is written. Men are expected to be the sexual aggressors, while women are the resistors. The double standard still judges women who are sexually expressive more harshly than men, so many women learn to behave as if they need to be "swept away." Real resistance is sometimes mistaken for the token resistance that is expected of women. More than 1 in 3 college women admit to having said "no" when they did not mean it and might have given mixed signals (Muehlenhard & McCoy, 1991).

Organized presentations are influential in defining rape-related issues.

Cases in which a woman says "no" and clearly means it are relatively easy to place at the "no consent" end of the continuum, but much sexual communication is nonverbal, without clearly articulated requests nor clearly stated responses. It is in this gray area that many cases fall, and they contribute to the difficulty of finding out how much rape exists. The amount depends heavily on how rape is counted, and for what purpose (see Finding Out 10.1).

Learning Individual Scripts

Through **sexualization,** individuals learn and develop their personal sexual scripts in much the same way they learn and develop in other areas of their lives (Gagnon, 1977). The process of developing a sexual script continues throughout one's lifetime, but is a more consuming task during adolescence. It is during this period that young persons deal with the question of premarital sexuality, and the time that most Americans have their first complete experience with coitus. For some, there is the issue of developing a sexual identity that is different from the norm; some of these eventually develop a homosexual self-image. It is with these issues that this section deals.

Premarital Sexuality

In the United States, a wide variety of influences help determine whether and when a young person will become sexually active, what he or she will do, and whether he or she will risk pregnancy and sexually transmitted disease.

Valid studies of sexual behavior are very difficult to conduct. Finding large numbers of persons who are willing to talk about such personal matters, or even to answer anonymous questionnaires, is not easy. When such individuals are found, it is not always true that they represent the larger population accurately. It is possible that only the more sexually "liberal" will feel comfortable answering questions about their sexuality, so surveys might overstate the sexual permissiveness of the population (Hunt, 1974). This is especially likely when

---

Acquaintance rape: Nonconsensual intercourse imposed by a person known by the victim.　**Date rape:** Nonconsensual sexual intercourse when the perpetrator and victim are voluntarily in a close relationship.　**Sexualization:** The process of learning one's individual sexual script; sexual socialization.

the survey does not use a randomly selected sample (Laumann et al., 1994).

Most researchers have concluded that there was a relatively rapid increase in the amount of premarital sexual behavior in the late 1960s and the 1970s. Both attitudes and behavior continued to become more permissive in the 1980s, but the change was slower than in the 1960s and 1970s. Throughout this period, change was more rapid for women than for men, reducing the sexual double standard (Darling, Kallan, & VanDusen, 1984; Hofferth, Rahn, & Baldwin, 1987; Laumann et al., 1994).

Sexual activity varies by race as well as gender (see Table 10.2). Black adolescents are more likely to have had intercourse than Whites or Hispanics. Hispanic females have about the same rate of activity as White females, but Hispanic males have considerably higher rates than their White counterparts. While more young men have sex at early ages, by the time all adolescents are out of high school nearly two thirds of them have had intercourse at least once.

Laumann and others (1994), conducted a major study of sexuality based on a nationally representative sample of 3,432 persons. They found that, among married individuals in their 20s, 16.3% of the men and 20.1% of the women were virgins at marriage. For those in their 50s, figures were 21.9% of men and 54.4% of women. In most cases, the premarital sex for women was with the man they ultimately married.

Laumann also found the median total number of partners for heterosexual men to be seven, while the median for women was two. For both men and women, sexual patterns were different for those whose first union was marriage compared to those whose first union was cohabitation. Those who married rather than cohabiting were far more likely to have no previous sexual partners and far less likely to have had five or more partners prior to the union.

Changes in premarital sexual attitudes and behavior seem to have slowed considerably in the 1990s. On the one hand, average age of marriage has increased, which increases the likelihood of premarital sexual activity. As we saw in chapter 7, the practice of having children out of wedlock has become more common and more acceptable, especially among the poor. Factors operating to reduce the amount of premarital sexual behavior include fear of AIDS and increasing activism by conservative political and religious forces.

Demographic, political, and religious factors are not the only ones that influence sexual behavior. Parents influence the sexual behavior of adolescents, but perhaps not in as direct a manner as might be thought.

Table 10.2	Percentage of High School Students Who Had Intercourse, by Gender, Race, and Grade in School, 1999	
Category	**Female**	**Male**
Race/Ethnicity		
White	44.8	45.4
Black	66.9	75.7
Hispanic	45.5	62.9
Grade in School		
9th	32.5	44.5
10th	42.6	51.1
11th	53.8	51.4
12th	65.8	64.9

Source: Centers for Disease Control, 2000. "Youth Risk Behavior Surveillance—United States, 1999." *CDC Surveillance Summaries, MMWR Morbidity and Mortality Weekly Report, June 9.* Table 30. Atlanta, GA.
http://www2.cdc.gov/mmwr/mmwr_ss.html
ftp://ftp.cdc.gov/pub/Publications/mmwr/ss/ss4905.pdf.

Finding Out | 10.1

Measurement of Rape, Politics, and Feminism

Counting human events on a societywide scale is a difficult thing to do, and counting crime is particularly troublesome. Definitions change over time; those changes are both the effect and cause of changes in the moral, normative, and political system. Changes in the way rape is perceived and counted provide an example. Estimates about how much rape there is in America vary widely, depending upon who does the counting, how the counting is done, and the purpose of the study. Measurements of rape have political implications regarding the roles of men and women in society.

Two major government counts of crime in the United States are compiled by the Justice Department. The FBI Uniform Crime Report counts incidents of rape and attempted rape, along with other serious crimes, that are reported by police departments annually. They found 89,110 cases of rape and attempted rape in 1999 for a rate of 32.7 per 100,000 population (http://www.fbi.gov/ucr/99cius.htm). The National Crime Victimization Survey (NCVS) uses a sample of about 50,000 households annually. The NCVS estimated 383,000 cases of rape, attempted rape, and sexual assault in 1999, for a rate of 170 per 100,000 people over 12 years of age (http://www.ojp.usdoj.gov:80/bjs/pub/pdf/cv99.pdf).

A Louis Harris (1993) study concluded that about 2% of American women had been raped in the previous 5 years. The Justice Department estimates that about 8% of women will be the victims of rape or attempted rape sometime during their lives (Harlow, 1991).

Estimates about the incidence of rape can go much higher than the official reports, especially when broad definitions of rape are used. Some feminist scholars have been particularly critical of official counts of rape incidence, claiming that lower counts understate the magnitude and severity of the rape problem. Catharine MacKinnon (1989), a feminist legal scholar, claimed that almost half of American women will be raped at least once in their lifetimes. One study reported that 27.5% of college women had been the victims of rape as the crime is legally defined (Koss, Gidycz, & Wisniewski, 1987). Koss concluded, "Rape rests squarely in the middle of what our culture defines as 'normal' interaction between men and women" (p. 169).

As with any major social research, Koss's study has been challenged. Although the sample included 6,159 women and men and was representative of college students nationwide, the way she posed her questions has been criticized. Her questionnaire asked several questions about various degrees of sexual victimization. A women who responded "yes" on any one of the following three questions was counted as a rape victim (Koss et al., 1987:167):

8. Have you had sexual intercourse when you didn't want to because a man gave you alcohol or drugs?

9. Have you had sexual intercourse when you didn't want to because a man threatened or used some degree of physical force (twisting your arm, holding you down, etc.) to make you?

10. Have you had sex acts (anal or oral intercourse or penetrations by objects other than the penis) when you didn't want to because a man threatened or used some degree of physical force (twisting your arm, holding you down, etc.) to make you?

Of the women surveyed, 15.4% of the respondents answered "yes" to one or more of the above questions.

Positive responses to either of the two following questions qualified a respondent to be a victim of attempted rape (Koss et al., 1987:167):

4. Have you had a man attempt sexual intercourse (get on top of you, attempt to insert his penis) when you didn't want to by threatening or using some degree of force (twisting your arm, holding you down, etc.), but intercourse did not occur?

5. Have you had a man attempt sexual intercourse (get on top of you, attempt to insert his penis) when you didn't want to by giving you alcohol or drugs, but intercourse did not occur?

In addition to the women who gave a positive reply to the "rape" questions, 12.1% of respondents answered "yes" to one or more of the "attempted rape" questions. This is a total of 27.5% of respondents who, by Koss's measure, had been victims of either rape or attempted rape.

Koss (1987:167) claimed that the "rape" victims had been through experiences that "met legal definitions of these crimes." While some of the experiences were certainly rape as legally defined, not all were. For one thing, it is not legally sufficient that a person "didn't want to" have sex. The objection has to be communicated to the other person unless the attack is such that it is clear that he or she would not want to, as when a knife, gun, or other serious threats are used. Alcohol- or drug-induced sex is generally classified as rape only when the drugs are given without the knowledge of the other person; when the victim is clearly not in a state of mind competent to resist; and when the drugs or alcohol were given with the intent of taking sexual advantage of the victim.

Another criticism is that different surveys were given to men and women. The women were asked victim-oriented questions, while the men were asked victimizer-oriented questions. Using the same questions for men and women might have prompted different conclusions. Another study used a very broad definition of "sexual aggression": "sexual intercourse through threats, pressure, lying; getting someone drunk or stoned; using or threatening to use physical force, a knife, or a gun; or raping." Fully 64% of women had experienced sexual aggression as that study defined it, but so had 47% of the men (Gwartney-Gibbs, Stockard, & Bohmer, 1987).

Sommers (1994) pointed to inconsistencies in the results of the Koss study. The "rape" categories in the study did not mention the word *rape* on the questionnaire, but respondents were also directly asked whether they had ever been raped and whether they had ever reported it to the police. Only 27% of the women Koss defined as rape victims responded "yes" when asked if they had ever been raped and only 5% had reported to the police. Koss attributed the discrepancy between her definition of rape and the respondent's self-definitions to the false consciousness of the sexual script, arguing that women often do not recognize their own victimization.

Roiphe (1993a) argued that the women themselves were better judges of whether they had been victims than were the researchers. There are a number of scenarios about which a woman might answer "yes" to one of Koss's questions but not consider herself a victim of rape. She might have willingly consumed the alcohol or drugs even though the man provided them. She might have been an active participant in the sex act to please him, even though she did not really want to. She could have decided the next day, rather than at the time, that she had not really wanted to. She might have known at the time that she didn't want to but didn't convey that fact to him. In the case of "attempted rape," the man might have stopped when she finally expressed her objections. She might have been a nonresisting partner as they disrobed and got into a situation where he could actually attempt to insert his penis.

In reaction to criticism, Koss later agreed that the drug and alcohol question, at least, was not necessarily a good indicator of rape, and if the two questions involving that condition were dropped, the "one in four" victimization rate would drop to one in nine (Sommers, 1994).

Sommers (1994) called Koss's work **advocacy research** because it was designed to advance the cause of what she called "gender feminists." Groups with special interests and ideologies fund much social research; when the results advance the cause of the funding source, they are open to criticism. Koss's research was funded and supported by *Ms* magazine and its editor Gloria Steinem, strong supporters of the feminist view that women are victims of men and of the patriarchy. Sommers argued that such views are enhanced when high rates of rape are reported. Not only is the ideological position bolstered, but more money will be appropriated for feminist organizations, rape crisis centers, battered wife shelters, and other causes.

In response to concerns about the underreporting of rape, the Department of Justice (Fisher et al., 2000) conducted a new study of rape on college campuses, using the Koss study as a model. The department concluded that over 3% of college women had been a victim of rape or attempted rape, by their definition, in the past academic year. Unlike Koss, this study included unwanted or forced oral sex as rape. Included in the 3% were unsuccessful attempts to perform, or have the women perform, oral sex. Like Koss, they asked only women the questions. Like Koss, they found that most of the women who were rape victims by the researcher's definition did not consider themselves to have been a victim of a crime. Finally, also like Koss, they found that fewer than 5% of the rapes as they defined them were officially reported.

Roiphe, Sommers, Paglia, and other equity feminists worry that poorly measured rape victimization statistics will result in legislation that treats women as victims in need of special protection, rather than equal treatment; laws preventing women from equal participation in the workforce have often been justified as "special protection." Finally, there is concern that broadening the definition of rape will trivialize the act.

In defense of their work, Koss and other researchers respond that men have always been the ones to define what rape is, and those definitions have always favored the male perspective. They argue that both research and public perceptions must change as women define rape from women's perspective. Rape of any kind, they argue, is a serious matter at both the personal and societal levels and needs to be treated as such.

Advocacy research: Study done primarily to advance a political cause or point of view.

Observing parental affection is valuable "sex education" for children.

A common belief is that parents who are sexually conservative themselves, who do not freely express affection in front of children, and who impose rigid expectations will have children who are less sexually active. Studies do not appear to confirm this hypothesis. One study of 1,200 college students found no significant relationship between perceived parental conservatism and premarital involvement for either men or women (Spanier, 1976b).

An alternative hypothesis is that, if parents are open and have good sexual communication, their children will be less sexually active and, if active, will be more likely to use contraceptives. Miller (1999) confirmed that good parental monitoring and positive general communication between mother and adolescent led to less frequent intercourse and fewer partners. Mothers with permissive sexual attitudes have adolescents who have more frequent intercourse and more partners. Hutchinson and Cooney (1998) found that talking about sexual risks with parents, especially mothers, was associated with greater condom use and better sexual communication with partners. By the 10th grade,

however, the influence of good parental monitoring significantly decreases (Whitbeck et al., 1999).

Two separate studies of teenagers and their mothers, however, failed to confirm the "good communication" hypothesis. Children who had little communication with their mothers were as likely to have sex, and to effectively use contraceptives, as those with good parental communication (Newcomer & Udry, 1985; Furstenberg et al., 1984). Parental disciplinary approaches seem to have some influence on their children's sexual behavior, but in a complicated way. When adolescents believed that their parents were not strict and had no dating rules, the adolescents were more sexually permissive. When parents were seen to be extremely strict and to have many dating rules, adolescents also were more sexually permissive. Parents who were seen as moderately strict had teenagers who were the least sexually permissive (Miller et al., 1986).

The presence of parents makes a difference. The more teenagers and parents see of each other, and the closer their relationship in general, the more restricted will be the sexual behavior of the teens (De Lamater & Mac-Corquodale, 1979). Adolescents who are not living with both of their biological parents are likely to become sexually active at younger ages than children in intact families (Newcomer & Udry, 1986; Upchurch et al., 1999). An intact family unit, especially one that is close-knit, seems to have a conservative influence on sexual behavior.

A study of 566 Black and 1,286 non-Black girls confirmed the relationship between living in a single-family home and premarital sexual experience (Billy, Brewster, & Grady, 1994). For White teenagers, having a mother employed outside the home was also associated with increased premarital sexual activity. The father's employment was not considered. For both Black and White girls, religious commitment decreased the amount of premarital activity.

Community composition, not just family characteristics, made a difference in premarital sexual activity (Billy, Brewster, & Grady, 1994). Communities with high social disorganization as measured by high crime rates, high divorce rates, and high rates of school dropout had higher rates of teen premarital sexual activity. In neighborhoods with high rates of out-of-home maternal employment, there was more permissive sexual behavior. This community influence held true regardless of the composition of the individual adolescent's family.

Historically, there has probably been more premarital activity among persons in the lower social classes, for whom such matters as legitimacy and inheritance are of less concern. Kinsey (1948; 1953) found that college-educated persons were more likely to be virgins at marriage and that they began sexual experimentation at a later age. Surveys since the 1960s found that the higher classes have about caught up with the lower classes in rates of nonvirginity at time of marriage; the upper classes are more likely to have engaged in masturbation and oral sex. Those in the lower classes, however, still become sexually active at younger ages and have more premarital partners (Hunt, 1974; Weinberg & Williams, 1980).

There has been considerable debate in this country in recent years about the effect of formal sex education programs in schools and elsewhere. Opponents of such programs have feared that they will encourage adolescents to become more sexually promiscuous. Supporters hope that it will teach the teens to become more responsible, especially in the use of contraceptives and the practice of safe sex.

Kirby (2001) conducted a comprehensive review of numerous types of sexuality-related school programs. He found that very few abstinence-only programs had been properly evaluated. Those that had undergone valid program reviews produced no overall positive effect on sexual behavior, and did not affect contraceptive use among those students who already were sexually active. Because of the small number of reviews programs, Kirby concluded that the evidence about abstinence-based programs remains inconclusive.

Much more information is available about the effectiveness of other sex and HIV education programs. While some of these stress abstinence as the wisest choice, they also provide information about contraception and other sexually related topics. These programs clearly do not result in earlier onset of sex, do not increase the frequency of adolescent sex, and do not increase the number of partners adolescents have. In fact, some such programs delay the first sexual experience. Such programs also tend to increase condom or other contraceptive use and thus reduce teen pregnancy (Kirby, 2001).

Some schools have health clinics that provide condoms or other contraceptives. Kirby (2001) found that such programs do not increase sexual activity. They might not, however, actually increase condom use. It is probable that some students simply substitute the school-provided contraception for that they were previously getting elsewhere. Providing better education, along with the contraception, might be more effective.

Perhaps the most important influence on the premarital sexual behavior of adolescents is their peer culture. Where parents and peers disagree about sexual behavior, peers seem to have the greater influence (Shah & Zelnik, 1981). Peers also share attitudes and behaviors

related to drug use which, in turn, is related to sexual experiences. Reported use of cigarettes and alcohol, marijuana, and other illicit drugs is significantly associated with early sexual behavior for both females and males (Rosenbaum & Kandel, 1990).

While teenagers who are strongly integrated into peer groups that condone drugs and alcohol have higher rates of premarital intercourse, so do teens who lack long-term peer connections. Stack (1994) found that young persons with high rates of geographical mobility have higher rates of premarital sexual activity.

Initial Sexual Scenes

The scripts developed by individuals, especially the "why" of sex, are major determinants of when they will become sexually active. The "real reasons" persons do things are quite difficult to determine, but the reasons they give to themselves and others are more easily accessible to research. D'Augelli and D'Augelli (1977) constructed a framework that connects premarital sexual behavior with sexual philosophies, at the root of which are individual "whys" of sex.

Adolescent Options. Not all teenagers are sexually active. Adolescents include *inexperienced virgins* who have not dated much and have not yet had to deal much with sexual issues. *Adamant virgins* firmly believe that premarital sexual activity is wrong. These young persons generally accept repressive sexual scripts, usually based on religion. *Potential nonvirgins* are not as adamant in their beliefs opposing premarital sexual activity, but they have not yet found the right partner or circumstance for loss of their virginity. They often have real fears about the possibility of pregnancy and other pitfalls of premarital sexuality.

D'Augelli and D'Augelli (1977) included nonvirgins in their typology, one group of which they called *engaged nonvirgins*. These young persons adopted a "sex for love" or "sex with commitment" why of sex, and had engaged in coitus only with a person with whom they had a mutual commitment. *Liberated nonvirgins* engaged in sexual activity with one or more partners to whom they were not committed. They tended to adopt a script based on "sex for pleasure." Finally, there are the *confused nonvirgins* who drift into sexual activity without a clearly thought out motivation or understanding of the place of sexuality in their lives. They would tend to answer, "I don't know" when asked why they do, or refrain from doing, things. They might go along with sex if they think it will help develop a relationship, but they feel ambivalent about having had sex when the relationship ends.

Context of First Intercourse. Individuals are likely to remember their first act of intercourse for the rest of their lives. Whether it is remembered as a positive or negative experience depends on a number of factors. Although individuals might fantasize about intercourse, or see movies of couples having coitus, or have considerable practice with the sexual response cycle as a result of masturbation, the "real thing" usually contains elements of surprise.

In humans, knowing how to have intercourse is a learned phenomenon and gets better with practice. Technically, one's first act of intercourse is not likely to be a virtuoso performance. It is not unusual that the man ejaculates quickly, or not at all, or loses his erection. Orgasm is rare in the woman's first sexual experience, which can even be uncomfortable or painful. If individuals are not aware that such outcomes are common, it is possible that they might begin to worry that there is something wrong with them. In extreme cases, worrying about the "performance" can result in long-term problems such as premature ejaculation for the man or orgasmic difficulties for the woman. Fortunately, with time, trust, and the relaxation that develops with practice, most couples can become quite satisfactory sexual partners (Masters, Johnson, & Kolodny, 1992).

The first sexual act generally occurs with the verbalized "why" of love, affection, or intimacy. A study of American university women found that they considered themselves to be in a "serious" relationship with their first sexual partners. Of those surveyed, only 5.1% lost their virginity on the first date with their partner; 27.3% had been in the relationship 3 to 6 months; 22.7% for 6 months to a year; and 16.7% had been in the relationship for more than 1 year. While 12.9% of the women had only one sex act with that particular partner, most continued in the relationship; 48.4% went on to have 20 or more sex acts with the same partner. Most (78% or more on all categories) considered their first sexual partner to have been gentle, caring, loving, and tender and not rough, inconsiderate, impatient, or insensitive (Schwartz, 1993).

The most common locations for a woman's first coital experience was her boyfriend's parents' home (33.2%) and her own parents' home (16.6%). In one third of the cases, the event was planned, while in the remaining two thirds it was self-labeled a spontaneous occurrence. Contraception was used in 56.7% of the cases, most commonly the condom (40.1%). At the time of their first intercourse, 26.3% of women were using alcohol; 10.1% reported that they were intoxicated (Schwartz, 1993).

Reactions to First Intercourse. Considerable research has been done on frequency and incidence of first coitus, but studies of how individuals feel about their loss of virginity have been rare (Brick, 1989). Perhaps because it is simply assumed that men will have overwhelmingly positive feelings about their first sexual experience, virtually no research has been done in that area. Qualitative interviews of women report a considerable amount of ambiguous and negative feelings about their first act of coitus (Thompson, 1990).

Weis (1983) examined both the positive and negative feelings held by women about their first sexual experience. The highest pleasure and other positive affect, and lowest anxiety, guilt, and other negative affect occurred under three conditions: women who reported that their lover was tender, loving, and considerate; women who had engaged in a considerable amount of noncoital sexual activity prior to the occasion of their first coitus; and women who held permissive attitudes about premarital sex.

The degree to which women have negative feelings about their first sexual feelings is partly associated with a discrepancy between their own behaviors and the sexual script of the society of which they are a part. Applying what is called the "theory of relative consequences," Christensen (1969) claimed that cultural norms "intervene between behavior and its own effect [i.e., consequences]" (p. 220). A person's emotional reaction is not a simple, direct result of his or her action but is also the result of how his or her action might be judged by the cultural norms.

The theory of relative consequences was tested by Schwartz (1993), who compared the feelings of American and Swedish women about their first coital experience. The theory would predict that American women would have more negative responses than would Swedish women, who live in a more sexually permissive society. Results of the study largely verified the hypothesis (see Table 10.3).

The sample of college and university women was asked to indicate "the degree to which they had experienced the . . . feelings in reaction to their first coitus at the time that it occurred" (Schwartz, 1993:20). Thirteen feelings were listed, each followed by a 7-point response choice ranging from 1 (not experienced the feeling at all) to 7 (strongly experienced the feeling).

The rank order of feelings shows more ambivalence among American women. Their two strongest reactions were "anxious" and "fearful," while the top five Swedish responses were all positive. The least common reaction among women in both countries was "exploited." A comparison of absolute differences in the scores finds the largest difference between the American and Swedish women for the score on "guilty."

A key factor in support of the theory of relative consequences is the fact that American women had their first coital experience at an age that they believed was almost 2 years younger than was socially acceptable. Swedish women, by contrast, actually waited almost a full year beyond the age at which they thought it was acceptable in their society. The fact that they believed they were violating the norms of the societal script apparently contributed to the negative feelings American women reported about their first act of coitus (Schwartz, 1993).

Impact of Premarital Sex on Marital Relationships. Some couples still refrain from coitus until they are married. Ard (1990) looked at marriages over a 20-year period to determine what effect having premarital sex with the eventual spouse had on the subsequent marriage. Of those who had premarital intercourse, about two thirds said it had no effect on the marriage. A favorable effect was reported by most of the remaining couples. Of those who did not have premarital sex, a little over half reported no effect, while one third said the effect of waiting was positive. These couples all married before 1970, however, when premarital intercourse was less acceptable than it is now, so caution must be taken in applying the findings to couples struggling with the issue today.

While Ard's study (1990) was concerned with couples who had engaged in premarital sex with their eventual spouse, many persons also have premarital sex with other partners. Kahn and London (1991; 1993) looked at those who had any premarital sexual partner. Individuals who had premarital sex ended up with higher divorce rates than those who did not. This confirmed earlier studies that found that individuals with premarital sexual experience were more likely to have affairs once they were married, and that the more premarital partners a person had, the greater the likelihood of unhappy marriages (Athanasiou & Sarkin, 1974).

Kahn and London (1991) concluded that, although there was a correlation between premarital sex and divorce, it would not be accurate to say that premarital sex caused the divorce. Rather, both premarital sex and divorce are considered unconventional behavior, so it is

Table 10.3	Rank Order and Score of Reactions to First Coitus for Women in the United States and Sweden	
Rank	**Score in the United States**	**Score in Sweden**
1.	Anxious (4.75)	Happy (4.58)
2.	Fearful (4.70)	Excited (4.26)
3.	Excited (4.34)	Relieved (3.80)
4.	Happy (4.33)	Romantic (3.78)
5.	Romantic (4.17)	Pleasurable (3.46)
6.	Guilty (4.10)	Anxious (3.41)
7.	Confused (3.86)	Fearful (3.17)
8.	Relieved (3.65)	Satisfied (3.03)
9.	Pleasurable (3.62)	Embarrassed (2.93)
10.	Embarrassed (3.60)	Confused (2.88)
11.	Sorry (3.65)	Sorry (2.09)
12.	Satisfied (3.35)	Guilty (1.89)
13.	Exploited (3.04)	Exploited (1.74)

Source: Adapted from Table 2, Schwartz, Israel M. 1993. "Affective Reactions of American and Swedish Women to Their First Premarital Coitus: A Cross-Cultural Comparison." *Journal of Sex Research* 30:18–26.

unconventional persons who would be more likely to do both.

The debate about the "unconventionality hypothesis" is similar to the discussion of the relationship between cohabitation and divorce rates (see chapter 8). In contrast to Kahn and London, analysis by Heaton (1993) concluded that there was sufficient evidence to assume that premarital sexuality activity itself contributed to divorce.

Homosexual Scripts

While forms of homosexual behavior might universally be found (Ford & Beach, 1951), an exclusively homosexual identity as it is thought of today is culturally specific. Each culture provides a script that furnishes meaning about homosexual acts for that particular culture and for the individuals in that culture.

Social Construction of Homosexuality

Scripting theorists see the cultural diversity of homosexuality as evidence that categories of sexual preferences are entirely socially constructed and learned (Blumstein & Schwartz, 1990). We saw in chapter 3 that the custom of the *berdache* was relatively widespread among native North Americans (Callender & Kochems, 1993), but it was not a role in which the actor assumed a "normal" identity in all ways except for choice of sexual partner, nor were the *berdache's* same-sex partners considered homosexual.

In Sambian culture there was a considerable amount of same-sex behavior, the "why" of which was given in terms of semen transmission (Herdt, 1993). No individuals were identified as homosexuals, but there were times in the life cycle when homosexual activity was expected. Such developmental patterns of homosexual behavior have also been found in the Melanesian culture known as East Bay (Davenport, 1976) and other cultures.

We have also seen that homosexual relationships between a powerful older man and a younger apprentice were common in ancient Greece, yet most participants saw no contradiction between that and their family life

of marriage and having children. Today in parts of Africa, Brazil, and other cultures there are many men who occasionally engage in homosexual behavior but marry and live generally heterosexual lives. The spread of AIDS is more difficult to deal with in those cultures (Sills, 1994).

American culture has used the term "homosexual" as a **master status.** Any person holds several positions in society at the same time. A man might, for example, be a carpenter, a father, a son, a musician, a fisherman, and a lay minister in his church. If it is discovered that the same person is also a homosexual, that can tend to become the status that determines the way others interact with him. If that man had 3,000 sex acts with 50 women, but one same-sex act that became public knowledge, a homosexual label might well be applied to him.

Although those who engage in homosexual activity have suffered considerable oppression in Western societies, the term itself is of relatively recent historical origin. The phrase "masculine love" was used in Europe during the renaissance (Cady, 1992), but this is a description of a particular type of relationship rather than the person in the relationship. Karl Kertbeny in Germany coined the terms *heterosexual* and *homosexual* in 1868, and their first documented use in the United States was in 1892 (Katz, 1990).

Judgments about the appropriateness of homosexual acts vary over time. We have seen that the Judeo-Christian tradition was harsh toward homosexuals; so were many secular agents of social control. The American Psychiatric Association held homosexuality to be a mental illness until 1973 (Bootzin et al., 1991).

Also in 1973, George Weinberg popularized the term **homophobia** to refer to the strong negative reaction many Americans had toward homosexuality. Some scholars rejected this term because it contains the root *phobia,* which in psychiatry is a persistent, powerful, and unreasonable fear (American Psychiatric Association, 1987). Because some individuals who have negative attitudes about homosexuality do not consider themselves to have an unreasonable fear, the phrase "antihomosexual prejudice" has been suggested (Haaga, 1991). The same connotation is intended by **heterosexism,** a term designed symbolically to connect, by

Master status: A social position that tends to override every other position a person holds (Hughes, 1945). **Homophobia:** A strong negative reaction to homosexuals and homosexuality (*homosexual* plus Greek *phobos,* fear). **Heterosexism:** Discrimination against homosexuals.

association with the terms *racism* and *sexism,* with the civil rights and feminist movements.

What all of the terms point to is a relatively rapid shift in the boundaries of acceptability of homosexuality in the mental health field. While homosexuals were thought 30 years ago to be mentally ill, they are now considered to be normal while persons who are opposed to homosexuality are now often thought to be the ones in need of help. Although antihomosexual feelings remain strong in the general population, they are rapidly changing (see Table 10.1).

How Many Gays and Lesbians?

According to social construction theory, it is partly because the term *homosexual* has been given such power in our society that there is pressure for an either-or definition of a person's sexual preferences. Kinsey (1948, 1953) tried to avoid dichotomizing sexual preference by categorizing sexual behavior on a continuum (see Figure 10.4). A person who had had only heterosexual experience would be a "Kinsey 0." At the other extreme, someone with only homosexual experience would be a "Kinsey 6." Categories one through five represent different combinations of same-sex and opposite-sex behavior.

Kinsey's (1948) research concluded that more than one third of men would have at least one homosexual experience in their lifetime, but his work was criticized for oversampling homosexuals. For some years after Kinsey, it was an accepted figure that about 10% of males are homosexual and about 5% of women. Gay-rights groups liked the 10% figure because it meant that

they were a large group whose voices needed to be listened to. Antihomosexual groups liked the numbers because it made the "danger" of homosexuality look more frightening. Both groups, it turns out, were probably overestimating the numbers.

One study of 3,224 men between the ages of 20 and 39 found that only 2.3% of the men reported any homosexual activity in the past 10 years; only 1.1% of them had been exclusively homosexual during the previous decade (Billy et al., 1993). Another study of adults found that about 5 to 6% of men have engaged in a homosexual act at least once since adolescence; the comparable figure for women is 2 to 3% (Diamond, 1993).

Throughout the 1990s, the General Social Surveys asked questions about the sex of respondents' intimate partners during the past 5 years. As Figure 10.5 indicates, the vast majority of Americans are heterosexuals. Only 2.8% of men and 1.6% of women had solely same-sex partners over the past 5 years, and even fewer were practicing bisexuals (see Figure 10.5).

The most comprehensive national survey of sexuality in recent years found that 7.1% of men had experienced a homosexual act at some time since puberty; 2.7% of sexually active men had done so in the past year. Among women, 3.8% had a homosexual encounter since puberty, and 1.3% had done so in the past year (Laumann et al., 1994).

Most definitions we have seen count behaviors. That, however, is not the only issue; self-definition is also important. Some individuals have homosexual experiences without defining themselves as homosexuals. Young male hustlers have historically made themselves available, for a fee, to gays who wish to perform oral

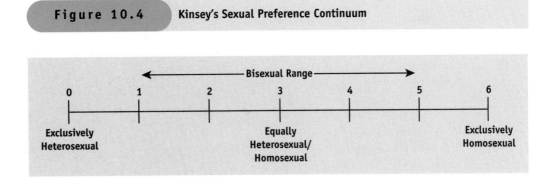

| Figure 10.4 | Kinsey's Sexual Preference Continuum |

Source: Adapted from Kinsey, Pomeroy, and Martin, 1948. *Sexual Behaviour in the Human Male.* Philadelphia: Saunders.

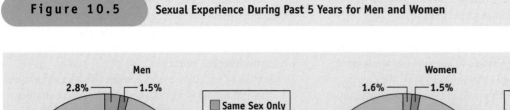

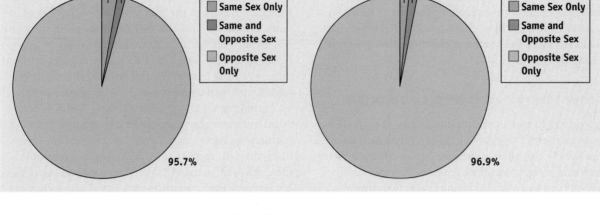

Figure 10.5 Sexual Experience During Past 5 Years for Men and Women

Source: Davis, James Allan, and Tom W. Smith: General Social Survey(s). (Machine-readable data file). Principal investigator, James A. Davis; director and co-principal investigator, Tom W. Smith; co-principal investigator, Peter V. Marsden, NORC ed. Chicago: National Opinion Research Center, producer, 1998; Storrs, CT: The Roper Center for Public Opinion Research, University of Connecticut, distributor. Microcomputer format and codebook prepared and distributed by MicroCase Corporation, Bellevue, WA. Analysis by Gene H. Starbuck.

sex on the hustler; the hustlers typically maintain a heterosexual identity (Reiss, 1961). In closed one-sex societies such as prisons, situational homosexuality for men often takes the form of violent sexual assaults. For women, lesbian activity is more likely to be seen as companionship among equals sharing a difficult experience (Reid, 1985). Many men and women who engage in homosexual acts in prison retain heterosexual self-identities, which they resume once they are out of prison.

Other individuals might consider themselves homosexual but not engage in sexual acts for long periods. Some people might fantasize about same-sex behavior while engaged in heterosexual acts; others might fantasize about heterosexual behavior while engaged in homosexual acts. Some might particularly enjoy very close same-sex friendships but not opposite-sex ones, while never engaging in gay or lesbian sexual behavior. Some people are actually asexual; they just have no sexual interest or behavior at all. Some people who enjoy same-sex intimate relationships might never consider having a long-term, live-in, committed relationship with anyone. Finally, some people have different sexual and relationship preferences over their life

course. All these variations make counting difficult indeed (Patterson, 2000).

The "Why" of Homosexuality

The reason some persons engage in homosexual acts and define themselves as homosexuals, especially in an antihomosexual culture, is not well understood. Various theories have been developed about the "causes" of homosexuality, including explanations rooted in heredity, hormonal influences, social learning, and psychodynamic processes. Each of these perspectives has some supporting evidence but none has overwhelming support (McCammon, Knox, & Schacht, 1993).

The theoretical perspectives do provide frameworks for individuals who are seeking to explain the "why" of their own or someone else's sexual orientation. Heterosexuals are not generally called upon to explain the "why" of their sexual orientation; it is assumed to be natural. Homosexuals, however, generally are compelled to explain to themselves and to others the reason for their orientation.

The process of "coming out of the closet" is one of announcing one's homosexuality to oneself, one's family, friends, and others. This is often stated in terms of acknowledging one's "true self" or recognizing what was there all along. Often someone who has come out will say that he or she has "always been homosexual." The "why" is given in terms of forces over which the person had no control.

Sometimes combined with the "born homosexual" identity component is a pleasure-based "why" of homosexual orientation. This is reflected in statements like "it feels better" or "it is more exciting for me." Love and affection are also part of the homosexual "why"; the term **homophilia** is sometimes used to emphasize the fact that there is an emotional, not just sexual, component to same-sex erotic relationships.

Lesbians are more likely than gay men to frame the "why" of their sexual preference in relationship and emotional terms (Peplau & Gordon, 1991). Lesbians also have access to a "why" not used by gay men. For a few, being lesbian is a political statement. Adrienne Rich (1980) wrote that, because of the oppression of women by men, heterosexuality is "sleeping with the enemy." To her, lesbianism is an act of political rebellion against the access and domination men have over women. For most, however, a lesbian orientation is a positive attraction to women, not an avoidance of men.

Of the available options, the "born homosexual" explanation seems to result in more acceptance by society as a whole. Believing that homosexuality is an inborn trait generates more tolerance than does the belief that it is learned or is a chosen lifestyle (Ernulf, Innala, & Whitam, 1989). In addition to asking whether people thought homosexuality was wrong, the General Social Surveys (Davis & Smith, 1972–98) have asked whether people thought homosexuality was something people choose to be or something they cannot change. Of those who believed that homosexuality is a choice, 82% also thought it was always wrong. Of those who thought it could not be changed, only half thought it was always wrong.

Homosexual "Whats"

The sexual "whats" of homosexuals tend to follow the general/genital difference of heterosexual women and men. Lesbians, like heterosexual women, tend to become sexual in a relationship context and "come out" more slowly than gays. One study found that 93% of lesbians said their first homosexual experience was

emotional, and physical expression came later (Corbett & Morgan, 1983). For gay men, as for heterosexual men, the sexual interest occurred first (McCammon, Knox, & Schacht, 1993).

Of those in new relationships, gay men have sexual activity more frequently than do cohabiting or married heterosexuals. Lesbians appear to have the least frequent sexual activity, although that may be because they define "having sex" differently than other couples (Christopher & Sprecher, 2000). The high frequency of gay men drops off rapidly, however, in longer relationships; after 10 years in the relationship, gay couples have sex with each other less frequently than do heterosexual married couples (Blumstein & Schwartz, 1983).

As demonstrated both by attitude and behavior, monogamy in a relationship is considerably less important for gay men than for lesbians or heterosexuals (Blumstein & Schwartz, 1983; Christopher & Sprecher, 2000). Gay men, like heterosexual ones, appear to be more genitally oriented in their sexual encounters; Lesbians, like heterosexual women, like to include more nongenital touching (Blumstein & Schwartz, 1983; Patterson, 2000).

Oral sex is the most common sexual activity for gay men, although anal sex also occurs frequently. In most couples, each partner at various times assumes both the "passive" and "active" roles in anal and oral stimulation. The most popular intimate acts of lesbians include hugging, kissing, touching, and oral sex (Van Gelder & Brandt, 1996).

Constructing Marital Scripts

Whether they have their initial sexual scene before or after the wedding, couples who are ongoing sexual partners gradually negotiate a mutual script that is unique to that particular couple. Their own script will be based on the societal script, each person's individual scripts, and the meanings they work out together. Their mutual script will include its own "who, what, where, when, and why" of sex.

The "Who" of Marital Sex

For nearly all American couples, the agreed-upon "who" of intercourse is one's spouse only. The Judeo-Christian

---

Homophilia: Intimate love for a person of the same sex.

tradition has long opposed adultery or, although it has sometimes been considered a less serious offense when engaged in by a married man than by a married woman. At other times, it has been the unfaithful wife's husband who receives social disapproval for an inability to keep his wife satisfied or under control. The word **cuckold** has long been applied as a form of derision to a man whose wife has an affair. There is no comparable word for a wife whose husband strays.

A person's religion is related to the likelihood of extramarital coitus. Kinsey found that the most religiously devout, whether Protestant, Catholic, or Jewish, were least likely to have affairs. Virtually all studies report higher rates of adultery among men than women, although that gap may have closed in recent years. Partly this is because women in the workforce have more opportunity to have extramarital contacts, and there are increasing numbers of women in the workforce (Hall, 1987).

There is a wider gap between husbands and wives on rates of brief extramarital encounters than for more "meaningful" affairs (Spanier & Margolis, 1983). Although most women who have extramarital involvements enjoy the sexual aspect (Hurlbert, 1992), their extramarital affairs are more likely to involve emotional ties. When wives have affairs, it is more likely to be a sign of marital dissatisfaction than when husbands do (Yablonsky, 1979; Schaefer, 1981).

Extradyadic relationships are not limited to marriage; couples who are cohabiting have higher rates of infidelity than married couples (Blumstein & Schwartz, 1983). Sexual infidelity also occurs during dating. "Whys" given for affairs during dating are dissatisfaction with the relationship, boredom, revenge, anger or jealousy, being unsure of the relationship, and variety (Roscoe et al., 1988). These probably also apply to reasons for cohabiting and marital infidelity; in addition, a few have affairs as a way to force an end to the relationship (McGinnis, 1981).

Several variables are associated with extramarital coitus. Based on a review of studies that had been done up to the time, Thompson (1983) concluded that the best predictor of extramarital sex was premarital sexual permissiveness. Attitudes favorable toward extramarital sex are more likely to be found among persons in large cities than in small towns, among those who are

unhappily married, and among those with the highest levels of formal education (Weeks & Jurich, 1985). Women with feminist orientations are more likely to see extramarital coitus as a viable option for themselves than are women with more traditional attitudes (Atwater, 1982).

Estimates about the frequency of extramarital sexual coitus vary considerably, depending on how the sample was chosen for the study. While some studies report rates as high as one half of men and women (Thompson 1983), national random samples find lower incidence. Greeley, Michael, and Smith (1990) found that 96% of married respondents said they had been monogamous for the past year. Ard (1990) followed couples over 20 years of marriage and found that only 7% of husbands and 4% of wives had an extramarital sexual experience in that time.

Two major surveys done in the 1990s came up with similar results. Laumann and others (1994) found that nearly 75% of men and 85% of women reported they had always remained faithful. The General Social Surveys (Davis & Smith, 1991–1998) found that 23.0% of men and 13.1% of women who had been married at some time admitted that they had engaged in extramarital sex.

It is probable that much extramarital sex occurs toward the end of a bad marriage, either as a cause for divorce or a response to other problems in the relationship. An unknown but probably fairly high amount of what is technically extramarital sex actually occurs after the couple has split up but before the divorce is legally final.

Most extramarital sexual activity is done without the knowledge of the spouse, but in some cases both knowledge and consent by the partner are present. Nena and George O'Neill (1972), a wife/husband team, popularized the concept of **open marriage** in the 1970s as an alternative to what they saw as unnecessary lack of freedom in marriage. As one part of self-fulfillment, they claimed, secure individuals should be free of jealousies and possessiveness and should be pleased when their partners experience pleasure with others.

Later developments indicate the difficulty of making such arrangements work. Two years after their original book, Nena O'Neill (1974), writing without her former collaborator and husband, explained why she no longer

---

Cuckold: A man whose wife has extramarital coitus.   **Open marriage:** Arrangement in which married partners allow each other to have extramarital sexual affairs and other freedoms not commonly associated with marriage.

supported such arrangements. Jealousy arises in spite of agreements to avoid it. Part of the problem is that a woman who is willing to have affairs has a good deal more opportunity to do so than does a man. Her husband in an open marriage is likely to see this as unfair, making the jealousy worse. Such marriages tend either to end in divorce or in renegotiating a more traditional "who" of marital sex.

Another form of consensual extramarital sexual activity has been called "swinging" or **comarital sex.** Usually with another couple, but sometimes with just a third person, a married couple engages in sexual activity. This is typically scripted as something a couple does together, so comarital sex might be less threatening to the relationship than other types of extramarital coitus. However, the fact that it is also referred to as "wife-swapping" hints at the fact that it is usually instigated by the man (Bringle & Buunk, 1991). A study of ex-swingers found that the most commonly stated reason for quitting the activity was the wives' dissatisfaction (Murstein, Case, & Gunn, 1985). All things considered, nearly all research finds that the vast majority of couples who remain in satisfactory marriages develop a spouse-only "who" of sex. The couples who revise the traditionally exclusive script tend to return to it, if their relationship survives, after a period of experimentation.

The "When" of Marital Sex

Because marriage legitimizes two individuals as a sexual couple, general consent to be sexual partners is assumed in nearly all marriages. What the couple must do is to develop a script that determines how often they will have sex, and what system they will use to negotiate having sex each time.

There are 24 hours in each day; even the most active newlyweds do not make love during all those hours for days on end. Some time is defined as sexual time and is set apart from other activities. Sexual scenes, like other activities that have a definable purpose, have a more-or-less clearly defined beginning and ending, and a certain set of behaviors that occur between those points in time. This **bracketed scene** allows behaviors that are not normative at other times and precludes actions that might be expected in other kinds of interactions.

Couples have other kinds of bracketed scenes, such as dinnertime, watching television, and going for a walk. Like dramatic productions, these call for their own roles and scripts that can include different costumes, lighting, lines, and actions. Each of these is negotiated by the couple in ways that have elements unique to that particular couple. Mutual scripts, which help guide the couple's interactions, develop over time.

Since sexual scenes must be carved out of the time that might otherwise be used for other activities, there needs to be an understanding about what is a sexual scene, how one partner indicates interest at a particular time, and how the other partner indicates agreement to have sex or declines the offer. Over time, most couples develop sets of nonverbal and indirect ways of deciding whether a particular time will become a sexual scene (Starbuck, 1985).

Some couples develop rituals that indicate sexual interest; one partner might announce that he or she is going to bed early, or will wait up, or will be home at a certain time. The way the other partner responds determines whether there will be a sexual scene or not. Another couple might get very good at reading each other's feelings as expressed by a goodnight kiss. Still other couples develop ritualized times, such as every Wednesday and Saturday night. These patterns develop over time, usually without actually discussing the matter; many couples are not consciously aware of the mutual script they have negotiated (Starbuck, 1985).

Whatever the set of signals a couple develops, the result is usually a declining frequency of intercourse over time. Couples in their 20s and 30s typically have intercourse two or three times each week. This frequency declines so that after age 50, once each week or less is typical. There is some evidence that marital sexual frequency has increased for all age groups in the past 3 decades (Masters, Johnson, & Kolodny, 1992).

A large study of randomly selected respondents over the age of 60 in Sweden found that 61% of the 60–80 age group still expressed sexuality by intercourse, mutual sexual stimulation other than intercourse, and masturbation. Of those in the 60–65 age group, 58% had intercourse at least once each month. This proportion declined to 23% of those in the 75–79 age group (Bergstrom-Walan & Nielsen, 1990).

Comarital sex: Extramarital sex in which the married couple participates together.   **Bracketed scene:** An interaction set apart from other day-to-day behavior by a definable beginning and end, during which particular roles and scripts apply.

These averages, however, hide considerable variation among couples. Some couples never have a very active sex life, while others are still frequently active when they are in their 90s. For some older couples, the genital focus of sexuality is replaced by a greater emphasis on nongenital intimacy (Weg, 1983). This is part of continued development of conjugal love and the "pleasure bond" (Masters & Johnson, 1976).

Couples who are the most sexually active during the first year of marriage tend to remain more active than their peers later on. A host of variables is associated with decreased frequency of sexual expression, including increased job and housework responsibility, having children, financial worries, and familiarity (Eshleman, 1994; Morris & Udry, 1983; Bogren, 1991).

There is a correlation between a couple's reported sexual satisfaction and the satisfaction of their relationship as a whole. There is also a relationship between sexual frequency and overall sexual satisfaction (Blumstein & Schwartz, 1985). The relationship between sexual frequency and overall relationship satisfaction, however, is indirect and affected by many other variables. Some couples are sexual only rarely but are very happy in their marriage. Others have good and frequent sex in an otherwise miserable marriage. Perhaps the worst problems can arise when one partner desires sexual activity much more frequently than the other. For these couples, negotiation of the "when" element of the mutual sexual script can become quite problematic.

The "What" of Marital Sex

The kinds of sexual things couples do have changed as the societal script has become less repressive. If the sole purpose of sex is reproduction, penile-vaginal thrusting until the man ejaculates is all that is necessary. As such "whys" as emotional closeness or pleasure evolve, however, the sexual scene can include more touching and a variety of stimulation (D'Emilio & Freedman, 1988; Weinberg et al., 1980).

Studies of marital coitus find that, for men, orgasm is part of most sexual scenes. Hunt (1975) found that only 7% of men 24 to 28 years old failed to reach orgasm in at least one quarter of their coital experiences; for older men, their figure went up somewhat. This is not necessarily considered a problem, however, unless a strict "why" of reproduction is maintained.

Kinsey found that the likelihood of wives experiencing orgasm went up over time. By the 15th year of marriage, 45% of women had orgasms in 90 to 100% of their sex acts, and nearly all had orgasms at least occasionally. By the 20th year of marriage, however, 11% of the wives had still not experienced coital orgasm. The *Redbook* survey (Tavris & Sadd, 1977), which probably oversampled more sexually expressive women, found that, in marriages that had lasted 15 years, 53% of wives had orgasms in all, or almost all, of their sexual scenes; only 7% had never had a coital orgasm.

The importance of orgasm, or the lack thereof, varies considerably from one couple to another. For many, especially those who can have orgasms in other ways, lack of coital orgasm is relatively unimportant; for others it is experienced as a serious problem (Masters, Johnson, & Kolodny, 1992).

More couples today than in Kinsey's time experiment with alternative sexual positions and activities. Laumann and others (1994) found that 67.7% of women and 78.7% of men had ever experienced **fellatio,** while 76.6% of men and 73.1% of women reported ever experiencing **cunnilingus.** Anal sex had been experienced by 25.6% of men and 20.4% of women.

Kinsey reported almost no foreplay among those with the lowest levels of education and an average of about 12 minutes for the college-educated sample; he also estimated that three fourths of married men typically ejaculated within 2 minutes of penetration. By contrast, Hunt (1975) found about 15 minutes in

Lighting is part of the "what" of sex. This couple always has sex in the dark.

Fellatio: Oral stimulation of the penis.   **Cunnilingus:** Oral stimulation of the clitoris or vulva.

Families in the **NEWS**

Politics and Sex Education

In the last year of the Clinton administration, Surgeon General David Satcher began preparing an extensive report on sexual attitudes and education. The report could have been published before George W. Bush's inauguration, but was not. Now it will probably never see the light of day.

Satcher's report is said be a far-reaching call for action, based on research about sex education. It apparently calls for comprehensive sex education, including information about contraception, in all schools in the country. Satcher reportedly hoped that "all people would be empowered, regardless of orientation, to be sexually responsible." This is not the kind of message likely to be favored by Bush and others who advocate "abstinence only" sex education.

So why wasn't the report issued before Bush took office? One theory is that a report on sexual responsibility would lose credibility coming from Bill Clinton. Another theory is that Satcher did not want to alienate the incoming president.

The report, which could have been highly influential in the public policy debate about sex education, will now probably never be officially released. Satcher's 4-year term as surgeon general does not expire until 2002, but he lost his post as assistant secretary of health and human services. That post had a staff of 200 persons. Satcher now has a staff of four.

Source: Diana Jean Schemo. **www.nytimes.com**, April 21, 2001.

foreplay, with no difference by educational level. He also reported that penile-vaginal intercourse lasted an average of 10 minutes.

The apparent changes all indicate increased acceptance of a "sex for pleasure" "why" of sex. Most research, however still finds a social class difference in marital scenes. Weinberg and Williams (1980) looked at social class and sexual behavior in the period from 1938 to 1970. Throughout that period, couples in the middle and upper classes were more likely to have sex while completely nude, engage in oral-genital contact, use a variety of sexual positions, and react positively to

masturbation. These finding were generally confirmed by the Laumann (1994) study.

Some impact of the societal script on a couple's mutual script is unavoidable. Even what is defined as a sexual problem or dysfunction is affected by societal expectations. Neither premature ejaculation nor lack of female orgasm would be considered a problem on the island of Inis Beag. In American society, however, both are defined as sexual dysfunctions because mutual pleasure is considered an appropriate "why" of sex, and orgasm for women has become an expected part of sexual scenes. The power of culture extends even into the privacy of the marital bed.

Summary and Conclusion

Sociological theories such as functionalism, feminism, and symbolic interactionism provide explanations of sexuality. Humans rely heavily on learning to become sexual. In the process, according to a social learning, scripting theoretical framework, they construct scripts at four levels. At each level, a script contains a "who, what, where, when," and most importantly, a "why" of sex.

The most abstract level of scripting contains the institutions, values, and norms of society as a whole. While some societies have widespread agreement about the "who, what, where, when, and why" of sexuality, complex societies like the United States have a variety of competing scripts. Control-repression models have been highly influential in American culture, both of the Christian and of the secular variety. There have been some proponents of full expression scripts, but most Americans adopt some intermediate form such as Christian joy, sex with love and commitment, or sex with affection.

Through the process of sexualization, individuals learn the societal scripts as influenced by their own personal experiences; this is the second scripting level. When a couple engages in what they might call sexual behavior, they are enacting roles in the form of a sexual scene. If they continue to be a sexual couple, they gradually construct their own mutual script, completing the fourth scripting level.

Changes in sexual scripts have contributed to the spread of AIDS, especially among homosexual men. American women are less likely to have AIDS; most of them get it either from sharing IV needles or having unprotected sex with men who are drug users.

A gendered double standard, although much less prevalent today than in the past, still exists in the United States today. So does rape. Like other kinds of deviance, rape has a variety of definitions. Measuring the amount of rape, or even agreeing on what is to be measured, is a difficult and partly political process. Various theoretical perspectives would generate different research results; even different branches of feminist thought reach different conclusions.

Individuals learn from the society around them as they develop their own scripts. Increasing numbers of young Americans have incorporated premarital sexual experience into their personal scripts. Some adopt a homosexual identity and are faced with developing "whys" of their sexual orientations.

In conclusion, a social learning-based scripting approach provides a much different explanation of sexuality than do biology-based perspectives. While biology might put the gas in the engine, scripting says where to drive. It provides a much more nuanced set of sociological questions.

This scripting approach can also be applied to other aspects of relationship life, as will be shown in chapter 12: Negotiating Marriages. First, though, we will look at the consequences of reproductive sexual behavior.

Rethinking in Context Consider the sexual norms you proposed before reading the chapter. Do they still seem appropriate? How closely do they match your personal script? Where did you learn that? Do the norms you propose fit the economic and political realities of postindustrial America? Which norms would you like to see become laws, and which enforced informally? Why?

Additional Resources

Diverse societal scripts

Marshall, Donald S., & David N. Suggs, eds. 1971. *Human Sexual Behavior: Variations in the Ethnographic Spectrum*. New York: Basic Books.

Suggs, David N., & Andrew W. Miracle, eds. 1993. *Culture and Human Sexuality*. Pacific Grove, CA: Brooks/Cole.

Key American studies

Hunt, Morton. 1974. *Sexual Behavior in the Seventies*. Chicago: Playboy Press.

Kinsey, Alfred, Wardell B. Pomeroy, & Clyde E. Martin. 1948. *Sexual Behaviour in the Human Male*. Philadelphia: Saunders.

Kinsey, Alfred, Wardell B. Pomeroy, & Clyde E. Martin. 1953. *Sexual Behaviour in the Human Female*. Philadelphia: Saunders.

Laumann, Edward O., John H. Gagnon, Robert T. Michael, & Stuart Michaels. 1994. *The Social Organization of Sexuality: Sexual Practices in the United States*. Chicago: University of Chicago Press.

Feminist views

Dworkin, Andrea. 1987. *Intercourse*. New York: Free Press.

Sprecher, Susan & Kathleen McKinney. 1993. *Sexuality*. Newbury Park, CA: Sage.

Stan, Adele M., ed. 1995. *Debating Sexual Correctness: Pornography, Sexual Harassment, Date Rape, and the Politics of Sexual Equality*. New York: Delta.

Special topics

Abelove, Henry, Michele Aina Barale, & David M. Halperin, eds. 1993. *The Lesbian and Gay Studies Reader*. New York: Routledge.

Centers for Disease Control and Prevention. 2000. *Surveillance Report* Vol. 11 # 2, Table 5. http://www.cdc.gov/hiv/stats/hasr1102/table5.htm.

Kirby, Douglas. 2001. "Emerging Answers: Research Findings on Programs to Reduce Teen Pregnancy." Washington, DC: The National Campaign to Prevent Teen Pregnancy. www.teenpregnancy.org/05001/emeranswsum.pdf.

LeVay, Simon. 1993. *The Sexual Brain*. La Jolla, CA: MIP Press.

Masters, William H., Virginia E. Johnson, & Robert Kolodny. 1994. *Heterosexuality*. New York: HarperCollins.

Rossi, Alice S., ed. 1994. *Sexuality Across the Life Course*. Chicago: University of Chicago Press.

Van Gelder, L., & P. R. Brandt. 1996. *The Girls Next Door: Into the Heart of Lesbian America*. New York: Simon & Schuster.

Weinberg, Martin S., Colin J. Williams, & Douglas W. Pryor. 1994. *Dual Attraction: Understanding Bisexuality*. New York: Oxford University Press.

Internet Sites

Kinsey Institute bibliography
http://www.indiana.edu/~kinsey/bib-methods.html

Society for the Scientific Study of Sexuality
http://www.ssc.wisc.edu/ssss/

Gay and lesbian
http://www.gayagenda.com/

Gay and lesbian youth
http://www.outproud.org/

Human sexuality and sex therapy
http://www.mastersandjohnson.com/

History and sociology of sexuality, feminist view
http://www.isis.aust.com/stephan/writings/sexuality/

For links to these sites and additional resources, visit the *Families in Context* Web site at
http://sociology.wadsworth.com

Chapter 11

Population and Family Planning

Prelude

Mitra, 10, lives in Calcutta, India. She was the fourth of six surviving children who live with their aging mother and father. They belong to a laboring caste, and her father is not able to work as hard as he used to. Although Mitra gets hungry sometimes, her family usually has enough rice to eat, and they are able to pay the rent on their two-room apartment.

Mitra is usually happy. She likes playing with the other children in the neighborhood. She is glad she is not in the untouchable caste, and she hopes that next time she will be born to a Brahmin, the upper caste.

When Mitra's oldest brother got married and they had a baby, the apartment seemed too crowded. But she was unhappy when they moved out; she misses having the baby around. She wants lots of children when she grows up and hopes that her father will find her a good man to marry.

Mitra has heard about places where only a few people live and where married couples only have one or two children. Mitra can't understand how people could live like that. Maybe they had done something horrible in their last life.

Are you as influenced by your social context as is Mitra?

The previous chapter mentioned that one of the functions of sexuality is reproduction. Earlier chapters demonstrated ways in which societies have attempted to influence the rate of reproduction among its members. This chapter provides more information about reproduction, society, and individual choice. It will also mention the host of new technologies available today and the challenge to our social and personal values and norms raised by the technological changes.

Thinking Ahead How many children would you like to have? Why? What social forces have affected this very personal decision of yours? Would adopting a child serve the same purposes for you as having a biological offspring? Why, why not? Is finding someone with similar views on these issues important in your mate-selection decisions?

Our sociological imagination would help us place ourselves in a particular sexual script at a particular time. It would help us see that even such a personal thing as how many children we would like to have is affected by the society in which we live. In turn, the number of children we, collectively, give birth to significantly affects our society.

In this chapter, we will first look at the issue of reproduction from a macro-social level in terms of forces that affect population growth and control. We will then cover the methods available today either to reduce fertility or to increase the chances of having a child. The chapter ends with an introduction to some of the legal, moral, and ethical issues involved with family planning.

Culture and Reproductive Regulation

As macro-level measures of reproduction, the **fertility** rate is the actual number of births while **fecundity** is a potential. Rarely does the fertility rate approach the fecundity rate, although it comes close among some groups. The Hutterites, a communal religious group in the northern Great Plains of the United States and in

southern Alberta, Canada, have approached the maximum reproduction rate. In 1954, Eaton and Mayer found that Hutterite women between 45 and 54 years of age had averaged 10.6 children per woman. Only for short periods of time have entire societies maintained such high fertility rates.

Preindustrial societies tended to have lifetime fertility levels of 6 or 7 children per woman, well below the fecundity rate (Haub & Riche, 1994). Both conscious and nonconscious birth control practices limited the actual number of offspring. The unconscious, or hidden, practices that lower fertility rates constitute **latent fertility regulation.** Practices used with the conscious purposes of limiting fertility are referred to as **manifest fertility regulation.**

Latent Fertility Regulation

Family formation norms are one form of latent fertility regulation. Polygyny, for example, may tend to reduce overall fertility rates because each married woman would be less likely to have sexual intercourse as often (Hern, 1991). Polygyny was not instituted for the purpose of reducing fertility, so that is latent fertility regulation.

Marital economic exchanges and age at first marriage also affect fertility rates. It takes time to accumulate a

---

Fertility: Actual number of births to a woman.   **Fecundity:** A biological potential of lifetime childbearing.   **Latent fertility regulation:** Cultural practices that affect fertility without conscious intent by individuals.   **Manifest fertility regulation:** Practices used by persons with the conscious intent of affecting fertility.

dowry or bridewealth. Some families are never able to accumulate enough to provide their offspring enough wealth to afford the marriage. When that was combined with a sexual morality that prohibited nonmarital sexual intercourse, lowered fertility for the society resulted. Even when a couple did marry, the average age at first marriage would be relatively old. This would reduce the numbers of children a woman would have in a lifetime. Societies with higher divorce rates also tend to have lower fertility rates, especially where remarriage rates are low (Clark, 1992).

Norms that make sexual intercourse forbidden at various times can lower the fertility rate. Many societies have had taboos about having sexual relations when women are breast feeding. While breast-feeding itself provided some contraceptive protection, the taboo would further reduce the odds of conception. This increased the time that would pass before a woman would have another child, and hence lower her lifetime fertility.

Throughout the Middle Ages, bishops and popes in the Catholic Church, while generally pronatalist, imposed several temporal bans on sexual intercourse. Christians were to abstain during Lent, the 40 days before Easter; during Advent, the 4 weeks before Christmas; on various Ember Days; on Sundays, the Lord's Days; and on Fridays (Kissling, 1994). Couples who followed all these rules would abstain about 180 days each year—almost half of the year.

Latent forms of fertility control have always affected fertility rates. So have other factors, such as maternal death rates and the supply of nutritional requirements. While these were all unintentional, some actions were taken specifically to affect population levels.

Manifest Fertility Control

Individuals in most societies have practiced various forms of manifest fertility control, or family planning. Some practices were designed to increase fertility; many cultures have potions, spells, prayers, charms, rituals, saints, or other customs to which individuals could turn when children were desired. Other practices were designed to limit fertility. For the most part, neither fertility-enhancement nor fertility-limiting practices were extremely effective until modern times.

Although the discovery of sperm and its exact part in conception did not occur until the late 17th century, earlier human groups recognized that sexual intercourse and semen were somehow necessary for procreation. This knowledge was applied in several ways in attempts to prevent conception. Egyptian sources from as long ago as 1850 BC describe vaginal plugs of honey, gum acacia, and crocodile dung (Fathalla, 1994). The acidity of the mixture probably had some spermicidal effect, and the plug would operate like the modern sponge in both absorbing sperm and acting as a barrier.

Coitus interruptus is a very old form of birth control. This and many other methods had at least some effectiveness, and their availability meant that there was some desire, especially among women, to regulate fertility. Abortion and infanticide have also long been used for fertility regulation (Daly & Wilson, 1984; Tannahill, 1980).

While family planning decisions are personal, social forces such as modes of production influence the decisions made by individuals and couples. In less industrialized countries, pronatalist attitudes remain prominent. This has implications for the entire world as concern grows about overpopulation and environmental depletion.

Demographic Transition Theory

Thomas Robert Malthus is sometimes called the father of demography. He was born in 1776, as the industrial revolution dawned. Already productivity was increasing and many social analysts were optimistic about improvements in the human condition. Not so Mr. Malthus. In his "Essay on the Principle of Population" he argued that a society's ability to produce children will always exceed the society's ability to increase the production of food and other products necessary for survival. As a consequence, overpopulation would always be a problem, and wars, disease, and starvation would be a permanent part of human life (Elwell, 1999).

Malthus's pessimistic essay was published in 1798 and went through seven editions, each one using more mathematics to prove his point. His argument was an influence on much of early demography and on the ecological-evolutionary theories of the Lenskis

---

Coitus interruptus: The practice of attempting to prevent contraception in which the penis is withdrawn from the vagina before ejaculation.

(chapters 2–4) (Elwell, 1999). His perspective is also echoed by Paul Ehrlich (1976; 1997) and others who today are concerned about the "population explosion."

Later demographers began to develop more sophisticated analyses. The initial version of a theory of demographic transition was advanced in 1929 by Warren Thompson. He suggested that the more industrialized nations were able to increase their production fast enough to keep up with increasing populations, but that the rest of the world was likely to remain in the conditions predicted by Malthus.

Several versions of a theory of demographic transition were later developed. All used the two basic facts of birthrates and death rates to determine overall population levels. European nations had gone through three stages of economic development; the suggestion is that other societies, too, might go through the same process (see Figure 11.1).

In the primary economic stage, all productive activity was directed toward providing basic necessities like food and shelter. This stage included hunting-gathering and agricultural modes of production. In these societies, there was a precarious balance between birthrates and death rates, both of which were high. Population levels were low and unstable for some groups. Agricultural societies were generally able to support a larger population than hunting-gathering ones, but at the global level populations were relatively sparse and constant for most of human history.

Because of the constant threat that a society would die out if death rates exceeded birthrates for any significant period, successful agrarian societies became quite pronatalist. This value was espoused in the major world religions. Christianity, Judaism, Islam, and Hinduism all have mechanisms to encourage families to have large number of children. Commands such as "be fruitful and multiply" developed in the primary stage.

In the secondary economic stage, increasing amounts of productive activity were directed toward manufacturing. In Western Europe, the death rate began to fall in about 1750, which roughly coincides with the beginning of the industrial revolution (Handwerker, 1986). Increased productivity provided better nutrition, and urban areas began to provide more sanitary living conditions.

In the next century, great strides were made in preventative medicine by such scientists as Louis Pasteur (1822–1895). The germ theory of disease replaced older ideas about what caused sickness. Widespread vaccines against smallpox, polio, and other killers followed over the next half century. The United States and other nations required that milk be pasteurized to prevent spread of disease. Penicillin and other antibiotics were developed.

The germ theory of disease also led to better sanitation systems in the major cities. Sewer systems were installed or improved, and concerted efforts were made to get rid of the conditions that bred rats, fleas, and other carriers of disease. In addition, nutrition and working conditions were improved.

These changes accelerated the drop in death rates while birthrates remained relatively high. A population explosion resulted. Between the time Malthus wrote and the beginning of World War I in the 20th century, the population of the United Kingdom grew from 10 million to 42 million. Had it not been for the mass migrations of millions to the Americas and elsewhere in the world, Europe might not have been able to increase its production enough to feed its growing population (Haub & Riche, 1994).

In about 1850, and considerably earlier in some parts of Europe, the fertility rate began to decline. In the 20th century, with the exception of the baby boom, the gradual decline continued. Several factors played a part. More and more people needed increasing number of years of formal education; this resulted in postponed marriages for many. Since they got married later, these women would have fewer children in a lifetime. Separation of women and men in the workforce and increasing numbers of women working outside the home played a part. The institutionalization of social security and other retirement plans reduced the necessity of the elderly to rely on large numbers of children to support them.

Perhaps the most important contributor to the decline in fertility rates was the fact that, especially in the cities, having children became a net economic cost, rather than a net labor benefit. On farms and ranches, children could begin to be economically productive at a fairly young age. This was not true in the cities, especially after the passage of child labor laws. Children still needed clothes, food, and school supplies; once they became self-supporting, they moved out of their parents' home.

Also, the drop in infant mortality meant that children were more likely to survive to adulthood, so fewer births were required to produce the same number of adult children. Increasingly wanting to limit their family size, couples used the technology available to do so. Fertility levels in Europe dropped from 7–10 lifetime births per woman in early 19th century to 2–4 by 1950 (Handwerker, 1986).

| Figure 11.1 | Theory of Demographic Transition |

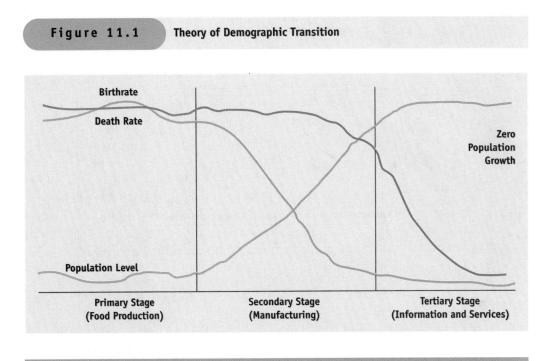

Source: Suggested by Thompson, Warren. 1929. "Population." *American Journal of Sociology* 34(6): 959–75 and Handwerker, W. Penn. 1986. "Culture and Reproduction: Exploring Micro & Macro Linkages." Pp. 1–29 in *Culture and Reproduction: An Anthropological Critique of Demographic Transition Theory*, edited by W. Penn Handwerker. Boulder, CO: Westview Press.

By the arrival of the tertiary economic stage, with economic activity focused on information and services, population growth had leveled off in most of the highly industrialized societies. Some countries have now apparently reached a point of zero population growth. This requires a prolonged period of time at replacement level, or about two children per couple.

Demographic transition theory predicted that, if industrialized societies would help the rest of the world to become more industrialized, other countries would go through the same kind of demographic transition. For a variety of reasons, however, many demographers now question that assumption (Cole, 1973; Handwerker, 1986; Goldscheider, 1992; Mazur, 1994).

At a global level, the world is still in the midst of a population explosion. In the thousands of years of human habitation of the earth, the total population did not reach 1 billion persons until about 1800 (see Figure 11.2). It reached 1.6 billion by 1900 and grew even more rapidly after that, reaching 2.5 billion in 1950 (Haub & Riche, 1994). World population now stands at 7.0 billion (Haub & Yanagishita, 1999). It is projected to reach 8.2 billion by 2025 (Haub & Yanagishita, 1996). Although birthrates have fallen in most of the countries of the world, they have not yet fallen to replacement level.

If the world's population continues to grow at the present rate, it will double in 51 years. That growth, however, will not be uniform throughout the world. Europe as a whole has stopped growing. **Doubling time** will be 124 years in North America, but only 42 years in South America and 23 years in Central Africa, already the poorest region (see Table 11.1).

Doubling time: The number of years it would take a particular population to double in size if it continued to grow at a given rate. Doubling time at low rates of growth can be approximated by the formula (69/annual percentage growth rate) = doubling time in years.

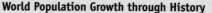

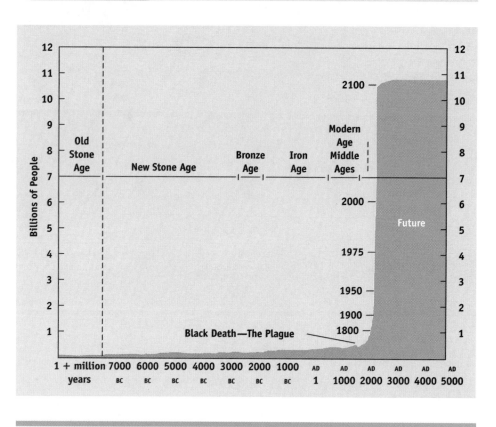

Source: Population Reference Bureau; and United Nations, *World Population Projections to 2100.*

The population explosion in poorer nations is a result not of increased birthrates but of rapidly decreasing death rates. Part of the problem stems from good intentions. The western world introduced modern vaccinations, sanitation, and other life-saving techniques to nations all over the world. The death rates dropped, but those nations were not able to increase their production of food and other necessities fast enough to feed the rapidly growing populations. The kinds of agricultural production in the United States are not feasible in many other parts of the world, either because of cultural differences or climatic differences.

While poorer societies as a whole might be better off if they had lower fertility rates, individual couples often see large families as the only chance they have of being supported in their old age. In addition, pronatalist religious and cultural beliefs encourage large families in many parts of the world. Table 11.1 reveals that the highly industrialized societies are at or near zero population growth; they have low infant mortality rates, low birthrates, and high consumption rates. Third World countries tend to have rapid growth rates, high infant mortality rates, high birthrates, and low consumption. Demographic transition has not occurred as many demographers had anticipated in most of the Third World.

Availability of family planning technology has allowed families in some Third World countries to plan their family size more accurately. Because many couples want large numbers of children, however, families remain larger than replacement level.

While not intentional, development attempts have sometimes increased the fertility rate by raising families' hopes of being able to provide for more children

| Table 11.1 | Population Data by Region and Selected Countries, Midyear 2000 |

Region	Population Mid-1996 (Millions)	Births Per 1,000	Deaths Per 1,000	Infant Mortality Per 1,000	Natural Increase Annual %	Doubling Time, Years	Per Capita GNP, 1998 U.S. $
World	6,067	22	9	57.0	1.4	51	$ 4,890
North America	306.4	14	9	7.0	0.6	124	28,230
United States	275.6	14.5	8.7	7.0	0.6	120	29,240
Canada	30.7	11.2	7.3	5.5	0.4	178	19,170
Central America	136.5	26	5	34.0	2.1	33	3,270
Mexico	99.6	23.9	4.4	31.5	1.9	36	3,840
Nicaragua	5.1	36.1	5.9	40.0	3.0	23	370
East Asia	1,492.6	15	7	29.0	0.8	85	3,880
China	1,264.6	15.2	6.4	31.4	0.9	79	750
Japan	126.9	9.4	7.9	3.5	0.2	462	32,350
Northern Africa	173	27	7	51.0	2.0	34	1,200
Western Africa	234.5	42	14	89.0	2.8	25	340
Eastern Africa	246.2	42	18	102.0	2.4	29	—
Middle Africa	96.4	46	16	106.0	3.0	23	320
Southern Africa	49.9	26	13	51.0	1.3	52	3,100
Europe	727.5	10	11	9.0	− 0.1	—	13,420
Sweden	8.9	9.9	10.7	3.5	− 0.08	—	25,580
United Kingdom	59.8	12.0	10.7	5.7	0.13	546	21,410
Germany	82.1	9.4	10.3	4.7	− 0.1	—	26,570
Spain	39.5	9.2	9.1	5.7	0.0	6931	14,100
South America	344.8	23	6	34.0	1.7	42	4,270
Brazil	170.1	21.3	5.9	38.0	1.5	45	4,630
Oceana	31	18	7	29.0	1.1	65	15,400
Australia	19.2	13.1	6.8	5.3	0.6	110	20,640
Papua-New Guinea	4.8	34.0	10.0	77.0	2.4	29	890

Source: Selected and adapted data from "World Population Data Sheet 2000." Population Reference Bureau, Washington, DC. **http://www.prb.org/pubs/wpds2000/.** Reprinted by permission.

(Abernethy, 1993). Further complicating the issue is the provision of more western medicine and sanitation that lowers infant mortality but causes populations to grow even faster.

Rather than simply advocating more development money, some demographers are taking a closer look at exactly what might cause a demographic transition in poorer nations. Handwerker (1986:1) argued "Fertility transition in the contemporary world comes about when personal material well-being is determined less by personal relationships than by formal education and skill training." This view advocates educational access for women, not only on grounds of gender equality but to help lower fertility rates (Sadik, 1994; De Barbieri, 1994). Pronatalism most directly affects women, since they are the ones who bear the children and provide most of their direct care. Lower fertility rates would improve the health of women, but in many societies, having children is the major source of a woman's status (McLaren, 1992).

The desire to limit family size is at least as important in regulating fertility rates as is the availability of modern contraceptive technology. That desire is influenced by a number of manifest and latent cultural factors. In the United States and other developed countries the desire to separate the pleasure function of

Finding Out | 11.1

Gathering Demographic Information

Most of the developed countries have a government agency that gathers and disseminates demographic information. In the United States there are a number of agencies that are involved, but the Census Bureau **http://www.census.gov** is the agency primarily responsible for that task. In addition to the national census taken every 10 years, the Census Bureau conducts hundreds of other studies related to population. Because the Census Bureau, a part of the U.S. Department of Commerce, is a government agency, the data it develops was not copyrighted and may be used without permission.

The Population Reference Bureau **http://www.prb.org** collects demographic data from all over the world. This is an important task because, in their words, "Population shapes almost every aspect of our lives. Population defines the need for resource allocations—where to build roads, schools, or hospitals. Population shapes political systems and helps determine economic vitality" **http://www.prb.org/inside/about_prb.htm.**

The Population Reference Bureau employs social scientists, health care professionals, computer programmers, and other experts from around the world. Information is collected in a large library and serves as the basis for a number of publications distributed by the PRB. Information is made available to other researchers, journalists, government officials, middle school and high school educators, among others. The organization provides technical support to both government and private agencies.

The PRB is governed by a diverse board of trustees. Its funds come from a number of sources including government contracts, foundation grants, individual and corporate contributions, and the sale of its publications. The PRB has copyrights on its material, which may not be reprinted without permission.

---

sexuality from the reproductive function has increased the demand for effective family planning technology (Giddens, 1992).

Fertility Choice in Contemporary America

Important fluctuations have occurred in the American birthrate in the 20th century. The birthrate experienced a downturn in the 1930s, during the Great Depression. Because of the hard times, couples intentionally limited their births. In addition, couples were often separated for long periods of time as one partner, usually the husband, searched for work in other locations. The birthrate increased in the 1940s as the economy improved. The upward trend was interrupted briefly during America's heaviest involvement in the war, but it resumed sharply in 1946, after the war. This was the beginning of the baby boom. The boom tapered off in the mid-1960s. As Figure 11.3 indicates, the birthrate has generally continued to fall since 1950. There was a slight increase in the 1980s, peaking in 1990, as children of the baby boomers had their

own children, and then a continuing decline since then.

In contemporary North America and other postindustrial societies, the questions of whether to have children and how many to have are increasingly seen as matters of choice. Results of surveys asking about "ideal" family size find that two children is the most common ideal in other postindustrial societies (Vandenheuvel, 1991). In the United States, also, two children is the most common ideal. Because a few people prefer large families, the mean average ideal is just over three children (Davis & Smith, 1998).

Pronatalism has weakened in the United States. Among all American women 18 to 34 years of age, 9.3% expect to have no births during their lifetime. That same figure applied to both Black and White women; 5.7% of Hispanic women expected to bear no children. The most highly educated women were most likely to expect to remain childless (Census Bureau, 1993:81).

Some who do not wish to have children have advocated replacing the term "childless" with the more positive-sounding term "child-free." While being child-free by choice is increasing, there are couples who are

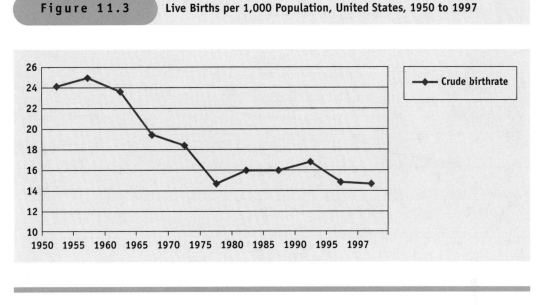

Figure 11.3   **Live Births per 1,000 Population, United States, 1950 to 1997**

Source: U.S. Census Bureau, 1999. *Statistical Abstract of the United States: 1999,* 19th ed. Table 91. Washington, DC: U.S. Government Printing Office.

involuntarily childless. More commonly, a couple drifts into childlessness (Heaton, Jacobson, & Holland, 1999). They are waiting until they are absolutely certain they want a child, or until they get their careers established, or for some other future event. Eventually, they wait so long that they become, or believe themselves to be, too old to have a child.

As Figure 11.4 indicates, the percentage of women remaining childless through their prime childbearing years has increased rapidly in postindustrial America. The percentage of childless women in their late 30s almost doubled from 1976 to 1995, when the figure stood at 19.7. In the early 40s group, 17.5% of women remained childless; very few of these will have their first child at a later age. We can soon expect that 20% or more of American women will never bear a child, and that a large proportion of these will be the most highly educated, economically well off women.

Polenko, Scanzoni, and Teachman (1982) compared women who had children with various categories of childless women. Some had voluntarily decided to be child-free; some had not yet decided; some wanted children but were postponing the event; and some wanted children but were unable to have them. Compared with mothers, women without children in the voluntary, undecided, and postponing categories had somewhat greater marital satisfaction. These were often women who had other sources of satisfaction such as fulfilling careers. In couples who were involuntarily childless, both the husbands and wives felt considerable marital stress. The infertility issue created problems that spread to other aspects of their relationship (Abbey, Andrews, & Halman, 1992).

For fertile couples, remaining child-free requires the continued use of some form of contraception. In the next section, we will explore some of the common family planning methods used by couples to reduce the number of children they might have, and to influence timing of childbirth. The section following that one covers methods used to increase family size.

Fertility Reduction Methods

Manifest forms of fertility reduction can be divided into two major types. **Contraception** is designed to prevent conception from occurring, while **abortion** prevents a

Contraception: Intentional prevention of impregnation.   **Abortion:** Termination of a pregnancy before the fetus can survive outside the uterus. **Spontaneous abortions** occur naturally and unintentionally; **induced abortions** are done intentionally.

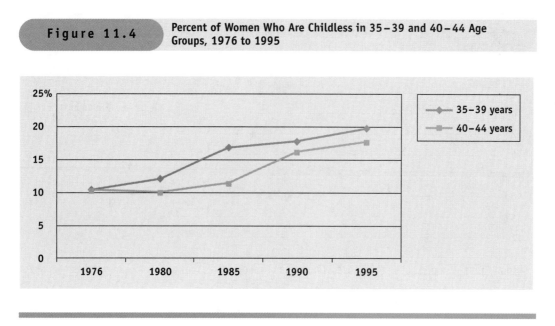

Figure 11.4 Percent of Women Who Are Childless in 35–39 and 40–44 Age Groups, 1976 to 1995

Source: U.S. Census Bureau, 1997. Current Population Survey Reports, Historical Time Series Tables. Table H1. **http://www.census.gov/population/www/socdemo/fertility.html.**

fertilized egg from going through the full developmental process to live birth. In addition, although births are not prevented, family size can be limited by giving an infant up for adoption. Each of these approaches has a variety of specific techniques, and varying degrees of social acceptability.

Abstinence-Based Methods

Some approaches to reducing the probability of pregnancy rely on avoidance of some or all sexual activity, some or all of the time. Also known as *coitus abstentia,* **general abstinence** is the attempt to avoid sexual intercourse completely. This is not a practical method for married couples or others who wish to have a sexual relationship, but it is the approach most American parents would prefer their unmarried adolescents would use.

Contrary to popular belief, general abstinence is not 100% effective in the prevention of pregnancy. Every type of contraception has both a method failure

rate and a user failure rate. Method failure occurs when a person using a contraceptive method does everything the method calls for, yet pregnancy still results. User failure rates are based on the experience of typical users of the method in real life. Both failure rates are calculated as the percentage of women who get pregnant in a year while using the method (see Table 11.2).

In the case of general abstinence, a woman can practice the method perfectly but become pregnant as a result of rape or incest. Pregnancy that results from user failure of abstinence is much more common. A couple or individual might plan to practice abstinence but have sexual intercourse anyway because they get "carried away." Failure rates of this type are not typically calculated, but it is quite probable that user failure of general abstinence is a major cause of unwanted pregnancy among American adolescents. Since about one third of all births in the United States are to unmarried mothers, it would appear that abstinence user failure is quite high.

Abstinence: The practice of refraining from indulging some appetite such as food, drink, or a particular sexual practice.
General abstinence: The practice of completely avoiding sexual intercourse.

Table 11.2	Contraceptive Failure Rates and Usage, Two Studies				

	Study A			Study B	
Method	**Method Failure %**	**User Failure %**	**% of All Users**	**Method Failure %**	**User Failure %**
No method	85.0	85.0			
Total abstinence	*	*		0	?
Periodic abstinence	9.0	19.0	2.3	1–9	20.0
Spermicide	6.0	30.0	<1	6.0	26.0
Withdrawal	4.0	24.0	3.0	4.0	19.0
Diaphragm	6.0	18.0	1.9	6.0	20.0
Cervical cap	9.0–26.0	18.0	<1.0	6.0	18.0
Male condom	3.0	16.0	20.4	3.0	14.0
Female condom	*	*	*	5.0	21.0
Pill	0.1	6.0	26.9	0.1–0.5	3.0
IUD	0.8	4.0	0.8	0.1–1.5	0.1–2.0
Tubal sterilization	0.5	0.5	27.7	0.5	0.5
Injectable (Depo-Provera)	0.3	0.4	3.0	0.3	0.3
Vasectomy	0.1	0.2	10.9	0.1	0.15
Implant	0.05	0.05	1.3	0.05	0.05
Sponge	*	*	*	9–20	20–40

Sources: Study A: The Alan Guttmacher Institute; **http://www.agi-usa.org/pubs/fb contr use.html**. Accessed Feb. 1, 2001.
Study B: Hatcher, Richard, et al. 1998. *Contraceptive Technology*, 17th ed. Decatur, GA: Ardent Media.

Also known as "natural family planning," "fertility awareness," and the "rhythm method," **periodic abstinence** is a very old family-planning technique. The basic idea of the method is to avoid sexual intercourse on and around the day of ovulation, so determining the time of ovulation is crucial. In the least restrictive of cases, use of the rhythm method would require abstinence for at least 7 out of every 28 days, or one fourth of the couple's time together. Even longer periods of abstinence are suggested if the woman's period varies from a regular 28-day cycle.

Coitus Interruptus. While abstinence methods generally assume that a couple does without sexual intercourse, it is technically only the ejaculation of sperm into the vagina that must be avoided for contraception to be successful. Coitus interruptus, now more commonly called early withdrawal, theoretically allows for sexual intercourse with decreased risk of pregnancy. While this is more effective than no contraception at all, it has a relatively high failure rate.

In what might also be considered a form of abstinence, a couple might engage in a number of noncoital sexual activities. Oral stimulation, manual stimulation, anal sex, and other activities that lead to noncoital orgasm are not usually considered contraceptive methods. They have very low method failure rates, but user failure rates are probably fairly high. Only if couples learn to define their sexual scripts in noncoital ways can alternative sexual expression be effective.

Coital Methods

For persons who want to enjoy less limited sexual behavior than the abstinence methods allow, a range of

Periodic abstinence: The practice of attempting to avoid conception by refraining from intercourse at certain times of the menstrual cycle.

This clinic in Gambia, Africa, provides the knowledge necessary to make family-planning techniques successful.

contraception techniques is available. These attempt to prevent pregnancy while allowing complete sexual intercourse, including ejaculation in the vagina.

Spermicide is designed to kill sperm before they can produce conception. It is available in a variety of forms, including foam, jelly, cream, and suppository. Creams and gels should be used in conjunction with a diaphragm, while foam and suppositories are intended to be used alone or in conjunction with a condom.

Barrier methods are designed to block sperm from reaching the ovum. The most common of these is the male condom, varieties of which have been used for centuries. The diaphragm, another barrier method, is worn internally by the woman and is designed to block the sperm from passing through the cervix. A more recent product in the family of barrier methods is the female condom. Like the male version, the vaginal condom provides some protection against HIV infection and other STDs.

Centuries ago, Arab and Turkish camel drivers placed a pebble into a camel's uterus to prevent pregnancy on long desert trips. This was the first known use of an **intrauterine device (IUD)**. The first human model, made of silkworm gut, was introduced in 1909, and the German physician Grafenberg produced an IUD made of gut and silver wire in the 1920s. Around the world today, it is estimated that 60 million women

use an IUD; it is especially common in China, where there are an estimated 40 million users (Masters, Johnson, & Kolodny, 1992; Piotrow, Rinehart, & Schmidt, 1979).

Oral contraceptives, often referred to simply as "the pill," are available in two basic types. The combination pill contains synthetic versions of the hormones estrogen and progesterone. The most popular are the low-dosage combination pills, which contain considerably lower dosages of hormones than the original pills that revolutionized contraception when they were first made available in the 1960s. The less common and less effective minipill contains only the low-dosage progesterone-like compound.

In effect, the primary action of the pill is to trick the body into thinking it is pregnant so that ovulation does not occur. Conception is prevented because no egg is available for the sperm to find. Secondarily, the pill causes cervical mucus to become thick and acidic, creating a hostile environment for sperm so that even if an egg is released, live sperm is unlikely to reach it. Finally, the hormones render the uterine lining unsuitable for implantation of a fertilized egg, should the other two effects fail (Knox & Schacht, 1994). This last effect, although probably quite rare, does make the pill a possible **abortifacient,** if preventing a fertilized egg from implanting is considered abortion.

Spermicide: An agent that kills sperm, especially as a contraceptive.   **Intrauterine device (IUD):** An object inserted into the uterus for the purpose of preventing pregnancy.   **Abortifacient:** A substance or device that causes abortion.

Although some are in the testing stage, there are no chemical contraceptives on the market designed for men. This is at least partly because it is easier to stop the release of one egg monthly than to stop the production of millions of sperm daily. Research has, however, found some chemicals with contraceptive promise. When taken by men, for example, Depo-Provera does decrease sperm production. Drawbacks are that production of sperm is not usually stopped completely. More seriously, the sex drive is significantly reduced (Bromwich & Parsons, 1990). Because of the effect of Depo-Provera on the libido, the drug has been referred to as "chemical castration" and has been suggested as a treatment or punishment for rapists. Because of such side effects, it likely to be several years before an acceptable male chemical contraceptive is on the market in the United States.

When both female and male methods are included, permanent sterilization is the most popular method of birth control for American couples today. Women can become surgically sterile as a result of **hysterectomy** or **ovariectomy,** but these operations are generally used only for treatment of serious infections, cancer, or other major problems.

When surgery is done only for birth control, some variation of a **tubal ligation**, designed to make passage of an ovum through the Fallopian tube impossible, is generally used. This popular "band-aid" surgery is relatively simple and leaves only a tiny scar in the navel. Although it is one of the safest forms of surgery, it is still surgery and can result in risk from the anesthetic, infection, bleeding, or from other rare complications.

Vasectomy, or surgical sterilization of the male, is cheaper, quicker, safer, and more effective than tubal ligation. General anesthetic is not necessary; the scrotum, not the abdominal cavity, is breached. There is, consequently, less chance of infection or dangerous bleeding.

Using methods that amount to major surgery, some physicians have reported a reversal rate for vasectomies of more than half; reversal for tubal ligations is more difficult and less often successful. Surgical sterilization of either type should be considered permanent. Individuals who think there is a chance that they might someday want more children are not good candidates for sterilization.

Postcoital Family Planning

A variety of methods, used after sexual intercourse occurs, exist for preventing unwanted births. With the exception of douching, which is largely ineffective, postcoital methods primarily interrupt the development of a fertilized egg rather than preventing conception.

Several "morning after" pills have been available, but it is generally advised that they be used only in emergencies such as rape. They must be taken within 72 hours of intercourse and have higher risks than most contraceptive methods (Hatcher et al., 1990).

RU-486, used for several years in Europe, was approved in 2000 for use in the United States. A synthetic steroid, RU-486 prevents the implantation of a fertilized egg or induces menstruation in the event that implantation has already occurred. As used in France, this "abortion pill" requires four separate visits to a medical facility: a preliminary evaluation, two separate supervised dosages of drugs, and a follow-up examination. Under these conditions, RU-486 is about 95% effective in inducing abortion (Klitsch, 1991). Similar procedures and results are expected in the United States.

The Abortion Issue

Abortion has been practiced throughout human history. Its acceptance has varied, but even in cultures that disapproved, termination of pregnancy has not generally been placed in the same category as murder. Much controversy, however, remains.

One major abortion issue centers on the question about the point at which a separate human life, entitled to rights under the law, begins. From some religious perspectives, the question is the precise time in the gradual fertilization and developmental process that the organism acquires a soul. Some anti-abortionists believe that life starts at the "moment of conception." This is currently the position of the Roman Catholic Church, although until 1869 the position was that life begins 40 days after conception (Esterbrook, 2000).

Many supporters of the "pro-life" position also hold that women who have sexual intercourse have a moral responsibility to carry a resultant fetus to term. By

---

Hysterectomy: Surgical removal of the uterus.   **Ovariectomy:** Surgical removal of the ovaries.   **Tubal ligation:** "Tying the tubes"; surgically cutting and tying the Fallopian tubes to prevent the passage of an ovum from the ovary to the uterus.
Vasectomy: A surgical procedure designed to make the transmission of sperm through the *vas deferens* impossible.

contrast, supporters of the "pro-choice" position, who believe that abortions should be a woman's legal choice, argue that the zygote and fetus are another part of the woman's body over which she should have control. These persons argue that a separate human life begins at the moment of birth.

One historical position has been that a unique human life begins, or the soul enters the organism, at the time of "quickening." This is the time, usually toward the end of the fifth month of pregnancy, that the pregnant woman begins to feel movement of the fetus.

In 1973, the abortion issue in the United States took a major turn when the Supreme Court handed down its famous Roe v. Wade decision. Based on the right to privacy between a woman and her physician, the Roe decision established that states could not interfere during the first trimester of pregnancy. In the second trimester, state interference could only be for purposes of protecting the woman's health. States were allowed to regulate or prohibit abortion during the third trimester.

A variety of court cases since that time have refined the original Roe decision, but the basic right to an abortion remains even if access to the procedure has been limited. In some states, teenagers must either notify their parents prior to having an abortion or get a judge's approval. As matters currently stand, the male progenitor has no legal rights in matters of abortion, although a live birth can legally obligate him to provide financial support until the infant becomes an adult.

The abortion issue sometimes appears to be highly polarizing, with very strong opinions on both the "pro-choice" and "pro-life" sides. Most Americans, however, are ambivalent about the issue, approving of abortion in some situations but not others. A majority of Americans approve of abortion in cases of rape or incest and when carrying the fetus to term would result in major risk to the health of the mother or the likelihood of serious defect in the child. Fewer than half, however, approve of abortion in cases where the woman is having the abortion solely because she already has too many children, is unmarried, or would have financial problems (see Table 11.3).

Having Abortions

Because it has been legal in the United States for 3 decades, abortion has become a relatively safe procedure. Although women who have abortions have somewhat more complications than women who do not get

The legal and political debate about abortion is not likely to end soon.

pregnant in the first place, legal abortions are safer than childbirth, using an IUD, or taking the pill. Major complications occur in less than 1% of abortions (*Facts in Brief,* 1992).

Although the decision to have an abortion is a difficult one for many women, Adler et al. (1990) found that most stress occurred before the abortion and that severe negative reactions occurred in only 5 to 10% of women. It is hard to measure the difficulties these women experienced compared to the stress and psychological trauma of having and raising an unwanted child. It would appear that negative postabortion psychological problems are less common than is postpartum depression in women who give birth, even including women who wanted the child. Little information exists about the psychological impact of abortion on the male progenitor.

In 1996, there were 1,366,000 abortions in the United States, or 351 abortions for every 1,000 live births (*Statistical Abstract* 1999: t. 114). Both figures are down considerably from the peak years in the mid-1980s. In 1985, there were 1,589,000 abortions, or 422 abortions per 1,000 live births.

The decrease is partly because there are relatively fewer women in the age groups most likely to have abortions. Although more abortions are performed on women age 20 to 24, women who get pregnant are most likely to get abortions if they are younger than 15; more than half of the known pregnancies of girls in this young age group end in induced abortion (Henshaw & Van Vort, 1992).

Table 11.3	Percentage of Americans Who Approve of Legal Abortion under Certain Circumstances, 1998

Abortion should be legal if. . .	Percentage Agreeing
The woman's own health is seriously endangered by the pregnancy	87.9%
She became pregnant as a result of rape	80.1
There is a strong chance of serious defect in the baby	78.6
The family has a very low income and cannot afford any more children	44.3
She is married and does not want to marry the man	42.3
The woman wants it for any reason	42.3

Source: Davis, James Allan, and Tom W. Smith: General Social Survey(s), year(s). (Machine-readable data file). Principal investigator, James A. Davis; director and co-principal investigator, Tom W. Smith; co-principal investigator, Peter V. Marsden, NORC ed. Chicago: National Opinion Research Center, producer, 1998; Storrs, CT: The Roper Center for Public Opinion Research, University of Connecticut, distributor. Microcomputer format and codebook prepared and distributed by MicroCase Corporation, Bellevue, WA. Analysis by Gene H. Starbuck.

About 80% of reported induced abortions are performed on unmarried women. The **abortion ratio,** which is the number of abortions for every 1,000 known pregnancies, is only 94 for married women and 466 for those who are unmarried. Although 59% of abortions are performed on White women, their abortion ratio is 206 compared to 412 for women of color (*Statistical Abstract* 1999: t. 124).

Postnatal Options

Abortion is only one option for an unmarried pregnant woman (see Figure 11.5). Single parenting is the most rapidly growing option and was chosen by about 21% of unwed pregnant American women in the late 1980s. The most common option cross-culturally and historically, marrying the father of the child-to-be, is sometimes not even mentioned today as an option for unmarried teens. Although it was once virtually the only viable option, in the 1980s only about 24% of never-married pregnant women got married before the birth of their child (Bachrach, Stolley, & London, 1992).

A relatively rare choice for a pregnant woman to make is to give birth and then give up her rights of motherhood. Sometimes called the "adoption option," it is more correct to refer to it as **relinquishment,** since

adoption refers to the relationship between the adoptive parents and the child (Strong & Devault, 1994).

Almost no married women relinquish their infants, and only about 2% of unmarried women do so (Strong & Devault, 1994). This figure is down from the unmarried mother relinquishment rate of about 14% in the early 1970s (Bachrach, Stolley, & London, 1992). In the late 1980s, there were about 33,000 infant relinquishments annually (Strong & Devault, 1994). At the same time, an estimated 200,000 women were seeking infants to adopt (Bachrach, London, & Maza, 1991).

Part of the reason for the declining popularity of relinquishment is the increased safety and availability of abortion. Also, there has been increasing social acceptance of single mothers, as well as accessibility of welfare benefits that make single motherhood more feasible (Daly, 1994). Perhaps reflecting the unpopularity of relinquishment and perhaps contributing to its unpopularity is the fact that it is not generally mentioned on a par with abortion in formal discussions of pregnancy resolution. As with other sources of information, marriage and family textbooks generally give considerably less coverage to relinquishment than to abortion (Stolley & Hall, 1994).

Although teenagers tend to have positive feelings about adoption and adopted children in general, they

---

Abortion ratio: Number of abortions for every 1,000 known pregnancies.   **Relinquishment:** A giving up or surrender of something; to give up legal rights to a child.   **Adoption:** Taking into one's own family and raising as one's own child.

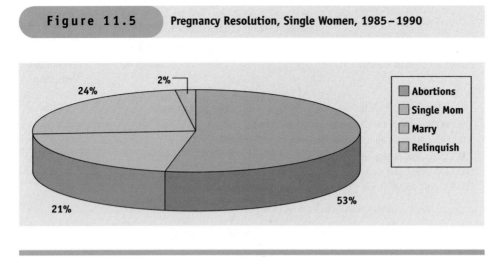

Figure 11.5 **Pregnancy Resolution, Single Women, 1985–1990**

Source: Recalculated using data from Strong and Devault, 1994; U.S. Bureau of the Census, 1995; Bachrach, Stolley, and London, 1992.

do not often consider it a viable option for themselves. They are much more likely to have talked with their friends, parents, and dating partners about single parenting and abortion than about relinquishment. Adolescents fear that choosing to relinquish would subject them to rejection from parents and peers, who might view their choice as "selfish, unloving and even incomprehensible" (Resnick et al., 1990:583).

While fear of peer rejection is important, other concerns are a stronger barrier to giving a child up for adoption. In one study, 80% of teenagers expressed concern about "feelings of abandoning the baby," and another 63% were concerned about "not knowing what is involved and what to expect with adoption" (Daly, 1994:339). Young persons know more about the proper use of birth control and how to get an abortion than they do about relinquishing parental rights.

Some recent research indicates that fear of negative consequences of relinquishment is partially unfounded. Placing for adoption does have some positive outcomes, especially as compared to single parenthood (Daly, 1994). The differences in outcome of parenting and relinquishment might partially be accounted for by social class variations, however. White unmarried pregnant teens are more likely to choose relinquishment than are minority youths (Kalmuss, Namerow, & Cushman, 1991). Women with higher socioeconomic status and higher academic ambitions are more likely to give up

their parental rights (Resnick et al., 1990). Women who hold more traditional attitudes about family life are more likely to relinquish (Hayes, 1987). Religious fundamentalists, who face both the prohibition of abortion and the social stigma of illegitimate birth, are more likely to resolve an unintended pregnancy by giving the child up for adoption (Medoff, 1993).

To determine the influence that government policy might have, Medoff (1993) compared relinquishment rates of the various states. He found that the higher the Aid to Families with Dependent Children payment, the more likely women in poverty were to keep their child. Price and availability of abortions appeared to have no statistically significant effect on adoption decisions. Studies have not yet been done on the effect of recent changes in welfare laws on abortion decisions.

State regulations about relinquishment and adoption vary considerably. Medoff (1993) looked at four separate issues to see if they influenced relinquishment rates. First, while all states have social services departments and nonprofit, licensed adoption agencies, some allow private adoptions through intermediaries and some do not. Second, states vary in terms of the extent to which they allow open adoptions, in which relinquishing mothers, adoptive parents, and adopted children know the identities of each other. Third, some states allow prospective adoptive parents to pay expenses of birth mothers, while other states forbid such practices. Finally, the length of time birth mothers are allowed to change their mind about relinquishment varies from state to state. While each of the four policy variations is important for other reasons, Medoff (1993) found that none has a statistically significant influence on relinquishment rates.

Contraception, abortion, and relinquishment are all methods of family planning designed to reduce the likelihood of unwanted parenthood. We turn now to family planning methods designed to do the opposite.

Childbirth and Fertility Enhancement

Childbirth in hunting-gathering societies was often a truly family affair. Women of the clan, often collectively, assisted in childbirth and the immediate postpartum phase. Fathers, too, often had a part, if only in ceremony.

The **couvade** provided participation for the men in the birthing process. The practice has been found among peoples in the Americas, Africa, Europe, India, and China (Wolf, 1996). When their wives are in labor, men appear to be going through the same process, including labor pains.

In some societies, the couvade is connected to a system of magic or religion; the man is drawing the attention of evil spirits away from his wife. It might allow the man to identify with the mother, thereby expressing his sympathy for the feminine role (Munroe & Munroe, 1989). It also appears to help establish the claim of the man to the legitimate fatherhood of the child (Broude, 1988).

The practice is more common in matrilocal societies and those in which motherhood is granted great importance (Broude, 1989). Even where the couvade was practiced, though, participation in the birth itself was primarily by women. Historically, this appears to be true almost universally (Rothman, 1993). In more specialized societies, a **midwife** presided over the birth. In most cases, the midwife got her expertise by having

children herself, through folk knowledge, and by experience (Burtch, 1994).

Over time, midwifery became a more specialized position. During the Middle Ages in Europe, the Catholic Church appointed and licensed midwives, who were expected not only to provide care for women, but also to prevent abortions, infant substitutions, and infanticide (Bohme, 1984). Many midwives continued to operate independently, however, and their craft was not infrequently the target when witch hunts were fashionable (Donnison, 1988).

In the American colonies, midwives were more independent from the church than in Europe, but in both places considerable friction developed between midwifery and the emerging field of medical science. By mid-20th century, licensed physicians had taken over the child-delivery business and midwives had all but disappeared. Feminist scholars have documented the process that not only moved childbirth from the home to the hospital, but also moved it from the care of women to the care of physicians, nearly all of whom were men (Donnison, 1988; Oakley, 1984; Rothman, 1993).

Modern medicine did contribute to a decline in fatalities among both mothers and infants. It also, however, removed control of the process not only from the mother but from all women. It also removed control of childbirth from the family and excluded the father from the process (Burtch, 1994).

In recent decades, a reaction to the impersonal "medicalization" of the birthing process resulted in several alternative methods. These include Lamaze's "natural" or "prepared" approach; the Dick-Read method, and Bradley's "husband-coached childbirth." The medical profession gradually responded by incorporating these methods into hospital delivery, and in providing family birthing rooms and other innovations. There has also been a resurgence of interest in home births and midwifery (Rothman, 1993).

Defining Infertility

Like childbirth, involuntary childlessness might sound like a primarily medical issue, but it has significant

---

Couvade: The practice in which the husband of a woman in labor takes to his bed as though he were bearing the child.   **Midwife:** A person, usually a woman, who provides specialized care during childbirth.

psychological, political, legal, and moral implications. Even defining the problem and looking at possible solutions are controversial.

While the term **infertility** is clear in its general meaning, like so many other terms its exact meaning and measurement are fuzzy. A typical figure is that about 10 to 15% of married American couples are infertile, but this might be misleading. Some persons are clearly incapable of achieving pregnancy because of aging or such intentional procedures as hysterectomy or vasectomy. A woman taking the pill would not be called infertile, even though she is not likely immediately to become pregnant. Some individuals do not wish to have additional children, so they might not be defined as infertile even if they cannot achieve pregnancy. The desire to achieve pregnancy, along with unsuccessful attempts to do so, are components of most precise definitions of infertility.

Specifying a certain amount of time during which unsuccessful attempts to achieve pregnancy occur is somewhat arbitrary, since few couples achieve pregnancy each and every time they have intercourse. Couples who have intercourse regularly without the use of contraception take an average of 5.3 months for pregnancy to occur (Shane, Schiff, & Wilson, 1976). Only 25% of women conceive after 1 month of unprotected intercourse, 63% after 6 months, and about 80% after 1 year (Masters, Johnson, & Kolodny, 1992:96). The 1-year rate has sometimes been used to report an infertility rate among American couples of 20%. Although it has long been known that infertility goes up as women get older, a 1982 study, using the 1-year cutoff, reported an infertility rate of close to 40% for women ages 31–35 (Schwartz & Mayaux, 1982). At least in the popular press, the implication of this figure was that women who might wish to have children someday should think about doing so sooner rather than later, even at some sacrifice to career development.

To refute the 40% infertility figure, Faludi (1991) cited a British study of more than 17,000 women that found 91% of women of all ages were able to achieve pregnancy after 39 months (Bongaarts, 1982). In fact, the two studies are not necessarily contradictory since they deal with different ages of women and different definitions of infertility.

Perhaps the best summary of fertility incidence would be that about 10% of American couples are infertile, and

another 10% are "underfertile," and that these rates begin to rise for women in over-30 age groups. Infertility is not the same as sterility, however, so even many of the over-30 infertility group might still achieve pregnancy.

Causes of Infertility

The Mayo Clinic reports that, in infertile couples, the man is infertile about 30% of the time, the woman about 50% of the time, and mutual problems exist the remaining 20% of the time (Larson, 1990). Other sources report that 40% of problems are attributed to women, 40% to men, and the remaining 20% to both (Derwinski-Robinson, 1990).

The two major causes of infertility in women are failure to ovulate and blockage of the Fallopian tubes. Failure to ovulate can be treated with hormones that are popularly referred to as fertility drugs. This is a relatively successful approach, with reported pregnancy rates as high as 70% for women with failure to ovulate but who have otherwise healthy-appearing ovaries. The drugs do not increase the risk of spontaneous abortion nor birth defects, but they can over-stimulate the ovaries to the point of rupture. The most noticeable side effect of ovulation-stimulating drugs is the greatly increased incidence of multiple births. As many as 15% of resultant births are twins, and another 5% are triplets, quadruplets, quintuplets, or sextuplets (Masters, Johnson, & Kolodny, 1992).

The problem of blocked Fallopian tubes is often caused by endometriosis, sometimes by scarring from sexually transmitted diseases or other infections. In some cases, microsurgery or laser technology can repair the damaged tube. Where endometriosis is the cause, laser surgery yields pregnancy rates in the 40 to 65% range (Berger, Goldstein, & Fuerst, 1989).

The most common immediate cause of male infertility is low sperm count. Temporarily low sperm counts have been attributed to a number of causes, including long-distance bicycling, wearing tight underwear, spending too much time in hot baths or hot tubs, and ejaculating too frequently. Permanently low sperm counts can be the result of testicular injury, high fever, infection, radiation, and undescended testes. With the exception of behavior changes to

---

Infertility: Inability to achieve pregnancy or to carry a pregnancy to live birth.

reduce the short-term causes of low sperm counts, direct treatment of infertility in men has not been as successful as treatment for women (Masters, Johnson, & Kolodny, 1992).

Assisted Reproductive Techniques

The last few decades have witnessed rapid changes in reproductive technology. Different techniques can now be used, alone or in combination with other procedures, depending on the type of infertility problem the couple has.

Artificial Insemination. When the fertility problem is one of low sperm count, **artificial insemination** with the husband's sperm (AIH) can be used. The advantage over sexual intercourse is that the fresh semen can be applied directly to the cervix, where sperm will have the best chance of reaching the Fallopian tubes. Knowledgeable and willing couples can actually perform this procedure themselves. With professional assistance, several sperm samples can be quick-frozen and injected all at once, but this reduces the mobility of the sperm and might not actually increase the odds of conception.

If AIH does not work, or if the sperm count approaches zero, artificial insemination with a donor's sperm (AID) can be tried. The procedure is the same as for AIH except that the sperm does not come from the husband. Several sperm banks exist in North America, including one in Escondido, California, that accepts sperm only from men who have both IQs of over 140 and significant intellectual accomplishments. Many medical schools have sperm banks and pay students for sperm samples.

In Vitro Fertilization. If a woman ovulates normally but has Fallopian tubes that are blocked, **in vitro fertilization** can be used. The woman is usually given hormones to increase ovulation. The eggs are then surgically removed and placed in a container with a controlled culture and live sperm. One or more fertilized eggs can then be implanted directly into the woman's uterus. Sometimes extra fertilized eggs are frozen for possible use at a later time.

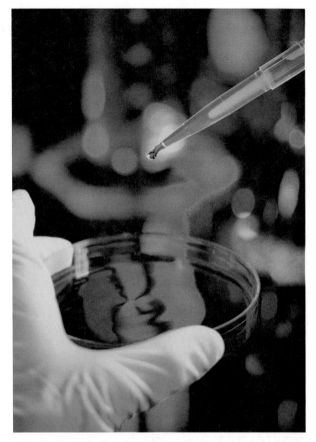

Reproductive technology is moving more rapidly than is legal and ethical knowledge. What might become of this Petri-dish zygote?

Surrogate Mothers. Surrogate parenthood is actually a very old practice. The Biblical practice of the Levirate essentially required that a man should serve as a surrogate progenitor for his dead brother's child. The Bible also reports that Sarah's maid Hagar gave birth to a child for Sarah and her husband, Abraham. These reports imply that the practice was not only considered acceptable at one time, but also might have been an obligation.

Today's **surrogate mothers** are usually paid to carry and give birth to a child who would then be given to someone else. The surrogate is typically impregnated, through artificial insemination, by the sperm of the husband of the couple who wants the child.

Artificial insemination: Placing semen in the vagina or uterus by means other than sexual intercourse. **In vitro fertilization:** Joining of sperm and egg outside the body. **Surrogate mother:** A woman who is paid for the use of her uterus to produce a baby.

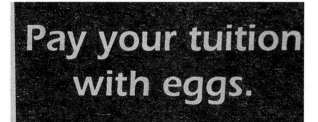

Pay your tuition with eggs.

If you're a woman between 18 and 35, you can earn money easily, anonymously. Donate your eggs to an infertile couple.

$3,500 and up, depending on you education and other qualifications. Call Today.

THE CENTER FOR EGG OPTIONS
310/546-6786

Women have an opportunity to pay their college expenses.

Combinations of techniques, however, are possible. A woman who ovulates but has no uterus could have her egg fertilized *in vitro* by her husband's sperm, then implanted in the surrogate's womb. Alternately, a donor's sperm could be used.

A surrogate woman could also be artificially inseminated; the egg can then be flushed from the surrogate's uterus and placed in the womb of the woman who wished to have the child. Either her husband's or a donor's sperm can be used.

The more steps in the assisted reproduction process, the lower the success rate and, generally, the more expensive the process. The cost of using artificial insemination and a surrogate mother can run well over $50,000, and some other technologies cost more and have relatively low success rates.

Reproductive Technology and Culture Lag

In 1950, William F. Ogburn introduced the term **culture lag.** He had noticed that social change such as that brought on by industrialization often resulted in the development of technologies with which the legal, moral, religious, and other elements of nonmaterial culture were not equipped to deal. Such appears to be the case with reproductive technology today, when few legal, ethical, and moral guidelines are available.

The Catholic Church has resolved the matter by firmly opposing any reproductive approach that directly involves anyone other than the husband and wife who wish to achieve pregnancy; this applies to surrogates and donors. The church also calls "morally unacceptable" such approaches as AIH because a third party is involved (*Catechism of the Catholic Church,* 1994). Although this is a very conservative approach, the Catholic Church has at least attempted to wrestle with the issues, something many other churches have not done.

In addition to religious concerns, reproductive technology has produced a good many unanswered legal questions. Where court cases and legislation exist, they are often contradictory and vary from one jurisdiction to another. Highlight 11.1 points to some of the issues.

| HIGHLIGHT 11.1 | **Issues in Reproductive Technology** Developments in reproductive technology have raised a number of questions in the United States in the last few decades. Read each case and try to answer each question. For even more fun, try to reach agreement on the issues with a group of friends.

1. In 1991, Arlette Schwartz served as a surrogate for her daughter, Christa, and gave birth to twins, who became Christa's legal children. What kinship term properly applies between the twins and Schwartz? Were the twins a product of incest?

2. In 1987, in the celebrated "Baby M" case, Mary Beth Whitehead was artificially inseminated with the sperm of William Stern. Although Whitehead signed a surrogate contract with William and his

---

Culture lag: A time discrepancy between technological change and change in nonmaterial aspects of culture such as law and values.

Families in the NEWS

Missing Girls in India

Early tabulations from India's 2001 census are confirming what many demographers suspected — there are not as many girls as there should be. Ultrasound testing is increasingly widespread and is being used to determine the sex of the fetus. The widespread Indian preference for boys is resulting in many more abortions of female fetuses than male ones.

In 1982, prior to widespread availability of ultrasound, there were 962 female births for every 1,000 male births. This is about the number that would be expected naturally. But in 2001, that number had dropped to 927 female births for every 1,000 males.

In Punjab, the most prosperous farming state in India, the new figure is only 793 girls per 1,000 boys; in Gujarat, a major industrial state, 878 girls are born per 1,000 boys.

Amartya Sen, a Nobel Prize–winning economist at Cambridge University, says that India is catching up with China, South Korea, and other Asian nations in the decreasing sex ratio. Even though health care is improving and women are living longer, the cultural preference for sons has not changed. Boys carry the family name and inherit the property. In addition, boys have the responsibility for caring for aging parents. Couples fear that if they do not have sons, they will have no one to look after them when they get older.

Within the next 20 years, when today's babies are of marriage age, the sex imbalance is likely to affect traditional mate-selection practices. When there are not enough potential brides to go around, they will become more valuable. Grooms' families might have to pay dowries to brides' families, rather than the present arrangement in which brides' families provide the dowries.

Source: Celia W. Dugger. www.nytimes.com, April 22, 2001.

---

wife, Elizabeth, she later changed her mind. She turned down the $10,000 fee she had agreed to take from the intended parents and determined to keep the child. A judge upheld the surrogate contract, removed the child from Whitehead, and presided over Elizabeth Stern's adoption of the child. On an appeal, the New Jersey Supreme Court ruled that surrogacy for hire was like selling a baby and invalidated the contract. The court further ruled that Whitehead could have visitation rights as a parent, but that Richard Stern, whose sperm was used, was the primary custodial parent.

Which court's decision do you think was correct? Should states honor and enforce surrogacy contracts, or should the contracts be outlawed like slavery is?

3. In a 1991 case, similar to the Baby M situation, the surrogate mother, Elvie Jordon, decided she wanted 17-month-old Marissa back when she found out that Bob and Cindy Moschetta, the intended parents, were getting divorced. The California superior court ruled that the two biological parents, Jordon and Bob Moschetta, should share joint custody of the child, and that Cindy Moschetta was to have no legal rights or visitation privileges.

Do your agree with the judge's decision? Is the strong bias toward biological parents, found throughout North American law, appropriate?

4. Mary Sue Davis and Junior Davis had frozen embryos, the result of *in vitro* fertilization, in storage when they filed for divorce. They disagreed over the custody of the embryos. Junior Davis wanted to have them destroyed because he did not want to become a father, at least of Mary Davis's child. Mary Davis wanted the embryos because she might want to be impregnated with them. The judge ruled in favor of Mary Davis.

Do you agree with the judge? If Mary Davis had become impregnated with the embryos and given birth, could she have successfully sued her ex-husband for financial support as the legal father of the child?

5. Suppose a couple uses donor sperm and donor eggs for *in vitro* fertilization. The fertilized egg

is then implanted into an unrelated surrogate mother, who gives birth.

If the intended parents both die in a car wreck before the baby is born, and the surrogate mother, egg donor, and sperm donor all want custody, who should get it?

If the baby is born severely disabled and the parents change their mind about accepting the child, should they be able to? If none of the parties want the child, who should be liable for its support?

6. Researchers search for the most effective laboratory environment for *in vitro* fertilization. In the process, they often dispose of eggs that have been fertilized.

If abortion became illegal, should the researchers be arrested? Would the sperm and egg donors also be guilty?

7. In January 2001, a University of Kentucky professor announced that he will work with a group of fertility researchers attempting to produce the first cloned human within 2 years.

Should human cloning research be allowed? What might the legal and moral consequences of such research be?

The following issues will probably continue to be controversial for some time:

Should *in vitro* fertilization research be publicly funded? Should it be done at all?

Should the cost of assisted reproductive techniques be covered by insurance policies?

Should reproductive assistance such as donor sperm be provided for intended single parents?

Can sperm banks, or individual sperm donors, be held liable if their sperm infects a woman with AIDS?

Is it racist if intended parents shop for a sperm donor or surrogate of a particular race? Could a sperm bank be sued if the child turns out to be of a different race than that promised as a "match" for the parents?

Is it ethical to have sperm banks solely for certain kinds of donors, such as Nobel Prize winners or outstanding athletes? Is it ethical for "supermodels"or other exceptional women to auction their eggs to the highest bidder?

What other issues are likely to arise because of cultural lag in reproductive technology?

Perhaps most importantly, who should answer these question? Judges? Legislators? Presidents? Religious leaders?

Adoption

Assisted reproductive technology can provide a means of producing a child who is biologically parented by at least one member of the couple. Adoption can also provide a child for a couple, but that child is usually a genetic stranger. Because they are chosen, however, there are no accidental, unwanted adopted children.

We have seen that infant relinquishments in the United States fall far behind the demand for adopted children. There are about 33,000 infant relinquishments and about 114,000 adoptions annually. This includes adoptions of older children and children from foreign countries (Strong & DeVault, 1994). About 2.1% of married couple households with children contain adopted children (U.S. Bureau of the Census, 1995: t. 77), but many more would adopt if more healthy infants were available.

Children who are more available are generally older ones who have been removed from highly abusive homes, or have physical, mental, or emotional disabilities. As many as 25% of children adopted in some states might have been prenatally exposed to drugs (Barth, 1991). Also, more Black children are available than White ones, and there is considerable controversy about the ethics of cross-racial adoption. These and other factors often make attempted adoption a difficult, expensive, and frustrating experience that is made more difficult by the high abortion rate.

Although difficult and not totally accepted in the United States, adoption is a common cross-cultural and historical event (Terrell & Modell, 1994). In many hunting-gathering societies, it was common for persons to be "adopted" by applying kinship terminology to nonrelatives, or by applying terms of close kinship to more distant relatives.

In ancient Rome, heirs were often adopted, even by single men. Both formal and informal adoption continued in many agrarian societies. In most societies it has been conduct and performance, care and reciprocity, which has defined kinship, not biological closeness. In the contemporary United States, however, there is an unusual bias against fictive kinship and relations other than those by marriage or blood (March & Miall, 2000; Wegar, 2000). Marshall (1977) refers to this as a "biogenic" bias in kinship characteristics, a bias also found in legal decisions involving child custody.

Summary and Conclusion

Cultural practices affect fertility rates in both latent and manifest ways. The theory of demographic transition provides a framework for understanding historical population patterns. At a global level, fertility regulation historically produced a relatively sparse population, but the industrial revolution resulted in a worldwide population explosion. Societies that went through the revolution first saw not only gradual reductions in death rates, but also subsequent reduction in birthrates. Many are now at or near zero population growth. Contemporary Third World countries still have rapidly growing populations.

At least in postindustrial countries, a wide range of methods is available for reducing the odds of pregnancy. Abstinence, historically the major option, is decreasingly effective because of user failure. Spermicides, barrier methods, the IUD, hormonal systems, and surgical sterilization are commonly used to prevent pregnancy.

Also available are methods of preventing unwanted births after sexual intercourse. These include "morning after" pills, RU-486, and various abortion procedures. Unplanned pregnancies can also be carried to birth and either relinquished for adoption or raised by one or both biological parents.

Control of childbearing has been an important historical issue. Couples now have several choices of childbirth techniques. Many couples want to have children but are faced with fertility problems. Techniques are available for couples, with and without assistance from medical professionals, to increase the odds of achieving pregnancy. Some of the newer approaches are accompanied by legal, religious, moral, and ethical concerns. Although there is a shortage of available infants, some couples are able to solve their fertility problem by adopting a child.

In conclusion, this chapter once again demonstrates the inter-relationship between macrosociological forces and individual choices. The economy and religion, among other factors, structure choices about the number of children a people want to have. The technology affects how easy it is for couples to meet their reproductive goals. And the number of children couples have, in turn, affects the economy.

Today's family size is seen more as a choice than has been the case in the past. That is but one of the many issues couples must negotiate in their relationships. The next chapter is devoted to that issue.

Rethinking in Context Do you believe that there is an overpopulation problem in the world? If so, what should American foreign policy be with respect to the problem? How do personal, individual, and family decisions influence national and international demographic variables?

Additional Resources

Adoption

Bartholet, Elizabeth. 1993. *Family Bonds: Adoption and the Politics of Parenting.* Boston: Houghton and Mifflin.

Bates, J. Douglas. 1993. *Gift Children: A Story of Race Family and Adoption in a Divided America.* New York: Ticknor & Fields.

Groze, Victor K. 1996. *Successful Adoptive Families: A Longitudinal Study of Special Needs Adoption.* Westport, CT: Praeger.

Simon, Rita J. 1993. *The Case for Transracial Adoption.* Washington, DC: American University Press.

Conception

Lasker, Judith N., & Susan Borg. 1994. *In Search of Parenthood: Coping with Infertility and High-Tech Conception,* Rev. ed. Philadelphia: Temple University Press.

Mattes, Jane. 1994. *Single Mothers by Choice: A Guidebook for Single Women Who Are Considering or Have Chosen Motherhood.* New York: Random House.

Ragone, Helena. 1989. *Surrogate Motherhood: Conception in the Heart.* Boulder, CO: Westview Press.

Robertson, John A. 1994. *Children of Choice: Freedom and the New Reproductive Technologies.* Princeton, NJ: Princeton University Press.

Demography and population growth

Ehrlich, Paul. 1997. *The Population Explosion.* New York: Buccaneer Books.

Goldschieder, Calvin. 1992. *Fertility Transition, Family Structure, and Population Policy.* Boulder, CO: Westview Press.

Mazur, Laurie Ann, ed. 1994. *Beyond the Numbers: A Reader on Population, Consumption, and the Environment.* Washington, DC: Island Press.

Fertility reduction:

Hatcher, R. A., J. Trussell, F. H. Stewart, G. K. Stewart, D. Kowal, F. J. Guest, W. Cates, & M. S. Policar. 1994. *Contraceptive Technology,* 16th ed. New York: Irvington.

Tribe, Lawrence H. 1990. *Abortion: The Clash of Absolutes.* New York: Norton.

History

Blanchard, Dallas A. 1994. *The Anti-Abortion Movement and the Rise of the Religious Right: From Polite to Fiery Protest.* New York: Twayne.

Burtch, Brian. *Trials of Labor: The Re-emergence of Midwifery.* Buffalo, NY: McGill-Queen's University Press.

Chesler, Ellen. 1992. *A Woman of Valor: Margaret Sanger and the Birth Control Movement in America.* New York: Simon & Schuster.

Riddle, John M. 1992. *Contraception and Abortion from the Ancient World to the Renaissance.* Cambridge: Harvard University Press.

Feminist reference

Rothman, Barbara Katz. 1993. *Encyclopedia of Childbearing: Critical Perspectives.* Phoenix: Oryx Press.

Internet Sites

Interactive population site—find out how many people were alive when you were born, etc., in French or English

http://www.popexpo.net/

The United States Census Bureau

http://www.census.gov

The Population Reference Bureau

http://www.prb.org/

Contraceptive technology, family planning, from Family Health International

http://www.fhi.org/

The Alan Guttmacher Institute, family planning advocate; online journal on family planning, research reports, etc.

http://www.agi-usa.org/

Planned Parenthood International

http://www.ippf.org/

A pro-life site

http://www.prolife.com/

Abortion rights

http://www.naral.org/

For links to these sites and additional resources, visit the *Families in Context* Web site at:

http://sociology.wadsworth.com

Chapter 12

Negotiating Marriages

Prelude

Jarrad and Kallia were married 10 years ago. So were Lou and Marina. Although the couples lived in the same city, they did not know each other.

Both couples had children, and were reasonably well off financially. Each couple was admired by their friends for having solid marriages. Their children did well in school; the couples were active in their respective religious groups; and they both had supportive family networks.

As nearly as anyone else could tell they were perfect couples. Things were not going as well, however, in the privacy of their homes. The two couples grew increasingly quarrelsome with each other. The couples still did not know each other, but their situations were similar.

Kallia and Jarrad finally decided that they had better get some help or their marriage would be in trouble. They finally found a marriage counselor who would see them on Sunday, which was about the only time they had free. They could drop their kids off at Sunday school and see the therapist.

After their first tense session with the counselor, Kallia went outside and looked at the congregation leaving the church across the street. The families looked so close and so happy; the couples all seemed like they had no problems in the world. Kallia wished her marriage could be like that of the couples across the street. She admired them.

By coincidence, Lou and Marina were in the congregation across the street. Marina glanced at the counselor's office and saw a woman and man leaving. The couple looked troubled but sincere and determined. Marina wished she and Lou had the nerve to see a counselor about their troubled marriage, like that couple did. She admired them.

Which couple is more likely to improve their marriage?

Even if you love someone, getting used to living with him or her is a major life adjustment. Issues of decision making and power must be worked out, and a variety of role relationships must be developed. Marital quality can be defined and measured in a variety of ways. While all couples would like to have happy, satisfying, and stable marriages, several factors decrease the chances that they will do so. Throughout a marriage, there are a number of developmental challenges that must be faced. Couples continually develop and renegotiate their scripts as they live out their marriages.

> **Thinking Ahead** How much independence do you think husbands and wives should have from each other? Which partner, if either, should have the final say in such matters as how to raise children, purchasing new furniture, or where to live? If you think they should have equal say, how will the matter get resolved when they disagree? Says who? How can you measure whether a marriage is good or bad?

The fact that we can find an institution in all societies that we can call marriage does not necessarily mean that the institution has the same meaning for all the participants. Meanings change as societies change.

From the range of roles available in the societal script, couples construct their own mutual marital scripts, making each family somewhat different from others (Edgar & Glezer, 1994). This chapter will focus primarily on the husband-wife dyad. Chapter 13 will consider the addition of children to the family unit.

Changing Meanings of Marriage

A wedding creates a marriage between a bride and a groom. These two partners are now legitimately called husband and wife. While both the newlyweds and the community understand that their roles are to change, exactly what those new roles will be varies by time and place.

A wedding finalizes a type of contract, not only between the bride and groom but also among members of their extended families and the entire community. All agree to change their role expectations in accord with the socially acceptable meanings associated with marriage. In late agrarian European societies, for example, young persons who were not married were not supposed to engage in sexual intercourse. After the wedding ceremony, however, it was virtually required that they do so because of strong pronatalist expectations.

Changes in modes of production have brought different ways of enforcing the marriage contract. In hunting-gathering societies, the contractual expectations were informal and were generally enforced by the extended families of the husband and wife. Agrarian societies added the strong influence of religious institutions, some extrafamilial political control, and community sanctions. While such forces continue to operate in industrial and postindustrial societies, the marital contract has become increasingly formalized and enforced by courts and other facets of the political institution.

In many aspects of their married lives, couples are considerably freer from social control now than was the case earlier in American history. Informal controls have weakened, and political laws do not regulate details of everyday married life. As a consequence, the dynamics of marriage have changed. These changes can be illustrated by use of the gender role continuum that was introduced in chapter 1 (see Figure 12.1).

As the left extreme of the gender role continuum indicates, the wedding ceremony in traditional societies carried with it a relatively complete set of instructions about the role relationship between the husband and wife. Couples reached agreement about their roles on the basis of **spontaneous consensus** rather than by discussion and negotiation (Fox, 1974; Scanzoni, 1979). In such a traditional marriage, the parties never discussed the division of labor that might assign home care tasks such as cooking to the woman, and provider tasks like earning a living to the man. Yet this might be what the marriage contract calls for. It was simply assumed that the husband and wife would behave in accord with the expected division of labor.

As laws replaced community pressure, the normative marital expectations were sometimes formalized as part of the legal system. The doctrine of *coverture* (see chapter 3), which assigned responsibility of property ownership to the husband and deprived married women of the right to own many kinds of property, was once part of the Western marital legal contract.

In the United States and other postindustrial societies, the gender-biased expectations of marriage have largely been removed from the legal system. Informal expectations, partly perpetuated by religious beliefs, still have influence, but fewer and fewer role decisions are based on spontaneous consensus. Instead, as there is movement toward the right-hand side of the gender role continuum, wives and husbands increasingly negotiate their decisions. The gender role distinctions are increasingly blurred and unclear.

Conjugal Power

Family power has long been of interest to social scientists. We will look at some early sociological perspectives on the topic, then move to more current definitions, measurements, and theories about power.

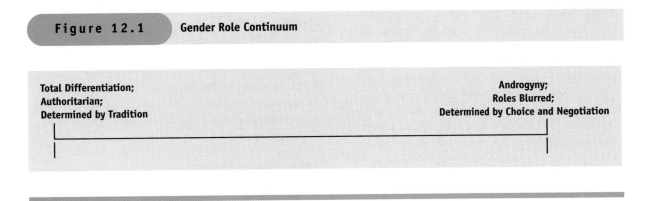

| **Figure 12.1** | **Gender Role Continuum** |

**Total Differentiation;
Authoritarian;
Determined by Tradition**

**Androgyny;
Roles Blurred;
Determined by Choice and Negotiation**

Source: Adapted from Adams, Bert N. 1995. *The Family: A Sociological Interpretation*. Fort Worth: Harcourt Brace. Page 108.

Spontaneous consensus: Agreement arrived at without consideration by the parties involved, based on commonly held assumptions that are often derived from tradition.

Family Power and Early Sociology

The changes brought about by industrialization, including those involving conjugal power, were a major topic for 19th-century social theorists. In 1855, the French sociologist Frederic Le Play wrote about what he saw as a rapid decline of the traditional, male-dominated peasant family. He called on the French government to adopt policies that would shore up the patriarchal stem family form.

In 1884, Friedrich Engels argued that the first historical class conflict resulted from the power gained by men over women in the monogamous family. In his view, only the communist revolution would finally enable women to have equal power with men.

Max Weber defined **power** as "the probability that one actor within a social relationship will be in a position to carry out his own will despite resistance" (1925/1964:152). The "probability" part of the definition implies that a powerful person need not always exercise power, and might not always be successful at getting his or her own way. If the probability is high, however, power is high.

There has been debate about whether overcoming resistance is an essential component of power. If a wife wants her husband to go to a church service with her, and he does so rather than watching a football game, she got her way. If he actually wanted to go and was just waiting to be asked, there was no resistance. By Weber's definition, no power was exerted. On the other hand, the husband might have "wanted to" only because the wife talked him into it. In this case, it could be argued that she had power even though there was no overt resistance.

Alternately, he might have worked out a deal that he would go with her to church if she would cook his favorite meal. Now do both have the power, or one more than another, or is it a situation in which both win?

Weber distinguished between **illegitimate power,** which is exercised without permission of the governed or any institutional approval, and **legitimate power** or **authority.** Illegitimate power typically involves force, coercion, or threat, while legitimate power operates in ways that are considered socially acceptable.

Weber was primarily addressing the issue of political power at the macro-social level, but his distinctions

This is illegitimate power.

have relevance to the issue of **conjugal power.** If the husband uses force or threat of force to get his favorite dinner, for example, this would be a form of illegitimate power. Other concepts related to power are useful at both the macro and micro levels. Someone with **influence** does not have authority to make the actual decision, but can help sway the outcome. At the conjugal level, even if the husband and wife both agree that the husband should make the final decision about what kind of car to buy, the wife can strongly influence the choice.

In spite of considerable theoretical speculation about conjugal power, there were few attempts precisely to define and measure it until the work of Robert O. Blood, Jr., and Donald M. Wolfe in the late 1950s. Although their research method has been criticized, they made a major contribution to the study of family power (see Finding Out 12.1).

Resource Theory

Social exchange theory (see chapter 2), originally developed by George C. Homans (1961) and Peter Blau

---

Power: The probability that one actor within a social relationship will be in a position to carry out his or her own will [despite resistance] (Weber).   **Illegitimate power:** Power exercised without the consent of the governed, or in socially unapproved ways, usually by coercion.   **Authority:** Power exercised in socially approved ways; legitimate power.   **Conjugal power:** The ability of spouses to affect each other's behavior.   **Influence:** The ability to shape the thinking and behavior of a decision maker.

(1964) to explain social interaction in general, has been applied to issues of marital power and decision making. A key assumption of the perspective is that humans seek to maximize their own rewards, and seek relationships that help them do that. Consideration of resources is an important component of the mate-selection process (see chapter 9).

As individuals interact, they develop a sense of trust and abide by a "norm of reciprocity," which prescribes that favors be repaid (Gouldner, 1960). Some sense of equity is established whereby each party to the agreement believes he or she is receiving a fair deal.

Ability to influence others is dependent, in part, on the resources available to reward compliance. The resources might be money, ownership of goods, knowledge, providing services, or even love. If the resources are unequal between the partners, power differences might develop that favor the partner with the most resources. An early application of this perspective was the development of Waller's (1951) "principle of least interest." Among the dating couples he observed, the person most committed to the relationship had the least power. The least-committed person used the other's love as a resource in the social exchange between the two.

Rather than consider emotions, Blood and Wolfe looked at income and social status as resources that could be used to gain power in a marriage. This "resource theory of marital power" has since been widely tested. While Blood and Wolfe found that power was associated with resources such as occupation, educational level, income, and age, other studies have found more complicated, and even contradictory, results (Brinkerhoff & Lupri, 1992; Lamousé, 1969; Michel, 1967; Safilios-Rothschild, 1970). Rodman (1972) suggested that the resource model might work in egalitarian family system, but not in a patriarchal society.

Rank (1982) found that women with high levels of income, education, and occupational prestige had more power in their marriages than women with low levels of such resources. This seems to confirm resource theory. For men, however, increases in resources were actually associated with less marital power. The explanation was that, in the United States, egalitarian norms are more commonly accepted among men in higher class positions.

Brinkerhoff and Lupri (1992) found a clear link between socioeconomic status and the type of egalitarian decision making. As education, occupation, and income of couples increased, a higher percentage of couples were characterized by autonomic rather than syncratic decision making. Rather than making decisions together, married individuals at high socioeconomic status levels were more likely to have independent but equal decision-making authority.

The Brinkerhoff and Lupri (1992) results confirmed other studies finding that having more resources at her disposal does increase the wife's autonomous decision-making authority, but add that husband's autonomy is increased as well. The joint decision making, as exemplified by the notion of "pooling" resources, is reduced.

Because they studied homosexual couples as well as heterosexual ones, Blumstein and Schwartz (1983) provided an interesting perspective on gender differences, resources, and power. Higher income was a better predictor of power holding in gay male couples than other types; the partner with the highest income had the most power. Among lesbian couples, perhaps because of a conscious effort to establish an egalitarian relationship, income imbalance did not affect the balance of power.

Married heterosexuals fell between the extremes. Husbands were rated more powerful in 33% of cases in which their incomes exceeded their wives' incomes by $8,000 or more. Husbands were more powerful in 18% of cases in which the income was about equal to their wives' income. When the wife's income exceeded her husband's by $8,000 or more, husbands were still rated more powerful in 15% of cases (Blumstein & Schwartz, 1983:54).

Gender-Based Conceptions of Power

The resource theory of power has been criticized from several perspectives. Feminists agree that control of resources influences power. They take exception, however, to Blood and Wolfe's assumptions that social structural variables are no longer relevant and that resources are individual matters (Gillespie, 1971; Glenn, 1987). Feminist scholars point out that men have greater access to high-paying jobs and high status positions in society. In addition, they argue that patriarchal norms still provide more authority to men in general and to husbands in particular. These structural variables give men, by virtue of being born male, resources and power in marriage. The result is gender inequity.

Other researchers have pointed out that, in the context of social exchange and resource theory, equity and equality are different concepts and must be distinguished from each other (Cate et al., 1982). An exchange might be considered equitable, or fair, in spite of the fact that exactly the equal amount of each type of reward is not provided to each participant. One partner might get more access to leisure time, for example, while the other gets more access to spending money.

Finding Out | 12.1

Blood and Wolfe's Studies of Conjugal Power

All contemporary studies of conjugal power acknowledge their debt to the pioneering work of Blood and Wolfe, published in 1960 as *Husbands and Wives: The Dynamics of Married Living*. Their study brought representative survey research to the study of the family and developed the resource theory that remains a cornerstone of thinking about marital power (Szinovacz, 2000).

Blood and Wolfe believed that, by the late 1950s, American marriages had moved so far in the direction of egalitarianism that traditional patriarchal norms no longer determined the distribution of conjugal power. To test their views, they developed a measure of power that they used to collect data from a sample of 731 urban wives and 178 farm wives in greater Detroit. They asked each wife who made the final decision in each of eight areas of married life.

On each item, respondents were given five choices, each of which was assigned a point value: husband always (5 points); husband more than wife (4 points); husband and wife exactly the same (3 points); wife more than husband (2 points); and wife always (1 point). Each couple, then, had a score ranging from 8 (1 point on each question) to 40 (5 points on each question). This was their "relative authority score." For the entire sample, the relative authority score averaged 26.08, or 3.26 per question. A score of 24, or 3.00 per question, would have been exactly egalitarian. Less than one half of 1% of

husbands made the final decision in all eight areas (a score of 40), and about the same portion of wives made the final decision in all areas (a score of 8).

The following questions, along with their aggregate relative authority scores, were given in order from most to least husband authority (Blood & Wolfe, 1960:21).

Who usually makes the final decision about:

- What job the husband should take (4.86);
- What car to buy (4.18);
- Whether or not to buy some life insurance (3.50);
- Where to go on a vacation (3.12);
- What house or apartment to take (2.94);
- Whether or not the wife should go to work or quit work (2.69);
- What doctor to have when someone is sick (2.53);
- How much money your family can afford to spend per week on food (2.26).

In addition to the relative authority score, Blood and Wolfe also calculated a "shared authority score" for each couple. This score was determined by the number of times the option "husband and wife exactly the same" was chosen. This score could range from 0, with no egalitarian choices, to 8, where egalitarian decision making was used in all areas.

Wives spend considerably more time doing housework than do husbands, even when wives are employed. Feminists see this as inequitable because the husband and wife are not doing exactly the same thing. Many couples might see the exchange as equitable, however, because the man is spending more time in paid labor, and the two activities offset each other (see chapter 5).

Some gender researchers have pointed out that, when role expectations are different, power might be approached in different ways. Lipmen-Blumen (1984) concluded that oppression by men in the public sphere of life resulted in the development of different power strategies by women in the private sphere. Called

"micromanipulation," women's strategy is a less direct form of power than that used by men and is based on the woman's superior interpersonal skills. Women might learn to behave as if they are maintaining the husband-dominated definition of marital power, while circumventing, influencing, and subverting that power in interpersonal interaction.

This might help explain why wives report overall satisfaction with their marital role structure in spite of the appearance that men have more power (Biernat & Wortman, 1991; Major, 1993). It might also help explain why men often do not feel like they have the power in relationships (Cancian, 1989; Farrell, 1993).

Using a combination of the "relative authority score" and the "shared authority score," each couple could be assigned to one of four categories of conjugal power (Gelles, 1995):

1. *Wife Dominant.* The wife had greater decision-making authority if the relative authority score was less than 19.

2. *Husband Dominant.* The husband had greater decision-making authority if the relative authority score was over 28.

3. *Syncratic.* This style was relatively egalitarian and had considerable shared decision making. The relative authority score was between 20 and 28 while the shared authority score was 4 or more.

4. *Autonomic.* This style was also relatively egalitarian, but differed from the syncratic style in that husband and wife each had areas in which they had more authority, but the couple had few decisions that were made together. The relative authority score was between 20 and 28, while the shared authority score was 3 or less.

As Blood and Wolfe predicted, most couples (71%) had one of the relatively egalitarian styles. There were, however, more couples in the "husband dominant" category (25%) than in the "wife dominant" classification (3%). To conclude "men have more marital power than women" did not mean that all, or even most, husbands had more power than their wives; 75% did not. Instead, the conclusion means that, when there was a power difference between husbands and wives, it was much more likely to be in favor of the husband.

Since they rejected the idea that patriarchal norms determined power, Blood and Wolfe explained the discrepancy between husband- and wife-dominant marriages by using the "resource theory" of power. They found that husbands who had the most resources, such as money, education, and status, tended to have the most decision-making authority. Similarly, wives who were in the paid labor force were likely to have more power than those who were not. Controlling resources provided a power base.

Although it is still referred to in the literature on family power, Blood and Wolfe's study has been severely criticized from several perspectives. The survey approach itself has been questioned as a way of studying marital power. A second set of criticisms relates to the specific survey approach used by Blood and Wolfe. In their study, and in most follow-up studies, only wives were asked about decision making in their marriages. Other studies have found that, when both husbands and wives are asked, they provide significantly different reports (Safilios-Rothschild, 1969; Cromwell & Cromwell, 1978).

Another concern with the method used by Blood and Wolfe is the number and type of questions used to indicate decision-making processes. They used only eight specific issues, which might not be indicative of the full range of variables in the actual interaction of married couples. The specific issues about which respondents are asked can make a difference in the outcome.

Finally, Blood and Wolfe have been criticized on the grounds that their measure directly concerns decision making, not power, and the two things might not be the same. Some definitions of power require an element of overcoming resistance. On the other hand, Blood and Wolfe generally referred in their study to "authority," as a kind of power in which the wife might not like the outcome, but does not reject the right of the husband to make that decision. In their interviews, most respondents in the Blood and Wolfe study reported that, even when one party makes the "final decision," the other party usually agrees. In other words, agreement has somehow already been arrived at before the "final decision" is made.

We discussed Cancian's concept of "feminization of love" in chapter 8. As a counterpart to that concept, Kranichfeld (1987) derived the "masculinization of power." She argued that the resource theory has defined and measured power in a male-biased way by focusing on resources that have traditionally been associated with men. Women have tremendous power over socialization of children and over the kin-keeping role that binds generations of families together. Kranichfeld pointed out that this kind of power has received little attention in the research literature; the result has been the inaccurate image that women are powerless.

From this perspective, it might not be true that employed women, or women with more income, have more power than full-time family workers. Instead, the employed woman's power base and style would be more similar to a man's, and she would appear more powerful by the measures and definitions currently in use. At the same time, the employed wife risks losing her traditionally feminine power base and style.

Little research has been done on the "selection factor" and marital power. The kinds of resources thought to bring power, especially money, status, and age, are precisely the kinds of resources women have traditionally looked for in the process of mate selection (see chapter 10). In effect, women choose men who, by standard measures, are likely to develop more power than they themselves do. A complete exchange theory would look at the characteristics women possess that make them desirable and presumably serve as their power base.

Human Capital and Empowerment Theories

The human capital analysis of marriage overlaps both functionalism and resource theory. Gary Becker (1991), the major proponent of this perspective, argued that specialization is more efficient in the family, just as it is in corporations and government. It is a rational choice by couples to maximize their combined rewards by specializing in different activities.

Becker argued that the traditional division of labor maximized rewards from the human capital invested in both household/family labor and wage labor. Wives specialized in family activities partly because biology made them more efficient feeders and tenders of children and because they received less reward from the paid labor force. This left the husband to dedicate himself to maximizing the reward from paid labor. When the couple attempted to develop a parallel role script, both household and paid labor suffer.

Using mathematical models to determine optimum efficiency, Becker concluded that, even in a society that provided truly equal opportunity for men and women, couples would specialize. Although some mixture of roles is efficient, the maximum reward occurs when one partner focuses primarily on wage labor and the other primarily on family work. The primary worker is therefore able to work overtime, to advance in a career more rapidly, and to move to a better job if necessary. The primary family worker could better organize the household, prepare meals more efficiently, and be available to take care of child emergencies. Even in an equal-opportunity society the primary income earner would still make more money than the primary family worker, and the distribution of decision making would still be affected by the division of labor. It would not necessarily be the case, however, that the roles would always be determined by gender.

In an effort to reformulate the concept of conjugal power, Jack O. Balswick and Judith K. Balswick (1995) proposed an "empowerment model." They pointed out that most theories assume that power is a matter of winners and losers; if one person is to get his or her way, the other person fails to get his or her way. Conjugal power,

however, can be viewed as a process in which each partner uses resources to increase the resources of the other partner. Rather than viewing relationships as a series of *quid pro quo* (one thing for another) exchanges, this perspective assumes that relationships can be seen as a condition in which both partners are mutually enhanced.

With the empowerment perspective, home-related tasks can take on a greater value. Cooking nutritious and delicious meals improves life for all family members—and the person doing the cooking can receive the reward of knowing he or she is providing a benefit that does not reduce either partner's power. Likewise with other tasks that families do with and for each other. All are empowered when all are helping.

Another attempt to reformulate questions of power and equity makes a distinction between the "justice perspective" and the "care perspective" (Gilligan, 1982; Noddings, 1984; Thompson, 1991; Giles-Sims, 1994). These theorists associate most traditional analysis with the justice principle, with focus on autonomy, self-interest, rational thoughts, and abstract standards of rights and justice. Such attributes are traditionally associated with men.

The "care perspective," in contrast, sees justice as derived from interactions that meet one's own and one's family's needs through cooperation and empathy in a particular context. The "care perspective" emphasizes elements of mutual script maintenance such as nurturing, understanding, and interdependence. These attributes are more commonly associated with women (Giles-Sims, 1994).

Marital Roles and Scripts

As society moves from rigid, traditional role expectations to egalitarian, negotiated relationships, the individuals involved must make an increasing number of the decisions. Several different role relationships need to be constructed, using communication and negotiation skills that were not as necessary before the postindustrial era. As couples establish these roles, they construct a mutual script that guides various areas of their relationship.

Couple Role Relationships

In chapter 10, we saw how couples construct a sexual script for themselves. Each person draws on the societal script and his or her own experiences to construct individual scripts. Two such scripts come together in scenes by which couples develop a mutual script that has features unique to that couple.

A Role Typology. It is not only in the sexual sphere that this process occurs. Nye (1976), along with Bahr, Chappell, and Leigh (1983), developed a typology of eight family roles that couples must consider in scripting their marriage:

- *The housekeeper role* includes both management and task aspects of running a household, from meal planning and deciding on cleanliness standards to doing laundry and tidying the house (Mederer, 1993).

- *The provider role* focuses on supplying the money and material goods necessary to support the family.

- *The sexual role* involves satisfaction of the sexual wants of the couple.

- *The kinship role,* also called the kin-keeper role, maintains the place of the couple's nuclear family in a network of extended families.

- *The recreational role* involves the leisure activities of the couple.

- *The therapeutic role* deals with emotional and instrumental needs of the couple, providing sympathy, understanding, and advice.

- *The child-care role* is primarily involved with the physical care of children, including feeding, bathing, and protecting infants and young children.

- *The child-socialization role* involves the responsibility of instilling the values, attitudes, skills, and behaviors required by the children for success in society at large.

Important additions to the list of role relationships are the *religious role,* which includes the responsibility for formal and informal religious practices, and the *friendship role,* which locates the couple in a network of extrafamilial social relationships.

Not all couples are involved in the child-care and child-socialization roles, and some do not make religion part of their role set, but these three roles can be of major importance in other marriages. All couples must deal with the other roles in one way or another. Some of these roles are discussed in considerable detail in other parts of this book. We will consider the two child-related roles in chapter 13. The sexual role was covered in chapters 10 and 11.

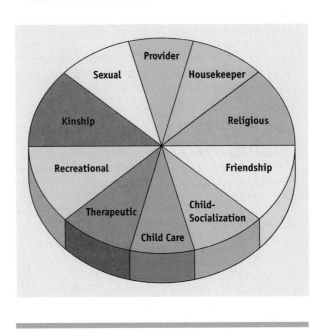

Figure 12.2 Marital Role Relationships

The Provider and Kinship Roles. We saw in chapter 6 how couples incorporate the provider and housekeeper roles into their relationship. The options ranged from completely complementary ones, in which each person performed a specific role, to completely parallel ones, in which the two were essentially interchangeable.

The provider and housekeeper roles interact in several ways. Money has to be brought into the household, but decisions about how to spend the money also need to be made. Pahl (1989) found five major distributive systems used by couples:

- *The female whole wage system* gives wives sole responsibility for household finances. The husbands hand over all of their wages, except perhaps a personal allowance, to their wives.

- *The male whole wage system* is the reverse of the female whole wage system. If the wife has no independent income, she may or may not receive a personal allowance. Very few couples use this system (Vogler & Pahl, 1994).

- *The housekeeping allowance system* is the second most common system. The husband, who brings in all or nearly all of the money, turns over a fixed amount of money to the wife for specified household expenses. He pays for other items out of his share, which includes his personal spending money. To the extent that the wife has personal spending money, it is the amount she might be able to save from the household expenses account.

■ *The independent management system* is relatively rare, but it might be increasing in popularity, especially for couples that include remarried individuals. It is probably the most common system for cohabiting couples. Each partner has an independent income and is responsible for certain expenses. They typically have separate checking and savings accounts but sometimes shift money back and forth between them.

■ *The pooling system* is the most common, found in over half of a large sample of British couples (Vogler & Pahl, 1994). The partners pool their resources, usually by a joint checking account, and each has access to the pool. Decision making tends to be egalitarian. Vogler and Pahl further divided their sample into a male-managed pool, a female-managed pool, and a joint pool. The joint pool included about 20% of all couples, while the male-managed and female-managed types included about 15% of couples each.

Vogler and Pahl (1994) found that joint control over pooled resources was associated with the most egalitarian decision making and with the smallest difference between the amount of personal spending money for husbands and wives. The housekeeping allowance system resulted in the greatest discrepancy in personal spending money.

It is not clear exactly how couples decide which financial allocation style to use. When wives have independent incomes, the couple is more likely to use one of the pooled systems or the independent management system. Blumstein and Schwartz (1983) found that wives were slightly less likely to favor pooling. The explanation was that it has long been part of the provider role that the man turn over his earnings to the family. Women are less likely to be socialized to the provider role, so they are more likely to believe that the money they earn should fall outside the joint account.

The Recreation Role. The issue of independence is also relevant to the recreation role. Orthner (1975) investigated the amount of time couples spent in each of three kinds of recreational activities:

■ *Individual activities,* such as reading books or taking solitary walks, do not involve interaction with others and might even discourage togetherness.

■ *Joint activities* require active participation with others. Playing card games and taking weekend trips together are examples.

■ *Parallel activities,* while being done with another person, do not require significant interaction. Watching television or listening to music can be like individual activities done in the company of others.

The distinction is not the activity itself; listening to music or walking can be a joint activity. The important difference is in the amount of interaction. All three types of recreation can provide benefits to individuals and families. Orthner (1975) found particular benefits from joint activities because they encourage communication between partners.

The Therapeutic Role. Good communication is a key component of the therapeutic role. Perhaps more than any of the role issues, the importance of the therapeutic role has increased in the postindustrial marriage. Partners in the modern "companionate marriage" (Blood & Wolfe, 1960) are expected to be friends with each other. They are expected to understand each other's problems and provide empathy, reassurance, and affection. Since 1970, hundreds of marital advice books have stressed the importance of marital communication, providing suggestions on how to listen and talk to each other. The theme of such books has been that therapeutic communication is particularly a problem for men who have been socialized into instrumental rather than expressive roles. Although there are inconsistent results, most studies find that women are somewhat better at self-disclosing, picking up nonverbal clues, empathizing, and listening (Basow, 1992). All of these qualities are important to the therapeutic role.

Constructing Postindustrial Marital Scripts

Constructing a marriage today involves an extraordinary number of adjustments and re-definitions of reality, many of which are never consciously addressed by the participants. Individuals receive images of marriage from a variety of sources including their own parents, other relatives, their religion, friends, and the media. These images must be reconciled with the images held by their partners as the two construct their own scripts for marriage.

Couples negotiate flight plans as part of their mutual script.

Even during courtship, couples begin to agree to "secret contracts" about how they would behave during marriage, and how they would expect their partner to behave (Stuart & Jacobson, 1985). These tacit agreements are often based on idealized images of each other and of marriage itself. After they marry, the couple cooperate in the construction of a marital reality of their own (Berger & Kellner, 1964). During their first year of marriage, successful couples are likely to tell each other stories about their courtship. These recollections help to construct a couple-based view of the world that increases the stability of the relationship (Orbuch, Veroff, & Holmberg, 1993). A vast variety of matters must be negotiated and made real for the couple (see Highlight 12.1).

Berger and Kellner (1964) use an example from the friendship role to illustrate their point that individuals revise their definitions of reality in favor of a mutually constructed, marital definition of the situation. It usually happens that each married partner gradually interacts less and less with persons who were good friends prior to the marriage. Each person begins to look at former friends through the eyes of his or her spouse. Gradually, the couple will begin to interact with other married dyads rather than with single former "best friends."

HIGHLIGHT 12.1 **Negotiating Flight Plans** Married couples have a host of major issues with which to deal: handling finances, the division of power and labor in the household, having and raising children, how frequently and in what ways to make love, and what kind of relationships to have with in-laws. In addition to these issues is a dazzling array of decisions about how to go about living together day to day.

Often a set of rules is gradually established about how to handle a particular matter, then there is constant monitoring to see if the rules are followed or if they need to be changed. One such issue could be called the "filing of flight plans."

Before they take off, airplane pilots file a flight plan that indicates their destination, route, and projected time of arrival. If they do not arrive at their destination, rescuers will have some idea about where to begin a search. If they do not arrive roughly when they plan to, they might be asked to account for their tardiness.

Family members file "flight plans" with each other, following a set of rules that they negotiate, often without consciously talking about the rules. One rule prescribes the occasions on which filing a plan is expected. If a husband is simply going outside to pick up the newspaper, he may or may not be expected to file a verbal plan by saying, "I think I'll go get the newspaper." If he is going shopping, he probably will have to let his wife know, especially if she is home when he leaves. If she is not, he might or might not be expected to file a written flight plan in the form of a note on the refrigerator or other predetermined location. Over time, couples develop unspoken norms that are taken for granted but that were initially problematic. The husband might have found out that he was expected to file a flight plan only after he got back from the store one day and was questioned regarding his whereabouts. After that, he filed a flight plan to avoid a disruption in the couple's definition of their marriage as cooperative and happy.

Another issue deals with the length of time covered by particular flight plans. If the wife files a "go to the store" flight plan, and returns in the normative time, her absence will not be questioned. If she returns 6 hours later, she will probably be expected to provide an account for her long absence by filing an amended flight plan explaining what took her so long. A new set of procedures for filing amended plans via telephone might be instituted. Anytime an account is called for, it is an indication that expectations have not been met

(Scott & Lyman, 1968). The result will be negotiation about whether the account will be honored, and perhaps a questioning of the expectation itself.

Another issue is the specificity expected of the flight plan. Some couples expect an almost minute-by-minute, detailed plan: "I'm going to the dentist for a check-up, then I'll drop the cleaning off, then to the mall to look for shoes, then to the post office to buy stamps, then . . ."; for other couples, a loose "I'll be gone all afternoon" will suffice.

Finally, there is the issue of "debriefings," or discussions after the event is over. In some cases, discussion is neither offered nor expected. At other times, the traveling partner is expected to indicate whether the original flight plan was followed exactly or if there were any changes not already noticed.

The husband and wife are not the only family members to file flight plans. Children must also learn the flight plan rules of their family, which change regularly as the child gets older. Flight plans, like other aspects of mutual scripts, are never finally settled, but continue to be changed and negotiated throughout the life of the relationship.

Berger and Zellner argue that the negotiation of a shared reality takes place almost automatically, extending not only into the future but into the past as well. In effect, the past is changed because it is seen through the newly created marital lens. Some events become more important, some less so, and the meaning of others is altered. An event that might once have been seen as "a good time" can become "an irresponsible act." Meanings are continually negotiated as a couple cooperate to construct a life together.

Generalized Mutual Scripts

Couples do not take each new day and each event as a totally new phenomenon; they give it meaning in accord with the generalized marital script they have developed over time. We saw in chapter 11 that the most important element of the sexual script is the "why" of the script. The same might be said for the typology, developed by Cuber and Haroff (1965), of more general marital scripts. They found two basic marriage types, **intrinsic marriages** and **utilitarian marriages,** each of which has subtypes. Intrinsic marriages exist for the love and intimacy they provide to the partners. This type of marriage, which has both vital and total varieties, is a relatively recent historical ideal.

Vital marriages are, as the term implies, full of life; the word *vital* comes from the Latin *vita,* meaning life. The recreational script of these couples includes considerable joint activity, but it is the togetherness rather than the activity itself that provides the pleasure. There are genuine sharing and excitement in their relationship, which supplies the central meaning in life for both of them. Similarities rather than differences between the two are emphasized, and when conflict does occur it tends to be settled quickly and without lasting rancor.

Total marriages are like vital marriages except that there are even more areas of sharing. In these rare marriages, all possible activities are joint. If people do not actually work together, they share their work extensively by talking to each other, having lunch together, and traveling together when possible. It is as if the two partners do not have, nor ever had, a truly separate existence. Infidelity would be virtually unthinkable for these couples. Although the matter has not been studied, partners in total marriages probably file more detailed flight plans than other couples, but have them challenged less often.

Utilitarian marriages exist for economic cooperation, maintaining the extended family line, establishing alliances among *familia,* or other purposes not related to couple intimacy. Until the late industrial period, most marriages were of this type. Cuber and Haroff found three varieties among contemporary utilitarian couples: conflict habituated, devitalized, and passive-congenial.

Conflict-habituated marriages are a utilitarian type in which the purpose seems to be tension and conflict. A central theme of these marriages is to control and channel the conflict, which rarely exhibits itself in public. It largely consists of verbal arguments, some of which provide running battles for the duration of the marriage. Although it is negative, there is a high energy level in these relationships that might be missed by a partner who got into a more passive, less conflicted, relationship.

Intrinsic marriages: Marriages with the "why" of maintaining the intimacy of the relationship between husband and wife.
Utilitarian marriages: Marriages with a "why" other than intimate expression; a marriage of convenience for economic or other reasons.

Devitalized marriages were once intrinsic, but have lost their spirit. Most marriages change over time, but in these there is a clear discrepancy between young marriage expectations and the middle-aged reality. The marriage still serves as a base of operations for each partner, and the couple have their children or other memories. Although the partners sometimes miss the earlier intimacy, they largely accept the changes without developing strong antagonisms.

Passive-congenial marriages are similar to devitalized marriages except that there never was a strong emotional component. Congenial means having similar tastes and habits, or being friendly and sociable. Although there is little strong emotion in these relationships, there is also little conflict. This style fits well with dual-career or parallel kinds of marriages.

Cuber and Haroff (1965) did not claim that all marriages, even among the upper-class couples they studied, fit clearly into one of their five types. There are borderline cases, and couples can move from one type to another over time. Cuber and Haroff stressed, too, that they did not see any one type as superior to any other, or that the participants of any type are more or less happy than other types. None of the couples they used for their typology had ever seriously considered divorce, even the conflict-habituated ones.

It is possible that, since divorce is much more common now than when they did their study, some of the "bad" marriages would be more likely to end and the "good" ones remain. We would not know that for sure, however, until we developed a valid way of determining what a good marriage is.

Marital Quality

We all know that some marriages seem very good, some seem very bad, and most seem somewhere in between. Family researchers are interested in finding valid ways of measuring the quality of marriages so that variables associated with good marriages can be found. This might help find ways to improve the quality of specific marriages or to help avoid bad marriages.

Measuring Marital Quality

Several concepts are related to measuring good marriages. One approach is to ask whether the partners in the marriage are **happy**. The root of the term relates to a matter of luck, as in mis*hap*, *hap*penstance, and *hap*hazard. This implies that happiness is not something that a person can aim directly for, but is an accidental byproduct of other phenomena.

To find the variables that are associated with happiness requires a way to measure the elusive concept. Typically, surveys are used to ask someone a question like, "Taken all together, how would you describe your marriage? Would you say your marriage is very happy, pretty happy, or not too happy?" (Davis & Smith, 1972–98; Glenn & Weaver, 1977). Sometimes the happiness question is asked about one's life in general, or one's job. It can also be asked about more specific aspects of marriage such as the household division of labor, the couple's sex life, or their financial situation. Another kind of variation is to word the answer differently, perhaps by having six categories ranging from "Extremely happy" to "Extremely unhappy."

It is easy to think of happiness as something that varies from one person to another. There are, indeed, individual differences; some people just seem happier than others regardless of the position they are in. There are, however, differences based on the role and status of the individual.

Because the concept of happiness seems so elusive, some researchers prefer to ask about marital **satisfaction** instead. As used in surveys, the approach is basically identical except the word "satisfied" is substituted for "happy." Even though the two words have slightly different meanings, they are often used interchangeably in the research. Both concepts tend to tap into the degree to which a person perceives his or her individual needs to be met in the marriage (Bahr, 1989).

Marital **adjustment** is both an ongoing process and an assessment of a marriage at a particular time. Although several measures preceded it, the best known measure is now the Dyadic Adjustment Scale developed by Graham B. Spanier (1976a), along with his colleagues Robert Lewis, Charles Cole, and Erik E. Filsinger (see Finding Out 12.2).

A final kind of measurement of marital quality is marital **stability** or instability, typically defined as a

---

Happy: Characterized by good luck, pleasure, satisfaction, or joy.   **Satisfaction:** Fulfillment of a desire, need, or appetite; contentment derived from having needs met.   **Adjustment:** The act or means of adapting, corresponding, or conforming.
Stable: Resistant to change, self-restoring, consistently dependable.

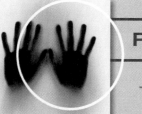

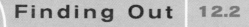

Finding Out | 12.2

The Dyadic Adjustment Scale

Graham B. Spanier and others developed a widely used measurement of the quality of marriage and similar relationships. To develop their scale, they began with a set of 300 questions that could be asked of couples about their marriage. Researchers added some questions of their own, and then got rid of duplicate questions and those that did not seem appropriate. This left a questionnaire with 225 items.

This set of questions was asked of a sample of 218 married persons in central Pennsylvania, as well as to every person who had gotten divorced in the same region in the preceding year. Answers were tabulated and scores for the married and divorced groups were compared. Any questions that did not receive significantly different answers from the two groups were thrown out. A pool of 32 questions remained; these became the Dyadic Adjustment Scale.

Each question was tabulated as part of one of four separate dimensions of the overall scale:

- *Dyadic satisfaction* is measured by asking how often the couple quarrels, gets on each other's nerves, or confides in their mates, and generally how happy they are in their relationship.

- *Dyadic cohesion* measures the couple's feeling of togetherness. They are asked how often they have a stimulating exchange of ideas, laugh together, or calmly discuss something.

- *Dyadic consensus* asks how frequently the partners agree on such items as handling family finances, recreation, and religious matters.

- *Affectional expression* asks how frequently partners agree on demonstrations of affection and sex relations, and whether these matters have been a problem in the past 2 weeks.

Based on the answers to each of the 32 questions, an overall score, as well as a score for each of the four dimensions, can be calculated. These scores can then be associated with other questions asked by the researchers about such things as the couple's income, religion, how long they have been married, whether they have children, and a number of other issues. Well over 1,000 separate studies have been reported that used the Dyadic Adjustment Scale to learn more about the quality of marriages.

Sources: Dyadic Adjustment Scale published in: Spanier, Graham B. 1976. "Measuring Dyadic Adjustment: New Scales for Assessing the Quality of Marriage and Similar Dyads." *Journal of Marriage and the Family* 38:15–28.
This summary is based largely on a copy of the scale found in: Miller, Delbert C. 1991. *Handbook of Research Design and Social Measurement*, 5th edition. Newbury Park, CA: Sage.

---

propensity to divorce. This might include serious contemplation of divorce, talking to friends about the possibility of divorce, or actually taking steps to get a divorce.

The least happy marriages are not necessarily the least stable. Udry (1981) found that a person's perception about marital alternatives was a better predictor of divorce than was marital dissatisfaction. A person in an unhappy marriage might stay with his or her partner if no alternative looks better, and one in a reasonably happy marriage might divorce if an even better alternative is seen. South and Lloyd (1985) tested this possibility using a large, nationwide sample. They found the highest risk of divorce where the husband or wife encountered an abundance of spousal alternatives.

Increased labor force participation of women and high geographic mobility both increase marital instability.

Correlates of Quality: Identifying Marital Strengths

Although rates of marital happiness have declined somewhat since the early 1970s, American couples remain quite satisfied with their current marriage. When asked to characterize their marriage as "very happy," "pretty happy," or "not too happy," well over 60% now respond "very happy" (Davis & Smith, 1998). Men (65.9%) are slightly more likely to report "very happy" marriages than are women (62.5%), but only 2.2% of men and

3.5% of women said "not too happy" (Davis & Smith, 1998). These figures vary in ways that help determine correlates of quality.

As chapter 9 indicated, married men and women have greater happiness with their lives than any category of single people. In fact, marital status is a better predictor of overall life happiness than any variable included in Table 12.1. Income is second as a predictor when other factors are held constant.

Many researchers have worked to find out what makes people happy in their marriages and their lives as a whole. Table 12.1 summarizes data about married Americans from the General Social Survey (GSS). One clear finding is that married individuals are considerably happier with their marriages than with their lives in general. It also appears that, while men rate their marriages as slightly happier than do women, married women report slightly happier lives than do their husbands.

Data in the table reflect the association between other variables and happiness. This information is valuable, but it is not as sophisticated as other studies cited below, and should be interpreted with some caution. We must

	Marital Happiness		Life Happiness	
Table 12.1 Marital Happiness and Life Happiness of Married Persons, by Selected Variables and Gender, Percentage Reporting "Very Happy"				
Variable	**Men**	**Women**	**Men**	**Women**
Family Income				
Lower Third	64.3	54.7	35.6	33.0
Middle Third	64.7	63.1	35.8	40.4
Upper Third	67.6	65.0	42.4	45.6
Educational Level				
Not High School Graduate	64.5	56.4	31.7	28.5
High School Graduate	65.4	63.4	30.1	33.2
College Graduate	67.2	65.3	32.6	36.1
Religious Affiliation				
Liberal Protestant	68.4	64.3	41.5	43.2
Conservative Protestant	66.2	61.0	40.1	41.3
Catholic	65.8	61.7	36.2	40.8
Jewish	68.4	67.4	41.3	42.9
None	55.3	57.9	30.7	32.3
Frequency of Attendance at Religious Services				
Never	57.6	58.7	32.7	37.8
Monthly-Yearly	64.0	59.0	35.3	36.6
Weekly	72.5	67.3	46.0	47.9
Age				
Under 30	65.5	67.3	32.9	40.2
30 to 49	63.1	60.4	35.9	40.0
50 and up	69.2	62.7	43.4	44.7
Race				
White	67.0	64.0	39.2	43.0
Black	53.5	46.1	29.1	27.2
Working Status, Self				
Full Time	64.8	61.5	37.7	40.0
Part Time	62.4	60.9	35.9	40.9
Unemployed	57.0	54.1	23.6	26.9
Retired	70.4	64.0	46.1	46.9

continued

| Table 12.1 | continued | | | |

	Marital Happiness		Life Happiness	
Variable	Men	Women	Men	Women
In School	64.6	56.6	38.6	40.9
Keeping House	63.9	62.9	31.3	42.3
Working Status, Spouse				
Full Time	63.3	63.7	37.4	42.0
Part Time	65.2	55.1	35.4	37.4
Unemployed	62.3	47.9	23.4	28.7
Retired	72.4	61.1	49.2	44.5
In School	65.2	68.9	34.9	38.8
Keeping House	66.9	54.3	39.2	36.5
Number of Children				
None	69.7	73.7	40.0	44.5
One or Two	64.4	61.6	37.8	41.9
Three or More	66.5	59.5	38.9	40.2
Overall:	65.9	62.5	38.6	41.6

Source: Davis, James Allan, and Tom W. Smith: General Social Survey(s), year(s). (Machine-readable data file). Principal investigator, James A. Davis; director and co-principal investigator, Tom W. Smith; co-principal investigator, Peter V. Marsden, NORC ed. Chicago: National Opinion Research Center, producer, 1998; Storrs, CT: The Roper Center for Public Opinion Research, University of Connecticut, distributor. Microcomputer format and codebook prepared and distributed by MicroCase Corporation, Bellevue, WA. Analysis by Gene H. Starbuck.

also remember that correlation does not prove causality. We might assume, for example, that having more money "causes" people to be happier. This might be true, but it is also possible that happy people make more money, that is, happiness "causes" the income change. It could also be true that some other variable such as level of education "causes" both more income and more happiness.

Socioeconomic Status. Lower income and educational levels are generally related to lower rates of marital stability (i.e., more divorce), but the effect of money and social status on marital satisfaction is less clear. Although some studies find no relationship (Bahr et al., 1983; Nye & McLaughlin, 1982), others find a slight positive correlation between social status and marital satisfaction (Lewis & Spanier, 1979; Piotrokowski, Rapoport, & Rapoport, 1987). Unemployment is associated with both lower marital stability and lower marital satisfaction (Larson, 1984).

Conger et al. (1990) concluded that economic hardship could reduce warmth and supportive interaction which, in turn, reduce marital quality. In a longitudinal study, Conger et al. (1999) found that, over time, economic pressure predict individual distress and marital conflict, which in turn predict marital distress. However, high marital support and effective couple problem solving reduced the negative effect of economic distress.

GSS results also find a correlation between family income and happiness. Higher incomes are associated with higher levels of both marital happiness and overall life happiness. These data also indicate that income appears to make more difference to women than it does to men. This might be a fruitful line of inquiry for future research. Education and income are clearly related variables, and have a similar association with happiness. Education makes some difference, more for women than for men.

Race. As with Whites, married Blacks have higher levels of happiness than single ones, although not as high as White marrieds (Taylor et al., 1991). This is partly related to lower average levels of economic and educational resources, since Black couples with higher income have greater satisfaction with family life than do Black couples with low incomes (Staples, 1988). GSS data confirm these conclusions.

Religion. Religious beliefs and participation are associated with marital satisfaction. Couples who attend religious services regularly have higher levels of marital satisfaction and stability than those who do not identify with a religion (Heaton & Pratt, 1990). The causality is unclear. Religious beliefs and participation themselves might directly increase happiness in individuals. Since religious services are a form of social interaction, though, it might be the connection with a supportive group of like-minded individuals, more than the religious beliefs themselves, that improves satisfaction. It might also be true that religious participation does not increase happiness, but rather that happy people are more likely to attend gatherings such as religious services.

The GSS findings (Table 12.1) confirm the relationship between frequent involvement in religious activities and higher marital and life happiness. In addition, there appear to be only small denominational differences, except that persons with no religious affiliation have considerably lower happiness levels than those with an affiliation of any kind.

Most studies find that religious homogamy increases marital satisfaction (Heaton & Pratt, 1990). Lower satisfaction with interreligious marriages appears more likely among men than women, perhaps because children tend to be raised in the faith of the mother, which could reduce the father's interaction in the family (Shehan et al., 1990).

Class, Age, and Racial Homogamy. As with religion, homogamous marriages of other types are generally characterized by higher quality, couple satisfaction, and stability than heterogamous ones (Lewis & Spanier, 1979). The association between social class heterogamy and marital satisfaction is difficult to research because social class is difficult to define and because hypergamy is an accepted part of the mate-selection process (Glenn, Hoppe, & Weiner, 1974). Large social class differences, however, can result in difficulties with in-laws, friends, and leisure interests.

Age seems to be an exception to the general rule about homogamy and marital quality. Large age difference between partners might create difficulties for some couples, but if so the difference apparently creates offsetting strengths. Analysis of two large sets of data found no significant differences in marital quality as associated with age discrepancies of partners (Vera, Berardo, & Berardo, 1985).

Racial and ethnic heterogamy are more acceptable now, so they might not have as big an effect on marital quality as was once the case. Research in Hawaii found some evidence that mixed marriages were less stable, but only under certain conditions and spousal combinations. Marriages in which the bride came from a higher income ethnic group than the groom, for example, were more likely to end in divorce than the reverse case (Ho & Johnson, 1990).

Carter and Glick (1976) looked at census data to determine how many of the marriages of the 1950s were still intact in 1970. Ninety percent of White-White marriages were intact, as were 78% of the Black-Black marriages. By contrast, 63% of Black husband–White wife marriages survived and only 47% of the White husband–Black wife couples were still together. Noting that survival rates of the marriage types are in order from most to least common, Reiss and Lee (1988) suggested that the survival rates reflect the differential in social support that each type receives. In the 1970s, at least, interracial couples faced difficulties of finding appropriate places of residence, lack of close emotional ties toward kin, and negative responses from the public (Golden, 1975). All of these factors can increase marital stress and reduce marital satisfaction.

Part of the difficulty faced by couples from different backgrounds is the possibility of a lack of **role consensus,** or agreement about how the various roles associated with marriage should be played. The greater the degree of role consensus, and the better each spouse meets the role expectations of the other, the better the marital quality (Bahr, Chappell, & Leigh, 1983; Burr, Leigh, Day, & Constantine, 1979). Mutual scripts are easier to construct and maintain if the two partners have similar assumptions about appropriate marital and familial roles. This general finding apparently applies to housekeeping, child socialization, and other marital roles mentioned earlier in this chapter.

Work/Family Arrangements. The entry of large numbers of women into the co-provider role in recent

---

Role consensus: Agreement between actors about how a role should be played.

years has led to considerable research on the effect of this trend on family and individual satisfaction. One question was whether wives who were employed outside the home were happier than homemakers. A careful review of six large national studies found no evidence to support the popular assumption that women who worked outside their homes were generally happier and more satisfied with their lives (Wright, 1978). Instead, each option has costs and benefits, and the negative images of homemaking have been emphasized in the research (Eshleman, 1994). Shehan's (1984) study of the mental health of homemakers and wage workers found the majority of both groups to be "well off" psychologically, with no significant differences between the groups in terms of depression, health anxiety, or life satisfaction.

More detailed study, however, revealed that the woman's life goals affected the relationship between homemaking and life satisfaction. Homemakers who wanted careers were less satisfied with their lives than those who never wanted outside careers. Women without career aspirations, however, were happier in general than employed women (Townsend & Gurin, 1981). A review of studies compiled by Spitze (1988) found that the effect of women's employment on marriage and family depended on whether the work was full or part time, whether there were children, the ages of the couple, how long they had been married, their income, and several other factors.

According to the GSS, the most desirable work status, for both men and women, is "retired," while the least desirable is "unemployed." The effect of being in school, or having a spouse in school, is complex. Beyond that, it would appear that both husbands and wives are happiest when the husband works for pay full time and the wife is a housekeeper. Perhaps surprisingly, the few men who are housekeepers appear much happier about their situation than are the women whose husbands do the housekeeping.

The kind of job, and amount of time a wife works, has an impact on marital stability. In both postindustrial societies like the United States and less developed countries like Thailand, the more hours a wife works outside the home, the higher the rates of marital instability for some types of marriages (Greenstein, 1990; Edwards et al., 1992). Women who work in jobs that are not traditionally held by women have divorce rates almost twice that for women in more traditional positions. Women who make considerably more income than their husbands, and who hold professional jobs requiring advanced levels of education, have less stable

marriages (South, 1985; Cooney & Uhlenberg, 1989; Houseknecht, Vaughn, & Macke, 1984).

Role consensus is difficult for couples to achieve in these situations, partially because they are departures from the traditional way of handling the provider role in marriage. Wives in the labor force reported higher marital quality if their husbands were less traditional (Vannoy-Hiller & Philliber, 1989). These attitudes apparently matched the role expectations of the less traditional women.

Quality is affected when gender-role attitudes change during the course of the marriage, according to a longitudinal study by Amato and Booth (1995) of 2,033 married individuals. Wives who developed less traditional attitudes over time believed that their marriage quality went down; they reported less happiness, less interaction, more disagreements, more problems and higher divorce proneness. When husbands developed less traditional attitudes, however, their marital quality went up slightly. Perhaps increasing nontraditionalism by wives distances them from their husbands, making role consensus more difficult, while increasing nontraditionalism by men brings the couple's views closer together.

Presence of Children. Whether or not the parenthood role is enacted makes a difference in marital quality. Women without children, in general, report higher levels of marital satisfaction than mothers (Polenko, Scanzoni, & Teachman, 1982). The GSS results (not shown) confirm that both men and women under 30 who have never had children report much higher levels of marital happiness than those who are parents. For women, this difference remains large throughout the life span. For men over 30, however, there is almost no difference in marital happiness between those who have fathered children and those who have not.

Voluntarily childfree women score especially high on the "marital cohesion" portion of the Dyadic Adjustment Scale. They report more outside interests, more work on projects with their husband, more frequently having a good exchanges of ideas, and more quiet discussions (Houseknecht, 1979).

Couples who do not yet have children, or those whose children have grown up and left home, have higher marital satisfaction than those with children currently in the home (Rollins & Feldman, 1970). Parenting stress negatively affects psychological well-being and perceived marital quality for both husbands and wives. Parenting stress increases as numbers of children increase and as economic problems grow. The household division of labor and whether the wife works or not do not appear to affect parenting stress (Lavee, Sharlin, & Katz, 1996).

On the other hand, presence of preschool children in the home does have at least a temporary effect on marital stability (Bradbury et al., 2000). Couples with very young children rarely get divorced. They will apparently suffer higher levels of marital unhappiness before they end a marriage than will childfree couples (White & Booth, 1985). Among elderly couples, those who had children reported significantly greater satisfaction with family life, an association particularly strong for women (Singh & Williams, 1981; Greil, Leitke, & Porter, 1988).

Communication, Support, and Sexuality.
Good communication, both in the therapeutic role and for purposes of negotiating marital roles, is strongly related to marital quality. A review of 20 years of research found that several aspects of communication are associated with high marital satisfaction: higher rates of self-disclosure, expression of love, support and affection, laughter and positive nonverbal communication involving good listening skills and body posture (Boland & Follingstad, 1987). Research specifically on Black couples has reached similar conclusions (Thomas, 1990). When the conflict management style is collaborative rather than competitive, marital happiness is happier (Greef & de Bruyne, 2000).

It is not completely clear whether good communication skills "cause" happy marriages or whether the happy marriages result in good communication. There is some evidence that teaching good communication skills such as self-disclosure to couples can increase the perceived intimacy of their marriage (Waring, Schaefer, & Fry, 1994).

Marital success is associated with the support each partner gives the other in nonmarital matters. This might be particularly true with dual-working couples, who like to see their partner as someone who can support them in their work activities and feelings (Bradbury et al., 2000). When a person turns to a friend, negative feeling about the relationship might actually increase, especially if the friend makes negative comments about the relationship. When individuals believe that their social network is positive about their relationship, however, relationship happiness is higher (Bryant & Conger, 1999; Julien et al., 1994). Wives' marital satisfaction appears to be more affected by their social support than does husbands' (Acitelli & Antonucci, 1994).

The communication that arises from joint leisure activities is important to marital satisfaction (Orthner, 1975). Joint decision-making and egalitarian communication styles are associated with higher levels of marital satisfaction. Of the nonegalitarian styles, wife-dominant marriages are less happy than husband-dominant ones, especially for women (Olson & DeFrain, 1994).

The sexual role is important to marital quality. Blumstein and Schwartz (1983) concluded that a good sex life is central to marital satisfaction. For people in the same age group, sexual frequency is strongly correlated with marital happiness (Christopher & Sprecher, 2000; Davis & Smith, 1972–98). Again, more frequent sexual activity might not, in itself, cause the happiness. Instead, couples who are getting along well and are otherwise happier probably feel more like having frequent sex than couples the same age who are otherwise miserable.

Satisfaction with sexual communication is probably more strongly associated with overall sexual satisfaction than is frequency of sex, frequency of orgasm, or other aspects of sexuality (Byers & Demmons, 1999; Cupach & Comstock, 1990; Sarrel & Sarrel, 1980). As with other role relationships, it was the perceptions of communication quality that was important, not objectively measured communication skills, although the two are probably related.

Maintenance Behaviors.
Relationship maintenance behaviors help to continue marriages by preventing their decline, by enhancing them, or by their repair and re-establishment. Canary and Stafford (1992) developed a typology of five common types. *Positivity* involves maintaining positive, cheerful, and uncritical interaction with one's spouse. *Openness* includes communication that directly addresses the nature of the relationship. *Assurances* are behaviors that stress one's interest in continuing the relationship. *Network* means interacting with common friends and relatives. *Sharing* tasks involves doing one's fair share (as each individual defines it) of such responsibilities as household tasks.

Canary and Stafford (1994) found that couples who engage in these maintenance behaviors have higher perceptions of such indicators of relationship quality as satisfaction, commitment, and liking each other. Dainton et al. (1994) and Weigel and Ballard-Reisch (1996) have found an association between maintenance behaviors and the love husbands and wives feel for each other.

Relationship maintenance behaviors: Actions taken by participants to preserve ongoing relationships.

Research on maintenance behaviors continues. Haas and Stafford (1998) found that same-sex couples use maintenance behaviors that are similar to those used by heterosexual couples. Their use is probably different for men and women. While wives' use is associated with events that occur within the relationship, husbands' use may be more connected to events outside the marriage (Weigel & Ballard-Reisch, 1999). While there is an association between marital quality and use of maintenance behavior, it is not clear which causes what. People in good relationships might be more inclined to engage in the helpful actions. On the other hand, using the behaviors might make the relationships better. Weigel and Ballard-Reisch (1999) suggest that the latter is true, and that couples might be able to intentionally improve their relationships by learning and using the five types of maintenance behaviors.

Marriage in the Middle and Later Years

The process of constructing a life together is not something that occurs early in the marriage and is then forgotten. Marital adjustment is a process that lasts throughout the marriage as situations change and are defined and redefined. One way of looking at this process is by use of the developmental perspective.

The Life Cycle of a Marriage

As we saw in chapter 2, the developmental perspective looks at family relations in terms of definable stages, each of which is associated with particular **developmental tasks.** Successful completion of the task leads to greater life satisfaction and success in later tasks, while failure is associated with unhappiness, failure at later stages, or social disapproval (Havighurst, 1953). For example, if a couple does not successfully adapt to the birth of their first child, the family may well be in jeopardy throughout the remaining stages.

The stages constituting a family life cycle are usually divided by discrete events that typically occur with married couples, but various theorists have used different events to differentiate the stages. For purposes of analysis, the family life cycle has been divided into as many as

24 stages (Rodgers, 1962) and as few as four (Sorokin, Zimmerman, & Galpin, 1931; Rubin, 1976).

Perhaps the most widely used typology was that developed by Duval (1957). Although other terminology is sometimes used, the eight basic stages are:

1. *Couples without children*: from the wedding until the birth of the first child.
2. *Infant*: until the first child is 30 months old.
3. *Preschooler*: oldest child is 30 months to 6 years old.
4. *Elementary school*: oldest child is 6 to 13 years old.
5. *Teenager*: oldest child is 13 to 20, or leaves home.
6. *Launching*: from the time the first child leaves home until the last child leaves home.
7. *Empty nest*: from the time the last child leaves the home until the husband's retirement.
8. *Retirement*: from the time the husband retires until the death of one or both spouses.

The development model remains a useful framework, but it does have serious shortcomings when applied to postindustrial American families (Mattessich & Hill, 1987). The biggest problem is that the model accurately describes only a minority of marriages. Some couples never have children, so their stage is impossible to determine. Perhaps half of couples divorce before either dies, so they have a "truncated" life cycle. Some have no "launching" stage because they have only one child. Others, including blended families, have children before the wedding, so they have no "childless" stage. Still other couples have no, or little, "empty nest" stage because their adult children continue to live with them. Some middle-aged couples have their elderly parents living with them; and in the increasing number of dual-career couples the wife's retirement is important but not reflected in the typology. Many of these family variations, however, still conform to certain characteristics of the life cycle, so the concept remains a useful tool for family analysis.

Marital Satisfaction and the Life Cycle

The most widely quoted study about marital satisfaction and the life cycle was done by Rollins and Feldman (1970) using an eight-stage developmental typology. Their

---

Developmental tasks: Undertakings or objectives associated with a particular stage in the life of an individual or life cycle of a family.

conclusion is referred to as the "U-shaped" relationship between family stages and life satisfaction. The majority of husbands and wives are very satisfied in the childless and into the infant stage, with the wives being slightly happier than husbands. After that, satisfaction goes down, with the wives' declining slightly faster than the husbands' through the "teenager" stage. After that, satisfaction goes up for both spouses through the retirement stage.

GSS data in Table 12.1 do not directly test the U-shaped hypothesis, but the age group with the greatest marital happiness is over 50. The middle age group is slightly least happy, with the youngest group next. This appears to slightly confirm the U-shaped hypothesis, as do the data that "retired" is the happiest job status. This is typical of cross-sectional research, that is, studies done at one time rather than across time. Longitudinal studies, where couples are followed over time to compare their happiness levels, tend to get different results.

Bossard and Boll (1955) found no relationship between marital unhappiness and the marital life cycle. In contrast, Blood and Wolfe (1960) found that marital satisfaction generally declined throughout the course of marriages. White and Booth (1985) followed couples for a 3-year period from the childless stage through birth of the first child. The U-shaped hypothesis would predict a decline in happiness during this period, but no such decline was found.

A more comprehensive study followed couples for 40 years. No evidence for a general U-shaped curve was found. Instead, marital satisfaction was relatively stable over time with a slight decrease at about the 20-year period. The researchers concluded that the U-shaped curve is largely an illusion (Vaillant & Vaillant, 1993). Glenn's (1998) longitudinal work found a general decline of happiness early in marriages, but no convincing evidence of a general upturn of happiness in older marriages. He concluded that, perhaps, the older people with happier marriages had happier marriages all along than did people who are currently middle aged.

Whether the U-shaped hypothesis or the gradual decline hypothesis is accurate, it has been argued that marriages for love are likely to become less happy after the romance wears off. They would "start off hot and get cold." Arranged marriages, since they are not based on emotional attachment, might be expected to "start off cold and get hot." Robert Blood (1967) tested this hypothesis with a study in Japan. He found no evidence that the arranged marriages got hotter with time; both arranged and love marriages demonstrated a gradual decline in happiness.

A similar study was done in China (Xiaohe & Whyte, 1990). Women who had married for love reported higher levels of satisfaction throughout the life cycle than those in arranged marriages. There was evidence for neither a general decline nor a U-shaped relationship. In both types of marriages, satisfaction was greatest for couples married 20–25 years, with a slight decline in older marriages.

Even studies that do find a general trend regarding marital satisfaction over the life cycle find only small differences, and they find that marital satisfaction for

Shared activities provide opportunities for communication and closeness throughout a marriage.

couples at all stages is relatively high (Rollins & Cannon, 1974; Gelles, 1995). Several factors appear to be more important determinants of marital satisfaction than the couple's stage in the marital life cycle.

Postparental Couples

A major change for most couples in middle age is the decreasing amount of time, energy, and money devoted to the child-care and child-socialization roles. For this reason, the term **postparental period** is sometimes applied to this stage of married life. Neither the name, nor most of the research, applies to the small number of couples who never had children. Even for parents, however, the name is slightly misleading. They really do not stop being parents even if they have "launched" their last child. There are sometimes "re-entries" of children, and ties are maintained to children who do not move back home. Whether in the home or living independently, their children are now adults and the role relationships change. The major characteristic of these couples is the return to the two-person conjugal family and ultimately to one partner living alone.

Length of time couples spend in postparental families has significantly increased during the 20th century. In 1900, the typical couple did not have a postparental period because at least one spouse died before the last child left home. Today, men and women typically marry in their early to mid-20s. The last child is launched in their mid- to late 40s, and a spouse is not likely to die until his or her early to mid-70s. This leaves the stable couple a postparental period of 20 to 25 years (Eshleman, 1994).

The majority of noninstitutionalized men today continue to live with their spouse until death. Even in the 75 years and over category, 70% of men are still living with their wives. By contrast, the percentage of women living with their spouses declines rapidly with age. In the 75 and older category, 52% of women live alone compared to 21% of men. About 5% of all elderly live in nursing homes at any given time, but 21% of those over 85 reside in such places (Soldo & Agree, 1988).

Most persons 65 and older continue to live with their spouses. Because of higher marriage rates and longer life expectance, Whites (56%) are more likely than Hispanics (50%) and Blacks (36%) to live with their wives or husbands (see Figure 12.3). Elderly Blacks (34%) are more likely to live alone are than Whites (31%) or Hispanics (22%).

The percentage of the population that is in the postretirement years has increased since 1970 and is

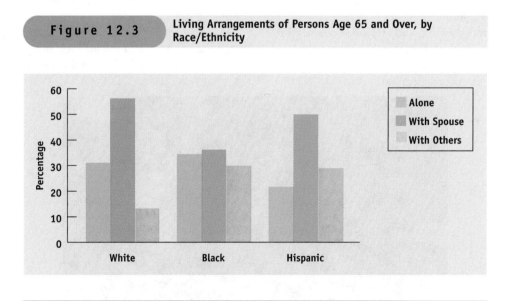

Figure 12.3 Living Arrangements of Persons Age 65 and Over, by Race/Ethnicity

Source: U.S. Bureau of the Census, 1999. *Statistical Abstract, 1999,* Table 61. Washington, DC: U.S. Government Printing Office.

Postparental period: Time in the family life cycle after the children leave home as adults.

projected to continue to increase well into the future. Part of this increase is the result of increasing life expectancy. In 2011, however, the first year's crop of baby boomers will hit age 65, bringing an even more rapid increase in the elderly population (see Table 12.2).

The increase in the numbers of elderly is expected to strain the Social Security system and perhaps other retirement programs. At the macroeconomic level, there will be fewer persons of working age supporting a larger number of post-working-age individuals. This is partially offset, however, by a decrease in the percentage of population that has not yet reached age 18. The total percent in the two nonworking age groups, then, remains relatively low until, in 2050, it is once again at the level it was in 1970. Since more of the nonworking population is elderly rather than young, there will be a shift of social resources from the very young to the very old. The net burden on the working population will continue to rise somewhat until about 2040, and then decrease slightly (see Table 12.2).

An increasingly older population will influence the employment market in the next few decades. Through 2005, the three fastest growing occupations are expected to be home health aides, human services workers, and personal and home care aides, all related to the aging population. Computer engineers and scientists will be the fourth in terms of rapid growth, but physical and corrective therapy assistants, physical therapists, and occupational therapy assistants and aides are also in the top 10 (U.S. Bureau of Census, 1994:394).

The aging population will not grow at the same rate in all ethnic groups. The non-Hispanic White population will shrink slightly as a percentage of the aged,

Table 12.2	Percent of U.S. Population in Young and Old Nonworking Age Groups, 1970 to 2050		
Year	Under 18	Over 64	Total
1970	34.2	9.8	44.0
1980	28.2	11.3	39.5
1990	25.7	12.3	38.0
2000	25.9	12.8	38.7
2010	24.6	13.4	38.0
2020	23.9	16.3	40.2
2040	23.4	20.7	44.1
2050	23.5	20.4	43.9

Source: U.S. Bureau of the Census, 1994. *Statistical Abstract of the United States, 1994.* 114th ed. Washington, DC: U.S. Government Printing Office. Tables 13 and 16.

while Hispanics, Blacks and Asians will become a slightly larger proportion. Perhaps more important is the growth in the absolute number of the aged. In the 30-year period between 1995 and 2025, the over-64 population is expected almost to double, from 33,648,000 to 62,149,000 (see Table 12.3).

Postlaunch Transitions

The postparental period can be divided into two developmental stages: the postlaunch stage and the

Table 12.3	Projections of the Age 65 and Over Population of the United States, 1995 to 2025, by Race and Ethnicity, in 1,000s and Percentages								
	1995		2000		2005		2010		2025	
	1,000	%	1,000	%	1,000	%	1,000	%	1,000	%
Non-Hispanic										
White	28,705	85.3	29,574	83.7	30,321	82.0	32,284	80.5	47,323	76.1
Black	2,660	7.9	2,825	8.0	2,999	8.1	3,278	8.2	5,540	8.9
Native Amer.	127	0.4	148	0.4	171	0.5	198	0.5	321	0.5
Asian	624	1.9	849	2.4	1,111	3.0	1,427	3.6	2,887	4.6
Hispanic	1,532	4.6	1,936	5.5	2,367	6.4	2,918	7.3	6,078	9.8
Total	33,648	100.1	35,332	100.0	36,969	100.0	40,105	100.1	62,149	99.9

Source: U.S. Bureau of the Census, 1994. *Statistical Abstract of the United States, 1994.* 114th ed. Washington, DC: U.S. Government Printing Office. Table 24.

postretirement period. The popular press, and popular wisdom, report several problems associated with both stages, for both men and women.

Men in the launch and postlaunch stage are often reported to suffer "midlife crises" involving dissatisfaction with career, family, social position, or self-perception. While men at all ages have issues of some kind to face, careful research finds little support for widespread midlife crises among Americans. Farrell and Rosenberg (1981) compared 300 men entering middle age with men in their 20s. They found some discontent and reassessment of their lives, but only 12% of the men displayed the signs generally associated with midlife crisis. Unskilled laborers were more likely to show psychological distress. Skilled workers and other lower-middle-class men exhibited what might be called denial mechanisms, allowing them successfully to maintain their worldview. Upper-middle-class men had neither identity problems nor denials and were generally satisfied with their careers and their families.

While many men are temporarily saddened by the departure of their children, it is rarely a serious problem. Exceptions might be rural or farm fathers at the departure of their youngest child. The return of an adult child who has already left the home might actually cause more distress than the launch itself (Lewis, Volk, & Duncan, 1989).

It was once thought that the **empty nest syndrome** was widespread among women whose children had left home, especially when their husbands were still in the workforce. Harkins (1978) found that, in the 1960s and 1970s, belief in the empty nest syndrome was so pervasive that medical journals ran ads for antidepressants to combat the alleged problem.

Attempts to verify the existence of an empty nest syndrome have been mixed. There are certainly some women who are extremely affected by their children's departure. Blood and Wolfe (1960) found evidence of increased marital discord during this stage, and Bart (1971) found some reported depression and feelings of maternal role loss among women who had been overly involved with their children. Other studies found unchanged or increased overall happiness and marital satisfaction at the time of the empty nest (Deutcher, 1969; Rollins & Feldman, 1970).

Norvel Glenn (1975) reviewed results from six national studies. He found that middle-aged women whose

The lives of parents and children change significantly when the children first leave home.

children had left home reported greater happiness and well-being than women the same age who still had children in the home. Harkins (1978) found no evidence of effect on physical well-being of the empty nest, and only a small and temporary negative effect on psychological well-being. Apparently belief in the existence of an empty nest syndrome has evaporated; there has been virtually no research on the subject in the past 20 years.

Postretirement Couples

The concept of retirement as an expected part of the life cycle is relatively new. In most hunting-gathering societies, persons who did live to older ages, perhaps 40 or so, were revered for their knowledge and participated

---

Empty nest syndrome: Role loss after a child has left the home resulting in depression, identity crisis, and lowered well-being. Actually a rare phenomenon.

in production as much as possible until their deaths. In agrarian societies, the elderly who were the owners of land and other means of production maintained their authority and social standing. Persons generally worked until they died or were no longer physically able; they were then supported by their families as their capacities waned. Government and religious positions were typically lifetime appointments, and women employed in such positions as midwives often continued working well into their 70s (Demos, 1986).

It was not until the 17th century that the English word **retirement** was used to describe withdrawal from a position for purposes of more leisure (*American Heritage Dictionary*, 1992). Even then, it was something reserved largely for the wealthy.

As industrialization proceeded, the elderly began to lose their social standing at the same time life expectancy was increasing. Rapid social change renders the knowledge base of the elderly less valuable, at least in terms of economic production. Further, elderly workers in factories did not own the means of production, and might actually be less productive than younger, more nimble, workers.

In Europe, beginning in England with the Elizabethan Poor Law of 1601, a larger governmental entity began to assume some responsibility for the infirm elderly and others in poverty (Trattner, 1979). This began to remove some of the responsibility of elderly support from children and other family members.

In the United States, it was not until the Great Depression of the 1930s that the federal government assumed major responsibility for older workers. The Social Security Act of 1935 had two goals in this regard: it provided an income that enabled older workers to retire, and it strongly encouraged, even forced, retirement so that more jobs would become available for younger workers. As mandatory retirement became an issue, older workers lobbied to set the age at 70; younger workers wanted the age to be 60. Age 65 became the arbitrary compromise for the mandatory retirement age (Bassis, Gelles, & Levine, 1991). In 1979 federal legislation outlawed mandatory retirement at 65, and now, with a few exceptions, all mandatory retirement policies have been eliminated.

Although life expectancy is going up, average retirement age is going down. In spite of the fact that workers must stay in the labor force until age 65 if they wish to receive full Social Security benefits, many retire early. The average age of retirement for men working in companies of more than 1,000 employees is 59 years (Bassis, Gelles, & Levine, 1991). Many companies have policies that encourage early retirement so they can fill positions with younger employees who make less money. These factors contribute to the fact that, since 1960, the portion of the over-64 age group that remains in the workforce has been reduced considerably (see Table 12.4).

Adjustment to retirement includes, for most persons, a reduction in income. Although this becomes a severe problem for some, poverty rates for the elderly are actually lower than for the country as a whole. In 1997, 13.3% of all Americans were living below poverty level, compared to 10.5% of those 65 and over. While 9.0%

Table 12.4	Labor Force Participation of Persons 65 and Older, by Sex and Marital Status, in Percentages, 1960 to 1998			
	Single		Married	
Year	Male	Female	Male	Female
1960	31.2	24.3	36.9	6.7
1970	25.2	19.7	29.9	7.3
1980	16.8	13.9	20.5	7.3
1990	15.7	12.1	17.5	8.5
1998	15.2	9.7	17.5	8.9

Source: U.S. Bureau of the Census, 1995. *Statistical Abstract of the United States, 1995*, Table 636. Ibid. 1999, Table 657. Washington DC: U.S. Government Printing Office.

Retirement: A withdrawal from one's paid occupation.

of elderly Whites were poor, the poverty rate for elderly Blacks was 26.0% and for elderly Hispanics was 23.8% (U.S. Bureau of Census, 1999: t. 762). Because the pensions of many retired persons do not keep up with the rate of inflation, poverty rates increase significantly for older retirees.

For married people, retirement is a joint concern. Retirement decisions are usually the result of joint decision making. The timing of retirement influences the adjustment of married couples, as Brubaker's (1985) typology of "traditional," "synchronized," and "dissynchronized" retirements suggests. The most common "traditional" or "single" type involves the retirement of the sole breadwinner, usually the husband. The loss of the breadwinner role is a significant adjustment for the husband, and the two partners must renegotiate the housekeeping and other roles. The wife might have difficulty with what she sees as interference with her household sphere of influence.

"Synchronized retirement" occurs when dual breadwinners retire simultaneously (Brubaker, 1985). Both partners suffer the loss of their breadwinner role at the same time, but these couples are probably accustomed to considerable negotiation regarding the housekeeping role.

Two types of dissynchronized retirements are possible. Because men's careers tend to start earlier and be more continuous, and because of age hypergamy, husbands in two-earner couples are more likely to retire first. This results in the "dissynchronized husband initially" couple. Less commonly, perhaps because of ill health or work dissatisfaction, the wife will retire first, resulting in a "dissynchronized wife initially" couple (Brubaker, 1985).

Because the breadwinner role no longer takes the time it once did and no longer ties the couple to their homes, the recreational role expands considerably. It becomes more important whether the couple has developed individual, joint, or parallel leisure activities.

Some of the adjustments associated with retirement are related to changing physical capability and the way older persons are perceived in America. Butler (1975) coined the term **ageism** to refer to discrimination against the elderly. He refers to the "myth of senility," which portrays all elderly persons as mentally disabled. When a teenager or young adult forgets where the car keys are, it is attributed to being busy, to being in love, or to other age-acceptable causes. When the same thing happens to a 70-year-old, it might be attributed to the age-acceptable cause of senility, even when the person is not senile.

In the United States, the elderly are thought to be

Many couples find that the postretirement stage is the happiest time of their lives.

less competent and intelligent, and to have low activity levels and poor health (Levin, 1988). While it is unfair to stereotype all the elderly in this way, health issues are important. Poor health and declining physical abilities do affect many retirees, and are a major concern and topic of conversation. Retirement does not cause poor health, however; poor health is more likely to cause retirement (Atchley & Miller, 1983).

In spite of role transitions and health concerns, Atchley (1992) found no evidence that retirement has a direct overall effect on marital satisfaction (Atchley, 1992). Spanier, Lewis, and Cole (1975) found levels of marital satisfaction equivalent to the earlier stage before the couple had children. We have seen the GSS data indicating that retirement is associated with higher levels of life and marital happiness than any other work status.

Myers and Booth (1996) found several connections between men's retirement and marital quality. Leaving a high-stress job increased marital satisfaction. Gender-role reversals and decreased social support, however, reduced marital quality.

Ageism: Discrimination or prejudice based on age, especially against the elderly.

First Couples Make Changes

As Bill Clinton moves to his wife's "home town" for job related reasons, Laura Bush moves to Washington, where her husband's new job is located. The Bush move is more typical, as wives are more likely to move to their husband's job than vice versa.

As with millions of other couples, once their new location is determined, it is the wife who takes charge of making a White House a home. In her first interview in the White House, except for a brief discussion about her education initiatives, Laura Bush declared questions about policy off-limits. Instead, she wanted to talk about decorating changes, food preparation, and the choice of china for the first official dinner.

In a brief tour, Mrs. Bush pointed out the changes that were being made. The second-floor office once occupied by Bill Clinton and soon to be used by President Bush was stripped to bare walls awaiting paint. Gone were the mahogany paneling and red, blue, and gold fabrics. In the Lincoln sitting room, the layers of patterned draperies and a trompe l'oeil coffered ceiling were also reduced to bare walls.

Mrs. Bush said that they would be having Mexican food at least once each week; they are especially fond of burritos. And the new president, just like his dad, will eat broccoli on occasion. It has to be all heads and no stalks, and covered with a great cheese sauce.

When the Clintons lived there, the kitchen stayed open until midnight in case anyone wanted a snack. The Bushes will close the kitchen right after dinner. They have to protect their weight, Mrs. Bush explained.

And they'll be using the new millennium china to host the president's dinner.

Source: Marian Burros. **www.nytimes.com**, February 23, 2001.

Generally, satisfaction with family life is high for both sexes, and most of the elderly are well integrated into the social and religious life of the community. Contrary to the images that their children and other family members forget the elderly, most have considerable contact. Women are especially likely to have family and religious contacts (Dorfman & Mertens, 1990).

The elderly often adjust by redefining their family situation (Allen et al., 2000). They sometimes add fictive kin to their support system. They also upgrade kin, such as treating a niece "like a daughter." Perhaps because such survival skills were more necessary for Blacks, they are more likely to convert friends into kin than are aging Whites (Johnson & Barer, 1997).

Death, Grief, and Mourning

All marriages that do not end in divorce eventually end in the death of one or both spouses. While this can occur at any age, it is more common among the elderly. **Bereavement** is accompanied by the emotional response of **grief**. Describing this response is perhaps better left to poets, psychiatrists, or clergy, rather than sociologists, but it can include shock, disbelief, overwhelming sorrow, depression, numbness, disbelief, loss of appetite, loss of desire to live, a questioning of the meaning of life or of one's god, a sense of total isolation, inconsolable sadness, anger, guilt, relief, remorse, regret, fear, and a number of other feelings.

Emotional and behavioral reactions are guided by **mourning** customs that vary from one culture to another. The wearing of black armbands for a time is a simple mourning practice. Others are more complex and depend on the culture's meanings of death and the roles expected before and after the loved one's death. The most formal expectations are signified by funeral practices that virtually all societies have but construct differently.

From a functionalist perspective, the funeral is an important ritual with personal, familial, religious, and social functions. A funeral is a rite of passage for the deceased, who is typically believed to be transported to a different form and status. It is also a rite of passage for the survivors because it signifies change in role and status. A wife becomes a **widow** and a husband becomes a **widower**. These roles redefine the place of the person with respect to other family members and the community at large. In most societies, remarriage is allowed after a specified period has elapsed.

There are considerably more widows than widowers in the United States. In 1992 there were 8.6 million

---

Bereavement: The condition of being deprived of a loved one by death.   **Grief:** Deep mental and emotional anguish.
Mourning: The socially constructed expectations regarding reactions to death.   **Widow:** A woman whose husband has died.
Widower: A man whose wife has died (this term reflects the fact that male family terms are typically derived from female terms).

widows and 1.9 million widowers. Average age at widowhood is 66.1 years for women and 68.4 years for men. Widows average another 14.3 years of life, while widowers average 6.6 remaining years (Kart et al., 1988).

In addition to the difficulties associated with grieving, widows often face financial hardship. Average standard of living for women dropped 18% after the death of their husbands, and 10% of women who were above the poverty line before dropped into poverty after their husbands died (Bound et al., 1991). While it is often assumed that widows have more economic problems, some studies have found that widowers are as likely to have economic hardships as widows (Benokraitis, 1993). Children and others are sometimes less likely to offer assistance to widowers because they assume the men have planned and managed their financial affairs better (Smith & Zick, 1986).

Loneliness can be a problem for both, but is more severe for men. Widows are more likely to be connected to family, peer, and religious groups than are widowers, who suffer more from depression and other mental illness (Gove, 1972). Widowers have higher suicide rates, and overall death rates, during the year following the death of their spouses than do widows (Smith, Mercy, & Conn, 1988).

The death of a spouse is an extraordinarily difficult life transition. After a period of adjustment, however, most widows and widowers go on to lead highly satisfying lives. Women often make the adjustment by turning inward and becoming more self-confident, assertive, and independent. Men often adjust by becoming more externally oriented and being more appreciative of friends and relationships (Silverman, 1988). For both, there remains the possibility of forming love relationships with new partners.

Summary and Conclusion

A wedding announces role changes for the bride and groom. How that happens changes from one time and place to another, and has become increasingly vague in the postindustrial era. Today's couples are increasingly free to negotiate their own role relationships rather than arriving at agreement by spontaneous consensus.

Blood and Wolfe conducted pioneering studies of conjugal power. Their resource theory of power remains important. It seems to provide good explanations for differences in power among women, but is less explanatory for men. Gender-based theories of conjugal power also have adherents, as do human capital and empowerment theories. Married relationships have also become increasingly egalitarian, as determined by different measures of, and theories about, conjugal power.

Newlyweds negotiate several role relationships, working out their own marital scripts using social expectations as a starting point. Utilitarian and intrinsic marriages are determined by the "why" of the marital relationship.

Couples have a number of role relationships to negotiate: sexual, provider, housekeeper, religion, friendship, child socialization, child care, therapeutic, recreational and kinship. Couples also develop a generalized script based on the basic "why" of their relationship.

Family scholars have developed a number of indicators of marital quality, including marital happiness and marital stability. Several factors are associated with marital happiness and life satisfaction.

Developmental theories look at the "life cycle" of marriages. Specific points in the life cycle, such as the "empty nest" period and retirement, pose challenges for couples. Considerable research has been done on the effect of life-cycle changes on marital quality, with confusing and sometimes contradictory results.

In conclusion, this chapter focused more on the micro-sociological processes and outcomes involved in marriages. It should be apparent that measuring the "goodness" or "badness" of relationship is difficult, and not all measures get the same results. Some unhappy marriages, for example, are nonetheless quite stable.

Just as a couple negotiates a marriage, their negotiations continue when children must be taken into account. This is the topic of the next chapter.

Rethinking in Context If you could ask a couple five questions to find out how good their marriage is, what would those questions be? Why? Would your questions be different for young than for old couples? Why, why not? Assuming you get married, what would you like to be able to say about your marriage when you look back at it at age 85?

Additional Resources

Couples processes

Blumstein, Philip, & Pepper Schwartz. 1983. *American Couples*. New York: Pocket Books.

Duck, Steve. 1994. *Meaningful Relationships: Talking Sense, and Relating*. Newbury Park, CA: Sage.

Fitzpatrick, Mary Anne. 1988. *Between Husbands and Wives: Communication in Marriage*. Newbury Park, CA: Sage.

Gottman, John. 1994. *Why Marriages Succeed or Fail*. New York: Simon & Schuster.

Johnson, Walton R., & D. Michael Warren, eds. 1993. *Inside the Mixed Marriages: Accounts of Changing Attitudes, Patterns, and Perceptions of Cross-Cultural and Interracial Marriages*. Lanham, MD: University Press of America.

Noller, Patricia, & Mary Anne Fitzpatrick. 1993. *Communication in Family Relationships*. Boston: Allyn and Bacon.

Schwartz, Pepper. 1994. *Peer Marriage: How Love Between Equals Really Works*. New York: Free Press.

Aging and care giving

Albert, Steven M., Maria G. Cattell, & Albert Cattell. 1994. *Old Age in Global Perspective: Cross-Cultural and Cross-National Views*. New York: G. K. Hall.

Brubaker, Timothy H., ed. 1990. *Family Relationships in Later Life*. Newbury Park, CA: Sage.

Hooyman, Nancy. 1995. *Feminist Perspectives on Family Care*. Newbury Park, CA: Sage.

Power and decision making

Becker, Gary S. 1991. *A Treatise on the Family*. Cambridge: Harvard University Press.

Kupers, Terry Allen. 1993. *Revisioning Men's Lives: Gender, Intimacy, and Power*. New York: Guilford.

Scanzoni, John. 1982. *Sexual Bargaining: Power Politics in the American Marriage*, 2nd ed. Chicago: University of Chicago Press.

Internet Sites

The American Association of Marriage and Family Therapy
http://www.aamft.org/

The Coalition for Marriage, Family and Couples Education
http://www.smartmarriages.com/

A British relationship study group
http://www.oneplusone.org.uk/

Marriage support
http://www.couples-place.com/

For links to these sites and additional resources, visit the *Families in Context* Web site at:
http://sociology.wadsworth.com

Chapter 13

Parents and Children

Prelude

Thomas grew up an only child in a middle-class home. He was seldom around younger children when he was growing up and didn't give much thought to raising children of his own. His wife, Terri, was the middle child of three in a working-class home. She was frequently around the smaller children in her neighborhood and, at a young age, baby-sat her younger cousins.

After Thomas and Terri had their two children, Terri could call her mom or aunt or cousins when she had concerns about parenting. Thomas read a few books about parenting, but the books sometimes contradicted what Terri did.

Terri was a strict parent, as hers had been. She never doubted that her father loved her, but he had believed that "children should be seen and not heard." The most important thing to him was to get the children to behave, and he meted out harsh punishments when they didn't.

Compared to Terri, Thomas was a very permissive parent. Whatever the children wanted to do was pretty much okay with him. He admired the children's creativity, even if it took the form of drawing on their bedroom wall with crayons. It was their room, after all, and it could always be repainted later.

Thomas usually let Terri have her way in decisions about the children, but occasionally the two would get into serious arguments. With help from friends and frank discussions with their relatives, they decided that maybe Terri was too authoritarian and Thomas was too permissive. They worked on finding a different approach that they could both agree on. And the children turned out fine.

When a father and mother have learned very different approaches to child rearing, how do they decide what to do?

Thinking Ahead What things about the way you were raised would you like to change if you raise (or have raised) children? What things would you like to do the same way? What things have changed about society since your parents were young that call for different ways of raising children today?

everal theoretical perspectives have organized our thinking about the socialization process, and have influenced parenting scripts that develop among today's couples. Not all children are raised by both of their biological parents. Some are raised by one parent, others by grandparents or other relatives, and some by foster parents. Some are raised by parents who are lesbian or gay. A discussion of the influence of those diverse families on children will conclude this chapter. First, we will put the socialization process in its historical and social context.

Socialization in Context

The socialization process operates quite differently in different times and places. We will first look at a continuum that helps define the kinds of socialization processes, then take a more detailed look at a history of the way the parent-child interaction has been perceived.

The Socialization Continuum

A major function of the family institution is socialization of the young, teaching them the roles, values, and norms of their society. Most socialization occurs in interaction with other individuals, either in a **primary relationship** or a **secondary relationship**.

The family is the most common example of primary relationships, where persons interact in more than one role. A married man and woman might interact together in such roles as friends, child-care givers, lovers, economic consumers, co-therapists, recreators, game players, housekeepers, social analysts and debaters. Together they would be the major socializers of their children.

Primary relationship: Continuing interaction by individuals in more than one role; characterized by personal, direct, and intimate interaction. **Secondary relationship:** Continuing interaction by individuals in only one role; characterized by impersonal interaction for a specific, practical purpose.

Individuals also form secondary relationships, where the interaction is in a specific role relationship such as teacher-student, customer-clerk, and worker-boss. These relationships can also be important in the socialization process, especially as individuals get older.

The socialization process varies from one society to another, as Figure 13.1 portrays. Very traditional, slowly changing societies would be close to point A on the socialization continuum. This would be the case in hunting-gathering and many agrarian societies. Socialization resulted in **orderly replacement**, which means that children grew up to have virtually the same values and norms as their parents and grandparents. There were no generation gaps in these societies. The elderly family and kin members, who controlled the socialization process, provided the role models with which the young identified. The elderly were respected and admired for their knowledge.

Movement toward point B on the continuum results in decreasing control of socialization by the family. The process is increasingly controlled by such extrafamilial agencies as education, government, religion, the military, and the media. Younger persons no longer fully identify with their parents and other family members, so finding role models is difficult. In these faster-changing societies, the elderly might be seen as outdated.

The United States and other postindustrial societies are somewhere near point B. In most two-parent families, both parents work. The increasing number of single parents also need paid employment. Increasingly, then, socialization is done by day-care centers, baby-sitters, and other extrafamilial agencies.

At point C on the continuum there is essentially no socialization. Each generation would redefine the culture for itself. Although some societies go through short periods of rapid change, such as the United States did in the 1960s, no society could sustain itself at this extreme end of the continuum; it is a hypothetical ideal type.

Historical Images of Parents and Children

Images of children, and how they are to be raised, change from one time and place to another. In most hunting and gathering societies, the responsibility of raising a child is spread among several adults. As we saw in chapter 3, a child might have several adults who are referred to as "mother" and "father." The idea that just one or two adults should have the full responsibility for a child is a relatively recent notion.

In hunting-gathering societies, keeping track of one's exact age was probably uncommon. In many pre-agrarian cultures, individuals were thought to belong to one of only two major age groups—children or adults. With a rite of passage, often associated with puberty, they moved from one group to another.

According to many historians, the idea of "childhood," as a phase distinct from infancy, adolescence, and

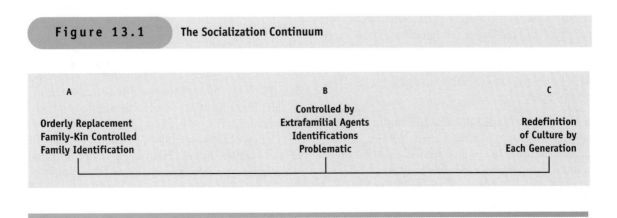

Figure 13.1   **The Socialization Continuum**

A	B	C
Orderly Replacement Family-Kin Controlled Family Identification	Controlled by Extrafamilial Agents Identifications Problematic	Redefinition of Culture by Each Generation

Source: Adams, Bert N. 1995. *The Family: A Sociological Interpretation.* Fort Worth: Harcourt Brace. Page 108.

Orderly replacement: Socialization in which each generation is an essential duplicate of the preceding generation.

In this 10th-century European painting, like others of its time, the infant has an adult-looking face and body.

adulthood, is a social construction not found until the industrial revolution. Ariès (1962) concluded that the idea of childhood did not exist in medieval Europe, and developed only slowly since then (see Finding Out 13.1).

The Emergence of Modern Childhood

Demos (1970) concluded that children in the early American Plymouth Colony were little different than the medieval European children studied by Ariès. More modern ideas about children began to appear in the middle part of the 18th century and became widespread during the 19th century (Carlson, 1990). Rousseau, a Swiss philosopher, introduced a new perspective in his 1762 book *Emile.* He wrote that children have several stages of development, each requiring special attention from parents and educators. Treating children in a way not appropriate to their age, by expecting moral reasoning from a 6-year-old, for example, could damage the child.

Another indication of the change in the way children were perceived was development of a literature designed especially for children. These books were not just for educational purposes, but also provided entertainment. (Degler, 1980; Greenleaf, 1978). At the same time, advice books for parents began to appear. Although the 19th-century advice varied from one book to another, just as it does today, all agreed on two related points: children required special treatment and care because they were different from adults, and traditional child-rearing approaches, handed down from generation to generation, were no longer adequate (Carlson, 1990).

The exact causes of the shift in the view of children, and child raising, is not fully understood. Earlier historians, including Ariès (1962), believed that a decline in mortality rates of children allowed parents to develop closer emotional ties to their children, with less fear of having to face the grief of a child's death. More recent investigation, however, has found that changes in views of childhood occurred more than 100 years before significant declines in death rates. Shorter's (1975) conclusion reversed the traditional explanation. He argued that changes in the view of children resulted in better care, which in turn lowered the death rate.

A third school of thought is that industrialization required a separation of parents, especially fathers, from children. Although early factories employed children, that practice was virtually ended by the early part of the 20th century (Carlson, 1990). Children were sent to school rather than to work, which postponed their assumption of adult responsibilities. As educational requirements increased, a longer period of adolescence developed, further postponing the assumption of work roles and increasing the dependence of adolescents on their parents. The "invention" of adolescence in North America was largely a result of the industrial revolution (Fasick, 1994). Along with the change in modes of production came better scholarship and research on children.

Whatever the cause, today's parents have a different view of children and of child rearing than was prevalent just a few generations ago. Harkness, Super, and Keefer (1992) found that today's parents rely heavily on the belief that children go through several "stages" when they describe their children.

American parents also refer frequently to degrees of "independence" demonstrated by their developing offspring. Middle-class American parents, at least, refer frequently to child-rearing "experts" who write books and appear on television talk shows providing advice and explanations about children. They also learn from a

13.1 | Finding Out

Centuries of Childhood

Philippe Ariès (1962), a French demographic historian, accomplished a ground-breaking study of the history of childhood in Europe. He concluded that the concept of "childhood" gradually evolved in Europe, not reaching anything like its present meaning until the 18th or 19th century.

Ariès used content analysis of diaries, theological and philosophical works, and personal letters written during the time in question. Perhaps his most impressive analysis was based on medieval and Renaissance paintings. He found that in the 10th century, artists depicted a child only as a small-scale adult.

Ariès also found that there was no distinction in the way young persons and adults dressed. There were separate toys for infants, but not for older children or adolescents. Children as young as 8 years old worked alongside adults and were even employed as soldiers. Others were apprenticed to craftsmen and worked for board and room. In fact, where a word such as "child" did appear, it did not refer solely to a young person but also to a servant or other worker who performed menial tasks. This implies that a young person, even of the upper classes, was put in the same category as the less-skilled servants.

For most persons, all household events occurred in the same room. Paintings show children and adults together engaged in singing, conversation or eating, without respect to age differences.

Perhaps because children were not believed to occupy a separate stage of life, they were not singled out for abuse. Ariès (1962:128) wrote, "In medieval society the idea of childhood did not exist; this is not to suggest that children were neglected, forsaken, or despised." Because of the high infant mortality rate, however, he did find some evidence that very young infants "did not count" when human interactions were considered.

Ariès's conclusion that "childhood" did not exist until the era of industrialization has not been without its critics. His method had a built-in class bias, since only the wealthy could afford to hire artists, or learn to read and write. His sources provided little way to know whether the masses shared the worldview of the privileged class.

Even using similar methods, other researchers have formed different opinions. Shahar (1990) concluded that medieval children were perceived as different from adults and that parents did make an emotional investment in infants. Shahar also argued that medieval adults recognized a period of infancy lasting until about age 7, a stage of childhood lasting until age 12 for girls and 14 for boys, and adolescence from then until marriage or assumption of other adult responsibilities. Like other researchers, however, Shahar concurs that medieval children were not seen in exactly the same way as today's youngsters. Although Ariès might have overstated the case, all historians of the family and of childhood are in his debt.

---

network of friends who are experiencing, or have gone through, the same "stages" with their children (Harkness, Super, & Keefer, 1992).

Becoming Parents: Rescripting the Conjugal Unit

Increasing numbers of marriages involve children from the very beginning. Divorced parents and never-married parents, and their new marital partners, find themselves in blended families immediately. We will discuss these families later in chapter 15. In the more traditional marriage, partners have some period of time for just the two of them before the arrival of the first child, an event that is associated with major changes for the couple.

Reasons for Having Children

A good many children are conceived because a sex act with recreational purpose becomes procreative by accident or bad planning. Nonetheless, most of these children are valued once they are born, and the vast majority of first-married couples wish to have at least one child.

Historically, most couples agreed to become parents by spontaneous consensus, following the pronatalist expectations of their environment. Declining family size and an increase in the age at which women bear their first child both indicate that pronatalism has decreased somewhat in the postindustrial era. America has not, however, become an antinatalist society. A recent poll found only 4% of adult respondents who said they did not have children, did not want them, and were glad they did not have them. Professional women with nontraditional gender expectations and several years of post–high school education are most likely to fall into this group (Gallop & Newport, 1990).

When asked the ideal number of children to have, only 3.7% of married respondents answered zero or one. Nearly 65 percent preferred two children, and just over 31% preferred three or more (Davis & Smith, 1998). There was no significant difference in the answers given by men and women. A component of pronatalism has been the belief that it was bad for a youngster to be an only child. That belief continues to exist in the United States today, in spite of evidence to the contrary. "Onlies" have considerably higher educational and intellectual achievement than do children with siblings. They have no more health or adjustment problems than children from larger families (Gee, 1992; Blake, 1981, 1989, 1991).

Religion is related to pronatalism. Catholics (47%) are most likely to prefer three or more children, followed by conservative Protestants (42%) and Jews (41%). Persons with no religion were least likely (25%) to want three or more children (Davis & Smith, 1972–98). People from large families of orientation are more likely to want large families of procreation; 48% of respondents with four or more siblings preferred having three or more children. Less than 30% of only children wanted three or more children of their own (Davis & Smith, 1972–98).

Race is also a factor. Among married individuals, Blacks (54.5%) are more likely than Whites (38.6%) to prefer having three or more children. Hispanics have more children than do either Whites or Blacks.

Although negative aspects of having children exist, today's parents generally see more advantages than disadvantages. Neal, Groat, and Wicks (1989) asked a random sample of 600 adults in their early years of marriage about their views of having children. Respondents valued children highly because they were thought to be necessary for "having a real family life" and because they were seen as "sources of love and affection." Children were also seen as a protection against loneliness and the impersonality of the world at large. Only a few

respondents valued children as a way of achieving spiritual fulfillment or achieving adult status.

Although family size is declining, the majority of couples still have more than one child. Although onlies might be subject to more pressure to achieve, at least part of the reason for the difference in achievement level of only compared with other children is that family resources are diluted by additional children. This includes not only money and material goods, but parents' time, emotional and physical energy, attention, and enrichment opportunities such as travel and music lessons (Blake, 1989; Rossi & Rossi, 1990).

Yamaguchi and Ferguson (1995) tested several variables that might affect a woman's decision to have a second or subsequent birth. Women who stopped after the first child were more likely to be highly educated, older, and White. Married women were more likely to have a second child than were unmarried women. The sex of the first child was not related to the decision.

If forced to choose, Americans would still prefer to have a boy baby than a girl, just as they did several decades ago. The Gallup Poll in both 1941 and 2000 asked respondents "Suppose you could only have one child. Would you prefer that it be a boy or a girl?" The "Doesn't Matter" option was not provided as a possible answer, but 23% of the respondents volunteered that answer in 1941; in 2000, 25 % did so. In 2000, 55% of men and 32% of women preferred a boy, while 18% of men and 35% of women preferred a girl. These figures are similar to the ones found in 1941 (see Table 13.1). Perhaps surprisingly, the youngest respondents (ages 18–29) had by far the strongest preference for boys of any age group.

A large part of the preference for boys is accounted for by the belief that boys are easier to raise than girls. In 2000, 53% of adults thought boys were easier to raise while 28% thought girls were. Most respondents who thought boys were easier to raise preferred to have a boy, while most who thought girls were easier would prefer to have a girl.

The Expense of Having Children

Becoming a parent is a tremendous commitment in time, emotion, and money. The dollar cost is easiest to calculate, and can seem staggering. Medical delivery expenses can easily exceed $5,000; adoptions are typically even more costly (Johnston, 1994).

Total-cost estimates of raising a child to maturity vary considerably. One general guideline is that the total cost of raising a child, not including a college education, is

Table 13.1	Response to a Question, "Suppose You Could Only Have One Child. Would You Prefer That It Be a Boy or a Girl?," by Sex and Age, in Percentages, 1941 and 2000			

Category	Boy	Girl	Doesn't Matter (Volunteered)	Not Sure, No Opinion
Total, 1941	38	24	23	15
Total, 2000	42	27	25	6
Gender, 2000				
Men	55	18	21	6
Women	32	35	28	5

Source: Simmons, Wendy W. 2000. "When It Comes to Having Children, Americans Still Prefer Boys." Gallup Poll, December 26. http://www.gallup.com/poll/releases/pr001226.asp.

about three times the parents' annual income (McLeod, 1991; in Rice, 1993).

Somewhat more accurate estimates are provided by the U.S. Department of Agriculture (1999). Table 13.2 provides estimates of the total cost of raising a child who was born in 1999 until the child's 18th birthday. These estimates vary by the income level of the parent; those in the highest third of income will spend nearly twice as much per child ($344,800) as parents in the lowest one third of income ($174,090). These are costs to the parents only, and do not include money spent by schools, grandparents, welfare agencies, and other entities. Nor do the estimates include college expenses, the cost of large weddings, or other expenses that might occur after the child's 18th birthday.

The figures in Table 13.2 are for the youngest child in a two-parent, two-child family. An only child would generally incur more expenditures; the amount spent per child goes down for each additional child the couple has, although total child expenditures go up with more children. Expenditures for an only child will amount to about 26% of household expenditures. If a couple has three children in their home, about 48% of household expenditures will be spent on the children (USDA, 1999:t. 11).

Table 13.3 breaks the expenditures down by category. Housing is the biggest expense included. Parents might not think of including housing as a cost per child, but bigger apartments and homes, as well as additional furniture, utilities and other items, make housing more costly for parents than for nonparents. Food is the next most expensive item, followed by clothing.

Annual expenditures per child vary considerably from one region of the country to another. A middle-income, husband-wife, two-child family will average $9,530 for a child 15–17 years old. For such families living in cities, expenditures were $9,090 in the midwest, $9,740 in the south, $10,010 in the northeast, and $10,360 in the west. The same family's expenditures in rural areas averaged $9,140 (USDA, 1999).

Quite clearly, raising children is an expensive proposition. In purely economic terms, the money spent is a poor investment for couples in postindustrial societies; the parents will never recoup the expenditures when their children are grown. For most parents, however, the money spent is well worth it for the other rewards that children bring.

The Transition to Parenthood

As we saw in chapter 12, negotiation is necessary for couples to develop their mutual marital script. The arrival of a child requires considerable renegotiation of the role relationship. During the 1950s, a decade sometimes considered the "golden age" of the American nuclear family, E. E. LeMasters (1957) interviewed couples about the transition to parenthood. Eight of every 10 couples reported a severe or extensive crisis in their adjustment to the birth of their first child.

Table 13.2	Estimated Annual Family Expenditures on Children Born in 1999, by Income Group, Average for the United States

| | | Income Group | | |
Year	Age of Child	Low	Middle	High
1999	<1	$6,080	$8,450	$12,550
2000	1	6,340	8,810	13,090
2001	2	6,610	9,190	13,650
2002	3	7,050	9,830	14,570
2003	4	7,350	10,250	15,200
2004	5	7,670	10,690	15,850
2005	6	8,120	11,200	16,360
2006	7	8,470	11,680	17,070
2007	8	8,840	12,180	17,800
2008	9	9,250	12,630	18,400
2009	10	9,640	13,180	19,200
2010	11	10,060	13,740	20,020
2011	12	11,850	15,560	22,290
2012	13	12,360	16,230	23,250
2013	14	12,890	16,930	24,250
2014	15	13,260	17,920	25,950
2015	16	13,830	18,690	27,070
2016	17	14,420	19,500	28,230
Total		**$174,090**	**$236,660**	**$344,800**

Note: Cost is for the youngest child in a husband-wife family with two children.
Source: U.S. Department of Agriculture, Center for Nutrition Policy and Promotion. 1999. "Expenditures on Children by Families: 1999 Annual Report," Table 12. Online at
http://www.usda.gov:80/cnpp/Crc/crc1999.PDF.

The LeMasters study was done at a time when most women became stay-at-home moms. Difficulties new mothers experienced include chronic tiredness, a sense of being too socially isolated and confined in the home, and, for many, the loss of fulfillment from the work role. New fathers were concerned about the reduced amount of intimacy and sexual responsiveness from their wives, some general displeasure from parenthood, and dealing with the costs of parenthood (LeMasters, 1957).

While the transition to parenthood is a joyful time for many couples, more recent studies generally confirm LeMasters's view that the transition is highly stressful. In general, studies find that birth of the first child is associated with declining satisfaction with marriage, with sex life, and with life in general for both husbands and wives (Belsky, Spanier, & Rovine, 1983; Cowan et al.,

1985; LaRossa & LaRossa, 1989). Women who remain in the labor force generally experience a decrease in job satisfaction (Holtzman & Glass, 1999).

Whether parents are generally gratified or are bothered by their new status, they consistently report that dealing with new time constraints is a major issue. LaRossa (1983) found that not only was there less time for sleep and sex, but there was also less time for television watching and couple communication. Time management and role conflict become more crucial, just when there is less time for couples to negotiate solutions.

Some children who are the result of unwanted pregnancies become quite wanted after they are born, but the birth of an unwanted child is especially related to a negative and long-term effect on the mother. Mothers with unwanted births had higher levels of depression

Table 13.3	Estimated Annual Family Cost of a 15–17-Year-Old Child, by Expenditure Type, Type of Parent, and Before–Tax Family Income, 1999

	Single-Parent Family		Husband-Wife Family		
Type of Expenditure	Income Less Than $36,800	Income $36,800 or More	Income Less Than $36,800	Income $36,800– $61,900	Income over $61,900
Housing	$2,560	$4,960	$1,800	$2,620	$4,470
Food	1,600	2,340	1,680	2,000	2,400
Transportation	910	2,140	1,350	1,720	2,180
Clothing	850	1,120	680	800	1,030
Health Care	470	910	550	700	800
Child Care, Education	270	930	360	730	1,330
Miscellaneous	580	1,720	630	960	1,590
Total	$7,240	$14,120	$7,050	$9,530	$13,800

Notes: Cost is for the youngest child in a two-child family. To estimate total cost for two children, multiply above total by 2. For cost of an only child, multiply total by 1.24. For per child cost of three or more, multiply total by 0.77.

Source: U.S. Department of Agriculture, Center for Nutrition Policy and Promotion. 1999. "Expenditures on Children by Families: 1999 Annual Report," Tables 1 and 7. Online at **http://www.usda.gov:80/cnpp/Crc/crc1999.PDF**.

and lower levels of happiness than did other mothers. Quality of relationship with the child remains lower well beyond adolescence, and even relationships with other children suffer when one is unwanted. Mothers of unwanted children spank more and spend less leisure time with their children, who have more health problems than wanted children (Barber, Axinn, & Thornton, 1999). It is quite possible, however, that a woman who does not want a child at a particular time might be in difficulty in ways, such as unemployment, poverty, or an abusive relationship, that make some of the difference (Kost, Landry, & Darroch, 1998).

Alice Rossi (1968) wrote a classic study of the transition to parenthood, comparing it to other kinds of role changes such as job changes or getting married. She concluded that, in modern society, the parenthood transition is more difficult for five reasons. First, pronatalist cultural sentiments lead some persons to become parents when they might actually prefer not to.

Second, parenthood is virtually irrevocable and pervasive. A person can quit a job or divorce a spouse, but parenthood is for life. Not only is it forever, it is for 24 hours each day, 7 days each week, 52 weeks each year. Parents are obviously not with their children all that time, but they are "on call" and must take the children

into consideration in all their plans. Even when the child goes to school, a parent has to be available, or must make child-care arrangements, when the child is sick and during school vacations. Even after children grow up and leave home, a commitment to them remains.

Thirdly, the transition to parenthood is abrupt. An official marriage is abrupt also, but a couple has generally spent some time interacting and getting to know each other before the wedding. With childbirth, the child is suddenly there. The child is expected, but the implications of its arrival often are not.

Fourth, child-raising norms are not as clear and well known as they once were. Social, legal, and economic changes, as well as a proliferation of "expert" advice givers, often leave parents without clear guidance.

Finally, the transition to parenthood affects the husband-wife relationship more directly and pervasively than most other role changes. The time stress and role changes forever alter the relationship that had been developed by the couple. Even their friendship roles are likely to change. They will begin to interact less with friends who remain childless, while increasing their interactions with other couples who also have children.

Breast feeding provides health benefits to infants, along with an opportunity for special bonding between mother and child.

The extent to which the transition to parenthood might be experienced as a crisis is not the same for couples in all social classes. LeMasters (1957) found the most severe crises among women who held professional positions prior to childbirth. Presumably, they felt the greatest loss if they gave up or interrupted their professional and career plans.

More recent studies confirm LeMasters's findings (McLanahan & Adams, 1989; Voydanoff, 1989). Middle-class families have more difficulty with the transition than do working-class ones. This probably is because middle-class persons, especially women, are more career-oriented than working-class persons, have less experience caring for children, and begin with less traditional expectations about gender roles. In addition, the husband-wife bond might be stronger, so its disruption might result in a greater sense of loss (Jacoby, 1969). Finally, middle-class couples generally wait longer before the birth of their first child (Rubin, 1976), giving them an opportunity to develop a well-established mutual script that is more difficult to renegotiate.

In earlier societies, the transition to parenthood was probably not as difficult because responsibility for children was diffused through a network of extended family and community members. Adults would have continual exposure to children. The arrival of their own first child would not occasion as abrupt a change in their lifestyles.

In spite of the stress, the transition to parenthood is certainly not all bad. While romance might decrease, the sense of partnership with one's spouse is likely to increase (Belsky, Spanier, & Rovine, 1983). Fathers might get a greater sense of being in a family, and the mother's overall life satisfaction can improve (Grossman, Eichler, & Winikoff, 1980).

Couples find a variety of ways of dealing with the stress of the transition to parenthood. For some, the increased love and affection the arrival of their infant brings can be resources on which the couple can draw. Couples who have close contact with extended family members can get practical support in the form of occasional child care, as well as emotional support and child-rearing guidance. Such extended networks do, however, often encourage more traditional gender expectations and child-rearing practices than the young parents themselves might prefer (Riley, 1990).

Some couples find support through their religious affiliations or through quasi-kin groups arranged by mental health professionals or other parents. There is some evidence that these groups are helpful in reducing the feelings of social isolation, and they might help increase marital satisfaction and stability (Cowan, 1988).

Ultimately, adjustment to parenthood is most successful for those couples who had the best relationship before childbirth (Wallace & Gotlib, 1990). Strong relationships, good communication, and good problem solving before childbirth predict higher marital and personal happiness after the transition to parenthood (Feldman, 1987). For mothers more than fathers, having marital difficulties before the first birth shows less sensitivity, warmth, and involvement with infants (Cox et al., 1999). In the other direction, when fathers are more positively involved in caregiving, marital satisfaction is likely to be higher (Levy-Schiff, 1994).

Parenting satisfaction is significantly higher for married parents, especially those with high marital satisfaction. Greater satisfaction is also experienced by those who are parenting their own children rather than stepchildren, and by mothers more than by fathers (Rogers & White, 1998). For parents who adopted a young child, parental well-being is similar to that of biological parents (Borders et al., 1998).

The Traditionalizing Influence of Parenthood

When couples have a child, their role relationships tend to become more traditional. Fathers in two-parent families spend less time in child care than do mothers (Aldous, Mulligan, & Bjarnason, 1998; Barnett & Shen, 1997). This is particularly true with preschoolers, when fathers handle about one third as much of the child care as do mothers; with older children, fathers do about two thirds as much as the mothers (Aldous, Mulligan, & Bjarnason, 1998).

A considerable body of research has found this **traditionalizing influence of parenthood** on couples (Cowan et al., 1985; Cowan & Cowan, 2000; Collins & Coltrane, 1995; Entwisle & Doering, 1981; LaRossa & LaRossa, 1981). Women assume more of the responsibility for child and home care and less of the economic responsibility. Men increase their responsibility for working outside the home but do less of the child care than their wives.

Today about 73% of single mothers with children under 18 are in the paid labor force. In about 64% of married couples with children, both parents work; only the father works in about 29% of the cases and only the mother does so in 4%. Working mothers include 62% of married women with a child less than 1 year old. By contrast, about 96% of men the same age are working. Of those in paid labor, mothers are much more likely to work part time than are fathers (*Statistical Abstract 1999*: t. 659, 657, 660).

The traditionalizing effect of parenthood is related to different images of the roles of women and men in general, and of mothers and fathers in particular. The "sex-irreducible role," in which men impregnate and women menstruate, gestate, and lactate (see chapter 1), has no direct bearing on the role division for a couple until they experience a pregnancy. The woman carries the fetus and bears the child. If breast-feeding is to be done, the woman will do it. As these role distinctions are played out by a couple, the sex-related and sex-arbitrary roles are likely to become more traditional as well.

No society has ever assigned primary child-care responsibility to men (Popenoe, 1996). If one parent is expected to become the primary caregiver, that parent will be the mother. Although there has been considerable role change, that remains the expectation in the United States today. Images of a "good mother" change over time (Thurer, 1994), but mothers in the United States today believe that they, not the fathers, other relatives, or unrelated day-care providers, are the ideal caregivers, at least until the children enter first grade (Mason & Kuhlthau, 1989). Most college women indicate a desire to interrupt their careers for child rearing. Both male and female college students have a more positive image of a woman who interrupts her employment or remains unemployed after childbirth (Bridges & Orza, 1993).

Explanations for Gender-Divergent Parenting

The fact that mothers and fathers approach parenting differently is related to virtually all other gender differences, and it has a variety of theoretical explanations in the social sciences. Sociobiologists and structure-functionalists focus on the importance of the sex-irreducible and sex-related roles. Concepts such as the "maternal instinct" have been used to argue that women are naturally more nurturing and better at child care. Explanations of this sort have historically been used not just to explain the role differences, but also to prescribe them. Appeals to biological differences have been used to exclude women from the opportunity to compete on an equal footing with men in the economic, religious, and political realms (Tavris & Wade, 1984), and to exclude men from equality in caretaker roles.

Partly because of the political uses to which biology-based explanations have been put, social scientists have more recently embraced explanations that assume that nurturing, empathy, commitment to paid labor, and virtually all other personal attributes are learned characteristics. Both social learning theorists and symbolic interactionists stress the learned and socially constructed nature of gender and parenting roles.

Feminist explanations add that the learning of parental roles occurs in a particular social-political system. From this perspective, the housewife/mother role consists primarily of mundane, low-status tasks. In a patriarchal society, women are forced into an unfair share of the burden because they lack equal power in families as well as in society at large. From this perspective,

---

Traditionalizing influence of parenthood: The tendency of couples to develop more traditional, gender-specific, roles once they have a child.

The term "Mr. Mom" implies that mothering and fathering are different activities.

women express their gendered selves by being nurturing and child-oriented, while men become work-oriented and largely insensitive to the emotional needs of women and children (Collins & Coltrane, 1994).

Because of the historical connection between women and the parenting role, the importance of the mother to the welfare of children has long been recognized, and perhaps even overemphasized in 20th-century America. Freudian and other psychological approaches appeared to blame the mother for practically everything that could possibly go wrong with a child. An influential series of studies was done on 45 institutionalized infants who were orphaned during World War II in England (Spitz, 1945; 1946). The infants were fed by nurses and their other physical needs were met, but there was little physical contact or evidence of emotional ties between the nurses and the children. Average developmental

scores of the infants deteriorated rapidly. Within 2 years after their institutionalization began, one third of the infants had died. Nine had left the hospital, but the 21 who remained were severely retarded. This study dramatically demonstrated the importance to infants of having warm, close, stable relationships with caring adults (Michener & Delamater, 1994).

Although the general finding of the study remains largely unchallenged, it was reinterpreted in ensuing years. Some scholars concluded that there must be a warm, continuous, nearly exclusive relationship with the mother, without which a child would suffer from serious **maternal deprivation** (Burchinal, 1963; Bowlby, 1953). Fear of the consequences of maternal deprivation prevented many women from returning to the labor force after they became mothers, and it was used by many to formulate social policy designed to keep women in their homes.

Just as the overly deterministic view about the influence of mothers is declining somewhat, the view of the father's role is also changing. A traditional belief is that fathers have little involvement in parenting (LaRossa & Reitzes, 1995), but that is not entirely the case. A somewhat biased view of father-child interaction might have resulted from omitting fathers from studies on parenting; when letters from men as well as women are included in analyses of early 20th-century parenting, an image of more active fathering emerges (LaRossa & Reitzes, 1995).

Another problem in the research is the way parenting has been defined. The instrumental role of providing food, clothing, and shelter is essential to the well-being of children; that has been a father's responsibility. These contributions, however, have sometimes not been counted as "active parental participation" but the "good provider" role remains an important one, both for fathers and their children (Christiansen & Palkovitz, 2001).

While the importance of the mother's interaction with children has long been established, there are two schools of thought about the importance of close relationships between children and their fathers (Amato, 1994). One camp argues that father involvement is very important in several areas of a child's development (Lamb, 1987; Snarey, 1993; Williams & Radin, 1999). The other school believes that, while the economic

---

Maternal deprivation theory: The theory, now largely discredited, that a child must have a warm, continuous, exclusive, and virtually full-time emotional involvement with its mother.

participation of fathers is an important contribution, the presence or absence of a father's interaction and nurturing makes little difference in the way children turn out.

Several recent studies have attempted to resolve the question of father importance. Amato (1994) studied a nationwide sample of young adults. He measured their general happiness with life, the satisfaction they got from their friends, the amount of psychological distress, and their self-esteem. Young adults who had a close relationship with their mother had significantly better scores in all four categories. Those who had a close relationship with their fathers had better scores in happiness, life satisfaction, and lack of distress. The self-esteem scores showed no statistically significant difference for closeness to father. Both men and women had more positive scores when they had higher father closeness; even after divorce a close relationship to the father had positive effects, and closeness to stepfathers was also related to positive outcomes for young adults.

Children living in father-present families have fewer problems in school and better math and reading scores (Teachman et al., 1998). Other research confirms that having involved, nurturing fathers is associated with greater intellectual development of the children, better academic outcomes, better social adjustment, and greater ability to empathize (Lamb, 1987; Radin & Russell, 1983; Snarey, 1993; Amato, 1994). The father's financial contribution accounts for many of the advantages of father-present homes.

Positive outcomes do not require that fathers be equally involved with the children. In fact, there is some evidence that completely equal marriages might have adverse effects on children. Booth and Amato (1994) compared adults who had been raised in families with more traditional parenting roles with those in which their father and mother were essentially androgynous. While there was little or no difference in most of the measured variables, older children of nontraditional (egalitarian) marriages were less likely to reside with their parents and had slightly poorer relationships with their fathers. This was largely because the nontraditional parents were more likely to get divorced. Children of nontraditional marriages were also more likely to have nontraditional gender attitudes, and daughters were more likely to cohabit.

For the marriages that do not end, however, nontraditional parenting roles do not appear to have a negative effect on children. A review of the few major studies that have been done on primary-care-giving fathers in intact families concluded that there was no demonstrated harm, and perhaps some benefits, in having a "Mr. Mom." One fairly consistent, but not surprising, finding is that children who have caregiving fathers tend to develop nontraditional gender roles themselves (Radin, 1994).

It would appear that children in America today are best off when there is a sense of closeness with both mother and father. As long as the closeness exists, there is no solid evidence that either the traditional or egalitarian work and family division of labor is generally better as a socializing agent.

Because the social construction of parenting is different for men and women, maintaining close relationships with children may be more difficult for fathers than for mothers. From conception to birth, the incipient mother has rights that the father does not have. Because the fetus is part of her body, she has the right to decide whether to get an abortion or not; he has no legal voice in that matter. In only about one third of nonmarital births is there any legal action to determine fatherhood (Adams, Landsbergen, & Hecht, 1994). In virtually all such cases, even if paternity were established, the mother would become the legal custodian of the child.

Mothers are the custodial parents in about 85% of all cases of divorce involving children (*Statistical Abstract 1999*:t. 637). Communication between fathers and their noncustodial children tends to decrease over time. Mothers, and sometimes grandmothers, often serve as "maternal gatekeepers" for the father's interaction with the children (Allen & Doherty, 1996; Wattenburg, 1993). Even among married partners, mothers sometimes regulate the father-child interaction (De Luccie, 1995).

Men who consider nurturing to be central to their sense of self are significantly more involved with their children than are other men, and mothers' behaviors affect fathers' views of nurturing (Rane & McBride, 2000). As part of their maternal gatekeeper role, most women do at least some emotions work to strengthen the father-child relationship (Seery & Crowley, 2000). In particular, support for father involvement may be stronger among women with nontraditional gender role attitudes, a high sense of trust, and low hostility toward men (Hoffman & Moon, 1999).

It appears that fatherhood and motherhood are constructed differently. Mothers tend to maintain parenthood throughout life, regardless of their relationship to the child's father. Fathers, on the other hand, tend to have close relationships with children as long as they have a relationship with the child's mother, but often drift away from the child if the adult relationship ends

(Ahrons & Miller, 1993; Furstenburg & Cherlin, 1991). As Doherty, Kouneski, and Erickson (1998) put it, "in American culture, a woman is a mother all of her life, but a man is a father if he has a wife." And even if he has a wife, a poor relationship with her is quite likely to mean he will have a poor relationship with the child. Doherty et al. (1998) further suggested that, while both motherhood and fatherhood are largely socially constructed, fatherhood is more subject to environmental and cultural influences than is motherhood.

Nonparental Child Care

Child care has become more complicated now that the dual-earner family is the most common form of two-parent families with children. In most cases the mothers and fathers are gone at the same time, so nonparental child care is needed for significant periods of time. More than 25% of working couples have schedules in which the hours do not overlap because one or both are doing shiftwork or they work different days of the week. In most of these cases, fathers do the child care while they are home and the mothers are at work, while mothers do the child care when they are home, whether the father is working or not (Brayfield, 1995; Glass, 1998). Even in these situations, however, nonparental

child care is often required for part of the time because father-care covers less than 60% of the period of mothers' work hours (Glass, 1998). For only 7% of single working moms do the fathers provide the primary child care (O'Connell, 1993).

Users of Nonparental Care

In the United States nearly 13 million children under the age of 6 (60%), spend at least part of their time in a nonparental child-care arrangement of some kind. As Figure 13.2 indicates, Hispanics are least likely to use nonparental care; 54% of the children had no arrangement for child care other than parents. Whites are most likely to use nonparental child care, especially that of nonrelatives such as baby-sitters, *au pairs*, or neighborhood sitters. Blacks (31%) are most likely to have their preschoolers cared for by relatives. About a third of Black and White preschoolers, but only 17% of Hispanics, are in day-care centers, Head Start programs, or other early childhood programs.

The working status of the mother and the family income make a difference in how much nonparental care is used. When mothers work full time (35 hours per week or more), 88% of their preschoolers use some nonparental care, compared to 75% of children of mothers who work part time. Perhaps surprisingly, 32% of children whose mothers are not in the labor force have some amount of regular nonparental child care. The higher

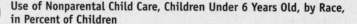

Figure 13.2 Use of Nonparental Child Care, Children Under 6 Years Old, by Race, in Percent of Children

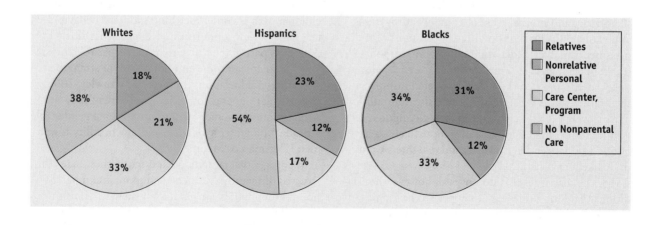

Source: *Statistical Abstract,* 1999, Table 639.

the family income, the more likely parents are to use nonparental care. Of those making $75,000 or more, 77% use nonparental care, while 50% of those making $10,000 or less do so (*Statistical Abstract 1999*: t. 639).

For children 6 years old and older, the school provides the bulk of nonparental child care. Still, nonparental care is often necessary before school, after school, or during school vacations. About 21% of 6- to 9-year-olds are primarily in the care of relatives, while another 21% use before-school or after-school day-care programs of some kind. Use of such care drops for 10- to 12-year-olds, with 17% primarily relying on relatives and 10% using before- or after-school programs (Capizzano, Tout, & Adams, 2000).

Significant numbers of children have no care from an adult for at least some of the time, usually before or after school. Such self-care, as Capizzano et al. (2000) call it, is the primary nonparental care for 5% of 6- to 9-year-olds and 24% of 10- to 12-year-olds. Ten percent of the younger group is in self-care at least some of the time, as is 35% of the older group. For the 10- to 12-year-old children, Whites (30%) are much more likely to be in self-care than Hispanics (15%) or Blacks (11%).

Consequences of Nonparental Care

Changes in patterns of child care have had economic consequences. The ability of the American economic system to sustain its productivity and maintain the high standard of living has been due in large part to the social transformation to the two-wage-earner family. This, in turn, has been made possible by the rapid growth of nonparental child care (Wojnilower, 1998). Most couples probably do not actually need to work a combined total of 80 hours per week, but they may choose to do so if good child care is available (Siegel, 1998).

One consequence has been the rapid growth in the child-care industry. Caregiving has traditionally been more a woman's role than a man's. The child-care industry reflects that expectation in that 98% of workers are women (Whitebook, 1999). While the work may be emotionally satisfying, it is generally low paid. A disproportionate number of child-care workers are non-White, many of whom are recent immigrants and have low levels of formal education. Their employers, especially of the private individual workers, are disproportionately White, well educated, and well paid. In some cases, then, the lower-paid minority workers are making it possible for middle- and upper-class couples to significantly increase their standard of living over what it

would be with just one wage-earner (Uttal & Tuominen, 1999). Consumers of public programs and child-center day care are more likely to be single mothers or couples who are struggling to make ends meet even with two incomes.

Considerable debate has ensued about the consequences of nonparental care for children. Clearly, millions of children who were exposed to nonparental care grow up with no ill effects. Nonparental care can even be positive if the parent(s) provides a destructive environment while alternative care provides an enriching one. Because of the importance of the issue, hundreds of studies have been conducted about the effect of nonparental, or more often nonmaternal, child care.

Russell (1999) conducted a meta-analysis of 101 published studies. She compared children whose mother was their care provider with children who spent at least some time in nonmaternal care. She looked at cognitive development, social-emotional qualities, behavioral outcomes, and the attachment of the children to their mothers. Differences were found in all four areas, with the nonmaternal care children having more negative outcomes. Boys fared more poorly in nonmaternal care than did girls; non-White children fared worse than did White children. The differences between the two groups of children were often small, but they were persistent and significant.

It is probably true that children in high-quality nonparental care compare favorably to those in parental care (Brown, Wood, & Harris, 1999). Several studies have found that quality of day care makes a difference in child cognitive, social, emotional, and behavioral development. In particular, better child outcomes are associated with better child-staff ratios (fewer children per staff member), smaller group size, and more caregiver training and education. Parents looking for child care are advised to pay attention to these factors (Gottfried, Bathurst, & Gottfried, 1994; National Institute of Child Health and Human Development, 1999; Burchinal, 1999; Blau, 2000).

Unfortunately, too little nonparental care is of high quality. Many parents cannot afford to pay large sums, and the low-paid work of child care is typically characterized by high turnover and a poorly educated workforce (Morris, 1999). The National Institute of Child Health and Human Development (1999) found that only 10% of providers of care to 6-month-old children met their quality standards; 34% of care for 3-year-olds did so. After reviewing several studies of child-care quality, Morris (1999:130) concluded that most child-care quality in the United States is "mediocre or worse." This might be in part because the United States lags behind other postindustrial countries in government and corporate policy about child care (Blau, 2000; Gornick, Meyers, & Ross, 1998; Morris, 1999). On a more positive note, there are a number of approaches to child care that do appear to work (Secret, Sprang, & Bradford, 1998).

Theoretical Images of Socialization

It is a primary function of families to guide the early socialization of children. Most parents would refer to this as child rearing; most social and behavioral scientists include it as part of the socialization process. We will first look at the psychological perspectives, then sociological and social-psychological ones.

Psychological Theories of Socialization

Many psychologists have studied socialization and human development. Major contributions were made by Sigmund Freud, Eric Erikson, and Jean Piaget.

The Psychoanalytic View: Sigmund Freud. Freud's image of the human personality is inherently pessimistic. He thought that humans have innate drives, especially a sexual drive known as the **libido**. It strives for immediate gratification, is selfish, and can be aggressive. Socialization is largely a process of teaching the individual to restrain his or her natural drives and to channel that energy into socially acceptable directions.

To Freud, socialization follows an individual through several stages of development named after the primary focus of the libido at each stage. Parents, especially mothers, are extremely important in successful negotiation of the developmental process. Most adult problems, Freud believed, result from things that went wrong very early in the child's life.

Because of the importance Freud placed on early infant training in the development of personality characteristics, Sewall (1952) attempted to test these elements of psychodynamic theory. He found that personality adjustment was almost totally unrelated to the heavily discussed issues of timing and type of weaning, bowel and bladder training, on-demand versus timed feeding schedules, and other issues (Eshleman, 1994).

Freud's dominance in psychiatry, socialization theory, and child rearing has waned, but his influence can still be felt. The idea that children go through discrete stages, each of which requires special guidance and understanding, is still common. His idea that many human motivations are hidden, latent, or unconscious is still widely believed.

Socialization as a Lifelong Process: Eric Erikson. Erik Erikson (1963, 1968) was a student of Freud's and built upon his theories. A major difference between the two was that, while Freud focused on socialization as a phenomenon of infancy and youth, Erikson thought human development and socialization were a lifelong process. Throughout their lives, according to Erikson, individuals go through stages in which the resolution of certain conflicts determines their ability to cope with life. Each of the eight stages involves the resolution of an issue.

Like Freud, Erikson placed great importance on the early developmental stages. Early development of a sense of self-confidence and self-worth can go a long way toward resolving some of the conflicts that arise later. Erikson's image of human nature is not quite as grim as Freud's, however, and Erikson considers more sociological variables.

Cognitive Development: Jean Piaget. Jean Piaget (1896–1980) also arrived at a developmental theory. Rather than focusing on personality development or the influence of parents on children, however, Piaget was interested in the changing thought processes of young children (Piaget & Inhelder, 1969). Piaget believed that there were some individual variations in the exact age at which children were able to do certain tasks, but the stages were fixed and could not be skipped. He allowed for some cultural and social influence on the content of development and the level of development that children might ultimately reach.

Physical development theories and research remind us that children will naturally grow out of some behaviors about which parents worry. Because young children lack the hand-eye coordination of adults, they are likely to spill their milk from time to time. Regardless of how they are treated after their spills, spilling will decrease

---

Libido: To Freud, the basic energy, primarily sexual in nature, that provides the driving force of all human behavior.

The volume conservation test is an indicator of the developmental level in Piaget's stages.

with age. Similarly, kitchen cupboards seem to be unavoidably attractive to toddlers. Whether they are scolded, spanked, ignored, hugged, pleaded with, or sent to time out, all children eventually stop playing in the cupboard. It is probably easier for everyone if the cupboards are "child-proofed" with latches or other devices until the child grows out of the urge to wreak cupboard havoc.

Sociological and Social-Psychological Theories

Some theorists put socialization more into its social context. Freud did this to some extent, but Travis Hirschi does so more. So too do Albert Bandura, George Herbert Mead, and Charles Horton Cooley.

Social Control and Bonding Theory: Travis Hirschi.
Travis Hirschi (1969) was interested in the relationship between socialization and juvenile delinquency. His view is more sociological than psychological but, like Freud, Hirschi assumed that young persons would tend to commit delinquent or deviant acts unless socialization prevented it. To Hirschi, prevention came in the form of both inner and outer forms of social bonding.

Belief. Inner bonding consists of learning the appropriate norms of a society and of developing a sense of belief in the appropriateness of the norms. Knowing right from wrong does not always result in appropriate behavior, however; the outer dimensions of social bonding are necessary also. These have three essential components: attachment, commitment, and involvement.

Attachment. The stronger the sense of attachment, or bond, between the youth and other members of society, especially law-abiding ones, the less likely the youth is to become delinquent. Early in the child's life, strong attachments to parents and other family members are particularly important. In adolescence, attachment to peers who conform to the rules becomes increasingly important.

Commitment. An investment in legitimate activities, and the rewards those activities can bring, reduces the likelihood of delinquency. The more individuals believe they stand to gain by behaving in the normatively prescribed fashion, the more they have to lose by deviating. A young person who sees no hope of rewards from "doing the right thing" is more likely to do the wrong thing.

Involvement. The expenditure of time and energy in legitimate activity reduces time and energy available for illegitimate activity. This increases conformity to the norms.

A variety of factors affect the external bonds that children develop. Rapid social or familial change can alter the attachment, commitment, and involvement of children. Parents are very important to the formation of the child's bonds; they influence not only the child's bonds to the parents themselves but to other relatives, friendship groups, and religious or social organizations. Success in school increases commitment to conventional avenues of success and achievement.

While Hirschi's theory was intended specifically as an explanation of juvenile delinquency, it serves as a more comprehensive theory of socialization. The implication of the theory is that proper parenting by adults committed to conventional values and norms, which included supervision and discipline, would significantly reduce the probability that a child would become delinquent. Successful involvement in schools and other agents of socialization also helps prevent delinquency. Hirschi's theory is not without its critics, but research done to test it has generally confirmed its validity (Pfohl, 1994).

Toward Social Learning Theory: B. F. Skinner and Albert Bandura.
Freud and Erikson were interested in the development of personality and dynamics within individuals, Piaget dealt with the development of cognitive processes, and Hirschi was concerned

with bonds and attachments between individuals and society. Behaviorists, as the name implies, are interested not in internal states, abilities, or attachments, but in observable behavior.

B. F. Skinner (1953, 1974) developed the principles of behaviorism mostly by working with pigeons and rats in the laboratory. He was interested in the impact of the **contingencies** on behavior. The basic principles of behaviorism are known to most parents who attempt to discipline their children by means of **rewards** and **punishments**. To the extent that parents are thought to control the contingencies, behaviorism confirms the importance of parental influence.

When contingencies are provided by another person or group, they are said to be social contingencies, the study of which provides the foundation of the social learning perspective. Albert Bandura (1965, 1971; Bandura & Jourden, 1991) was a pioneer in this perspective. He noted that humans are different from rats and pigeons in the way they learn. Behavioral conditioning requires that a response occur before it can be either rewarded or punished.

Through **observational learning**, however, humans can benefit from watching others. One form of this is simple **imitation**, where the child simply copies someone else's behavior. Another form of observational learning, called **modeling**, is more complex. It involves observational learning not just of discrete behaviors but of entire role performances. Rather than simply copying behavior, it is as if a child says, "What would Mother do in this situation?" This concept can also be approached from a symbolic interactionist perspective.

Symbolic Interactionism: Cooley and Mead.
The symbolic interactionist approach has been discussed previously in this text. The present section focuses on the perspective's image of socialization. The development of the **self** was central to the views of both Cooley and Mead, pioneers of the symbolic interactionist school.

Charles Horton Cooley (1902) is credited with developing the first sociological model of socialization. In his view, the "self" is developed in interaction with other persons. With a mirror as an analogy, Cooley believed that our image of "self" is the result of how we think others react to us. Others, especially family members, are the mirror through which our **looking-glass self** develops.

Children who believe that their parents see them as smart, attractive, and capable are likely to see themselves the same way. Children who believe that their parents see them as stupid, ugly, and worthless are likely to believe it of themselves. These perceptions can sometimes become a self-fulfilling prophecy. A child who believes himself or herself to be a troublemaker, because that is what his or her parents said, might behave in accord with the self-image and in fact become a troublemaker.

More recent studies tend to confirm Cooley's general perspective. Parental support has been found to affect the self-esteem of children and adolescents, but the effect is bidirectional; the amount of self-esteem children have affects how much support their parents give them (Gecas & Schwalbe, 1986; Felson & Zielinski, 1989). Young people who believe their parents reject them are much more likely to develop low self-esteem and to be depressed (Robertson & Simons, 1989).

George Herbert Mead (1934) observed that we become active participants and do not simply behave in response to stimuli in our environments. We develop our "self" through symbolic interaction with others. The symbols include smiles, frowns, and other movements, but more importantly the symbols are found in language.

Mead believed that children go through a developmental process with three overlapping **stages of observation**. The first is the **preparatory**, or preverbal stage. The infant is unable to view his or her own behavior. Some actions of others are imitated, and random babbling is sometimes rewarded by hugs and smiles if it sounds something like a word the parents want to hear.

Contingency: To Skinner, a change in the environment that affects the behavior preceding it. **Reward:** A contingency that increases the probability that a preceding behavior will recur. **Punishment:** A contingency that decreases the probability that a preceding behavior will recur. **Observational learning:** Changes in behavior that result from watching others, without direct rewards or punishments to oneself. **Imitation:** The repetition of an observed behavior. **Modeling:** Repetition of an observed set of behavior patterns. **Self:** An individual's sense of identity. **Looking-glass self:** To Cooley, the concept that we come to see ourselves as we think other persons see us. **Stages of observation:** To Mead, the developmental socialization process by which children learn from others. **Preparatory stage:** To Mead, the time during which the infant lacks the capacity for extensive language use.

The beginnings of language are learned in this fashion (Skinner, 1957).

The second observational period is the **play stage**. Children begin to imitate "people in roles" rather than simply mimicking discrete behaviors. They play "dress up," "school," "doctor," "mommy and daddy," and other roles. They learn to switch from one role to another, getting practice seeing the world from different perspectives.

At around age 7 or 8, children begin increasingly to enter the **game stage**. Rather than playing at roles, they actually assume roles in interaction with others. This is a more complicated process than we might imagine, because assuming a role in an interactive script requires a knowledge not only of our own role but of the roles of others in the interaction.

To illustrate the nature of interaction in the game stage, Mead liked to use the analogy of a baseball game. To play the game well, each player must have some idea of what all the other players are expected to do. A good shortstop must know what the pitcher, batter, center fielder, and base runner are likely to do on any given play. Only by understanding the role of each of the other players can the shortstop play the game well. This involves a mental process of "taking the role of the other."

In everyday life, as in baseball games, Mead saw interaction as a complicated process. Before we speak or perform other actions, it is as if we imagine what effect that action will have on the other person or persons involved. Based upon that image we have of their reaction, we adjust our own anticipated behavior. Other persons in the interaction are doing the same thing. In all likelihood, none of the students reading this text wore a Speedo swim suit or string bikini the last time they went to class. Should such a thought have even occurred, it would quickly have been dismissed. Students could easily imagine the reaction of others to their behavior, and anticipate how they would feel about those reactions. Instead, everyone chose to wear clothes deemed more appropriate to the role they were about to play. The reaction to their imagined role performance might have focused on how one or two specific persons might respond, but it might also involve a more abstract "they."

As the child develops, the "role of the other" becomes more abstract. A **generalized other** develops in

In baseball as in life, playing one's role well means anticipating how others will play their roles.

the young person's mind. Rather than ask, "What would Mom think?" it is as if the child thinks, "What would society think?" Imagined responses to this question provide guidelines that help the child know how to interact in his or her society.

Although both Freud and Mead developed stage theories, there are major differences between the two. While Freud saw the socialization process as a perpetual conflict between the basic needs of individuals and the needs of the society, Mead saw the process primarily as one of cooperation. Socialization is necessary to give direction to life and to help the individual meet his or her needs.

In addition to having a more optimistic view of human nature, the symbolic interactionist perspective of

---

Play stage: To Mead, the second stage of observational development, up to about age 7 or 8, characterized by playing at being other persons.   **Game stage:** To Mead, the third stage of observational development, beginning about age 7 or 8, in which children actually assume roles in interaction with others.   **Generalized other:** To Mead, the internalized image persons have of the expectations of society as a whole.

socialization differs from the psychoanalytic view in another important respect. To Freud, the early years of a child's life were by far the most important, and personality was typically fixed by the time of adolescence. To Mead and Cooley, however, socialization was a lifelong process of learning new roles and adapting to life through constant social interaction. Mead, Cooley, and other symbolic interactionists explain how societal scripts, personal scripts, scenes, and mutual scripts all interact.

Like Freud, Erikson, and Piaget, Mead proposed a developmental model with various stages. Mead's are less rigidly defined, however, and overlap more. Table 13.4 provides a comparison of the various stage theories.

The Genetics Critique

Socialization is central to the theories discussed above. The way a child is raised by his or her parents is assumed to play a large part in the kind of adult a child eventually becomes. While most psychologists and sociologists interested in socialization fall on the "nurture" side of the argument over nature versus nurture, other perspectives do exist.

David C. Rowe (1994) is one of many who believe genetics is more important than environment in determining child outcomes. Rowe argues that most studies about socialization have a major flaw. Such studies often find that certain kinds of parents are likely to produce certain kinds of children. Certain parenting styles are found to be associated with particular personality traits in children (Baumrind, 1967); researchers find that parents who are good readers, or have high education success, or smoke or drink, or any number of other characteristics, tend to have offspring who mirror those characteristics.

According to Rowe, socialization theorists assume that the environment provided by parents' home life is the cause of the children's traits, and ignore the possible influence of genetic inheritance. Rowe argues that genetics provides a better explanation for the association between parents' and children's traits than does socialization. He further asserts that, except in extreme cases where there is abuse, neglect, or limited opportunity, parents' influence on their children is quite limited.

To Rowe, such variables as social class, ethnic identification, parental warmth, parenting style, and whether the child grows up in a single-parent or two-parent home do not much affect how a child turns out. Parents have little influence on the child's intelligence, school

success, personality, psychopathology, criminal behavior, addictive behavior, or other important characteristics. The genetic influence, according to Rowe, is the major contribution parents make to their children's lives.

Rowe's position is based partly on a critique of psychological theories and socialization science. It is also partly based on the observation that siblings who essentially share the same environment still often turn out quite differently. At the same time, identical twins who happen to be raised in different homes often turn out to be quite similar.

As one might guess, Rowe's argument has not gone unchallenged. Bradley (1994) pointed out that few socialization theorists totally dismiss the influence of genetics, so Rowe is arguing with a straw man. In addition, Rowe makes a serious error when he excludes such influences as neglect, abuse, and limited opportunities. These things happen, to a greater or lesser degree, in a sizable proportion of families, and their presence or absence can significantly affect children.

Bailey (1994) pointed out that rates of some behaviors change significantly over time. The divorce rate, crime rates, rates of cigarette smoking, school achievement test scores, and a number of other variables have significantly changed in the last few decades. The crime rate, for example, increased rapidly from 1960 to about 1992, then dropped rapidly. It is difficult to attribute these trends to changes in the gene pool; this demonstrates the importance of environmental forces.

It is clear that both nature and nurture play a part in child development. Perhaps sociologists and psychologists need to be more aware of genetic influences, while behavioral geneticists need to keep environment influence in mind.

Socialization in Practice

There are several points of agreement between the symbolic interactionist and the social learning perspectives. They have similar views about the early learning of language by children. Both would tend to agree that part of the socialization process is the acquisition of **role models** that help guide behavior.

Because humans can learn by watching and interpreting others, they do not have to make all the mistakes themselves. They can also learn from what might

---

Role model: A person who provides an image with which an observer identifies and may wish to emulate.

be called "negative role models." In real life and in stories, movies, and other forms of entertainment there are abundant images of how not to play life's roles.

Stories are often told with the specific purpose of illustrating what happens to persons who behave inappropriately. When parents gossip or say negative things about real or fictional characters, children learn behavioral norms. The function of fictional villains is to provide negative role models without damaging the social interaction with real persons.

Discipline and Punishment

Part of the role of parents is to **discipline** their children. While many individuals think of punishment when they consider discipline, the word derives from the same root as "disciple," a pupil who learns from someone. Punishment might be part of the process, but children learn the boundaries of acceptability from their parents in a number of other ways, including rewards, imitation, and modeling (see Highlight 13.1).

There has been considerable debate in recent years about the proper place of punishment in general, and spanking or other corporal punishment in particular, in child rearing. Some American experts even consider spanking to be a form of child abuse (Straus & Gelles, 1990), and spanking has been made illegal in Sweden as a way of attempting to change parents' minds about physical punishment (Gelles & Edfeldt, 1986). In the United States, spanking itself is not legally considered to be child abuse unless it leaves long-lasting marks or becomes too frequent and severe.

Psychologists note that punishment must clearly be associated with the undesired behavior if it is to be effective at all. The longer the time between the undesired behavior and the punishment, the less effective punishment is (Aronfreed & Reber, 1965).

Symbolic interactionists point out the importance of understanding the meanings of actions. With punishment, it is the meanings of the offender, not those of the punisher, that determine whether a particular contingency operates as a punishment or not.

| | **Table 13.4** | **Comparison of Stage Theories** | | | |

	Stage			
Age	**Psychosexual (Freud)**	**Psychosocial (Erikson)**	**Cognitive (Piaget)**	**Observational (Mead)**
1–2	Oral	Trust vs. mistrust	Sensorimotor	Preparatory
2–3	Anal	Autonomy vs. shame and doubt	Preoperational	Play
3–6	Phallic	Initiative vs. guilt		
6–12	Latent	Industry vs. inferiority	Concrete operational	Game
Adolescence	Genital	Identity vs. role confusion	Formal operational	
Young Adult		Intimacy vs. isolation		
Middle Age		Generativity vs. stagnation		
Aging		Integrity vs. despair		

Discipline (verb): To train by instruction and practice; especially to teach self-control.

Parents, Children, and Social Acceptability Part of the task of parents is to teach their children the behaviors which the larger society defines as acceptable as compared with the acts defined as immoral, illegal, or otherwise inappropriate. To illustrate the process, put a number of dots in the box below:

Now imagine that each dot in the box represents a behavior of a child. Some of these behaviors are acceptable while others are not. By looking at each dot, can you tell which are which? Of course not, unless you are cheating, which is a behavior represented by one of the unacceptable dots.

Now, draw a circle that takes up about half the space inside the box. Arbitrarily, decide that all dots inside the circle represent socially acceptable behavior, while other dots are unacceptable. Now can you tell the difference? But of course. What you have done is to draw a boundary of acceptability, which is what parents attempt to do with their children. Without boundaries, children would not learn the difference between appropriate and inappropriate behavior.

The boundaries are constantly changing because of maturation of the child. Five-year-old children can get away with some things that teenagers cannot, and vice versa. At any given time, however, children learn where the boundaries are by rewards, punishments, imitation, modeling, direct instruction, and other means. Unless there is some consistency, it will be difficult for the child to figure out the boundaries; there is likely to be even more boundary-testing than would otherwise be the case.

A parent might scold a child who has a tantrum, expecting to reduce the probability of future tantrums. If the goal of the child is to get attention, however, the scolding will provide that attention and operate as a reward rather than a punishment. It will then actually increase the probability that another tantrum will occur.

Sometimes, while punishment is effective in its narrow purpose, it has unintended consequences (Bandura, 1969; 1986). In accord with the looking-glass self, if punishment is constant or composed of harsh criticism, a child might come to believe that he or she is worthless. One study found that the more individuals were subjected to physical punishment as children, the more likely they were as adults to experience depression and suicidal thoughts (Straus, 1994a).

In the case of physical punishment, overgeneralization might lead the child to see the spanking as an aggressive and violent act, and the child might come to believe that aggression and violence are proper ways by which adults solve problems. Children who have been physically punished are generally more aggressive (Straus, 1994b) and might be more likely to see violence as an acceptable part of the individual's script for the interaction of loved ones as well as strangers (Straus, Gelles, & Steinmetz, 1980).

A variety of studies have found a correlation between being spanked and depression, criminal behavior, psychological maladjustment, and other negative effects on children (Straus, 1994; Straus & Stewart, 1999). Boys who receive frequent physical punishment from their fathers are more likely than other boys to abuse animals (Flynn, 1999). While the research finds a correlation between spanking and certain negative outcomes, a clear causal relationship is difficult to prove (Graziano, 1996). It could be that extreme spanking and other abusive physical punishments are related to the negative outcomes, but that occasional and mild spanking is not. It could also be true that problem children are more likely to be spanked, so that bad behavior causes spanking, rather than spanking causing the bad behavior.

While punishment can, under certain conditions, be effective in preventing the recurrence of a particular behavior, it cannot be used by itself to teach new behavior. It provides no hint as to what should be done instead of the punished behavior. Punishment is probably more effective when an opportunity for an alternative response, which can then be rewarded, is provided (Bandura, 1969).

Whatever the effects of spanking, it remains popular. About 90% of parents spank their children at some time or another (Straus, 1994b). Parents who spank weekly or more believe that it reduces child misbehavior in both the short and long term (Holden et al., 1999). The General Social Surveys found that almost three fourths of adult Americans agree that "it is sometimes necessary to discipline a child with a good, hard spanking." Over time, however, there has been some decline in support for spanking (see Figure 13.3).

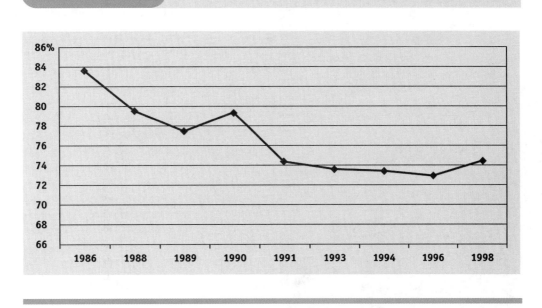

Figure 13.3 Percentage Agreeing That a Hard Spanking Is Sometimes Necessary, by Year

Source: Davis, James Allan, and Tom W. Smith: General Social Surveys, 1986–1998. (Machine-readable data file). Principal investigator, James A. Davis; director and co-principal investigator, Tom W. Smith; co-principal investigator, Peter V. Marsden, NORC ed. Chicago: National Opinion Research Center, producer, 1998; Storrs, CT: The Roper Center for Public Opinion Research, University of Connecticut, distributor. Microcomputer format and codebook prepared and distributed by Microcase Corporation, Bellevue, WA. Analysis by Gene H. Starbuck.

Parenting Scripts

A widely used typology of parenting scripts was developed by Diana Baumrind (1967, 1968, 1971, 1972, 1980, 1989), who identified three approaches used by parents in child rearing and discipline: authoritarian, permissive, and authoritative.

The Authoritarian Style. Authoritarian parents have rigid expectations about proper behavior and see unquestioned obedience to these expectations as the most important quality of their children. Respect for authority is emphasized, and punishment is often used to achieve that goal. Children's obedience, not discussion and good communication, is seen as the solution to problems.

Some research has found children of authoritarian parents to be less happy and more susceptible to stress than other children. They might also be more moody and more easily annoyed (Belsky, Lerner, & Spanier, 1984).

The Permissive Style. Permissive parents see children as persons who have the right to have their emotional and physical needs met. Parents deal with their children nearly as equals, being nonpunitive and accepting. They see themselves as "resources" for their children, who, they believe, will turn out fine on their own without a lot of guidance or discipline. There are frequent hugs and other physical touching of children, and an absence of physical punishment. Parents attempt to use reason and persuasion with their children. This approach is similar to that suggested by the first edition of Benjamin Spock's influential child-rearing book, *Baby and Child Care* (1945).

By some measures, children of permissive parents are somewhat more likely to have trouble controlling their impulses and tend to be more impulse-aggressive. They also have lower levels of self-reliance. They are, however, more cheerful than children of authoritarian parents (Baumrind, 1967; Belsky, Lerner, & Spanier, 1984).

The Authoritative Style. The authoritative style is somewhere on the continuum between authoritarian and permissive. It is also referred to as "strictness with affection"; Spock (1989) refers to it as "democratic child rearing." It is the apparent choice of current child-rearing experts.

Authoritative parents are the most nurturing and generally use rewards rather than punishment. They respond to their children's demands for attention. They are somewhat democratic yet controlling and demanding. They are also warm, receptive, and rational in their interactions with

Authoritarian parents rely heavily on punishment child rearing.

their children (Arendell, 2000). Children are allowed to express their feelings to their parents (White, 1985).

Baumrind (1968) believed children of authoritative parents to be the most socially competent, energetic, friendly, self-reliant, and cheerful. Most of the more recent studies tend to support Baumrind's conclusions. Children of authoritative fathers have more positive outcomes, including greater life satisfaction, than children whose fathers use other styles of parenting. This holds true both for fathers in intact homes and for non-resident fathers (Amato & Gilbreth, 1999; Marsiglio et al., 2000; Young et al., 1995). Authoritative mothers are more satisfied with parenting, and likewise have children with better outcomes. Again, this holds true both for single and for married mothers (Arendell, 2000; Rogers & White, 1998; Stewart et al., 1997).

Most studies of authoritative parenting, however, were done on White, middle-class families. There is some question whether this type of parenting is as effective with Black children or with poor children (Demo & Cox, 2000). The concept "authoritative" and "authoritarian" might not even apply to Chinese and other Asian child-rearing patterns, where the idea of "training" might make more sense (Chao, 1994).

The kind of child rearing a parent prefers is heavily influenced by the approach his or her own parents used. Parenting styles are also affected by social class and race. A pioneering study of social class and parenting was accomplished by Melvin Kohn (1963; Kohn & Schooler, 1983). His general finding was that parenting styles are affected by the nature of the parents' work in the paid labor force. More specifically, authoritarian parenting is more typical of agricultural societies and among working-class or poor families in the industrial United States.

To be successful, workers in blue-collar jobs must learn to work under conditions of close supervision, must follow directions, and must perform routine tasks. Creativity and independent thinking are more likely to be punished than rewarded. These same qualities are associated with authoritarian child rearing.

One indicator of authoritarian parenting is a belief that the primary task of child rearing is to teach the child to be obedient. The General Social Survey asked respondents whether they thought it was more important that children learn to be obedient or that they learn to think for themselves. While "thinking for themselves" was chosen by a majority of all groups, it was more likely to be the choice of those with higher incomes, with more education, and by Whites rather than Blacks (see Figure 13.4).

In contrast to blue-collar work, white-collar work is more likely to involve skill in interpersonal relationships, creativity, initiative, and manipulation of mental images. There are less likely to be "right" and "wrong" ways of doing things, and more likely to be "reasoned" ways of doing things. For both blue-collar and white-collar workers, socialization of children is in accord with what is thought to be necessary for occupational success. Working-class parents are more likely to judge an event based on the behavior itself. They are more likely to apply strict discipline, enforced with physical punishment. Middle-class parents are more likely to try to figure out the reason for a child's behavior, rather than react to the behavior itself. They are more likely to use rewards and psychological, rather than physical, punishments.

Multigenerational Grandparent Families with Children

Perhaps the standard traditional image of the American family is a mother and father, neither of whom has ever been divorced, living in the same house as their own minor children, while the husband/father works outside the home and the wife/mother is a full-time homemaker. As

Figure 13.4	Percent Saying It Is More Important for Kids to Learn to Think for Themselves Than to Be Obedient

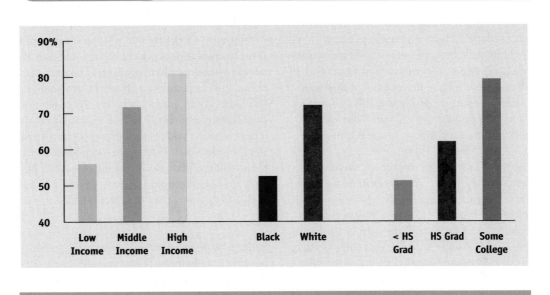

Source: Davis, James Allan, and Tom W. Smith: General Social Surveys, 1986–1998. (Machine-readable data file). Principal investigator, James A. Davis; director and co-principal investigator, Tom W. Smith; co-principal investigator, Peter V. Marsden, NORC ed. Chicago: National Opinion Research Center, producer, 1998; Storrs, CT: The Roper Center for Public Opinion Research, University of Connecticut, distributor. Microcomputer format and codebook prepared and distributed by Microcase Corporation, Bellevue, WA. Analysis by Gene H. Starbuck.

we saw in chapter 1, most families in the United States do not fit that description. We will look at other forms in this section, with a focus on the children of such relationships.

Parents and Their Adult Children

In chapter 12 we noted that marriages change, not end, when children leave the home. It is likewise true that parent-child relationships continue after the children leave the home. The arrival of grandchildren once again alters family relationships. Socialization and interaction generally continue among the family members, in spite of changing roles and scripts.

A number of family members assist the elderly. Children of the elderly and children-in law have similar experiences with caregiving (Peters-Davis et al., 1999). Stronger obligations are generally felt toward elderly parents than to stepparents (Ganong et al., 1998). Adult grandchildren, too, often provide assistance to their grandparents (Dellman-Jenkins et al., 2000).

Because most elderly caretaking is done by women, the term **daughter track** has been created to refer to the stresses and burdens associated with caring for an elderly parent in addition to other roles like wife and employee (Abel, 1991; Murphy et al., 1997; Sheehan & Nutthall, 1988).

Caring for elderly parents can be stressful and, for some adult children, can lead to disrupted work, depression, frustration, helplessness, emotional and physical exhaustion, and other symptoms (Faison et al., 1999; Mancini & Bliesner, 1989; Snyder & Keefe, 1985). Caregiving is especially difficult when the parent has a serious physical disability or dementia such as that produced by Parkinson's disease or Alzheimer's disease (Deimling & Bass, 1986; Caserta et al., 1996).

The negatives of elderly caregiving have probably been somewhat exaggerated (Stull, Bowman, & Smerglia, 1994). Much research on caregiving, as well as the popular press, has focused on the most difficult situations and has often ignored positives. As was true when their parents raised them, the stress of caring for an older parent is real, but it can also bring gratification. Many caregivers report that they feel appreciated by the parent they care for, and that they receive other rewards even when the parent suffers from dementia (Lawton et al., 1989; Montenko, 1989). One study of the relationship between daughters and the elderly mothers for

Daughter track: Role expectation that a daughter will have primary responsibility for familial elder care, in addition to other tasks.

whom they cared found that most caregivers reported that the care had either a positive or neutral influence on their relationship. A negative impact was reported by only 5.4% of daughters (Walker, Shin, & Bird, 1990).

Research on the elderly sometimes appears to forget that, throughout their lives, parents provide aid to their adult children. They provide emotional support and advice in difficult times such as divorce and widowhood (Johnson, 1988; Greenberg & Becker, 1988). They act as a "safety net" by providing such material goods as money, food, and housing during times of transition (DeVanzo & Goldscheider, 1990).

Assistance is not limited to emergency situations. Many older parents provide everyday help in the form of money and personal advice, either in person or via letter or telephone (Spitze & Logan, 1992). Child-rearing assistance is often given directly or in the form of anecdotes. Often simply knowing that there is a sympathetic ear to call on can be quite helpful. Especially in the urban Black community, grandparents and even great-grandparents are often an essential part of the everyday child-care network (Malson, 1983; Gelles, 1996). In addition, the elderly provide a good deal of assistance to their remaining siblings and to the community through volunteer work (Gallagher, 1994).

As the parent-child unit ages, aid and assistance become more reciprocal. Expectations about filial responsibility combine with the sense of parental responsibility to maintain some degree of intergenerational solidarity (Bengtson & Roberts, 1991).

Lee, Netzer, and Coward (1994) studied the assistance given by elderly parents to their adult children, including financial help, advice, and practical assistance of various kinds. They also looked at the amount of assistance provided to the aged by their adult children. The reciprocal relationship was demonstrated in the statistical relationship between the amount of aid given to adult children and that received from adult children.

As would be expected, a major determinant of the amount of personal assistance rendered is the geographical proximity of the parent and adult child (Lee, 1980). In general, assistance also varies with need and resources available. Older parents with higher levels of education, income, and health provide more assistance to their adult children, and receive somewhat less. Married parents receive less aid from their children, but do not necessarily give more than unmarried ones (Lee, Netzer, & Coward, 1994).

Gender is strongly associated with receiving aid as well as giving it. Elderly mothers give slightly more aid to their children, and receive significantly more, than elderly fathers. This is partly because mothers live longer and therefore might be in more need of help. They are also more likely to be alone. Adult daughters both give more aid and receive more from their parents than do adult sons (Lee, Netzer, & Coward, 1994).

Not only do elderly parents and their adult children form reciprocal networks of caring, but they also sometimes co-reside, or live together. Characteristics of both the parents and children affect the probability of co-residence. Aging parents who are the oldest and most disabled are most likely to live with their children. Those who are widowed or divorced are also more likely to co-reside. Black elderly are more likely to live with their children than are White elderly. Adult children who are not employed full time are more likely to live with their parents (Lee & Dwyer, 1996).

Grandparenting

Perhaps as many as 94% of older adults with children become grandparents (Hooyman & Kiyak, 1993), but the scripts involving the three generations of grandparent, parent, and child are varied. A useful typology of grandparenting styles was developed by Cherlin and Furstenberg (1986) as a result of interviews with a national sample of 510 grandparents. Three styles were identified: companionate, remote, and involved.

Companionate. The majority (55%) of grandparents saw their relationship with their grandchildren as friendly, close, affectionate, and playful. They saw their grandchildren regularly, but did not see themselves as responsible for setting rules or disciplining the children. They did not take on a "parent" role with respect to their grandchildren.

Remote. About 29% of grandparents were not intimately or closely involved in the lives of their grandchildren. Their interactions tended to be ritualistic and symbolic. The remoteness was usually the result of geographical separation rather than choice.

Involved. About 16% of grandparents had close contact and assumed some parental functions with respect to grandchildren. In a few cases, they were the functional parents of the children, at least for a period of time. More than 2 million children live with their grandparents in a home where no biological parent is present (Smith et al., 1998).

Extremely involved relationships are somewhat more likely to experience conflict among the three generations. This is in part explained by the fact that it is often a crisis of some kind, rather than a choice, which precipitates a highly involved grandparent-grandchild role relationship. Hospitalization of the child's mother, or her death, or her incarceration often precede the grandparental acceptance of the parenting role. In addition, part of the benefit of the grandparent role is that it involves voluntary, rather than required, interaction. Both grandparents and grandchildren are more likely to express dissatisfaction about the relationship when the grandparents are forced into a custodial role (Shore & Hayslip, 1994).

The grandparenting role is generally seen as mutually beneficial to grandparents and grandchildren. It helps the children develop a sense of self and of belonging to a large family network, aids in the socialization of the child, and can help children understand their own parents. By serving as a backup or emergency baby-sitter, grandparents can take some pressure off the middle generation (Flaherty, Facteau, & Garver, 1991).

In return, having grandchildren can contribute to a sense of immortality and provide a social connection for the grandparents. Acting as teacher and "expert" on family history can enhance the self-esteem of the grandparent, as long as grandchildren listen and respect the status. Having young children around also keeps grandparents current with fads in music, clothing, and language. When grandchildren get older, they can assist in chores such as shopping, lawn care, and transporting (Barranti, 1985).

The grandparent-grandchild relationship is a positive experience for most (Timberlake, 1980; Robertson, 1977). Grandmothers generally get more satisfaction from the role than do grandfathers (Thomas, 1986). Maternal grandparents have more contact with their grandchildren than do paternal grandparents, and grandchildren feel the closest to their maternal grandmother (Matthews & Sprey, 1985).

High rates of divorce and out-of-wedlock births account for at least a part of the higher rates of maternal grandparenting. Most out-of-wedlock children have little interaction with their father, let alone their father's parents. Mothers usually get custody of children after divorce. For paternal grandparents, both the quality and quantity of interaction with grandchildren go down after their son divorces, while the relationship for maternal grandparents often gets more intense as the older parents operate as an emotional, financial, and child-care safety net for their divorced daughter (Cherlin & Furstenberg, 1986).

While the problem of "too many" grandparents can affect blended families, the problem of "too few" grandchildren affects other families. A declining birthrate results in fewer grandchildren per grandparent. The "one-child" policy in China (see chapter 4) results in what has been called the 4-2-1 problem, where there are four grandparents, two parents, and one grandchild. In cultures where grandchildren are counted upon to provide considerable assistance to their aging grandparents, this can create a tremendous burden for the lone grandchild. In the United States, with increasing numbers of one- and two-children families, a similar situation could arise, although most Western societies have developed social security systems that do not make the elderly quite so dependent upon their offspring.

There remain in the United States, however, differences in grandparenting based on ethnicity. African Americans, Asian Americans, Italian Americans, Latinos, and Native Americans all have more grandparent involvement than is average for Americans (Cavanaugh, 1993; National Indian Council on Aging, 1981). In some cases these are cultural preferences associated with more extended family relations in general; in other cases it is an adaptation to poverty and other social forces.

Single Parents and Children

In the United States there are 16.4 million children living with single mothers and another 2.9 million living with single fathers (*Statistical Abstract 1999*: t. 83). Millions of others either have lived with single parents or will do so before their 18th birthdays. Most of these single parents do an excellent job of parenting, raising well-adjusted, happy, productive children, while some two-parent families do a poor job of raising children. Virtually every study on the matter, however, indicates that children are generally better off being raised by two loving parents than by one.

Silverstein and Auerbach (1999) concluded, after a comprehensive review of the literature, that fathers are not "essential" to the well-being of children. They did report that it is important that children have a continuous, stable, long-term relationship with two or more adults. As advocates for nontraditional families, Silverstein and Auerbach were making the point that children do not necessarily have to have parents who are lifelong, heterosexual marital partners. To this extent they are probably correct. The stable partners might just be living together, or they might be living apart but in close touch, or they might be a mother and grandmother, or they might be a homosexual couple.

Using the same logic, Silverstein and Auerbach might also have said that mothers are not essential to the well-being of children, but that was not their agenda. What they fail to point out is that the long-term marital unit is the arrangement most likely to provide the kind of close relationships that benefits children. No one, including Silverstein and Auerbach, has ever found otherwise.

Research over the last 50 years has found a generally modest but persistent and pervasive relationship between juvenile delinquency and single-parent homes. The relationship holds for both boys and girls and for all crimes and all forms of drug use, but the correlation is stronger for less serious offenses. Similar correlations are found for all racial and ethnic groups, for all religions, and in both rural and urban residence (Bahr, 1979; Wilkinson, 1980; Demo & Acock, 1988; Wells & Rankin, 1991; Regoli & Hewitt 1994). Living in anything but a two-parent family reduces the chance that a child will leave home to attend college and increases the odds that a child will leave home early for other reasons such as getting a job, joining military service, getting married, or cohabiting (Goldscheider & Goldscheider, 1998).

Bronstein, Clauson, Stoll, and Abrams (1993) reported typical results. They compared parenting styles in three types of families: those with two biological or infant-adoption parents, those with a single mother, and those with a mother plus a stepfather or father surrogate. The researchers looked at several child-outcome variables of the fifth-grade children in the study, including self-concept, psychological problems, classroom behavioral problems, academic performance, and peer relations.

Parenting behavior and the parent-child relationship were perceived more positively in the traditional family. There was more conflict in both the single-parent and father-surrogate families. Both boys and girls from non-traditional homes had more psychological problems, more classroom behavior problems, and lower grades. In addition, boys from nontraditional homes had poorer self-concepts; girls from nontraditional homes were less popular with their peers (Bronstein et al., 1993).

When comparing children of single-mother homes with those containing a father surrogate, the results are somewhat mixed. Bronstein et al. (1993) found that girls with father surrogates had fewer behavioral problems, higher grades, better adjustment, and more popularity with their peers than those from single-mother homes. There were no statistically significant differences for boys in the two types of homes. Amato and Rivera (1999), however, found a positive impact for father involvement for both boys and girls, by biological fathers and by stepfathers; this held true for Black, White, and Latino families.

Bogenschneider (1995) found a strong correlation between the amount of involvement parents had in schools and their children's grades. This generally holds true regardless of the parent's gender and educational level and for students of both genders and all races. Single mothers who were involved in their children's schools also had a positive impact on their children's grades. However, only 20% of single mothers were able to be highly involved in the schools, compared to 51% of mothers in biological two-parent families.

Not all single-parent families have the same kind of households, and some of these seem to affect children more positively than do others. Many children live in homes with their mother and grandmother. These

children start school with better skills than do children in other types of single-parent families (Entwisle & Alexander, 2000). In addition, some children have "surrogate fathers" (Allen & Connor, 1997) in extended kin or friendship networks who may provide the kind of school involvement that benefits children (Marks, 2000).

While children of unmarried young mothers have lower overall school success than other children, some do well. Single mothers of the more successful children were more likely to be employed, had fewer children, lived in more desirable neighborhoods, and were more likely to be living with a male partner (Luster et al., 2000).

Overall, children in two-biological parent homes are the best off, with those in father-surrogate homes slightly better off than are those in mother-only homes. Much of the difference between outcomes for traditional and nontraditional children, however, is accounted for by socioeconomic status. In other words, the fact that single-mother families are poorer than traditional ones accounts for most, but not all, of the difference between the two groups (Bronstein et al., 1993). Further, poverty is not equally distributed. Among single-mother households, Blacks, Mexican Americans, and Puerto Ricans have poverty rates almost twice as high as Whites (Manning & Smock, 1997; Walker, 2000).

Another major difference in child outcomes is accounted for by the fact that two-parent families generally provide more supervision for their children. In addition, it might be the number of family transitions a child makes, rather than the family structure at any given time, that causes some of the problems for children in nontraditional homes (Capaldi & Patterson, 1991).

To understand how single parents saw their own lives, Richards and Schmiege (1993) interviewed a small sample of single mothers and custodial fathers. The most commonly mentioned problem, affecting 78% of single women, was money. Fewer than 20% of single fathers had this concern. The mothers were also more likely to mention role and task overload and problems with their social lives. Men were more likely to report problems with their ex-spouse.

Nearly all single parents can identify some strengths in their family situation. About 60% of both mothers and fathers thought that their parenting skills were a strength, and about 40% thought they were strong in family management. About 20% identified personal growth and communication as strengths. In addition, 69% of mothers and 64% of fathers thought single parenting got easier over time, while 23% of women and 27% of men thought it got harder. The remainder thought it stayed about the same (Richards & Schmiege, 1993).

Families in the NEWS

Tiny Twins in Tangled WWWeb

Infant twins have had two sets of names and four sets of parents. They have lived in two countries and three American states, and their future remains uncertain.

In August 2000, Tranda Wecker gave birth in Missouri to twins at a time she was negotiating a divorce from a man she claimed had been a cocaine addict. She named the twins Kiara and Keyara, variant spellings of a character from a *Lion King* sequel.

With three older children, she decided she would not be able to care properly for the twins, so she contacted an Internet adoption broker she found in the yellow pages. In October 2000, Richard and Vickie Allen of California paid the adoption "facilitator" $6,000 and took control of the twins.

Adoption brokering is legal and lightly regulated in California, which also allows 90 days for a birth mother to change her mind about adoption. Either because the adoption facilitator was afraid she would not get the rest of the money promised by the Allens, or because their check bounced, or because she got a better offer, or because Wecker decided the Allens would not be good parents, the birth mother went to California. She apparently said she wanted to see the twins to say goodbye, but she then turned them over to Judith and Alan Kilshaw.

The Kilshaws, who are British citizens, had paid $12,000 to the same Internet adoption agency. They took the twins to Arkansas, which has only a 30-day residency requirement for adoptions. Wecker used an aunt's address, the adoption was finalized, and the Kilshaws took the twins to their farmhouse in North Wales.

The Allens fought the Arkansas adoption, which a judge ultimately revoked on the grounds that proper residence was not established. The court requested that the twins be returned. In Britain, where private adoption brokering is not legal, even the Prime Minister publicly announced his disapproval.

In the meantime, Tranda Wecker decided she wanted the twins back. She was assisted by a high-profile feminist lawyer, Gloria Allred of California.

The Allens dropped out of the case. Richard Allen was charged with molesting the young baby-sitter who sometimes cared for the twins during their stay with the Allens. A previously adopted child of the Allens was removed from their home while the investigation continued, and the Allens said they wanted to spend their energies getting that child returned. The outcome of that trial was not known when this account was written.

On April 18, 2001, three British social workers accompanied the twins from their foster home in Britain to a foster home in Missouri. Their biological mother and father have each spent some time with the well-traveled infants.

The Allens, the Kilshaws, and the Weckers have appeared on a number of American television shows, including *Oprah* and *Today*. Allred and other attorneys have also received national attention.

Aaron Wecker, who apparently now wants custody, accused Tranda Wecker of inflicting emotional abuse on the twins. The custody dispute will now be resolved as part of the Weckers' divorce settlement.

Sources: Sarah Lyall, **www.nytimes.com**, January 18, 2001; The Associated Press, **www.latimes.com**, March 8, 2001; Bettina Boxall, **www.latimes.com**, March 11, 2001; The Associated Press, **www.nytimes.com**, April 20, 2001.

Gay and Lesbian Parents and Their Children

Historically, nearly all children of same-sex couples arrived in their situation as a result of a divorce of a heterosexual marriage. Most frequently, a woman would marry a man and have children, then find her lesbian identity either before or after a divorce. She would get custody of the children, and, at some point, move in with her lover.

Today, however, increasing numbers of lesbian couples are having a child through donor insemination. It is quite likely that children in these two types of homes would have different kinds of experiences (Patterson, 2000). In the first case, there is an identifiable father, who may or may not remain active in the child's life. In the second case, there is no father figure at all.

This practice challenges many ideas about marriage, family, and parenting (Dunne, 2000). One member of the lesbian pair is the biological mother of the child, but the status of the other member of the couple is unclear. New legal issues are emerging. In 2000, the Colorado Supreme Court upheld the right of a lesbian couple to put both the women's names on the birth certificate of a baby that one of the women had through donor insemination (Associated Press, 2000).

Lesbian and gay parenting raises a number of other theoretical, legal, moral, and research issues. The percentage of children directly involved, however, is probably quite small. Only about 1% of children have parents who self-identify as lesbian or gay, and only a portion of those parents have live-in lovers while raising their children (Black et al., 2000; Stacey & Biblarz, 2001). Because the numbers are small, and because of privacy concerns, it is difficult to get a large national sample of lesbigay parents that is representative of the whole group.

Most research on lesbigay parenting is done on small convenience samples consisting of White lesbian mothers who are better educated than the general public and live in more progressive urban centers, especially in California or the Northeastern states. They are commonly found in and around major university communities (Stacey & Biblarz, 2001). It is reasonable to expect that such mothers, lesbian or heterosexual, would have different mothering skills and child outcomes than lesbian mothers in general.

Much of the research on lesbigay parenting has been done by advocates of gay and lesbian rights for the purpose of providing testimony in child custody cases. This research typically reports a "no difference" finding that children raised by lesbian couples are identical to children raised in two-parent, heterosexual couples. Falk (1994) reviewed and summarized the available social science research on seven issues often raised in court proceedings, essentially reaching a "no difference" conclusion. Keeping in mind the research concerns mentioned earlier, as well as the fact that many children of lesbians are also children of divorce and single mothers, the evidence points to the following conclusions:

1. *Mental health of lesbian mothers.* The American Psychological Association has not considered homosexuality itself to be a mental illness since 1972. Studies since then have generally found lesbian mothers to have the same or lower incidence of psychiatric disorders as heterosexual mothers; on some measures of mental health, lesbian mothers score higher.

2. *Parenting ability of lesbian mothers.* Available research generally finds either that lesbians are similar to heterosexual mothers in maternal attitudes and caregiving behaviors, or that lesbian mothers are more child-oriented.

3. *Mental health of children raised by lesbian mothers.* While children of lesbian mothers might have more adjustment problems than children of heterosexual couples, there are generally no significant differences between overall mental health of children of lesbian mothers compared with children of single heterosexual mothers.

4. *Sexual molestation of children raised by lesbian mothers.* Child molestation by lesbians is quite uncommon, and by lesbian mothers it is even more rare.

5. *Gender-role development of children raised by lesbian mothers.* Gender measures typically look at choices of toys and games, or are based on observations of play and interaction. Several studies confirm that there are no major gender effects on children of lesbians. There is some tendency for daughters of lesbian mothers to have less traditional, more egalitarian gender roles. Boys were found to be either traditionally masculine or, in a few studies, slightly overmasculinized.

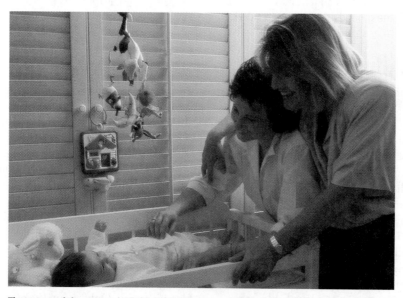

These two adults cannot both be the biological parents of the child, but they can both be motherly.

6. *Sexual orientation of children raised by lesbian mothers.* There is no evidence for the "contagion" view of homosexuality, that children of homosexuals are themselves likely to be homosexual. The vast majority of children of homosexuals turn out to be heterosexuals.

7. *Social stigma of children of lesbian mothers.* There is evidence that most children of lesbians face teasing and other negative interactions, mostly from peers. Perhaps because virtually all children get teased about one thing or another, levels of self-esteem of children of lesbians are generally the same as with other children. Those with lesbian mothers reported being liked by peers as much as did children of heterosexual parents.

Even less information is available about children of gay fathers than about children of lesbian mothers. In their review of the literature, Barret and Robinson (1994) essentially concluded that what little evidence there was suggests that the findings regarding lesbian parenting (Falk, 1994) also apply to gay parenting. Other research points to the conclusion that no significant differences have been found between children of homosexual and children of heterosexual parents (Allen & Burrell, 1996; Brewaeys & Van Hall, 1997; Fitzgerald, 1999; Patterson, 1997, 2000; Tasker & Golombok, 1997).

There is not, however, universal agreement on this point. Some critics report serious flaws in the research, others point to contradictory findings, and still others find that lesbigay parenting has a number of dangers for children (Cameron & Cameron, 1996, 1997; Cameron, 1999; Lerner, 2000; Wardle, 1997). Stacey and Biblarz (2001) suggest that these researchers, too, have their political agendas. They tend to be associated with conservative groups who strongly favor the traditional family.

Stacey and Biblarz (2001) claim that nearly all research suffers from a "hetero-normative presumption" which uses heterosexual parenting and lifestyles as the measuring rod by which to judge same-sex practices. Both the "no difference" and the "bad outcome" perspectives are guilty of this error. Instead, Stacey and Biblarz argue that sometimes, different is just different—not necessarily better or worse.

The most controversial finding appears to deal with the sexual orientation of children, especially girls, raised in lesbian families (Kunin, 1998). In their comprehensive review of the literature, Stacey and Biblarz (2001) find considerable evidence that children of same-sex couples, especially daughters of lesbians, are much more likely to adopt a lesbian adult orientation than are daughters of heterosexuals. They found that even research with a "no difference" conclusion, when the raw data are analyzed, supports the "difference" conclusion in this regard. Stacey and Biblarz also found evidence of gender roles differences, especially among girls of lesbian mothers; the girls were less likely to adopt traditional gender role expectations than girls with heterosexual mothers.

There might be some parenting differences, too. Compared with stepfathers or fathers whose wives were impregnated by donor insemination, lesbian "stepmothers" had higher levels of closeness with the child, greater co-parental compatibility, and high quality parenting skills. However, these were probably more related to gender differences (mothers "parent" differently than fathers) than to sexual orientation. Also, lesbian co-parental couples, lacking institutional marriage, are more likely to break up than heterosexual co-parents. This is potentially damaging to the children (Stacey & Biblarz, 2001).

Stacey and Biblarz (2001) conclude that there probably are differences in parenting and child outcomes of same-sex compared with opposite-sex couples, but no differences that warrant social or legal disapproval of same-sex parenting in general. More research is clearly needed on the topic of diverse family forms such as those involving homosexual parents. Such research does, however, pose difficult methodological and ethical questions. It is difficult for researchers on both sides of the question to set aside their political preconceptions (Clarke, 2000).

Summary and Conclusion

In traditional societies, children become virtually identical replacements for their parents in terms of values, norms, language, and occupational roles. In today's society, extrafamilial agencies conduct much of the socialization, and children are different from their parents because the society is different. Still, parents remain the primary socializers of young children.

Preindustrial societies had different views of children and of child rearing than exist in the United States today. The idea that children are a qualitatively different kind of person, with special needs at particular stages of development, is relatively new.

Adults want children for a variety of reasons, but once they become parents their lives change forever. Couples' mutual scripts change when they have children. Increased role conflict, stress, and money concerns can become a problem. Many couples find themselves developing more traditional gender roles after the birth of a child. Fathers and mothers often experience parenthood in different ways. Few couples regret having children, and many have more than one.

Because both the husband and wife in most parenting couples work, nonparental child care has become increasingly important. Unfortunately, not all such care is of high quality.

Several theories about socialization have affected both the social-science literature and the way children are raised today. Some theorists of socialization, such as Freud, Erikson, and Piaget, use approaches that are primarily psychological. Others, like Hirschi, Bandura, and Mead, prefer approaches grounded in sociology or social psychology. Considerable debate has occurred, both in the scholarly journals and in everyday life, about the role of punishment in child rearing. Most research does agree, however, that authoritative parenting has better outcomes than either authoritarian or permissive approaches.

Not all families consist of children living with a biological mother and father who have traditional work-family gender roles. Although it is important that children form attachments to a caring adult in the early stages of life, the fact that a mother works appears to have little direct impact on child outcomes if quality nonparental care is available. Grandparents generally enjoy their time with grandchildren, but the relationships are more difficult if grandparents assume full-time parenting responsibilities.

Children raised with both a mother and father in the home are generally better off than those raised by single parents, partly because of financial pressures. Available research suggests that children raised by gay or lesbian parents may not be significantly different in important ways than other children.

In conclusion, both being a parent and being a child are, to some extent socially constructed in a context involving economics, religion, politics, and educational systems. While children can prosper in a variety of family forms and under a variety of parenting styles, some are generally more likely to produce positive outcomes than others. On average, the best outcomes occur when a child is raised by the same two stable, loving parents who can afford to buy their child at least the necessities of life and who use authoritative parenting styles.

Rethinking in Context Have you changed any of your opinions about raising children as a result of reading this chapter? Do you think children should have all the same rights as adults? If not, which should they not have? Should parents be made legally responsible for the criminal acts of their children? If such laws were passed, how, from the various theoretical perspectives, would the socialization process be affected? If you ran an adoption agency, would you give preference in adoptions to married couples over single individuals or gay couples? Why or why not?

Additional Resources

The Transition to parenthood

Cowan, Carolyn Pape, & Philip A. Cowan. 2000. *When Partners Become Parents: The Big Life Change for Couples.* Mahway, NJ: Erlbaum.

General parenting

Berry, Mary Frances. 1993. *The Politics of Parenthood: Child Care, Women's Rights, and the Myth of the Good Mother.* New York: Penguin.

D'Augelli, Anthony R., & Charlotte J. Patterson, eds. 1995. *Lesbian, Gay, and Bisexual Identities Over the Lifespan: Psychological Perspectives*. New York: Oxford University Press.

Demo, David H., Anne-Marie Ambert, & Jay A. Mancini, eds. 1995. *Parents and Adolescents in Changing Families*. Minneapolis: National Council on Family Relations.

Lerner, Richard M. 1995. *America's Youth in Crisis: Challenges and Options for Programs and Policies*. Newbury Park, CA: Sage.

Mason, Mary Ann, & Eileen Gambrill. 1993. *Debating Children's Lives*. Newbury Park, CA: Sage.

Rossi, Alice S., & Peter Rossi. 1990. *Of Human Bonding*. New York: Aldine de Gruyter.

Thurer, Shari L. 1994. *The Myths of Motherhood: How Culture Reinvents the Good Mother*. Boston: Houghton Mifflin.

Fathers and mothers

Frank, Robert. 1999. *The Involved Father: Family-Tested Solutions for Getting Dads to Participate More in the Daily Lives of Their Children*. New York: St. Martin's Press.

Aging families

Binstock, Robert H., & Linda K. George, eds. 1990. *Handbook on Aging and the Social Sciences*, 3rd ed. New York: Academic Press.

Brubaker, Timothy H. 1990. *Family Relationships in Later Life*, 2nd ed. Newbury Park, CA: Sage.

Cherlin, Andrew J., & Frank F. Furstenberg, Jr. 1992. *The New American Grandparent: A Place in the Family, a Life Apart*. Cambridge: Harvard University Press.

Gay and lesbian parents and their children

Black, Dan A., Gary Gates, Seth Sanders, & Lowell Taylor. 2000. "Demographics of the Gay and Lesbian Population in the United States: Evidence from Available Systematic Data Sources." *Demography* 37:139–154.

Stacey, Judith & Timothy J. Biblarz. 2001. "(How) Does the Sexual Orientation of Parents Matter?" *American Sociological Review* 66:159–183.

Tasker, Fiola L., & Susan Golombok. 1997. *Growing Up in a Lesbian Family: Effects on Child Development*. New York: Guilford.

Wardle, Lynn D. 1997. "The Potential Impact of Homosexual Parenting on Children." *University of Illinois Law Review* 1997:833–919.

Internet Sites

On generative fathering
http://fatherwork.byu.edu/

The Fatherhood Project
http://www.familiesandworkinst.org/fatherhood/index.html

The Families and Work Institute
http://www.familiesandworkinst.org

The Alliance for Children and Families
http://www.alliance1.org/

Children, Youth, and Families Consortium
http://www.cyfc.umn.edu/

Single-parent support
http://www.family.org/spfmag/lifeskills/

Gay Parent Magazine
http://www.gayparentmag.com

For links to these sites and additional resources, visit the *Families in Context* Web site at:
http://sociology.wadsworth.com

Chapter 14

Crisis and Violence in Families

Prelude

Jim's mother, struggling to make it, often lost her temper and physically abused her four children. Jim never know his dad except for the negative things his mother said about him. Jim was popular in school, though, and grew up to be a good-looking, charming guy.

When he was 19 he fell in love with, impregnated, and married Judy. She had been raised by her mom and dad, who frequently got into loud arguments. Especially when they were drinking, her parents got into physical fights. On more than one occasion, Judy's mom had to go to the hospital with injuries she got from her husband, but she always lied about the cause of the injuries and neither she nor her husband was ever arrested.

Jim and Judy had gotten into fights before they got married, but thought it would stop after the wedding. It didn't. It got worse instead. With their new baby looking on, they yelled at each other, hit, shoved, and kicked each other, and otherwise abused each other. Judy finally spent a week in the hospital with broken bones and severe bruises. Jim was arrested.

What should happen next?

Family life does not always go as smoothly as everyone would like. Individuals change, societies change, and sometimes things just go wrong. Stress affects individuals and the family unit as a whole. This chapter takes a look at crisis in families with particular focus on family violence. We will see that family-related issues, like other aspects of society, are socially defined and constructed. These definitions change over time, partly as a result of social movements.

Thinking Ahead **What are the most serious problems in families today? If you had to measure the amount of family violence in America, how would you go about it? What is your definition of child abuse? In what ways should the government be involved in reducing family violence? How would your answers be likely to differ from those given by your parents when they were your age? Your grandparents?**

The kinds of things that result in crisis for one family at one time and place might not be considered serious by another family in another time and place. Several theories have been developed to account for such differences, some of which focus on the way certain couples deal with the world as they construct mutual scripts.

Other approaches look at the ways social meanings and scripts change over time. Role expectations, values, and norms evolve in response to social conditions and in response to intentional efforts by groups of concerned individuals. As people focus on issues and come to define them as problematic, new ways of looking at "social problems" emerge. Family violence, for example, is considered a serious problem today, but that has not always been the case. Changes in definitions of family problems, and the research these changes have generated, will serve as a major focus of this chapter.

Defining Family Crisis

A number of models exist for understand family problems. After defining basic terms, we will consider two well-known models of dealing with stress in families.

Coping with Stress

Family systems theory provides the context for understanding research concerning what stress is and the way families deal with it. Robert Angell (1936), as well as Ruth Cavan and Katherine Ranck (1938), conducted pioneering studies in this field. These researchers examined how families handled stress associated with the Great Depression in the 1930s.

Cavan and Ranck (1938) found that families that were better organized before the depression handled the problems better. These families had clearly defined boundaries about who was a family member and who was not. They also had more clearly defined roles and routines that individuals and subsystems were expected to follow when dealing with events. Families without these characteristics were less able to maintain their stability when faced with economic hardship. Having well-defined family scripts helps.

While economic problems can be difficult for families, research since the depression has looked at other kinds of problems as well. A wide variety of events, called **stressors,** can threaten a family's equilibrium. These can range from relatively minor events, such as making vacation plans, to major events such as the death of a family member. Although faced regularly with minor stressors, successful families develop ways of

---

Stressors: Events with the potential of causing major change in a family system.

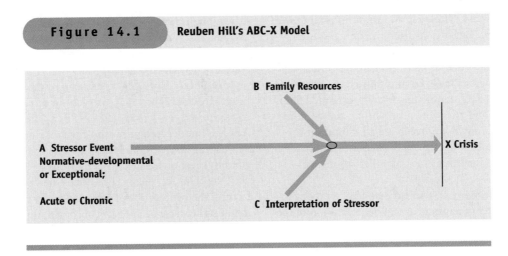

Figure 14.1   Reuben Hill's ABC-X Model

coping that prevent most stressors from seriously disrupting the system. If not, a family **crisis** can develop. If the family system survives, the period of disorganization is followed by the establishment of a new level of reorganization that can be below, equal to, or even above the original level of functioning (Boss, 1987, 1988).

Hill's ABC-X Model

Reuben Hill (1949, 1958) studied family separation during World War II and developed the classic ABC-X model of family crisis and stress. "A" represents the stressor event; "B" equals the resources the family has for dealing with the stress; "C" stands for the family's subjective interpretation of the stressor event; and "X" is the extent of the crisis (see Figure 14.1).

A: The Stressor Event. There are several sources and types of stressors (Boss, 1988). First, a stressor can be external, originating outside the family, or it can be more internal in origin. Economic cycles, wars, natural disasters, and urban renewal projects that displace families are among the possible external sources. Illness and a change in life goals are more likely to be categorized as internal to the family.

Stressors can be either normative-developmental or exceptional in nature. The birth of a child, sending a child to school for the first time, having the last child leave the home, and retirement are all predictable, normative events. They do represent change in the family

system, however, so they are sources of stress that can have either positive or negative outcomes. Exceptional stressors, such as the death of a child, are not a normal part of the family life cycle, at least in postindustrial societies.

Stressors can also be characterized as either acute or chronic. Acute ones, like having one's house robbed, happen suddenly and are then over. Chronic stressors, such as having to take care of a family member with Alzheimer's disease, can drag on. A family that is barely surviving because of low income can experience chronic stress, as can groups facing racial prejudice and discrimination (McAdoo, 1983). While some issues can be resolved and forgotten, others provide potential sources of stress throughout a marriage. Straus, Gelles, and Steinmetz (1980) provided survey respondents with five general categories of potential conflicts that can run throughout the life cycle of the marriage. Respondents said that the categories of relationship issues most likely to produce conflict, in order, were housekeeping, sex, social activities, money, and children. While housekeeping caused the most frequent conflict, arguments over children were most likely to result in serious conflict and violence, with disagreements over money a close second. It would appear that housekeeping matters are nagging and continuous, while children and money provide more serious but less frequent sources of conflict.

B: Resources. The presence of stressors might not result in crisis if the family has sufficient resources for

---

Coping: Management of stressors without detrimental effects to the family system.   **Crisis:** The period of disorganization resulting from a stressor that ordinary coping mechanisms have trouble dealing with.

dealing with them. Money is important in dealing with some problems, but it is far from the only resource. Characteristics such as good health, a good sense of humor, problem-solving skills, communication skills, optimism, religious faith, common interests, knowledge about marriage and family life, friends, extended family support, love and affection, adaptability, and commitment to the family relationship are all important resources on which a family can draw. Some families use counselors or therapists as extrafamilial resources.

C: The Definition of the Stressor. Symbolic interactionist theory reminds us that the definition of the event, not some objective view of the event, determines human reactions. For one couple a third pregnancy might be occasion for joy, but for another, a catastrophe. One couple might interpret the launch of the youngest child or retirement as a severe role loss, while another see it as a welcome increase in freedom and opportunity. If a couple see a job loss as internally caused, the result of the worker's laziness or incompetence, they will react differently than the couple who see the job loss as part of a widespread, externally produced economic downturn.

X: The Crisis. The combination of A, B, and C determines whether there is a crisis in the family and how serious the crisis might be. A severe crisis includes disequilibrium, instability, or disorganization of the family system. This affects the success of attempts at reorganization of the family system. Some families might operate better than ever after dealing with a crisis, but others might never again operate as well as before. In extreme cases, the particular family system might be so reorganized that it can no longer be considered the same system. Divorce has this effect.

McCubbin developed a variation of the ABC-X model (McCubbin, 1979; McCubbin & Dahl, 1985; McCubbin & Patterson, 1982, 1983). This "double ABC-X" model recognizes the effect of time on a family's coping ability. Going through one crisis can change a family's resource base and definitions of later events. This can result in "pileup," in which a new stressor is faced in the context of a previous crisis. An event that might earlier have been easily coped with might now result in a crisis (Clark, 1999). One period of unemployment, for example, can quickly use up savings so that another layoff has more serious consequences. An episode of adultery, even if it does not end the marriage, can reduce the amount of love and trust that would otherwise be available to deal with less serious day-to-day stressors.

It is possible that going through one crisis actually improves a family's coping mechanisms. They might learn new communication skills, for example, that can help when the next stressor appears. Confidence that problems can be dealt with can also serve as a resource.

McCubbin's model suggests that adaptation is one outcome of a crisis. Nonadaptation, in which the system breaks down or remains in stress, is also a possibility. Maladaptation, too, can result. A family might respond to a crisis by becoming violent or by using drugs or alcohol. This could allow the system to continue, but in a destructive or dysfunctional way.

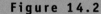

Figure 14.2   **McCubbin's Double ABC-X Model**

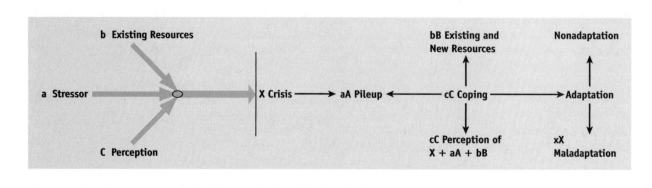

Source: McCubbin, Hamilton, and Joan Patterson. 1982. "Family Adaptation to Crisis." Pp. 26–47 in *Family Stress, Coping, and Social Support.* Edited by A. Elizabeth McCubbin. Springfield IL: Charles Thomas.

The Social Construction of Child Abuse

While definitions of reality affect how individuals respond to situations, the meanings are not constructed in a vacuum. The social context in which people find themselves helps shape their personal reality, and these contexts change. Chapter 13 suggested that images of children vary culturally and historically and that the boundaries of acceptability have changed with respect to child-rearing practices. Changes such as this often result from intentional social change.

Social Movement Theory

The scripting perspective has been applied to several topics in this text, most often in terms of the ways societies affect individuals and groups or in how individuals interact in groups. In the present section, we will look at the way powerful individuals and groups can change the social reality.

Armand Mauss (1975) proposed that some changes could be looked at as **social movements** that have a natural history, career, or developmental cycle. The civil rights movement is one American example, but social movements do not always lead to such positive change. The Nazi movement in Germany was a social movement with destructive consequences. Regardless of whether the changes are seen as positive or negative, Mauss proposed that movements go through five stages: incipiency, coalescence, institutionalization, fragmentation, and demise.

Incipiency means "a beginning." At this stage, there is a general sense among several persons that something is wrong. As they communicate, they begin to see the matter as a common problem that might have a solution. The media occasionally get involved, writing exposés or exploiting sensational cases to sell newspapers or to popularize television shows. In spite of cycles of interest, some issues never go beyond this point.

Coalescence means "coming together." At this stage, groups form to advance the movement by soliciting more public support. Sides of the issue are redefined, and opposition arises, attempting to advance its own definition of the situation.

Successful movements are able to convince large numbers of persons that their side of the issue is correct for moral, legal, or religious reasons. They also convince large numbers in the public that their side "deserves" support. Successful movements generally are able to convince the public of three things.

First, the **claims makers** and **moral entrepreneurs** must convince people that there is some "widespread social evil." Second, movements are more successful if they demonstrate that there are "deserving victims." These are typically persons who are perceived to be in a bad situation through no fault of their own. Since children are largely thought to be innocent, they make good "victims" for social movements. Other victims used lately are victims of car wrecks caused by drunken drivers and victims of second-hand cigarette smoke. Finally, people must be convinced that something can be done about "the widespread evil done to deserving victims." There are many ways of making these three points, including the use and misuse of statistics, lobbying public officials, protesting, boycotting, publicizing extreme anecdotal data, and staging mass rallies.

Mauss (1975) was referring to *institutionalization* of the movement itself, but the goals and specific programs can also become part of the formal legal system. As it gains public acceptance and becomes institutionalized, the movement may lose momentum. Supporters increasingly disagree about goals and approaches to use. Some leaders of the movement become part of new government agencies, task forces, and programs, while others go on to different causes. This contributes to the fourth stage of social movements.

Fragmentation occurs when some individuals in the movement drop out because they see the movement as a success. Some who remain in the movement might become part of a permanent watchdog group that attempts to make sure the advances are not lost. Others will see institutionalization as "selling out" before the full platform of the movement is achieved. These persons will be seen as extremists or radicals both by the general public and by former movement members who are now part of the establishment. Sometimes a movement that has been relatively successful finds that it has given rise to a countermovement.

Demise occurs when a movement dies out, which movements do even if they have changed society in an

---

Social movement: A large number of persons who join together to bring about or resist some social or cultural change. **Claims maker:** Person who puts forth a particular view of reality in support of, or in response to, a social movement. **Moral entrepreneurs:** People who risk moral capital to produce social change (Howard Becker).

enduring way. When this occurs, the natural history of the social movement, as Mauss (1975) saw it, is over.

One lasting result of a successful social movement is a shift in the way the public views a particular phenomenon. What was once considered appropriate might no longer be. Something that once was informally considered wrong might become formally considered illegal, or vice versa. Symbolic meanings change and so does the way persons view their world.

When worldviews change, standards for judging behavior change. When people judge the past using the standards of today, they are engaging in what historians sometimes call **presentism.** Some behaviors once considered appropriate child-raising practice, for example, are now defined as child abuse. Social movement theory sheds light on the process by which child abuse came to be seen as a social problem in the 1960s.

History of Child Abuse

Until the 1960s, there was no institutionalized social problem called child abuse, but there have probably always been parents who treated their children in ways that would now be considered wrong. As Ariès pointed out (see chapter 13), childhood was seen differently before the industrial revolution. Children were not especially singled out for special positive treatment, but they were probably not often singled out for extreme negative treatment either. Physical punishment of children might be seen as abusive by today's standards, but much of life was dangerous by today's standards. Accident, disease, injury, hunger, and death were a much more intimate part of life in preindustrial societies than in today's developed world. Play was dangerous, travel was dangerous, work was dangerous, and life in general was dangerous. A small welt from a whipping might not have had the same symbolic meaning as it would today.

Presentism sometimes results in the conclusion that "parents in the past had the right to abuse their children." In some respects this was true. Except in extreme cases, child raising was not seen as an appropriate matter for intervention by the state; it was a family matter. There is no evidence, however, that extreme brutality toward children, in the context of the time in which it occurred, was ever widely supported. When it did occur, intervention might come in the form of rebukes by the church, neighbors, or other family members. Informal norms, rather than formal ones, governed child raising.

Child labor such as in this glass factory was once quite common. Now it would be considered abusive.

Presentism: Seeing and judging the past or future using today's definitions.

Early in the 17th century, American Puritans adopted the "rebellious sons" law, taken from the Bible (Deuteronomy 21:18-21), which allowed for the death penalty by stoning for sons older than 16 who cursed or hit a parent. No American children were ever executed under the law, which was repealed in 1681, but it indicated the symbolic support of the state for parents. Other laws existed that regulated household violence, including wife abuse, child abuse, and servant abuse. Possible punishments included fines and public whippings, but prosecutions were rare (Pleck, 1987). Most family matters were dealt with informally by neighbors, pastors, or extended family members. The incipiency phase of the child abuse movement really came and went several times without moving to the next stage.

In the United States, the coalescence and institutional stages of the child protection movement were first reached in New York City in 1874, when public perception of what was then called "child cruelty" was changed as a result of the case of Mary Ellen. She was a 10-year-old illegitimate child being raised by a couple not directly related to her. Her foster mother apparently whipped Mary Ellen frequently with a leather thong, cut her with scissors, and consistently failed to dress her properly during cold weather. Several months of complaints and concern by neighbors finally resulted in legal action.

Later mythology of the child-protection movement held that, because laws protecting children were nonexistent, Mary Ellen had to be legally defined as an animal so she could be removed from the home through ASPCA (American Society for the Prevention of Cruelty to Animals) laws. In fact, however, Mary Ellen was ultimately removed from her home under an old English writ, *de homine replegando*. This procedure allowed a magistrate to remove one person from the custody of another (Thomas, 1972, in Pleck, 1987). She was sent to another foster home, where she received much better care. She had a fruitful life, living to the age of 92 (Lazoritz, 1990). Her abusive foster mother received the maximum sentence available at the time, one year at hard labor in the penitentiary.

The fact that the Mary Ellen case made the newspapers in the first place indicates that it represented unusual and unacceptable parental behavior. It sparked the formation in several American cities of the Society for the Prevention of Cruelty to Children, modeled after the older Society for the Prevention of Cruelty to Animals. Although the issue died down again after a relatively short time (Nelson, 1984), "child cruelty" had been defined as a matter that justified government

intervention into the privacy of the family. The institutionalization of "child abuse" had begun.

The Mary Ellen case was probably not as severe as some cases that had been reported in the media earlier, but it came at a time when there was "structural readiness for change" (Smelser, 1962). Friendship and sentiment were increasingly being seen as an expected part of the American family structure (Shorter, 1975). Also, the reconstruction period following the Civil War saw an extension of civil rights to former slaves; some reformers extended the concept to argue that children had at least some rights (Nelson, 1984). Finally, the concern about factory working conditions for children could easily be extended to worry about home living conditions.

As with many social movements, concern about child abuse waxed and waned for several decades, with only occasional change in public perception or government action. Congress established the U.S. Children's Bureau in 1912. As the first federal child welfare agency, the bureau initially dealt primarily with delinquency and institutionalized youth and only occasionally concerned itself with child cruelty. The Great Depression and two world wars turned America's attention elsewhere.

When concern about child abuse arose again, the medical community, with assistance from social workers, led the movement. The fledgling field of radiology reported the existence of children's broken bones that could not be accounted for by the parents' explanations. The first report of this "new" problem was presented to the Children's Bureau in 1946. That was followed throughout the late 1940s and 1950s by occasional mentions in the medical literature and the popular press (Nelson, 1984).

In the 1960s the child protective movement quite rapidly moved through the coalescence and institutionalization stages of mass movements. This was another period in American history with a "structural readiness to change." The civil rights movement of the 1950s was followed by the peace movement of the 1960s. Both of these provided an audience for stories of child abuse, the first because of concern for equality and the second because of concern about violence.

A major event in the movement came in 1962 when C. Henry Kempe, a pediatrician at the University of Colorado Medical School, published an article in the prestigious *Journal of the American Medical Association*. The research, first presented at a conference organized by the Children's Bureau, was a collaboration by Kempe, a psychiatrist, an obstetrician, and two radiologists (Nelson, 1984).

The article's title, "The Battered Child Syndrome," fit the problem into the medical view of the world, implying that a few parents with a psychological disorder of some kind committed abuse. Social movement researchers Spector and Kitsuse (1977) explained that the acceptance of a new term, or new meaning for an old term, signals an important step in the life cycle of a social movement. Developing the concept of the "battered child syndrome" was such an event in the construction of the "child abuse" movement.

The term "syndrome" implies a set of symptoms associated with a disease, in this case inadequate parenting (Pleck, 1987). The medical field had recently enjoyed tremendous successes with polio and smallpox vaccinations, saving millions of children, and the hope was that the medical community could do the same for other ailments. The prestige of the medical community was eventually used to overcome the traditional reluctance of government to get involved with internal family matters, and the resistance by citizens to what they saw as governmental meddling in private affairs.

Even given the climate of the times, the Kempe article might have gone relatively unnoticed had the journal's accompanying editorial not become public. The journal warned, solely on the basis of speculation, that the battered child syndrome might cause more deaths than leukemia, cystic fibrosis, and muscular dystrophy. Within a few weeks, this warning had been repeated in nearly all major newspapers and magazines in the country (Nelson, 1984). This alarmed large numbers of citizens who grew increasingly concerned with the "social problem" of child abuse as a major cause of death of children. To reach the institutionalization phase, leaders of a movement must demonstrate that their issue is both damaging and widespread. In the approach typical of mass movements, the damage is illustrated with reference to the most grotesque, severe possible examples. This is followed by an official-appearing statement about how widespread the problem is. For child abuse, the *Journal of the American Medical Association's* speculations provided the latter. Evidence and pictures of extreme cases could easily be obtained. When accompanied by reports that large numbers of children were victims, a powerful case was made for the existence of a serious social problem.

When child abuse gained public attention as a growing social problem, concerned individuals and groups worked to generate even greater public attention and to obtain political support for institutionalization. Although claims makers assumed that child abuse was widespread, no one knew how much child abuse existed; there lacked even agreement about exactly what child abuse was. Despite its vagueness, politicians found child abuse to be a powerful issue, and the movement was institutionalized in relatively rapid fashion.

Unlike what had happened on previous occasions, the child protective movement did not die after the initial flurry of activity. A number of organizations continued to press until Congress passed the 1974 Child Abuse Prevention and Treatment Act (CAPTA). This act provided a formal definition of child abuse:

> "Child Abuse and Neglect" means the physical or mental injury, sexual abuse, negligent treatment, or maltreatment of any child under the age of eighteen by a person who is responsible for the child's welfare under circumstances that indicate the child's health or welfare is harmed or threatened thereby (PL 93-247, 1974, Sec. 2; in Nelson, 1984:14).

CAPTA also provided for a variety of offices and programs regarding child abuse, but states could not receive funding unless they adopted certain policies, including provisions for removing children from their homes if abuse was suspected (Hoffman, 1978). In addition to the criminal laws already on the books, most states developed a separate apparatus for dealing with child abuse; this usually became part of the welfare, social services, family protective services, or similar branch of state and local government (Michaelis, 1993).

The child protective movement was institutionalized with little opposition. Only a few political conservatives, concerned about intrusion of government into private family matters, objected to child-abuse legislation. In recent years, however, the movement began to suffer some fragmentation, and there is debate in the field today. One area of disagreement has been the exact definition of child abuse, and what kinds of things count as abuse and what do not. Some advocates prefer the Swedish approach of including spanking and other corporal punishment as child abuse; others think this is going too far. If spanking is included, the vast majority of American children are victims; if spanking is not included, the number of victims drops considerably (Gelles & Straus, 1987).

There is also disagreement about the process by which child abuse is reported and investigated. In most states, reports of abuse are investigated by the Child Protective Services or similarly named agency, although police might also be involved in investigation of serious allegations. Because Protective Services is designed to look after the interests of the child, parents are not entitled to the same legal protections they get in criminal investigations. Some experts find that there is not always enough concern for the rights of parents (Fincham et al., 1994).

Some researchers claim that child abuse is still not taken seriously enough and that more reporting, investigation, and removal of children from abusive homes are called for (Finkelhor, 1993). Others are concerned that unnecessary reporting and investigation can damage the child as well as the parents. These researchers point to evidence that between 60 and 65% of reports of child abuse turn out to be unfounded and that family relationships are often harmed by the investigation itself (Besharov, 1993). In spite of the fragmentation in the child protective movement, no one seriously proposes that American society go back to the pre-1962 nonintervention practice. Although the boundaries remain unclear, some cases are clearly abusive, and most Americans still believe that children need some protection from truly abusive parents.

Types and Frequency of Child Abuse

Child mistreatment can conceptually be divided into neglect and abuse. **Neglect** is an act of omission; it is the failure of a parent or parent-surrogate to do something he or she should have done. Failure to dress children properly in cold weather, or to provide them with a properly nutritious diet, or even the failure to provide sufficient hugs and positive support might be considered neglect. Because of the difficulty of knowing where the exact boundary is, knowing how much neglect there is in the United States today is virtually impossible.

Abuse is an act of commission that occurs when parents or someone acting in the role of a parent harms or places a child in a harmful situation. There are three types of abuse: emotional, sexual, and physical. Like neglect, emotional abuse can be extremely difficult to define and measure. It could include yelling at a child, making mean comments, or locking a child in a dark closet for long periods. While definitions of neglect, sexual abuse, and physical abuse are often included in child maltreatment laws, emotional abuse is generally not included (Michaelis, 1993).

Because children are assumed not to be competent to consent to sexual acts with an adult, any sexual activity between an adult and a child is considered abusive

(Finkelhor, 1979, 1984). Only a small fraction of sexual abuse cases involve penetration of a vagina by a penis. Most involve fondling, inappropriate touching, or voyeurism and other noncontact behaviors with sexual implications. Because of the difficulties of definition and measurement, estimates of the portion of children who are victims range from 6% to 62% for girls and from 3% to 31% for boys (Peters, Wyatt, & Finkelhor, 1986; Fincham et al., 1994).

Most verified cases of child abuse fall into the broad category of physical abuse, which is somewhat easier to define and measure than emotional abuse or neglect. One source of information about physical abuse is the National Family Violence Surveys that were conducted in 1976 and 1985 (Gelles & Straus, 1987, 1988; Straus & Gelles, 1986; Straus, Gelles, & Steinmetz, 1980). These surveys asked parents with children under 18 whether they had engaged in specific abusive behaviors during the past year. In 1985, a total of 54.9% of parents said they had "slapped or spanked" their child in the past year; 30.7% had "pushed, grabbed, or shoved" their child.

The surveys found that the most severe forms of violence were not common. Severe abuse was defined as those behaviors with a high probability of injuring a child, including kicking, biting, punching, hitting or trying to hit with an object, beating up, burning or scalding, and threatening to use or using a gun or a knife. One or more of these behaviors was admitted to by 2.3% of parents. Seven out of 1,000 children under age 18 were injured by a parent in the year preceding the survey. If these percentages are applied to the number of children in the country, about 1.5 million are severely abused annually and about 450,000 are injured by their parents (Gelles, 1995).

The National Family Violence Surveys found a 47% decrease in child abuse from 1976 to 1985 (Gelles & Straus, 1987). By contrast, advocacy groups such as the American Association for Protecting Children (1989) and the National Center on Child Abuse and Neglect (1988) reported rapidly increasing rates of child abuse. The perception of increasing rates was probably a result of increased reporting and redefining abuse rather than of changing parental behavior. In the long view, the images that individuals have about the proper raising of children, and the role of government in that process, have changed quite rapidly in the last three decades. The same is true with the topic of "spouse abuse" or

---

Child neglect: Failure of a parent or parent-surrogate to do something he or she should have done for his or her child.
Child abuse: Action by a parent or parent-surrogate that should not have been done because of potential harm to the child.

As a child welfare investigator, in which of these photos might you suspect child abuse?

"wife battering." Not all child abuse comes at the hands of parents. Anyone in a position of trust or authority over a child can legally be charged with child abuse. Much of the sexual abuse or molestation is committed by nonparental individuals who gain the trust of the child, then threaten the child not to tell anyone. It is in cases such as this that Bikers Against Child Abuse (see Highlight 14.1) gets involved.

Spouse Abuse

The movement to identify a social problem called "wife battering" was somewhat intertwined with child protective movements. The most recent mass movement about spouse abuse began in the 1970s, but there is a much longer history of concern about this form of family violence.

Spouse Abuse before the Postindustrial Era

Examples of severe abuse of wives by their husbands can be found throughout Western history, but it has never been a socially acceptable practice. The **charavari,** a form of public ridicule, was found throughout Europe. People yelling, banging on pots and pans, and generally making a disturbance would surround the home of wayward persons, usually at night. They might chant the

Charavari: "A noisy public demonstration to subject wayward individuals to humiliation in the eyes of the community" (Shorter, 1975:218).

HIGHLIGHT 14.1 **BIKERS AGAINST CHILD ABUSE** The unique organization Bikers Against Child Abuse (BACA) was formed in Provo, Utah, in 1995. It now has chapters in 24 states and in Canada, and is growing world wide. BACA's mission is to create a safer environment for abused children. On the streets, BACA members look like a motorcycle gang—hogs, leather jackets, and all. But like many bikers, they have a soft spot for children.

Although there was some initial difficulty in gaining acceptance, BACA now works with law enforcement and other officials. When a BACA chapter is informed of a child abuse or molestation case in the area, members ask the child and his or her parents for permission to get involved. If the answer is yes, the membership of the group rides, en masse, to the home of the child.

They make the child a "member" of their club and let the child know that they are willing to shield him or her from further harm. In the process, perpetrators are likely to become aware that the child has the protection of a high-profile group.

The child is given a vest with the BACA patch; he or she decides whether to wear it. After the initial contact, the child is given the names of the two fully authorized BACA members who live the closest. BACA does not condone violence or physical force but stands ready to be an obstacle to further harm to the child. If afraid, children can call the bikers who will provide an escort for them in their neighborhood, ride by their homes regularly, support the children at court and parole hearings, and stay with them if they are alone and frightened.

BACA members will be available as long as the child needs them, but the goal of the group is to empower the child so that he or she does not need permanent help. BACA demonstrates that there are a number of ways people can get involved in helping while also doing what they enjoy—in this case sharing the camaraderie of a biking group.

Source: http://www.bacausa.com/ and personal communication with "HarleyThor," the group's treasurer.

person's alleged crime, which often related to marriage or sexuality. Unwed mothers and the fathers of their children were charavaried, as were those who committed adultery, especially the women (Shorter, 1975).

Men who failed to work were charavaried, as were men who beat their wives. Because husbands were supposed to control their wives, men whose wives cheated on them were charavaried. So, too, were men whose wives abused them. In a region of France, a man whose wife had abused him was forced to ride backward through the village on a donkey, carrying women's implements while the villagers mocked him (Shorter, 1975).

Prior to the 19th century, husbands were legally responsible for the behavior of their wives. Blackstone, whose 18th-century compendium of English common law became the basis of much American law, allowed men power to restrain their wives using "domestic chastisement," but "the husband was prohibited from using any violence to his wife" (Blackstone, 1826, v. 1 p. 36; in Sommers, 1994:205). The exact boundary between domestic chastisement and violence is not clear, but punishment was exacted upon some who stepped across the line. Among the Puritan communities of colonial Massachusetts, family violence was thought to jeopardize the standing of the entire community in the eyes of God. The Puritan leader Cotton Mather preached that a man who defiled the institution of the family by beating his wife would be better off being buried alive than to show his head among his neighbors (Pleck, 1987:18).

Actual penalties were not as harsh as Mather suggested, but both husbands and wives were sometimes brought before the courts on charges of spouse abuse. More often, less formal remedies were used. Neighbors, religious leaders, relatives, and other community members kept an eye on families that disturbed the peace. Shame, public and church confessions, and informal counseling helped curb family violence and other unwanted behavior.

Formal prosecutions for wife abuse were rare in colonial and early U.S. history, but occasional severe cases encouraged the emergence of a wife-protective movement. The 19th-century prohibitionist movement argued that violence against women was caused by alcohol, using the image of the drunken, abusive, working-class man in its anti-alcohol campaigns (Pleck, 1987).

The term "wife beating" was first used in England in 1856 during a campaign for divorce reform. After the Civil War, American feminists and others used this powerful label in the divorce reform movement. Arguing that women should have the right to divorce in cases of both drunkenness and wife beating, they were somewhat successful in producing reforms (Pleck, 1987).

Early feminists were not the only ones concerned about wife beating; strong "law and order" supporters also got involved. In addition, beginning in the 1870s, the Ku Klux Klan included in its targets of informal punishment both Black and White men thought to be guilty of severe child abuse or wife abuse; a few abusive husbands were lynched (Pleck, 1987).

Formal action was also taken. In 1885 there began a call to resurrect old Puritan punishments in cases of wife abuse and other crimes. Offenders were to be tied to a whipping post in the town square and given a prescribed number of lashes. The matter was seriously debated by the American Bar Association, in Congress, and in several state legislatures. Laws prescribing the whipping post for wife beaters were passed and applied in three states, and came close to passage in several others (Pleck, 1987). These provided some early examples of institutionalization of the wife-abuse movement.

Although the first two decades of the 20th century saw numerous advances in the rights of women, including the right to vote, the social movement regarding wife beating essentially died out. It was revived in the late 1960s and 1970s along with the new feminist movement and the shelter movement.

The Shelter Movement

The most significant part of the new wife-protective movement was the effort to establish shelters for battered women. The first shelters were established in England by a group led by Erin Pizzey, who also wrote the influential book *Scream Quietly, or the Neighbors Will Hear* (1974). Pizzey later became active in the American shelter movement, and several Americans visited English shelters. These visitors included journalists from *Ms.* and *Newsweek*, among other magazines. In 1976, *Ms.* could find only 20 shelters for battered women in the United States; four years later there were around 200.

The shelter movement gained support from a broad spectrum of groups and individuals. Funding for the shelters came from federal, state, and local governments; church and other nonprofit groups; feminist organizations; and local fund-raising activities such as bake sales. The common goals were to provide a safe, temporary place to stay for abused women and their children and to define the problem of battered women for the public (Pleck, 1987). Shelters are now institutionalized in virtually all American cities, and the image of domestic violence portrayed by the shelter movement is often the "official" version presented by police officers, prosecutors, and family counselors (Starbuck, 1997).

The feminist movement, which helped generate definitions of abuse and delineate causes, has been a sustaining force for the shelter movement and the wife-abuse movement in general. The foundation of the theoretical feminist analysis of wife abuse came from two books. *Violence against Wives*, by R. Emerson Dobash and Russell Dobash (1979), provided a conflict-theory analysis of wife abuse.

According to the Dobashes, wife abuse is not surprising in male-dominated societies that produce such male-dominated institutions as marriage. Patriarchal family structures, they held, allow wife beating as a way for men to keep women in line. They argued that wife beating was not caused by mental illness, but was "normal" behavior in a patriarchal society like the United States. It was unlikely to change without major social changes.

While the Dobash and Dobash book was theoretical, Del Martin (1976) provided more practical organizational advice in *Battered Wives*. Martin had been a founder of NOW (National Organization for Women) and was especially active as an advocate of lesbian rights. In her view, wife beating resulted from a long tradition in which wives were considered to be the property of their husbands. Martin's book gave birth to the belief that the phrase "rule of thumb" originated from the English common law that a man had the right to beat his wife as long as the stick he used was no bigger around than his thumb. Although this account has since been discredited (Sommers, 1994), it remains a widely circulated myth in the domestic violence literature (Barnett, Miller-Perrin, & Perrin, 1997; Kaplan, 1996).

Lenore Walker was probably the most influential claims maker in the battered women's movement. Her 1979 book *The Battered Woman* and 1984 follow-up *The Battered Woman Syndrome* provided a prototype of

Advocates for social causes might be very caring and committed, but they do not always get the facts straight.

victim believes that she deserves the battering and is powerless to stop it. In extreme cases, in one last attempt to save herself, she kills her abuser. In Walker's view, which has been upheld in some court cases, women are justified in killing their abusive husbands if they reasonably believed that they had no other choice.

Loseke (1992) characterized Walker's battered woman syndrome as a "woman as pure victim" perspective, which became very important to the shelter movement. Walker's description helped overcome political objections that shelters were interfering in family privacy, and it helped counter the perspective that women "deserved" their beatings. It was politically important to show that battered women were helpless victims who deserved help, not abuse. Walker's description provided that image.

While Walker's "battered woman" provided a useful framework, it also provided a stereotype into which some advocates tried to fit all cases. Shelters often defined success as helping victims gain enough independence to leave their abusive relationships. Walker's description left little hope that the marriage could improve, since she argued that abuse would only get more severe and more frequent (Loseke, 1992).

The "woman as pure victim" became the dominant model promoted by women's shelter advocates, who strongly objected to suggestions that some women might have contributed to problems in their own relationships (Stacey et al., 1994). Staff workers in some shelters were forbidden from asking residents whether

the battered woman's "cycle of violence" that trapped women. Walker contended that abused wives were trapped in a cycle of violence. Because of economic and emotional dependence, wives were vulnerable to violent episodes that were cyclical and predictable. Walker's cycle of violence begins with a period of rising tension, when abuse does not occur but the threat is present (see Figure 14.3). After a period of tension, an abusive incident occurs and tensions are released. Shortly after an abusive incident, husbands sincerely regret their behavior. During this "honeymoon phase" husbands try to make the situation right by apologizing, buying gifts, and treating wives with extra care. Wives often like this phase very much and believe that the abusive incidents will end. Walker argued, however, that the tension inevitably begins again, followed by violent incidents and again the honeymoon stage. Over time, incidents become more severe and more frequent.

In some cases, according to Walker (1989), the woman develops a sense of "learned helplessness"; the

Figure 14.3 | **Lenore Walker's Model**

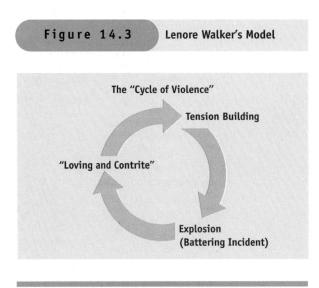

they had ever abused their husbands; there was concern that workers, or the records they kept, might be used against the female residents in later court proceedings. Shelter workers saw themselves as advocates for women, not as neutral observers. In some shelters, residents were forbidden to talk about good times they had enjoyed with their abuser and were instructed instead to focus on how bad the relationship was and how happy they should be to leave it (Loseke, 1992).

Suggestions that women could sometimes also be violent were strongly rejected by those in the shelter movement (Straus, 1993). Specific examples of violence by wives were dismissed as rare, as not serious, or as only being committed in self-defense. This was done partly because of concerns that the movement would lose ground if the "pure victim" image were weakened and attention diverted from the pressing concern of wife battering (Kurz, 1993).

The shelter movement's focus on the "pure victim" was gradually replaced by the "victim-oriented stage of women and children" (Stacey et al., 1994). Because shelters housed children as well as women, advocates could claim that they were preventing the transmission of violence from one generation to another. The shelters were serving innocent children, in addition to innocent women.

As more counselors and law enforcement agencies got involved, the "male-perpetrator-oriented phase" developed (Stacey et al., 1994). During this stage, programs for male batterers were established. Until that time, little research had been done on the men who abused their wives. Lenore Walker never interviewed men, nor did most of the workers in the shelter movement know much about the men's perspective. This

emphasis led to new counseling programs that might reduce marital violence and help save marriages (Buzawa & Buzawa, 1993). These goals were contrary to goals held by some people in the shelter movement, who sought social change in the institution of marriage itself, not adjustment to what they saw as patriarchal families.

The battered women's movement has altered the way society perceives domestic violence. Laws and court procedures have changed; police officers, prosecutors, and judges in many jurisdictions have been required to receive training to be more sensitive to the problems of battered women. This training is usually done by activists in the battered-women movement who support the Walker/women's shelter view of domestic violence. Several federal laws have been changed; the Violence Against Women Act, passed by Congress in 1994, requires the federal government to commit more resources to understanding and stopping the forms of violence in which women are the victims. The Violence Against Women Office (http://www.ojp.gov/vawo/about. htm) was established, and from 1995 through 2000 $1.79 billion was spent under the authority of that act (U.S. Department of Justice, 2000).

Public attitudes, too, have changed (see Table 14.1). In 1968, about 20% of Americans could imagine a situation in which they would approve of a husband's slapping a wife or a wife's slapping a husband. By 1994, the percentage who could imagine approving a husband slapping a wife had been reduced by half, while the percentage who could approve of husband slapping increased slightly. Table 14.2 provides a gender breakdown of the 1994 data. Men are more likely than women to approve of slapping, but both are now much

Table 14.1	Gallup Poll Data, Percentage Approving of Spouse Slapping, Trend			
Approve	**1968**	**1985**	**1992**	**1994**
Husband Slapping Wife	20	13	12	10
Wife Slapping Husband	20	21	22	23

Response "Yes" to question "Are there any situations that you can imagine in which you would approve of a husband slapping his wife's face" or "a wife slapping her husband's face?" "Yes" or "No."
Source: Moore, David W. 1994. "Approval of Husband Slapping Wife Continues to Decline." *The Gallup Poll Monthly* #341, February, p. 2.

Table 14.2	Gallup Poll Data, Percentage Approving of Spouse Slapping, by Gender, 1994		
	Total	Male	Female
Approve of Husband Slapping Wife	10%	14%	7%
Approve of Wife Slapping Husband	23%	27%	18%

Source: Moore, David W. 1994. "Approval of Husband Slapping Wife Continues to Decline." *The Gallup Poll Monthly* #341, February, p. 2.

more likely to approve of wives slapping their husbands than husbands slapping their wives.

Fragmentation of the Battered Women's Movement

The battered women's movement never fully overcame its opposition. Although President Jimmy Carter established the federal Office of Domestic Violence in 1979, it was abolished in 1981 under the Reagan administration (Pleck, 1987). Some opponents objected to what they saw as unwarranted interference in the family institution. Others objected that the shelters were too focused on divorce and not enough on saving troubled families. These and other objections contributed to fragmentation in the movement.

Among those who remain concerned about spousal abuse, there is disagreement about how best to handle the problem. Some argue that mandatory arrest of abusers is the best solution (Berk, 1993). Supporters of this position cite a controlled study in Minneapolis by Sherman and Berk (1984), who tentatively concluded that automatically arresting a man when there is reasonable cause to believe he abused his wife actually reduced the amount of repeat abuse. Although the researchers cautioned against generalization of their results to other situations, abuse movement leaders were able to use the tentative conclusions to get mandatory arrest laws passed in many jurisdictions.

Later research challenged the validity of the Minneapolis study (Binder & Meeker, 1988; Sheptycki, 1991). Attempts to replicate the original study in Atlanta, Charlotte, Colorado Springs, Miami, Omaha, and Milwaukee produced different findings. These studies found that, while mandatory arrest reduced violence in some situations, it increased abuse in others (Buzawa & Buzawa, 1993).

Stacey et al. (1994) suggested that the view of spouse abuse has moved past the "wife as pure victim," the "women and children as victim," and "male as perpetrator" phase. It has shifted toward the "systemic" phase in which the couple is seen as part of a system in which abuse occurs. In this view, Walker's "battered woman's syndrome" is only one of several mutual scripts in which violence can occur. Although Steinmetz (1977–78) encountered serious opposition from the battered women's movement when she first reported finding some men who were victims of a "battered husband syndrome," that possibility is now more widely recognized (Straus & Gelles, 1990; Straus, 1993).

Supporters of the systemic approach claim that there are a variety of abusive scripts in which couples can find themselves (Stacey et al., 1994). Steinmetz (1987) documented the existence of various types of mutual abuse, including a "Saturday night brawler" script. These couples would, regularly and predictably and often after using alcohol or drugs, get into fights in which both were violent. Even in these situations, of course, the wife is more likely to suffer injury, even though the two might have been equally guilty of "starting" the fight.

Other violent marital scripts are also possible. In some cases, a couple that has not previously used violence will do so at the end of a relationship. This is a very stressful time, and one or both might become violent. In other relationships, violence might occur once or twice during periods of high stress, such as unemployment, but never happen again. The systemic approach allows for the discovery and treatment of a wide variety of violent scripts.

Another disagreement in the field is whether alcohol causes marital violence. Flanzer (1993) claimed that alcohol and other drugs are direct causes of family violence. Gelles (1993) maintained that, while alcohol and drug use are highly associated with family violence, they

Finding Out | 14.1

Measuring Domestic Violence with the Conflict Tactics Scale

There are three primary sources of information about family violence: official government statistics, case studies and advocacy groups, and independent surveys. Each has its advantages and disadvantages, and each shows a different side of the family violence issue.

The best-known independent surveys are the National Family Violence Surveys conducted in 1976 and 1985 by Richard J. Gelles and Murray A. Straus. Their measure of what couples do when they experience conflict is called the Conflict Tactics Scale. The survey asked men and women whether they had engaged in a variety of behaviors in a couple-conflict situation and a child discipline situation. Possible responses fell into the general categories of rational discussion, verbal aggression, and physical aggression. The survey asked about the more acceptable responses, such as engaging in a calm discussion, first.

Responses in the physical aggression questions have become the most widely used measure of family violence; by 1990 the Conflict Tactics Scale had been used in over 100 articles and several books and applied in many countries (Straus, 1990).

The violence portion of the scale asks whether couples have used specific categories of violent behavior. These range from "pushing, grabbing, or shoving" and "slapping" to "used knife or gun." Results of the two studies are summarized in Table 14.3.

Figures on Table 14.3 represent the percentage of persons in each category who committed the act in question. For example, in both 1975 and 1985, 2.8% of husbands "threw something" at their wives in the context of a conflict tactic. These figures represent the incidence, not the frequency. The act in question could have happened once or several times during the past 12 months.

Most of the violence fell into the first three categories, which were referred to as "minor violent acts." Categories 4 through 8 were combined into the "severe violent acts" category. These were not direct measures of injury, but were rough indicators of the potential for serious injury.

If the percentage of women in the survey were extrapolated to the general population, it would mean about 2 million women annually are victims of severe violent acts as defined by the survey. This works out to an average of one every 15 seconds and is a source of the

| Table 14.3 | Comparison of 1975 and 1985 National Survey of Family Violence, Percentage Incidence in the Past Year |

Item	Parent-to-Child		Husband-to-Wife		Wife-to-Husband	
	1975	1985	1975	1985	1975	1985
1. Threw something	5.4	2.7	2.8	2.8	5.2	4.3
2. Pushed/grabbed/shoved	31.8	30.7	10.7	90.3	8.3	8.9
3. Slapped/spanked	52.2	54.9	5.1	2.9	4.6	4.1
4. Kicked/bit/hit with fist	3.2	1.3	2.4	1.5	3.1	2.4
5. Hit or tried to hit with object	13.4	9.7	2.2	1.7	3.0	3.0
6. Beat up	1.3	0.6	1.1	0.8	0.6	0.4
7. Threatened with gun or knife	0.1	0.2	0.4	0.4	0.6	0.6
8. Used gun or knife	0.1	0.2	0.3	0.2	0.2	0.2

Source: Straus, Murray A., and Richard J. Gelles. 1990. *Physical Violence in American Families: Risk Factors and Adaptations to Violence in 8,145 Families.* New Brunswick, NJ: Transaction Publisher. Adapted from pp. 118 and 121.

widely quoted statement, "a woman is severely beaten in this country every 15 seconds." It is not often mentioned, however, that the exact same measure could lead to the conclusion that "a man is severely beaten in this country every 15 seconds" since the numbers of men and women victimized in those ways are about the same.

The mix of male and female victims and perpetrators was nearly identical in the two surveys. Overall, about 16% of couples experienced one or more of the violent acts. Of these, both parties were violent in 49% of the cases; only the men were violent in 23%; and only the women were violent in the remaining 28% of cases (see Figure 14.2). When both had been violent, the women were slightly more likely to have hit first; this finding held true whether the men or women were asked. In response to an initial violent act, women (24.4%) were more likely than men (15.0%) to hit back. Also in response to being assaulted, more women (8.5%) than men (0.9%) called the police (Stets & Straus, 1990).

Several studies using the Conflict Tactics Scale to measure domestic violence have reached similar conclusions about the distribution of violence in dating, cohabiting, and married couples. Schafer et al. (1998), using both partners' reports, developed a range of estimates of intimate partner violence in the United States. Of couples living together, from 5.2% to 13.6% experience male-to-female violence. Female-to-male violence is slightly more common, occurring in 6.2% to 18.2% of couples. Partner violence of some kind occurs in 7.8% to 21.5% of couples.

Archer (2000) combined the results of several studies. He found that women were slightly more likely to use these forms of intimate violence than were men, but that men were more likely to cause injury. All told, 62% of those injured by partner violence were women.

The National Family Violence Survey is subject to criticism. Like other surveys, it relies on the honesty of the persons answering the questions. Archer (1999) compared answers given by men and women about the violence they had committed and the violence of which they had been victims. Both men and women understated the violence they had committed as compared to the violence their partners attributed to them. Generally, though, Archer concluded that the Conflict Tactics Scale was a reliable measure of couple violence.

The original survey studied only couples who were married or cohabiting at the time of the survey. Including cohabitants, who tend to have rockier relationships, might have led to an overestimation of the amount of marital violence. On the other hand, the survey would have missed the violence that occurred in relationships involving couples who no longer live together.

Another criticism is that not all possible acts of violence were included in the survey. In response to this and other concerns, the Conflict Tactics Scale has recently been revised (Straus et al., 1996). The new version includes such categories as "choked partner," "burned or scalded partner," and "used force to have sex." Frieze (2000) suggested that stalking should be added. Results based on the new scale are not yet available.

| Figure 14.4 | **Distribution of Couples by Violence Type** |

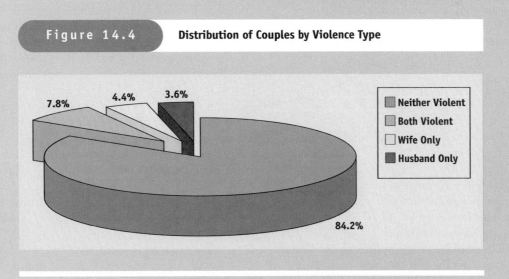

Source: Straus, M. A., and R. J. Gelles (1990). *Physical Violence in American Families: Risk Factors and Adaptations to Violence in 8,145 Families.* New Brunswick, NJ: Transaction Publishers.

Another limitation of the survey method is that acts of extreme violence are relatively rare and might easily be missed by a survey such as this. Perpetrators and victims of extreme violence might be more likely to lie or to refuse to answer the questions; they might not even be available for a survey because they have no telephone, have no permanent address, or are in jail.

Some critics are concerned that the data about violence committed by women might set back efforts to reduce violence committed by men (White et al., 2000). Others, while agreeing that researchers and politicians should pay more attention to female-initiated couple violence, still find fault with the use of the Conflict Tactics Scale (O'Leary, 2000).

In spite of the flaws in the method, the National Family Violence Surveys and other applications of the Conflict Tactics Scale remain the best source of information about the national picture of family violence. They are probably less valid as an indicator of the dynamics of extreme cases of family violence; perhaps the horror of extreme cases can best be understood anecdotally.

are not direct causes. They are, this argument goes, sometimes used by perpetrators to justify the violence once it occurs.

Finally, it has not yet been settled what name to call the problem. Feminists and those in the shelter movement prefer descriptors like "wife battering" or "wife beating" because the terms indicate a more serious problem that is placed in the broader context of gender relationships, power, and patriarchal institutions including marriages (Yllo, 1993). Other advocates prefer the terms "domestic violence," "family violence," or "intimate violence" that put the problem into the context of a violent society that can include the victimization of husbands and sons, as well as wives and daughters (Pleck, 1987). How the phenomenon is defined and framed affects the way researchers approach the topic.

Research on Family Violence

It is clear that good information about the incidence and dynamics of family violence is difficult to obtain. Abuse is often hidden by family privacy, is poorly defined, and is illegal. A variety of sources, however, continue to provide information of varying degrees of reliability. This issue is explored in Finding Out 14.1. Information obtained from reliable sources can be used to sort out some of the causes and correlates of family violence and to test theories about the phenomenon. It can also be used to generate more social movements.

The image of couple violence portrayed by Lenore Walker and the shelter movement is different than the picture painted by surveys using the Conflict Tactics Scale. Women's shelters maintain that violence is virtually always committed by a man on an innocent female victim and that violence is likely to get worse as time goes by unless there is intervention in the relationship. Research using the Conflict Tactics Scale finds that women are as likely to be as violent as men, that mutual violence is common, and that violence declines with age. Both agree that women are more likely to be injured than are men.

In an attempt to resolve those differences, Michael Johnson (1995, 1999, 2000; Johnson & Ferraro, 2000) suggested that the national surveys and the women's shelters were finding two different types of violence. Johnson first called the type found by women's shelters "patriarchal terrorism." Although men are usually the perpetrators of this type, Johnson (2000) changed the name to "intimate terrorism" because a few women in both heterosexual and lesbian relationships commit this type. The violence is used as a form of control over the partner. It probably will get worse over time as control becomes more complete. Johnson suggested that type of domestic violence found by national surveys was more likely to be "common couple violence." It is the result of a specific argument in which one or both partners become physically violent. This type of violence is less likely to escalate over time, it usually involves less serious violence, and it is more likely to be mutual than the intimate terrorism type.

Another type of violence, according to Johnson (2000), is "violent resistance." This is almost always perpetrated by women, in response to being long-term victims of intimate terrorism. It includes not only women who kill their husbands, but also those who do not go quite as far as that. Some women might engage in this type of violence as a prelude to leaving the relationship (Jacobson & Gottman, 1998). Johnson's (1999, 2000) fourth type of violence is "mutual violent control." In this pattern, both the husband and wife are controlling and violent. The relationship dynamics are like two "intimate terrorists" trying to gain control over each other. The violence can become quite serious and constant.

Johnson contributed a great deal to an understanding of couple violence by pointing out that there is more than one type. Each type probably calls for different responses from law enforcement and the counseling community, but those responses have not yet been established. We do not know, either, what the relative frequency of each of these types might be.

It is important for social scientists to continue to study family violence, but to focus solely on it can be misleading. It would be easy to conclude that families are a dangerous place to be and that maybe people are better off without them. Such is decidedly not the case, as Figure 14.5 indicates.

Widows and widowers are least likely to be victims of violent crimes, primarily because of their higher average age. Married adults have considerably lower victimiza- tion rates than either the divorced or separated category or the never married category. Men are more likely to be victims in all categories except the divorced/separated, where women are slightly more likely. For both men and women, being married is a safer condition, in spite of the unacceptable rates of couple violence.

Correlates of Family Violence

Child abuse and spouse abuse occur in all social classes, but the poor are more likely to find themselves in courts and jails for their acts. This is partly because the poor are more visible and have fewer resources to avoid being labeled as abusers, but there is also evidence that those lower in socioeconomic status actually commit more abuse. Survey data find that rates are higher among those with lower educational level, among blue-collar rather than white-collar workers, and in homes where the husband is unemployed (Gelles, 1995).

Most studies report higher rates of family violence for Hispanics than for Whites, and yet higher rates for Blacks (Straus & Smith, 1990). The racial difference is at least partly accounted for by social-class variables like income, unemployment, and occupational level

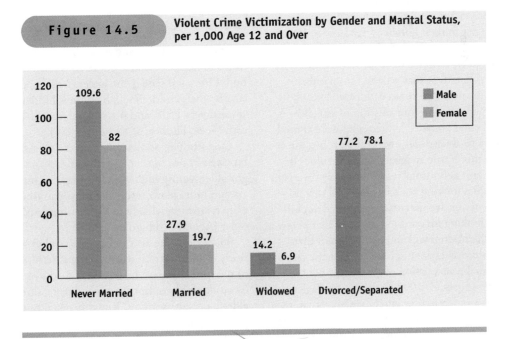

Figure 14.5 Violent Crime Victimization by Gender and Marital Status, per 1,000 Age 12 and Over

Source: United States Department of Justice, Bureau of Crime Statistics. 1997. *Criminal Victimization in the United States, 1994.* Table 12. Washington DC: Government Printing Office.

(Cazenave & Straus, 1990). Even within a racial and ethnic group, the amount of family violence varies by immigration status (Kane, 1999). Sorenson and Telles (1991) found no overall difference in spousal violence rates between Mexican Americans and non-Hispanic Whites. The rate for Mexican Americans born in the United States, however, was 2.4 times the rate for Mexican Americans who were born in Mexico.

Social isolation is also associated with child and partner abuse. Families that have little contact with other people have a higher abuse rate. Families that are part of a larger kin network, friendship groups, community organizations, or religious organizations have lower rates of violence (Cazenave & Straus, 1990; Miller & Chilamkurti, 1991).

To some extent, violent behavior, like many other traits, is passed from one generation to the next. Persons who were exposed to any kind of violence in their families of orientation are more likely to be part of violence in their families of procreation. Children who watched one parent abuse the other are more likely to be abusive, and more likely to be abused, than children who were not exposed to such violence (Straus, Gelles, & Steinmetz, 1980). One sample of abusive husbands found that 80% of them reported either being abused as children or witnessing their fathers abusing their mothers (Roy, 1977). In dating relationships, men and women alike are more likely to be both victims and perpetrators if they witnessed violence in their homes as children (Gwartney-Gibbs, Stockard, & Bohmer, 1987). Domestic violence of all types seems to be associated with a general antisocial orientation that is passed from one generation to the next (Simmons & Johnson, 1998).

The "intergenerational transmission of violence" is also seen with child abuse. Children who were abused are more likely to abuse their own children, but the extent to which this is true is debatable. Difficulties in measurement and definitions result in widely divergent estimates. Studies looking back in time find that as many as 90% of abusive parents were abused as children. Studies looking forward in time find that as few as 18% of abused children will abuse children of their own. More common estimates indicate that the rate of intergenerational transmission of violence is between 30% and 40% (Egeland, 1993; Kaufman & Zigler, 1993). This is a much higher rate of violence than the rate found in the general public (Gelles, 1995), but it still explains only a small amount of the difference in family violence (Johnson & Ferraro, 2000).

Age is a factor in family violence. Rates of both child abuse and spousal abuse are higher for younger parents and partners (Cazenave & Straus, 1990). The additional economic stresses and immaturity of youth-headed families appear to increase the likelihood of abuse. It is also possible, however, that abusive marriages are more likely to end in divorce than nonabusive ones and that they would be less likely to become old marriages.

It has been widely reported that wives are more likely to be abused when they are pregnant. Gelles (1990) found, however, that the important factor was age, not pregnancy. Younger women are more likely to be abused, and younger women are more likely to be pregnant. Pregnant women are not more likely to be abused than other women their own age.

Couple violence occurs in homosexual relationships too. Some studies have indicated that there is more partner abuse in lesbian relationships than in either gay male or heterosexual relationships (Lie & Gentlewarrior, 1991; Lie et al., 1991; Renzetti, 1992). Tjaden et al. (1999) found instead that abuse is most likely in gay male relationships, least likely in lesbian ones. Because of the amount of abuse in same-sex relationships, Dutton (1994) concluded that there is reason to question the theoretical link between "patriarchy" and heterosexual wife abuse; it might be stretching believability to argue that oppression of women causes abuse among lesbian and gay male couples.

Other Forms of Family Violence

After the child-abuse and wife-abuse movements, other forms of family violence began to receive public attention. One such type is the violence directed toward parents by their children. Such abuse is hidden, has been studied very little, and has generated little public concern (Peek, Fischer, & Kidwell, 1985).

One study of adolescents found that about 5% had hit one or both of their parents in the past year. As they got older, young men were less likely to hit their mothers and more likely to hit their fathers. Young women were increasingly likely to hit their parents as they got older (Agnew & Huguley, 1989).

The elderly are also victims of family violence. One study found that about 2% of the elderly were victims of physical abuse in the past year. Some of the abuse was by adult children, but the most likely culprits were the elderly person's spouses. Roughly equal numbers of men and women were victims, but women received the most severe injuries (Pillemer & Finkelhor, 1988).

Sibling violence is also common. According to the first National Family Violence Survey, 16% of children had "beat up" a sibling. In addition, 40% had hit a sibling with an object, and 42% had kicked, bit, or punched a brother or sister. A few had even used knives or guns (Straus, Gelles, & Steinmetz, 1980). Although fights between siblings are by far the most common form of family violence, it is rarely considered a social problem (Gelles, 1995).

The newest area of research in family violence is pet abuse. Since some people see pets as being members of their family, pet abuse can be dealt with as another type of family violence in itself (Raupp, 1999). Other researchers report finding a high correlation between pet abuse and partner violence (Flynn, 2000; Weber, 1999). Combined interest by family violence interests and animal rights interests could thrust this issue into social problems status.

Alternative Theoretical Explanations of Family Violence

Social movements theory provides an excellent way of looking at the way societies change their definitions and evaluative judgments. It does not, however, explain why some persons are violent even when the norms have clearly defined it as unacceptable behavior.

A social-exchange perspective would argue that, although violence is against the norms, the costs of violating the norms are relatively low. The benefits, in terms of control derived or stress released, might be higher than the costs (Gelles, 1983). In a similar vein, resource theory would predict that persons with more resources are less likely to resort to violence because they can get their way by other means (Goode, 1971). Finally, resource theory correctly predicts that women with more resources, in the form of education and independent sources of income, are more likely to leave an abusive relationship (Gelles, 1976).

Social learning theory can account for the intergenerational transmission and other aspects of family violence for both male and female perpetrators (Giordano et al., 1999). Although many who are abused do not later abuse their own children or spouses, they had the obstacle of prior conditioning to overcome and had to be more conscious of their own actions and definitions the situation to avoid repeating what they had learned.

Scripting perspectives of family violence could incorporate all the other theories. Accordingly, social movements theory helps explain the societal boundaries of behavior found in the societal scripts. Feminist and other structural theories address issues of power in society. Social learning theory explains the development of individual scripts. Symbolic interactionist perspectives help explain how couples develop scripts of their own.

For most couples, violence is never part of their mutual script. Other couples construct roles and scripts that incorporate violence. For some couples, a violent episode may be defined as a crisis, in accord with the

There is sometimes a fine line between children playing appropriately and children abusing each other.

Church Members Refuse to Spare the Rod

An Atlanta church was the center of a child abuse scandal in 2001. Child welfare agencies claimed that almost 60 children were victims of beatings by their parents and church leaders. The Rev. Arthur Allen, Jr., apparently supervised the actions that caused open wounds and large bruises and welts.

Allen and other church leaders were charged with cruelty to children, and 41 children were sent to foster care. This is not Allen's first brush with the law. Eight years ago he spent 30 days in jail for ordering a 16-year-old to be whipped with belts. Allen admitted that the whippings might have lasted as long as half an hour.

One former church member claimed that teenage girls who had sex were whipped during church services after their dresses or skirts were removed. Allen denied any sexual abuse, but he said the girls were better off being whipped than becoming whores.

Allen allegedly forced several 14- and 15-year-old girls to marry after they got pregnant or, sometimes, after they had just become sexually active. Georgia law specifies a minimum age of 16 for marriage, so the girls were married in neighboring Alabama, where 14 is the legal age.

Like all the church members, Allen is Black. He claims that White society can do what it wants with White children, but it shouldn't try to make him and his congregation White.

Chief Judge Sanford Jones offered to release 41 children from foster care if their parents would agree to certain conditions. The parents were to spank only with their hands, to do so only at home rather than at church, and to prevent girls under 16 from being married.

The parents refused the offer on the grounds that they had the right to "raise our children according to the Bible." The children remained in foster care.

Source: David Firestone. **www.nytimes.com.** March 30, 2001.

ABC-X model. In other cases, the violence might become part of a fairly predictable pattern and would not be as likely to precipitate a crisis unless it were a particularly injurious episode. In either case, one or both partners might seek help from extrafamilial sources, as they might for other kinds of family problems. It is certainly true that more—probably considerably more—injury is caused to women by men than vice versa, but there is ample evidence that women, too, can be violence in relationships. Little is known about the dynamics of cases in which women initiate violence against their male partners; most theoretical work is directed toward male-to-female violence. Some scholars report political and academic pressure against doing research on female-to-male violence (Archer, 1999; Cook, 1997; Straus, 1990).

Abuse of elderly, frail, institutionalized, and gay men has been confirmed (Kosberg, 1998). In cases of heterosexual intimate violence, some men probably protect themselves without hitting back because it is part of their cultural learning never to hit a woman (Steinmetz, 1978). Men are less likely to report such abuse to authorities because they are less likely than women to be seriously injured. They may also be afraid, probably with good reason, that their reports will not be taken seriously or that their masculinity would be challenged.

The presence and frequency of such possibilities would require more research, but abused men are unlikely victims around which to start a social movement.

Other Family Troubles and Responses

Family violence is far from the only problem families can have. Alcohol and drug abuse are common family concerns. There are a variety of possible responses to trouble and crisis in families. Some families muddle along the best they can, some improve, and others experience divorce or other reorganization. Others seek help from formal or informal extrafamilial resources. Still others focus on making changes in society.

Responses to Spouse Abuse

Considerable research has addressed the issue of what women do in response to violence. Gelles (1976) found three factors that were associated with the probability that a woman would stay in an abusive relationship rather than leave. First, the less frequent and severe the violence, the more likely she is to stay. Second, women who experienced violence as children were more likely to stay in an abusive marriage. Third, the fewer resources the woman had, such as occupational skills and educational attainment, the more likely she was to stay. These same factors probably affect the decision of abused men to leave relationships, but virtually no research has been done on that question. In at least some abusive relationships, the abuser might be the one who wants to leave, but no research has taken that direction either. The women's shelter image assumes that the male perpetrator always wants the relationship to continue. That is probably true in most cases, but we do not know in what percentage.

Other factors are involved. Women might actually fear for their lives if they try to leave. In fact, attempting to leave can be a dangerous time in a relationship that already has been violent. They might also fear social rejection as a "failed wife." Their religious and personal values might strongly oppose divorce. Women who have a strong commitment to their marriage and to their husbands might also believe that they can help him change (Herbert, Selver, & Ellard, 1991). A woman might see him as a good provider and husband except for the abuse. To ask why she does not leave is to imply that she should, and the woman herself might not believe that leaving is in the best interests of herself or her children.

To ask why a woman (or man) does not leave an abusive relationship also reduces a complex interaction to only one of its elements. Abuse might be a part of the relationship, but in the eyes of the woman the positive aspects of the relationship might still outweigh the negative, especially if the abuse is rare and minor or if the woman believes that she contributes to a case of mutual abuse. In this respect, an abusive relationship is like any other kind of relationship that is not the most desirable possible. The question becomes, "How bad does a relationship have to get before it should be ended?" This question is relevant to all kinds of relationships, not just those that are abusive.

Alcohol Abuse

The damage that alcohol can do to individuals is well known; it can also be destructive to families. Both victims and perpetrators of spouse abuse are more likely to abuse alcohol and other drugs (Brookoff et al., 1997; Gelles, 1993; Maiden, 1997).

Alcohol abuse is associated with several other destructive behaviors as well, including rape and other crimes (Koss et al., 1987; Inciardi, 1993). A study of college students found that one fourth of them were under the influence of alcohol the first time they had sex (Moore & Davidson, 1994). Excessive drinking by pregnant mothers can have negative effects, including mental retardation, on the fetus (Roeleveld et al., 1992). Alcoholism can result in job loss and serious deterioration of family functioning.

Alcoholism can be seen as an individual problem, and it may well have genetic causes; it can also be seen as a family problem. Some family systems theorists have looked at the scripts that can be developed in families with one or more problem drinkers. A spouse of a drinker might take on the "enabler" role by covering up the problem, making excuses, and preventing the alcoholic from facing the full consequences of his or her drinking (Iber, 1991). The children can assume various predictable roles as well (Wegscheider, 1981).

System theorists point out that, if the alcoholic quits drinking, all the roles in the script will be disturbed. There may be resistance to this change, and there might even be subtle attempts to restore the role relationships to their previous condition (Higgins, 1998; Zuska & Pursch, 1988).

Counseling

Sometimes individuals or couples seek outside help for their problems. Friends and relatives provide a major source of informal support for persons, but there exist a range of more formal kinds of assistance. Religious practitioners, psychiatrists, psychologists, and a variety of counselors and self-help groups are part of the community resources available for families or individuals in crisis. Unfortunately, it is difficult to accurately measure the comparative effectiveness of the different approaches, and the field has many competing claims. One important controversy is between advocates of individual counseling, where one or more family members are treated separately, and supporters of family counseling, which treats all family members as a system.

Individual Counseling and Therapy. One source of support for the individual approach is the medical model in which an individual is considered to be "sick" and in need of a cure. Freudian psychoanalysis is an example, with its assumption that difficulties are caused by childhood traumas that must be worked through with the help of a therapist. A wide variety of other approaches also treat the individual, whether a batterer, a poor communicator, or an unhappy spouse. Sometimes this counseling takes place in a group of people with similar problems, but the focus is still on changing one individual in the family, not the family system. Several batterers, victims, alcoholics, or persons with other labels might attempt to change themselves through group support and interaction.

Another form of individual counseling comes from feminist therapists who object to traditional family counseling. These criticisms are especially strong in cases of abuse, but also apply to other situations in which it is believed that the wife is not being allowed to achieve her full potential because she is part of a male-dominated relationship (Hansen, 1993; Cheatham et al., 1993). Advocates of this approach argue that family therapists often fail to see the inherent power differential between men and women and so do not take this differential into account in therapy (McLellan, 1999; Wright & Fish, 1997). From this perspective, therapy becomes political and consciousness-raising work (Bender & Ewashen, 2000).

Family Counseling. Rather than have a goal of maximizing the function of one individual (Flemons, 1989), family therapy attempts to restore the optimal functioning of the entire family unit. Based on a systems model, family therapy believes that changes in the family system's functioning will effect change in its subsystems and individuals (Huber & Driskill, 1993).

An ideal-typical family therapist would work with all members of the family system at once. This would reduce the problem of individualist approaches where there is no check on the perceived reality maintained by the client. Hearing only one side of the story might result in therapeutic techniques that do not address the real problem. In family therapy, the dynamics of interaction provide a reality check on clients' alternative perceptions of problems. (Hackney & Cormier, 1996).

Family therapists argue that not much is accomplished by working to change one individual, when that person is put back into the same unbalanced system he or she was in before (Foley, 1989; Hackney & Cormier, 1996). Even where the problem might appear to more clearly be found in one individual, such as with alcoholism or nonmutual violence, the undesirable behavior has become part of a family system that might, in unconscious ways, actually perpetuate the poor adaptation.

Seagull and Seagull (1991) suggested that, in some marital abuse cases, there is a psychological payoff of being a victim. "Victims" gain some power by continuing to suffer in what Seagull and Seagull call "accusatory suffering." To end the abuse would change much of the dynamic of the couple's interaction. The roles in their mutual script would change, and family therapists argue that all family members must participate in the desired changes to prevent someone from sabotaging the effort.

Many abusers and abuse victims grew up in homes where violence was common, and they feed into each

Family counseling can become an extrafamilial resource that helps a family cope.

other's expectations about marital scripts. They might not know any other script, and they might not know how to change their own or their partner's behavior (Hotaling & Sugarman, 1986). Even if the relationship ends, there is a chance they will find another partner with whom to play similar roles unless they find new ways of interacting and alter their individual scripts.

Family therapists argue that blaming one person or another is not usually effective in improving the dynamics of a system. Quite probably the roles and scripts of all parties involved need to be changed. After all, the reason for seeking extrafamilial help is that the system has been unable to correct itself. It is quite possible that all persons involved lack the skills needed to improve their situation (Hansen & Goldenberg, 1993). The therapist can serve as an extrafamilial resource to help the system improve.

It is difficult to judge the relative effectiveness of types of therapy, partly because the goals are different. In the case of marital violence, some individual feminist therapists might consider therapy to be a success only if the woman left the abuser. A family therapist might consider that outcome to be a failure, while defining success as stopping the abuse and saving the marriage.

Individuals or couples who seek counseling must take care. Only some kinds of counselors or therapists are licensed by states. Because psychiatrists are physicians, they are licensed in all states. Psychologists are licensed in most states. Marriage counselors are registered in about half of the states (Lamanna & Riedmann, 1994). There is a national association of marriage counselors, called the American Association for Marital and Family Therapy, that requires a certain amount of training. Certification is available for social workers and for drug and alcohol treatment counselors.

In most states, anyone who wishes to become a counselor of some type may do so; some of these are self-trained, and some have no training at all. Being certified increases the chances that the therapist is responsible, but it is no guarantee. Lack of certification, on the other hand, does not necessarily mean that the counselor is not good.

Social Change

While individuals, couples, and families deal with their trouble in a variety of ways, many theorists suggest that considerable change is necessary at the societal level. A variety of suggestions have been made about social changes that might help families cope with the stressors they face.

In response to social causes of family violence, Straus, Gelles, and Steinmetz (1980) suggested several changes that they believed would reduce many kinds of stress in families. Among their suggestions were elimination of the glorification of violence in American society; gun control; reduction of unemployment; adequate health and dental care for every citizen; integration of families into kin and community networks; elimination of sexism; and prevention of the intergenerational transmission of violence.

The correlates of family difficulties suggest other social changes. Among these are reducing unwed teen pregnancies, eliminating institutional racism, improving educational opportunities, and providing role models of successful marriages and effective conflict resolution. Some advocates for children have proposed that parents should be required to demonstrate their fitness and be licensed by the state before having children, which would presumably reduce child abuse (Westman, 1994).

Summary and Conclusion

Most families cope with some degree of stress regularly, but only sometimes does a crisis result. Hill's ABC-X and McCubbin's double ABC-X models help conceptualize the potential for crisis in family systems.

Social construction and social movement theory helps in understanding how the ideas about what is right and wrong in families can change over time. Both child abuse and spouse abuse can be understood from the perspective of social movement theory.

Although it had been a public issue at previous times in history, child abuse began to be considered a major social problem in the 1960s, in response to Kempe's research and the efforts of various claims makers. Laws were fairly quickly passed. Both child abuse and child neglect were defined, and social responses were institutionalized. There do, however, remain debates about how child abuse should be defined, measured, and dealt with.

Although it, too, had been an issue in various historical times, wife abuse began to be seen as a social problem a few years later than did child abuse. The feminist and shelter movements were major influences in defining spouse abuse, often using Walker's "cycle of violence" construct. Several phases of the spouse abuse movement followed, and much of the movement has been institutionalized.

Research on family violence takes different approaches and reaches different conclusions. National surveys such as those using some version of the Conflict Tactics Scale result in much different images of spouse abuse than do feminist approaches. Johnson suggested that more than one type of spouse abuse exists. Future research on the topic will probably adopt that perspective.

Most social scientists agree, that certain kinds of social and personal conditions are associated with higher rates of abuse. Persons and families respond differently to abuse and other family crises such as alcoholism. Individual and family counseling have somewhat different approaches to dealing with family problems.

In conclusion, social movements theory provided a framework in this chapter for an overview of family violence. In a sense, such things as family violence are social constructs developed by opinion leaders, claims makers, and moral entrepreneurs. Real people, however, are harmed by what we now call family violence, and research in the areas needs to be as accurate as possible in order to reduce the damage done by violence while also minimizing the damage done by a particular political construction of family violence.

Talk of family violence is important but not cheery. We continue the not-always-happy coverage in the next chapter by discussing divorce, remarriage, and stepfamilies.

Rethinking in Context What family-related issues might become social problems in the future? What groups would be likely advocates for the issue? Should the legal authorities become more or less involved in family violence than is now the case? Why or why not should spanking be considered a form of child abuse? Would you turn your parents in if you thought they were abusing you?

Additional Resources

Family violence

Bart, Pauline B., & Eileen Geil Moran, eds. 1993. *Violence against Women: The Bloody Footprints*. Newbury Park, CA: Sage.

Gelles, Richard J., & Donileen R. Loseke, eds. 1993. *Current Controversies on Family Violence*. Newbury Park, CA: Sage.

Stacey, William A., Lonnie R. Hazlewood, & Anson Shupe. 1994. *The Violent Couple*. Westport, CT: Praeger.

Westman, Jack C. 1994. *Licensing Parents: Can We Prevent Child Abuse and Neglect?* New York: Plenum.

Stressors and counseling

Burr, Wesley R. 1994. *Reexamining Family Stress: New Theory and Research*. Thousand Oaks, CA: Sage.

Elkind, David. 1994. *Ties That Stress: The New Family Imbalance*. Cambridge: Harvard University Press.

Hackney, Harold L., & L. Sherilyn Cormier. 1996. *The Professional Counselor: A Process Guide to Helping*. Boston: Allyn and Bacon.

Hester, Reid K., & William R. Miller, eds. 1995. *Handbook of Alcoholism Treatment Approaches: Effective Alternatives*. Boston: Allyn and Bacon.

Ivey, Allen E., Mary Bradford Ivey, & Lynn Simek-Morgan, eds. 1993. *Counseling and Psychotherapy: A Multicultural Perspective*, 3rd ed. Boston: Allyn and Bacon.

Leeder, Elaine J. 1994. *Treating Abuse in Families: A Feminist and Community Approach*. New York: Springer.

Street, Eddy. 1994. *Counselling for Family Problems*. Thousand Oaks, CA: Sage.

Internet Sites

Feminist view of domestic violence

http://www.umn.edu/mincava/

Men and domestic violence

http://www.vix.com/men/domestic-index.html

Family resiliency site

http://www.glue.umd.edu/~fraz/Welcome.html

Federal Violence Against Women Office

http://www.ojp.usdoj.gov/vawo/laws/vawa/vawa.htm

Alcoholics Anonymous

http://www.alcoholics-anonymous.org/

Bikers Against Child Abuse

http://www.bacausa.com/

Marriage and Family Therapy

http://www.aamft.org/

The Conflict Tactics Scale

http://darkwing.uoregon.edu/~rlweiss/473/section4/cts.htm

CTS New Version

http://darkwing.uoregon.edu/~rlweiss/473/section4/ctsx.htm

For links to these sites and additional resources, visit the *Families in Context* Web site at:

http://sociology.wadsworth.com

Chapter 15

Divorce and Rescripted Families

Prelude

Jose and Julie started their marriage as a happy couple very much in love. They both adored their three children. But over time, they grew apart. They increasingly got into fights and didn't make up the way they used to.

Jose began spending more and more time after work with his pals at the bar. Julie developed a close friendship with a man at work; one night, after a few drinks, that friendship became a sexual relationship. She broke off the friendship, and Jose never found out about it. But things were never the same.

Finally Jose and Julie got a divorce. Their dreams of lifelong love and joy were shattered. Their children now lived with a single mother and saw their father less and less frequently. Jose remarried in a few years; Julie never did.

Thousands of couples, and their children, go through similar experiences every year. Over time, most go on to live happy, normal lives. Some never fully recover.

Under the circumstances, did Jose and Julie do the right thing in getting a divorce?

Difficulties such as those mentioned in the last chapter sometimes result in the end of a marriage. This chapter will put the topic of divorce in its social and historical context. Some of the causes of divorce will be examined. We will also look at what happens in the lives of couples and children who are involved in divorce, remarriage, and the construction of stepfamilies.

> *Thinking Ahead* **What do you think has happened to the divorce rate in the United States in the last 30 years? Why? How does this compare to other countries? What kinds of social changes would be likely to lower the divorce rate? Would these changes be desirable? In what ways do stepfamilies differ from intact families? How would family systems theorists answer these questions? Feminist theorists? Scripting theorists?**

For most societies and times, marriages were more likely to end by death than by divorce. Today's American marriages are more likely to end in divorce than death (Whitehead, 1996). The process of divorce, long and complicated, significantly affects adults and children who go through it. After divorce, individuals must rescript their personal lives and redefine their family systems and subsystems. For most who remarry, another major rescripting process is required. This often results in stepfamilies that have their own unique problems and opportunities.

Divorce in Comparative Context

This section begins with definition of terms, followed by discussion of divorce as affected by modes of production, especially the industrial revolution. A review of the history of divorce in the United States follows. The section also includes a comparison of ways to calculate divorce rates.

Ending the Marital Union

Not all people believe that death completely ends a marriage. As we saw in chapter 5, Mormons believe that marriage can be for "time and eternity," surviving the death of both partners. The "ghost father," a practice common in many African groups, and the case of the Biblical Levirate in which a dead man was able to "impregnate" his wife with a little help from his living brother, are other cases in which, socially, a marriage did not really end at death.

For most purposes, however, it is assumed in Western societies that marriages end when one partner dies. Provisions are made, either legally or by custom, for the transfer of property. After a "suitable" time, the surviving partner is free to remarry.

A divorce enables the former partners to carry on separate lives legally although the former partners might continue to interact if they had children. Considerable rescripting of roles is often necessary for couples to change from spouses to nonintimate coparents.

Partly to reduce the stigma attached to the term *divorce*, it is now sometimes called **dissolution of marriage**. In some societies that do not allow absolute divorce, and in others as an alternative to divorce, there is the possibility of a "divorce from board and bed," or **legal separation**. This is the same as an absolute divorce, except that remarriage cannot legally occur and sometimes certain inheritance rights are maintained.

Today, it is more common for couples to have an **informal separation**. Like the legal separation, this is typically used as either a prelude to divorce or a "time

---

Dissolution of marriage: Divorce.   **Legal separation:** A condition in which a married couple separates, has a legally recognized property and custody settlement, lives apart, but may not remarry.   **Informal separation:** A condition in which married couples maintain separate residences because of problems living together.

out" during which marital problems will be worked on. As many as one in six American marriages undergoes a temporary informal separation of 48 hours or more because of discord at some time (Kitson, 1985).

Legal annulments, relatively rare today, are generally included with divorces when divorce rates are calculated. Where divorces are not legally possible, annulments are more common. The Catholic Church, which does not approve of absolute divorces, does recognize annulments. Some Catholics get a divorce through the civil process and then pursue an annulment via the formal church process.

Although an annulment legally means that a marriage "never happened," the participants and the community know that something occurred. A child from the marriage is considered legitimate, and the "nonhusband" can be ordered to provide child support (Eshleman, 1994).

With both formal and informal separations, the married partners generally know where each other can be found. In the case of **desertion**, however, one partner leaves without saying where he or she will be living. The marriage is still intact in that neither partner can legally remarry, but marital interaction ends. For many, especially the poor, desertion has historically served as the functional equivalent of divorce. For those who want a more formal end of the relationship, desertion has been one of the most widely accepted grounds for divorce (Riley, 1991).

Modes of Production and Divorce

The process of divorce has changed as modes of production have changed. Industrialization seems to have had a homogenizing effect on divorce rates and processes in many of the world's countries.

Hunting-Gathering Divorce. Something like divorce has been available in most societies as a way of ending unsatisfactory marriages. Although divorces were difficult to get in some hunting-gathering societies, they were generally easier than in horticultural and agrarian societies. One example is provided by the Inuit, often called Eskimos, in what is now northern Alaska.

Burch (1970) found that both marriage and divorce traditionally occurred among the Inuit with little or no ceremony. Either partner could accomplish a divorce simply by ceasing to live with and have sexual intercourse with the spouse. The spouse desiring the divorce could simply depart or put the partner's belongings

Traditional Eskimos had a stable high-divorce, high-remarriage system. This is a Siberian Eskimo family in about 1910.

Desertion: Legally or culturally unjustified abandonment of a spouse, children, or both.

outside the door of the dwelling. Divorced couples frequently remarried by moving back in with each other, but they were free to form other marriages.

Such arrangements characterize what Goode (1993) referred to as "stable high-divorce-rate" systems. These societies have consistently high divorce rates; Burch (1970) estimated an almost 100% divorce rate among the Inuit. Rather than being considered a problem, however, the high rate is institutionalized as part of the marriage and family system. Such matters as child custody and division of property have normative and fairly clearly defined solutions.

Stable high-rate divorce systems typically have high remarriage rates. Individuals quickly either remarry their old partner or find a new one. The household division of labor and economic organization of the group thus are relatively unaffected by the high divorce rate.

Divorce in Agrarian Societies.

As we saw in chapter 4, ancient Rome had relatively high divorce and remarriage rates. Although the *pater familias* had considerable control, at least in later Roman times divorce could be realized by mutual consent of the married partners (Goode, 1993).

As Catholicism spread throughout the Roman Empire and all of Europe, divorce rates gradually declined. Just before the industrial revolution, divorce was nearly impossible to get anywhere in Europe. Although King Henry the Eighth (1509–1547) of England broke with the Roman Catholic Church in order to get a divorce, the new Anglican Church was almost as strict as the Catholic Church. In all of England there were only 375 recorded divorces in the years 1670–1857. Only recently have Italy (1970), Portugal (1974), Spain (1981), and Ireland (1995) allowed divorce, and even now there is a waiting period of up to seven years in some cases (Goode, 1993).

Divorce was rare in advanced-agrarian China, although the rates varied depending on which of the three types of marriage was involved (Wolf & Huang, 1980). In the "standard" or "major" type, the bride was essentially absorbed into the extended family of the groom. This was the most common form of marriage in most of China and had an extremely low divorce rate (Wolf & Huang, 1980).

A stable-high-rate system was found in Japan before its major industrialization. As in China, the traditional Japanese marriage form was patrilineal and patrilocal, but the Japanese bride had more independence than did her Chinese counterpart. After the wedding, she moved into her husband's family for what, in effect, was a trial

period. If divorce occurred, it was usually because the groom's parents sent the bride back to her own parents. The marriages that ended in this way usually did so within the first year or two. Remarriage rates were close to total, however, and later marriages lasted longer than did first marriages (Beardsley, Hall, & Ward, 1939; Goode, 1963, 1993; Smith & Wiswell, 1982; Yanagida, 1957).

Much of the Arab world has also had relatively high divorce rates. Islamic law allowed a husband to get a divorce simply by repeating, "Go, I divorce you" three times ("Talak. Talak. Talak."). It was rare and much more difficult for a woman to initiate a divorce (Goode, 1993). Young children went to their mother's family home with her, but they were considered to be part of their father's lineage and were returned to his home at a certain age. The woman's father was responsible for her support until she could be remarried (Goode, 1993).

Industrialization and Divorce.

William J. Goode (1963, 1970, 1993) proposed that the industrial revolution resulted in higher divorce rates. A person's status is defined more by achievement than by ascription in industrial systems. Individuals increasingly rely on their own educational achievements and work experiences, and they become less dependent upon their families of orientation for adult status and livelihood.

As individual freedom increases in the economic sphere, there is pressure to increase it in the personal and family spheres as well. Persons begin to believe they have the "right" to seek their own happiness, rather than follow the script laid out by tradition and by their families. Marriage begins to be seen more as a matter of individual development than as a lifelong spiritual or family commitment. The result is the "desacralization" of the social institution of marriage (Goode, 1993).

Industrialization and individualism have led to a steady increase in divorce rates. In North America, after a long-term increase, divorce rates peaked in the United States in about 1980. In other countries, rates have continued to climb.

The industrialized world shares other divorce-related characteristics. Wives file for divorce in two thirds to three fourths of the cases, and custody of minor children goes to the mothers in 80% to 90% of cases. Although fathers are expected to provide child support after divorce, all countries have difficulty enforcing this expectation (Goode, 1993).

With the possible exception of Russia, the United States retains the highest divorce rates in the modern world, but other countries are catching up. Popenoe (1988) argued that Sweden has surpassed the

United States in the effective, if not the reported, divorce rate. Cohabitation before marriage is almost universal in Sweden, and cohabiting relationships have a considerably higher break-up rate than do marriages.

Goode (1964, 1993) intended his model not only as a description about what has happened in countries that have already gone through the industrial revolution, but also as a prediction about what will happen as other countries industrialize. Central and South America, which always had very low rates, have recently begun to see their divorce rates climb. Similar patterns can be found in Africa, although less is known about patterns in the sub-Saharan region (Goode, 1993).

Societies that had stable-high-rate systems just before industrialization provide apparent exceptions to Goode's hypothesis that industrialization increases divorce rates. This was the case in Taiwan, Japan, Malaysia, and Indonesia (Wolf & Huang, 1980; Yanagida, 1957; Kumagai, 1983; Goode, 1993). In virtually all of the societies with initial high-rate systems, however, divorce rates reached some low point, and then began to creep back up in the pattern previously seen in European societies.

In the Muslim Arab countries there seems to be no clear association between industrialization and divorce. Part of the reason, Goode (1993) argued, is that industrialization has not yet fully affected these countries. While the petroleum industry has become highly industrialized, the Arab societies are still largely organized around preindustrial patterns.

Divorce in the United States

Glenda Riley (1991) found that the United States has always had a fairly high divorce rate, at least compared to Europe. Immigrants usually left their extended families behind, so older relatives had less influence on their marital selection and behavior. The continual westward movement of earlier European-Americans had the same effect.

Early Protestant teachings emphasizing individualism ultimately influenced divorce. Martin Luther argued that marriage should not be a sacrament of the church and that religion should be a matter between an individual and God, not to be regulated by church or state. This individualism took root in the American colonies more strongly than in Europe, and it contributed to the development of capitalism and the industrial revolution,

along with higher divorce rates (Weber, 1958; Goode, 1963; see chapter 4).

In the New England colonies, divorce was rare. The Massachusetts Bay Colony granted the first divorce in 1630. In the Plymouth colony, a total of nine absolute divorces and several "divorces from bed and board" were granted in the first 72 years (Riley, 1991).

New England initially followed the English pattern requiring an act of parliament for a bill of divorce. As colonial and state legislatures became busier, however, authority to grant divorces was transferred to the courts. The last state to have legislative divorces was Delaware, where the practice ended in 1897 (Blake, 1962).

From the beginning, divorce in the colonies took on the adversarial nature of legal proceedings used in civil suits. One partner sued to prove that the other was "at fault" for breaking the marriage contract. The plaintiff attempted to prove that the defendant had done something that was a ground for divorce.

The first formal list of grounds for divorce in colonial America was in a statute passed by the Court of Magistrates in New Haven in the 1650s: adultery, desertion, and male impotence (Cohn, 1970; in Riley, 1991). Grounds for divorce varied considerably from one jurisdiction to another. In South Carolina, there were no grounds for absolute divorce; only divorce from bed and board was allowed until 1949. In New York, divorce was allowed only on the Biblically acceptable ground of adultery until 1968 (Riley, 1991). In early America, the "guilty" party in a divorce suit could be punished by fines, whipping, the stocks, or banishment. The guilty party was often forbidden from remarriage. If a wife was the successful plaintiff, she could receive **alimony.** This term was first applied to the money paid by the husband to the wife during a legal separation or divorce from bed and board, and was later applied to divorce. In early Massachusetts, a woman could receive her dower rights, or one third of her husband's property, only if she were the "innocent" party (Riley, 1991).

Early Americans followed the patrilineal European tradition that generally left the children with their father after divorce. In the 19th century, this custom gave way to the **tender years rule,** which states that children, especially if they were young, were better off staying with their mother. From 1887 to 1906, mothers got custody by a 3 to 1 ratio over fathers (Riley, 1991).

Alimony: Support paid to a spouse by the former spouse after divorce or separation.   **Tender years rule:** The legal guideline that young children are better off living with their mothers.

Throughout American history, women have filed for divorce more than have men. In the 19th century, women were the plaintiffs in about two thirds of the divorces. Part of the reason for this might be that, as mothers increasingly got custody, some fathers were reluctant to ruin the reputation of the woman who would be raising their children (Riley, 1991; Steinmetz, 1987).

Another possibility is that husbands' behavior was more likely to be defined as grounds for divorce. Men were probably more likely to commit adultery and to be alcoholics. Only men could be impotent, and only men were required to provide support to their spouse and children. Men were more likely to commit the kind of injurious physical abuse that would provide grounds under the cruelty statutes.

Although it could be defined as desertion if a wife refused to move to a new location with her husband (Liss, 1987), this was seldom actually used as grounds for divorce. It was established in law that if a husband's actions drove his wife from their home, he was considered the deserter (Riley, 1991).

The wife's role in marriage was primarily to perform the labor in and near the home, to be a sexual partner, and to bear and care for children. Unlike the case in some other cultures, failure to fulfill these traditional expectations has not been formal grounds for divorce in the United States.

The federal government has generally stayed out of marriage and divorce regulation, leaving each state to define its own divorce laws. The U.S. Constitution contains a "full faith and credit" clause (Article IV, section 1) that obligates each state to accept acts of the other states, so a divorce in any state is considered legal in all other states.

As the country expanded, divorce laws were often more liberal in the newer western states. Because of the different laws, a number of major cities in the newer states developed the reputation of being "divorce mills," including Indianapolis, Indiana; Fargo, North Dakota; Guthrie, Oklahoma; and Salt Lake City, Utah. The most recent and famous "divorce mill" was Reno, Nevada. Some local citizens lobbied to increase business by maintaining the laws that made divorce easier (Riley, 1991).

Although many "divorce mills" later changed their laws to make divorce more difficult, the general direction of change was toward more liberal laws. In some cases, the law itself did not change, but the interpretations of the law did. One example is the change in the meaning of "cruelty." Initially, the term referred only to the most serious physical abuse. Less serious physical abuses and "mental abuses" gradually were included. In some jurisdictions, the cruelty ground was so broadly defined that it included almost anything.

These changes, perhaps driven by the forces of industrialization mentioned by Goode, resulted in a gradual increase in the divorce rate. The American divorce rate grew steadily from the colonial period until 1980, after which it leveled off and even declined slightly (see Figure 15.1).

At one time, being a "divorce mill" was good business for Reno.

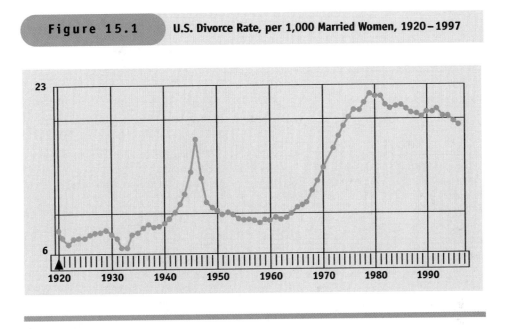

| **Figure 15.1** | **U.S. Divorce Rate, per 1,000 Married Women, 1920–1997** |

Source: 1970 and before, Series B217, *Historical Abstracts of the United States, Colonial Times to 1970*, published by the Department of Commerce after 1970, Table 156, Statistical Abstract 1998, Table 156. Accessed by Gene H. Starbuck from the Microcase Trendsmp database.

There were noticeable peaks and valleys in the general upward trend. Divorce rates increased briefly after every major war. The rate almost doubled after the Civil War ended (1865). There was a small peak in about 1920, just after World War I. The most noticeable peak occurred around 1945, at the end of World War II. Wars resulted in hasty marriages, social disorganization, and separation of young spouses for long periods (Cherlin, 1992; Pavalko & Elder, 1990).

A significant decline in divorce occurred during the Great Depression of the 1930s. Jobs and housing became scarce, and many couples who might otherwise have gotten divorced could not afford to do so (Cherlin, 1992). In addition many men were forced to leave their families in search of work, rendering a divorce unnecessary since there was an informal separation anyway.

A clear reversal of the general upward trend occurred in the 1950s and early 1960s; a period sometimes referred to as the "Golden Age of the American Nuclear Family." The baby boom had begun, America was at the zenith of world power, suburbs were proliferating, and economic times were generally good. Then, beginning in the mid-1960s, the divorce rate began a rapid increase that lasted until about 1980. Much of this rise was accounted for by the demographic variable of the baby boom. In 1964, the first of the "boomers" reached age 18, the high-risk time for early marriage

and divorce. In 1980, the last of the boomers was growing out of the high-risk age group. Because a relatively large share of the population was in the high-risk age group between 1964 and 1980, the divorce rate for the country as a whole increased.

Related to the baby boom, the 1960s and 1970s was a time in which all social institutions, including marriage and the family, were being questioned and challenged. A number of other structural and economic factors, including rapidly changing gender roles, also contributed to the increase in divorce rates (Beeghley & Dwyer, 1989; South, 1985).

Since 1980, the divorce rate has trended slightly downward. Among the reasons for this decline are the continued aging of the baby boomers and the smaller percentage of the population that is in the age group at greatest risk for divorce. The increased average age at first marriage might also be important. The general trends discussed here show up regardless of the way the divorce rate is measured. The exact amount of increase and decrease depends on how the rate is calculated (see Finding Out 15.1).

The Divorce Revolution

As Riley (1991) noticed, divorce has always been controversial in the United States; some advocates

Finding Out | 15.1

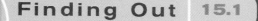

Calculating the Divorce Rate

There are at least five ways to calculate and report divorce rates, each with advantages and disadvantages (Crosby, 1980). These methods lead to slightly different conclusions about recent U.S. trends in divorce, as Table 15.1 reveals.

1. One way to report divorces is simply to provide the **absolute number of divorces** for a particular jurisdiction for a given time period. A one-year period is used for most purposes. The figures are initially gathered at the county level, and then aggregated to provide totals for states, regions, or the entire country. For many purposes, a sample of counties is selected rather than collecting data from all counties in the country.

   The absolute number of divorces, although easier to calculate, does not reveal information about the actual risk of divorce because it does not consider the population base. The absolute number might go up simply because there are more persons in the population.

   In the United States, the year with the largest absolute number of divorces was 1981, when there were 1,213,000 (see Table 15.1). Even by 1998, that number had not yet been surpassed.

2. Another way to report divorce is to use some **comparisons of number of divorces with number of marriages** in a given jurisdiction and time period. Both numbers can fairly easily be obtained from official records.

   In 1970, there were 2,159,000 marriages and 708,000 divorces. If we divide the former by the latter we get a marriage-to-divorce ratio of 3.05 to 1. More commonly, the number of marriages is divided by the number of divorces; in 1970, this resulted in a divorce-to-marriage ratio of .328 to 1.

   As Table 15.1 indicates, the divorce-to-marriage ratio peaked in 1981 at .500 to 1, dropped back down, and then peaked again in 1994 at .508 to 1.

Although there were considerably fewer divorces in 1994 than 1981, the ratio was higher in 1994 because there were considerably fewer marriages in that year. The number of divorces and the number of marriages continued to fall through 1998.

Many persons read these figures as saying that .50, or 50%, of all marriages will end in divorce. This is not necessarily the case, because the divorces in any given year are from marriages from many previous years and are being compared to the marriages from only one year.

A divorce figure such as this can be especially misleading if applied to smaller jurisdictions. A rapidly growing area, for example, attracts persons who have gotten married somewhere else. The divorce counts in the growing area, the marriage in the other region. Over time, the divorce-to-marriage ratio will be artificially higher in regions to which families are moving and artificially lower in areas from which they come.

3. Perhaps the most common way that divorce is reported in statistical sources is the **crude divorce rate.** This is the number of divorces per year for a jurisdiction, per each 1,000 persons in that same jurisdiction. In 1970, there were 708,000 divorces and 203,302,031 individuals in the United States. The former figure divided by the latter yields 0.00348; multiplied by 1,000, this rounds to 3.5, the figure reported in Table 15.1.

   The highest crude divorce rate was reached in 1981, at 5.3 per 1,000 population. Since 1981, the figure has gradually been going down. The crude divorce rate stood at 4.2 in 1998.

   Although it is sometimes difficult to know exactly how many persons live in a particular area at a certain time, this measure provides at least some indication of the actual risk of divorce in a population. However, not all persons in a population are married; the population includes infants and single adults, who are not at risk for divorce.

Crude divorce rate: Number of divorces per year per 1,000 persons in the population.

4. A more precise approach is to use the **refined divorce rate,** which is the number of divorces per 1,000 married women who are 15 years of age and older. In 1970 there were 708,000 divorces and 47,516,778 married women. Dividing the former by the latter yields 0.0149; multiplied by 1,000 that yields 14.19, the figure reported in Table 15.1. The highest refined divorce rate in U.S. history was 22.6, reported in both 1980 and 1981. The rate for 1994 was 21.8.

   This is a more accurate figure because only those at risk for divorce are included in the base figure. It is very difficult in many populations, however, to find out how many married women there are at any given time. Current national and international comparisons, therefore, more often use the crude divorce rate.

5. The rate that many persons wish to know is **average marital risk.** This would be some figure that would indicate what percentage of marriages begun in a given year would eventually end in divorce. Although that would be nice to know, it involves seeing into the future or relying on very old information. To calculate this rate correctly would require a longitudinal study. All marriages registered in 1996, for example, would be followed until they ended either in divorce or death. After all marriages had ended, the percentage ending in divorce could be calculated. This would take at least until 2076, however, because a few marriages from 1996 will last 80 or more years. Alternatively, we could go back to 1916 and see how many marriages of that year ended in divorce. However, since the divorce rate has gone up since then, that figure would not be very useful for predicting the stability of today's marriages.

   Calculations not using one of the two methods suggested above are estimated by demographers. The National Center for Health Statistics (1980) estimated that marriages begun in 1952 would have a lifetime dissolution rate of 32.1%; those begun in 1962 would be about 40%; and those begun in 1972 would be about 50%. Norton and Moorman (1987) estimated that about 56% of current first marriages would end in divorce. Perhaps the most extreme of the estimates came from Martin and Bumpass (1989), who estimated that as many as two thirds of today's marriages will end in divorce. This figure, however, included remarriages. The most widely accepted estimate today is that about 50% of first marriages initiated in recent years will end in divorce (Amato, 2000; Cherlin, 1992).

| Table 15.1 | Various Divorce Calculations for Selected Years, United States |

Year	Absolute Number of Divorces	Current Divorces Divided by Current Marriages	Crude Divorce Rate	Refined Divorce Rate
1970	708,000	div./2,159,000 = .328	3.5	14.9
1980	1,189,000	div./2,390,000 = .497	5.2	22.6
1981	1,213,000	div./2,422,000 = .500	5.3	22.6
1988	1,167,000	div./2,396,000 = .487	4.7	20.7
1994	1,182,000	div./2,329,000 = .508	4.6	21.8
1997	1,163,000	div./2,384,000 = .488	4.3	N.A.
1998	1,135,000	div./2,256,000 = .503	4.2	N.A.

Sources: 1994 data from National Center for Health Statistics, in Famighetti, 1995. 1970–1988 from *Statistical Abstract 1999.* 1998 divorces from http://www.cdc.gov/nchs/fastats/divorce.htm. 1988 marriages from http://www.cdc.gov/nchs/fastats/marriage.htm. Accessed February 14, 2001.

Refined divorce rate: Number of divorces per year per 1,000 married women age 15 and older.

wanted to make divorce more difficult to get, others wanted it to be easier. The easy-divorce faction argued that the whole process of finding one parent "guilty" of something, and the antagonism that often resulted from the adversarial process, ultimately harmed the children involved in the divorce. Reformers looked for a way to allow couples to divorce with as little rancor as possible.

"No-fault" divorce laws were an attempt to solve this problem. The idea of divorce by "mutual consent" had been around for many years; the idea that either partner could initiate a divorce simply by declaring the irremediable breakdown of a marriage was a more recent innovation. Divorce would become more an administrative matter than an issue battled out in the courts.

The first "no-fault" divorce law became effective in California in 1970. The idea spread quickly; by 1977, all but three states had either replaced all their divorce grounds with the no-fault rule or had added a no-fault clause to the traditional fault-based grounds. The last holdout, South Dakota, accepted a no-fault clause in 1985 (Kay, 1990). There is now discussion in some states about rescinding the no-fault laws.

In some jurisdictions a couple may, if there are no children or other major issues involved, get divorced by mail. In other places, there is a provision for **divorce mediation**. Although such processes might reduce conflict, the results tend to follow the traditional outcome, in which the mother has custody and the father is expected to pay child support and get visitation rights (Teachman & Polonko, 1990).

Other changes in divorce law have happened in the postindustrial era, although considerable differences remain from state to state. One change has been the removal of the tender-years rule in child custody in favor of "gender neutral" criteria such as "the best interests of the child." In spite of the legal changes, mothers retain custody in about 90% of cases. Most of these are ones in which the father does not fight the mother's desire for custody, but even when their desires clash, mothers get custody twice as often as do fathers. Most of these decisions are made during divorce mediation or other negotiation processes. In California, a judge settles the matter in fewer than 2% of cases. In these, mothers and fathers are about equally likely to get custody (Maccoby & Mnookin, 1992).

Rather than award sole custody to one or the other parent after divorce, many states now allow, or even encourage, **joint custody**. This has two separate types, legal and residential. With joint legal custody, each parent retains the right to make legal decisions about such

For some attorneys, divorce is just another routine process.

Divorce mediation: A conflict-resolution process in which a third party helps a couple resolve divorce issues. **Joint custody:** The awarding of shared residential or legal custody to both parents after divorce.

things as medical care, to be informed by schools about the child's progress, and other matters. Joint legal custody might be accompanied by joint residential custody, in which the child is expected to spend roughly equal time living with each parent. Joint custody appears to be associated with better father-child relationships and better child outcomes (Arditti, 1992; Buchanan, Maccoby, & Dornbush, 1996), but it is unclear whether the joint custody itself makes the difference or if the kinds of couples who can make joint custody work are the kinds who would maintain good relationships anyway (Amato, 2000).

Changes have also occurred in the division of marital property. The traditional, or common law, procedure was to assume that the property belonged to the husband, but that in certain cases some of it could be given to the divorcing wife. Some states have adopted community-property laws, in which property acquired during marriage, with such exceptions as inheritance and gifts, belonged equally to both partners. In practice, the two approaches now have similar results; common-law states now prescribe "equitable" division, while community-property states adhere to an "equal" division of property standard (Goode, 1993; Fineman, 1989).

A major dispute today concerns what is counted as property. Weitzman (1985) and others argued that such things as pensions and insurance should be considered property; in some cases that view has prevailed. The status of educational and occupational licenses and degrees is also disputed. Suppose one partner sacrifices his or her own education to support the other partner, who earns an M.D. degree. Some argue that the degree should be considered an asset, marital property that partly belongs to the supporting partner. Others argue that it cannot be treated as an asset because it has no direct market value. Since women are typically in the supporter role in this situation, many feminists argue for the "shared asset" position (Rhode & Minow, 1990).

Alimony, now usually referred to as "spousal support awards," was never common; it is even less common now. Rather than a continual obligation, spousal support now more often takes the form of a short-term obligation or payment for a certain period of training (Kay, 1990).

Whether child support is ordered, and the amount of the award, historically has varied widely among jurisdictions and even among judges within a jurisdiction. To combat this problem, the federal government began in 1984 to require the states to use more consistent guidelines. All states now have formulas that include such variables as the predivorce income of the couple, the percentage of that income made by each partner, and the estimated monetary needs of the children at certain income levels. Although some ambiguity and variability in the application of guidelines still exist, consistency has improved significantly (Pirog-Good & Brown, 1996).

In 92% of cases, it is the father who is ordered to pay child support to the custodial mother. Of those ordered to pay, fathers are more likely to comply than mothers. About 76% of women receive all or part of the amount they are owed, compared to about 63% of men. Even though the amount of child support received by women averaged about one third more money than that received by men, the total income of custodial women is only about 55% of that for custodial men (Bureau of the Census [HTTP], 1995).

The problem of "deadbeat dads" rivals that of "welfare moms" in much of the popular press, but only recently has there been research explaining the lack of payment. Virtually no research has been done on "deadbeat moms" or "welfare dads."

Some men decline to pay because they do not take their obligation seriously and can get away without paying (Aulette, 1994; Weitzman, 1985). Other researchers have pointed out that some men cannot afford to pay the amount ordered (Meyer & Bartfeld, 1996). Meyer (1999) found that the total income of the father, along with his total financial burden, were the strongest factors in whether a father paid child support or not. Remarried men virtually always contribute to the support of their new wife and any children she might bring into the marriage, or children they have together, leaving less money for his children in his previous marriage. Custodial mothers can get Temporary Assistance to Needy Families (TANF) and other funds if they are poor, but there is no comparable program to help poor noncustodial fathers meet their obligation of support.

If their former wives are on welfare, some men argue, their payment will not help their children; the child-support payment is deducted from the mother's welfare amount without improving the child's standard of living (Krouse, 1990). Some fathers object to paying support when they cannot be personally involved in their children's lives. A common complaint is that their former wives will not follow the court's visitation order, so they will not follow the court's payment order. In some cases, fathers believe their remarried ex-wives are living better than they themselves are and see no need to provide additional money. Finally, some men doubt that the support they do provide actually is spent on the children (Krouse, 1990).

Whatever the reason, recent legal changes have made it possible to garnish the wages of fathers who do not meet their obligations and to withhold income tax refunds and licenses. These programs do increase the amount of child support paid, but if a man feels too burdened by the collection he can quit his job, making him even less able to pay (Meyer, 1999).

Some legal analysts have argued that there should be more shared community support for all children, including those of divorce (Krause, 1990). Sweden, for example, provides day care and medical care to all children and pays a child-support stipend to all parents, whether divorced or not (Popenoe, 1988). These procedures help Sweden remain a stable-high-divorce society. Although the United States is a high-divorce society, the institutional arrangements remain those of a low-divorce system.

The impact on society of continuing high divorce rates is significant. High rates become a self-perpetuating cycle. As more couples divorce, it becomes more acceptable, and as it becomes more acceptable, more divorce occurs. In addition, high rates of divorce reduce the marriage rate. One of the traditional advantages of marriage was the near-certainty that one could count on having a permanent relationship. High rates of divorce significantly reduce that certainty, reducing the potential reward of marriage and increasing the potential pain. Consequently, fewer people choose to get married (Waite & Gallagher, 2000).

The Postdivorce Society

A high divorce rate affects individuals, but it also has significant social implications as well. Amato (1999) describes these new conditions as a "postdivorce society." He found three major areas in which society has changed along with high divorce rates.

Family Bonds. First, family bonding has changed in a variety of ways. Intimate relationships have different meanings than they once did. Fewer relationships are seen as potentially permanent. More couple cohabit before, or instead of, marrying. People have more sexual partners, both in and out of marriage, than was previously true.

Intergenerational ties have weakened. Children of divorce and their parents generally have weaker ties with one another, and grandparents of those children often end up with very weak relationships, especially on the father's side. Elderly divorced fathers are less likely to get support from their children than never-divorced fathers.

The number of stepfamilies has grown significantly, along with the percentage of children who will live in a stepfamily at some time in their lives. This creates a family structure that is more complex and often less stable.

Inequality. The nature of social inequality has changed with the emergence of a high-divorce-rate society. The number of children living in single-mother homes has increased poverty for both women and children. This, in turn, has generated more gender inequity than would be the case if more of the working women were married rather than single. In spite of increasing equality in the workplace, there has been a net decline in the standard of living of women compared to men in recent decades (Spain & Bianchi, 1996).

Structural and Cultural Factors. Increased divorce has led to the necessity for more women to enter the labor force. Some find themselves needing to work after the divorce; other want to work to be prepared in case of a divorce. In addition, increased numbers of women in the labor force increase the number of divorces. With increasing numbers of working wives, both married men and married women have an opportunity to meet alternative partners. This increases the perceived benefit of a divorce.

A high divorce rate is both a cause and an effect of changes in American values. Americans have become increasingly individualistic and decreasingly familialistic. The norm of lifelong marriage sometimes conflicts with the norm of increased personal and economic development, in spite of the fact that individuals with the strongest commitment to lifelong marriage have the happiest lives and the most successful marriages (Glenn, 1996; Amato & Rogers, 1997).

In addition, high divorce rates bring numbers of people who would otherwise not do so into contact with the legal system. This creates a greater demand for lawyers. Other professionals, such as marriage counselors and mediators, are also needed in greater numbers. Finally, politicians and other policy makers have had to develop a new set of rules and procedures for dealing with issues raised in a postdivorce society (Amato, 1999).

In response to concern about the high rate of divorce, some states have considered enacting "covenant marriage" laws. Louisiana did so in 1997. There are several versions of such laws, but they basically allow couples the option of choosing a form of marriage that is both more difficult to get into and to get out of. Premarital counseling is required. More proof of fault, and more counseling, is required before a divorce is allowed. While such a law indicates a societal concern about divorce, its effectiveness is not yet established. Very few couples are choosing the covenant marriage in Louisiana. Some observers suggest that it is attacking only the symptoms, not the causes, of high divorce rates (Brinig, 1998; Nock et al., 1999).

Divorce "Whys"

The question "What causes divorce?" can be addressed at various levels of analysis. At each level, a set of "causes" or "reasons" can be constructed in response to relevant questions. At the macrosociological level, the question is about rates of behavior. At the microsociological level, the "whys" for divorce are constructed from the set of reasons considered acceptable in a particular society at a particular time.

Macrosociological and Demographical Variables

At the most macrosociological level, the question becomes "What causes some societies to have different divorce rates than others?" or "What causes divorce rates to change over time?" We have mentioned Goode's macro-level studies of the effect of industrialization on the divorce rate. At this level the divorce rate is not a measure of how miserable marriages are; marital stability is not the same as marital satisfaction or happiness. The fact that divorce rates in the United States were higher in 1996 than in 1956 does not necessarily mean that marriages were "better" or "happier" in 1956. It could mean that couples were more likely to remain in miserable marriages in 1956. Of course, the possibility remains that marriages were happier in the past.

At a somewhat less abstract level of analysis than Goode's, discussions about "causes" of divorce are often given in terms of correlations between various social variables and the divorce rate. While it is sometimes assumed that these variables represent causes, it is safer to call them "correlates," since causality is so difficult to prove. Among these correlates are ethnicity, socioeconomic status, type of employment, age at marriage, duration of marriage, geographic residence, religion, and presence of children.

Race and Ethnicity. Most studies find that African Americans have a much higher divorce rate than Whites. The rate for Latinos is between the other two, but closer to that for Anglos (Martin & Bumpass, 1989; Sweet & Bumpass, 1987; White, 1990). This association

is affected by many other variables, including income levels, educational levels, and urban residence. When these variables are controlled, racial differences decrease substantially and might even disappear (Raschke 1987).

Socioeconomic Status. In general, higher socioeconomic status is associated with lower divorce rates. Highest rates are found among couples with low incomes, low educational levels, and low status jobs (Kitson & Raschke, 1981; Raschke, 1987). Similarly, those with higher and more stable incomes have lower divorce rates (Glick & Norton, 1977; Raschke, 1987; Cherlin, 1978; Ross & Sawhill, 1975).

In general, the higher the educational level the lower the divorce rate (Furstenberg, 1990). For men, each additional level of education has a correspondingly lower divorce rate, but the same is not quite true for women. High school dropouts have relatively high rates. Lower rates are found for high school graduates, and rates are even lower for college-educated women. For women with five or more years of college, however, divorce rates go back up. Professional women, with degrees beyond the bachelor's level, are more likely to get divorced and less likely to remarry than women with only a bachelor's degree. This relationship is especially strong for women who started graduate school after they were married (Houseknecht, Vaughn, & Macke, 1984; Cooney & Uhlenberg, 1989).

Employment Type. Steadily employed husbands have lower divorce rates than those who are unemployed or have unstable employment histories (Martin & Bumpass, 1989; Raschke, 1987; Kitson & Raschke, 1981). Couples in which one or both partners are employed in shift work have increased probabilities of divorce (White & Keith, 1990).

Women employed more than 35 hours per week have more than twice the risk of marital disruption compared with women employed 20–35 hours weekly, although the negative effect is at least partly offset by the positive effect of the added family income (Greenstein, 1990). The relationship between hours worked and divorce is strong for women with nontraditional gender ideology; there is no relationship for women with traditional gender views (Greenstein, 1995).

Age at Marriage. The age of a person when he or she gets married is strongly associated with the probability of divorce. Martin and Bumpass (1989) concluded that age at marriage was the strongest predictor of divorce during the first five years of a marriage and remained a strong predictor even in marriages of longer duration. Women who marry at ages 14 to 17 are three times as likely to divorce as those who wait until their 20s. Eighteen- and 19-year-old brides are twice as likely as their 20-something counterparts to divorce. Teenage grooms are twice as likely as those who marry in their 20s to divorce (Spanier & Glick, 1981).

After about age 26 for men and 23 for women, marrying later no longer reduces the divorce rate (Glenn & Supancic, 1984). Persons who marry for the first time in their 30s might even have a slightly higher divorce rate than those who first marry in their 20s (Glick & Norton, 1977).

Duration of Marriage.   Partly because of the waiting period required by most states, few couples (less than 4% of all divorces) get divorced in their first year of marriage. Rates climb sharply through the second, third and fourth years, which are the modal, or most common, times to get divorced. After that, each year of marriage reduces the risk of divorce. The median duration of marriages that end in divorce is about seven years (National Center for Health Statistics, 1988:t. 11).

Religion.   Of the three most commonly compared American religions, homogamous Jewish marriages have the lowest divorce rates, followed by Catholics and then Protestants. The highest rates are found among those with no religious affiliation. Mixed-faith marriages have higher rates than do homogamous ones (Glenn & Supancic, 1984; Raschke, 1987).

Among Protestants, the most conservative and fundamentalist groups such as Nazarenes, Pentecostals, and Baptists, have higher rates than do more mainstream Protestant groups like Methodists, Episcopalians, and Presbyterians (Glenn & Supancic, 1984). This might be the result of nonreligious factors. Members of conservative Protestant groups have lower average socioeconomic status, which contributes to higher divorce rates (Roberts, 1995).

Children.   Although having children is generally associated with lower levels of marital satisfaction, the presence of children does not necessarily increase the divorce rate. The birth of the first child reduces the divorce rate almost to zero in the year following the birth (White, 1990). Couples with preschool children have considerably lower rates of marital dissolution than couples with no children (Fergusson, Horwood, & Lloyd, 1990; Waite, Haggstrom, & Kanouse, 1985).

Older children have the opposite effect. The presence of adolescent children in both first marriages and remarriages increases the possibility of divorce (Waite & Lillard, 1991; White & Booth, 1985). Having young children in the home would appear to postpone divorces, not prevent them (Rankin & Maneker, 1985). White and Booth (1985) referred to this as the "Braking Hypothesis."

Other Factors.   A large number of other factors have been found to be associated with higher divorce rates:

- Couples who cohabit before marriage are more likely to divorce than those who do not (Amato, 2000).

- Divorce rates are lowest in the northeast, led by Massachusetts, Connecticut, New York, and New Jersey. The highest rates are in the west, led by Nevada. It has a divorce rate nearly 10 times that of the United States as a whole, largely because people go there with the specific purpose of getting a divorce (*Statistical Abstract*, 1999).

- Urban couples have higher divorce rates than rural ones (Glick & Norton, 1977; Norton & Glick, 1976).

- Lower divorce rates are found among couples whose friends and family approve of the marriage and share attitudes about marriage (Goode, 1956).

- Divorce is more likely among those who had children before marriage, but premarital conception itself does not appear to affect the divorce rate (Billy, Landale, & McLaughlin, 1986; Wineberg, 1988; Bumpass & Sweet, 1972). The relationship between premarital childbearing and later divorce has been found to be especially strong for Black women (Teachman, 1983).

- Adults whose parents divorced are more likely to end their own marriage by divorce (McLanahan & Bumpass, 1988). This "intergenerational transmission" of divorce is partly because children of divorce marry earlier and are somewhat more likely to be struggling financially. It is also possible that children of divorce lacked good role models for marriage but did have role models for divorce.

Personal "Whys"

Individuals are called upon to give accounts for their behaviors, especially when those behaviors are considered deviant (Lyman & Scott, 1970). The reasons tend to be given in terms intended to make the behavior more socially acceptable. Whether these are the "real" reasons for the actions is difficult to ascertain, but sociologists can report what individuals say about their behavior.

The grounds given by plaintiffs in divorce actions provide one source of information about the "whys" that have historically been given for divorce. In systems requiring fault, plaintiffs in each state had a short list of statutory grounds from which to choose.

In the period 1887–1906 the most common grounds offered when women filed were desertion (33.6%), cruelty (27.5%), and adultery (10.0%). The same three grounds were most popular for men, but with a different distribution: desertion (49.4%), adultery (28.7%), and cruelty (10.5%) (Riley, 1991:124).

As the definition of cruelty expanded and became easier to demonstrate, it became the grounds of choice for most plaintiffs. In a typical jurisdiction in the period 1928–1944, 88% of women and 78% of men used "cruel and inhuman treatment" as the ground for their divorces. Desertion, second most common at that time, was used by 8% of women and 19% of men (Riley, 1991:149).

While stated grounds provided "official whys" of divorce, individuals also have reasons they tell to friends, to themselves, to other family members, and to researchers. The "whys" might vary, depending on the audience to whom the individual is providing his or her account, and depending upon the questions asked.

A Gallup poll questionnaire (Colasanto & Shriver, 1989) found that the leading reported cause of marital breakup, given by 47% of respondents, was "basic personality differences" or "incompatibility." This "why" is consistent with the no-fault grounds of the postindustrial era; respondents essentially said, "It was nobody's fault, we were just too different."

The second leading cause of divorce was reported to be infidelity (17%), followed by drug or alcohol problems (16%), disputes about money, family, or children (10%), and physical abuse (5%). Women were more likely to report alcohol or drug problems (24% compared to 6%); men were more likely to name family disputes (15% to 6%) (Colasanto & Shriver, 1989).

Another survey found that "communication problems" were the number one reported reason for divorce. Infidelity was second, followed by constant fighting and emotional abuse. "Falling out of love" was fifth (Patterson & Kim, 1991).

Spanier and Thompson's (1987) study asked separated individuals about their marital problems.

Economic and work issues were frequently mentioned as sources of conflict: amount of money available (56%); respondent's or spouse's working hours (54%); time away from home because of job (40%); the kind of job held by respondent or spouse (39%); and work colleagues (35%).

Spanier and Thompson (1987) found that 60% of separated respondents reported an extramarital sexual relationship. Fifty-six percent of the separated women reported being dissatisfied with their husband's contribution to housework. Dissatisfaction with their spouse's parenting skills was reported by 40% of women and 20% of men.

This list provides a reminder that accounts, or explanations about the reasons for divorce, come from a temporal and cultural context. In the year 1900, men were not expected to contribute significantly to housework. Although wives might have complained about lack of their husband's help in the home, it certainly would not have provided socially or legally acceptable grounds for divorce. Personality differences, communication problems, or falling out of love are also modern "whys" for marital problems and divorces.

Some accounts are more acceptable today than are others in reducing the stigma felt by divorced persons. Few blame the woman who has been the victim of severe physical abuse if she gets a divorce; in fact, she is likely to be stigmatized if she does not leave (see chapter 15).

Reasons given for divorce vary somewhat from one society to the next. Although the divorce rate in China is small today compared to that of the United States, their large population means there are many divorces. As elsewhere, women file the majority (82%) of petitions (Ziaxiang, Xinlian, & Zhahua, 1987).

The most common general reason for divorce in China, cited by 21% of respondents in one study, was a hasty marriage. This category included marrying quickly for love at first sight and premarital pregnancy. An overconcern for materialism, noted by 15%, was the second leading "why." This included a preoccupation with money and pleasure, a reason constructed in the context of China's communist ideology (Ziaxiang, Xinlian, & Zhahua, 1987; in Benokraitis, 1993).

The Divorce Process and Outcomes

The decision to divorce is not an easy one; it involves the end of a set of hopes and dreams, and often a sense of failure. Deciding just how bad a marriage has to get before a divorce is considered the appropriate remedy is a personal choice made in a community and society. How easy the divorce will be to get, what one's friends and family would think, and whether there is a socially and legally acceptable "why" are among the many factors a person or couple considers.

How life might be after the divorce is also a consideration: the probability of remarriage or surviving as a single person, and the effect on children and others (Amato, 2000). Levinger (1965), following an exchange theory approach, argued that persons consider both their pushes and pulls in favor of divorce, balanced against the pushes and pulls in favor of remaining in the marriage. As we saw in chapter 14, sometimes a person will elect to remain in a poor marriage because the alternatives are thought to be even worse. The divorce decision, usually arrived at slowly, involves detaching from several role involvements.

At the beginning of a relationship, two persons whose realities previously did not include each other redefine themselves and construct a mutual identity (Berger & Kellner, 1964). If the relationship does not work out, each person must once again redefine himself or herself. Diane Vaughan (1988) referred to this process as "uncoupling." The end of a marriage is not only painful; it is a long, difficult, complicated process.

The Stations of Divorce

Anthropologist Paul Bohannan (1970) conceptualized divorce as a process involving six "stations." These are not to be seen as rigid stages in a clearly defined series of events; not all stations apply to every case, nor is there an empirically established amount of time for each station. The two partners involved might not proceed at the same pace. Still, Bohannan provides a useful framework for looking at the divorce process (see Figure 15.2).

The Emotional Divorce.   At least one marital partner typically withdraws emotionally from the marriage long before there is legal action. Love is gradually replaced by indifference or by more negative emotions like anger, rejection, depression, or unhappiness.

There are ups and downs in nearly all marriages, and it is difficult for partners to know for sure whether the current condition is a low point in an otherwise good relationship, or part of a long-term downward trend. Some marriages continue for a lifetime after an emotional divorce if a legal divorce is not obtained.

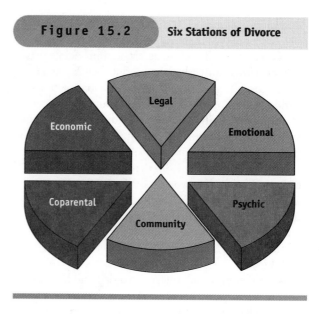

Figure 15.2   Six Stations of Divorce

Source: Concept from Bohannan, Paul. 1970. "The Six Stations of Divorce." Pp. 29–55 in *Divorce and After,* edited by Paul Bohannan. New York: Doubleday.

The Legal Divorce.   Although a legal divorce does occur at a specific time, after which the partners are free to remarry, the legal process can be a long and difficult one. States require a waiting period between the initial filing and final decree, and practical delays often slow the process even more. Negotiation over details of the settlement occurs, often with the involvement of attorneys. Under the no-fault system, divorces themselves are not contested, but property and custody settlements can be complicated, especially when the negotiations occur in the context of the emotional wounds associated with divorce. A couple may be separated, legally or informally, for a long period before the divorce is final.

The Economic Divorce.   This station of divorce involves resolving matters such as division of property and debt, alimony, and child support. While there is an agreement at the time of the legal divorce, many couples continue to negotiate long after the divorce is final. This is especially true for child support; changing circumstances or a failure to abide by the divorce decree brings matters of the economic divorce back into court.

The economic divorce affects men and women differently, with women generally getting the worst of the deal. Married men and women with complementary role divisions of labor share the benefits and costs of a woman who devotes time to her family rather than to her career.

Because she shares her husband's income, insurance, and other marketplace benefits, the wife is shielded from the disadvantages of not fully participating in the paid labor force. Once she is divorced, however, those disadvantages are fully felt (Rhode & Minow, 1990).

Stroup and Pollock (1994) concluded that, among White divorcees, women experienced an average income loss of 22% while men's income dropped an average of 10%. Peterson (1996) used Weitzman's (1996) raw data to estimate a 27% decline in women's standard of living and a 10% increase in men's standard of living following divorce. More extreme differences were found by Bianchi et al. (1999). By their estimate, custodial mothers experienced a 36% decline in standard of living, while noncustodial fathers had a 28% increase. Whatever the exact figure, divorce is a major cause of poverty among women and their custodial children (Amato, 2000).

The Coparental Divorce. For couples with children, the divorce changes the interaction between the former spouses. The inability to clearly define the former partner as a coparent but not a spouse is a major source of coparental conflict after divorce (Madden-Derdich et al., 1999). At the same time, continued attachment between the former partners may be a natural outcome of shared parenting (Madden-Derdich & Arditti, 1999).

New boundaries of intimacy and power must be established between the former spouses, and among former spouses and their children (Emery & Dillon, 1994). Negotiation occurs directly between the adults and, if children are in contact with both, they often become agents of negotiation for their parents. The custodial mother has a powerful influence on how the children perceive the father, and on the father's relationship with the children. He has less influence on the child's relationship with the mother (Nielsen, 1999).

Although custody issues are technically resolved by the final divorce decree, considerable negotiation goes into that decision. Further, both formal and informal changes in children-related arrangements often continue long after the legal divorce is granted (Ganong, Coleman, & Mistrina, 1995). Physical mobility, remarriage, and the preferences of children themselves are among the variables that change coparental arrangements.

Couples who divorce later in life, or after long marriages, often find that their adult children provide social and emotional support (Gander, 1991). Divorced mothers are more likely to receive such support than are divorced fathers (Wright & Maxwell, 1991).

The Community Divorce. When a couple marry, they undergo a rite of passage that informs the community that their roles have changed and that they are now to be treated as husband and wife. They develop mutual friends and community ties.

When the couple divorce, there is no formal rite of passage that clearly defines their new roles with respect to the community. The more the couple interacted as a dyad in the community, the more difficult is the process of the community divorce. Couples who have been active together in a religious organization must redefine their religious roles. Recreation, too, is often affected.

Dyadic friends of the divorcing couple often feel as though they have to "choose sides" or they wish not to become involved at all (Weiss, 1975). One study found that more than three fourths of divorced women reported losing friends as a result of the divorce (Arendell, 1986); presumably, divorced men lose friends also.

As part of the community in which a couple is located, kin networks are affected. Generally each former partner retains ties to the kin network of his or her family of orientation; this affects the intergenerational relationships. Divorced women with custody of minor children have more contact with their own parents than do married women with children, and they get more help from their parents. Divorced men, on the other hand, get less help, and their children see the paternal grandparents less often (Spitze et al., 1994).

The Psychic Divorce. The psychic divorce, which can be a lifetime effort for some persons, involves complete psychological recovery from the divorce and the development of a self completely apart from the previous mutual script. For many, this involves a grieving process similar to that felt after the death of a spouse.

Some counselors say that the psychic process is complete only when the individual forgives both the former mate and himself or herself and when there is no longer anger or bitterness (Masheter, 1991). Although counselors sometimes say that persons cannot remarry successfully until the psychic divorce is complete, this expectation may be too high for many persons, and the suggestion lacks empirical support.

As Bohannan's six-station conceptualization of divorce implies, divorce is typically a long, difficult process. Extreme moods, from depression to euphoria, are common. Those who see themselves as the ones who initiated the divorce fare better emotionally than do those who believe the marriage should not be ended (Weiss, 1975). Contrary to their expectations, Sheets and Braver (1996) found that women were more satisfied with the divorce process than were men. Women reported greater satisfaction with custody and visitation outcomes, as well as all economic arrangements except child support. Women were more likely to believe the divorce process was fair.

Outcomes of Divorce

Several studies have found that, compared with married individuals, divorced men and women have lower levels of psychological well-being. This includes lower happiness, more symptoms of psychological distress, and poorer self-concepts (Amato, 2000; Demo & Acock, 1996; Simon & Marcussen, 1999). Divorced adults have more health problems and higher death rates (Aldous & Ganey, 1999; Waite & Gallagher, 2000). Divorced individuals report more social isolation, less satisfying sex lives, and more negative life events than their married counterparts (Joung et al., 1997; Laumann et al., 1994; Lorenz et al., 1997; Mastekaasa, 1997).

There is some question whether the divorce causes the negative outcomes, or whether people with negative outcomes are more likely to be divorced. Longitudinal studies find that unhappiness and stress do increase over time for well-being people who get divorced. However, the decreases in well-being actually begin before the divorce actually occurs (Booth & Amato, 1991; Mastekaasda, 1997). These studies would support the idea that divorce itself, and the immediately preceding period of time, cause much of the distress.

The "selection effect" suggests that people with various indicators of poor well-being are more likely to get divorced. This has been found true for problems with alcohol (Mastekaasa, 1997). Depression in women as much as ten years earlier increases the probability of divorce (Davies et al., 1997; Hope et al., 1999). The safest conclusion is that both explanations are true; divorce does generate negative well-being, but there is some selection effect also (Amato, 2000).

In spite of the generally negative findings, some individuals are better off after divorce. As with most crises, divorce can also provide opportunities. Divorce allows persons to end a poor and even destructive marriage (Lund, 1990). Higher levels of autonomy and personal growth characterize divorced compared to married individuals (Amato, 2000; Marks, 1996).

Recently divorced women speak of personal growth in management of daily life, in social relationships, and in developing an individual identity (Reissman, 1991).

Many divorced women experience improvements in their careers, and report higher levels of happiness than before the divorce (Acock & Demo, 1994). Most studies of positive outcomes of divorce focus on women. If more such studies were done on both men and women, more positive outcomes would probably be found (Amato, 2000).

Several factors moderate the impact of divorce for adults. Individuals fare better if they have higher educational levels, more money, better job security, and a large support network of family and friends (Amato, 2000; Booth & Amato, 1991; Demo & Acock, 1996). Getting support from a new intimate partner or spouse appears to be especially beneficial (Funder et al., 1993; Demo & Acock, 1996). The individual who initiates the divorce has better postdivorce adjustment (Kitson, 1992). Finally, individuals who report a large number of problems during the marriage have better postdivorce adjustment than those who saw few marital problems (Booth & Amato, 1991).

Children of Divorce

Between 1960 and 1980, the number of children involved in divorce each year almost tripled. Although the numbers have dropped somewhat since the early 1980s, divorce affects more than 1 million new children annually in the United States (*Statistical Abstract 1999*:t.159). As many as 40% of all children will spend at least part of their childhood living with a single parent as a result of divorce (Peters et al., 1993).

Divorce-Related Stressors

Emory's (1999) review of studies done on the impact of divorce on children reached five conclusions. First, divorce creates a number of stressors on families and children. Relationships with parents change and there is exposure to conflict of several kinds. Children of divorce are more likely than other children to change residences, and the move is usually to a poorer neighborhood (South et al., 1998). Moving to a new home and other factors often result in changes in friendship patterns. Financial insecurity is often one of the stressors. As Figure 15.3 demonstrates, while children with single divorced parents are less likely to be in poverty than children in never-married homes, they are much more likely to be poor than children in two-parent homes. This holds true with all racial/ethnic groups. Again, causality is an issue in the data; poor people are more likely to divorce, so the divorce does not cause all the poverty. There is no doubt, though, that financial standing of children drops when their parents divorce.

As McCubbin's (1979) ABC-X model reminds us, existence of stressors does not necessarily lead to a problem. The kinds of stressors precipitated by divorce, however, are quite likely to lead to "pileup" of stressors that can lead to a crisis.

Children at Risk

Emery's (1999) second point about the impact of divorce on children is that the stressors associated with divorce can lead to adjustment problems of various kinds. Children are at risk for social, psychological, educational, and vocational problems.

Judith Wallerstein and Joan Kelly began a longitudinal study of divorce in 1971. They published results of 5-year and 10-year follow-up studies of children of divorce (Wallerstein & Kelly, 1976, 1980; Kelly & Wallerstein, 1976; Wallerstein & Blakeslee, 1989).

Wallerstein found that children reacted to the news of divorce with shock, shame, anger, disbelief, and grief. Rather than blame themselves for the divorce, as popular literature often reports, children tended to blame one parent or the other. Five years later, nearly 40% of the children remained moderately or severely depressed; the majority still hoped that their parents would get back together. Even 10 years later, the children of divorce continued to have difficulties forming intimate relationships.

The children in the study have now been interviewed 25 years after their parents' divorce (Wallerstein & Lewis, 1998). Effects of the divorce were still apparent. The subjects' childhood memories were of abandonment, terror, and loneliness. Adolescence was, for many, characterized by early sexual activity and drug and alcohol use. The subjects, now in their late 20s and early 30s, continue to have some fears of intimacy.

The Wallerstein studies were limited by a small sample that was selected from a wealthy area. The respondents had been referred to a mental health clinic, and many of the children's parents suffered from mental health ailments; these children might have had more problems than other children even if they had been from intact homes. The conclusion that children of divorce can experience long-term negative effects, however, is borne out by other research.

Baker, Barthelemy, and Kurdek (1993) found that fifth- and sixth-grade children of divorce were less likely to be popular with their peers and were more at risk for long-term maladjustment. Canadian research found that children who lived through a parental divorce had lower levels of self-efficiency, self-esteem, and social support and had less effective coping styles (Kurtz, 1994).

Younger children of divorce have more problems in school than children in intact homes. Most of the problems are related to the poverty often associated with single motherhood (Duncan, Brooks-Gunn, & Klebanov, 1994). Even when the student's race, socioeconomic status, sex, age, and ability are held constant, however,

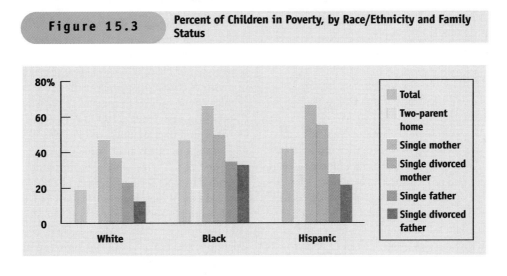

Figure 15.3   **Percent of Children in Poverty, by Race/Ethnicity and Family Status**

Source: U.S. Census Bureau. 1996. "Marital Status and Living Arrangements: March 1994." *Current Population Report* (P20–484). Washington, DC: Government Printing Office. In Emery, 1999.

Some moments in life are indelibly imprinted in memories.

adolescents from divorced homes are 1.7 times more likely to drop out of school (McNeal, 1995).

Among adolescent boys, higher rates of delinquency and incarceration were found for those who had divorced parents (Matlock et al., 1994). A study in Great Britain found that adolescent children of divorce were more likely to impregnate or conceive children out of wedlock than were their peers from intact homes (Russell, 1994). A very high correlation exists between parental divorce and incidence of depression among women (Rodgers, 1994).

A research project in New Zealand followed 935 children over 15 years. Children of divorce were found to have more frequent illegal drug usage, earlier and more premarital sexual activity, and more disruptive behaviors. Most, but not all, of the correlation was explained by the socioeconomic status of the parents (Fergusson, Horwood, & Lynsky, 1994). Higher divorce rates also appear to be correlated with higher suicide rates (Krull & Trovato, 1994; Lester & Abe, 1993; McCall & Land, 1994).

The negative effects of divorce appear to extend into adulthood. Adults who grew up in divorced, single-parent families report less solidarity with their parents, see them less often, and perceive less support from their parents. Although these findings apply more strongly to noncustodial parents, they apply to custodial parents also (White, 1994). Relationships with parents suffer even if the divorce occurs after the young persons have left the home (Aquilino, 1994).

Resilience

Emery's (1999) third conclusion is that, in spite of the stressors and risks, most children of divorce are **resilient**. Most "bounce back" to function as well on commonly used measures of adjustment as do those from married-couple households. This seems to contradict the research about risks, but it actually does not. Those studies must be interpreted with some care. Although differences between children of divorce and those in intact families are consistently found, the differences are generally relatively small. The minority of children who do have significant negative reactions can bring down the average scores for the whole group of children of divorce.

Also, even a doubling of risk may only affect a small minority of the group. McLanahan and Sandefur (1994) found that teen pregnancy and dropping out of school were about twice as common in children of divorce as in children of married-couple families. Although this is a significant difference between the two categories of children, most in each group neither drop out nor get pregnant.

In addition, most of the studies find correlations, but that does not prove causal relationships between parents' divorce and negative child outcomes. Much of what appears to be the result of divorce itself might be the result of the conflict that occurs before the divorce. Many of the problems were present in some of the children before the divorce occurred (Emery, 1999). Amato and Booth (1996) found that marital quality is related to parent-child relationships as much as 12 years before the parental divorce occurs. Children who live with significant amounts of marital conflict for long periods of time would likely be troubled even if their parents did not separate. Some problems might be the result of a self-fulfilling prophesy resulting from attitudes held by teachers, counselors, neighbors, and others about the impact of divorce (Smith, 1990; Amato & Keith, 1991; Dawson, 1991).

Resilient: Marked by an ability to recover quickly from misfortune.

Distress Without Disorders

Emery's (1999) fourth point confirms Wallerstein's finding of long-lasting effects. Even when there are little overall difference between children of divorce and others in terms of particular measured disorders, there are nonetheless some distress and even pain associated with a parental breakup. Not all people who have distress show that by dropping out of school, using drugs, or engaging in risky sexual behavior. Although resilient, children of divorce still have to deal with issues that children in married-couple households do not.

Laumann-Billings and Emery (1999) found that half of a divorced group of college students worried about events, such as graduation, where both parents would be in attendance. Only 10% of students from married parents had such concerns. Twenty-nine percent of the divorce group wondered whether their fathers really loved them; 10% of the children of married couples were concerned about that. Forty-six percent from the divorce group compared with 19% from married families wished they could have spent more time with their father. While these matters might not indicate serious problems in the children of divorce, Emery (1999) concluded, they are matters that we might prefer our children would not have to worry about.

Diverse Outcomes in Children of Divorce

Emery's (1999) final conclusion was that child outcomes following divorce depend on a variety of circumstances. Perhaps most important is the relationship between the child and the residential parent. Whether the mother or father is the residential parent makes little difference in the child's adjustment (Guttmann & Lazar, 1998).

Compared to married parents, divorced custodial parents "have fewer rules, dispense harsher disciplining, provide less supervision, and engage in more conflict with their children" (Amato, 2000:1279). Children have poorer adjustment if their divorced custodial parent is depressed. Good parenting skills and parental adjustment of the custodial parent predict better outcomes for the children.

It is helpful if the primary parent gets along well with the child, provides proper supervision, and is authoritative rather than authoritarian or permissive. As with other families, resilience is most likely when there are parental competence, shared values, good communication, and parental receptiveness toward the child (Daly, 1999; Hauser et al., 1989; McCubbin et al.,

This child would miss his father's helping hand.

1999; Pett et al., 1999). Evidence suggests that the noncustodial parent level of contact and involvement with his or her children, and parenting cooperation between the former spouses, reduces risk for children (Bronstein et al., 1994).

Children's adjustment is also related to the amount of parental conflict, both before and after the divorce. Some marriages are high in conflict before the divorce occurs, while others appear to have very little conflict before the breakup. Children subject to high levels of predivorce conflict handle the divorce relatively well. They actually did better as adults than did children whose high-conflict parents remained together. Children whose parents had low-conflict marriages before divorce, by contrast, suffered a great deal more. The divorce came as unexpected and unwelcome. It affected their ability to trust and to form relationships of their own well into adulthood. In fact, children whose low-conflict parents divorced had higher divorce rates in their own adult marriages (Amato & Booth, 1996; Booth, 1999; Booth & Amato, 2001).

Conflict during and after the divorce has the opposite effect. Children whose parents have acrimonious conflict over such issues as child custody, child support, and visitation, have poorer parent-child relationships.

Such children are more likely to have emotional and behavioral problems (Johnston, 1994). The impact is particularly destructive to the child if the conflict includes domestic violence or child maltreatment (Ayoub, Deutsch, & Maraganore, 1999).

Children's adjustment is also related to economic standing. When income differences are taken into account, much of the disadvantage of children of divorce statistically goes away. Parenting quality, however, suffers in lower income families, and the children consequently suffer (Emery, 1999).

The child's relationship with the noncustodial parent might also affect his or her adjustment. Many studies find that frequency of visitation and perceived closeness with the noncustodial parent do not matter much in the child's long-term resilience. After a survey of all available data, however, Emery (1999) concluded that children will adjust better if they have a good relationship with both parents. After a review of 63 studies, Amato and Gilbreth (1999) concluded that authoritative parenting on the part of noncustodial fathers improves their children's academic achievement and reduces other difficulties.

Not all adjustment-related influences come directly from parents. Children who use active coping skills do better than those who withdraw or avoid dealing with problems (Sandler, 1994). Getting social support from their peers helps children cope with parental divorce (Samera & Stolberg, 1993). At least some school-based

support programs and other therapeutic interventions can benefit children of divorce (Emery et al., 1999). Finally, children who blame themselves for their parents' divorce are more poorly adjusted (Bussell, 1995).

Remarriage and Stepfamilies

Most men and women reenter the singles scene after divorce, although the idea of "dating" is awkward for those who have been married for some time. Many eventually do so to relieve loneliness, reassure their self-worth, enjoy themselves, and meet intimate needs (Weiss, 1975). Formerly married persons who date or cohabit have better adjustments than those who do not (Tschann, Johnston, & Wallerstein, 1989), but doing so quickly after divorce can disturb the relationship with his or her children (Rodgers & Conrad, 1986). Those who cohabited before their first marriage are more likely to engage in postmarital cohabitation, although cohabiting seems to make remarriages less stable (Wu, 1995).

Remarriage Data

The United States and Western Europe have always had high rates of remarriage. In earlier times, the remarriages followed death of a spouse; in the

Double remarriages come with a whole new set of challenges and opportunities for everyone.

postindustrial era the remarriages have more typically followed divorce (Cherlin, 1992; Furstenberg, 1990). Remarriage rates have gone down somewhat since 1970, partly because of the increased incidence of postmarital cohabitation, but still about 70% of divorced men and 60% of divorced women eventually remarry. Half of these occur within four years of the divorce (Wilson & Clarke, 1992). About half of remarriages involve creating a stepfamily with minor children (Wineberg & McCarthy, 1998).

National data reveal that 46.3% of American marriages involve remarriage for one partner (21.9%) or both partners (19.7%). It is the first marriage for both bride and groom 53.7% of the time (see Table 15.2). Remarriages involving widows or widowers are only a small percentage of the total (see Table 15.2).

A variety of factors, including gender, influence the probability of remarriage. Men are more likely to remarry, and do so more quickly, than women. As we saw in earlier chapters on the data on first marriages and widowhood, longer life expectancy and age hypergamy work against women in the marriage market. It might also be true that fewer women want to remarry.

The younger a woman is at divorce, the more likely she is to remarry, but age is not a factor in probability of remarriage for men (Ahlburg & De Vita, 1992; Bumpass, Sweet, & Martin, 1990). However, a divorced person of any age is more likely to marry than is a person the same gender and age who has never married (Goode, 1993).

Studies about the impact of having children on the likelihood of remarriage are mixed (Bumpass, Sweet, & Martin, 1990). The best guesses are that the more children a woman has custody of, the less likely she is to remarry (Spanier & Glick, 1981), but that the relationship is complicated by the age of the mother (Koos & Suchindran, 1980).

Race and ethnicity make considerable difference in remarriage rates. One study of remarriage among women found the five-year remarriage rate for White women to be 53%, while the rate for Latinas was 30% and that for African American women was 25% (U.S. National Center for Health Statistics, 1991:t. 4).

The influence of education on remarriage rates differs by gender. Better-educated women are less likely to remarry, especially if they have more than four years of college. Better-educated men are more likely to remarry (Bumpass, Sweet, & Martin, 1990).

Remarriage Process and Quality

The mate-selection process is different the second time around. For one thing, it appears to be quicker. Divorced persons are intimate sooner in a relationship than never-married persons. They also spend less time dating and have shorter engagements before marriage than never-married singles (O'Flaherty & Eels, 1988).

Remarriages are likely to be somewhat less homogamous than first marriages. The age difference for remarriages is about twice that for first marriages, and the age gap increases with the age of the groom. Educational differences are also greater in remarriages (U.S. National Center for Health Statistics, 1990), and religious differences are probably greater as well (Lamanna & Riedmann, 1994).

Interviews revealed that remarried couples see marriage differently than those in their first marriages. They have different perceptions of love and believe that they

Table 15.2	Distribution of Marriages by Previous Marital States, by Percentage		

	Husband's Previous Status		
Wife's Previous Status	**Never Married**	**Divorced**	**Widowed**
Never Married	53.7	10.9	0.3
Divorced	11.0	19.7	1.3
Widowed	0.5	1.4	1.2

Source: Centers for Disease Control and Prevention. 1995. *Monthly Vital Statistics Report* 43(12). Table 7.

are more likely to leave a bad marriage than couples in their first marriage (Furstenberg & Spanier, 1984).

Remarried couples also report having a more flexible household division of labor, and more shared decision making (Furstenberg, 1980). Although financial problems are common, remarried partners are less likely to think of money as "ours," and more as "his" and "hers," than is the case in first marriages (Fishman, 1983).

Several studies have compared the quality of remarriages with that of first marriages (Coleman, Ganong, & Fine, 2000). In general, such studies find little or no difference in terms of marital happiness or satisfaction (White & Booth, 1985; Vemer et al., 1989; Glenn, 1990, 1991). MacDonald and DeMaris (1995) found, contrary to expectation, that there was less marital conflict in remarriages; the least conflict was found in the double remarriages. Other studies, however, find lower relationship quality in remarriages (Brown & Booth, 1996).

Remarried spouses are more likely to openly express criticisms, anger, and irritation than first-married couples (Bray & Kelly, 1998), and they report somewhat higher levels of tension and disagreement (Hobart, 1991). The most common source of disagreement is matters dealing with children (Pasley et al., 1993; Clingempeel et al., 1994).

While some studies find a slight negative effect on marital satisfaction of the presence of children (White & Booth, 1985), others find a slight positive effect (Vemer et al., 1989). Kurdek (1999) concluded that children born to first marriages lowered the marital quality more than did having stepchildren in remarriages. MacDonald and DeMaris (1995) found that in the early years of remarriages with stepchildren, there was less marital conflict than in families with biological children only. Over time, however, the couples with stepfamilies began to have more conflict.

All things considered, remarriages appear able to achieve about the same level of marital satisfaction as first marriages (Coleman & Ganong, 1990). In stepfamilies, both men and women adjust better if they bring children of their own into the new household; women adjust better when the only children in the household are theirs (Coberly, 1996).

Although remarriages are about as happy as first ones, they are not as stable. Overall, they are about 10% more likely to end in divorce than are first marriages (Furstenberg, 1987; Martin & Bumpass, 1989), and those that end do so more quickly (U.S. National Center for Health Statistics 1991b:t. 10).

It seems inconsistent that remarriages are as happy as first ones while being less stable. Part of the reason for this apparent discrepancy is that those who have divorced once will recognize a bad marriage more quickly than first marrieds and consider it more acceptable to terminate the marriage by divorce (White & Booth, 1985; Booth & Edwards, 1992).

Lynn White and Alan Booth (1985) addressed the apparent inconsistency between happiness and stability in remarriages. They noted that remarriages containing stepchildren are more likely to end in divorce than those that do not. Some couples who are generally satisfied with their marriage and their partner are dissatisfied with the entire family group that includes the stepchildren. They might have high marital satisfaction but low family satisfaction, a situation that sometimes leads to divorce.

White and Booth (1985) found that when only one partner was in a remarriage, divorce rates were about the same as for first marriages. Marriages that were remarriages for both partners were about twice as likely to break up as first marriages. To put this in perspective, Wilson and Clarke (1992) found that couples who entered double remarriages between ages 25 and 44 still had lower divorce rates than those who entered first marriages as teenagers.

Stepfamilies

Andrew Cherlin (1978) referred to remarriage as an "incomplete institution." Role conflict is more common in stepfamilies. Conflict over parenting roles is especially common in stepfamilies compared to first marriage families (Grizzle, 1999). The media, the culture, and the society reinforce a view of family life that is based on the intact nuclear family (Coleman & Ganong, 1997). The image of stepparents is often negative, as evidenced by the "wicked stepmother" often found in fairy tales.

Stepfamilies differ from intact families in several ways. Stepfamilies lack a shared family history, have more stress, are less cohesive, and have more loyalty conflicts (Visher & Visher, 1988). Further, stepfamily relationships can become extremely complicated, as Figure 15.4 illustrates.

Figure (a) in Figure 15.4 depicts an intact nuclear family, living in one household. Figure (b) symbolizes the effect of a divorce in which the children live with their mother in their primary household. They visit their father regularly in what could be called a secondary household. This results in a binuclear family. Both adults

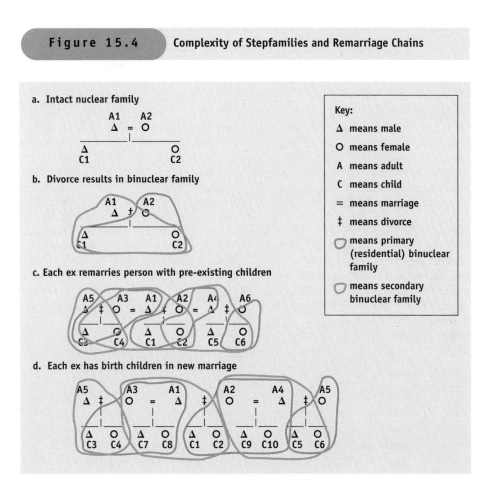

Figure 15.4 Complexity of Stepfamilies and Remarriage Chains

a. Intact nuclear family

b. Divorce results in binuclear family

c. Each ex remarries person with pre-existing children

d. Each ex has birth children in new marriage

Key:

Δ means male

O means female

A means adult

C means child

= means marriage

‡ means divorce

means primary (residential) binuclear family

means secondary binuclear family

(A1 and A2) are heads of a household that, at least part of the time, includes the two children (C1 and C2).

In figure (c), matters get considerably more complicated. The children's mother and father each remarry. Each new spouse is also a divorced parent. Children C1 and C2 remain part of the secondary household of their father, but that household now serves as the primary household of a new stepmother (A3), stepbrother (C3), and stepsister (C4). In addition, the primary household for C1 and C2 is now the secondary household of their stepfather's children, C5 and C6, who regularly visit their own father.

Figure (d) represents a still more complicated situation. Both of the C1 and C2's birth parents become birth parents with their new spouses. This adds half brother (C7) and half sister (C8) to their secondary household. It also adds C9 and C10 to their primary

household. Rather than existing in discrete household units, these stepfamilies have formed **remarriage chains** that connect them across households (Cherlin, 1996).

The roles of all the individuals in figure (d) are not clear, nor is it clear exactly how many families are represented, nor what kinship term everyone should call everyone else. Imagine how complicated the diagram would be if the families of origin of each of the adults were included, especially if these adults had also been children of divorce. The lack of institutional support for stepfamilies is reflected in the absence of role names. It is more difficult to know how to behave toward someone when the role relationship is unclear (Beer, 1992).

Figure 15.4 seems confusing; that is the point. Many real-life stepfamilies are confusing. Systems theorists would point out that stepfamilies have more potential for subsystem conflict. In addition, stepfamilies are

---

Remarriage Chains: Connections that link individuals across households through ties of disrupted and new unions (Cherlin, 1996).

Families in the **NEWS**

Genetic Test Reveals Good News and Bad News

When Morgan Wise and Wanda Fryer got divorced, in 1996, he fought for and won custody of their four children. In 1999, because of the travel demands of his job, he gave custody back to his ex-wife. He was granted the same visitation rights she previously had and was ordered to pay $1,110 per month in child support.

One of his children had cystic fibrosis. Just after returning custody to his ex, Mr. Wise had genetic testing done to see if he was a carrier. The good news for him was that he was not a carrier of the disease. The bad news was that children should not get cystic fibrosis unless both parents are carriers. Further genetic testing revealed that Mr. Wise was the biological father of only one of his children. The other three resulted from affairs Ms. Fryer had conducted while they were married.

Mr. Wise went to court to end his financial support obligation, while retaining visitation rights. Judge Robert Moore III, following the longstanding tradition that all children born in a marriage are legally the husband's responsibility, declined to change the support order. In addition, he barred any further child visitation by Mr. Wise.

State laws vary considerably in the allowed use of genetic paternity testing. The law apparently lags behind the technology. Harry Tindall, who helped draft a law designed to be a model for several states, claims that as many as 5 or 10% of marital children are not the biological children of their legal, marital father. In any case, genetic paternity testing has raised a whole new set of issues about the legal and social meaning of fatherhood.

Source: Tamar Lewin. **www.nytimes.com**, March 11, 2001.

---

often characterized by **boundary ambiguity**, which leaves family membership and interaction guidelines unclear. Unlike intact nuclear families, stepfamilies have both pre-existing subsystems, consisting of adults and children, and subsystems that cross the boundaries of the new stepfamily.

Such things as flight plans and dinner time rituals must be negotiated. So must financial matters. Resource distribution is complicated by the obligations established in the entire remarriage chain. A stepfamily might have child-support payments coming in through the mother and going out through the stepfather, in addition to two or more paychecks and child allowances and decisions about who pays what.

Stepfathers typically assume at least some financial responsibility for the new household without reducing the amount of child support due to their biological children. The more children there are in the new household, especially if they are new biological children, the less frequent in-person contact a father has with his nonresident children (Manning & Smock, 1999).

Even though they have suffered though a divorce, a biological parent and his or her child have established a script that defines their roles and prescribes certain behavioral boundaries. Introduction into the household of another adult, who might have his or her own set of boundaries in mind, requires considerable boundary and role negotiation. Stepparents and biological parents generally think that the stepparent should assume an active parental role. Stepchildren, by contrast, think the stepparent should be less like a parent and more like a friend (Fine et al., 1998). This is reflected in the practice of calling the stepparent by his or her first name, as equals in a relationship typically do, rather than using a title that signifies a dominant-subordinate relationship.

The law is not particularly helpful in establishing stepfamily boundaries, nor in defining the role of stepparents. For the most part, the law ignores the stepparent-stepchild relationship. Often, the stepparent has no legal right to the child's school records or to be involved in such matters as making legal medical decisions for the child. Even criminal incest laws often do not apply to the stepparent-stepchild relationship, although child-abuse laws generally do apply because the stepparent is in a position of authority over the child (Chambers, 1990).

Boundary ambiguity: Uncertainty about who is considered pat of a particular family system, or what roles the members should play.

There is a lack of research on the well-being of stepfathers. Mothers in stepfamilies, however, fare as well as mothers in first marriages. Never-married mothers and those who have divorced but not remarried are least happy and well off (Demo & Acock, 1996).

Even if they have a long-term relationship with a stepchild, stepparents generally have no parental rights in the event that they divorce the child's biological parent. In most states, the stepparents have no more legal standing to get custody, or even visitation, than would a stranger. There are also no grounds to expect them to pay child support (Chambers, 1990).

Research on behavioral problems and adjustment of stepchildren gets mixed results. Overall, children in intact homes have the fewest behavioral problems and the best life adjustment, while those in divorced-single homes have more problems and poorer adjustment. Children in remarried families are often found to be more like divorced children with single parents (Amato, 2000). When differences are found, children in stepfamilies generally are between the other two groups in behavioral problems and adjustment (Pasley, Ihinger Tallman, & Lofquist, 1994).

Research has attempted to understand how children, especially adolescents, are parented in stepfamilies. Studies consistently find that stepparents are less active in both support (warmth, acceptance, and nurturance) and control (supervision and discipline) than are biological parents (Amato, 1987; Fine, Voydanoff, & Donnelly, 1993; Kurdek & Fine, 1993).

Adolescent adjustment is somewhat lower when stepparents punish more (Fine, Donnelly, & Voydanoff, 1991) and somewhat higher when stepparents are perceived by stepchildren to exhibit warmth (Fine & Kurdek, 1992). In stepfather families, better adolescent adjustment is found when mothers are the primary disciplinarians and the stepfathers play only a small part in discipline (Bray, 1988). Consistency in the scripted boundaries of the biological unit apparently eases adjustment for the child.

As is true in intact families, better child adjustment is generally found with parents using authoritative than with authoritarian parenting styles. Crosbie-Burnett and Giles-Sims (1994) found better adolescent adjustment when the stepparent had a parenting style high in supportive behaviors but low in control behaviors.

Summary and Conclusion

With the exception of those societies with stable high-divorce systems, industrialization had the nearly universal effect of increasing the divorce rate. This was true for the United States, where the divorce rate was nearly always higher than in most of Europe.

Over time, divorce in the United States became both more common and easier to get. Divorce in the postindustrial era is usually conducted under no-fault provisions, which replaced the traditional adversarial system. The United States today could be called a "postdivorce society," which affects family bonds, inequality, and structural and cultural factors.

A host of variables is associated with divorce rates, including geographical mobility, individualism, race, age at marriage, cohabitation, educational level, and income level. Most persons see the cause of their own divorce, however, in more personal terms that are constructed in terms compatible with social acceptability.

Divorce is a long process with several stages of detachment from previous role relationship: legal, emotional, economic, coparental, community, and psychic. Adults suffer from divorce, but so do children. Most children of divorce adjust, but divorce is associated with risks such as school problems, delinquency problems, and relationship problems. Most children are resilient, but they still suffer some distress. Several factors, such as economic hardship, determine how well the parents deal with divorce, and support from extrafamilial sources influences children's adjustment.

Almost half of marriages are now remarriages for one or both partners, and many of those involve children. In spite of the difficulties, remarriages are about as happy as first marriages, but are more likely to end in divorce. Presence of stepchildren, especially adolescents, is one contributor to remarriage instability. Stepfamilies are different from intact nuclear families in several ways, including their complexity. Some ways of constructing stepparent/stepchild relationships are more effective than are others.

In conclusion, divorce rates in the United States have held relatively steady since 1980. Still, millions of adults and children are directly affected every year. The divorce rate is a response to a number of social variables, but the rate itself affects schools, the workforce, and other social factors. In some respects, the United States has become a high-divorce-rate society but is attempting to deal with the issue using low-rate solutions. The next chapter will consider social policies, some of which deal with divorce.

> *Rethinking in Context* Should the government take steps to try to lower the divorce rate? If so, what should those steps be? What might be the consequences of getting rid of no-fault divorce? Should couples have to get counseling before divorcing? Should joint custody be considered? At what age should children's preferences be honored in making custody decisions? What could schools do to ease the adjustment of children in stepfamilies?

Additional Resources

Divorce

Ahrons, Constance. 1994. *The Good Divorce: Keeping Your Family Together When Your Marriage Comes Apart*. New York: HarperCollins.

Berner, R. Thomas. 1992. *Parents Whose Parents Were Divorced*. New York: Haworth Press.

Cherlin, Andrew J. 1992. *Marriage, Divorce, Remarriage*, rev. ed. Cambridge, MA: Harvard University Press.

Ebaugh, Helen Rose Fuchs. 1988. *Becoming an Ex: The Process of Role Exit*. Chicago: University of Chicago Press.

Everett, Craig A., ed. 1992. *Divorce and the Next Generation: Effects on Young Adults' Patterns of Intimacy and Expectations for Marriage*. New York: Haworth Press.

Goode, William J. 1993. *World Changes in Divorce Patterns*. New Haven, CT: Yale University Press.

Parkman, Allen M. 1992. *No-Fault Divorce: What Went Wrong?* Boulder, CO: Westview Press.

Remarriage and stepfamilies

Bray, James, & John Kelly. 1999. *Stepfamilies: Love, Marriage, and Parenting in the First Decade*. New York: Broadway.

Ganong, Lawrence H., & Marilyn Coleman. 1994. *Remarried Family Relationships*. Thousand Oaks, CA: Sage.

Kelly, Patricia. 1995. *Developing Healthy Stepfamilies: Twenty Families Tell Their Stories*. New York: Haworth Press.

Papernow, Patricia L. 1993. *Becoming a Stepfamily: Patterns of Development in Remarried Families*. San Francisco: Jossey-Bass.

Pasley, Kay, & Marilyn Ihinger-Tallman, eds. 1994. *Stepparenting: Issues in Theory, Research, and Practice*. Westport, CT: Greenwood Press.

Internet Sites

Several scholarly articles on children of divorce, from a variety of perspectives

http://www.futureofchildren.org/cad

The Children of Separation and Divorce Center

http://www.divorceabc.com

Links to several divorce sites

http://www.divorceinfo.com

The Stepfamily Network

http://stepfamily.net

A feminist view of divorce

http://www.backlash.com/book/divorce.html

Alliance for Non-Custodial Parents Rights

http://www.ancpr.org/sitemap.htm

Men's perspective on divorce and custody issues

http://www.vix.com/men/single-dad.html

Advocates for divorce reform

http://www.divorcereform.org

For links to these sites and additional resources, visit the *Families in Context* Web site at:

http://sociology.wadsworth.com

Chapter 16

Family Perspectives,

Policy, and the Future

Prelude

In 1946, Aldous Huxley published his classic novel *Brave New World*. He painted a disturbing picture of life in some imagined future. The family unit had been abolished. Children were bred artificially and raised in common groups. Each child was genetically programmed to have a certain limited intellectual and physical ability so that he or she would do certain kinds of jobs and would be appropriately challenged and happy with them. In case someone would become upset with the system, a drug called "soma" was freely available; everybody was happy, partly because they were drugged and partly because they could imagine no other way of life. Only the elite group of Alphas were allowed the full human potentials to question, imagine, and fall in love.

Huxley was far seeing. The technology to construct such a world did not exist in 1946. It does now. New human fertilization procedures and a rapidly expanding knowledge of genetics would make that world possible in a few years, if it isn't already.

Could this be what the future holds? Would it be possible for people to be happier in a brave new world, without the challenges of family life?

A major theme of this book has been that the family must be seen in the context of the larger social system of which it is a part. Economic, political, religious, and family institutions have always affected each other. In the past, decisions made elsewhere have often affected the family institution more by accident than by intent.

Increasingly, scholars, policy makers, and politicians are intentionally considering the impact of their actions on the family. This chapter looks at the issue of public policies and the family. Images of the past and future of the family in America will also be considered.

> *Thinking Ahead* Based on what you have learned in this course, do you agree more with the pessimistic or optimistic view of the future of the family? List several political issues that directly affect the family. If you were president, how would you deal with these issues?

This chapter serves both as a review of what we know about the family in the past and present and as a framework for asking questions about the future of the family. Neither the past nor the future is what it used to be, but this is nothing new.

Images of the Past, Present, and Future

To imagine a vision of the future, science fiction writers often select a trend that has been going on for some time, then imagine what might happen if that trend continues. Similarly, family analysts sometimes project trends of family change into the future. This provides an opportunity to revisit the "family decline" debate that was introduced in chapter 1.

Family Continua, Change, and Interpretation

Throughout the book we have looked at continua used to analyze changes in the family form over time. We can now review those continua by illustrating how the pessimists and optimists can select data to bolster their case. We can also use the continua to project the direction of change into the future.

Change on the mate selection continuum (Figure 16.1) has been toward the "total choice" end. A high divorce and remarriage rate would indicate a position near the "universal, permanent availability" position. High rates of nonmarital cohabitation, such as found in Sweden and increasingly in the United States, might indicate that the system is approaching the "random liaisons-no marriage system" position.

Pessimists see these changes as evidence of the decline of the family, as indicated by Sorokin's characterization of marriage as a parking lot. The distinction between being legally married or not is being lost; cohabitants, heterosexual or homosexual, increasingly have many of the same rights as married persons and fewer of the responsibilities and commitments.

Optimists see the change as beneficial, opening the marital status to more options and allowing individuals the freedom to choose their marriage partners and to leave a relationship when it is destructive or no longer fulfilling.

If the direction of change continues, divorce rates will begin to increase again, while marriage and remarriage rates will continue to decline. Laws, policies, and practices will continue to redefine the marital state until it no longer has legal distinction. Perhaps some couples will continue to marry for personal or religious reasons.

Marriage rates are indeed going down, partly because of an increase in average age at first marriage. This average age, however, is about the same as it was in 1900. The lowest averages occurred in midcentury.

Perhaps the greatest change in the postindustrial era is reflected in the gender role continuum. Increasing numbers of women have entered the labor force, forming more two-income families. The traditional

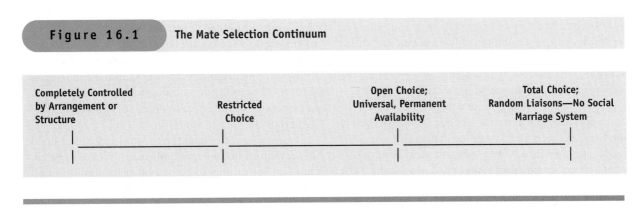

Figure 16.1 The Mate Selection Continuum

Completely Controlled by Arrangement or Structure

Restricted Choice

Open Choice; Universal, Permanent Availability

Total Choice; Random Liaisons—No Social Marriage System

Source: Adams, Bert N. 1995. *The Family: A Sociological Interpretation.* Fort Worth: Harcourt Brace. Page 108.

division of labor, in which the husband provides the economic sustenance and instrumental leadership, while the wife provides emotional sustenance and expressive leadership, is no longer taken for granted. Instead, each couple negotiates their own role relationship, influenced by financial and other considerations.

We have seen considerable evidence of these changes throughout this text, but we have also seen that the change toward androgyny is not complete. Even in Sweden, which has a long policy of encouraging androgyny, many women elect to work part-time rather than full-time and fewer men take advantage of family leave policies (Haas, 1992). Childbearing continues to have a "traditionalizing" influence on marriages.

Pessimists see the movement toward androgyny as evidence of the breakdown of the family. Additional stresses of two-earner families and the need constantly to agree to negotiate roles decrease marital happiness and stability, and take time and energy from children.

"Glad it changed" optimists are pleased about the move toward androgyny, but they often feel it has not gone far enough. They point to the facts that husbands are not doing an equal share of the housework and that women are not paid equally in the workforce.

Couples still tend to organize their division of labor such that men have the primary responsibility for economic support of the family, while women have the primary responsibility for home and children. Whether this is because of the continued force of tradition or because of negotiation and choice of the couple themselves is a matter of debate.

The direction of change appears to be toward more androgyny. If this continues, eventually there will be no social difference between men and women. Barring technological developments such as artificial wombs, and a cultural change making most persons willing to use such technology, androgyny is limited

Figure 16.2 Gender Role Continuum

Total Differentiation; Authoritarian, Determined by Tradition

Androgyny; Roles Blurred; Determined by Choice and Negotiation

Adapted from: Adams, Bert N. 1995. *The Family: A Sociological Interpretation.* Fort Worth: Harcourt Brace. Page 108.

by sex-irreducible gender roles. The increasing number of childless couples and longer life expectancies, which allow a long postchild lifespan, reduce the power of gender roles.

The direction of change on the socialization continuum (Figure 16.3) is away from family-kin controlled socialization. Day-care facilities, schools, the media, the Internet, and peers are more influential on children's socialization. Pessimists are quite concerned about this trend. Especially troubling is the **defathering of the family**. With increasing numbers of out-of-wedlock children and children of divorce, fathers are decreasingly involved in the socialization of children (Blankenhorn, 1995). This gap is often filled by other influences such as gangs, television, and other extrafamilial agencies. For many young persons, identification is indeed problematic.

"It has not really declined" optimists point to the alternatives that have evolved for child care, and the possibility that quality of time between parents and children has improved. Declining parental death rates also increase the chances that a child will have a living parent. "Glad it changed" optimists point to the need for more positive extrafamilial agencies such as day care at the workplace, so that working parents have a viable alternative for part of the socialization process.

Complete change in socialization could ultimately lead to institutional child rearing such as that portrayed in the novel *Brave New World* (Huxley, 1946). All children would be raised in orphanage-like institutions; parents would have no direct responsibility after the child's birth. Another alternative would be near-chaos, where youth-based cultures continually redefine society. Pessimists might argue that some inner-city areas already are approaching that position on the continuum. Without the family, the socialization options appear to be complete control by government or other powerful agency, or chaos.

Figure 16.4 introduces the Personnel Embeddedness Continuum. The concept "embedded" means to be enclosed by something, to be part of a surrounding whole, as a fossil might be embedded in a larger rock. When embedded, an object does not have a separate, independent existence. Personnel embeddedness deals with the extent that persons in a system are part of a larger family group.

The high value Americans place on individualism makes it difficult to imagine societies at point A on the personnel embeddedness continuum. The individual in such a society is not perceived to have an identity apart from his or her family. The interests and survival of the society are more important than the interests of the individual.

At point A, it is not even the nuclear family that is important, but the larger kin group. The nuclear family and individual serve the interests of the kin group or clan. Some hunting-gathering and horticultural groups were close to this position on the continuum.

At point B on the personnel embeddedness continuum, the extended family and kin group become less important and the nuclear family is the most important

---

Figure 16.3	**The Socialization Continuum**

Orderly Replacement;
Family-Kin Controlled;
Family Identification

Controlled by
Extrafamilial
Agencies
Identifications;
Problematic

Redefinition
of Culture by
Each Generation

Source: Adams, Bert N. 1995. *The Family: A Sociological Interpretation*. Fort Worth: Harcourt Brace. Page 108.

Defathering of the family: Declining involvement of the "father" role in the typical family unit.

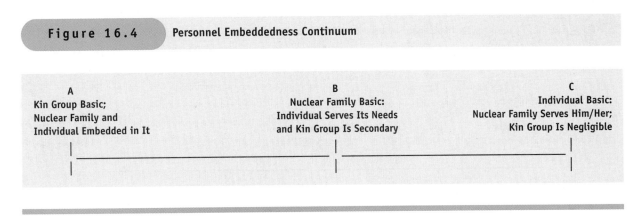

Figure 16.4 Personnel Embeddedness Continuum

A	B	C
Kin Group Basic; Nuclear Family and Individual Embedded in It	Nuclear Family Basic: Individual Serves Its Needs and Kin Group Is Secondary	Individual Basic: Nuclear Family Serves Him/Her; Kin Group Is Negligible

Source: Adams, Bert N. 1995. *The Family: A Sociological Interpretation*. Fort Worth: Harcourt Brace. Page 108.

social unit. The individual serves the needs of the nuclear family. The status, reputation, and survival of the nuclear family are the most important consideration. Parents who tell children, "Don't let the family down!" are referring to the central place of the family. They are examples of this point on the continuum.

Point C on the continuum is the ideal-typical point at which the individual is the most important element in society. The kin group has essentially no influence, and it is the task of the nuclear family to serve the individual. Parents worry about letting down their children, rather than the other way around. Partners leave marriages because their individual needs are not being met, rather than sacrificing their individual needs for the family.

Even the ideal family of the 1950s was at least as far to the right on the personnel embeddedness continuum as the "nuclear family is basic" point. Further movement has occurred in the direction of what Popenoe (1994) referred to as the "post-nuclear family." It is especially troubling to pessimists when it appears to be the adult individuals, rather than the children, whose needs are primarily being served.

Popenoe (1994) also refers to the "overindividualism" he sees in society. In the past, according to the pessimists, "doing one's duty" was more important than "self-fulfillment." Ralf Dahrendorf (1979) and Daniel Yankelovich (1994) expressed the same sentiment when they argued that there is always tension between "social bonds" and "personal choice," and that the pendulum has moved too far in the direction of personal choice. Interest in the collective forms of association, whether that is government, community, voluntary associations, or the family, is declining; individual fulfillment has become more

important. More Americans live by themselves today than at any other time in history (Popenoe, 1994).

"Glad it changed" optimists claim that, too often, collectivism stifled individual development, creativity, and freedom. Feminists suggest that women have always been asked to sacrifice the most for the family and the collective good, and changes have allowed them more complete individual expression.

"It has not really changed" optimists point to the fact that the vast majority of Americans still yearn to be involved in monogamous, long-lasting relationship that entails raising children. It is still true that men, women, and children all gain fulfillment from such relationships. The family ideal is intact, even if the reality is sometimes difficult to achieve.

Projecting continuing movement in the direction and rate of the recent past would result in relationships that lasted only as long as each person's immediate needs were met. No one would expect to make the sacrifices that are generally necessary to make a long-term relationship work. Whether society can actually move further in that direction and still remain viable is not known.

Figure 16.5 illustrates the Institutional Embeddedness Continuum. At point A, all necessary functions occur within the family institution. Many preindustrial societies would be close to this point. As societies became more complex they moved toward points B or even C on the continuum.

Society today is highly differentiated. The family is no longer the basic unit of economic production, and has long ago ceased to be the primary political power. Education and other institutions do much of the socialization that once was carried on in the family. Those

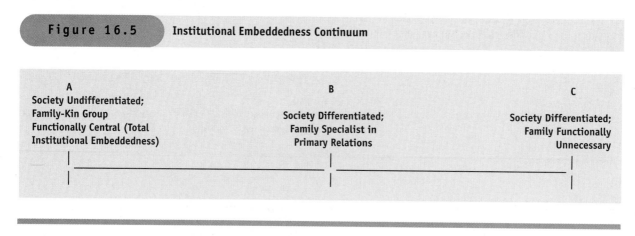

Figure 16.5 Institutional Embeddedness Continuum

A
Society Undifferentiated;
Family-Kin Group
Functionally Central (Total
Institutional Embeddedness)

B
Society Differentiated;
Family Specialist in
Primary Relations

C
Society Differentiated;
Family Functionally
Unnecessary

Source: Adams, Bert N. 1995. *The Family: A Sociological Interpretation*. Fort Worth: Harcourt Brace. Page 108.

who are religious might attend services as a family, but the family and home itself are rarely at the center of religion. Few Americans practice ancestor worship in their homes. Medicine is generally controlled by specialists, as are childbirth and much food production and preparation. We listen to music performed by others, rather than making music as a family or community.

Pessimists see many of these trends as evidence of family decline. Geographic mobility, relative prosperity, and cultural complexity have removed most of the functions previously performed in the family. Several science fiction writers have imagined a society in which the family did not exist or was dominated by the state, and the portrayals were typically grim (Huxley, 1946; Orwell, 1949; Zamyatin, 1972). No known society has managed to survive without some institutionalized arrangements that could be called a family.

"Glad it changed" optimists point out that having some functions performed by extrafamilial specialists is more efficient, and allows more free time for individual and family activities. It is no longer common or necessary for a family to bake all their own bread, make their own clothes, and raise their own food. That time is freed for tasks considered more enjoyable.

Other Future Considerations

Not all considerations about the future fit neatly into the five continua we have been considering. For one thing, the discussion tends to imply that families in all social groups are similarly affected. This is not the case.

The American economy is creating an increasingly large gap between the well off and the poor. Professionals with careers in high-tech and other areas of the postindustrial economy are doing quite well. Those in the working classes, however, might be the first generation of Americans to be worse off economically than their parents.

Assortive mating is a part of this widening gap in family incomes. Women are increasingly employed in the higher paying professions, and these women tend to marry even higher paid men. Often such dual-career couples remain childless or have only one child in whom to invest their resources. Children of such marriages are economically and educationally privileged.

At the other extreme are the families headed by single mothers who are often poorly educated and unskilled. They and their children face grim economic prospects. Even working very hard, it is difficult to support a family on the wages of one minimum-wage job.

The increasing gap between the rich and poor hits particularly hard in the Hispanic community and is disastrous in the Black portion of central cities. Black single mothers are generally embedded in a stable, functional network of kin and pseudo-kin, often centered around mothers, grandmothers, aunts and sisters, with less involvement by husbands and fathers (Cherlin & Furstenberg, 1983). That family form seems adaptive for providing survival, but not in building toward a more affluent and secure future.

The postindustrial, global economy does not appear likely to furnish large numbers of low-skill, high-wage jobs. The "underclass," characterized by unstable families, is likely to remain a serious concern unless institutional arrangements, including institutional racism, change. At the same time, educated couples who have few children and remain married may well have more opportunities than any class in history.

※ use this

Pessimists might take heart about some changes that have occurred since the early 1990s. Rates of unwed births are going down, although they remain at near-record levels. Crime rates are going down significantly. Abortion rates, too, are down; they now stand at the lowest rate in two decades (Census Bureau, 2000). The economy is strong, with the lowest unemployment rates since the late 1960s. This paragraph was written in June 2001; whether the trends are of the short-term or long-term variety remains to be seen.

Family Policy

Many of the macro-level changes in the family occurred without intentional effort by groups or individuals. In some respects, the industrial and postindustrial revolutions are forces beyond individual influence. Intentional effort on the part of individuals or government might not have much effect on such social variables as average age at first marriage, the percentage of the workforce employed in high-paying jobs at a given time, or even the divorce rate.

Some family variables are influenced by the actions of governments, large corporations, or religious organizations. These effects sometimes occur unintentionally; income tax provisions that effectively penalize persons who marry rather than live together, for example, might affect the marriage rate.

Requirements that spouses be economically liable for bills accumulated for each other's health care are a major factor when widows or widowers consider remarriage; for most elderly Americans, it would, from a purely financial standpoint, be foolish to remarry rather than to cohabit. Similarly, a single mother on welfare gets Medicaid, which covers the health needs of her children. She might be economically foolish to marry a low-income partner if it meant losing her welfare and health benefits. These are examples of policies that have unintentional anti-family consequences.

Almost any policy has some influence on the family institution or upon large numbers of families. Policies on drug use and other crimes, availability of contraception and abortion, and quality of schools affect families. The elimination of institutional racism, reduction of

unemployment, and creation of more living-wage jobs would help millions of poor families. Although these policies affect families, they are not usually viewed as intentional family policies.

Sometimes, however, government will formulate plans with the specific intent of influencing families; these intentional plans become **family policy** (Moen & Schorr). Most family scholars agree that the United States is well behind most other postindustrial nations in the development of explicit family policy but that interest in such policies has increased significantly in recent years (Wisensale, 1993). *how recent?*

Part of the reason the United States has been slower to develop family policy is that the process involves not only issues but values as well (Moen, 2001; Zimmerman, 1988). Americans are a long way from agreeing on the values surrounding the family, and they do not always agree on what specific issues need to be addressed.

Attempts to formulate family policy are sometimes stymied over basic disagreements. One such example was the fate of the White House Conference on Families, called for by Jimmy Carter during his 1976 presidential campaign. Although Carter won the election, the conference was not held until 1980, the year Ronald Reagan won the next election.

Controversy prevented the conference from accomplishing much. Political conservatives objected to the proposed naming of a divorced Black mother to chair the conference; she resigned. Liberals proposed a functional definition of "family" that would have included homosexual couples; that proposal was defeated after bitter debate (Gelles, 1995).

Family Policy Roles

In spite of setbacks, family issues remain an important topic of political discussion. Professionals in family studies contribute to the discussion in various ways. F. Ivan Nye and Gerald W. McDonald (1979) delineated four major roles that can be assumed by family professionals: research for family policy, family evaluation research, family impact analysis, and family policy advocacy.

Research for Family Policy. In the family policy role, a researcher would gather data that might be used to

---

Family policy: A definite course or method of action with the intent of influencing forms of family organization, behaviors, and decisions (Eschleman, 1994).

make policy decisions. Such a person might, for example, attempt to perform objective research about children who grow up with a homosexual parent (see chapter 14). Results of the research would be provided to politicians and others who make decisions about family policy. Objective research could help determine what, if any, policy changes are called for. Legislation might be necessary on such topics as same-sex couple adoption.

Family Evaluation Research. Family evaluation research attempts to find out whether a particular policy or program has achieved its goal. A family evaluation researcher might study a school program designed to reduce teen pregnancy to see if students in the program were less likely to get pregnant than students who were not in the program (see chapter 11). The effect of mandatory arrest on repeated wife abuse is another area that has been studied by family evaluation researchers (see chapter 14).

Family Impact Analysis. Policies and programs often have unintended consequences for families. Family evaluation research focuses on whether a program meets its goal, while family impact analysis takes a broader view. It looks at all possible consequences of an intended or actual policy or program. A program might be started in a school to allow children of divorced parents to get together in a group to discuss their feelings. Family evaluation researchers might find that, indeed, the children got together; family impact analysis might discover that identifying children of divorce in such a way only added to the stigma they felt among their peers (see chapter 15).

Family Policy Advocacy. Advocates are active supporters of a particular policy or point of view. They are essential to the success of any policy change, but there is debate about whether researchers should also be advocates. Nye and McDonald (1979) contended that advocacy is never a proper role for researchers, who are supposed to maintain objective neutrality. Advocates' actions are based on a set of beliefs and values that might not be supportable by the actual evidence. There might be a temptation to conduct or report only research that supports the advocate's position (Gelles, 1996).

To the four roles suggested by Nye and McDonald, Karen Bogenschneider (1995) added a fifth option called *family policy alternative education*. The role of these professionals is to educate the general public about the latest family research. They attempt to maintain neutrality and objectivity, and let the public determine what the actual policies should be.

Family Policy Issues

One set of issues has to do with the sources of family policies. Some advocates want public, or governmental, policies; others call for the private sector to handle family matters. For example, many observers believe that more attention needs to be paid to the mutual influence of family and work, and that policies are needed to make the work world more "family friendly." Especially with the large number of mothers in the workforce, day care and family leave become more crucial issues (Moen, 2001).

Those who favor government interventions think that laws should require employers to provide more day care, better leave practices, and more flexible work schedules. Sweden, where lengthy paid leaves are guaranteed for childbirth and other family matters, might be a model.

Advocates for private action think that government requirements impose an unnecessary burden on employers, and that the employers and their employees should be allowed to work out their own arrangements for more worker-friendly policies. Employers who provide the best family-friendly policies, free-enterprise supporters argue, should attract better and more loyal employees, so the market system should take care of the problem. Perceived job flexibility, for example, improves work-family balance while allowing a worker to actually work longer and better hours (Hill et al., 2001).

Some conservatives are certainly in favor of better child care, but think parents are best able to provide that. Government regulations or more family-friendly private sector policies might have the effect of encouraging even more parents to put the care of their children in the hands of strangers. In cases of both private and public action, however, the programs instituted thus far tend to benefit middle-class professionals more than they help working-class or poor families (Baker, 1995b).

Among those who advocate government action, there remains the question as to what level of government should formulate family policy. Historically, the states have had more to do with family laws, policies, and programs than has the federal government (Wisensale, 1993).

States determine most marriage and divorce laws. Where the federal government has gotten involved, it has often been the courts as well as the legislature, as in the Supreme Court's upholding of the Edmunds-Tucker

Act that ended polygyny among the Mormons (see chapter 6). Although the federal government provides guidelines and some funding, state laws actually deal with child abuse and spouse abuse (see chapter 14). Only recently has the federal government gotten involved in such matters as fathers who do not pay their court-ordered child support (see chapter 14). Federal funding for the Violence Against Women Act also frames the issue of family violence in a feminist direction and influences state and local responses to family violence.

Specific topics of concern are also varied. It is difficult to imagine what family-related issues might surface in the next 25 years or so, but there are some unresolved matters that will need to be settled. An important issue continues to be the moral and legal definition of marriage and family.

The increasing incidence and acceptance of cohabitation have blurred the line between married and unmarried conditions. Some legal distinctions remain in tax codes and other formal areas. Courts and legislatures will clarify these.

A controversy remains about whether homosexual marriages should be allowed. Because of the "full faith and credit" clause in the United States Constitution, if any state changed its laws to allow homosexual marriages, all other states would presumably be bound to recognize the marriages as valid. Many states, however, have passed legislation that forbids the recognition of same-sex marriages.

Another emerging set of issues involves the balancing of the right of parents and the rights of children, as enforced by the state. Some advocates want harsher child abuse laws, even to the extent of defining spanking or smoking cigarettes near children as child abuse. Other advocates believe the state already has too much power to regulate child rearing.

Several highly public court cases have revolved around the rights of biological parents versus those of adoptive or stepparents. Blood ties have long had a strong presumption in American law when custody cases are decided. Even when parents relinquish their children for adoption, they often have the right to change their minds later. These issues are likely to be debated for some time.

The abortion issue is likely always to be controversial, but there are also other concerns involving conception and contraception. The use of surrogate mothers, cloning, and a variety of artificial devices are issues that will have to be decided (see chapter 11). It is not even widely agreed who should decide these issues.

The Family in Advanced Postindustrialism

There has been little indication that the postindustrial revolution has slowed the movement toward increased individualism and the atomization of the family. Increased use of telecommunication and computers, however, hints at the possibility of a different future for the family.

Industrialization removed production from the home, creating a "family world" and a separate "work world." Postindustrial technology could reverse that trend. As increasing numbers of persons make their living in the information and services sectors of the economy, more workers are able to make their living in their homes.

A Scenario

One can imagine a college professor who writes all her articles at home, accessing all her references via the Internet. She prepares her lectures on the computer. When ready, she presents the lecture; it is digitally

"Does the brave new world beckon?"

Families in the NEWS

Social Research, Child Care, Politics, and Policy

A report about the effects of out-of-home child care has created controversy among the study's authors and the press. Preliminary results from a study by the National Institute of Child Health and Human Development were presented by Jay Belsky, a principal investigator for the study, at a biennial meeting of the Society for Research in Child Development.

Belsky, who is also a professor at the University of London, said results indicate that children in high-quality day care develop superior language and memory skills compared with those who have stayed at home. The study also found, according to Belsky, that children who had been in day care more than 30 hours per week were more at risk for such behavioral problems as aggressiveness and disobedience.

More specifically, 17 percent of children with more than 30 hours per week of day care were judged by caregivers, mothers, and school teachers as being aggressive in kindergarten. By contrast, only 6 percent of children with fewer than 10 hours of day care weekly were so identified.

These results were published in several national newspapers, usually as bad news about the effects of nonmaternal care on children and on society. But some people objected, claiming it was just another attempt to make working mothers feel guilty. Kathleen McCartney, also a principal investigator of the study, responded that Belsky had overstated the findings.

Belsky suggested that the study calls for policies that would help families reduce the amount of time their children spend in child care. These might include longer parental leave after childbirth, tax breaks for stay-at-home moms, or more part-time work opportunities.

Others suggest that more government spending to improve the quality of child care would be a more appropriate policy response. And still others say more analysis is needed before any decisions about policy should be made.

Sources: Linda Jacobson. **www.washingtonpost.com**, April 23, 2001. Jessica Garrison. **www.latimes.com**, April 26, 2001. Peggy Orenstein. **www.latimes.com**, April 29, 2001.

"filmed" and recorded. When students are ready, they can log in from their computers, simultaneously watching her lecture and reading the material. If they miss a point, they can "rewind" and view the section again. They can ask her questions by e-mail.

While the professor is at work on her computer, her husband, an accountant, has accessed his day's work on his computer and is doing his client's taxes.

Meanwhile, their oldest child is doing her homework on her own computer. They can stop and have lunch together, then get back to their respective computers. The baby, too young to have a computer lesson, spends much of his time in his room playing and being monitored electronically for wet diapers, cries, and other concerns. At any time, of course, mom or dad can go play with Junior for a while.

When they run low on groceries, they access the warehouse food market's World Wide Web page and order what they need. Their order is automatically filled and shipped that afternoon.

In the evening, the family has dinner and then selects a program or two to watch on their 3-D-vision in the living room. They call Grandma, who lives in another country, and set the interactive tele-unit so that she can watch a program with them. Family members then go to their respective pods for more work or recreation. The teenage girl calls her boyfriend, whom she met through Compudating; they simul-watch a concert together while chatting on the Net.

Later in the evening, one of the children begins to feel sick. A parent logs on to the Medi-net program and types in the list of symptoms. The child's arm is inserted into the Compumedi-net attachment, which takes a temperature, counts the pulse, and performs a quick blood analysis. Fortunately the treatment called for is a simple one, and the drug is automatically made from the Compumed's internal supply source.

With telecommunication, it does not much matter where on the earth a person is. Families could live anywhere and work from any site. The above family could live in Bozeman, Montana. The professor's "home" college could be in Florida, the accountant's "home" office in New York, and the children's "home" schooling program monitored in California. Grandma lives in Belize, the "doctor's office" is in Boston, and the grocery store is in Utah.

Most of this scenario is now technologically possible, but there are problems with it. First, it is not clear that most individuals would want the kind of life described. Some want to personally interact with people outside the family, and might tire of interacting only with family. This is, however, probably a learned value. As we have seen, for most of history, people interacted with a relatively small number of others. Further, with telecommunication, a person can interact with thousands of others.

Other problems might be more serious than the decrease in personal, physical contact. There would be a massive relocation of the workforce. A process of "de-urbanization," already occurring, would accelerate. There would be increased environmental demand on the few remaining "unspoiled" parts of the world. Pollution due to automobiles, however, could decrease because of less commuting.

Millions of employees would lose their jobs. One teacher's lecture, for example, could be viewed by thousands of students, and the tests could be graded by computer. Most other teachers would be jobless, although some of them would find work in other fields. Some workers would get jobs delivering goods and other relatively low-paid positions, while the incomes of the well-educated professional families would probably increase. What the workforce would actually look like is difficult to imagine.

The Author's Conclusion

Several issues regarding the future of the family have been dealt with in this text and in this chapter in particular. A few specific possibilities are mentioned in Highlight 16.1.

HIGHLIGHT 16.1 **Speculations about Family Issues of the Future: Things That Might — or Might Not — Happen** Debate about the legality of homosexual marriage is likely to continue. At some point, one state will make such marriages legally indistinguishable from heterosexual marriages, causing something of a constitutional crisis when other states refuse to accept them. Or, "domestic partnership" laws in most states will be a politically acceptable alternative.

The baby boomers will continue to age, resulting in a large population requiring care but also opening up job opportunities for younger workers as baby boomers retire.

In the next few years, as the country diversifies and multiculturalism grows, the laws forbidding polygamy will be challenged on the grounds of religious freedom, probably by a Muslim.

The Human Genome Project will develop the ability to test a fetus, very early in gestation, for a number of diseases, conditions, and abilities predisposed by heredity. This will make the abortion issue more controversial. Also, cures for various diseases will follow, greatly extending the life expectancy. This will significantly affect Social Security and other retirement programs.

An artificial womb will soon be developed, allowing the maturation of a fetus to viability without a uterus. The process will be very expensive, however, and few will use it.

Before 2002 ends, a human being will be cloned. This will allow individuals to have a child that is an exact genetic duplicate — without a partner. It will also raise a number of moral and legal issues.

Many states will tighten their divorce laws, making divorce more difficult to get. The results will include increased cohabitation and fewer marriages.

Catholic priests will be allowed to marry. Women will not be allowed to become priests, but an essentially equivalent role will be created, allowing them to do everything priests do.

A jurisdiction in Minnesota, California, or Massachusetts will legally define spanking as child abuse.

A "one-time permanent" contraceptive pill, requiring that another pill be taken to restore fertility, will be developed.

More countries will adopt China's "one child only" policy.

Several students now reading this book will become family sociologists.

Regardless of how these and other issues are decided, the vast majority of individuals will continue to form relatively enduring relationships. They will continue to find much of their happiness, joy, and fulfillment in such relationships and in their families. Maintaining marriages and families will continue to be difficult, and perhaps it will become even more so because of the economic and social forces we have examined in this text. Consequently, much unhappiness is also likely to be associated with familial relationships. The institutions of marriage and family will remain embattled but strong into the foreseeable future.

Summary and Conclusion

Even among the experts, there is wide disagreement about the current status and the future of the family. Pessimists think the family institution has declined and is likely to decline further. They are particularly concerned with the increased number of children who do not have an active father in their lives.

"Glad it changed" optimists agree that there has been decline, but the decline is a good thing because the traditional family was patriarchal and oppressive. These analysts believe that still more change is called for.

"It has not really changed" optimists think that the decline is an illusion created by comparisons to romanticized images of the past. The family today, these observers assert, is really no more troubled than it has historically been. It might continue to be troubled, but will remain strong and adaptive.

Many family scholars call for clearer and more active family policy in its many roles. Issues involving the family of the future will be resolved one way or another, and it is better to resolve them in accord with some well-thought-out plan than to rely on chance. The problem might not be the lack of plans, but rather too many plans because Americans disagree on most aspects of family policy.

In conclusion, the long journey through *Families in Context* is at an end. It is unlikely, gentle reader, that you can say you enjoyed the trip. But we hope it was a learning experience that you will appreciate. May you have long life, happy memories, and great families.

Rethinking in Context Would you like to live in the kind of family depicted in the "postindustrial family" scenario? Why or why not? What kind of future do you see for the family in America and the world?

Additional Resources

Trends in marriage and the family and the future

Booth, Alan, ed. 1991. *Contemporary Families: Looking Forward, Looking Back.* Minneapolis, MN: National Council on Family Relations.

Kagan, Sharon L., & Bernice Weissbourd, eds. 1994. *Putting Families First: America's Support Movement and the Challenge of Change.* San Francisco: Jossey-Bass.

Popenoe, David, Jean Bethke Elshtain, & David Blankenhorn. 1996. *Promises to Keep: Decline and Renewal of Marriage in America.* Lanham, MD: Rowman and Littlefield.

Settles, Barbara H., Roma S. Hanks, & Marvin B. Sussman, eds. 1993. *American Families and the Future: Analyses of Possible Destinies.* New York: Haworth Press.

Family policy

Anderson, Elaine A., & Richard C. Hula, eds. 1991. *The Reconstruction of Family Policy.* New York: Greenwood Press.

Brubaker, Timothy, ed. 1993. *Family Relations: Challenges for the Future.* Newbury Park, CA: Sage.

Cantor, Marjor, ed. 1994. *Family Caregiving: Agenda for the Future.* San Francisco: American Society on Aging.

Chow, Esther Ngan-ling, & Catherine White. 1994. *Women, the Family, and Policy: A Global Perspective.* Albany, NY: State University of New York Press.

Haas, Linda. 1992. *Equal Parenthood and Social Policy: a Study of Parental Leave in Sweden.* Albany: State University of New York Press.

Kendrigan, Mary Lou. ed. 1991. *Gender differences: Their Impact on Public Policy.* New York: Greenwood Press.

Zimmerman, Shirley L. 1995. *Understanding Family Policy: Theories and Applications.* Newbury Park, CA: Sage.

Internet Sites

CYFERNet: Children, Youth and Families Education and Research Network, on Family Policy, with links to several other sites

http://www.nnfr.org/fampolicy/home.html

The World Future Society

http://www.wfs.org/

Michael Finley on Alvin Toffler and other futurists

http://www.mfinley.com/toffler.htm

Find and write your U.S. representative

http://www.house.gov/writerep/

Find your U.S. senator

http://www.senate.gov/

Working Mother magazine; see its list of Top 100 mother-friendly companies to work for

http://www.workingwoman.com/wwn/magazine/wm_magazine.jsp

For links to these sites and additional resources, visit the *Families in Context* Web site at:

http://sociology.wadsworth.com

Glossary

Abortifacient: A substance or device that causes abortion.

Abortion ratio: Number of abortions for every 1,000 known pregnancies.

Abortion: Termination of a pregnancy before the fetus can survive outside the uterus. **Spontaneous abortions** occur naturally and unintentionally; **induced abortions** are done intentionally.

Abstinence: The practice of refraining from indulging some appetite such as food, drink, or a particular sexual practice.

Acculturation: Process by which immigrant groups assimilate into a dominant or host culture and change their values, language, and practices (Silverstein, 2000).

Achieved status: A social position that results from a person's own life events.

Acquaintance rape: Non-consensual sexual intercourse imposed by a person known by the victim.

Adjustment: The act or means of adapting, corresponding, or conforming.

Adoption: Taking into one's own family and raising as one's own child.

Advocacy research: Study done for the primary purpose of advancing a particular political cause or point of view.

Agape (ah-GAH-pay): Love style characterized by nurturing concern and self-sacrifice.

Ageism: Discrimination or prejudice based on age, especially against the elderly.

AIDS (Acquired Immune Deficiency Syndrome): Fatal condition in which the body loses its natural ability to protect itself from disease.

Alimony: Support paid to a spouse by the former spouse after divorce or separation.

Analysis of existing statistics: Use of previously completed analysis as the raw data in an original study. This differs from secondary analysis of data, where someone else's raw data are used for a new analysis.

Androcentric: With men at the center of interest.

Androgyny: A social condition in which there is no gender role differentiation.

Anecdote: A short account of an interesting or humorous event; the **anecdotal method** is the attempt to prove a point by telling a story.

Animism: The belief that spirits can reside in all aspects of nature (Latin *anima*, soul).

Annulment: Official declaration that a supposed marriage was never valid.

Arranged marriage: Mate selection by someone other than the potential mates.

Artificial insemination: Placing semen in the vagina or uterus by means other than sexual intercourse.

Ascribed status: A social position that is assigned to the individual at birth or other life stage, based on criteria over which the individual has no control.

Ascription: Assignment to a position because of characteristics, such as race, sex, or family ancestry, over which the individual has no control.

Assortive mating: The phenomenon that persons marry others like themselves more often than would be expected by chance.

Authority: Power exercised in socially approved ways; legitimate power.

Authority: The socially granted right to control and influence others.

Bachelor: An unmarried man.

Banns: A proclamation that a marriage was agreed to and would occur.

Berdache: "A person, usually male, who was anatomically normal but assumed the dress, occupations, and behavior of the other sex to effect a change in gender status" (Callender and Kochems, 1993:367).

Bereavement: The condition of being deprived of a loved one by death.

Bias: A perception or process that results in systematic misrepresentation of reality.

Bilateral: Tracing descent and inheritance through both male and female lines.

Boundary ambiguity: Uncertainty about who is considered part of a particular family system, or what roles the members should play.

Bourgeoisie: The social class that, in Marxist theory, controls the means of production and uses capital, natural resources, and exploited labor to make profits.

Braceros: Workers who are expected to return to Mexico after a temporary period of employment.

Bracketed scene: An interaction set apart from other day-to-day behavior by a definable beginning and end, during which particular roles and scripts apply.

Bundling: A courting custom by which a couple would spend an evening together in bed, but fully clothed, separated by a "bundling board" or other material.

Calling: In Protestant theology, an occupation to which one could be "called" by God.

Capitalism: An economic system in which production and distribution are controlled by private individuals or groups and guided by the profit motive.

Career: A long-term professional or occupational path with commitment and opportunities for promotion, advancement, and change.

Charavari: "A noisy public demonstration to subject wayward individuals to humiliation in the eyes of the community" (Shorter, 1975:218).

Chicanos: Alternative name for Mexican-Americans. A contraction of *Mexicanos,* pronounced "meschicanos" in Nahuatl, an ancient language of Mexico (Eshleman, 1994).

Child abuse: Action by a parent or parent surrogate that should not have been done because of potential harm to the child.

Child neglect: Failure of a parent or parent surrogate to do something they should have done for their child.

Chivalry: Medieval norms of knighthood, including bravery, courtesy, honor, and gallantry toward women.

Claimsmaker: Person who puts forth a particular view of reality in support of, or in response to, a social movement.

Clan: A group of kin who believe themselves related to a common, sometimes mythological, ancestor.

Closed mobility system: A ideal-typical system of social stratification in which there is no mobility; all status is by ascription.

Cohabiting: Living together, especially as an intimate couple in a marriage-like relationship.

Coitus interruptus: Practice of attempting to prevent contraception in which the penis is withdrawn from the vagina prior to ejaculation.

Comarital sex: Extramarital sex in which the married couple participates together.

Common-law marriage: A union legally recognized as a marriage in spite of not having been solemnized by the state.

Commuter marriages: Dual-career marriages in which husband and wife live separately.

Compadrazgo: A traditional Mexican custom of co-parenthood that developed from God-parenthood.

Complementary scripts: A role relationship where actors assume different roles, but those roles mesh with and support each other.

Concordia: A state of harmony and lack of disagreement between Roman husband and wife.

Concubine: A women who cohabits with a man; a live-in mistress.

Conjugal power: The ability of spouses to affect each other's behavior.

Conjugal unit: The husband-wife pair.

Content analysis: The study of recorded human communications, such as book, Web sites, paintings, and laws (Babbie, 2001).

Contingency: To Skinner, a change in the environment that affects the behavior preceding it.

Continuum: Unbroken degrees of measurement between two extremes.

Contraception: Intentional prevention of impregnation.

Controlled experiment: A form of data gathering in which variables are controlled and manipulated by the researcher.

Coping: Management of stressors without detrimental effects to the family system.

Courtly love: A code of romantic behavior idealized among the aristocracy of medieval Europe.

Courtship: Socially scripted process by which potentially sexual pairs interact to form relationships that can result in marriage.

Couvade: Practice in which the husband of a woman in labor takes to his bed as though he were bearing the child.

Coverture: The doctrine that a man and woman became one flesh at marriages, with the consequence that a wife's property rights are controlled by her husband.

Crisis: The period of disorganization resulting from a stressor that ordinary coping mechanisms have trouble dealing with.

Cross cousins: One's mother's brother's or father's sister's children.

Cross-sectional studies: Studies based on observations representing a single point in time.

Crude divorce rate: Number of divorces per year per 1,000 persons in the population.

Cuckold: A man whose wife has extramarital coitus.

Cultural capital: The general cultural background, knowledge, disposition, and skills that are passed from one generation to the next.

Cultural survival: A culture trait that has survived after its original function has disappeared.

Culture lag: A time discrepancy between technological change and change in non-material aspects of culture such as law and values.

Culture traits: The simplest functional units into which a culture is divided for purposes of analysis (Fairchild, 1970:83).

Cunnilingus: Oral stimulation of the clitoris or vulva.

Date rape: Non-consensual sexual intercourse when the perpetrator and victim are voluntarily in a close relationship.

Daughter track: Role expectation that a daughter will have primary responsibility for familial elder care, in addition to other tasks.

De-fathering of the family: Declining involvement of the "father" role in the typical family unit.

Democracy: Government by the people.

Demography: The study of the characteristics of populations, including birth rates, death rates, growth, and vital statistics. **Demographics** are characteristics of human populations.

Desertion: Legally or culturally unjustified abandonment of a spouse, children, or both.

Developmental paradigm: Explanations of social behavior emphasizing stages of life cycles.

Developmental tasks: Undertakings or objectives associated with a particular stage in the life of an individual or life cycle of a family.

Dichotomy: 1. Divided into two parts. 2. The division of a continuum into two mutually exclusive parts.

Discipline (verb): To train by instruction and practice, especially to teach self control to.

Dissolution of marriage: Divorce.

Divorce mediation: A conflict-resolution process in which a third party helps a couple resolve divorce issues.

Divorce: An official end of a marriage.

Donatio: A payment at marriage from the groom's *familia* to the bride.

Doubling time: The number of years it would take a particular population to double in size if it continued to grow at a given rate. Correct doubling time at low rates of growth can be approximated by the formula (69/annual percentage growth rate) = doubling time in years.

Dramaturgy: The study of interaction as impression management by an actor for an audience.

Dysfunctions: Those observed consequences that lessen the adaptation or adjustment of the system (Merton 1957:51).

Economic determinism: The theory that the economic base of society determines the general character of social structure and culture.

Emigration: Movement *out of* a native country or region.

Emotion work: "Efforts to shape and control one's emotions by socially defining them, through conversations or personal reflections on one's feelings" (Collins and Coltrane, A-3).

Empty nest syndrome: Role loss after a child has left the home resulting in depression, identity crisis, and lowered well-being. Actually a rare phenomenon.

Endogamy: Mate selection from within the group.

Erogenous zones: Parts of the body which, when stimulated, can lead to sexual arousal.

Eros (AIR-ohs): Love style with intense emotional and sexual attachment, but without possessiveness.

Ethnicity: Group distinction based on national origin or distinctive cultural patterns such as religion, language, or region.

Ethnography: A type of field research on a specific culture or subculture.

Eufunction: A positive impact on society of a trait or institution.

Eugenics: The study of hereditary improvement of the human species by controlled selective breeding.

Exogamy: Mate selection from outside the group.

Extended family: A family composed of the nuclear family plus additional relatives, usually a third generation.

Extramarital sex: Sexual intercourse between a married person and someone not his or her spouse; adultery.

Familia: Latin word for the group of slaves and servants in the household; came to refer to the household as a whole.

Familism: "The belief in a strong sense of family identification and loyalty, mutual assistance among family members, a concern for the perpetuation of the family unit, and the subordination of the interests and personality of individual family members to the interests and welfare of the family group" (Popenoe, 1993:538).

Family career: The entirety of events and stages traversed by a family.

Family leave: A leave from employment for family matters, especially birth of a child.

Family of orientation: The family unit that includes one's parents and siblings.

Family of procreation: The family unit that includes one's spouse and, at least potentially, one's children.

Family policy: A definite course or method of action with the intent of influencing forms of family organization, behaviors, and decisions

Fecundity: A biological potential of lifetime childbearing.

Fellatio: Oral stimulation of the penis.

Feminization of poverty: The impression that women are increasingly likely to be poor because of the increasing concentration of poverty in female-headed families.

Fertility rate: The total number of children each woman is expected to have over a lifetime.

Fertility: Actual number of births to a woman.

Fictive kin: Persons treated "as if" they are related.

Field research: Gathering data by direct observation in the natural setting.

Filial piety: Central Confucian ideal involving devotion and reverence of a son to his father; extended to other dominant-subordinate relationships.

Foraging: Collecting plants and animals for subsistence.

Formal norms: Behavioral expectations that are written and enforced by specialized social mechanisms; laws.

Function: Consequence of an action or trait.

Functional definition: Definition based on how the family serves the participating individuals (**microfunctional**) or how it serves society (**macrofunctional**).

Functionalism: A paradigm that focuses on the way various parts of society have consequences that maintain the stability of the whole.

Game stage: To Mead, the third stage of observational development, beginning about age 7 or 8, in which children actually assume roles in interaction with others.

Gender: The social fact of being feminine or masculine.

General abstinence: The practice of completely avoiding sexual intercourse.

General marital desirability: The desirability of a person as a mate based on socially agreed-upon resources.

Generalized other: To Mead, the internalized image persons have of the expectations of society as a whole.

Gens: Roman clan; group of persons of both **gen**ders who believe themselves to share a common **gen**esis for many **gen**erations, and who treat each other **gen**tly.

Glass ceiling: An alleged invisible barrier to women's advancement in the workforce.

Grief: Deep mental and emotional anguish.

Group marriage: A marriage involving more than one husband and more than one wife.

Gynocentric: With women at the center of interest.

Happy: Characterized by good luck, pleasure, satisfaction, or joy.

Heterogamy: Selection of mates from among those with different social characteristics.

Heterosexism: Discrimination against homosexuals.

HIV (Human Immunodeficiency Virus): The virus that causes AIDS.

Homeostasis: The tendency of an organism to maintain internal equilibrium by making adjustments to changing conditions.

Homogamy: Selection of mates from those with similar social characteristics.

Homophilia: Intimate love for a person of the same sex.

Homophobia: A strong negative reaction to homosexuals and homosexuality (homosexual plus Greek *phobos,* fear).

Household: A living unit; a group of persons sharing living quarters.

Human capital: Potential means of production held by an individual that was acquired through formal training, education, or experience.

Humanistic studies: Finding ways of improving the human condition.

Husband exclusion clause: Part of a rape law that makes it impossible to charge a husband with the rape of his wife.

Hypergamy: Marriage in which the woman marries into a higher social level.

Hypogamy: Marriage in which the woman marries into a lower social level.

Hypothesis: A testable educated guess, usually about the relationship among two or more variables.

Hysterectomy: Surgical removal of the uterus.

Ideal type: A hypothetical construct used for comparisons.

Illegitimate power: Power exercised without the consent of the governed, or in socially unapproved ways, usually by coercion.

Imitation. The repetition of an observed behavior.

Immigration: Movement *into* a non-native country or region; compare with **Emigration.**

Impression management: Process in which a person manipulates others' perceptions of himself or herself to achieve a desired outcome.

In vitro **fertilization:** Joining of sperm and egg outside the body.

Incest taboo: A rule forbidding marriage or sexual activity among closely related persons.

Infanticide: The killing of infants, usually as a population control mechanism.

Infertility: Inability to achieve pregnancy or to carry a pregnancy to live birth.

Influence: The ability to shape the thinking and behavior of a decision-maker.

Informal norms: Behavioral expectations that lack codified, enforceable sanctions.

Informal separation: A condition in which married couples maintain separate residences because of problems living together.

Institution: 1. A system of norms, values, statuses, and roles that develop around a basic social goal; 2. a regular and traditional way of meeting a society's needs.

Intrauterine device (IUD): An object inserted into the uterus for the purpose of preventing pregnancy.

Intrinsic marriages: Marriages with the "why" of maintaining the intimacy of the relationship between husband and wife.

Issei: First generation Japanese immigrants to the United States, mostly between 1890 and 1920.

Joint custody: The awarding of shared residential or legal custody to both parents after divorce.

Kin group: Network of persons related by blood, marriage, or adoption.

Kinkeeper: Role that serves to hold family and relationships together by communication and organization.

Kinship system: The way in which a society defines the relationships of those who are inter-related by blood, marriage, or adoption.

La Casa: House, immediate family, household.

Latent fertility regulation: Cultural practices that affect fertility without conscious intent by individuals.

Legal separation: A condition in which a married couple separates, has a legally recognized property and custody settlement, lives apart, but may not remarry.

Libido: To Freud, the basic energy, primarily sexual in nature, that provides the driving force of all human behavior.

Life chances: The probability a person has of sharing in the economic and cultural goods of a society.

Life course: A developmental perspective that focuses on individuals' lives, in their entirety, in historical and social context.

Longitudinal study: A study involving the collection of data at different points in time.

Looking glass self: To Cooley, the concept that we come to see ourselves as we think other persons see us.

Love contract: Expectations partners in a love-appropriate relationship have for each other and themselves.

Love-appropriate relationship: An affiliation in which the partners mutually accept the use of the word "love."

Ludus (LEWD-us): Love as play and recreation.

Machismo: Ideal-typical characteristics of manliness in a highly differentiated Mexican or Mexican-American gender role structure.

Macrosociology: The study of the large-scale structures and processes of society.

Maiden: An unmarried girl or woman, usually assumed to be virgin.

Mania (MAY-nee-ah): Love style with strong emotional intensity, sexual attraction, jealousy, and moodiness.

Manifest fertility regulation: Practices used by persons with the conscious intent of affecting fertility.

Marriage (a) (Legalistic definition): The legal union of a man and woman as husband and wife. (b) A socially sanctioned sexual and economic union between two (or more) members of opposite sexes (occasionally between members of the same sex) (From Howard, Michael C., 1989:454). (c) A socially approved sexual union of some permanence between two or more individuals (Robertson Ian, 1981:630).

Marriage market: The concept that individuals or their families shop and bargain for mates in a way similar to economic transactions.

Marriage squeeze: A demographic condition in which there are considerably more eligible mates for one sex than for another.

Master status: A social position that tends to override every other position a person holds (Hughes, 1945).

Maternal deprivation theory: The theory, now largely discredited, that a child must have a warm, continuous, exclusive, and virtually full-time emotional involvement with its mother.

Mating gradient: Result of a tendency to have more hypergamy than hypogamy in a mate-selection system.

Matriarchy: A system in which women have the authority.

Matrifocal family: "A family in which the mother-child bond takes precedence over the husband-wife bond and in which the day-to-day problems of family living (especially child care and socialization) are managed by women" (LaRossa, 1984:142).

Matrilineal: Tracing descent and inheritance through female lines.

Matrilocal residence: A custom that newlyweds are expected to live with the bride's relatives.

Meritocracy: Government by persons found to be most capable.

Mésalliance: Marriage with a person of lower social position.

Microsociology: The study of small-scale social processes like face-to-face interaction.

Midwife: A person, usually a woman, who provides specialized care during childbirth.

Miscegenation laws: Formal norms against marriage of persons of different races.

Mixed marriage rate for individuals: The percent of individuals of a particular group who are married to an individual who is not in the group in question.

Mixed marriage: Marriage between individuals with characteristics that society generally defines as grounds for homogamy.

Mixed marriages rate: The percentage of marriages involving members of a particular group that includes a partner who is not in that group.

Modeling: Repetition of an observed set of behavior patterns.

Modes of production: The method by which the majority of a society's members produce or develop the goods needed by the society.

Modified-extended family: Nuclear family that retains considerable autonomy but maintains emotional and economic ties to other related groups.

Mommy track: Career path that would allow more time for families.

Monogamy: Marriage with one husband and one wife. Gr. *mono* (one) and *gamy* (marriage).

Monotheism: Belief in only one god.

Moral entrepreneurs: People who risk moral capital to produce social change (Howard Becker).

Mourning: The socially constructed expectations regarding reactions to death.

Mutual script: Expectations developed from interaction between specific actors.

Myth: A sacred tale expressing the unobservable realities of religious belief in terms of observable phenomena.

Neolocal residence: A custom that newlyweds are expected to live separately from either's family.

Nisei: Second generation Japanese Americans, mostly born between 1910 and 1940.

Nomadic: Moving as a group from place to place in search of food, water, or grazing land.

Norms: Widespread expectations governing behavior. *Prescriptive norms* determine what *should* be done; *proscriptive norms* determine what *should not* be done.

Nuclear family: A two-generation group that includes parents and their children.

Objectivity: The assumption that truth resides in the object or phenomenon being studied. **Object:** something perceptible by one or more of the senses. **Objective:** based on observable phenomena.

Observational learning: Changes in behavior that result from watching others, without direct rewards or punishments to oneself.

Open marriage: Arrangement in which married partners allow each other to have extramarital sexual affairs and other freedoms not commonly associated with marriage.

Open mobility system: An ideal-typical system of social stratification in which there is total mobility; all status is by achievement.

Orderly replacement: Socialization in which each generation is an essential duplicate of the preceding generation.

Organismic analogy: The view that society is like an individual life form, with parts that work together to carry on the various processes of life.

Ovariectomy: Surgical removal of the ovaries.

Panel study: A type of longitudinal study in which the same people or other cases are observed at different points in time.

Parallel cousins: One's mother's sister's or father's brother's children.

Parallel scripts: A role relationship in which actors assume the same, identical, interchangeable roles.

Pater familias: The male head of household.

Patriarchy: A system in which men have the authority.

Patrician: member of the Roman aristocracy; the ruling class from which Senators came.

Patrilineal: Tracing descent and inheritance through male lines.

Patrilocal residence: A custom that newlyweds are expected to live with the groom's relatives.

Periodic abstinence: The practice of attempting to avoid conception by refraining from intercourse at certain times of the woman's menstrual cycle.

Personal script: Expectations learned by socialization and shaped by an individual's unique experiences.

Person-specific marital desirability: The desirability of a person as a mate based on another individual's particular preferences.

Play stage: To Mead, the second stage of observational development, up to about age 7 or 8, characterized by playing at being other persons.

Polyandry: A marriage involving one wife and more than one husband.

Polygamy: Any marriage with more than two partners. Gr *poly* (many) and *gamy* (marriage).

Polygyny: A marriage with one husband and more than one wife. Gr *poly* (many) and *gyny* (woman).

Polytheism: The belief in many gods.

Pool of eligibles: The group of individuals constituting realistic potential mates.

Population: A specified set of study units, such as all students attending a certain college.

Positivism: Doctrine emphasizing use of the senses, measurement, and science as a basis for knowledge.

Poverty threshold: An annual income amount that separates the poor from the non-poor.

Power: The actual ability to exercise one's will over others.

Power: The probability that one actor within a social relationship will be in a position to carry out his or her own will [despite resistance] (Weber).

Pragma (PRAG-mah): Love style emphasizing practical elements in relationships and rationality in partner selection.

Praxis: Combining social research and theory with the active attempt to improve society.

Preparatory stage: To Mead, the time during which the infant lacks the capacity for extensive language use.

Prescriptive mating system: A set of norms that specify whom a person should marry.

Prescriptive norms: Expectations about what *should* be done.

Presentism: Seeing and judging the past or future using today's definitions.

Prestige: Respect or favorable regard attached to a person because of his or her position in the social system.

Primary relationship: Continuing interaction by individuals in more than one role; characterized by personal, direct, and intimate interaction.

Primogeniture: The right of the eldest child, especially the eldest son, to inherit all property of the parents.

Principle of least interest: Idea that the partner who cares the least about the relationship has the most power.

Proletariat: The social class that, in Marxist theory, labors as the instrument of production for the bourgeoisie.

Pronatalism: A belief system that encourages childbearing.

Pronuptialism: A belief system that encourages marriage.

Propinquity: Nearness; the tendency to select mates from persons who live nearby.

Proscriptive norms: Expectations about what *should not* be done.

Protestants: Christians who are the theological descendants of Martin Luther, John Calvin, or Ulrich Zwingli. For practical purposes, a member of any Christian denomination that is not Catholic.

Punishment: A contingency that decreases the probability that a preceding behavior will recur.

Qualitative analysis: Nonnumerical examination and interpretation of observations (Babbie, 1995:G6).

Quantitative analysis: Numerical representation and manipulation of observations (Babbie, 1995:G6).

Race: A group defined by socially selected physical characteristics.

Random sample: Sample in which all units in the population have an equal chance of being selected.

Referent: The something else for which a symbol stands.

Refined divorce rate: Number of divorces per year per 1,000 married women age 15 and older.

Regular: Customary, usual, or normal.

Relationship maintenance behaviors: Actions taken by participants to preserve ongoing relationships.

Relinquishment: A giving up or surrender of something; to give up legal rights to a child.

Remarriage chains: Connections that link individuals across households through ties of disrupted and new unions (Cherlin, 1996).

Replication: A copy or reproduction; repetition of an experiment or procedure using the same process.

Resilient: Marked by an ability to recover quickly from misfortune.

Retirement: To withdraw from one's paid occupation.

Reward: A contingency that increases the probability that a preceding behavior will recur.

Rite of passage: A public ceremony in recognition of a change in status.

Role: Expectations associated with a particular position in the social system.

Role conflict: Incompatibility between two or more roles that an individual is expected to play.

Role consensus: Agreement between actors about how a role should be played.

Role model: A person who provides an image with which an observer identifies and may wish to emulate.

Romanticism: An artistic and intellectual movement originating in Europe in the late 18th century.

Safe sex: Use of condoms or other practices that significantly reduce the risk of spreading the AIDS-causing virus. Perhaps better thought of as safer sex.

Sandwich generation: An age group with care-taking responsibilities both to their aging parents and their own offspring.

Sansei: Third generation Japanese Americans, mostly born after World War II.

Satisfaction: Fulfillment of a desire, need, or appetite; contentment derived from having needs met.

Scene: Interpersonal interaction among more than one individual.

Script: Expectations governing the interaction of two or more roles.

Secondary relationship: Continuing interaction by individuals in only one role; characterized by impersonal interaction for a specific, practical purpose.

Secularization: The process by which religious control over social institutions and individual behavior declines.

Sedentary: Remaining in one place; not migratory.

Self: An individual's sense of identity.

Self-fulfilling prophecy: A prediction that comes true because of the effect of the prediction itself.

Sex ratio: A demographic calculation of the number of males per 100 females in a given population.

Sex: The biological fact of being female or male.

Sex-arbitrary gender roles: Expectations that could as easily be the opposite.

Sex-influenced gender roles: Expectation influenced, but not fully determined, by secondary sex characteristics and other biological differences of men and women.

Sex-irreducible gender roles: Basic differences in expectations that define the differences between men and women.

Sexualization: The process of learning one's individual sexual script; sexual socialization.

Shaman: A person who acts as a medium between the visible world and the invisible world of the spirits.

Shift work: Any work schedule in which more than half of an employee's hours are before 8 A.M. or after 4 P.M. (Bureau of Labor Statistics).

Social differentiation: The division and specialization of social and cultural units such as groups, organizations, and institutions.

Social exchange paradigm: Explanations of social behavior based on calculation of resources, costs, and benefits of alternative actions.

Social movement: A large number of persons who join together to bring about or resist some social or cultural change.

Social power: The probability of controlling or influencing the behavior of other persons, even against resistance.

Social reproduction: The process whereby a society reproduces its system of inequality from one generation to the next.

Social stratification: The hierarchical ranking of individuals on the basis of wealth, power, or prestige.

Societal script: Society-wide, macro-social expectations.

Sociobiology: A scientific approach that attempts to use biological and evolutionary principles to explain the behavior of all social animals, including human beings.

Socio-cultural evolution: The process of social and cultural change in response to the environment, made possible by the accumulation of technical knowledge.

Sociological imagination: A way of understanding ourselves through locating our positions in society, and the social forces that affect us (Popenoe, 1986:584).

Spermicide: An agent that kills sperm, especially as a contraceptive.

Spinster: A woman who remains unmarried beyond the typical marriage age.

Spontaneous consensus: Agreement arrived at without consideration by the parties involved, based on commonly held assumptions that are often derived from tradition.

Stable: Resistant to change, self-restoring, consistently dependable.

Stages of observation: To Mead, the developmental socialization process by which children learn from others.

Status: A position in the social system.

Statutory rape: Having sexual intercourse, even if consensual, with a person not considered old enough to give consent. In some states only female victims are considered; others are gender-neutral (Inciardi, 1993:82).

Stem family: A type of extended family comprised of parents plus one, and only one, child who might marry and have children.

Stepfamily: Family unit consisting of a married man and woman, plus children from a previous relationship. A *simple stepfamily* includes children of one parent; a *complex stepfamily* includes children from both adults. Also called a *blended family* or a *reconstituted family.*

Storge (STOR-gay): Affectionate, companionate style of loving.

Stressors: Events with the potential of causing major change in a family system.

Structural definition: Definition describing the components and make-up of a family.

Subjectivity: The assumption that truth resides in the subject, or person doing the observing.

Surrogate mother: Woman who is paid for the use of her uterus to produce a live birth.

Survey research: A way of finding things out by asking a sample of persons a set of questions.

Symbol: A thing that stands for something else.

Symbolic interactionism: Study of the interaction between persons that takes place through symbols, such as signs, gestures, and language.

System: A functionally related group of interacting parts that form a complex whole.

Technology: The body of knowledge available to a society that is of use in fashioning implements, practicing arts and skills, and extracting or collecting materials.

Teleology: The study of final causes; the belief that events are determined by some ultimate design or purpose.

Tender Years rule: The legal guideline that young children are better off living with their mothers.

Tender years rule: The norm that, in divorce, a mother should automatically get custody of minor children unless proven unfit.

Testable: Able to be tested (some meanings are just obvious).

Theory: A systematic explanation for the observations about related phenomena.

Totem: Symbolic representation that links individuals or groups with human ancestors, plants, animals, or other natural phenomena.

Traditionalizing influence of parenthood: The tendency of couples to develop more traditional, gender-specific, roles once they have a child.

Trailing spouse: Husband or wife of an income-producer who relocates for employment purposes.

Transfer payments: Redistribution of something of value from one person or group to another person or group, not based on work the receiver is currently performing.

Trickle down economics: The view that increased wealth in the hands of the rich will result in an improved economy that will help the poor.

Trickle up economics: The view that directly helping the poor will create a demand for goods and services that will improve the economy.

Tsu: The Chinese version of the *gens* or clan.

Tubal ligation: "Tying the tubes"; surgically cutting and tying the Fallopian tubes to prevent passage of an ovum from the ovary to the uterus.

Typology: A systematic classification of related phenomena based on defined characteristics or traits.

Universal faith: A belief that there is only one appropriate religion for all people everywhere.

Universal permanent availability: A social condition wherein any individual is always a potential mate for anyone else.

Unmarried couple household: Two adults, not related and of opposite sex, but no additional adults; and any children present are under 15 years old (U.S. Bureau of the Census).

Unobtrusive research: Gathering data without influencing the thing being studied.

Urbanization: An increase in the percentage of a population living in cities.

Utilitarian marriages: Marriages with a "why" other than intimate expression; a marriage of convenience for economic or other reasons.

Value free: Unaffected by preconceived ideas about what is good, right, and proper.

Values: Shared ideas about what is good, right, or proper.

Variable: A concept that has more than one attribute.

Vasectomy: A surgical procedure designed to make transmission of sperm through the *vas deferens* impossible.

Victorianism: A value system emphasizing a strong sense of duty and strict sexual morality; after Queen Victoria of England.

Widow: A woman whose husband has died.

Widower: A man whose wife has died (This term reflects the fact that, unlike terms applying to other topics, male family terms are typically derived from female terms).

Yin-yang principle: Taoist unity of opposites: female-male; dark-light; passive-active; moon-sun.

References

A

Abbey, Antonia, Frank M. Andrews, and L. Jill Halman. 1992. "Infertility and Subjective Well-Being: The Mediating Roles of Self-Esteem, Internal Control, and Interpersonal Conflict." *Journal of Marriage and the Family* 54:408–17.

Abbott, J., R. Johnson, and S. R. Lowenstein. 1995. "Domestic Violence Against Women: Incidence and Prevalence in an Emergency Department Population." *JAMA: The Journal of the American Medical Association* (June 14) 273:1763–66.

Abel, Emily K. 1991. *Who Cares for the Elderly: Public Policy and the Experiences of Adult Daughters.* Philadelphia: Temple University Press.

Abelove, Henry, Michele Aina Barale, and David M. Halperin, eds. 1993. *The Lesbian and Gay Studies Reader.* New York: Routledge.

Abercrombie, Nicholas, Stephen Hill, and Bryan S. Turner. 1984. *Dictionary of Sociology.* New York: Penguin.

Abernathy, Virginia. 1993. *Population Politics: The Choices that Shape Our Future.* New York: Plenum Press.

Acitelli, Linda K., and Toni C. Antonucci. 1994. "Gender Differences in the Link between Marital Support and Satisfaction in Older Couples." *Journal of Personality and Social Psychology* 67:688–98.

Acock, Alan, and David H. Demo. 1994. *Family Diversity and Well-Being.* Thousand Oaks, CA: Sage.

Ackerman, Diane. 1994. *A Natural History of Love.* New York: Random House.

Adams, Bert N. 1968. *Kinship in an Urban Setting.* Chicago: Markham.

————. 1995. *The Family: A Sociological Interpretation.* Fort Worth: Harcourt Brace.

Adams, Charles F., David Landsberger, and Daniel Hecht. 1994. "Organizational Impediments to Paternity Establishment and Child Support." *Social Science Review* 72:109–26.

Adams, William Forbes. 1932. *Ireland and Irish Emigration to the New World, from 1815 to the Famine.* New Haven: Yale University Press.

Adelman, Robert M., and Charles Jaret. 1999. "Poverty, Race and US Metropolitan Social and Economic Structure." *Journal of Urban Affairs* 21(1):35–56.

Adler, Nancy E., Henry P. David, and Brenda Major. 1990. "Psychological Responses After Abortion." *Science* 248:41–44.

Agnew, Robert, and Sandra Huguley. 1989. "Adolescent Violence Toward Parents." *Journal of Marriage and the Family* 47:51:699–711.

Ahlander, Nancy Rollins, and Kathleen Slaugh Bahr. 1995. "Beyond Drudgery, Power, and Equity: Toward an Expanded Discourse on the Moral Dimensions of Housework in Families." *Journal of Marriage and the Family* 57:54–68.

Ahlberg, Dennis A., and Carol J. De Vita. 1992. "New Realities of the American Family." *Population Bulletin* 46:1–44.

Ahrons, Constance. 1994. *The Good Divorce: Keeping Your Family Together When Your Marriage Comes Apart.* New York: HarperCollins.

Ahrons, Constance R., and Richard B. Miller. 1993. "The Effect of the Postdivorce Relationship on Paternal Involvement: A Longitudinal Analysis." *American Journal of Orthopsychiatry* 63:441–50.

Akerlof, George A. 1998. "Men Without Children." *The Economic Journal* 108:287–309.

Alba, Richard D. 1985. "The Twilight of Ethnicity Among Americans of European Ancestry: The Case of Italians." *Ethnic and Racial Studies* 8:134–58.

Aldous, Joan. 1996. *Family Careers: Rethinking the Developmental Perspective.* Thousand Oaks, CA: Sage.

————. 2000. "Book Review of *World Revolution and Family Patterns.*" *Journal of Marriage and the Family* 62:857–58.

Aldous, Joan, and Rodney F. Ganey. 1999. "Family Life and the Pursuit of Happiness: The Influence of Gender and Race." *Journal of Family Issues* 20:155–80.

Allen, Katherine R. 2000. "A Conscious and Inclusive Family Studies." *Journal of Marriage and the Family* 62:4–17.

Allen, Katherine R., Rosemary Blieszner, and Karen A. Roberto. 2000. "Families in the Middle and Later Years: A Review and Critique of Research in the 1990s." *Journal of Marriage and the Family* 62:911–26.

Allen, Mike, and Nancy A. Burrell. 1996. "Comparing the Impact of Homosexual and Heterosexual Parents on Children: Meta-Analysis of Existing Research." *Journal of Homosexuality* 32(2):19–35.

Allen, William D., and M. Connor. 1997. "An African American Perspective on Generative Fathering." Pp. 52–70 in *Handbook of Family Diversity,* edited by A. J. Hawkins and D. C. Dollahite. Newbury Park, CA: Sage.

Allen, William D., and William J. Doherty. 1996. "The Responsibilities of Fatherhood as Perceived by African American Teenage Fathers." *Families in Society: The Journal of Contemporary Human Services* 77:142–55.

Allen, Walter R. 1970. "Class, Culture and Family Organization: The Effects of Class and Race on Family Structure in Urban America." *Journal of Comparative Family Studies* 10:301–13.

Alvarez, Robert. 1987. *Families: Migration and Adaptation in Baja and Alta, California from 1800 to 1975.* Berkeley: University of California Press.

Alwin, Duane F. 1986. "Religion and Parental Child Rearing Orientations: Evidence of a Catholic-Protestant Convergence." *American Journal of Sociology* 92:412–40.

Amaro, Hortensia. 1995. "Love, Sex, and Power: Considering Women's Realities in HIV Prevention." *American Psychologist* 50:437–47.

Amato, Paul R. 1987. "Family Processes in One-Parent, Stepparent, and Intact Families: The Child's Point of View." *Journal of Marriage and the Family* 49:327–37.

_____. 1994. "Father-Child Relations, Mother-Child Relations, and Offspring Psychological Well-Being in Early Adulthood." *Journal of Marriage and the Family* 56:1031–42.

_____. 1999. "The Postdivorce Society: How Divorce Is Shaping the Family and Other Forms of Social Organization." In *The Postdivorce Family: Children, Parenting, and Society,* edited by Ross A. Thompson and Paul Amato. Thousand Oaks, CA: Sage.

_____. 2000. "The Consequences of Divorce for Adults and Children." *Journal of Marriage and the Family* 62:1269–87.

_____. 2001. "What Children Learn From Divorce." *Population Today* 29(1):1,4.

Amato, Paul R., and Alan Booth. 1991. "The Consequences of Divorce for Attitudes Toward Divorce and Gender Roles." *Journal of Family Issues* 12:306–22.

_____. 1995. "Changes in Gender Role Attitudes and Perceived Marital Quality." *American Sociological Review* 60:58–66.

_____. 1996. "A Prospective Study of Divorce and Parent-Child Relationships." *Journal of Marriage and the Family* 58:356–65.

_____. 1997. *A Generation at Risk.* Cambridge, MA: Harvard University Press.

Amato, Paul A., and Joan G. Gilbreth. 1999. "Nonresident Fathers and Children's Well-Being: A Meta-Analysis." *Journal of Marriage and the Family* 61:557–73.

Amato, Paul R., and Bruce Keith. 1991. "Parental Divorce and Adult Well-Being: A Meta-Analysis." *Journal of Marriage and the Family* 53:43–58.

Amato, Paul R., and Fernando Rivera. 1999. "Paternal Involvement and Children's Behavior Problems." *Journal of Marriage and the Family* 61:375–84.

Amato, Paul R., and Stacey Jo Rogers. 1997. "Do Attitudes Toward Divorce Affect Marital Quality?" Paper presented at the meeting of the American Sociological Association, Toronto.

American Association for Protecting Children. 1989. *Highlights of Official Child Neglect and Abuse Reporting, 1987.* Denver, CO: American Humane Association.

American Psychiatric Association. 1987. *Diagnostic and Statistical Manual of Mental Disorders,* 3rd ed., rev. Washington, DC: American Psychiatric Association.

Anderson, Elaine A., and Richard C. Hula, eds. 1991. *The Reconstruction of Family Policy.* New York: Greenwood Press.

Anderson, Karen. 1991. "African American Families." Pp. 259–90 in *American Families: A Research Guide and Historical Handbook,* edited by Joseph M. Hawes and Elizabeth I. Nybakken. Westport, CT: Greenwood Press.

Angell, Robert C. 1936. *The Family Encounters the Depression.* New York: Scribner.

Aquilino, William S. 1994. "Later-Life Parental Divorce and Widowhood: Impact on Young Adults' Assessment of Parent-Child Relations." *Journal of Marriage and the Family* 56:908–22.

Archdeacon, Thomas. 1983. *Becoming American: An Ethnic History.* New York: Free Press.

Archer, John. 1999. "Assessment of the Reliability of the Conflicts Tactics Scale: A Meta-Analytic Review." *Journal of Interpersonal Violence* 14(12):1263–89.

_____. 2000. "Sex Differences in Aggression between Heterosexual Partners: A Meta-Analytic Review." *Psychological Bulletin* 126(5):551–80.

Ard, Ben Neal. 1990. *The Sexual Realm in Long-Term Marriages: A Longitudinal Study Following Marital Partners over Twenty Years.* San Francisco: Mellen Research University Press.

Arditti, Joyce. 1992. "Differences Between Fathers with Joint Custody and Noncustodial Fathers." *American Journal of Orthopsychiatry* 62:186–95.

Arendell, Terry. 1986. *Mothers and Divorce: Legal, Economic, and Social Dilemmas.* Berkeley: University of California Press.

_____. 2000. "Conceiving and Investigating Motherhood: The Decade's Scholarship." *Journal of Marriage and the Family* 62:1192–1207.

Aries, Philippe. 1962. *Centuries of Childhood: A Social History of Family Life*. Translated by Robert Baldiek. New York: Vintage Books.

Aron, A., D. G. Dutton, E. N. Aron, and A. Iverson. 1989. "Experiences of Falling in Love." *Journal of Social and Personal Relationships* 6:243–57.

Aronfreed, J., and A. Reber. 1965. "Internalized Behavior Suppression and the Timing of Social Punishment." *Journal of Personality and Social Psychology* 1:3–16.

Associated Press. 1996. "Mormon Leader Calls for Stay-at-Home Mothers." *The Daily Sentinel*, October 7, P. 3A. Grand Junction, CO.

_____. 2000. "State Supreme Court Upholds Listing Lesbian Couples on Birth Certificates." *The Daily Sentinel*, September 9, P. 3A. Grand Junction, CO.

Atchley, Robert C. 1992. "Retirement and Marital Satisfaction." Pp. 145–58 in *Families and Retirement*, edited by Maximilian E. Szinovacz, David J. Ekerdt, and Barbara H. Vinick. Newbury Park, CA: Sage.

Atchley, Robert C., and Sheila J. Miller. 1983. "Types of Elderly Couples." Pp. 77–90 in *Family Relationships in Later Life*, edited by Timothy H. Brubaker. Beverly Hills, CA: Sage.

Athanasiou, R., and R. Sarkin. 1974. "Premarital Sexual Behavior and Postmarital Adjustment." *Archives of Sexual Behavior* 3:207–25.

Atwater, Lynn. 1982. *The Extramarital Connection*. New York: Irvington.

Augustine. [c. 425] 1934. *The City of God, Book XIV*. Translated by J. Healey. New York: E. P. Dutton.

Auletta, Ken. 1982. *The Underclass*. New York: Random House.

Aulette, Judy Root. 1994. *Changing Families*. Belmont, CA: Wadsworth Publishing.

Aylette, Jennes. 1990. *Families: A Celebration of Diversity, Commitment, and Love*. Boston: Houghton Mifflin.

Ayoub, Catherine C., Robin M. Deutsch, and Andronicki Maraganore. 1999. "Emotional Distress in Children of High-Conflict Divorce: The Impact of Marital Conflict and Violence." *Family and Concilliation Courts Review* 37(3):297–314.

B

Babbie, Earl. 2001. *The Practice of Social Research*, 9th ed. Belmont, CA: Wadsworth.

Bachrach, Christine, Michelle J. Hindin, and Elizabeth Thomson. 2000. "The Changing Shape of Ties That Bind: An Overview and Synthesis." Pp. 3–16 in *The Ties That Bind: Perspectives on Marriage and Cohabitation*, edited by Linda J. Waite. New York: Aldine de Gruyter.

Bachrach, Christine A., Kathryn A. London, and Penelope L. Maza. 1991. "On the Path to Adoption: Adoption Seeking in the United States, 1988." *Journal of Marriage and the Family* 53:705–18.

Bachrach, Christine A., Kathy Shepherd Stolley, and Kathryn A. London. 1992. "Relinquishment of Premarital Births: Evidence from National Survey Data." *Family Planning Perspectives* 24:27–32.

Bahr, Howard M., and Bruce A. Chadwick. 1985. "Religion and Family in Middletown, USA." *Journal of Marriage and the Family* 47:407–14.

Bahr, Stephen J. 1979. "Family Determinants and Effects of Deviance." In *Contemporary Theories About the Family*, edited by Wesley Burr, Ruben Hill, F. Ivan Nye, and Ira Reiss. New York: Free Press.

_____. 1989. *Family Interaction*. New York: McGraw-Hill.

Bahr, Stephen J., Bradford Chappell, and Geoffrey K. Leigh. 1983. "Age at Marriage, Role Enactment, Role Consensus, and Marital Satisfaction." *Journal of Marriage and the Family* 45:795–803.

Bailey, B. L. 1988. *From Front Porch to Backseat: Courtship in Twentieth Century America*. Baltimore: The Johns Hopkins University Press.

Bailey, Michael. 1994. "Book review of *The Limits of Family Influence*." *The Quarterly Review of Biology* 70:256–7.

Baily, William C., Clyde Hendrick, and Susan S. Hendrick. 1987. "Relation of Sex and Gender Role to Love Sexual Attitudes, and Self-Esteem." *Sex Roles* 16:637–48.

Baize, Harold R., Jr., and Jonathan E. Schroeder. 1995. "Personality and Mate Selection in Personal Ads: Evolutionary Preferences in a Public Mate Selection Process." *Journal of Social Behavior and Personality* 10:3:517–36.

Baker, Angela K., Kimberly J. Barthelemy, and Lawrence A. Kurdek. 1993. "The Relation Between Fifth and Sixth Graders' Peer-Related Classroom Social Status and Their Perceptions of Family and Neighborhood Factors." *Journal of Applied Developmental Psychology* 14:547–56.

Baker, Robin L. 1995a. "Sociological Reflections: The Organization of Work and the Changing American Family." Paper presented at the meeting of the Western Social Science Association, April, Oakland, CA.

_____. 1995b. *Economic, Time, and Household-Task Satisfaction in Marriage: The Effects of Gender, Gender Ideology, and Type-of-Earner Marriage*. Unpublished Master's Thesis. Logan, UT: Utah State University.

Bakker, B. F. M. 1993. "A New Measure of Social Status for Men and Women: The Social Distance Scale." *Netherlands Journal of Social Sciences* 29:113–29.

Balswick, Jack O., and Judith K. Balswick. 1995. "Gender Relations and Family Power." Pp. 297–315 in *Families in Multicultural Perspective*, edited by Bron B. Ingoldsby and Suzanne Smith. New York: The Guilford Press.

Bandura, Albert, and Forest J. Jourden. 1991. "Self-Regulatory Mechanisms Governing the Impact of Social Comparison on Couples Decision Making." *Journal of Personality and Social Psychology* 60:941–51.

Bandura, Albert. 1965. "Influence of Models' Reinforcement Contingencies on the Acquisition of Imitative Responses." *Journal of Personality and Social Psychology* 1:589–95.

————. 1969. "Social-Learning Theory of Identificatory Processes." In *Handbook of Socialization Theory and Research*, edited by D. A. Goslin. Chicago: Rand-McNally.

————. 1971. *Psychological Modeling: Conflicting Theories.* Chicago: Aldine-Atherton.

————. 1986. *Social Foundations of Thought and Action.* Englewood Cliffs, NJ: Prentice-Hall.

Bane, Mary Jo. 1976. *Here to Stay: American Families in the Twentieth Century.* New York: Basic Books.

Bane, Mary Jo, and David T. Ellwood. 1994. *Welfare Realities: From Rhetoric to Reform.* Cambridge, MA: Harvard University Press.

Barber, Nigel. 1999. "Women's Dress Fashions as a Function of Reproductive Strategy." *Sex Roles* 40:5–6, 459–71.

Barber, Jennifer S., William G. Axinn, and Arland Thornton. 1999. "Unwanted Childbearing, Health, and Mother-Child Relationships." *Journal of Health and Social Behavior* 40(3):231–57.

Barich, Rachel Roseman, and Denise D. Bielby. 1996. "Rethinking Marriage: Change and Stability in Expectations, 1967–1994." *Journal of Family Issues* 17:139–69.

Barnett, Ola W., Cindy L. Miller-Perrin, and Robin D. Perrin. 1997. *Family Violence Across the Lifespan: An Introduction.* Thousand Oaks, CA: Sage.

Barnett, Rosalind C., and Yu-Chu Shen. 1997. "Gender, High- and Low-Schedule-Control Housework Tasks, and Psychological Distress: A Study of Dual-Earner Couples." *Journal of Family Issues* 18(4):403–28.

Barranti, Chrystal C., and R. Ramirez. 1985. "The Grandparent-Grandchild Relationship: Family Resources in an Era of Voluntary Bonds." *Family Relations* 34:343–52.

Barret, Robert L., and Bryan E. Robinson. 1994. "Gay Dads." Pp. 157–70 in *Redefining Families: Implications for Children's Development*, edited by Adele Eskeles and Allen W. Gottfried. New York: Plenum.

Barry, Herbert III, Irving L. Child, and Margaret K. Bacon. 1959. "Reliance of Child Training to Subsistence Economy." *American Anthropologist* 61:51–63.

Bart, Pauline B., and Eileen Geil Moran, eds. 1993. *Violence Against Women: The Bloody Footprints.* Newbury Park, Thousand Oaks, CA: Sage.

Bart, Pauline. 1971. "Depression in Middle-Aged Women." Pp. 163–86 in *Women in Sexist Society*, edited by Vivian Gornick and Barbara K. Moran. New York: Basic.

Barth, Richard P. 1991. "Adoption of Drug-Exposed Children." *Children and Youth Services Review* 13:323–42.

Bartholet, Elizabeth. 1993. *Family Bonds: Adoption and the Politics of Parenting.* Boston: Houghton Mifflin.

Basow, Susan A. 1992. *Gender Stereotypes and Roles*, 3rd ed. Pacific Grove, CA: Brooks/Cole.

Bassis, Michael S., Richard J. Gelles, and Ann Levine. 1991. *Sociology: An Introduction.* New York: McGraw-Hill.

Bates, J. Douglas. 1993. *Gift Children: A Story of Race Family and Adoption in a Divided America.* New York: Ticknor & Fields.

Baumrind, Diana. 1967. "Child Care Practices Anteceding Three Patterns of Preschool Behavior." *Genetic Psychology Monographs* 75:43–83.

————. 1968. "Authoritarian Versus Authoritative Parental Control." *Adolescence* 3:255–72.

————. 1971. "Current Patterns of Parental Authority." *Developmental Psychology Monographs* 4:1–102.

————. 1972. "Socialization and Instrumental Competence in Young Children." Pp. 202–24 in *The Young Child: Reviews of Research, Vol. 2,* edited by Willard W. Hartup. Washington, DC: National Association for the Education of Young Children.

————. 1980. "New Directions in Socialization Research." *American Psychologist* 35:639–52.

————. 1989. "Rearing Competent Children." Pp. 349–78 in *Child Development Today and Tomorrow,* edited by William Damon. San Francisco: Jossey-Bass.

Baxter, Janeen. 1991. "The Class Location of Women: Direct or Derived." Pp. 202–22 in *Class Analysis and Contemporary Australia*, edited by J. Baxter, M. Emmison, J. Western, and M. Western. Melbourne, Australia: Macmillan.

————. 1994. "Is Husband's Class Enough? Class Location and Class Identity in the United States, Sweden, Norway, and Australia." *American Sociological Review* 59:220–35.

Baxter, L. A., and W. W. Wilmot. 1985. "Taboo Topics in Close Relationships." *Journal of Social and Personal Relationships* 2:253–69.

Beardsley, Richard K., John W. Hall, and Robert E. Ward. 1939. *Village Japan*. Chicago: University of Chicago Press.

Becker, Gary S. 1991. *A Treatise on the Family*. Cambridge: Harvard University Press.

Becker, Penny Edgell, and Phyllis Moen. 1999. "Scaling Back: Dual-Earner Couples' Work-Family Strategies." *Journal of Marriage and the Family* 61:995–1007.

Beeghley, Leonard. 2000. *The Structure of Social Stratification in the United States*. Boston: Allyn and Bacon.

Beeghley, Leonard, and Jeffrey W. Dwyer. 1989. "Social Structure and the Divorce Rate." *Perspectives on Social Problems* 1:147–70.

Beer, William R. 1992. *American Stepfamilies*. New Brunswick, NJ: Transaction.

Belkin, Lisa. 1986. "The Mail Order Marriage Business." *New York Times Magazine* 28ff.

Bell, Allen P., and Martin S. Weinberg. 1978. *Homosexualities: A Study of Diversity among Men and Women*. New York: Simon and Schuster.

Bell, Daniel. 1973. *The Coming of Post-Industrial Society*. New York: Basic Books.

———. 1979. "The Social Framework of the Information Society." Pp. 163–211 in *The Computer Age: A Twenty Year View*, edited by M. Dertouzos and J. Moses. Cambridge, MA: MIT Press.

Bell, Robert R., and Kathleen Coughey. 1980. "Premarital Sexual Experiences among College Females." *Family Relations* 29:353–57.

Bellah, Robert N., Richard Madsen, William M. Sullivan, Ann Swindler, and Steven M. Tipton. 1985. *Habits of the Heart: Individualism and Commitment in American Life*. Berkeley and Los Angeles: University of California Press.

Belsky, Jay, Richard M. Lerner, and Graham B. Spanier. 1984. *The Child in the Family*. Reading, MA: Addison-Wesley.

Belsky, Jay, Graham B. Spanier, and M. Rovine. 1983. "Stability and Change in Marriage Across the Transition to Parenthood." *Journal of Marriage and the Family* 45:567–77.

Bem, Sandra L. 1974. "The Measurement of Psychological Androgyny." *Journal of Consulting and Clinical Psychology* 42:155–62.

Bender, Amy, and Carol Ewashen. 2000. "Group Work Is Political Work." *Issues in Mental Health Nursing* 21(3):297–308.

Benenson, Harold. 1984. "Women's Occupational and Family Achievement in the U.S. Class System: A Critique of the Dual-Career Family Analysis." *The British Journal of Sociology* 35:19–41.

Benet, William Rose, ed. 1987. *Benet's Reader's Encyclopedia*, 3rd ed. New York: Harper & Row.

Bengtson, Vern L., and Robert E. L. Roberts. 1991. "Intergenerational Solidarity in Aging Families: An Example of Formal Theory Construction." *Journal of Marriage and the Family* 53:856–70.

Bennet, Neal G., Ann Klimas Blanc, and David E. Bloom. 1988. "Commitment and the Modern Union: Assessing the Link Between Premarital Cohabitation and Subsequent Marital Stability." *American Sociological Review* 1988:127–38.

Benokraitis, Nijole B. 1993. *Marriages and Families: Changes, Choices, and Constraints*. Englewood Cliffs, NJ: Prentice-Hall.

Berger, Peter, and Brigitte Berger. 1984. *The War Over the Family: Capturing the Middle Ground*. Garden City, NY: Anchor.

Berger, Peter L., and Hansfried Kellner. 1964. "Marriage and the Construction of Reality." *Diogenes* 45:1–25.

Berger, G., M. Goldstein, and M. Fuerst. 1989. *The Couple's Guide to Fertility*. New York: Doubleday.

Bergstrom-Walan, Maj-Briht, and Helle H. Nielsen. 1990. "Sexual Expression Among 60–80-Year-Old Men and Women: A Sample from Stockholm, Sweden." *The Journal of Sex Research* 27:289–95.

Berk, Sarah. 1985. *The Gender Factory: The Apportionment of Work in American Households*. New York: Plenum Press.

Berk, Richard A. 1993. "What the Scientific Evidence Shows: On the Average, We Can Do No Better than Arrest." Pp. 323–36 in *Current Controversies on Family Violence*, edited by Richard J. Gelles and Donileen R. Loseke. Newbury Park, CA: Sage.

Berman, E., and D. R. Miller. 1967. "The Matching of Mates." In *Cognition, Personality and Clinical Psychology*, edited by R. Jesser and S. Fenschback. San Francisco: Jossey-Bass.

Bernard, Jessie. 1972. *The Future of Marriage*. New York: Bantam.

Berner, R. Thomas. 1992. *Parents Whose Parents Were Divorced*. New York: Haworth Press.

Bernstein, Basil. 1971–75. *Class, Codes, and Control*. 3 vols. London: Routledge and Kegan Paul.

Berry, Mary Frances. 1993. *The Politics of Parenthood: Child Care, Women's Rights, and the Myth of the Good Mother*. New York: Penguin.

Berscheid, Ellen, and Elaine Walster. 1974. "Physical Attractiveness." Pp. 158–216 in *Advances in Experimental Social Psychology, Vol. 7*, edited by L. Berkowitz. New York: Academic Press.

Besharov, Douglas J. 1993. "Overreporting and Underreporting Are Twin Problems." Pp. 257–72 in *Current Controversies on Family Violence*, edited by Richard J. Gelles and Donileen R. Loseke. Newbury Park, CA: Sage.

Bianchi, Suzanne M., and Lynne M. Casper. 2000. "American Families." *Population Bulletin* 55(4): 17. Washington, DC: Population Reference Bureau.

Bianchi, Suzanne M., Lekha Subaiya, and Joan R. Kahn. 1999. "The Gender Gap in the Economic Well-Being of Nonresident Fathers and Custodial Mothers." *Demography* 36:195–203.

Biddle, Ellen Horgan. 1981. "The American Catholic Irish Family." Pp. 86–114 in *Ethnic Families in America: Patterns and Variations*, 2nd ed., edited by Charles H. Mindel and Robert W. Habenstein. New York: Elsevier.

Biernat, Monica, and Camille B. Wortman. 1991. "Sharing of Home Responsibilities Between Professionally Employed Women and Their Husbands." *Journal of Personality and Social Psychology* 60:844–60.

Billingham, Robert E., Rachel Bland, and Amity Leary. 1999. "Dating Violence at Three Time Periods: 1976, 1992, and 1996." *Psychological Reports* 85(2):574–78.

Billingsley, Andrew. 1968. *Black Families in White America*. Englewood Cliffs, NJ: Prentice-Hall.

———. 1992. *Climbing Jacob's Ladder: The Enduring Legacy of African-American Families*. New York: Simon and Schuster.

Billy, John O., Karin L. Brewster, and William R. Grady. 1994. "Contextual Effects on the Sexual Behavior of Adolescent Women." *Journal of Marriage and the Family* 56:387–404.

Billy, John, Nancy Landale, and Steven McLaughlin. 1986. "The Effects of Marital Status at First Birth on Marital Dissolution Among Adolescent Mothers." *Demography* 23:329–49.

Billy, John O., Koray Tanfer, William R. Grady, and Daniel H. Klepinger. 1993. "The Sexual Behavior of Men in the United States." *Family Planning Perspectives* 25:52–60.

Binder, Arnold, and James W. Meeker, 1988. "Experiments as Reforms." *Journal of Criminal Justice* 16:347–58.

Binstock, Robert H., and Linda K. George, eds. 1990. *Handbook on Aging and the Social Sciences*, 3rd ed. New York: Academic Press.

Blackstone, Sir William. 1836. *Commentaries on the Laws of England*. New York: W. E. Dean.

Blackwood, Evelyn. 1993. "Breaking the Mirror: The Construction of Lesbianism and the Anthropological Discourse on Homosexuality." Pp. 328–40 in *Culture and Human Sexuality: A Reader*, edited by David N. Suggs and Andrew W. Miracle. Pacific Grove, CA: Brooks/Cole.

———. 1989. *Family Size and Achievement*. Berkeley: University of California Press.

———. 1991. "Number of Siblings and Personality." *Family Planning Perspectives* 23:272–74.

Blake, Nelson M. 1962. *The Road to Reno: A History of Divorce in the United States*. New York: Macmillan.

Blanchard, Dallas A. 1994. *The Anti-Abortion Movement and the Rise of the Religious Right: From Polite to Fiery Protest*. New York: Twayne.

Blankenhorn, David. 1995. *Fatherless America: Confronting Our Most Urgent Social Problems*. New York: Basic Books.

Blau, David. 2000. "The Production of Quality in Child-Care Centers: Another Look." *Applied Developmental Science* 4(3):136–48.

Blau, Francine, Marianne Ferber, and Ann E. Winkler. 1998. *The Economics of Women, Men, and Work*, 3rd ed. Upper Saddle River, NJ: Prentice-Hall.

Blau, Peter M. 1964. *Exchange and Power in Social Life*. New York: Wiley.

Blood, Robert O., Jr. 1967. *Love Match and Arranged Marriage*. New York: Free Press.

Blood, Robert O., Jr., and Donald M. Wolfe. 1960. *Husbands and Wives: The Dynamics of Married Living*. New York: Free Press.

Blumberg, Rae Lesser. 1984. "A General Theory of Gender Stratification." Pp. 23–101 in *Sociological Theory*, edited by Randall Collins. San Francisco: Jossey-Bass.

Blumer, Herbert. 1969. *Symbolic Interactionism: Perspective and Method*. Englewood Cliffs, NJ: Prentice-Hall.

Blumstein, Philip, and Pepper Schwartz. 1983. *American Couples: Money, Work, Sex*. New York: William Morrow.

———. 1990. "Intimate Relationships and the Creation of Sexuality." Pp. 96–109 in *Homosexuality/Heterosexuality: Concepts of Sexual Orientation*, edited by D. McWhirter, S. Sanders, and J. Reinisch. New York: Oxford University Press.

Bodnar, John. 1985. *The Transplanted: A History of Immigrants in Urban America*. Bloomington: Indiana University Press.

Bodovitz, Kathy, and Brad Edmondson. 1991. "Asian America." *American Demographics Desk Reference* (July)16–18.

Bogenschneider, Karen. 1995. "Roles for Professionals in Building Family Policy: A Case Study of State Family Impact Seminars" *Family Relations* 44:5–12.

Bogren, Lennart Y. 1991. "Changes in Sexuality to Women and Men During Pregnancy." *Archives of Sexual Behavior* 20:35–45.

Bohannan, Paul. 1970. "The Six Stations of Divorce." Pp. 29–55 in *Divorce and After*, edited by Paul Bohannan. New York: Doubleday.

Bohme, Gernot. 1984. "Midwifery as Science: An Essay on the Relations between Scientific and Everyday Knowledge." In *Society and Knowledge: Contemporary Perspectives in the Sociology of Knowledge*, edited by N. Stehr and V. Meja. New Brunswick, NJ: Transaction Books.

Boland, Joseph P., and Diana R. Follingstad. 1987. "The Relationship Between Communication and Marital Satisfaction: A Review." *Journal of Sex and Marital Therapy* 13:286–313.

Bongaarts, John. 1992. "Infertility After Age 30: A False Alarm." *Family Planning Perspectives* 14:75.

Booth, Alan, ed. 1991. *Contemporary Families: Looking Forward, Looking Back.* Minneapolis, MN: National Council on Family Relations.

_____. 1999. "Causes and Consequences of Divorce." Pp. 29–48 in *The Postdivorce Family: Children, Parenting, and Society,* edited by Ross A. Thompson and Paul R. Amato. Thousand Oaks, CA: Sage Publications.

Booth, Alan, and Paul R. Amato. 1994. "Parental Gender Role Nontraditionalism and Offspring Outcomes." *Journal of Marriage and the Family* 56:865–77.

_____. 1991. "Divorce and Psychological Stress." *Journal of Health and Social Behavior* 32:396–407.

_____. 2001. "Parental Predivorce Relations and Offspring Postdivorce Well-Being." *Journal of Marriage and the Family* 63:197–212.

Booth, Alan, Karen Carver, and Douglas A. Granger. "Biosocial Perspectives on the Family." *Journal of Marriage and the Family* 62:1018–34.

Booth, Alan, and John Edwards. 1985. "Age at Marriage and Marital Instability." *Journal of Marriage and the Family* 47:67–75.

_____. 1992. "Starting Over: Why Remarriages Are More Unstable." *Journal of Family Issues* 13:179–94.

Booth, Alan, and David Johnson. 1988. "Premarital Cohabitation and Marital Success." *Journal of Family Issues* 9:255–72.

Bootzin, Richard R., Gordon H. Bower, Jennifer Crocker, and Elizabeth Hall. 1991. *Psychology Today: An Introduction*, 7th ed. New York: McGraw-Hill.

Boss, Pauline G. 1987. "Family Stress." Pp. 695–723 in *Handbook of Marriage and the Family*, edited by Marvin B. Sussman and Suzanne K. Steinmetz. New York: Plenum.

_____. 1988. *Family Stress Management*. Newbury Park, CA: Sage.

Bossard, James H. S. 1932. "Residential Propinquity as a Factor in Mate Selection." *American Journal of Sociology* 38:219–24.

Bossard, James H. S., and Eleanore S. Boll. 1955. "Marital Unhappiness in the Life Cycle of Marriage." *Marriage and Family Living* 17:10–14.

Boulding, Kenneth. 1978. "Sociobiology or Biosociology?" Pp. 260–76 in *Sociobiology and Human Nature*, edited by Michael S. Gregory, Anita Silvers, and Diane Sutch. San Francisco: Jossey-Bass.

Bound, John, Greg Cuncan, Deborah Laren, and Lewis Oleinick. 1991. "Poverty Dynamics in Widowhood." *Journal of Gerontology* 46: S115–24.

Bourdieu, Pierre. 1977. "Cultural Reproduction and Social Reproduction." In *Power and Ideology in Education,* edited by Jerome Karabel and A. H. Halsey. New York: Oxford University Press.

_____. 1990. *The Logic of Practice..* Cambridge: Polity Press.

Bowen, Gary L., and Joe F. Pittman, eds. 1995. *The Work and Family Interface: Toward a Contextual Effects Perspective.* Minneapolis: National Council on Family Relations.

Bowlby, John. [1953] 1965. "Maternal Care and Mental Health." In *Child Care and the Growth of Love*, edited by John Bowlby. London: Penguin.

Bowles, Samuel, and Herbert Gintis. 1976. *Schooling in Capitalist America.* New York: Basic Books.

Bozett, Frederick W., and Marvin B. Sussman, eds. 1990. *Homosexuality and Family Relations.* New York: Harrington Park Press.

Bradbury, Thomas N., Frank D. Fincham, and Steven R. H. Beach. 2000. "Research on the Nature and Determinants of Marital Satisfaction: A Decade in Review." *Journal of Marriage and the Family* 62:964–80.

Bradley, Keith R. 1991. *Discovering the Roman Family: Studies in Roman Social History.* New York: Oxford University Press.

Bradley, Robert. 1994. "Book Review of *The Limits of Family Influence.*" *Journal of Marriage and the Family* 56:779–80.

Bray, James H. 1988. "Children's Development during Early Remarriage." Pp. 279–98 in *Impact of Divorce, Single Parenting and Stepparenting on Children*, edited by E. Mavis Hetherington and Josephine D. Arasteh. Hillsdale, NJ: Erlbaum.

_____. 1998. *Stepfamilies: Who Benefits? Who Does Not?* New York: Broadway.

_____. 1999. *Stepfamilies : Love, Marriage, and Parenting in the First Decade.* New York: Broadway.

Brayfield, April. 1995. "Juggling Jobs and Kids: The Impact of Employment Schedules on Fathers' Caring for Children." *Journal of Marriage and the Family* 57:321–32.

Brehm, Sharon S. 1992. *Intimate Relationships,* 2nd ed. New York: McGraw-Hill.

Brewaeys, A., and E. V. Van Hall. 1997. "Lesbian Motherhood: The Impact on Child Development and Family Functioning." *Journal of Psychosomatic Obstetrics and Gynecology* 18:1–16.

Brick, Peggy. 1989. "Toward a Positive Approach to Adolescent Sexuality." *SIECUS Report* 17:1–3.

Bridges, Judith S., and Ann Marie Orza. 1993. "Effects of Maternal Employment-Childrearing Pattern on College Students' Perceptions of a Mother and Her Child." *Psychology of Women Quarterly* 17:103–17.

Brightman, Joan. 1994. "Why Hillary Chooses Rodham Clinton: Women's Choices for Married Names." *American Demographics* 16:9–10.

Brinig, Margaret F. 1998. "Economics, Law, and Covenant Marriage." *Gender Issues* 16(1–2):4–33.

Brinkerhoff, Merlin B., and Eugen Lupri. 1983. "Conjugal Power and Family Relationships: Some Theoretical and Methodological Issues." In *The Canadian Family*, edited by K. Ishwaran. Toronto: Gage.

_____. 1992. "Power and Authority in the Family." Pp. 213–36 in *Family and Marriage: Cross-Cultural Perspectives*, edited by K. Ishwaran. Toronto: Thomson Educational Publishing.

Bringle, Robert G., and Bram T. Buunk. 1991. "Extradyadic Relationships and Sexual Jealousy." Pp. 135–52 in *Sexuality in Close Relationships*, edited by Kathleen McKinney and Susan Sprecher. Hillsdale NJ: Lawrence Erlbaum Associates.

Broke, Christopher N. L. 1991. *The Medieval Idea of Marriage*. New York: Oxford University Press.

Bromwich, P., and T. Parsons. 1990. *Contraception: The Facts*. Oxford: Oxford University Press.

Bronfenbrenner, Urie. 1977. "Nobody Home: The Erosion of the American Family." *Psychology Today* 10:41–47.

Bronstein, Phyllis, JoAnn Clauson, Miriam Frankel Stoll, and Craig L. Abrams. 1993. "Parenting Behavior and Children's Social, Psychological, and Academic Adjustment in Diverse Family Structures." *Family Relations* 42:268–76.

Bronstein, Phyllis, Miriam Frankel Stoll, and JoAnn Clauson. 1994. "Fathering after Separation or Divorce: Factors Predicting Children's Adjustment." *Family Relations* 43:469–79.

Brookoff, Daniel, Kimberly O'Brien, Charles S. Cook, Terry D. Thompson, and Charles Williams. 1997. "Characteristics of Participants in Domestic Violence." *JAMA: Journal of the American Medical Association* 277(17):1369–73.

Brooks, Nancy Rivera. 1994. "Study Says Asian Affluence a Myth." *Denver Post*, May 19, P. 2A.

Brown, Susan L., and Alan Booth. 1996. "Cohabitation Versus Marriage: A Comparison of Relationship Quality." *Journal of Marriage and the Family* 58:668–78.

Brubaker, Timothy H. 1985. *Later Life Families*. Beverly Hills, CA: Sage.

_____. 1990. *Family Relationships in Later Life*, 2nd ed. Newbury Park, CA: Sage.

_____, ed. 1990. *Family Relations: Challenges for the Future*. Newbury Park, CA: Sage.

Bryant, A. S., and Demian. 1994. "Relationship Characteristics of American Gay and Lesbian Couples: Findings From a National Survey." *Journal of Gay and Lesbian Social Services* 1:101–17.

Bryant, Chalandra, and Rand D. Conger. 1999. "Marital Success and Domains of Social Support in Long-Term Relationships: Does the Influence of Network Members Ever End?" *Journal of Marriage and the Family* 61:437–50.

Buchanan, Christy, Eleanor E. Maccoby, and Sanford M. Dornbush. *Adolescents After Divorce*. Cambridge, MA: Harvard University Press.

Bulcroft, Richard, Kris Bulcroft, Karen Bradley, and Carl Simpson. 2000. "The Management and Production of Risk in Romantic Relationships: A Postmodern Paradox." *Journal of Family History* 25:1:63–92.

Bullough, Vern L. 1976. *Sexual Variance in Society and History*. New York: Wiley.

Bumpass, Larry, and James A. Sweet. 1972. "Differentials in Marital Instability: 1970." *American Sociological Review* 37:754–56.

_____. 1989. "National Estimates of Cohabitation." *Demography* 26:615–25.

Bumpass, Larry L., and R. Kelly Raley. 1995. "Redefining Single-Parent Families: Cohabitation and Changing Family Reality." *Demography* 27:483–98.

Bumpass, Larry L., and H.-H Lu. 2000. "Trends in Cohabitation and Implications for Children's Family Contexts in the United States." *Population Studies* 54:29–41.

Bumpass, Larry L., James A. Sweet, and Andrew Cherlin. 1991. "The Role of Cohabitation in Declining Rates of Marriage." *Journal of Marriage and the Family* 53:913–27.

Bumpass, Larry, James Sweet, and Teresa Castro Martin. 1990. "Changing Patterns of Remarriage." *Journal of Marriage and the Family* 52:747–56.

Bunker, Barbara B., Josephine M. Zubek, Virginia J. Vanderslice, and Robert W. Rice. 1992. "Quality of Life in Dual-Career Families: Commuting Versus Single-Residence Couples." *Journal of Marriage and the Family* 54:399–407.

Burch, Ernest S. 1970. "Marriage and Divorce among North

American Eskimos." Pp. 152–81 in *Divorce and After*, edited by Paul Bohannon. New York: Doubleday.

————. 1982. "Marriage and Divorce Among the North Alaskan Eskimos." Pp. 105–131 in *Anthropology for the Eighties: Introductory Readings*, edited by Johnnetta B. Cole. New York: The Free Press.

Burchinal, Lee G. 1963. "Personality Characteristics of Children." Pp. 106–24 in *The Employed Mother in America*, edited by F. Ivan Nye and L. W. Hoffman. Chicago: Rand-McNally.

Burchinal, Margaret R. 1999. "Child Care Experiences and Developmental Outcomes." *The Annals of the American Academy of Political and Social Science* 563:73–97.

Bureau of Labor Statistics. 1995. *A CPS Supplement for Testing Methods of Collecting Racial and Ethnic Information: May, 1995*. Washington, DC: Bureau of Labor Statistics.

Burgess, Ernest W., and Harvey J. Lock. [1945] 1953. *The Family: From Institution to Companionship*. New York: American Book.

Burgess, Ernest W., and Paul Wallin. 1953. *Engagement and Marriage*. Philadelphia: Lippincott.

Burke, Meredith B. 1995. "Mexican Immigrants Shape California's Fertility, Future." *Population Today* 23(9): 4–6.

Burnham, Philip. 1993. "Selling Poor Steven." *American Heritage* (February-March).

Burr, Wesley R. 1994. *Reexamining Family Stress: New Theory and Research*. Thousand Oaks, CA: Sage.

Burr, Wesley R., Geoffrey K. Leigh, Randall D. Day, and John Constantine. 1979. "Symbolic Interaction and the Family." Pp. 42–111 in *Contemporary Theories About the Family*, edited by Wesley R. Burr, Reuben Hill, F. Ivan Nye, and Ira R. Reiss. New York: Free Press.

Burtch, Brian E. 1994. *Trials of Labour: The Re-emergence of Midwifery*. Buffalo: McGill-Queen's University Press.

Buss, David M. 1989. "Sex Differences in Human Mate Preferences: Evolutionary Hypotheses Tested in 37 Cultures." *Behavior and Brain Sciences* 12:1–49.

————. 1994. *The Evolution of Desire: Strategies of Human Mating*. New York: Basic Books.

Buss, David M., R. J. Larsen, D. Westen, and J. Semmelroth. 1992. "Sex Differences in Jealousy: Evolution, Physiology, and Psychology." *Psychological Science* 3:251–55.

Buss, David M., and David P. Schmitt. 1993. "Sexual Strategies Theory: An Evolutionary Perspective on Human Mating." *Psychological Review* 100:204–32.

Butler, Robert N. 1975. *Why Survive? Being Old in America*. New York: Harper & Row.

Buunk, Bram, and Ralph B. Hupka. 1987. "The Elicitation of Sexual Jealousy." *The Journal of Sex Research* 23(1).

Buys, Christian J. 1992. "Human Sympathy Groups: Cross-Cultural Data." *Psychological Reports* 71 (3):786.

Buzawa, Eva S., and Carl G. Buzawa. 1993. "The Scientific Evidence Is Not Conclusive: Arrest Is No Panacea." Pp. 337–56 in *Current Controversies on Family Violence*, edited by Richard J. Gelles and Donileen R. Loseke.

Byers, E. Sandra, and Staphanie Demmons. 1999. *The Journal of Sex Research* 36:180–89.

C

Cady, Joseph. 1992. "'Masculine Love,' Renaissance Writing, and the 'New Invention' of Homosexuality." *Journal of Homosexuality* 23:9–40.

Calahan, Don, and Robin Room. 1974. *Problem Drinking among American Men*. New Brunswick, NJ: Rutgers Center for Alcohol Studies.

Callender, Charles, and Lee M. Kochems. 1993. "The North American Berdache." Pp. 367–98 in *Culture and Human Sexuality: A Reader*, edited by David N. Suggs and Andrew W. Miracle. Pacific Grove, CA: Brooks/Cole.

Cameron, Paul. 1999. "Homosexual Parents: Testing 'Common Sense'—A Literature Review Emphasizing the Golombok and Tasker Longitudinal Study of Lesbians." *Psychological Reports* 85(1):282–322.

Cameron, Paul, and Kirk Cameron. 1996. "Homosexual Parents." *Adolescence* 31:757–76.

————. 1997. "Did the APA Misrepresent the Scientific Literature to Courts in Support of Homosexual Custody?" *The Journal of Psychology* 131:313–32.

Campbell, Joseph. 1949. *Hero With a Thousand Faces*. Cleveland: Meridian.

Campisi, Paul J. 1948. "Ethnic Family Patterns: The Italian Family in the United States." *American Journal of Sociology* 53:443–49.

Canary, Daniel J., and Laura Stafford. 1994. "Maintaining Relationships through Strategic and Routine Interaction." Pp. 3–21 in *Communication and Relational Maintenance*, edited by D. J. Canary and L. Stafford. San Diego: Academic.

Cancian, Francesca M. 1986. "The Feminization of Love." *Signs: Journal of Women in Culture and Society* 11:692–709.

————. 1987. *Love in America: Gender and Self-Development*. New York: Cambridge University Press.

————. 1989. "Gender Politics: Love and Power in the Private and Public Spheres." Pp. 219–35 in *Family in*

Transition, 6th ed., edited by Arlene S. Skolnick and Jerome H. Skolnick. Glenview, IL: Scott, Foresman.

Cantor, Marjorie, ed. 1994. *Family Caregiving: Agenda for the Future*. San Francisco: American Society on Aging.

Capaldi, D. M., and Gerald R. Patterson. 1991. "Relation of Parental Transitions to Boys' Adjustment Problems: I. A Linear Hypothesis: II. Mothers at Risk for Transitions and Unskilled Parenting." *Developmental Psychology* 27:489–504.

Capizzano, Jeffrey, Kathryn Tout, and Gina Adams. 2000. "Child Care Patterns of School-Age Children with Employed Mothers: Occasional Paper Number 41." Washington, DC: The Urban Institute. http://newfederalism.urban.org/html/op41/occa41.html.

Caplow, Theodore, Howard M. Bahr, Bruce A. Chadwick, Rueben Hill, and Margaret Holmes Williamson. 1982. *Middletown Families: Fifty Years of Change and Continuity*. Minneapolis: University of Minnesota Press.

Carlson, Christopher. 1990. *Perspectives on the Family: History, Class, and Feminism*. Belmont, CA: Wadsworth.

Carter, Hugh, and Paul C. Glick. 1976. *Marriage and Divorce: A Social and Economic Study*. Cambridge, MA: Harvard University Press.

Caserta, Michael S., Dale A. Lund, and Scott D. Wright. 1996. "Exploring the Caregiver Burden Inventory (CBI): Further Evidence for a Multidimensional View of Burden." *International Journal of Aging and Human Development* 43(1):21–34.

Casper, L. M., and L. C. Sayer. 2000. "Cohabitation Transitions: Different Attitudes and Purposes, Different Paths." Paper presented at the annual meeting of the Population Association of America, Los Angeles, March 2000.

Caspar, Lynne, Phillip N. Cohen, and Tavia Simmons. 1999. "How Does POSSLQ Measure Up: Historical Estimates of Cohabitation." Population Division, U. S. Bureau of Census, Washington, DC. http://www.census.gov/population/www/documentation/twps0036/twps0036.html.

Cate, Rodney M., and Sally A. Lloyd. 1992. *Courtship*. Newbury Park, CA: Sage.

Cate, Rodney M., Sally A. Lloyd, June M. Henton, and J. H. Larson. 1982. "Fairness and Reward Level as Predictors of Relationship Satisfaction." *Social Psychology Quarterly* 45:177–81.

Catechism of the Catholic Church. 1994. Mahwah, NJ: Paulist Press (Libreria Editrice Vaticana).

Catlett, Beth Skilten, and Patrick C. McKenry. 1996. "Implications of Feminist Scholarship for the Study of Women's Postdivorce Economic Disadvantage." *Family Relations* 45:91–97.

Cavan, Ruth S., and Katherine H. Ranck. 1938. *The Family and the Depression*. Chicago: University of Chicago Press.

Cavanaugh, John. 1993. *Adult Development and Aging*, 2nd ed. Pacific Grove, CA: Brooks/Cole.

Cazenave, Noel A., and Murray A. Straus. 1990. "Race, Class, Network Embeddedness, and Family Violence: A Search for Potent Support Systems." Pp. 321–40 in *Physical Violence in American Families: Risk Factors and Adaptations to Violence in 8,145 Families*, edited by Murray A. Straus and Richard J. Gelles. New Brunswick, NJ: Transaction.

Centers for Disease Control and Prevention. 1993. "HIV/AIDS Surveillance Report." February:1–23. U.S. Department of Health and Human Services. Atlanta, GA.

_____. 2000. "Youth Risk Behavior Surveillance—United States, 1999." *Morbidity and Mortality Weekly Report 49*: SS-5. U.S. Department of Health and Human Services. Atlanta, GA.

Chafetz, Janet Saltzman. 1984. *Sex and Advantage: A Comparative, Macrostructural Theory of Sex Stratification*. Totowa, NJ: Rowman and Allanheld.

Chambers, David L. 1990. "Stepparents, Biologic Parents, and the Law's Perceptions of 'Family' after Divorce." Pp. 102–29 in *Divorce Reform at the Crossroads*, edited by Stephen D. Sugarman and Herma Hill Kay. New Haven: Yale University Press.

Chambers, Mortimer, Raymond Grew, David Herlihy, Theodore Rabb, and Isser Woloch. 1979. *The Western Experience to 1715*, 2nd ed. New York: Alfred A. Knopf.

Chao, Paul. 1977. *Women under Communism: Family in Russia and China*. Bayside, NY: General Hall.

Chao, Ruth K. 1994. "Beyond Parental Control and Authoritarian Parenting Style: Understanding Chinese Parenting through the Cultural Notion of Training." *Child Development* 65:1111–19.

Chapman, Audrey B. 1994. *Entitled to Good Loving: Black Men and Women and the Battle for Love and Power*. New York: Holt.

Chapman, C. G. 1971. *Milocca: A Sicilian Village*. Cambridge, MA: Schenkman.

Cheatham, Harold E., Allen E. Ivey, Mary Bradford Ivey, and Lynn Simek-Morgan. 1993. "Multicultural Counseling and Therapy: Changing the Foundations in the Field." Pp. 356–78 in *Counseling and Psychotherapy: A Multicultural Perspective*, 3rd ed., edited by Allen E. Ivey, Mary Bradford Ivey, and Lynn Simek-Morgan. Boston: Allyn and Bacon.

Chen, Xiangming. 1985. "The One-Child Population Policy, Modernization, and the Extended Chinese Family." *Journal of Marriage and the Family* 47:193–202.

Chenoworth, Barbara, and Beth Spencer. 1986. "Dementia: The Experience of Family Caregivers." *The Gerontologist* 26:267–72.

Cherlin, Andrew J. 1978. "Remarriage as an Incomplete Institution." *American Journal of Sociology* 84:634–50.

_____. 1992. *Marriage, Divorce, Remarriage*, rev. ed. Cambridge, MA: Harvard University Press.

_____. 1996. *Public and Private Families: An Introduction*. New York: McGraw-Hill.

Cherlin, Andrew J., and Frank F. Furstenberg, Jr. 1983. "The American Family in the Year 2000." *The Futurist* 17:7–14.

_____. 1986. *The New American Grandparent: A Place in the Family, a Life Apart*. New York: Basic Books.

_____. 1992. *The New American Grandparent: A Place in the Family, a Life Apart*. Cambridge: Harvard University Press.

_____. 1994. *Divided Families: What Happens to Children When Parents Part*. Cambridge, MA: Harvard University Press.

Cherry, Robert. 1999. "Black Male Employment and Tight Labor Markets." *The Review of Black Political Economy* 27(1):31–45.

Chesler, Ellen. 1992. *A Woman of Valor: Margaret Sanger and the Birth Control Movement in America*. New York: Simon and Schuster.

Chin, Ko-Lin, and Douglas S. Massey. 1999. *Smuggled Chinese: Clandestine Immigration to the United States*. Philadelphia: Temple University Press.

Ching, C. C. 1982. "The One-Child Family in China." *Studies in Family Planning* 13:208–12.

Chodorow, Nancy. 1978. *The Reproduction of Mothering*. Berkeley: University of California Press.

Chow, Esther Ngan-ling, and Catherine White. 1994. *Women, the Family, and Policy: A Global Perspective*. Albany, NY: State University of New York Press.

Christensen, Harold. T. 1969. "Normative Theory Derived from Cross-Cultural Family Research." *Journal of Marriage and the Family* 31:209–22.

Christiansen, Shawn L., and Rob Palkovitz. 2001. "Why the 'Good Provider' Role Still Matters." *Journal of Family Issues* 22(1):84–106.

Christopher, F. Scott, and Mark W. Roosa. 1990. "An Adolescent Pregnancy Prevention Program: Is 'Just Say No' Enough?" *Family Relations* 39:68–72.

Christopher, F. Scott, and Susan Sprecher. 2000. "Sexuality in Marriage, Dating, and Other Relationships: A Decade Review." *Journal of Marriage and the Family* 62:999–1017.

Clark, Michael. 1999. "The Double ABCX Model of Family Crisis as a Representation of Family Functioning After Rehabilitation from Stroke." *Psychology, Health & Medicine* 4(2):203–20.

Clark, Roger D. 1992. "Family Structure, Liberty and Equality, and Divorce: A Cross-National Examination." Pp. 175–96 in *Fertility Transition, Family Structure, and Population Policy*, edited by Calvin Goldscheider. Boulder, CO: Westview Press.

Clark, Roger D., and Hatfield, Elaine. 1989. "Gender Differences in Receptivity to Sexual Offers." *Journal of Psychology and Human Sexuality* 2:39–55.

Clark, Victoria. 2000. "'Stereotype, Attack and Stigmatize Those Who Disagree': Employing Scientific Rhetoric in Debates about Lesbian and Gay Parenting." *Feminism and Psychology* 10(1):152–59.

Clayton, Richard R. 1979. *The Family, Marriage, and Social Change*, 2nd ed. Lexington, MA: D. C. Heath.

Clingempeel, Glen, M. Flescher, and E. Brand. 1987. "Research on Stepfamilies: Paradigmatic Constraints and Alternative Proposals." Pp. 229–51 in *Advances in Family Intervention: Assessment and Theory*, edited by John P. Vincent. Greenwich, CT: JAI.

Coale, Ansley. 1973. "The Demographic Transition Theory Reconsidered." *International Population Conference* (1):53–71.

Coberly, Frank Sheldon. "Marital Adjustment in Blended Families: The Effects of Stepchidren in the Home on Married Couples." *Dissertation Abstracts International: Section B: The Sciences and Engineering* 56(10-b):5831.

Cohen, Myron L. 1976. *House United, House Divided: The Chinese Family in Taiwan*. New York: Columbia University Press.

Colasanto, Diane, and J. Shriver. 1989. "Middle-Aged Face Marital Crisis." *Gallup Report* 284 (May): 34–38.

Cole, H. M. 1989. "Intrauterine Devices." *Journal of the American Medical Association* 261:2127–30.

Cole, William Graham. 1959. *Sex and Love in the Bible*. New York: Association Press.

Coleman, E. 1987. "Bisexuality: Challenging Our Understanding of Human Sexuality and Sexual Orientation." Pp. 225–42 in *Sexuality and Medicine Vol. 1*, edited by E. E. Shelp. New York: Reidel Publishing.

Coleman, E. M., P. W. Hoon, and E. F. Hoon. 1983. *Journal of Sex Research* 19:58–73.

Coleman, James S. 1990. *Foundations of Social Theory*. Cambridge, MA: Belknap.

Coleman, Marilyn, and Lawrence H. Ganong. 1990. "Remarriage and Stepfamily Research in the 1980s: Increased Interest in an Old Family Form." *Journal of Marriage and the Family* 52:925–40.

————. 1997. "Stepfamilies from the Stepfamily's Perspective." *Marriage and Family Review* 26(1–2):107–21.

Collins, Randall. 1985. *Three Sociological Traditions.* New York: Oxford University Press.

Collins, Randall, and Scott Coltrane. 1991, 1995. *Sociology of Marriage and the Family: Gender, Love, and Property.* Chicago: Nelson-Hall.

Coltrane, Scott. 2000. "Research on Household Labor: Modeling and Measuring the Social Embeddedness of Routine Family Work." *Journal of Marriage and the Family* 62:1208–33.

Comfort, Alex. 1972. *The Joy of Sex.* New York: Crown.

Conger, Rand, Glen H. Elder, Jr., Frederick O. Lorenz, Katherine J. Conger, Ronald L. Simons, Les B. Whitbeck, Shirley Huck, and Janet N. Melby. 1990. "Linking Economic Hardship to Marital Quality and Instability." *Journal of Marriage and the Family* 52:643–56.

Conger, Rand, Martha A. Rueter, and Glen H. Elder, Jr. 1999. "Couple Resilience to Economic Pressure." *Journal of Personality and Social Psychology* 76:64–71.

Congressional Quarterly Weekly Report. 1988. "Catastrophic Bill Is Sent to White House." *Congressional Quarterly* 46: 31–32.

Cook, Phillip W. 1997. *Abused Men: The Hidden Side of Domestic Violence.* Westport, CT: Praeger Publishers/Greenwood Publishing Group.

Cooley, Charles Horton. 1902. *Human Nature and Social Order.* New York: Scribner.

Coombs, Robert H. 1991. "Marital Status and Personal Well-Being: A Literature Review." *Family Relations* 40:97–102.

Cooney, Rosemary Santana, Jin Wei, and Mary G. Powers. 1991. "The One-Child Certificate in Hebei Province, China: Acceptance and Consequence, 1979–1988." *Population Research and Policy Review* 10:137–55.

Cooney, Teresa M. 1993. "Recent Demographic Change: Implications for Families Planning for the Future." *Marriage and Family Review* 18:37–55.

Cooney, Teresa M., and Peter Uhlenberg. 1989. "Family-Building Patterns of Professional Women: A Comparison of Lawyers, Physicians, and Postsecondary Teachers." *Journal of Marriage and the Family* 51:749–58.

————. 1992. "Support from Patents Over the Life Course: The Adult Child's Perspective." *Social Forces* 71:63–84.

Coontz, Stephanie. 1988. *The Social Origins of Private Lives: A History of American Families, 1600–1900.* New York: Verso.

————. 1992. *The Way We Never Were: American Families and the Nostalgia Trap.* New York: Basic Books.

————. 1998. *The Way We Really Are: Coming to Terms with America's Changing Families.* New York: Basic Books.

————. 2000. "Historical Perspectives on Family Studies." *Journal of Marriage and the Family* 62:283–97.

Corbet, S. L., and K. D. Morgan. 1983. "The Process of Lesbian Identification." *Free Inquiry in Creative Sociology* 11:81–83.

Côté, James E. 1998. "Much Ado About Nothing: The 'Fateful Hoaxing' of Margaret Mead." *Skeptical Inquirer* 23(4).

Cott, Nancy. 2000. *Public Vows: A History of Marriage in the U.S. as a Public Institution.* Cambridge; Harvard University Press.

Covello, Leonard. 1967. *The Social Background of the Italo-American School Child.* Leiden, Netherlands: E. J. Brill.

Cowan, Carolyn Pape, and Philip A. Cowan. 2000. *When Partners Become Parents: The Big Life Change for Couples.* Mahway, NJ: Erlbaum.

Cowan, Carolyn P., Philip A. Cowan, G. Heming, E. V. Garrett, W. S. Coysh, H. Curtis-Boles, and A. J. Boles. 1985. "Transitions to Parenthood: His, Hers, and Theirs." *Journal of Family Issues* 6:451–81.

Cowan, Philip A. 1988. "Becoming a Father: A Time of Change, an Opportunity for Development." In *Fatherhood Today*, edited by Phyllis Bronstein and Carolyn P. Cowan.

Cowan, Ruth Schwartz. 1983. *More Work for Mother: The Ironies of Household Technology from the Open Hearth to the Microwave.* New York: Basic Books.

Cox, Martha J., Blair Paley, C. Chris Payne, and Margaret Burchinal. 1999. "The Transition to Parenthood: Marital Conflict and Withdrawal and Parent-Infant Interactions." Pp. 87–104 in *Conflict and Cohesion in Families: Causes and Consequences,* edited by Martha J. Cox and Jeanne Brooks-Gunn. Mahway, NJ: Erlbaum.

Crépault, C., and M. Couture. 1977. "Erotic Imagery in Women." Pp. 267–83 in *Progress in Sexology*, edited by R. Gemme and C. C. Wheeler. New York: Plenum.

————. 1980. "Men's Erotic Fantasies." *Archives of Sexual Behavior* 9:565–81.

Cromwell, Vicky L., and Ronald E. Cromwell. 1978. "Perceived Dominance in Decision-Making and Conflict-Resolution Among Anglo, Black and Chicano Couples." *Journal of Marriage and the Family* 40:749–59.

Crosbie-Burnett, Margaret, and Jean Giles-Sims. 1994. "Adolescent Adjustment and Stepparenting Styles." *Family Relations* 43:394–99.

Crosby, John. 1980. "A Critique of Divorce Statistics and Their Interpretations." *Family Relations* 29:51–68.

Cuber, John H., and Peggy B. Harroff. 1968. *The Significant Americans: A Study of Sexual Behavior among the Affluent.* Baltimore: Penguin Books.

Cultural Indicators Research Project. 2001. http://nimbuis.ocis.temple.edu/~ggerbner/ci.html.

Cupach, W. R., and J. Comstock. 1990. "Satisfaction with Sexual Communication in Marriage: Links to Sexual Satisfaction and Dyadic Adjustment." *Jounal of Social and Personal Relationships* 7:179–86.

D

Dahrendorf, Ralf. 1979. *Life Chances: Approaches to Social and Political Theory.* Chicago: University of Chicago Press.

Dainton, Marianne, Laura Stafford, and Daniel J. Canary. 1994. "Maintenance Strategies and Physical Affection as Predictors of Love, Liking, and Satisfaction in Marriage." *Communication Reports* 7:89–98.

Dalmage, Heather M. 2000. *Tripping on the Color Line: Black-White Multiracial Families in a Racially Divided World.* New Brunswick: Rutgers University Press.

Daly, Kerri J. 1999. "Crisis of Genealogy: Facing the Challenges of Infertility." Pp. 1–40 in *The Dynamics of Resilient Families,* edited by Hamilton I. McCubbin, Elizabeth A. Thompson, Anne I. Thompson, and Jo A. Futrell. Thousand Oaks, CA: Sage Publications.

Daly, Kerri. 1994. "Adolescent Perception of Adoption: Implications for Resolving an Unplanned Pregnancy." *Youth and Society* 25:330–50.

Daly, Martin, and Margo Wilson. 1984. "Sociobiological Analysis of Human Infanticide." Pp. 487–502 in *Infanticide: Comparative and Evolutionary Perspectives,* edited by Glenn Hausfater and Sarah Blaffer Hardy. New York: Aldine.

Daniels, R. 1990. *Coming to America: A History of Immigration and Ethnicity in American Life.* New York: Harper Perennial.

Danziger, Sheldon, Robert Haveman, and Robert Plotnick. 1981. "How Income Transfer Programs Affect Work, Savings, and the Income Distribution." *Journal of Economic Literature* 19:975–1026.

Darling, Carol A., David J. Kallan, and Joyce E. Vandusen. 1984. "Sex in Transition, 1900–1980." *Journal of Youth and Adolescence* 13:385–99.

D'Augelli, Judith Frankel, and Anthony R. D'Augelli. 1977. "Moral Reasoning and Premarital Sexual Behavior: Toward Reasoning About Relationships." *Journal of Social Issues* 33:46–66.

D'Augelli, Anthony R., and Charlotte J. Patterson, eds. 1995. *Lesbian, Gay, and Bisexual Identities Over the Lifespan: Psychological Perspectives.* New York: Oxford University Press.

Davenport, William H. 1976. "Sex in Cross Cultural Perspective." Pp. 115–63 in *Human Sexuality in Four Perspectives,* edited by Frank A. Beach. Baltimore: The Johns Hopkins University Press.

Davies, Lorraine, William R. Avison, and Donna D. McAlpine. 1997. "Significant Life Experiences and Depression among Single and Married Mothers." *Journal of Marriage and the Family* 59:294–308.

Davis, Anthony. 1998. "Age Differences in Dating and Marriage: Reproductive Strategies or Social Preferences?" *Current Anthropology* 39(3):374–80.

Davis, James Allan, and Smith, Tom W. General Social Survey(s), year(s). (Machine-readable data file). Principal investigator, James A. Davis; director and co-principal investigator, Tom W. Smith; co-principal investigator, Peter V. Marsden, NORC ed. Chicago: National Opinion Research Center, producer, 1998; Storrs, CT: The Roper Center for Public Opinion Research, University of Connecticut, distributor. Microcomputer format and codebook prepared and distributed by MicroCase Corporation, Bellevue, WA. Analysis by Gene H. Starbuck.

Davis, Jennifer Nerissa, and Martin Daly. 1997. "Evolutionary Theory and the Human Family." *The Quarterly Review of Biology* 72(4):407–35.

Davis, Kingsley. 1971. "Sexual Behavior." Pp. 313–60 in *Contemporary Social Problems,* edited by Robert Merton and Robert Nisbet. New York: Harcourt Brace Jovanovich.

Davis, Kingsley, and Wilbert Moore. 1945. "Some Principles of Stratification." *American Sociological Review* 7:242–49.

Davis, Nancy, and Robert Robinson. 1988. "Class Identification of Men and Women in the 1970s and 1980s." *American Sociological Review* 53:103–12.

Dawson, Deborah. 1991. "Family Structure and Children's Health and Well-Being: Data from the 1988 National Health Interview Survey on Child Health." *Journal of Marriage and the Family* 53:573–84.

Day, Jennifer Cheeseman. 1993. *Population Projections of the United States, by Age, Sex, Race, and Hispanic Origin: 1993 to 2050.* U.S. Bureau of the Census, Current Population Reports, P25–1104. Washington, DC: U.S. Government Printing Office.

De Barbieri, M. Teresita. 1994. "Gender and Population Policy." Pp. 257–66 in *Beyond the Numbers: A Reader on Population, Consumption, and the Environment,* edited by Laurie Ann Mazur. Washington, DC: Island Press.

Degler, Carl N. 1980. *At Odds: Women and the Family in America from the Revolution to the Present.* New York: Oxford University Press.

Deimling, Gary T., and David M. Bass. 1986. "Symptoms of Mental Impairment Among Elderly Adults and Their Effects on Family Caregivers." *Journal of Gerontology* 41:778–84.

De Lamater, John, and Patricia MacCorquodale. 1979. *Premarital Sexuality.* Madison: University of Wisconsin Press.

Dellmann-Jenkins, Mary, Maureen Blankmeyer, and Odessa Pinkard. 2000. "Young Adult Children and Grandchildren in Primary Caregiver Roles to Older Relatives and Their Service Needs." *Family Relations: Interdisciplinary Journal of Applied Family Studies* 49(2):177–86.

De Luccie, M. F. 1995. "Mothers as Gatekeepers: A Model of Maternal Mediators of Father Involvement." *The Journal of Genetic Psychology* 156:115–31.

DeMaris, Alfred, and K. Vaninadha Rao. 1992. "Premarital Cohabitation and Subsequent Marital Stability in the United States: A Reassessment." *Journal of Marriage and the Family* 54:178–90.

DeMaris, Alfred, and William MacDonald. 1993. "Premarital Cohabitation and Marital Instability: A Test of the Unconventionality Hypothesis." *Journal of Marriage and the Family* 55:399–407.

DeMause, Lloyd. 1974. "The Evolution of Childhood." Pp. 1–73 in *The History of Childhood*, edited by Lloyd Demause. New York: Harper & Row.

D'Emilio, John, and Estelle B. Freedman. 1988. *Intimate Matters: A History of Sexuality in America*. New York: Harpers.

Demo, David, and Alan Acock. 1988. "The Impact of Divorce on Children." *Journal of Marriage and the Family* 50:619–48.

————. 1996. "Singlehood, Marriage, and Remarriage: The Effects of Family Structure and Family Relationships on Mothers' Well-Being." *Journal of Family Issues* 17:388–407.

————. 1996. "Family Structure, Family Process, and Adolescent Well-Being." *Journal of Research on Adolescence* 6:457–88.

Demo, David H., Katherine R. Allen, and Mark A. Fine, eds. 2000. *Handbook of Family Diversity*. New York: Oxford University Press.

Demo, David H., Anne-Marie Ambert, and Jay A. Mancini, eds. 1995. *Parents and Adolescents in Changing Families*. Minneapolis: National Council on Family Relations.

Demo, David H., and Martha J. Cox. 2000. "Families With Young Children: A Review of Research in the 1990s." *Journal of Marriage and the Family* 62:876–95.

Demos, John. 1970. *A Little Commonwealth: Family Life in Plymouth Colony*. New York: Oxford University Press.

————. 1971. "Demography and Psychology in the Historical Study of Family-Life: A Personal Report." Pp. 561–70 in *Household and Family in Past Time*, edited by Peter Laslett. Cambridge: Cambridge University Press.

————. 1986. *Past, Present, and Personal: The Family and the Life Course in American History*. New York: Oxford University Press.

Derwinski-Robinson, B. 1990. "Infertility and Sexuality." Pp. 291–304 in *Sexual Health Promotion*, edited by C. I. Fogel and D. Lauver. Philadelphia: W. B. Saunders.

Deutcher, Irwin. 1969. "From Parental to Post-Parental Life." *Sociological Symposium* 3:47–60.

DeVanzo, J., and F. K. Goldscheider. 1990. "Coming Home Again: Returns to the Nest in Young Adulthood." *Population Studies* 44:241–55.

Diamond, Milton. 1993. "Homosexuality and Bisexuality in Different Populations." *Archives of Sexual Behavior* 22:291–310.

Dickens, Wenda, and Daniel Perlmen. 1981. "Friendship Over the Life Cycle." Pp. 91–122 in *Personal Relationships, Vol. 2*, edited by Steve Duck and Robin Gilmour. London: Academic Press.

Dickinson, George E. 1995. *Understanding Families: Diversity, Continuity, and Change*. Fort Worth: Harcourt Brace.

Digest of Educational Statistics. 1999. U.S. Department of Education. Accessed through USTrends Dataset, MicroCase, Seattle, WA.

Divale, William Tulio. 1972. "Systemic Population Control in the Middle and Upper Palaeolithic. Inferences Based on Contemporary Hunter–Gatherers." *World Archaeology* 4:222–243.

Divale, William Tulio, and Marvin Harris. 1976. "Population, Warfare, and the Male Supremacist Complex." *American Anthropologist* 78:521–39.

Dixon, Suzanne. 1992. *The Roman Family*. Baltimore: Johns Hopkins University Press.

Dobash, R. Emerson, and Russell Dobash. 1979. *Violence Against Wives*. New York: The Free Press.

Doherty, William J., Edward F. Kouneski, and Martha F. Erickson. 1998. "Responsible Fathering: An Overview and Conceptual Framework." *Journal of Marriage and the Family* 60:277–92.

Dolan, Edwin G., and David E. Lindsey. 1991. *Microeconomics*, 6th ed. Chicago: Dryden Press.

Donnison, Jean. 1988. *Midwives and Medical Men: A History of the Struggle for the Control of Childbirth*. London: Historical Publications.

Doosje, Bertjan, Krystyna Rojahn, and Agneta Fischer. 1999. "Partner Preferences as a Function of Gender, Age, Political Orientation, and Level of Education." *Sex Roles* 40:1–2, 46–60.

Dorfman, Lorraine T., and Carol E. Mertens. 1990. "Kinship Relations in Retired Rural Men and Women." *Family Relations* 39:166–73.

Draper, Patricia, and Elizabeth Cashdan. 1975. "Contrasts in Sexual Egalitarianism in Foraging and Sedentary Contexts." Pp. 77–109 in *Toward an Anthropology of Women*, edited by Rayna Reiter. New York: Monthly Review Press.

Dror, Yuval. 1998. "Reducing Totality and Opening Residential Settings to Their Regions in the Israeli Kibbutz Artzi Educational Institutions in the 1980s and 1990s." *Journal of Adolescence* 21:529–41.

DuBois, W. E. B. 1899. *The Philadelphia Negro*. Philadelphia: University of Pennsylvania Press.

Dubois, Stephanie L. 1997. "Gender Differences in the Emotional Tone of Written Sexual Fantasies." *Canadian Journal of Human Sexuality Special Issue: Papers Presented at the 1997 Canadian Sex Research Forum* 6(4):307–15.

Duck, Steve. 1994. *Meaningful Relationships: Talking, Sense, and Relating*. Newbury Park, CA: Sage.

Dumont, Louis. 1970. *Homo Hierarchieus: The Caste System and Its Implications*. Chicago: University of Chicago Press.

Duncan, Greg, et al. 1984. *Years of Poverty, Years of Plenty: The Changing Economic Fortunes of American Workers and Families*. Ann Arbor: Institute for Social Research, the University of Michigan.

Duncan, Greg J., Jeanne Brooks-Gunn, and Pamela Kato Klebanov. 1994. "Economic Deprivation and Early Childhood Development." *Child Development* 65:296–318.

Duncan, Greg, and Willard Rodgers. 1987. "Single-Parent Families: Are Their Economic Problems Transitory or Persistent?" *Family Planning Perspectives* 19:171–78.

Dunne, Gillian A. 2000. "Opting Into Motherhood: Lesbians Blurring the Boundaries and Transforming the Meaning of Parenthood and Kinship." *Gender and Society* 14(1):11–35.

Dupaquier, Jacques, and Louis Jadin. 1971. "Structure of Household and Family in Corsica, 1769–71." Pp. 283–98 in *Household and Family in Past Time*, edited by Peter Laslett. Cambridge: Cambridge University Press.

Durkheim, Emile. [1893] 1966. *On the Division of Labor in Society*. Translated by G. Simpson. New York: Free Press.

———. [1897] 1964. *Suicide*. Glencoe, IL: Free Press.

———. [1912] 1954. *The Elementary Forms of Religious Life*. Translated by W. Swain. New York: Free Press.

Dutton, Donald. 1988. *The Domestic Assault of Women*. Boston: Allyn and Bacon.

———. 1995. "Patriarchy and Wife Assault: The Ecological Fallacy." *Violence and Victims* 9:167–82.

Dutton, Donald, and Arthur Aron. 1974. "Some Evidence for Heightened Sexual Attraction under Conditions of High Anxiety." *Journal of Personality and Social Psychology* 4:510–17.

Duval, Evelyn M. 1957. *Family Development*. Philadelphia: J. B. Lippincott.

———. 1967. *Family Development*, 3rd ed. Philadelphia: J. B. Lippincott.

Dworkin, Andrea. 1976. *Our Blood: Prophecies and Discourses on Sexual Politics*. New York: Harper & Row.

———. 1987. *Intercourse*. New York: Free Press.

E

Eaton, Joseph W., and Albert J. Mayer. 1954. *Man's Capacity to Reproduce: The Demography of a Unique Population*. New York: Free Press.

Ebaugh, Helen Rose Fuchs. 1988. *Becoming an Ex: The Process of Role Exit*. Chicago: University of Chicago Press.

Edgar and Glezer. 1994. "Family and Intimacy: Family Careers and the Reconstruction of Private Life." *International Social Science Journal* 139:117–39.

Edin, Kathryn, and Laura Lein. 1997. "Work, Welfare, and Single Mothers' Economic Survival Strategies." *American Sociological Review* 62:253–66.

Edwards, John N., Theodore D. Fuller, Sairudee Vorakitphokatorn, and Santhat Sermsri. 1992. "Female Employment and Marital Instability: Evidence from Thailand." *Journal of Marriage and the Family* 54:59–68.

EEOC (Equal Employment Opportunity Commission). 2000. http://www.eeoc.gov/stats/index.html.

Egeland, Byron. 1993. "A History of Abuse Is a Major Risk Factor for Abusing the Next Generation." Pp. 197–208 in *Current Controversies on Family Violence*, edited by Richard J. Gelles and Donileen R. Loseke. Newbury Park, CA: Sage.

Ehrenreich, Barbara. 1983. *The Hearts of Men: American Dreams and the Flight from Commitment*. Garden City, NY: Anchor/Doubleday.

Ehrenreich, Barbara, and Deirdre English. 1978. *For Her Own Good: 150 Years of the Experts' Advice to Women*. Garden City, NY: Anchor/Doubleday.

Ehrlich, Paul. 1997. *The Population Explosion*. New York: Buccaneer Books.

Eisen, Marvin, Gail L. Zellman, and Alfred L. McAlister. 1990. "Evaluating the Impact of a Theory-Based Sexuality and Contraceptive Education Program." *Family Planning Perspectives* 22:261–71.

Elkind, David. 1994. *Ties that Stress: The New Family Imbalance*. Cambridge: Harvard University Press.

Elkins, Stanley M. 1959. *Slavery: A Problem in American Institutional and Intellectual Life.* Chicago: University of Chicago Press.

Eller, T. J. 1994. *Household Wealth and Asset Ownership: 1991.* U.S. Bureau of the Census, Current Population Reports, Pp. 70–34. Washington, DC: U.S. Government Printing Office.

Ellis, Bruce J., and Donald Symons. 1990. "Sex Differences in Sexual Fantasy: An Evolutionary Psychological Approach." *Journal of Sex Research* 27:527–55.

Ellsworth, S. George. 1985. *The New Utah's Heritage.* Salt Lake City, UT: Peregrine Smith Books.

Elwell, Frank. 1999. *Malthus' Home Page.* http://www.faculty.rsu.edu/~felwell/Theorists/Malthus/Index.htm.

Emery, Robert E., 1999. "Postdivorce Family Life for Children: An Overview of Research and Some Implications for Policy." Pp. 3–28 in *The Postdivorce Family: Children, Parenting, and Society.* Thousand Oaks, CA: Sage Publications.

Emery, Robert E., and Peter Dillon. 1994. "Conceptualizing the Divorce Process: Renegotiating Boundaries of Intimacy and Power in the Divorced Family System." *Family Relations* 43:374–79.

Engels, Friedrick. [1884] 1972. *The Origin of the Family, Private Property and the State.* New York: International Publishers.

Entwisle, Doris R., and K. L. Alexander. 2000. "Diversity in Family Structure: Effects on Schooling." Pp. 316–37 in *Handbook of Family Diversity,* edited by D. H. Demo, K. R. Allen, and M. A. Fine. New York: Oxford University Press.

Entwisle, Doris R., and Susan G. Doering. 1981. *The First Birth: A Family Turning Point.* Baltimore: Johns Hopkins University Press.

Erikson, Erik K. 1963. *Childhood and Society,* 2nd ed. New York: W. W. Norton.

————. 1968. *Identity: Youth and Crisis.* New York: W. W. Norton.

Erikson, Kai T. 1966. *Wayward Puritans: A Study in the Sociology of Deviance.* New York: John Wiley and Sons.

Ernulf, Kurt E., Sune M. Innala, and Frederick L. Whitam. 1989. "Biological Explanation, Psychological Explanation, and Tolerance of Homosexuals: A Cross-National Analysis of Beliefs and Attitudes." *Psychological Reports* 65:1003–10.

Eshleman, J. Ross. 1994. *The Family: An Introduction,* 7th ed. Boston: Allyn and Bacon.

Esterbrook, Gregg. 2000. "Abortion and Brain Waves." *The New Republic,* January 1.

Estioko-Griffin, Agnes, and P. Bion Griffin. 1981. "Woman the Hunter: The Agta." Pp. 121–151 in *Woman the Gatherer,* edited by Frances Dahlberg. New Haven: Yale University Press.

Etaugh, Claire, and Joan Malstrom. 1981. "The Effect of Marital Status on Person Perception." *Journal of Marriage and the Family* 43:801–05.

Etzioni, Amitai. 1977. "The Family: Is It Obsolete?" *Journal of Current Social Issues* 14:4–9.

Everett, Craig A., ed. 1992. *Divorce and the Next Generation: Effects on Young Adults' Patterns of Intimacy and Expectations for Marriage.* New York: Haworth Press.

F

Facts in Brief: Abortion in the United States. 1992. New York: Alan Guttmacher Institute.

Fairchild, Henry Pratt. 1970. *Dictionary of Sociology and Related Sciences.* Totowa, NJ: Helix Books.

Faison, Karin J., Sandra Faria, and Deborah Frank. 1999. "Caregivers of Chronically Ill Elderly: Perceived Burden." *Journal of Community Health Nursing* 16(4):243–53.

Faltermayer, Edmund. 1990. "Who Are the Rich?" *Fortune* 122:95–96 Ff.

Falk, Patricia J. 1994. "The Gap between Psychosocial Assumptions and Empirical Research in Lesbian-Mother Child Custody Cases." Pp. 131–56 in *Redefining Families: Implications for Children's Development,* edited by Adele Eskeles Gottfried and Allen W. Gottfried. New York: Plenum.

Faludi, Susan. 1991. *Backlash: The Undeclared War Against American Women.* New York: Crown Publishers.

Family Caregiver Alliance Clearinghouse. 1998. www.caregiver.org/factsheets/caregiver_stats.html.

Famighetti, Robert, ed. 1993. *The World Almanac and Book of Facts 1994.* Mahwah, NJ: Funk & Wagnalls.

Farber, Bernard. 1964. *Family: Organization and Interaction.* San Francisco: Chandler.

Farley, Reynolds, and Walter R. Allen. 1987. *The Color Line and the Quality of Life in America.* New York: Russell Sage Foundation.

Farley, Reynolds, and S. Bianchi. 1991. "The Growing Racial Differences in Marriage and Family Patterns." Pp. 5–22 in *The Black Family,* edited by Robert Staples. Belmont, CA: Wadsworth.

Farrell, Michael P., and Stanley D. Rosenberg. 1981. *Men at Midlife.* Boston: Auburn House.

Farrell, Warren. 1993. *The Myth of Male Power: Why Men Are the Disposable Sex*. New York: Simon and Schuster.

Fasick, Frank A. 1994. "On the 'Invention' of Adolescence." *Journal of Early Adolescence* 14:6–23.

Fathalla, Mahmoud F. 1994. "From Family Planning to Reproductive Health." Pp. 144–49 in *Beyond the Numbers: A Reader on Population, Consumption, and the Environment*, edited by Laurie Ann Mazur. Washington, DC: Island Press.

Featherman, David L., and Robert Hauser. 1978. *Opportunity and Change*. New York: Academic Press.

Federal Bureau of Investigation. (1998). *Crime in the United States: Uniform Crime Reports*. Washington, DC: U. S. Department of Justice.

Feeney, Griffith, Feng Wang, Mingkun Zhou, and Baoyu Xiao. 1989. "Recent Fertility Dynamics in China: Results from the 1987 One Percent Population Survey." *Population and Development Review* 15:297–322.

Feldman, S. Shirley. 1987. "Predicting Strain in Mothers and Fathers of Six-Month-Old Infants: A Short-Term Longitudinal Study." In *Men's Transitions to Parenthood*, edited by Phyllis W. Berman and Frank A. Pederson. Hillsdale, NJ: Erlbaum.

Felson, Richard B., and Mary Z. Zielinski. 1989. "Children's Self-Esteem and Parental Support." *Journal of Marriage and the Family* 51:727–35.

Feminists, The. 1974. "The Feminists: A Political Organization to Annihilate Sex Roles." Pp. 101–10 in *Social Problems: The Contemporary Debates*, edited by John B. Williamson, Jerry F. Boren, and Linda Evans. Boston: Little, Brown.

Fergusson, David M., L. John Horwood, and Michael Lloyd. 1990. "The Effect of Preschool Children on Family Stability." *Journal of Marriage and the Family* 52:531–38.

Fergusson, David M., L. John Horwood, and Michael T. Lynsky. 1994. "Parental Separation, Adolescent Psychopathology, and Problem Behaviors." *Journal of the American Academy of Child and Adolescent Psychiatry* 33:1122–31.

Ferree, Myra Marx. 1976. "The Confused American Housewife." *Psychology Today* 10 (September):76–80.

———. 1991. "The Gender Division of Labor in Two-Earner Marriages." *Journal of Family Issues* 12:158–80.

Ferree, Myra Marx, and Patricia Yancey Martin (eds.). 1995. *Feminist Organizations: Harvest of the New Women's Movement*. Philadelphia: Temple University Press.

Field, Mark G. 1968. "Workers (and Mothers): Soviet Women Today." Pp. 7–50 in *The Role and Status of Women in the Soviet Union*, edited by Donald R. Grown. New York: Teacher's College Press.

Fincham, Frank, Steven R. H. Beach, Thom Moore, and Carol Diener. 1994. "The Professional Response to Child Sexual Abuse: Whose Interests Are Served?" *Family Relations* 43:244–54.

Fine, Mark A., Marilyn Coleman, and Lawrence H. Ganong. 1998. "Consistency in Perceptions of the Step-Parent Role Among Step-Parents, Parents and Stepchildren." *Journal of Social and Personal Relationships* 15(6):810–28.

Fine, Mark A., Brenda W. Donnelly, and Patricia Voydanoff. 1991. "The Relationhsip between Adolescents' Perception of Their Family Lives and the Adjustment in Stepfather Families." *Journal of Adolescent Research* 6:423–36.

Fine, Mark A., and Lawrence A. Kurdek. 1992. "The Adjustment of Adolescents in Stepfather and Stepmother Families." *Journal of Marriage and the Family* 54:725–36.

Fine, Mark A., Patricia Voydanoff, and Brenda W. Donnelly. 1993. "Relations between Parental Control and Warmth and Child Well-Being in Stepfamilies." *Journal of Family Psychology* 7:222–32.

Fineman, Martha. 1989. "Societal Factors Affecting the Creation of Legal Rules for Distribution of Property and Divorce." *Family Law Quarterly* 23:279–99.

Finkelhor, David. 1979. *Sexually Victimized Children*. New York: Free Press.

———. 1984. *Child Sexual Abuse: New Theories and Research*. New York: Free Press.

———. 1993. "The Main Problem Is Still Underreporting, Not Overreporting." Pp. 273–88 in *Current Controversies on Family Violence*, edited by Richard J. Gelles and Donileen R. Loseke. Newbury Park, CA: Sage.

Fisher, Helen. 1992. *Anatomy of Love: The Mysteries of Mating, Marriage, and Why We Stay*. New York: Fawcett Columbine.

Fisher, Wesley A. 1980. *The Soviet Marriage Market*. Cambridge, MA: Harvard University Press.

Fisher, Bonnie S., Francis T. Cullen, and Michael G. Turner. 2000. "The Sexual Victimization of College Women." U.S. Department of Justice, Bureau of Justice Statistics. http://www.ncjrs.org/pdffiles1/nij/182369.pdf.

Fishman, Barbara. 1983. "The Economic Behavior of Stepfamilies." *Family Relations* 32:359–66.

Fitzgerald, Bridget. 1999. "Children of Lesbian and Gay Parents: A Review of the Literature." *Marriage and Family Review* 19(1):57–75.

Fitzpatrick, Mary Anne. 1988. *Between Husbands and Wives: Communication in Marriage*. Newbury Park, CA: Sage.

Flaherty, Sr. Mary Jean, Lorna Facteau, and Patricia Garver. 1991. "Grandmother Functions in Multi-Generational Families: An Exploratory Study of Black Adolescent Mothers and Their Infants." Pp. 192–200 in *The Black Family*, edited by Robert Staples. Belmont, CA: Wadsworth.

Flanzer, Jerry P. 1993. "Alcohol and Other Drugs Are Key Causal Agents of Violence." Pp. 171–81 in *Current Controversies on Family Violence*, edited by Richard J. Gelles and Donileen R. Loseke. Newbury Park, CA: Sage.

Flemons, Douglas G. 1989. "An Ecosystemic View of Family Violence." *Family Therapy* 16:1–10.

Flynn, Clifton P. 1999. "Exploring the Link Between Corporal Punishment and Children's Cruelty to Animals." *Journal of Marriage and the Family* 61(4):971–81.

———. 2000. "Woman's Best Friend: Pet Abuse and the Role of Companion Animals in the Lives of Battered Women." *Violence Against Women* 6(2):162–77.

Foeman, Anita Kathy, and Teresa Nance. 1999. "From Miscegenation to Multiculturalism: Perceptions and Stages of Interracial Relationship Development." *Journal of Black Studies* 29:4, 540–57.

Foley, Vincent D. 1989. "Family Therapy." Pp. 46–87 in *Current Psychotherapies*, 4th ed., edited by Raymond J. Corsini and Danny Wedding. Itasca, IL: F. E. Peacock.

Ford, Clellan A., and Frank A. Beach. 1951. *Patterns of Sexual Behavior*. New York: Harper & Row.

Forste, Renate, and Koray Tanfer. 1996. "Sexual Exclusivity Among Dating, Cohabiting, and Married Women." *Journal of Marriage and the Family* 58:33–37.

Foshee, Vangie A., Karl I. Bauman, and G. Fletcher Linder. 1999. "Family Violence and the Perpetration of Adolescent Dating Violence: Examining Social Learning and Social Control Processes." *Journal of Marriage and the Family* 61:331–42.

Foster, Lawrence. 1991. *Women, Family and Utopia: Communal Experiments of the Shakers, the Oneida Community, and the Mormons*. Syracuse: Syracuse University Press.

Fox, A. 1974. *Beyond Contract: Work, Power, and Trust Relations*. London: Faber & Faber.

Fox, Greer Litton, and Velma McBride Murray. 2000. "Gender and Families: Feminist Perspectives and Family Research." *Journal of Marriage and the Family* 62:1160–72.

Frazier, E. Franklin. 1957. *The Negro Family in the United States*, rev. ed. New York: Macmillan.

Freed, Stanley A., and Ruth S. Freed. 1993. "One Son Is No Sons." Pp. 166–170 in *Culture and Human Sexuality*, edited by David N. Suggs and Andrew W. Miracle. Pacific Grove, CA: Brooks/Cole.

Freeman, Derek. 1983. *Margaret Mead and Samoa: The Making and Unmaking of an Anthropological Myth*. Cambridge, MA: Harvard University Press.

———. 1989. "Fa'apua'a Fa'amu and Margaret Mead." *American Anthropologist* 91:1017–22.

———. 1999. "On the Ethics of Skeptical Inquiry." *Skeptical Inquirer* 23:3, 60–61.

Freud, Sigmund. [1913] 1950. *Totem and Taboo*. Translated by James Strachly. London: Routledge and Kegan Paul.

———. [1930] 1961. *Civilization and Its Discontents*. Translated by James Strachly. New York: W. W. Norton.

———. [1953] 1974. *The Standard Edition of the Complete Psychological Works of Sigmund Freud*, rev. ed. Translated by J. Strachly in collaboration with Anna Freud, Alex Strachly, and Alan Tyson. London: Hogarth Press and the Institute of Psychoanalysis.

Frieze, Irene Hanson. 2000. "Violence in Close Relationships—Development of a Research Area: Comment on Archer." *Psychological Bulletin* 126(5):681–84.

Fugita, Stephen S., and David J. O'Brien. 1985. "Structural Assimilation, Ethnic Group Membership, and Political Participation Among Japanese Americans: A Research Note." *Social Forces* 63:986–95.

Fumento, Michael. 1989. *The Myth of Heterosexual AIDS*. New York: Basic Books.

Funder, K., M. Harrison, and R. Weston. 1993. *Settling Down: Pathways of Parents After Divorce*. Melbourne, Australia: Australian Institute of Family Studies.

Furstenberg, Frank F., Jr. 1980. "Reflections on Remarriage: Introduction to *Journal of Family Issues* Special Issue on Remarriage." *Journal of Family Issues* 1:443–53.

———. 1987. "The New Extended Family: The Experience of Parents and Children after Remarriage." Pp. 42–61 in *Remarriage and Stepparenting*, edited by Kay Pasley and Marilyn Ihinger-Tallman. New York: Guilford.

———. 1990. "Divorce and the American Family." *Annual Review of Sociology* 16:379–403.

Furstenberg, Frank F., Jr., Roberta Herceg-Baron, Judy Shea, and David Webb. 1984. "Family Communication and Teenagers' Contraceptive Use." *Family Planning Perspectives* 16:163–70.

Furstenberg, Frank F., and Graham B. Spanier. 1984. *Recycling the Family: Remarriage After Divorce*. Beverly Hills, CA: Sage.

G

Gabaccia, Donna R. 1993. "Southern Europeans." Pp. 783–94 in *Encyclopedia of American Social History, Vol. II*, edited by

Mary Kupiec Cayton, Elliott J. Gorn, and Peter W. Williams. New York: Charles Scribner's Sons.

Gagnon, John H. 1977. *Human Sexualities*. Glenview, IL: Scott, Foresman and Company.

Gallagher, Sally K. 1994. "Doing Their Share: Comparing Patterns of Help Given by Older and Younger Adults." *Journal of Marriage and the Family* 56:567–78.

Gallup, George, Jr., and Frank Newport. 1990a. "Americans Widely Disagree on What Constitutes 'Rich.'" *The Gallup Poll Monthly* 298:28–29.

_____. 1990b. "Americans Ignorant of Basic Census Facts." *The Gallup Poll Monthly* 294:11–13.

Gallup, George, Jr., and F. Newport. 1990. "Virtually All Adults Want Children, But Many of the Reasons Are Intangible." *The Gallup Poll Monthly* 8:9–22.

_____. 1996. "Which Sex Baby Would You Prefer?" *The Gallup Poll Monthly* (March) 5:3.

Gambino, Richard. 1974. *Blood of My Blood*. New York: Doubleday and Co.

Gander, Anita Moore. 1991. "After the Divorce: Familial Factors That Predict Well-Being for Older and Younger Persons." *Journal of Divorce and Remarriage* 15:175–92.

Gannett News Service. 1994. "Gender Gap Closing: A Woman Now Earns 71 Cents to Man's Dollar." *The Salt Lake Tribune*, February 24, P. 6A.

Ganong, Lawrence H., and Marilyn Coleman. 1994. *Remarried Family Relationships*. Thousand Oaks, CA: Sage.

Ganong, Lawrence H., Marilyn Coleman, Annette Kusgen McDaniel, and Tim Killian. 1998. "Attitudes Regarding Obligations to Assist an Older Parent or Stepparent Following Later-Life Remarriage." *Journal of Marriage and the Family* 60:595–610.

Ganong, Lawrence H., Marilyn Coleman, and Deborah Mistrina. 1995. "Home Is Where They Have to Let You In: Beliefs Regarding Physical Custody Changes of Children Following Divorce." *Journal of Family Issues* 16:466–87.

Ganong, Lawrence H., Marilyn Coleman, Aaron Thompson, and Chanel Goodwin-Watkins. 1996. "African American and European American College Students' Expectations for Self and for Future Partners." *Journal of Family Issues* 17(6):758–75.

Gans, Herbert J. 1962. *The Urban Villagers: Group and Class in the Life of Italian-Americans*. New York: The Free Press.

_____. 1979. "Symbolic Ethnicity: The Future of Ethnic Groups and Cultures in America." In *On the Making of Americans: Essays in Honor of David Riesman*, edited by Herbert Gans et al. Philadelphia: University of Pennsylvania Press.

Garbarino, James. 1992. *Future as If It Really Mattered*. Chicago: Noble Press.

Gardner, Jane, and Thomas Wiedeman. 1991. *The Roman Household: A Sourcebook*. New York: Routledge.

Gardner, Robert W., Bryant Robey, and Peter C. Smith. 1995. "Asian Americans: Growth, Change, and Diversity." *Population Bulletin, Vol. 40*. Washington, DC: Population Reference Bureau.

Gecas, Viktor, and Michael L. Schwalbe. 1986. "Parental Behavior and Adolescent Self-Esteem." *Journal of Marriage and the Family* 48:37–46.

Gee, Ellen M. 1992. "Only Children as Adult Women: Life Course Events and Timing." *Social Indicators Research* 26:183–97.

Gelles, Richard J. 1976. "Abused Wives: Why Do They Stay?" *Journal of Marriage and the Family* 38:659–68.

Gelles, Richard J. 1979. *Family Violence*. Newbury Park, CA: Sage.

_____. 1983. "An Exchange/Social Control Theory of Intrafamily Violence." Pp. 151–65 in *The Dark Side of Families: Current Family Violence Research*, edited by David Finkelhor, Richard J. Gelles, Gerald Hotaling, and Murray A. Straus. Beverly Hills, CA: Sage.

_____. 1990. "Violence and Pregnancy: Are Pregnant Women at Greater Risk of Abuse?" Pp. 279–86 in *Physical Violence in American Families: Risk Factors and Adaptations to Violence in 8,145 Families*, edited by Murray A. Straus and Richard J. Gelles. New Brunswick, NJ: Transaction Publishers.

_____. 1993. "Alcohol and Other Drugs Are Associated With Violence—They Are Not Its Cause." Pp. 182–96 in *Current Controversies on Family Violence*, edited by Richard J. Gelles and Donileen R. Loseke. Newbury Park, CA: Sage.

_____. 1995. *Contemporary Families: A Sociological View*. Thousand Oaks, CA: Sage.

_____. 1996. "Intimate and Interpersonal Violence: Politics, Policy and Practice." Paper presented at the National Council on Family Relations annual meeting, Kansas City, MO, November 7. Session #123. NCFL, Minneapolis, MN.

Gelles, Richard J., and Ake Edfeldt. 1986. "Violence Towards Children in the United States and Sweden." *Child Abuse and Neglect: The International Journal* 10:501–10.

Gelles, Richard J., and Donileen R. Loseke, eds. 1993. *Current Controversies on Family Violence*. Newbury Park, CA: Sage.

Gelles, Richard J., and Murray A. Straus. 1987. "Is Violence Toward Children Increasing? A Comparison of 1975 and 1985 National Survey Rates." *Journal of Interpersonal Violence* 2:212–22.

_____. 1988. *The Violent Home.* Newbury Park, CA: Sage.

Gerhart, Barry. 1990. "Gender Differences in Current and Starting Salaries: The Role of Performance, College Major, and Job Title." *Industrial and Labor Relations Review* 43:418–33.

Gibbons, Judith L., Randy R. Richter, Deane C. Wiley, and Deborah A. Stiles. 1996. "Adolescents' Opposite-Sex Ideal in Four Countries." *Journal of Social Psychology* 136(4):531–37.

Giddens, Anthony. 1992. *The Transformation of Intimacy: Sexuality, Love & Eroticism in Modern Societies.* Cambridge: Polity Press.

Gies, Frances, and Joseph Gies. 1987. *Marriage and the Family in the Middle Ages.* New York: Harper & Row.

Gilbert, Dennis, and Joseph A. Kahl. 1993. *The American Class Structure: A New Synthesis*, 3rd ed. Homewood, IL: Dorsey.

Giles-Sims, Jean. 1994. "Comparison of Implications of the Justice and Care Perspectives for Theories of Remarriage and Stepparenting." Pp. 33–50 in *Stepparenting: Issues in Theory, Research, and Practice*, edited by Kay Pasley and Marilyn Ihinger-Tallman. Westport, CT: Greenwood Press.

Gillespie, Dair L. 1971. "Who Has the Power? The Marital Struggle." *Journal of Marriage and the Family* 33:445–58.

Gilligan, Carol. 1982. *In a Different Voice: Psychological Theory and Women's Development.* Cambridge, MA: Harvard University Press.

Giordano, Peggy C., Toni J. Millhollin, and Stephen A. Cernkovich. 1999. "Delinquency, Identity, and Women's Involvement in Relationship Violence." *Criminology* 37(1):17–40.

Glass, Jennifer. 1998. "Gender Liberation, Economic Squeeze, or Fear of Strangers: Why Fathers Provide Infant Care in Dual-Earner Families." *Journal of Marriage and the Family* 60:821–34.

Gladwell, Malcolm. 1995. "Fundamental Ignorance About Numbers." *The Washington Post: National Weekly Edition*, October 16–22, P. 7.

Glenn, Evelyn Nakano. 1987. "Gender and the Family." Pp. 348–80 in *Analyzing Gender: A Handbook of Social Science Research*, edited by Beth Hess and Myra Marx Ferree. Newbury Park, CA: Sage.

Glenn, Norval D. 1975. "Psychological Well-Being in the Post-Parental Stage: Some Evidence From National Surveys." *Journal of Marriage and the Family* 37:105–10.

_____. 1982. "Interreligious Marriage in the United States: Patterns and Recent Trends." *Journal of Marriage and the Family* 44:555–68.

_____. 1990. "Quantitative Research on Marital Quality in the 1980s: A Critical Review." *Journal of Marriage and the Family* 52:818–31.

_____. 1991. "The Recent Trend in Marital Success in the United States." *Journal of Marriage and the Family* 53:261–70.

_____. 1993. "A Plea for Objective Assessment of the Notion of Family Decline." *Journal of Marriage and the Family* 55:542–44.

_____. 1996. "Values, Attitudes, and the State of American Marriage." Pp. 15–34 in *Promises to Keep: Decline and Renewal of Marriage in America*, edited by David Popenoe, Jean Bethke Elshtain, and David Blankenhorn. Lanham, MD: Rowman and Littlefield.

_____. 1998. "The Course of Marital Success and Failure in Five American 10-Year Marriage Cohorts." *Journal of Marriage and the Family* 60:569–76.

_____. 2000. "A Plea for Greater Concern About the Quality of Marital Matching." Paper presented at the Revitalizing the Institution of Marriage for the 21st Century Conference, Provo, UT, March 9–11.

Glenn, Norval D., and Marion Tolbert Coleman. 1988. *Family Relations: A Reader.* Chicago: Dorsey Press.

Glenn, Norval D., Sue Keir Hoppe, and David Weiner. 1974. "Social Class Heterogamy and Marital Success: A Study of the Empirical Adequacy of a Textbook Generalization." *Social Problems* 21:539–50.

Glenn, Norval D., and Michael Supancic. 1984. "The Social and Demographic Correlates of Divorce and Separation in the United States: An Update and Reconsideration." *Journal of Marriage and the Family* 46:563–75.

Glenn, Norval D., and Charles N. Weaver. 1977. "The Marital Happiness of Remarried Divorced Persons." *Journal of Marriage and the Family* 39:331–37.

Glick, Paul C. 1990. "American Families: As They Are and Were." *Sociology and Social Research.* 74:139–45.

Glick, Paul C., and Arthur J. Norton. 1979. "Marrying, Divorcing, and Living Together in the U.S. Today." *Population Bulletin* 32(5):1–39. Washington, DC: Population Reference Bureau.

Glick, Paul C., and Graham Spanier. 1980. "Married and Unmarried Cohabitation in the United States." *Journal of Marriage and the Family* 42:19–30.

Goffman, Erving, 1959. *The Presentation of Self in Everyday Life.* Garden City, NY: Doubleday.

_____. 1963. *Stigma: Notes on the Management of Spoiled Identity.* Englewood Cliffs, NJ: Prentice-Hall.

_____. 1967. *Interaction Ritual.* Garden City, NJ: Doubleday.

Goldberg, Carey. 2000. "Same-Sex Unions Draw Couples to Vt. From Afar." *The Denver Post*, July 23, P. 8A.

Goldberg, Gertrude Schaffner, and Eleanor Kremen. 1990. *The Feminization of Poverty: Only in America?* New York: Praeger.

Goldberg, Steven. 1973. *The Inevitability of Patriarchy*. New York: Morrow.

Golden, J. 1975. "Patterns of Negro-White Intermarriage." Pp. 9–16 in *Black Male/White Female*, edited by D. L. Wilkinson. Morristown, NJ: General Learning Press.

Goldschieder, Calvin. 1992. *Fertility Transition, Family Structure, and Population Policy*. Boulder, CO: Westview Press.

Goldscheider, Frances K. 1990. "The Aging of the Gender Revolution: What Do We Know and What Do We Need to Know?" *Research on Aging* 12:531–45.

Goldscheider, Frances K., and Calvin Goldscheider. 1989. "Family Structure and Conflict: Nest-Leaving Expectations of Young Adults and Their Parents." *Journal of Marriage and the Family* 51:87–97.

_____. 1991. "The Intergenerational Flow of Income: Family Structure and the Status of Black Americans." *Journal of Marriage and the Family* 53:499–508.

_____. 1998. "The Effects of Childhood Family Structure on Leaving and Returning Home." *Journal of Marriage and the Family* 60:745–56.

Goldthorpe, John. 1983. "Women and Class Analysis: In Defence of the Conventional View." *Sociology* 17:465–88.

_____. 1984. "Women and Class Analysis: Reply to the Replies." *Sociology* 18:491–99.

Gonzales, Marti Hope, and Sarah A. Meyers. 1993. "'Your Mother Would Like Me': Self-Presentation in the Personal Ads of Heterosexual and Homosexual Men and Women." *Personality and Social Psychology Bulletin* 19:131–42.

Goode, Erich. 1996. "Gender and Courtship Entitlement: Responses to Personal Ads." *Sex Roles* 343:3–4, 141–69.

_____. 1998. "Photographs as Sexual Advertisements: Responses to Personal Ads." *Sociological Focus* 31:4, 373–89.

Goode, William J. 1956. *After Divorce*. New York: Free Press.

_____. 1963, 1970. *World Revolution and Family Patterns*. New York: Free Press.

_____. 1964. *The Family*. Englewood Cliffs, NJ: Prentice-Hall.

_____. 1971. "Force and Violence in the Family." *Journal of Marriage and the Family* 33:624–36.

_____. 1993. *World Changes in Divorce Patterns*. New Haven: Yale University Press.

Gordon, Michael. 1981. "Was Waller Ever Right? The Rating and Dating Complex Reconsidered." *Journal of Marriage and the Family* 43:67–76.

Gordon, Tuula. 1994. *Single Women: On the Margins?* New York: New York University Press.

Gornick, Janet C., Marcia K. Meyers, and Katherin E. Ross. 1998. "Public Policies and the Employment of Mothers: A Cross-National Study." *Social Science Quarterly* 79(1):35–54.

Gottfried, Adele, Kay Bathurst, and Allen W. Gottfried. 1994. "Role of Maternal and Dual-Earner Employment Status in Children's Development: A Longitudinal Study from Infancy through Early Adolescence." Pp. 55–97 in *Redefining Families: Implications for Children's Development*, edited by Adele Eskeles Gottfried and Allen W. Gottfried. New York: Plenum Press.

Gottman, John. 1994. *Why Marriages Succeed or Fail*. New York: Simon and Schuster.

Gottman, John M., and Clifford I. Notarius. 2000. "Decade Review: Observing Marital Interaction." *Journal of Marriage and the Family* 62:927–47.

Gottman, John M., James Coan, Sybil Carrere, and Catherine Swanson. 1998. "Predicting Marital Happiness and Stability from Newlywed Interactions." *Journal of Marriage and the Family* 60:5–22.

Gough, Kathleen. 1960. "Is the Family Universal: The Nayar Case." Pp. 76–92 in *A Modern Introduction to the Family*, edited by Norman Bell and Ezra F. Vogel. New York: Free Press.

_____. 1992. "The Origin of the Family." Pp. 23–39 in *Family in Transition: Rethinking Marriage, Sexuality, Child Rearing, and Family Organization*, 7th ed., edited by Arlene S. Skolnick and Jerome H. Skolnick. New York: HarperCollins.

Gouldner, Alvin W. 1960. "The Norm of Reciprocity." *American Sociological Review* 25:161–78.

_____. 1970. *The Coming Crisis of Western Sociology*. New York: Avon Books.

Gove, Walter R. 1972. "Sex, Marital Status and Suicide." *Journal of Health and Social Behavior* 13:204–13.

Gove, Walter R., Carolyn Briggs Style, and Michael Hughes. 1990. "The Effect of Marriage on the Well-Being of Adults." *Journal of Family Issues* 11:4–35.

Graham, Lawrence Otis. 1999. *Our Kind of People: Inside America's Black Upper Class*. New York: HarperCollins.

Graham, Mary, Julie L. Hotchkiss, and Berry Gerhart. "Discrimination by Parts: A Fixed-Effects Analysis of Starting Pay Differences Across Gender." *Eastern Economic Journal* 26(1):9–19.

Grant, Nicole J. 1995. "From Margaret Mead's Field Notes: What Counted as 'Sex' in Samoa?" *American Anthropologist* 97:678–82.

Gray, Jeffrey S., and Michel J. Vanderhart. 2000. "On the Determination of Wages: Does Marriage Matter?" Pp. 356–67 in *The Tie That Binds: Perspectives on Marriage and Cohabitation*, edited by Linda J. Waite. New York: Aldine de Gruyter.

Gray-Little, Bernadette. 1982. "Marital Quality and Power Processes Among Black Couples." *Journal of Marriage and the Family* 44:633–46.

Graziano, Anthony M. 1996. "Book Review of *Beating the Devil Out of Them: Corporal Punishment in American Families* by Murray A. Straus." *Journal of Marriage and the Family* 58:1039–40.

Greeff, Abraham P., and Tanya de Bruyne. 2000. "Conflict Management Style and Marital Satisfaction." *Journal of Sex and Marital Therapy* 26(4):321–34.

Greeley, Andrew. 1971. *Why Can't They Be Like Us?* New York: Wiley.

————. 1974. *Ethnicity in the United States: A Preliminary Reconnaissance*. New York: John Wiley and Sons.

Greeley, Andrew M., R. T. Michael, and T. W. Smith. 1990. "Americans and Their Sexual Partners." *Society* (July/August): 36–42.

Greenberg, J., and M. Becker. 1988. "Aging Parents as Family Resources." *The Gerontologist* 28:876–91.

Greenleaf, Barbara Kaye. 1978. *Children Through the Ages: A History of Childhood*. New York: Barnes & Noble.

Greenstein, Robert, Jim Jaffee, and Toni Kayatin. 1999. "Low Unemployment, Rising Wages Fuel Poverty Decline." *Center on Budget and Policy Priorities*. www.cbpp.org/9–30–99pov.htm.

Greenstein, Theodore N. 1990. "Marital Disruption and the Employment of Married Women." *Journal of Marriage and the Family* 52:657–76.

————. 1995. "Gender Ideology, Marital Disruption, and the Employment of Married Women." *Journal of Marriage and the Family* 57:31–42.

————. 1996. "Husbands' Participation in Domestic Labor: Interactive Effects of Wives' and Husbands' Gender Ideologies." *Journal of Marriage and the Family* 58:585–95.

————. 2000. "Economic Dependence, Gender, and the Division of Labor in the Home: A Replication and Extension." *Journal of Marriage and the Family* 62:322–35.

Greil, Arthur L., Thomas A. Leitke, and Karen L. Porter. 1988. "Infertility: His and Hers." *Gender and Society* 2:172–99.

Grizzle, Gary L. 1999. "Institutionalization and Family Unity: An Exploratory Study of Cherlin's (1978) Views." *Journal of Divorce and Remarriage* 30(3–4):125–37.

Gross, Harriet Engle. 1980. "Dual-Career Couples Who Live Apart: Two Types." *Journal of Marriage and the Family* 42:567–76.

Grossberg, Michael. 1983. "Who Gets the Child? Custody, Guardianship, and the Rise of a Judicial Patriarchy in Nineteenth-Century America." *Feminist Studies* 9:235–60.

Grossman, Frances Kaplan, L. S. Eichler, and S. A. Winikoff. 1980. *Pregnancy, Birth and Parenthood*. San Francisco: Jossey-Bass.

Groze, Victor K. 1996. *Successful Adoptive Families: A Longitudinal Study of Special Needs Adoption*. Westport, CT: Praeger.

Gruber, James E., and Lars Bjorn. 1986. "Women's Responses to Sexual Harassment: An Analysis of Sociocultural, Organizational, and Personal Resource Models." *Social Science Quarterly* 67:814–26.

Gryl, Frances E., Sandra M. Stith, and Gloria W. Bird. 1991. "Close Dating Relationships among College Students: Differences by Use of Violence and Gender." *Journal of Social and Personal Relationships* 8:243–64.

Gutman, Herbert G. 1976. *The Black Family in Slavery and Freedom, 1750–1925*. New York: Pantheon.

Gutmann, Joseph, and Amnon Lazar. 1998. "Mother's or Father's Custody: Does It Matter for Social Adjustment?" *Educational Psychology* 18(2):225–34.

Gwartney-Gibbs, Patricia A., Jean Stockard, and Susanne Bohmer. 1987. "Learning Courtship Aggression: The Influence of Parents, Peers, and Personal Experiences." *Family Relations* 36:276–82.

H

Haaga, David A. F. 1991. "Homophobia." *Journal of Social Behavior and Personality* 6:171–74.

Haas, Linda. 1992. *Equal Parenthood and Social Policy: A Study of Parental Leave in Sweden*. Albany: State University of New York Press.

Haas, Stephen M., and Laura Stafford. 1998. "An Initial Examination of Maintenance Behaviors in Gay and Lesbian Relationships." *Journal of Social & Personal Relationships* 15:846–55.

Hackney, Harold L., and L. Sherilyn Cormier. 1996. *The Professional Counselor: A Process Guide to Helping*. Boston: Allyn and Bacon.

Halfpenny, Peter, and Peter McMylor. 1994. *Positivist Sociology and Its Critics*. Brookfield, VT: E. Elgar Publishing.

Hall, T. 1987. "Infidelity and Women: Shifting Patterns." *New York Times*, June 1, P. B8.

Halle, David. 1984. *America's Working Man, Work, Home, and Politics among Blue-Collar Property Owners*. Chicago: University of Chicago Press.

Handwerker, W. Penn. 1986. "Culture and Reproduction: Exploring Micro/Macro Linkages." Pp. 1–29 in *Culture and Reproduction: An Anthropological Critique of Demographic Transition Theory*, edited by W. Penn Handwerker. Boulder, CO: Westview Press.

Hannaford, Ivan. 1994. "The Idiocy of Race." *The Wilson Quarterly* 18(2):8–35.

Hansen, Marsali. 1993. "Feminism and Family Therapy: A Review of Feminist Critiques of Approaches to Family Violence." Pp. 69–81 in *Battering and Family Therapy: A Feminist Perspective*, edited by Marsali Hansen and Michele Harway. Newbury Park, CA: Sage.

Hansen, Marsali, and Irene Goldenberg. 1993. "Conjoint Therapy With Violent Couples: Some Valid Considerations." Pp. 82–91 in *Battering and Family Therapy: A Feminist Perspective*, edited by Marsali Hansen and Michele Harway. Newbury Park, CA: Sage.

Haraway, Donna. 1990. *Primate Visions: Gender, Race and Nature in the World of Modern Science*. New York: Routledge.

Hareven, Tamara K. 1987. "Historical Analysis of the Family." Pp. 37–57 in *Handbook of Marriage and the Family*, edited by Marvin B. Sussman and Suzanne K. Steinmetz. New York: Plenum.

_____. 1997. "Continuity and Change in American Family Life." Pp. 29–36 in *Family in Transition*, edited by Arlene S. Skolnick and Jerome H. Skolnick. New York: Longman.

Harjo, Suzan Shown. 1999. "The American Indian Experience." Pp. 63–71 in *Family Ethnicity: Strength in Diversity*, 2nd ed., edited by Hariette Pipes McAdoo. Thousand Oaks, CA: Sage.

Harkins, Elizabeth. 1978. "Effects of Empty Nest Transition on Self-Report of Psychological and Physical Well-Being." *Journal of Marriage and the Family* 40:549–56.

Harkness, Sara, Charles M. Super, and Constance H. Keefer. 1992. "Learning to be an American Parent: How Cultural Models Gain Directive Force." Pp. 163–78 in *Human Motives and Cultural Models*, edited by Roy D'Andrade and Claudia Strauss. Cambridge: Cambridge University Press.

Harlow, Caroline Wolf. 1991. "Female Victims of Violent Crime." Washington, DC: U.S. Department of Justice.

Harmatz, Morton G., and Melinda A. Novak. 1983. *Human Sexualities*. New York: Harper & Row.

Harris, Marvin. 1987. *Why Nothing Works: The Anthropology of Daily Life*. New York: Touchstone.

Harrison, Maureen, and Steve Gilbert, eds. 1992. *Landmark Decisions of the Supreme Court, Vol. 3*. Beverly Hills, CA: Excellent Books.

Harry, Joseph. 1983. "Gay Male and Lesbian Relationships." Pp. 216–34 in *Contemporary Families and Alternative Lifestyles: Handbook on Research and Theory*, edited by Eleanor D. Macklin and Roger H. Rubin. Newbury Park, CA: Sage.

Harvey, David L. 1993. *Potter Addition: Poverty, Family, and Kinship in a Heartland Community*. New York: Aldine de Gruyter.

Hassan, Fekri A. 1973. "On Mechanisms of Population Growth During the Neolithic." *Current Anthropology* 14:535–42.

Hatcher, Robert A., F. Stewart, J. Trussell, D. Kowal, F. Guest, G. K. Stewart, and W. Cates. 1990. *Contraceptive Technology 1990–1992*, 5th ed. New York: Irvington.

Hatcher, R. A., J. Trussell, F. H. Stewart, G. K. Stewart, D. Kowal, F. J. Guest, W. Cates, and M. S. Policar. 1994. *Contraceptive Technology*, 6th ed. New York: Irvington.

Hatcher, Richard, et al. 1998. *Contraceptive Technology*, 7th ed. Decatur, GA: Ardent Media.

Hatfield, Elaine. 1988. "Passionate and Companionate Love." Pp. 191–217 in *The Psychology of Love*, edited by Robert J. Sternberg and Michael L. Barnes. New Haven, CT: Yale University Press.

Hatfield, Elaine, and Richard L. Rapson. 1987. "Passionate Love: New Directions in Research." Pp. 109–39 in *Advances in Personal Relationships, Vol. 1*, edited by Warren H. Jones and Daniel Perlman. Greenwich, CT: JAI.

Hatfield, Elaine, and G. William Walster. 1978. *A New Look at Love*. Lantham, MA: University Press of America.

Haub, Carl, and Diana Cornelius. 1999. *World Population Data Sheet*. Washington, DC: Population Reference Bureau.

Haub, Carl, and Martha Farnsworth Riche. 1994. "Population by the Numbers: Trends in Population Growth and Structure." Pp. 95–108 in *Beyond the Numbers: A Reader on Population, Consumption, and the Environment*, edited by Laurie Ann Mazur. Washington, DC: Island Press.

Haub, Carl, and Machiko Yanagishita. 1996. *World Population Data Sheet*. Washington, DC: Population Reference Bureau.

Hauser, Robert M., and David L. Featherman. 1977. *The Process of Stratification: Trends and Analysis*. New York: Academic Press.

Hauser, St., M. A. B. Vieyra, A. M. Jacobson, and D. Wertlieb. 1989. "Family Aspects of Vulnerability and Resilience in Adolescence: A Theoretical Perspective." Pp. 103–33 in *The Child in Our Times: Studies in the Development of Resiliency*. New York: Brunner/Mazel.

Havighurst, Robert J. 1953. *Human Development and Education.* New York: Academic Press.

Hawkins, Alan J., Christina M. Marshall, and Kathryn M. Meiners. 1995. "Exploring Wives' Sense of Fairness About Family Work: An Initial Test of the Distributive Justice Framework." *Journal of Family Issues* 16:693–721.

Hayes, Cheryl D., ed. 1987. *Risking the Future: Adolescent Sexuality, Pregnancy, and Childbearing, Vol. 1.* Washington, DC: National Academy Press.

Haynes, Faustina E. 2000. "Gender and Family Ideals: An Exploratory Study of Black Middle-Class Americans." *Journal of Family Issues* 21(7):811–37.

Health and Human Services Department. 1996. "The HHS Poverty Guidelines: One Version of the [U.S.] Federal Poverty Measure." http://www.os.dhhs.gov/progorg/aspe/poverty/poverty.html.

Heaton, Tim B. 1993. "Comment on 'Premarital Sex and the Risk of Divorce.'" *Journal of Marriage and the Family* 55:240–41.

Heaton, Tim B., Cardell K. Jacobson, and Kimberlee Holland. 1999. "Persistence and Change in Decisions to Remain Childless." *Journal of Marriage and the Family* 61:531–39.

Heaton, Tim B., and Edith L. Pratt. 1990. "The Effects of Religious Homogamy on Marital Satisfaction and Stability." *Journal of Family Issues* 11:191–207.

Helin, Etienne. 1971. "Size of Households before the Industrial Revolution: the Cases of Liege in 1801." Pp. 319–34 in *Household and Family in Past Time*, edited by Peter Laslett. Cambridge: Cambridge University Press.

Hendrick, Susan S., and Clyde Hendrick. 1987. "Love and Sex Attitudes and Religious Beliefs." *Journal of Social and Clinical Psychology* 5:391–98.

——————. 1992. *Romantic Love*. Newbury Park, CA: Sage.

Hendrick, Susan S., Clyde Hendrick, and N. L. Adler. 1988. "Romantic Relationships: Love, Satisfaction, and Staying Together." *Journal of Personality and Social Psychology* 54:980–88.

Hennessee, J. A. 1983. "'Monkey See, Monkey Do' Dating." *Psychology Today* 17:74ff.

Henshaw, S. K., and J. Van Vort, eds. 1992. *Abortion Factbook, 1992 Edition: Readings, Trends, and State and Local Data to 1988*. New York: The Alan Guttmacher Institute.

Herbert, Tracy Bennett, Roxane Cohen Silver, and John H. Ellard. 1991. "Coping with an Abusive Relationship: I. How and Why Do Women Stay?" *Journal of Marriage and the Family* 53:311–25.

Herdt, Gilbert H. 1993. "Semen Transactions in Sambia Culture." Pp. 298–328 in *Culture and Human Sexuality: A Reader*, edited by David N. Suggs and Andrew W. Miracle. Pacific Grove, CA: Brooks/Cole.

Herlihy, David. 1985. *Medieval Households*. Cambridge, MA: Harvard University Press.

Hern, Warren. 1991. "Effects of Cultural Change on Fertility in Amazonian Indian Societies: Recent Research and Projections." *Population and Environment* 13:23–44.

Herring, R. D. 1989. "The American Native Family: Dissolution by Coercion." *Journal of Multicultural Counseling and Development* 17(1):4–13.

Hertz, Rosanna, and Joy Charleton. 1989. "Making Family Under a Shiftwork Schedule: Air Force Security Guards and Their Wives." *Social Problems* 36: 491–507.

Hester, Reid K., and William R. Miller, eds. 1995. *Handbook of Alcoholism Treatment Approaches: Effective Alternatives*. Boston: Allyn and Bacon.

Hiedemann, Bridgett, Olga Suhomlinova, and Angela M. O'Rand. 1998. *Journal of Marriage and the Family* 60:219–31.

Higgins, Maura P. 1998. "Alcoholic Families: The Crisis of Early Recovery." *Family Therapy* 25(3):202–19.

Higman, Howard. 1970. "Rings and Things." Class lectures in the sociology department at the University of Colorado.

Hill, Charles T., Zick Rubin, and Letitia A. Peplau. 1976. "Breakups Before Marriage: The End of 103 Affairs." *Journal of Marriage and the Family* 32:147–68.

Hill, Jeffrey, Alan J. Hawkins, Maria Ferris, and Michelle Weitzman. 2001. "Finding an Extra Day a Week: The Positive Influence of Perceived Job Flexibility on Work and Family Life Balance." *Family Relations* 50:49–58.

Hill, Jeffrey, Alan J. Hawkins, and Brent C. Miller. 1996. "Work and Family in the Virtual Office." *Family Relations* 45:293–301.

Hill, Reuben. 1949. *Families Under Stress*. New York: Harper & Row.

——————. 1958. "Generic Features of Families Under Stress." *Social Casework* 39:139–50.

Hill, Reuben, and R. H. Rogers. 1964. "The Developmental Approach." Pp. 171–211 in *Handbook of Marriage and the Family*, edited by H. Christensen. Chicago: Rand-McNally.

Hiller, Dana Vannoy, and Janice Dyehouse. 1987. "A Case for Banishing 'Dual-Career Marriages' from the Research Literature." *Journal of Marriage and the Family* 49:787–95.

Hilton, Jeanne, Laura Baird, and Virginia Haldeman. 1992. "Comparison of Finances, Stress, and Satisfaction in One-Earner and Two-Earner Rural Families." Paper, 54th annual conference, National Council on Family Relations, Orlando, FL.

Hirschi, Travis. 1969. *Causes of Delinquency*. Berkeley: University of California Press.

Ho, Fung Chu, and Ronald C. Johnson. 1990. "Intra-Ethnic and Inter-Ethnic Marriage and Divorce in Hawaii." *Social Biology* 37:44–51.

Hobart, C. 1991. "Conflict in Remarriages." *Journal of Divorce and Remarriage* 15:69–86.

Hochschild, Arlie. 1983. *The Managed Heart*. New York: Viking.

_____. 1989. *The Second Shift: Working Parents and the Revolution at Home*. New York: Viking/Penguin.

_____. 1998. *The Time Bind: When Work Becomes Home and Home Becomes Work*. New York: Owl.

Hodson, Randy, and Teresa A. Sullivan. 1990. *The Social Organization of Work*. Belmont, CA: Wadsworth.

Hoem, Britta, and Jan M. Hoem. 1988. "The Swedish Family: Aspects of Contemporary Developments." *Journal of Family Issues* 9:397–424.

Hofferth, Sandra L., and Cheryl D. Hayes, eds. 1987. *Risking the Future: Adolescent Sexuality, Pregnancy, and Childrearing, Vol. 2*. Washington, DC: National Academy Press.

Hofferth, Sandra L., Joan R. Rahn, and Wendy Baldwin. 1987. "Premarital Sexual Activity Among U.S. Teenage Women Over the Past Three Decades." *Family Planning Perspectives* 19:46–53.

Hoffman, Charles D., and Michelle Moon. 1999. "Women's Characteristics and Gender Role Attitudes: Support for Father Involvement with Children." *The Journal of Genetic Psychology* 160(4):411–18.

Hoffman, Ellen. 1978. "Policy and Politics: The Child Abuse Prevention and Treatment Act." *Public Policy* 26:72.

Hogan, Dennis P., David J. Eggebeen, and Clifford C. Clogg. 1993. "The Structure of Intergenerational Exchanges in American Families." *Social Forces* 68:797–812.

Holden, George W., Pamela C. Miller, and Susan D. Harris. 1999. "The Instrumental Side of Corporal Punishment: Parents' Reported Practices and Outcome Expectancies." *Journal of Marriage and the Family* 61:908–18.

Holtzman, Mellisa, and Jennifer Glass. 1999. "Explaining Changes in Mothers' Job Satisfaction following Childbirth." *Work and Occupations* 26(3):365–404.

Homans, George C. 1961. *Social Behavior: Its Elementary Forms*. New York: Harcourt Brace.

Hood, Jane C. 1986. "The Provider Role: Its Meaning and Measurement." *Journal of Marriage and the Family* 48:349–59.

_____. 1993. *Men, Work, and Family*. Thousand Oaks, CA: Sage.

Hooyman, Nancy. 1995. *Feminist Perspectives on Family Care*. Newbury Park, CA: Sage.

Hooyman, Nancy, and H. Asuman Kiyak. 1993. *Social Gerontology: A Multi-Disciplinary Perspective*, 3rd ed. Boston: Allyn and Bacon.

Hope, Steven, Chris Power, and Bryan Rodgers. 1999. "Does Financial Hardship Account for Elevated Psychological Distress in Lone Mothers?" *Social Science and Medicine* 29:381–89.

Horwitz, Allan V., and Helene Raskin White. 1998. "The Relationship of Cohabitation and Mental Health: A Study of a Young Adult Cohort." *Journal of Marriage and the Family* 60:505–14.

Hotaling, Gerald T., and David B. Sugarman. 1986. "An Analysis of Risk Markers in Husband to Wife Violence: The Current State of Knowledge." *Violence and Victims* 1:101–24.

Houseknecht, Sharon K. 1979. "Childlessness and Marital Adjustment." *Journal of Marriage and the Family* 11:259–65.

Houseknecht, Sharon K., Suzanne Vaughn, and Ann S. Macke. 1984. "Marital Disruption Among Professional Women: The Timing of Career and Family Events." *Social Problems* 31:273–84.

Hoyt, Homer. 1939. *The Structure and Growth of Residential Neighborhoods in American Cities*. Washington, DC: Federal Housing Administration.

Howard, Michael C. 1989. *Contemporary Cultural Anthropology*, 3rd ed. Glenview, IL: Scott, Foresman.

Huber, Charles H., and Patricia G. Driskill. 1993. *Equilibrium Family Therapy: A Basic Guide for the Helping Professions*. New York: Crossroad Publishing.

Hughes, Diane Owen. 1978. "From Brideprice to Dowry in Mediterranean Europe." *Journal of Family History* 3:262–96.

Hughes, Everett. 1945. "Dilemmas and Contradictions of Status." *American Journal of Sociology* 50:132–59.

Hummer, Robert A., Isaac W. Eberstein, and Charles B. Nam. 1992. "Infant Mortality Differentials Among Hispanic Groups in Florida." *Social Forces* 70:1055–75.

Hunt, Morton. 1974. *Sexual Behavior in the Seventies*. Chicago: Playboy Press.

Hupka, R. B. 1991. "The Motive for the Arousal of Romantic Jealousy: Its Cultural Origin." Pp. 252–70 in *The Psychology of Jealousy and Envy*, edited by R. E. Zambrana. Thousand Oaks, CA: Sage.

Hurlbert, David F. 1992. "Factors Influencing a Woman's Decision to End an Extramarital Sexual Relationship." *Journal of Sex and Marital Therapy* 18:104–14.

Hurst, Charles E. 1998. *Social Inequality: Forms, Causes, and Consequences,* 3rd ed. Boston: Allyn and Bacon.

Hurst, Norman, and Stephan B. Hulley. 1988. "Preventing the Heterosexual Spread of AIDS." *JAMA* 259:22–29.

Hutchinson, M. Katherine, and Teresa M. Cooney. 1998. "Patterns of Parent-Teen Sexual Risk Communication: Implication for Intervention." *Family Relations* 47:185–94.

Hutter, Mark. 1999. *The Family Experience: A Reader in Cultural Diversity*, 3rd ed. Boston: Allyn and Bacon.

Huxley, Aldous. 1946. *Brave New World.* New York: Harper & Row.

Hymowitz, Carol, and Michaele Weissman. 1978. *A History of Women in America.* New York: Bantam.

I

Iber, Frank. 1991. *Alcohol and Drug Abuse as Encountered in Office Practice.* Boca Raton, FL: CRC Press.

Inciardi, James A. 1993. *Criminal Justice*, 4th ed. New York: Harcourt Brace Jovanovich.

Ingoldsby, Bron B., and Suzanna Smith, eds. 1995. *Families in Multicultural Perspective.* New York: The Guilford Press.

Ishwaran, K. 1992. *Family and Marriage: Cross-Cultural Perspectives.* Toronto: Thomson Educational Publishing.

Israelsen, Craig L. 1991. "Family Resource Management." Pp. 171–234 in *Family Research: A Sixty-Year Review, Vol. 1*, edited by Stephen J. Bahr. New York: Lexington Books.

Ivey, Allen E., Mary Bradfor Ivey, and Lynn Simek-Morgan, eds. 1993. *Counseling and Psychotherapy: A Multicultural Perspective*, 3rd ed. Boston: Allyn and Bacon.

J

Jackman, Mary, and Robert Jackman. 1983. *Class Consciousness in the United States.* Berkeley, CA: University of California Press.

Jacoby, Arthur P. 1969. "Transition to Parenthood: A Reassessment." *Journal of Marriage and the Family* 31:720–27.

Jacquet, Constant H. 1989. *Yearbook of American and Canadian Churches.* Nashville, TN: Abingdon.

Jankowiak, William R., and Edward F. Fisher. 1992. "A Cross-Cultural Perspective on Romantic Love." *Ethnology* 31:149–55.

Jayakody, Rukmalie. 1998. "Race Differences in Intergenerational Financial Assistance: The Needs of Children and the Resources of Parents." *Journal of Family Issues* 19(5):508–33.

Jedlicka, Davor. 1984. "Indirect Parental Influence on Mate Choice." *Journal of Marriage and the Family* 46:65–70.

Jencks, Christopher, et al. 1972. *Inequality: A Reassessment of the Effect of Family and Schooling in America.* New York: Basic Books.

————. 1979. *Who Gets Ahead?* New York: Basic Books.

Johansson, Sten, and Ola Nygren. 1991. "The Missing Girls of China: A New Demographic Account." *Population and Development Review* 17:35–51.

John, Daphne, Beth Ann Shelton, and Kristen Luschen. 1995. "Race, Ethnicity, Gender, and Perceptions of Fairness." *Journal of Family Issues* 16:357–79.

Johnson, Colleen Leahy. 1988. *Ex Familia.* New Brunswick, NJ: Rutgers University Press.

Johnson, Colleen L., and Barbara M. Barer. 1997. *Life Beyond 85 Years: The Aura of Survivorship.* New York: Springer.

Johnson, David R. 1995. "Women's Marital Naming in Two Generations: A National Study." *Journal of Marriage and the Family* 57:724–32.

Johnson, Jan. 1993. "I Have a Mail-Order Marriage." *Ladies Home Journal* 110:22ff.

Johnson, Michael P. 1995. "Patriarchal Terrorism and Common Couple Violence: Two Forms of Violence Against Women." *Journal of Marriage and the Family* 57:283–94.

————. 1999. "Two Types of Violence Against Women in the American Family: Identifying Patriarchal Terrorism and Common Couple Violence." Paper presented at the National Council on Family Relations annual meetings, Irvine, CA.

————. 2000. "Conflict and Control: Images of Symmetry and Asymmetry in Domestic Violence." In *Couples in Conflict*, edited by Alan Booth, Ann C. Crouter, and Mari Clements. Hillsdale, NJ: Erlbaum.

Johnson, Michael P., and Kathleen J. Ferraro. 2000. "Research on Domestic Violence in the 1990s: Making Distinctions." *Journal of Marriage and the Family* 62:948–63.

Johnson, Otto, ed. 1992. *Information Please Almanac: Atlas & Yearbook 1993*, 46th ed. Boston: Houghton Mifflin.

Johnson, Walton R., and D. Michael Warren, eds. 1993. *Inside the Mixed Marriages: Accounts of Changing Attitudes, Patterns, and Perceptions of Cross-Cultural and Interracial Marriages.* Lanham, MD: University Press of America.

Johnston, Janet. 1994. "High-Conflict Divorce." *Future of Children* 4(1):165–82.

Johnston, Jo Ann. 1994. "The Cost of Children." *The Salt Lake Tribune*, September 19, P. D1.

Jones, Jacqueline. 1985. *Labor of Love, Labor of Sorrow: Black Women, Work, and Family from Slavery to the Present.* New York: Basic Books.

Jones, Elise F., Jacqueline Darroch Forrest, Noreen Goldman, Stanley K. Henshaw, Richard Lincoln, Jeannie I. Rosoff, Charles F. Westoff, and Deidre Wulf. 1986. *Teenage Pregnancy in Industrialized Countries*. New Haven, CT: Yale University Press.

Joung, I. M. A., K. Stronks, H. van de Mheen, F. W. A. van Poppel, J. B. W. van der Meer, and J. P. Mackenbach. 1997. "The Contribution of Intermediary Factors to Marital Status Differences in Self-Reported Health." *Journal of Marriage and the Family* 59: 476–90.

Julien, Danielle, Howard J. Markman, and Sophie Léveillé. 1994. "Networks' Support and Interference with Regard to Marriage: Disclosures of Marital Problems to Confidants." *Journal of Family Psychology* 8:16–31.

Juster, F. Thomas, and Frank P. Stafford. 1991. "The Allocation of Time: Empirical Findings, Behavioral Models, and Problems of Measurement." *Journal of Economic Literature* 29:471–522.

K

Kahn, Joan R., and Kathryn A. London. 1991. "Premarital Sex and the Risk of Divorce." *Journal of Marriage and the Family* 53:845–55.

————. 1993. "Reply to Comment on Kahn and London (1991)." *Journal of Marriage and the Family* 55:241.

Kain, Edward L., 1990. *The Myth of Family Decline: Understanding Families in a World of Rapid Social Change*. Lexington, MA: Lexington Books.

Kagan, Sharon L., and Bernice Weissbourd, eds. 1994. *Putting Families First: America's Support Movement and the Challenge of Change*. San Francisco: Jossey-Bass.

Kalmijn, Matthijs. 1991a. "Status Homogamy in the United States." *American Journal of Sociology* 97:496–523.

————. 1991b. "Shifting Boundaries: Trends in Religious and Educational Homogamy." *American Sociological Review* 56:786–800.

————. 1998. "Intermarriage and Homogamy: Causes, Patterns, Trends." *Annual Review of Sociology* 24:395–421.

Kalmuss, Debra, Pearila Brickner Namerow, and L. Cushman. 1991. "Adoption Versus Parenting among Young Pregnant Women." *Family Planning Perspectives* 23:17–23.

Kane, E. W. 1999. "Race, Ethnicity, and Beliefs about Gender Inequality." Paper presented at the Society for the Study of Social Problems, Chicago, August.

Kane, Paula M. 1993. "Irish Catholics." Pp. 743–55 in *Encyclopedia of American Social History, Vol. II*, edited by Mary Kupiec, Elliott J. Gorn, and Peter W. Williams. New York: Charles Scribner's Sons.

Kanin, Eugene J., Karen D. Davidson, and Sonia R. Scheck. 1970. "A Research Note on Male-Female Differentials in the Experience of Heterosexual Love." *Journal of Sex Research* 6:64–72.

Kanter, Rose M. 1977. *Work and Family in the United States: A Critical Review and Agenda for Research and Policy*. New York: Russell Sage.

Kaplan, N., J. K. Whitmore, and M. H. Choy. 1989. *The Boat People and Achievement in America: A Study of Family Life, Hard Work, and Cultural Values*. Ann Arbor: University of Michigan Press.

Kaplan, Sandra J., ed. 1996. *Family Violence: A Clinical and Legal Guide*. Washington, DC: American Psychiatric Press.

Kart, Cary S., Eileen Metress, and Seamus Metress. 1988. *Aging, Health, and Society*. Boston: Jones and Bartlett.

Katchadourian, Herant A., and Donald T. Lunde. 1975. *Fundamentals of Human Sexuality*, 2nd ed. New York: Holt, Rinehart and Winston.

Katz, Alvin M., and Ruben Hill. 1958. "Residential Propinquity and Marital Selection: A Review of Theory, Method, and Fact." *Marriage and Family Living* 20:27–35.

Katz, Donald. 1992. *Home Fires: An Intimate Portrait of One Middle-Class Family in Postwar America*. New York: Aaron Asher Books.

Katz, Michael. 1990. "The Invention of Heterosexuality." *Socialist Review* 59:7–34.

Kaufman, Joan, and Edward Zigler. 1993. "The Intergenerational Transmission of Abuse Is Overstated." Pp. 209–21 in *Current Controversies on Family Violence*, edited by Richard J. Gelles and Donileen R. Loseke. Newbury Park, CA: Sage.

Kay, Herma Hill. 1990. "Beyond No-Fault: New Directions in Divorce Reform." Pp. 6–36 in *Divorce Reform at the Crossroads*, edited by Stephen D. Sugarman and Herma Hill Kay. New Haven: Yale University Press.

Keenan, Julian Paul, Gordon G. Gallup Jr., Nicole Goulet, and Mrinmoyi Kulkarni. 1997. "Attributions of Deception in Human Mating Strategies." *Journal of Social Behavior and Personality* 12:1:45–52.

Kehoe, Alice B. 1993. "The Function of Ceremonial Sexual Intercourse Among the Northern Plains Indians." Pp. 262–68 in *Culture and Human Sexuality: A Reader*, edited by David N. Suggs and Andrew W. Miracle. Pacific Grove, CA: Brooks/Cole.

Keith, Verna M., and Cedric Herring. 1991. "Skin Tone and Stratification in the Black Community." *American Journal of Sociology* 97:760–78.

Kejing, Dai. 1991. "The Life Experience and Status of Chinese Rural Women from Observation of Three Age Groups." *International Sociology* 6:5–23.

Kelly, Joan B., and Judith S. Wallerstein. 1976. "The Effects of Parental Divorce: Experiences of the Child in Early Latency." *American Journal of Orthopsychiatry* 46:20–32.

Kelly, Patricia. 1995. *Developing Healthy Stepfamilies: Twenty Families Tell Their Stories*. New York: Haworth Press.

Kempe, C. Henry, Frederic N. Siversman, Brandt F. Steele, William Droegemueller, and Henry K. Silver. 1962. "The Battered Child Syndrome." *Journal of the American Medical Association* 181:107–12.

Kendrigan, Mary Lou, ed. 1991. *Gender Differences: Their Impact on Public Policy*. New York: Greenwood Press.

Kenrick, Douglas T., and R. C. Keefe. 1992. "Age Preferences in Mates Reflect Sex Differences in Reproductive Strategies." *Behavioral and Brain Sciences* 15:75–133.

Kenrick, Douglas T., Richard C. Keefe, Cristina Gabrielidis, and Jeffery Cornelius. 1996. "Adolescents' Age Preferences for Dating Partners: Support for an Evolutionary Model of Life-History Strategies." *Child Development* 67:4:1499–1511.

Kennedy, Paul. M. 1993. *Preparing for the Twenty-First Century*. New York: Random House.

Kennedy, Robert E., Jr. 1973. *The Irish: Emigration, Marriage, and Fertility*. Berkeley: University of California Press.

Kephart, William M., and William W. Zellner. 1994. *Extraordinary Groups: An Examination of Unconventional Life-Styles*. New York: St. Martin's Press.

Kerckhoff, Alan C. 1974. "The Social Context of Interpersonal Attraction." Pp. 61–78 in *Foundations of Interpersonal Attraction*, edited by L. Huston. New York: Academic Press.

Kern, Stephen. 1992. *The Culture of Love: Victorians to Moderns*. Cambridge, MA: Harvard University Press.

Kilbride, Philip Leroy, and Janet Capriotti Kilbride. 1990. *Changing Family Life in East Africa: Women and Children at Risk*. University Park, PA: The Pennsylvania State University Press.

Kindlund, Soren. 1988. "Sweden." Pp. 74–92 in *Child Support: From Debt Collection to Social Policy*, edited by Alfred Kahn and Shela B. Kamerman. Newbury Park, CA: Sage.

King, Charles E., and Andrew Christensen. 1983. "The Relationship Events Scale: A Guttman Scaling of Progress in Courtship." *Journal of Marriage and the Family* 45:671–78.

Kinsey, Alfred, Wardell B. Pomeroy, and Clyde E. Martin. 1948. *Sexual Behavior in the Human Male*. Philadelphia: Saunders.

————. 1953. *Sexual Behavior in the Human Female*. Philadelphia: Saunders.

Kirby, Douglas, Cynthia Waszak, and Julie Ziegler. 1991. "Six School-Based Clinics: Their Reproductive Health Services and Impact on Sexual Behavior." *Family Planning Perspectives* 23:6–16.

Kissling, Frances. 1994. "Theo-Politics: The Roman Catholic Church and Population Policy." Pp. 320–29 in *Beyond the Numbers: A Reader on Population, Consumption, and the Environment*, edited by Laurie Mazur. Washington, DC: Island Press.

Kitano, Harry H. L. 1976. *Japanese Americans: The Evolution of a Subculture*. Englewood Cliffs, NJ: Prentice-Hall.

Kitson, Gay C. 1985. "Marital Discord and Marital Separation: A County Survey." *Journal of Marriage and the Family* 47:693–700.

————. 1992. *Portrait of Divorce: Adjustment to Marital Breakdown*. New York: Guilford Press.

Kitson, Gay C., and Helen J. Raschke. 1981. "Divorce Research: What We Know, What We Need to Know." *Journal of Divorce* 3:1–37.

Klein, David M., and James M. White. 1996. *Family Theories: An Introduction*. Thousand Oaks, CA: Sage.

Klitsch, M. 1991. "Antiprogestins and the Abortion Controversy: A Progress Report." *Family Planning Perspectives* 23:275–82.

Kluegel, James R., and Eliot R. Smith. 1986. *Beliefs about Inequality: Americans' Views of What Is and What Ought to Be*. New York: Aldine de Gruyter.

Knapp, John L., and Brian D. Cunningham. 1991. *A Labor Supply Study for the City of Fredericksburg and the Counties of Stafford and Spotsylvania*. Charlottesville, VA: University of Virginia Center for Public Service.

Knox, David H., Jr. 1975. *Marriage: Who? When? Why?* Englewood Cliffs, NJ: Prentice-Hall.

Knox, David, and Caroline Schacht. 1994. *Choices in Relationships: An Introduction to Marriage and the Family*. Minneapolis: West.

Knudson-Martin, Carmen, and Anne Rankin Mahoney. 1998. "Language and Processes in the Construction of Equality in New Marriages." *Family Relations* 47:81–91.

Kohn, Melvin. 1963. "Social Class and Parent-Child Relationships: An Interpretation." *American Journal of Sociology* 68:471–80.

————. 1977. *Class and Conformity*. Chicago: University of Chicago Press.

Kohn, Melvin, and Carmi Schooler. 1983. *Work and Personality: An Inquiry Into the Impact of Social Stratification*. Norwood, NJ: Ablex.

Komarovsky, Mirra. 1962. *Blue-Collar Marriage*. New York: Random House.

———. 1976. *Dilemma of Masculinity*. New York: W. W. Norton & Co.

Koop, C. Everitt. 1989. "The U. S. Surgeon General on the Health Effects of Abortion." *Population and Development Review* 15:172–75.

Koos, Helen P., and C. M. Suchindran. 1980. "Effects of Children on Women's Remarriage Prospects." *Journal of Family Issues* 1:497–515.

Kornfield, Ruth. 1986. "Who's to Blame: Adolescent Sexual Activity." *Journal of Adolescence* 8:17–31.

Kosberg, Jordan I. 1998. "The Abuse of Elderly Men." *Journal of Elder Abuse and Neglect* 9(3):69–88.

Kosmin, Barry A., and Seymour Lachman. 1994. *One Nation Under God*. New York: Harmony.

Koss, Mary P., Christine A. Gidycz, and Nadine Wisniewski. 1987. "The Scope of Rape: Incidence and Prevalence of Sexual Aggression and Victimization in a National Sample of Higher Education Students." *Journal of Consulting and Clinical Psychology* 55:162–70.

Kost, Kathryn, David J. Landry, and Jacqueline E. Darroch. 1998. "The Effects of Pregnancy Planning Status on Birth Outcomes and Infant Care." *Family Planning Perspectives* 30(5):223–30.

Kotlowitz, Alex. 1991. *There Are No Children Here: The Story of Two Boys Growing Up in the Other America*. New York: Anchor Books.

Kovecses, Z. 1991. "A Linguist's Quest for Love." *Journal of Social and Personal Relationships* 8:77–97.

Kramarae, Cheris. 1992. "The Condition of Patriarchy." Pp. 397–405 in *The Knowledge Explosion: Generations of Feminist Scholarship*, edited by Cheris Kramarae and Dale Spender. New York: Teachers College Press.

Kramarae, Cheris, and Paula A. Treichler. 1985. *A Feminist Dictionary*. Boston: Pandora Press.

Kranichfeld, Marion. 1987. "Rethinking Family Power." *Journal of Family Issues* 8:42–56.

Krause, Harry D. 1990. "Child Support Reassessed: Limits of Private Responsibility and the Public Interest." Pp. 166–90 in *Divorce Reform at the Crossroads*, edited by Stephen D. Sugarman and Herma Hill Kay. New Haven: Yale University Press.

Krich, John. 1989. "Here Come the Brides: The Blossoming Business of Imported Love." Pp. 382–92 in *Men's Lives*, edited by M. S. Kimmel and M. A. Messner. New York: Macmillan.

Krokoff, Lowell J., John M. Gottman, and Anup K. Roy. 1988. "Blue-Collar and White-Collar Marital Interaction and Communication Orientation." *Journal of Social and Personal Relationships* 5:201–21.

Krull, Catherine, and Frank Trovato. 1994. "The Quiet Revolution and the Sex Differential in Quebec's Suicide Rate: 1931–1986." *Social Forces* 74:1121–47.

Kulis, Stephen Stanley. 1991. *Why Honor Thy Father and Mother? Class, Mobility, Family Ties in Later Life*.

Kumagai, Fumie. 1983. "Changing Divorce Rates in Japan." *Family History* (Spring):85–108.

Kunin, Julie Danielle. 1998. "Predictors of Psychosocial and Behavioral Adjustment of Children: A Study Comparing Children Raised by Lesbian Parents to Children Raised by Heterosexual Parents." *Dissertation Abstracts International: Section B: The Sciences and Engineering* Vol 59(6-B)3094.

Kupers, Terry Allen. 1993. *Revisioning Men's Lives: Gender, Intimacy, and Power*. New York: Guilford.

Kurdek, Lawrence A. 1991. "The Relations between Reported Well-Being and Divorce History, Availability of a Proximate Adult, and Gender." *Journal of Marriage and the Family* 53:71–8.

———. 1993. "The Allocation of Household Labor in Gay, Lesbian, and Heterosexual Married Couples." *Journal of Social Issues* 49:127–39.

———. 1995. "Lesbian and Gay Couples." Pp. 243–61 in *Lesbian, Gay and Bisexual Identities Over the Lifespan: Psychological Perspectives*, edited by A. R. D'Augelli and C. J. Patterson. New York: Oxford University Press.

———. 1998. "Relationship Outcomes and Their Predictors: Longitudinal Evidence from Heterosexual Married, Gay Cohabiting, and Lesbian Cohabiting Couples." *Journal of Marriage and the Family* 60:553–68.

Kurdek, Lawrence A., and Mark A. Fine. 1993. "Parent and Non-Parent Residential Family Members as Providers of Warmth and Supervision to Young Adolescents." *Journal of Family Psychology* 7:245–49.

Kurdek, Lawrence A., and J. Patrick Schmitt. 1986. "Relationship Quality of Partners in Heterosexual Married, Heterosexual Cohabiting, Gay, and Lesbian Relationships." *Journal of Personality and Social Psychology* 51:711–20.

Kurtz, Linda. 1994. "Psychosocial Coping Resources in Elementary School-Age Children of Divorce." *American Journal of Orthopsychiatry* 64:554–62.

Kutsche, Paul. 1983. "Household and Family in Hispanic Northern New Mexico." *Journal of Comparative Family Studies* 14:151–65.

L

Lalli, Michale. 1969. "The Italian-American Family: Assimilation and Change, 1900–1965." *Family Coordinator* 18:44–48.

Lamanna, Mary Ann, and Agnes Riedmann, 1994. *Marriages and Families: Making Choices Throughout the Life Cycle,* 5th ed. Englewood Cliffs, NJ: Prentice-Hall.

Lamb, Michael E. 1987. "The Emergent American Father." Pp. 3–26 in *The Father's Role: Cross-Cultural Perspectives*, edited by Michael E. Lamb. Hillsdale, NJ: Lawrence Erlbaum.

Lamousé, Annette. 1969. "Family Roles of Women: A German Example." *Journal of Marriage and the Family* 31:145–52.

Landale, Nancy S., and Katherine Fennelly. 1992. "Informal Unions among Mainland Puerto Ricans: Cohabitation or an Alternative to Legal Marriage?" *Journal of Marriage and the Family* 54:269–80.

Langman, Lauren. 1987. "Social Stratification." Pp. 211–49 in *Handbook of Marriage and the Family*, edited by Suzanne K. Steinmetz and Marvin B. Sussman.

LaRossa, Ralph. 1983. "The Transition to Parenthood and the Social Reality of Time." *Journal of Marriage and the Family* 45:579–89.

_____. 1984. *Family Case Studies: A Sociological Perspective.* New York: Free Press.

LaRossa, Ralph, and Maureen LaRossa. 1981. *Transition to Parenthood.* Beverly Hills, CA: Sage.

_____. 1989. "Baby Care: Fathers vs. Mothers." In *Gender in Intimate Relationships*, edited by Barbara J. Risman and Pepper Schwartz. Belmont, CA: Wadsworth.

LaRossa, Ralph, and Donald C. Reitzes. 1995. "Gendered Perceptions of Father Involvement in Early 20th Century America." *Journal of Marriage and the Family* 57:223–29.

Larson, David E., ed. 1990. *Mayo Clinic Family Health Book.* New York: William Morrow.

Larson, Jeffrey. 1984. "The Effect of Husband's Unemployment on Marital and Family Relations in Blue-Collar Families." *Family Relations* 33:503–11.

Lasch, Christopher. 1977. *Haven in a Heartless World: The Family Besieged.* New York: Basic Books.

Lasker, Judith N., and Susan Borg. 1994. *In Search of Parenthood: Coping With Infertility and High-Tech Conception*, rev. ed. Philadelphia: Temple University Press.

Laslett, Barbara. 1977. "Social Change and the Family." *American Sociological Review* 42:269–91.

Laslett, Peter, ed. 1972. *Household and Family in Past Time: Comparative Studies in the Size and Structure of the Domestic Group over the Last Three Centuries in England, France, Serbia, Japan and Colonial North America, with Further Materials from Western Europe.* London: Cambridge University Press.

_____. 1977. *Family Life and Illicit Love in Earlier Generations.* New York: Cambridge University Press.

Laumann, Edward O., John H. Gagnon, Robert T. Michael, and Stuart Michaels. 1994. *The Social Organization of Sexuality: Sexual Practices in the United States.* Chicago: University of Chicago Press.

Laumann-Billings, L., and R. E. Emery. 1998. *Young Adults' Painful Feelings about Parental Divorce.* Unpublished manuscript, University of Virginia. Reported in Emery, 1999.

Lavee, Yoav, Shlomo Sharlin, and Ruth Katz. 1996. "The Effect of Parenting Stress on Marital Quality: An Integrated Mother-Father Model." *Journal of Family Issues* 17:114–35.

Lawton, M. Powell, Morton H. Kleban, Miriam Moss, Michael Rovine, and Allen Glicksman. 1989. "Measuring Caregiver Appraisal." *Journal of Gerontology: Psychological Sciences* 44:61–71.

Lazoritz, Stephan. 1990. "What Ever Happened to Mary Ellen?" *Child Abuse and Neglect* 14:143–49.

Leavitt, Gregory. 1977. "The Frequency of Warfare: An Evolutionary Perspective." *Sociological Inquiry* 14 (January).

Lee, Gary R. 1980. "Kinship in the 1970s: A Decade Review of Research and Theory." *Journal of Marriage and the Family* 42:923–34.

_____. 1987. "Comparative Perspectives." Pp. 59–80 in *Handbook of Marriage and the Family*, edited by Marvin B. Sussman and Suzanne K. Steinmetz. New York: Plenum.

Lee, Gary R., and Jeffrey W. Dwyer. 1996. "Aging Parent-Adult Child Coresidence: Further Evidence on the Role of Parental Characteristics." *Journal of Family Issues* 17:46–59.

Lee, Gary R., Julie K. Netzer, and Raymond T. Coward. 1994. "Filial Responsibility Expectations and Patterns of Intergenerational Assistance." *Journal of Marriage and the Family* 56:559–65.

Lee, John A. 1973. *The Colors of Love: An Exploration of the Ways of Loving.* Don Mills, Ontario: New Press.

_____. 1988. "Love Styles." Pp. 38–67 in *The Psychology of Love*, edited by Robert J. Sternberg and Michael L. Barnes. New Haven, CT: Yale University Press.

Leeder, Elaine J. 1994. *Treating Abuse in Families: A Feminist and Community Approach.* New York: Springer.

LeMasters, E. E. 1957. "Parenthood as Crisis." *Marriage and Family Living* 19:352–55.

Lenski, Gerhard. 1961. *The Religious Factor.* Garden City, NY: Doubleday.

Lenski, Gerhard. 1994. "Societal Taxonomies: Mapping the Social Universe." *Annual Review of Sociology* 20:1–26.

Lenski, Gerhard, and Jean Lenski, 1987. *Human Societies: An Introduction to Macrosociology*. New York: McGraw-Hill.

Lenski, Gerhard, Jean Lenski, and Patrick D. Nolan. 1991. *Human Societies: An Introduction to Macrosociology.* New York: McGraw-Hill.

Lenski, Gerhard, and Patrick D. Nolan. 1984. "Trajectories of Development: A Test of Ecological-Evolutionary Theory." *Social Forces* 63:1–23.

Lenski, Gerhard, Patrick Nolan, and Jean Lenski. 1995. *Human Societies: An Introduction to Macrosociology*, 7th ed. New York: McGraw-Hill.

Lerner, Richard M. 1995. *America's Youth in Crisis: Challenges and Options for Programs and Policies*. Newbury Park, CA: Sage.

Lerner, Robert. 2000. "Out of Nothing Comes Nothing: Homosexual and Heterosexual Marriage Not Shown to Be Equivalent for Raising Children." Paper presented at the Revitalizing the Institution of Marriage for the 21st Century Conference, March 9–11, Provo, UT.

Leslie, Gerald R., and Sheila K. Korman. 1989. *The Family in Social Context*, 7th ed. New York: Oxford University Press.

Lester, David, and Kazuhiko Abe. 1993. "The Regional Variation of Divorce Rates in Japan and the United States." *Journal of Divorce and Remarriage* 1/2:227–30.

LeVay, Simon. 1993. *The Sexual Brain*. La Jolla, CA: MIP Press.

Levin, W. C. 1988. "Age Stereotyping." *Research on Aging* 10:134–48.

Levinger, George. 1965. "Marital Cohesiveness and Dissolution: An Integrative Review." *Journal of Marriage and the Family* 27:19–28.

Levy, Marion J. 1949. *The Family Revolution in Modern China*. Cambridge: Harvard University Press.

Lewis Harris and Associates. 1993. "Commonwealth Fund Survey of Women's Health." New York: Commonwealth Fund.

Lewis, Oscar. 1966. *La Vida: A Puerto Rican Family in the Culture of Poverty—San Juan and New York*. New York: Random House.

————. 1975. *Five Families: Mexican Case Studies in the Culture of Poverty*. New York: Basic Books.

Lewis, Robert A. 1973. "A Longitudinal Test of a Developmental Framework for Premarital Dyadic Formation." *Journal of Marriage and the Family* 35:16–27.

Lewis, Robert A., and Graham B. Spanier. 1979. "Theorizing About the Quality and Stability of Marriage." Pp. 268–94 in *Contemporary Theories About the Family, Vol. 1,* edited by Wesley R. Burr, Reuben Hill, F. Ivan Nye, and Ira L. Reiss. New York: Free Press.

Lewis, Robert A., Robert J. Volk, and Stephen F. Duncan. 1989. "Stresses on Fathers and Family Relationships Related to Rural Youth Leaving and Returning Home." *Family Relations* 38:174–81.

Lichter, Daniel T., Diane K. McLaughlin, George Kephart, and David J. Landry. 1992. "Race and the Retreat from Marriage: A Shortage of Marriageable Men?" *American Sociological Review* 57:781–99.

Lie, Guat-Yong, and Sabrina Gentlewarrior. 1991. "Intimate Violence in Lesbian Relationships: Discussion of Survey Findings and Practice Implications." *Journal of Social Service Research* 15:41–59.

Lie, Guat-Yong, Rebecca Schilit, Judy Bush, M. Montague, and L. Reyes. 1991. "Lesbians in Currently Aggressive Relationships: How Frequently Do They Report Aggressive Past Relationships?" *Violence and Victims* 6:121–35.

Lillard, Lee A., Michael J. Brien, and Linda J. Waite. "Premarital Cohabitation and Subsequent Marital Dissolution: A Matter of Self-Selection?" *Demography* 32:437–57.

Lin, Chien, and William T. Liu. 1993. "Intergenerational Relationships Among Chinese Immigrant Families From Taiwan." Pp. 271–86 in *Family Ethnicity: Strength in Diversity*, edited by Harriette Pipes McAdoo. Newbury Park, CA: Sage.

Lipmen-Blumen, Jean. 1984. *Gender Roles and Power*. Englewood Cliffs, NJ: Prentice-Hall.

Liss, Lora. 1987. "Families and the Law." Pp. 767–93 in *Handbook of Marriage and the Family*, edited by Marvin B. Sussman and Suzanne K. Steinmetz. New York: Plenum Press.

Litwak, Eugene. 1965. "Extended Kin Relations in an Industrial Democratic Society." Pp. 291 in *Social Structure and the Family: Generational Relations*, edited by Ethel Shanas and Gorden F. Streib. Englewood Cliffs, NJ: Prentice-Hall.

Litwak, Eugene, and Stephen Kulis. 1987. "Technology, Proximity, and Measures of Kin Support." *Journal of Marriage and the Family* 49:649–61.

Lizot, Jacques. 1985. *Tales of the Yanomami: Daily Life in the Venezuelan Forest*. New York: Cambridge University Press.

Lloyd, Sally A., and Beth C. Emery. 1999. *The Dark Side of Courtship : Physical and Sexual Aggression*. Newbury Park, CA: Sage.

Logan, Charles H. 1972. "General Deterrence, Effects of Imprisonment." *Social Forces* 51:63–72.

London, Katheryn A., and Barbara Foley Wilson. 1988. "Divorce." *American Demographics* 10:22–26.

Loomis, Laura Spencer, and Alan Booth. 1995. "Multigenerational Caregiving and Well-Being: The Myth of the Beleaguered Sandwich Generation." *Journal of Family Issues* 16:131–48.

Lopata, Helen Znaniecka. 1993. "Career Commitments of American Women: The Issue of Side Bets." *Sociological Quarterly* 34:257–77.

Lorber, Judith. 1984. *Women Physicians: Careers, Status, and Power*. New York: Free Press.

Lorenz, Frederick O., Ronald L. Simon, Rand D. Conger, Glen H. Elder, Jr., Christine Johnson, and Wei Chao. 1997. "Married and Recently Divorced Mothers' Stressful Events and Distress: Tracing Change Across Time." *Journal of Marriage and the Family* 59:219–32.

Loseke, Donileen R. 1992. *The Battered Woman and Shelters: The Social Construction of Wife Abuse*. Albany: State University of New York Press.

Lott, Juanita Tamayo. 1993. "Do United States Racial/Ethnic Categories Still Fit?" *Population Today* (Population Reference Bureau) 6:9.

Loury, Glenn C. 1996. "Are Jobs the Solution?" *Wilson Quarterly* 20(4):89–92.

Luhman, Reid, and Stuart Gilman. 1980. *Race and Ethnic Relations: The Social and Political Experience of Minority Groups*. Belmont, CA: Wadsworth.

Luker, Kristin. 1992. "Dubious Conceptions: The Controversy over Teen Pregnancy." Pp. 160–172 in *Family in Transition*, 7th ed., edited by Arlene S. Skolnick and Jerome H. Skolnick New York: HarperCollins.

Lund, Kristina. 1990. "A Feminist Perspective on Divorce Therapy for Women." *Journal of Divorce* 13:57–67.

Luster, Tom, Laura Bates, Hiram Girzgerald, Marcia Vanderbelt, and Judith Peck Key. 2000. "Factors Related to Successful Outcomes Among Preschool Children Born to Low-Income Adolescent Mothers." *Journal of Marriage and the Family* 62:133–46.

Lyman, Stanford M., and Marvin B. Scott. 1970. *A Sociology of the Absurd*. New York: Appleton-Century-Crofts.

Lynam, Donald R., Richard Milich, and Rick Zimmerman. 1999. "Project DARE: No Effects at 10-Year Follow-up." *Journal of Consulting and Clinical Psychology* v. 67(4):590–3.

Lynd, Robert S., and Helen M. Lynd. 1929/1956. *Middletown: A Study in American Culture*. Harcourt Brace Jovanovich.

M

Maccoby, Eleanor E., and Robert H. Mnookin. 1992. *Dividing the Child: Social and Legal Dilemmas of Custody*. Cambridge: Harvard University Press.

MacDonald, William L., and Alfred DeMaris. 1995. "Remarriage, Stepchildren, and Marital Conflict: Challenges to the Incomplete Institutionalization Hypothesis." *Journal of Marriage and the Family* 57:387–98.

MacKinnon, Catherine. 1989. "Sexuality, Pornography, and Method." *Ethics* 99:331.

MacLeod, Jay. 1995. *Ain't No Makin' It: Aspirations and Attainment in a Low Income Neighborhood*. Boulder: Westview Press.

Madden-Derdich, Debra A., and Joyce A. Arditti. 1999. "The Ties that Bind: Attachment between Former Spouses." *Family Relations* 48(3):243–49.

Madden-Derdich, Debra A., Stacie A. Leonard, and F. Scott Christopher. 1999. "Boundary Ambiguity and Coparental Conflict After Divorce: An Empirical Test of a Family Systems Model of the Divorce Process." *Journal of Marriage and the Family* 61(3):588–98.

Maiden, R. Paul. 1997. "Alcohol Dependence and Domestic Violence: Incidence and Treatment Implications." *Alcohol Treatment Quarterly* 15(2):31–50.

Mair, Lucy. 1962. *Primitive Government*. Baltimore: Penguin.

Major, Brenda. 1993. "Gender, Entitlement, and the Distribution of Family Labor." *Journal of Social Issues* 49:141–59.

Malson, M. R. 1983. "Black Families and Childrearing Support Networks." Pp. 131–41 in *Research in the Interweave of Social Roles: Jobs and Families*, vol. 3. Greenwich, CT: JAI Press.

Mancini, Jay A., and Rosemary Blieszner. 1989. "Aging Parents and Adult Children: Research Themes in Intergenerational Relations." *Journal of Marriage and the Family* 51:275–90.

Manning, Wendy D. 1993. "Marriage and Cohabitation Following Premarital Conception." *Journal of Marriage and the Family* 55:839–50.

Manning, Wendy D., and Pamela J. Smock. 1997. "Children's Living Arrangements in Unmarried-Mother Families." *Journal of Family Issues* 18:526–44.

————. 1999. "New Families and Nonresident Father-Child Visitation." *Social Forces* 78(1):87–116.

March, Karen, and Charlene Miall. "Adoption as a Family Form." *Family Relations* 49:359–62.

Mare, Robert D., and Christopher Winship. 1991. "Socioeconomic Change and the Decline in Marriage for Blacks and Whites." Pp. 175–202 in *The Urban Underclass*, edited by Christopher Jencks and Paul E. Peterson. Washington, DC: The Brookings Institution.

Margolis, Maxine. 1984. *Mothers and Such: Views of American Women and Why They Changed*. Berkeley: University of California Press.

Marks, Carole. 1985. "Black Workers and the Great Migration North." *Phylon* 46:148–61.

Marks, Stephen R. 2000. "Teasing Out the Lessons of the 1960s: Family Diversity and Family Privilege." *Journal of Marriage and the Family* 62:606–22.

Marshall, Donald S. 1971. "Sexual Behavior on Mangaia." Pp. 103–62 in *Human Sexual Behavior: Variations in the Ethnographic Spectrum*, edited by Donald S. Marshall and David N. Suggs. New York: Basic Books.

Marshall, Mac. 1977. "The Nature of Nurture." *American Ethnologist* 4:643–62.

Marsiglio, William. 1993. "Attitudes toward Homosexual Activity and Gays as Friends: A National Survey of Heterosexual 15- to 19-Year-Old Males." *Journal of Sex Research* 30:12–17.

Marsiglio, William, Paul Amato, Randal D. Day, and Michael E. Lamb. 2000. "Scholarship on Fatherhood in the 1990s and Beyond." *Journal of Marriage and the Family* 62:1173–91.

Marsiglio, William, and Frank L. Mott. 1986. "The Impact of Sex Education on Sexual Activity, Contraceptive Use and Premarital Pregnancy Among American Teenagers." *Family Planning Perspectives* 18:151–62.

Martin, Del. 1976. *Battered Wives*. San Francisco: Glide Publications.

Martin, M. Kay, and Barbara Voorhies. 1975. *Female of the Species*. New York: Columbia University Press.

Martin, Teresa Castro, and Larry Bumpass. 1989. "Recent Trends in Marital Disruption." *Demography* 26:37–51.

Marx, Karl. [1867] 1967. *Capital: A Critical Analysis of Capitalist Production*, vol. 1. New York: International Publishers.

Marx, Karl, and Friedrich Engels. [1848] 1964. *The Communist Manifesto*. Translated by Paul M. Sweezy. New York: Modern Reader.

Masheter, Carol. 1991. "Postdivorce Relationships between Ex-Spouses: The Roles of Attachment and Interpersonal Conflict." *Journal of Marriage and the Family* 53:103–10.

Mason, Karen Oppenheim, and Karen Kuhlthau. 1989. "Determinants of Child Care Ideals Among Mothers of Preschool-Aged Children." *Journal of Marriage and the Family* 51:593–603.

Mason, Mary Ann, and Eileen Gambrill. 1993. *Debating Children's Lives*. Newbury Park, CA: Sage.

Massey, Douglas S., and Nancy A. Denton. 1993. *American Apartheid: Segregation and the Making of the Underclass*. Boston: Harvard University Press.

Massey, Douglas, and Kumiko Shibuya. 1995. "Unraveling the Tangle of Pathology: The Effect of Spatially Concentrated Joblessness on the Well-Being of African Americans." *Social Science Research* 24:352–66.

Mastekaasa, Arne. 1994. "Marital Status, Distress, and Well-Being: An International Comparison." *Journal of Comparative Family Studies* 25:183–205.

————. 1997. "Marital Dissolution as a Stressor: Some Evidence on Psychological, Physical, and Behavioral Changes During the Preseparation Period." *Journal of Divorce and Remarriage* 26:155–83.

Masters, William H., and Virginia E. Johnson. 1976. *The Pleasure Bond*. New York: Bantam Books.

————. 1979. *Homosexuality in Perspective*. Boston: Little, Brown.

Masters, William H., Virginia E. Johnson, and Robert C. Kolodny. 1992. *Human Sexuality*, 4th ed. New York: HarperCollins.

————. 1994. *Heterosexuality*. New York: HarperCollins.

Matlock, M. Eileen, et al. 1994. "Family Correlates of Social Skill Deficits in Incarcerated and Nonincarcerated Adolescents." *Adolescence* 29:119–30.

Mattes, Jane. 1994. *Single Mothers by Choice: A Guidebook for Single Women Who Are Considering or Have Chosen Motherhood*. New York: Random House.

Mattessich, Paul, and Reuben Hill. 1987. "Life Cycle and Family Development." Pp. 437–69 in *Handbook of Marriage and the Family*, edited by Marvin B. Sussman and Suzanne K. Steinmetz. New York: Plenum Press.

Matthews, Sarah, and Jetse Sprey. 1985. "Adolescents' Relationships with Grandparents: An Empirical Contribution to Conceptual Clarification." *Journal of Gerontology* 40:621–26.

Mauss, Armand L. 1975. *Social Problems as Social Movements*. Philadelphia: J. B. Lippincott.

Maynard, Eileen, and Gayla Twiss. 1969. *Hechel Lena Oyate Kin Nipi Kte—That These People May Live: Conditions Among the Oglala Sioux of the Pine Ridge Reservation*. Pine Ridge, SD: Indian Health Service, U.S. Public Health Service.

Mattis, Mary Catherine. 1975. *The Irish Family in Buffalo, New York, 1855–1875: A Socio-Historical Analysis*. Unpublished Dissertation, St. Louis: Washington University.

Mazur, Allan, Carolyn Halpern, and J. Richard Udry. 1994. "Dominant Looking Male Teenagers Copulate Earlier." *Ethology and Sociobiology* 15:87–94.

Mazur, Laurie Ann, ed. 1994. *Beyond the Numbers: A Reader on Population, Consumption, and the Environment*. Washington, DC: Island Press.

McAdoo, Harriet Pipes. 1980. "Black Mothers and the Extended Family Support Network." Pp. 125–44 in *The Black Woman*, edited by L. Rodgers-Rose. Beverly Hills, CA: Sage.

_____. 1983. "Societal Stress: The Black Family."
Pp. 178–87 in *Stress and the Family: Volume 1. Coping With Normative Stress*, edited by Hamilton I. McCubbin and Charles R. Figley. New York: Brunner/Mazel.

_____. 1988. "Transgenerational Patterns of Upward Mobility in African-American Families." Pp. 148–68 in *Black Families*, 2nd ed., edited by Harriette Pipes McAdoo. Newbury Park, CA: Sage Publications.

_____, ed. 1993. *Family Ethnicity: Strength in Diversity*. Thousand Oaks, CA: Sage.

_____. ed. 1999. *Family Ethnicity: Strength in Diversity*, 2nd ed. Thousand Oaks, CA: Sage.

_____. 2000. "Transference of Values of African American Families and Children." *National Council on Family Relations Report* 45(2):F5.

McCall, Patricia L., and Kenneth C. Land. 1994. "Trends in White Male Adolescent, Young-Adult, and Elderly Suicide: Are There Common Underlying Structural Factors?" *Social Science Research* 23:57–81.

McCammon, Susan L., David Knox, and Caroline Schacht. 1993. *Choices in Sexuality*. Minneapolis/St. Paul: West Publishing.

McCarthy, Frederick D., and Margaret McArthur. 1960. "The Food Quest and the Time Factor in Aboriginal Economic Life." Pp. 28–43 in *Records of the American-Australian Scientific Expedition on Arnhem Land, Vol. 2: Anthropology and Nutrition*, edited by Charles P. Mountford. Melbourne: Melbourne University Press.

McCubbin, Hamilton I. 1979. "Integrating Coping Behavior in Family Stress Theory." *Journal of Marriage and the Family* 41:237–44.

McCubbin, Hamilton I., and Barbara B. Dahl. 1985. *Marriage and Family: Individuals and Life Cycles*. New York: John Wiley.

McCubbin, Hamilton I., and Joan Patterson. 1982. "Family Adaptation to Crisis." Pp. 26–47 in *Family Stress, Coping, and Social Support*, edited by Hamilton McCubbin, A. Elizabeth Cauble, and Joan Patterson. Springfield, IL: Charles C. Thomas.

_____. 1983. "The Family Stress Process: The Double ABCX Model of Adjustment and Adaptation." Pp. 7–37 in *Social Stress and the Family*, edited by Hamilton I. McCubbin, Marvin Sussman, and Joan Patterson. New York: Haworth.

McCubbin, Hamilton I., Elizabeth A. Thompson, Anne I. Thompson, and Jo A. Futrell, eds. 1999. *The Dynamics of Resilient Families*. Thousand Oaks, CA. Sage.

McElrath, Karen. 1992. "Gender, Career Disruption, and Academic Rewards." *Journal of Higher Education* 63:269–81.

McGinnis, T. 1981. *More Than Just a Friend: The Joys and Disappointments of Extramarital Affairs*. Englewood Cliffs, NJ: Prentice-Hall.

McLanahan, Sara S., and Julia Adams. 1989. "The Effects of Children on Adults' Psychological Well-Being: 1957–1976." *Social Forces* 68:79–91.

McLanahan, Sara, and Larry Bumpass. 1988. "Intergenerational Consequences of Family Disruption." *American Journal of Sociology* 94:130–52.

McLanahan, Sara, and Gary Sandefur. 1994. *Growing Up with a Single Parent: What Hurts, What Helps*. Cambridge, MA: Harvard University Press.

McLaren, Angus. 1992. *A History of Contraception: From Antiquity to the Present Day*. Cambridge, MA: Blackwell Publishers.

McLellan, Betty. 1999. "The Prostitution of Psychotherapy: A Feminist Critique." *British Journal of Guidance and Counselling* 27(3):325–37.

McNally, J. W., and W. D. Mosher. 1991. "Digest." *Family Planning Perspectives* 23:234–35.

McNeal, Ralph B., Jr. 1995. "Extracurricular Activities and High School Dropouts." *Sociology of Education* 68:62–81.

Mead, George Herbert. 1934. *Mind, Self, and Society*. Chicago: University of Chicago Press.

Mead, Margaret. 1928. *Coming of Age in Samoa: A Psychological Study of Primitive Youth for Western Civilisation*. New York: Blue Ribbon Books.

Mederer, Helen J. 1993. "Division of Labor in Two-Earner Homes: Task Accomplishment Versus Household Management as Critical Variables in Perceptions About Family Work." *Journal of Marriage and the Family* 55:133–45.

Medoff, Marshall H. 1993. "An Empirical Analysis of Adoption." *Economic Inquiry* 31:59–70.

Merkle, Erich R., and Rhonda A. Richardson. 2000. "Digital Dating and Virtual Relating: Conceptualizing Computer Mediated Romantic Relationships." *Family Relations* 49:187–92.

Merton, Robert K. 1957. *Social Theory and Social Structure*, rev. ed. Chicago: Free Press.

Messinger, J. C. 1971. "Sex and Repression in an Island Folk Community." Pp. 3–37 in *Human Sexual Behavior: Variations in the Ethnographic Spectrum*, edited by Donald S. Marshall and Robert C. Suggs. New York: Basic Books.

Meyer, Daniel. 1999. "Compliance with Child Support Orders in Paternity and Divorce Cases." Pp. 127–57 in *The Postdivorce Family: Children, Parenting, and Society*. Thousand Oaks, CA: Sage.

Meyer, Daniel R., and Judi Bartfeld. 1996. "Compliance with Child Support Orders in Divorce Cases." *Journal of Marriage and the Family* 58:201–12.

Michaelis, Karen L. 1993. *Reporting Child Abuse: A Guide to Mandatory Requirements for School Personnel.* Newbury Park, CA: Corwin Press.

Michel, A. 1967. "Comparative Data Concerning the Interaction in French and American Families." *Journal of Marriage and the Family* 29:227–44.

Michener, H. Andrew, and John D. DeLamater. 1994. *Social Psychology*, 3rd ed. Fort Worth: Harcourt Brace.

Michrina, Barry, and CherylAnne Richards. 1996. *Person to Person: Fieldwork, Dialogue, and the Hermeneutic Method.* Albany, NY: State University of New York Press.

Microsoft Encarta Encyclopedia. 1999. Compact disk. Redmond, WA.

Milkie, Melissa A., and Pia Peltola. 1999. "Playing All the Roles: Gender and the Work-Family Balancing Act." *Journal of Marriage and the Family* 61:476–90.

Miller, Brent C., J. Kelly McCoy, Terrance D. Olson, and Christopher M. Wallace. 1986. "Parental Discipline and Control Attempts in Relation to Adolescent Sexual Attitudes and Behavior." *Journal of Marriage and the Family* 18:503–12.

Miller, Delbert C. 1991. *Handbook of Research Design and Social Measurement,* 5th ed. Newbury Park, CA: Sage.

Miller, Joel S., and Chinni Chilamkurti. 1991. "Physical Child Abuse Perpetrator Characteristics: A Review of the Literature." *Journal of Interpersonal Violence* 6:345–66.

Miller, Kim S. 1999. "Adolescent Sexual Behavior in Two Ethnic Minority Samples: The Roles of Family Variables." *Journal of Marriage and the Family* 61:85–98.

Miller, R. K., and S. J. McNamee, eds. 1998. *Inheritance and Wealth in America.* New York: Plenum.

Mindel, Charles H. 1980. "Extended Familism Among Urban Mexican-Americans, Anglos and Blacks." *Hispanic Journal of Behavioral Sciences* 2:21–34.

Mintz, Steven, and Susan Kellogg. 1988. *Domestic Revolutions: A Social History of American Family Life.* New York: Free Press.

Modell, J. 1983. "Dating Becomes the Way of American Youth." Pp. 169–75 in *Essays on the Family and Historical Change*, edited by D. Levine, L. P. Mock, L. A. Tilly, J. Modell, and E. Pleck. College Station: Texas A & M University Press.

Moen, Phyllis. 1985. "Continuities and Discontinuities in Women's Labor Force Activity." Pp. 113–155 in *Life Course Dynamics*, edited by G. H. Elder, Jr. Ithaca, NY: Cornell University Press.

––––––––. 1989. *Working Parents: Transformation in Gender Roles and Public Policies in Sweden.* Madison: University of Wisconsin Press.

––––––––. 1992. *Women's Two Roles: A Contemporary Dilemma.* New York: Auburn House.

––––––––. 2001. "The Career Quandary." *Reports on America* 2(1). Washington, DC: Population Reference Bureau.

Moen, Phyllis, and Alvin L. Schorr. 1987. "Families and Social Policy." Pp. 795–814 in *Handbook of Marriage and the Family*, edited by Marvin B. Sussman and Suzanne K. Steinmetz. New York: Plenum.

Money, John. 1980. *Love and Love Sickness: The Science of Sex, Gender Difference, and Pair-Bonding.* Baltimore: Johns Hopkins University Press.

––––––––. 1985. *The Destroying Angel.* Buffalo, NY: Prometheus Books.

Montenko, Aluma K. 1989. "The Frustrations, Gratifications, and Well-Being of Dementia Caregivers." *The Gerontologist* 29:166–72.

Montgomery, Marilyn J., Edward R. Anderson, E. Mavis Hetherington, and W. Glenn Clingempeel. 1992. "Patterns of Courtship for Remarriage: Implications for Child Adjustment and Parent-Child Relationships." *Journal of Marriage and the Family* 54:686–98.

Moore, Barrington, Jr. 1958. *Political Power and Social Theory.* Cambridge, MA: Harvard University Press.

Moore, David W. 1994. "Approval of Husband Slapping Wife Continues to Decline: Approval of Wife Slapping Husband Remains Steady." *The Gallup Poll Monthly* 341 (February).

Moore, Joan W. 1971. "Mexican Americans and Cities," *International Migration Review* 5:292–308.

Morawska, Ewa. 1994. "Ethnicity." Pp. 240–42 in *Encyclopedia of Social History*, edited by Peter Stearns. New York: Garland.

Morgan, Barrie S. 1981. "A Contribution to the Debate on Homogamy, Propinquity, and Segregation." *Journal of Marriage and the Family* 43:909–21.

Morgan, Edmund S. 1975. *American Slavery, American Freedom: The Ordeal of Colonial Virginia.* New York: W. W. Norton.

Morgan, Laurie A. 1998. "Glass-Ceiling Effect or Cohort Effect? A Longitudinal Study of the Gender Earnings Gap for Engineers, 1982–1989." *American Sociological Review* 63:479–83.

––––––––. 2000. "Is Engineering Hostile to Women? An Analysis of Data from the 1993 National Survey of College Graduates." *American Sociological Review* 63:316–21.

Morgan, Myfanwy, and Hilda H. Golden. 1979. "Immigrant Families in an Industrial City: A Study of Households in Holyoke, 1880." *Journal of Family History* 4:59–68.

Morris, John. 1999. "Market Constraints on Child Care Quality." *The Annals of the American Academy of Political and Social Science* 563:130–45.

Morris, Naomi M., and J. Richard Udry. 1983. "Menstruation and Marital Sex." *Journal of Biosocial Science* 15:173–81.

Moynihan, Daniel Patrick. 1965. *The Negro Family: The Case for National Action.* Washington, DC: U.S. Government Printing Office.

Moynihan, Daniel Patrick, ed. 1970. *Toward a National Urban Policy.* New York: Basic Books.

Moynihan, Ruth B., Susan Armitage, and Christine Fischer Dichamp, eds. 1990. *So Much to Be Done: Women Settlers on the Mining and Ranching Farms.* Lincoln: University of Nebraska Press.

Muehlenhard, Charlene L., and Marcia L. McCoy. 1991. "Double Standard/Double Bind: The Sexual Double Standard and Women's Communication about Sex." *Psychology of Women Quarterly* 15:447–61.

Mullins, Elizabeth I., and Paul Sites. 1984. "The Origins of Contemporary Eminent Black Americans: A Three-Generation Analysis of Social Origin." *American Sociological Review* 49:672–85.

Murdock, George P. 1949. *Social Structure.* New York: Macmillan.

————. 1957. "World Ethnographic Sample." *American Anthropologist* 59:664–87.

————. 1967. *Ethnographic Atlas.* Pittsburgh: University of Pittsburgh Press.

Murdock, George P., and D. White. 1969. "Standard Cross-Cultural Sample." *Ethnology* 8:329–69.

Murstein, Bernard I. 1970. "Stimulus-Value-Role: A Theory of Marital Choice." *Journal of Marriage and the Family* 32:465–81.

————. 1974. *Love, Sex, and Marriage through the Ages.* New York: Springer.

————. 1976. *Who Will Marry Whom?* New York: Springer.

————. 1986. *Paths to Marriage.* Beverly Hills, CA: Sage.

————. 1987. "A Clarification and Extension of the SVR Theory of Dyadic Pairing." *Journal of Marriage and the Family* 49:929–47.

Murstein, Bernard I., David Case, and Steven P. Gunn. 1985. "Personality Correlates of Ex-Swingers." *Lifestyles* 8:21–34.

Myers, Scott M., and Alan Booth. 1996. "Men's Retirement and Marital Quality." *Journal of Family Issues* 17:336–57.

N

Nadeau, Serge, William D. Walsh, and Catherine E. Wetton. 1993. "Gender Wage Discrimination: Methodological Issues and Empirical Results for a Canadian Public Sector Employer." *Applied Economics* 25:227–41.

Nakosteen, Robert A., and Michael A. Zimmer. 1997. "Men, Money, and Marriage: Are High Earners More Prone than Low Earners to Marry?" *Social Science Quarterly* 78:1:66–82.

Nass, Gilbert D., and Gerald W. McDonald. 1982. *Marriage and the Family,* 2nd ed. Reading, MA: Addison-Wesley.

National Center for Health Statistics. 1980. *National Estimates of Marriage Dissolution and Survivorship.* Health and Vital Statistics, Series 3, No. 19 (November). Washington, DC: National Center for Health Statistics.

————. 1988. "Advance Report of Final Divorce Stastics, 1988." *Monthly Vital Statistics Report* 39(12). Washington, DC: National Center for Health Statistics.

————. 1990a. "Advance Report of Final Natality Statistics." *Monthly Vital Statistics Report* 39(4). Hyattsville, MD: Public Health Service.

————. 1990b. *Vital Statistics of the United States: 1988, Vol. 1, Natality.* Washington, DC: U.S. Government Printing Office.

————. 1991. "Advance Report of Final Natality Statistics, 1989." *Monthly Vital Statistics Report* 40(8) (supplment). Hyattsville, MD: Public Health Service.

National Center for Health Statistics. 1995. "Vital Statistics Report Shows Broad Gains in the Nation's Health." http://www.cdc.gov/nchswww/releases/nrbd1995.htm.

National Center on Child Abuse and Neglect. 1988. *Study Findings: Study of National Incidence and Prevalence of Child Abuse and Neglect: 1988.* Washington, DC: U.S. Department of Health and Human Services.

National Commission on AIDS. 1992. "The Challenge of HIV/AIDS in Communities of Color." January. Washington, DC: The Commission.

National Indian Council on Aging. 1981. "1981 White House Conference on Aging: The Indian Issues." *National Indian Council on Aging Quarterly* 4:1.

National Institute of Child Health and Human Development, Early Child Care Research Network. 1999. *American Journal of Public Health* 89(7):1072–7.

Neal, Arthur G., Theodore Groat, and Jerry W. Wicks. 1989. "Attitudes About Having Children: A Study of 600 Couples in the Early Years of Marriage." *Journal of Marriage and the Family* 51:313–28.

Nee, Victor, and Herbert Wong. 1985. "Asian-American Socioeconomic Achievement: The Strength of the Family Bond." *Sociological Perspectives* 28:281–306.

Nelson, Barbara J. 1984. *Making an Issue of Child Abuse.* Chicago: University of Chicago Press.

Newcomer, Susan F., and J. Richard Udry. 1985. "Parent-Child Communication and Adolescent Sexual Behavior." *Family Planning Perspectives* 17:169–74.

Newman, Katherine. 1988. *Falling from Grace: The Experience of Downward Mobility in the American Middle Class.* New York: Random House.

Nielsen, Joyce McCarl. 1990. *Sex and Gender: Perspectives on Stratification.* Prospect Heights, IL: Waveland Press.

Nielsen, Linda. 1999. "Demeaning, Demoralizing, and Disenfranchising Divorced Dads: A Review of the Literature." *Journal of Divorce and Remarriage* 31(3–4):139–77.

Nock, Steven L. 1995. "Spouse Preferences of Never-Married, Divorced, and Cohabiting Americans." *Journal of Divorce and Remarriage* 24:91–108.

_____. 1998. *Marriage in Men's Lives.* New York: Oxford University Press.

Nock, Steven L., James D. Wright, and Laura Sanchez. 1999. "America's Divorce Problem." *Society* 36,4(240):43–52.

Noddings, Nell. 1984. *Caring: A Feminine Approach to Ethics and Moral Education.* Berkeley, CA: University of California Press.

Noller, Patricia, and MaryAnn Fitzpatrick. 1993. *Communication in Family Relationships.* Boston: Allyn and Bacon.

Norton, Arthur J., and Paul C. Glick. 1976. "Marital Instability: Past, Present, and Furture." *Journal of Social Issues* 32:5–19.

Norton, Arthur J., and Jeanne H. Moorman. 1987. "Current Trends in Marriage and Divorce Among American Women." *Journal of Marriage and the Family* 49:3–14.

Norton, Sally Ann. 1999. "Reconciling Decisions Near the End of Life: A Grounded Theory Study." Ph.D. Dissertation, University of Wisconsin, Madison. *Dissertation Abstracts International Section B: The Sciences and Engineering* 60(6-B).

Nsamenang, A. Bame. 1992. *Human Development in Cultural Context: A Third World Perspective.* Newbury Park, CA: Sage Publications.

Nye, F. Ivan., 1976. *Role Structure and Analysis of the Family.* Beverly Hills, CA: Sage.

Nye, F. Ivan, and Gerald W. McDonald. 1979. "Family Policy Research: Emergent Models and Some Theoretical Issues." *Journal of Marriage and the Family* 41:473–85.

Nye, F. Ivan, and Steven D. McLaughlin. 1982. "Role Competence and Marital Satisfaction." Pp. 67–79 in *Family Relationships: Rewards and Costs*, edited by F. Ivan Nye. Beverly Hills, CA: Sage.

O

Oakley, Ann. 1984. *The Captured Womb: A History of Medical Care of Women.* London: Basil Blackwell.

_____. 1985. *Sociology of Housework.* New York: Pantheon.

O'Connell, Martin. 1993. "Where's Papa? Fathers' Role in Child Care." Report 20, *Population Trends and Public Policy.* Washington, DC: Population Reference Bureau.

O'Flaherty, Kathleen M., and Laura Workman Eels. 1988. "Courtship Behavior of the Remarried." *Journal of Marriage and the Family* 50:499–506.

Ogburn, William F. 1933. "The Family and Its Functions." Ch. 13 in *Recent Social Trends.* New York: McGraw-Hill.

_____. 1950. *Social Changes with Respect to Culture and Original Nature,* rev. ed. New York: Viking.

O'Hare, William P. 1992a. "America's Minorities—The Demographics of Diversity." *Population Bulletin* 47(3). Washington, DC: Population Reference Bureau.

_____. 1992b. *Can the Underclass Concept Be Applied to Rural Areas?* Washington, DC: Population Reference Bureau.

_____. 1996. "A New Look at Poverty in America." *Population Bulletin* 51(2):1.

O'Keefe, Maura. 1998. "Factors Mediating the Link between Witnessing Interparental Violence and Dating Violence." *Journal of Family Violence* 13:1:39–57.

O'Leary, K. Daniel. 2000. "Are Women Really More Aggressive than Men in Intimate Relationships? Comment on Archer." *Psychological Bulletin* 126(5):685–89.

O'Leary, K. Daniel, Julian Barling, Ileana Arias, Alan Rosenbaum, June Malone, and Andrea Tyree. 1989. "Prevalence and Stability of Physical Aggression between Spouses: A Longitudinal Analysis." *Journal of Consulting and Clinical Psychology* 57:263–68.

Olsen, Florence. 2001. "U. of Kentucky Professor Announces Project to Clone a Human Within 2 Years." *Chronicle of Higher Education.* http://chronicle.com/daily/2001/01/2001012904n.htm.

Olson, David H., and John DeFrain. 1994. *Marriage and the Family: Diversity and Strengths.* Mountain View, CA: Mayfield.

O'Neill, Nena. 1974. *Shifting Gears: Finding Security in a Changing World.* New York: Evans.

O'Neill, Nena, and George O'Neal. 1972. *Open Marriage.* New York: Avon.

Orbuch, Terri L., Joseph Veroff, and Diane Holmberg. 1993. "Becoming a Married Couple: The Emergence of Meaning the First Years of Marriage." *Journal of Marriage and the Family* 55:815–26.

Oropesa, R. S. 1993. "Using the Service Economy to Relieve the Double Burden: Female Labor Force Participation and Service Purchases." *Journal of Family Issues* 14:438–73.

————. 1996. "Normative Beliefs About Marriage and Cohabitation: A Comparison of Non-Latino Whites, Mexican Americans, and Puerto Ricans." *Journal of Marriage and the Family* 58:49–62.

Oropesa, R. S., and Bridget K. Gorman. 2000. "Ethnicity, Immigration, and Beliefs about Marriage as a 'Tie That Binds.'" Pp. 188–211 in *The Tie That Binds: Perspectives on Marriage and Cohabitation*, edited by Linda J. Waite. New York: Aldine de Gruyter.

Orthner, Dennis K. 1975. "Leisure Activity Patterns and Marital Satisfaction Over the Marital Career." *Journal of Marriage and the Family* 37:91–101.

Ortner, Sherry B. 1981. "Gender and Sexuality in Hierarchical Societies: The Case of Polynesia and Some Comparative Implications." Pp. 359–409 in *Sexual Meanings: The Cultural Construction of Gender and Sexuality*, edited by Sherry B. Ortner and Harriet Whitehead. Cambridge: Cambridge University Press.

Orwell, George. 1949. *1984*. New York: Harcourt, Brace, and Company.

Ostrander, Susan A. 1984. *Women of the Upper Class*. Philadelphia: Temple University Press.

Oxford Analytica. 1986. *America in Perspective*. Boston: Houghton Mifflin.

P

Paglia, Camille. 1990. *Sexual Personae: Art and Decadence from Nefertiti to Emily Dickinson*. New York: Vintage.

Pahl, Jan. 1989. *Money and Marriage*. London: Macmillan.

Papanek, Hanna. 1973. "Men, Women and Work: Reflections on the Two-Person Career." Pp. 90–110 in *Changing Women in a Changing Society*, edited by Joan Huber. Chicago: University of Chicago Press.

Papernow, Patricia L. 1993. *Becoming a Stepfamily: Patterns of Development in Remarried Families*. San Francisco: Jossey-Bass.

Parker, Karen F., and Matthew V. Pruitt. 2000. "Poverty, Poverty Concentration, and Homicide." *Social Science Quarterly* 81(2):555–70.

Parker, Stephen. 1990. *Informal Marriage, Cohabitation and the Law: 1750–1989*. New York: St. Martin's.

Parrinder, Geoffrey. 1984. *World Religions: From Ancient History to the Present*. New York: Facts on File Publications.

Parsons, Talcott, and Robert F. Bales. 1955. *Family Socialization and Interaction Process*. Glencoe, IL: Free Press.

————. 1956. *Family Socialization and Interaction Process*. London: Routledge and Kegan Paul.

Pasley, Kay, and Marilyn Ihinger-Tallman, eds. 1994. *Stepparenting: Issues in Theory, Research, and Practice*. Westport, CT: Greenwood Press.

Pasley, Kay, Marilyn Ihinger-Tallman, and Amy Lofquist. 1994. "Remarriage and Stepfamilies: Making Progress in Understanding." Pp. 1–14 in *Stepparenting: Issues in Theory, Research, and Practice*, edited by Kay Pasley and Marilyn Ihinger-Tallman. Westport, CT: Greenwood Press.

Pasley, Kay, M. Koch, and Marilyn Ihinger-Tallman. 1993. "Problems in Remarriage: An Exploratory Study of Intact and Terminated Remarriages." *Journal of Divorce and Remarriage* 20:63–83.

Patterson, Charlotte. 1997. "Children of Lesbian and Gay Parents." Pp. 235–282 in *Advances in Clinical and Child Psychology, Vol. 19,* edited by Thomas H. Ollendick and Ronald J. Prinz. New York: Plenum Press.

————. 2000. "Family Relationships of Lesbians and Gay Men." *Journal of Marriage and the Family* 62:1052–69.

Patterson, James, and Peter Kim. 1991. *The Day America Told the Truth: What People Really Believe about Everything that Really Matters*. Englewood Cliffs, NJ: Prentice-Hall.

Pavalko, Eliza, and Glen H. Elder, Jr. 1990. "World War II and Divorce: A Life-Course Perspective." *American Journal of Sociology* 95:1213–34.

Pedraza, Silvia, and Ruben Rumbault. 1995. *Origins and Destinies: Immigration, Race and Ethnicity in America*. Belmont, CA: Wadsworth.

Peek, Charles W., Judith L. Fischer, and Jeannie S. Kidwell. 1985. "Teenage Violence Toward Parents: A Neglected Dimension of Family Violence." *Journal of Marriage and the Family* 47:1051–58.

Peele, Stanton, and Archie Brodsky. 1975. *Love and Addiction*. New York: Taplinger.

Peplau, Letitia A. 1981. "What Homosexuals Want in Relationships." *Psychology Today* 15:28–38.

Peplau, Letitia A., and S. D. Cochran. 1990. "A Relationship Perspective on Homosexuality." Pp. 321–49 in *Homosexuality/Heterosexuality: Concepts of Sexual Orientation*, edited by David P. McWhirter. S. A. Sanders, and J. M. Reinisch. New York: Oxford University Press.

Peplau, Letitia A., and Steven L. Gordon. 1991. "The Intimate Relationships of Lesbians and Gay Men." Pp. 479–96 in *Marriage and Family in Transition*, edited by J. N. Edwards and D. H. Demos. Boston: Allyn and Bacon.

Peplau, Letitia Ann., R. C. Veniegas, and S. M. Campbell. 1996.

"Gay and Lesbian Relationships." Pp. 250–73 in *The Lives of Lesbians, Gays, and Bisexuals: Children to Adults,* edited by Ritch C. Savin-Williams and Kenneth M. Cohen. New York: Harcourt Brace.

Peters, H. Elizabeth, Laura M. Argys, Eleanor E. Maccoby, and Robert H. Mnookin. 1993. "Enforcing Divorce Settlements: Evidence from Child Support Compliance and Award Modifications." *Demography* 30:719–35.

Peters, Stephanie D., Gail E. Wyatt, and David Finkelhor. 1986. "Prevalence." Pp. 15–59 in *A Sourcebook on Child Sexual Abuse*, edited by David Finkelhor. Beverly Hills, CA: Sage.

Peters-Davis, Norah D., Miriam S. Moss, and Rachel A. Pruchno. 1999. "Children-in-Law in Caregiving Families." *Gerontologist* 39(1):66–75.

Peterson, Richard. 1996. "A Re-Evaluation of the Economic Consequences of Divorce." *American Sociological Review* 61:528–36.

Peterson, W. 1966. "Success Story, Japanese American Style." *New York Times Magazine* (January 6):20ff.

Pett, Marjorie A., Bruce E. Wampold, Charles W. Turner, and Beth Vaughan-Cole. 1999. "Paths of Influence of Divorce on Preschool Children's Psychosocial Adjustment." *Journal of Family Psychology* 13(2):145–64.

Pfeiffer, John. 1977. *The Emergence of Society: A Prehistory of the Establishment*. New York: McGraw-Hill.

Pfohl, Stephen. 1994. *Images of Deviance and Social Control: A Sociological History*, 2nd ed. New York: McGraw-Hill.

Phillips, Angela. 1994. *The Trouble with Boys*. New York: Basic Books.

Phizacklea, Annie, and Carol Wolkowitz. 1995. *Homeworking Women: Gender, Racism, and Class at Work*. Thousand Oaks, CA: Sage.

Piaget, Jean, and Barbara Inhelder. 1969. *The Psychology of the Child*. New York: Basic Books.

Pillemer, Karl, and David Finkelhor. 1988. "The Prevalence of Elder Abuse: A Random Sample Survey." *The Gerontologist* 28:51–57.

Pimentel, Ellen Efron. 2000. "Just How Do I Love Thee? Marital Relations in Urban China." *Journal of Marriage and the Family* 62:32–47.

Piotrkowski, Chaya, Robert N. Rapoport and Rhona Rapoport. 1987. "Families and Work." Pp. 251–83 in *Handbook of Marriage and the Family*, edited by Marvin B. Sussman and Suzanne K. Steinmetz. New York: Plenum Press.

Piotrow, P. T., W. Rinehart, and J. C. Schmidt. 1979. "IUDs: An Update on Safety, Effectiveness, and Research." *Population Reports,* Series B(3).

Pirog-Good, Maureen A., and Patricia R. Brown. 1996.

"Accuracy and Ambiguity in the Application of State Child Support Guidelines." *Family Relations* 45:3–10.

Pizzey, Erin. 1974. *Scream Quietly or the Neighbors Will Hear*. Milddlesex, England: Penguin Books.

Plath, David W., ed. 1983. *Work and Lifecourse in Japan*. Albany: State University of New York Press.

Pleck, Elizabeth. 1987. *Domestic Tyranny: The Making of Social Policy Against Family Violence from Colonial Times to the Present*. New York: Oxford University Press.

Polenko, Karen A., John Scanzoni, and Jay D. Teachman. 1982. "Childlessness and Marital Satisfaction." *Journal of Family Issues* 3:545–73.

Pollock, Linda. 1983. *Forgotten Children: Parent-Child Relations from 1500 to 1900*. Cambridge: Cambridge University Press.

Popenoe, David. 1987. "Beyond the Nuclear Family: A Statistical Portrait of the Changing Family in Sweden." *Journal of Marriage and the Family* 49:173–83.

_____. 1988. *Disturbing the Nest: Family Change and Decline in Modern Societies*. New York: Aldine de Gruyter.

_____. 1993. "American Family Decline, 1960–1990: A Review and Appraisal." *Journal of Marriage and the Family* 55:527–41.

_____. 1994. "The Family Condition of America: Cultural Change and Public Policy." Pp. 81–112 in *Values and Public Policy*, edited by Henry J. Aaron, Thomas E. Mann, and Timothy Taylor.

_____. 1996. *Life Without Father: Compelling New Evidence that Fatherhood and Marriage Are Indispensable for the Good of Children and Society*. New York: Free Press.

Popenoe, David, Jean Bethke Elshtain, and David Blankenhorn. 1996. *Promises to Keep: Decline and Renewal of Marriage in America*. Lanham, MD: Rowman and Littlefield.

Popper, Karl. 1959. *The Logic of Scientific Discovery*. New York: Science Editions.

Population Reference Bureau. 2000. *2000 World Population Data Sheet of the Population Reference Bureau*. Washington, DC. www.prb.org.

Portes, Alehandro, and Robert D. Manning. 1986. "The Immigrant Enclave: Theory and Empirical Examples." Pp. 47–68 in *Competitive Ethnic Relations*, edited by Susan Olzak and Joane Jagle. Orlando, FL: Academic Press.

Portes, Alehandro, and Ruben G. Rumbault. 1996. *Immigrant America: A Portrait*. Berkeley, CA: University of California Press.

Portes, Alehandro, and Ruben G. Rumbault. 2001. *Legacies: The Story of the Immigrant Second Genderation*. Berkeley, CA: University of California Press.

"Portrait of U. S. Fertility Shows Average Number of Births, Family-Size Differences Are Shrinking." 1985. *Family Planning Perspectives.* 17:37–38.

Potuchek, Jean. 1992. "Employed Wives' Orientation to Breadwinning: A Gender Theory Analysis." *Journal of Marriage and the Family* 54:548–58.

Presser, Harriet B. 1987. "Work Shifts of Full-Time Dual-Earner Couples. Patterns and Contrasts by Sex of Spouse." *Demography* 24:99–112.

_____. 2000. "Nonstandard Work Schedules and Marital Instability." *Journal of Marriage and the Family* 62:93–100.

Presser, Harriet B., and Virginia S. Cain. 1983. "Shift Work among Dual-Earner Couples with Children." *Science,* 219:876–79.

Pyke, Karen. 2000. "Ideology of 'Family' Shapes Perceptions of Immigrant Children." *National Council on Family Relations Report* 45(2):F12.

Q

Quadagno, Jill S. 1981. "The Italian American Family." Pp. 61–85 in *Ethnic Families in America: Patterns and Variations,* 2nd ed., edited by Charles H. Mindel and Robert W. Habenstein. New York: Elsevier.

Quale, G. Robina. 1988. *A History of Marriage Systems.* New York: Greenwood Press.

_____. 1992. *Families in Context.* New York: Greenwood Press.

R

Rabin, Albert I. 1982. *Twenty Years Later: Kibbutz Children Grown Up.* New York: Springer.

Radcliffe-Brown, A. R. 1930. "The Social Organization of Australian Tribes." *Oceania* 1:44–46.

Radin, Norma, 1994. "Primary-Caregiving Fathers in Intact Families." Pp. 11–54 in *Redefining Families: Implications for Children's Development,* edited by Adele Eskeles Gottfried and Allen W. Gottfried. New York: Plenum.

Radin, Norma, and G. Russell. 1983. "Increased Father Participation and Child Development Outcomes." Pp. 191–218 in *Fatherhood and Social Policy,* edited by M. Lamb and A. Sagi. Hillsdale, NJ: Lawrence Erlbaum.

Ragone, Helena. 1989. *Surrogate Motherhood: Conception in the Heart.* Boulder, CO: Westview Press.

Ramu, G. N. 1989. "Patterns of Mate Selection." Pp. 165–78 in edited by K. Ishwaran. *Family and Marriage: Cross-Cultural Perspectives.* Toronto, Canada: Wall and Thomson.

Rand, Michael R. 1997. "Violence-Related Injuries Treated in Hospital Emergency Departments." U.S. Department of Justice, Bureau of Justice Statistics. http://www. ojp.usdoj.gov/bjs/.

Rane, Thomas R., and Brent A. McBride. 2000. "Identity Theory as a Guide to Understanding Fathers' Involvement With Their Children." *Journal of Family Issues* 21:347–66.

Rank, Mark R., 1982. "Determinants of Conjugal Influence in Wives' Employment Decision Making," *Journal of Marriage and the Family* 44:591–604.

_____. 1994. *Living on the Edge: The Realities of Welfare in America.* New York: Columbia University Press.

Rank, Mark R., and Thomas A. Hirschl. 1999. "The Economic Risk of Childhood in America: Estimating the Probability of Poverty Across the Formative Years." *Journal of Marriage and the Family* 61:1058–67.

Rankin, Robert M., and Jerry S. Maneker. 1985. "The Duration of Marriage in a Divorcing Population: The Impact of Children." *Journal of Marriage and the Family* 47:43–52.

Raschke, Helen J. 1987. "Divorce." Pp. 597–624 in *Handbook of Marriage and the Family,* edited by Marvin B. Sussman and Suzanne K. Steinmetz.

Raupp, Carol D. 1999. "Treasuring, Trashing or Terrorizing: Adult Outcomes of Childhood Socialization about Companion Animals." *Society and Animals* 7(2):141–59.

Regoli, Robert M., and John D. Hewitt. 1994. *Delinquency in Society: A Child-Centered Approach.* New York: McGraw-Hill.

Reich, Wilhelm. [1933] 1946. *The Mass Psychology of Fascism.* Translated by Theodore P. Wolfe. New York: Orgone Institute Press.

_____. 1942. *The Function of the Orgasm.* Translated by Theodore P. Wolfe. New York: World.

Reid, Sue Titus. 1985. *Crime and Criminology,* 4th ed. New York: Holt, Rinehart and Winston.

Reigal, Betty Polisar, and Rita K. Spina. 1996. *Beyond the Traditional Family: Voices of Diversity.* New York: Springer Publishing.

Reinharz, Shulamit. 1984. *On Becoming a Social Scientist: From Survey Research and Participant Observation to Experiential Analysis.* New Brunswick, NJ: Transaction Books.

_____. 1992. *Feminist Methods in Social Science Research.* New York: Oxford University Press.

Reinisch, June Machover, and Stephanie Sanders. "Would You Say You Had Sex If …?" *Journal of the American Medical Association* 281:275–7.

Reiss, Albert J., Jr. 1961. "The Social Integration of Queers and Peers." *Social Problems* 2:102–20.

Reiss, Ira L. 1960. "Toward a Sociology of the Heterosexual Love Relationship." *Marriage and Family Living* 22:139–45.

_____. 1967. *The Social Context of Premarital Sexual Permissiveness.* New York: Holt, Rinehart and Winston.

_____. 1980. *Family Systems in America,* 3rd ed. New York: Holt, Rinehart and Winston.

_____. 1986. *Journey into Sexuality: An Exploratory Voyage.* Englewood Cliffs, NJ: Prentice-Hall.

_____. 1990. *An End to Shame: Shaping Our Next Sexual Revolution.* Buffalo, NY: Prometheus Books.

Reiss, Ira L., and Gary R. Lee. 1988. *Family Systems in America,* 4th ed. New York: Holt, Rinehart and Winston.

Reissman, Catherine. 1991. *Divorce Talk: Women and Men Make Sense of Personal Relationships.* New Brunswick, NJ: Rutgers University Press.

Renzetti, Claire M. 1992. *Violent Betrayal: Partner Abuse in Lesbian Relationships.* Newbury Park, CA: Sage.

Resnick, Michael D., Robert Wm. Blum, Jane Bose, M. Smith, and R. Toogood. 1990. "Characteristics of Unmarried Adolescent Mothers: Determinants of Child Rearing Versus Adoption." *American Journal of Orthopsychiatry* 60:577–84.

Rhode, Deborah L., and Martha Minow. 1990. "Reforming the Questions; Questioning the Reforms: Feminist Perspectives on Divorce Law." Pp. 191–210 in *Divorce Reform at the Crossroads,* edited by Stephen D. Sugarman and Herma Hill Kay. New Haven: Yale University Press.

Rich, Adrienne. 1980. "Compulsory Heterosexuality and Lesbian Existence." *Signs: Journal of Women in Culture and Society* 5:631–60.

Richards, Leslie N., and Cynthia J. Schmiege. 1993. "Problems and Strengths of Single-Parent Families: Implications for Practice and Policy." *Family Relations* 43:277–85.

Riddle, John M. 1992. *Contraception and Abortion from the Ancient World to the Renaissance.* Cambridge: Harvard University Press.

Riley, Dave. 1990. "Network Influences on Father Involvement in Childrearing." In *Extending Families: The Social Networks of Parents and Their Children,* edited by Moncrieff Cochran, Larner, Riley, Gunnarsson, Henderson, and Cross. Cambridge: Cambridge University Press.

Riley, Glenda. 1991. *Divorce: An American Tradition.* New York: Oxford University Press.

Rindfuss, Ronald R., and Elizabeth Hervey Stephen. 1990. "Marital Noncohabitation: Separation Does Not Make the Heart Grow Fonder." *Journal of Marriage and the Family* 52:259–70.

Risman, Barbara J., C. T. Hill, Z. Rubin, and L. A. Peplau. 1981. "Living Together in College: Implications for Courtship." *Journal of Marriage and the Family* 43:77–83.

Roberts, Keith A. 1995. *Religion in Sociological Perspective,* 2nd ed. Belmont, CA: Wadsworth.

Robertson, Ian. 1981. *Sociology,* 2nd ed. New York: Worth Publishers.

Robertson, Joan F., 1977. "Grandmotherhood: A Study of Role Conceptions." *Journal of Marriage and the Family* 39:165–74.

Robertson, Joan F., and Ronald L. Simons. 1989. "Family Factors, Self-Esteem, and Adolescent Depression." *Journal of Marriage and the Family* 51:125–38.

Robertson, John A. 1994. *Children of Choice: Freedom and the New Reproductive Technologies.* Princeton, NJ: Princeton University Press.

Robinson, John P. 1988. "Who's Doing the Housework?" *American Demographics* 10:26.

Robinson, John P., and Geoffrey Godbey. 1997. *Time for Life: The Surprising Ways Americans Use Their Time.* University Park, PA: The Pennsylvania State University Press.

Rodgers, Bryan. 1994. "Pathways Between Parental Divorce and Adult Depression." *Journal of Child Psychology and Psychiatry* 35:1289–1308.

Rodgers, Roy. 1962. *Improvements in the Construction and Analysis of Family Life Style Categories.* Kalamazoo: Western Michigan University Press.

Rodgers, Roy H., and Linda M. Conrad. 1986. "Courtship for Remarriage: Influences on Family Reorganization after Divorce." *Journal of Marriage and the Family* 48:767–75.

Rodgers, Willard L., and Arland Thornton. 1985. "Changing Patterns of First Marriage in the United States." *Demography* 22:265–79.

Rodman, Hyman. 1972. "Marital Power and the Theory of Resources in Cultural Context." *Journal of Comparative Family Studies* 3:50–69.

Roeber, A. G. 1993. "German Speakers." Pp. 719–27 in *Encyclopedia of American Social History, Vol. II,* edited by Mary Kupiec Cayton, Elliott J. Gorn, and Peter W. Williams. New York: Charles Scribner's Sons.

Roeleveld, N., E. Vingerhoets, G. Zielhuis, and F. Gabreels. 1992. "Mental Retardation Associated with Parental Smoking and Alcohol Consumption Before, During, and After Pregnancy." *Preventive Medicine* 21:110–19.

Rogers, Stacy J., and Lynn K. White. 1998. "Satisfaction with Parenting: The Role of Marital Happiness, Family Structure, and Parents' Gender." *Journal of Marriage and the Family* 60:293–308.

Roiphe, Katie. 1993a. *The Morning After: Sex, Fear, and Feminism.* Boston: Little, Brown.

_____. 1993b. "Date Rape's Other Victim." *New York Times Magazine* (June 13):26ff.

Rokach, Ami. 1990. "Content Analysis of Sexual Fantasies of Males and Females." *Journal of Psychology* 124:427–36.

Rollins, Boyd C., and Kenneth L. Cannon. 1974. "Marital Satisfaction Over the Family Life Cycle: A Reevaluation." *Journal of Marriage and the Family* 36:271–72.

Rollins, Boyd C., and Harold Feldman. 1970. "Marital Satisfaction Over the Family Life Cycle." *Journal of Marriage and the Family* 32:20–28.

Roof, Wade Clark, and William McKinney. 1987. *American Mainline Religion: Its Changing Shape and Future*. New Brunswick, NJ: Rutgers University Press.

Roosa, Mark W., and F. Scott Christopher. 1990. "Evaluation of an Abstinence-Only Adolescent Pregnancy Prevention Program: A Replication." *Family Relations* 39:363–67.

Roscoe, Bruce, Lauri E. Cavanaugh, and Donna R. Kennedy. 1988. "Dating Infidelity: Behavior, Reasons, and Consequences." *Adolescence* 13:35–43.

Rose, Suzanna, and Irene Hanson Frieze. 1989. "Young Singles' Scripts for a First Date." *Gender and Society* 3:258–68.

Rosen, Ellen I. 1987. *Bitter Choices: Blue-Collar Women In and Out of Work*. Chicago: University Press of Chicago.

Rosenbaum, Emily, and Denise B. Kandel. 1990. "Early Onset of Adolescent Sexual Behavior and Drug Involvement." *Journal of Marriage and the Family* 52:783–98.

Rosenblatt, Paul C. 1994. *Metaphors of Family Systems Theory: Toward New Constructions*. New York: Guilford.

Rosenblatt, Paul, Terri Karis, and Richard Powell. 1995. *Multiracial Couples: Black and White Voices*. Thousand Oaks, CA: Sage.

Rosencrantz, Helen Bee, Susan Voge, Inge Broverman, and Donald Broverman. 1968. "Sex Role Stereotypes and Self-Concepts in College Students." *Journal of Consulting and Clinical Psychology* 32:287–95.

Rosenthal, Carolyn J. 1985. "Kinkeeping in the Familial Division of Labor." *Journal of Marriage and the Family* 47: 965–74.

Ross, Catherine. 1995. "Reconceptualizing Marital Status as a Continuum of Social Attachment." *Journal of Marriage and the Family* 57:129–40.

Rossi, Alice S. 1968. "Transition to Parenthood." *Journal of Marriage and the Family* 30:26–39.

_____. 1978. "A Biosocial Perspective on Parenting." Pp. 1–31 in *The Family*, edited by Alice S. Rossi, Jerome Kagan, and Tamara K. Hareven. New York: Norton.

_____, ed. 1994. *Sexuality Across the Life Course*. Chicago: University of Chicago Press.

Rossi, Alice S., and Peter H. Rossi. 1990. *Of Human Bonding: Parent-Child Relations Across the Life Course*. New York: Aldine.

Rothman, Barbara. 1993. *Encyclopedia of Childbearing: Critical Perspectives*. Phoenix: The Oryx Press.

Rothman, Ellen K. 1984. *Hands and Hearts: A History of Courtship in America*. New York: Basic Books.

Rowe, David C. 1994. *The Limits of Family Influence: Genes, Experience, and Behavior*. New York: The Guilford Press.

Roxburgh, Susan. 1999. "Exploring the Work and Family Relationship: Gender Differences in the Influence of Parenthood and Social Support on Job Satisfaction." *Journal of Family Issues* 20:771–88.

Roy, M., ed. 1977. *Battered Women: A Psychosocial Study of Domestic Violence*. New York: Van Nostrand Reinhold.

Rubin, Lillian. 1976. *World of Pain: Life in the Working-Class Family*. New York: Basic Books.

_____. 1995. *Families on the Fault Line*. New York: HarperCollins.

Rubin, Zick. 1970. "Measurement of Romantic Love." *Journal of Personality and Social Psychology* 16:265–73.

_____. 1973. *Liking and Loving: An Introduction to Social Psychology*. New York: Holt, Rinehart and Winston.

Rubin, Zick, Charles T. Hill, Letitia Ann Peplau, and Christine Dunkel-Schetter. 1980. "Self-Disclosure in Dating Couples: Sex Roles and the Ethic of Openness." *Journal of Marriage and the Family* 42:305–17.

Ruggles, Steven. 1994. "The Origins of African-American Family Structure." *American Sociological Review* 59:136–51.

Rushton, Philippe J., Robin J. H. Russell, and Pamela A. Wells. 1984. "Genetic Similarity Theory: Beyond Kin Selection." *Behavioral Genetics* 14, 179–93.

Russell, Bertrand. 1929. *Marrriage and Morals*. New York: Horace Liveright.

Russell, Clare Marlane. 1999. "A Meta-Analysis of Published Research on the Effects of Nonmaternal Care on Child Development." *Dissertation Abstracts International Section A: Humanities and Social Sciences* 59(9-A)3362.

Russell, Diana. 1990. *Rape in Marriage*, 2nd ed. Bloomington: Indiana University Press.

Russell, Stephen T. 1994. "Life Course Antecedents of Premarital Conception in Great Britain." *Journal of Marriage and the Family* 56:480–92.

Ryan, Kathryn M. 1998. "The Relationship between Courtship Violence and Sexual Aggression in College Students." *Journal of Family Violence* 13:4:377–94.

Ryan, Kevin, and James M. Cooper, eds. 1988. *Kaleidoscope: Readings in Education,* 5th ed. Boston: Houghton Mifflin Company.

Ryan, Mary. 1979. *Womanhood in America*, 2nd ed. New York: New Viewpoint.

Ryan, William. 1976. *Blaming the Victim*. New York: Random House/Vintage.

S

Sacher, Jennifer A., and Mark A. Fine. 1996. "Predicting Relationship Status and Satisfaction After Six Months, Among Dating Couples." *Journal of Marriage and the Family* 58:21–32.

Sadik, Nafis. 1994. "Investing in Women: The Focus of the '90s." Pp. 209–26 in *Beyond Numbers: A Reader on Population, Consumption, and the Environment*, edited by Laurie Ann Mazur. Washington, DC: Island Press.

Safilios-Rothschild, Constantina. 1969. "Family Sociology or Wives' Sociology: A Cross-Cultural Examination of Decision Making." *Journal of Marriage and the Family* 30:290–301.

_____. 1970. "The Study of Family Power Structure: A Review 1960–1969." *Journal of Marriage and the Family* 31:290–301.

_____. 1977. *Love, Sex, and Sex Roles*. Englewood Cliffs, NJ: Prentice-Hall.

Sakai, Derek K., and Ronald Johnson. 1997. "Active Phenotypic Assortment in Mate Selection: Self-Descriptions and Sought-For Attributes of Mates in Dating Advertisements." *Social Biology* 44:3–4, 258–64.

Saks, Michael J., and Edward Krupat. 1988. *Social Psychology and Its Applications*. New York: Harper & Row.

Saller, Richard P. 1987. "Men's Age at Marriage and Its Consequences in the Roman Family." *Classical Philology* 82:21–34.

Salz, Beate R. 1984. "The Use of Time." Pp. 203–18 in *Work in Non-Market and Transitional Societies*, edited by H. Applebaum. Albany, NY: State University of New York Press.

Samera, T., and Arnold L. Stolberg. 1993. "Peer Support, Divorce, and Children's Adjustment." *Journal of Divorce and Remarriage* 20:45–64.

Sanchez, Laura, and Emily W. Kane. 1996. "Women's and Men's Constructions of Perceptions of Housework Fairness." *Journal of Family Issues* 17:358–87.

Sandler, Irwin N., Jen-Yun Tein, and Stephen G. West. 1993. "Coping, Stress and the Psychological Symptoms of Children of Divorce: A Cross-Sectional and Longitudinal Study." *Child Development* 65:1744–63.

Sandqvist, Karin. 1987. "Swedish Family Policy and the Attempt to Change Paternal Roles." Pp. 147–62 in *Reassessing Fatherhood*, edited by Charles Lewis and Margaret O'Brien. Newbury Park, CA: Sage.

_____. 1992. "Sweden's Sex-Role Scheme and Commitment to Gender Equality." Pp. 129–55 in *Dual-Earner Families*, edited by Susan Lewis, Dafna N. Izraeli, and Helen Hootsmans. Newbury Park, CA: Sage.

Sarrel, Philip, and Lorna Sarrel. 1980. "The Redbook Report on Sexual Relationships, Part I." *Redbook* (October):73–80.

Savane, Marie Angelique. 1986. "The Effects of Social and Economic Changes on the Role and Status of Women in Sub-Saharan Africa." Pp. 124–32 in *Understanding Africa's Rural Households and Farming Systems*, edited by Joyce Lewinger Moock. Boulder, CO: Westview Press.

Savin-Williams, Ritch C. 1994. "Dating Those You Can't Love and Loving Those You Can't Date." Pp. 196–215 in *Personal Relationships During Adolescence: Advances in Adolescent Development, Vol. 6*, edited by Raymond Montmayor, Gerald R. Adams, and Thomas P. Gullotta. Thousand Oaks, CA: Sage Publications.

Scanzoni, John. 1979. "Social Processes and Power in Families." Pp. 295–316 in *Contemporary Theories About the Family: Research-Based Theories, Vol 1.* edited by Wesley R. Burr, Reuben Hill, F. Ivan Nye, and Ira L. Reiss. New York: The Free Press.

_____. 1982. *Sexual Bargaining: Power Politics in American Marriage*, 2nd ed. Englewood Cliffs, NJ: Prentice-Hall.

Scarlet, Peter. 1994. "LDS Church Move for Gender Equity in Marriage Still Raises Questions." *The Salt Lake Tribune*, February 26, Pp. 1–2E.

Schaefer, L. 1981. "Women and Extramarital Affairs." *Sexuality Today* 4:3.

Schafer, John, Raul Caetano, and Catherine L. Clark. 1998. "Rates of Intimate Partner Violence in the United States." *American Journal of Public Health* 88(11):1702–4.

Schellenberg, James A. 1960. "Homogamy in Personal Values and the 'Field of Eligibles.'" *Social Forces* 39:157–62.

Scheper-Hughes, Nancy. 1984. "The Margaret Mead Controversy: Culture, Biology and Anthropological Inquiry." *Human Organization: Journal of the Society for Applied Anthropology* 43:85–93.

Schillinger, Liesl. 1994. "Bride and Seek." *The New Republic* 210:15–17.

Schoen, Robert. 1990. "First Unions and the Stability of First Marriage." *Journal of Marriage and the Family* 54:281–84.

Schoen, Robert, and Robin M. Weinick. 1993. "Partner Choice in Marriages and Cohabitation." *Journal of Marriage and the Family* 55:408–14.

Schor, Juliet B. 1993. *The Overworked American: The Unexpected Decline of Leisure.* New York: Basic.

Schrier, Arnold. 1958. *Ireland and the American Emigration 1850–1900.* Minneapolis: University of Minnesota Press.

Schroeder, Karen A., Linda L. Blood, and Diane Maluso. 1993. "Gender Differences and Similarities between Male and Female Undergraduate Students Regarding Expectations for Career and Family Roles." *College Student Journal* 27:237–49.

Schwartz, Daniel, and M. J. Mayauz. 1982. "Female Fecundity as a Function of Age." *The New England Journal of Medicine* 306:424–26.

Schwartz, Felice N. 1989. "Management Women and the New Facts of Life." *Harvard Business Review* 67:65–76.

_____. 1992. *Breaking with Tradition: Women and Work, the New Facts of Life.* New York: Warner Books.

Schwartz, Israel M. 1993. "Affective Reactions of American and Swedish Women to Their First Premarital Coitus: A Cross-Cultural Comparison." *Journal of Sex Research* 30:18–26.

Schwartz, Mary Ann, and Barbara Marliene Scott. 1994. *Marriages and Families: Diversity and Change.* Englewood Cliffs, NJ: Prentice-Hall.

Schwartz, Miguel, Susan G. O'Leary, and Kimberly Kendziora. 1997. "Dating Aggression among High School Students." *Violence and Victims* 12:4:295–305.

Schwartz, Pepper. 1994. *Peer Marriage.* New York: Free Press.

Scott, Marvin, and Stanford Lyman. 1968. "Accounts." *The American Sociological Review* 33:46–62.

Secret, Mary, Ginny Sprang, and Judith Bradford. 1998. "Parenting in the Workplace." *Journal of Family Issues* 19(6):795–815.

Seery, Brenda, and M. Sue Crowley. 2000. "Women's Emotion Work in the Family: Relationship Management and the Process of Building Father-Child Relationships." *Journal of Family Issues* 21:100–27.

Seagull, Elizabeth Ann, and A. A. Seagull. 1991. "Healing the Wound that Must Not Heal: Psychotherapy with Survivors of Domestic Violence." *Psychotherapy* 28:16–20.

Seigel, J. S., and C. M. Taeuber. 1986. "Demographic Perspectives on the Long-Lived Society." *Daedalus* 115:77–117.

Seltzer, Judith. 2000. "Families Formed Outside of Marriage." *Journal of Marriage and the Family* 62:1247–68.

Settles, Barbara H., Roma S. Hanks, and Marvin B. Sussman, eds. 1993. *American Families and the Future: Analyses of Possible Destinies.* New York: Haworth Press.

Sewall, William H. 1952. "Infant Training and the Personality of the Child." *The American Journal of Sociology* 58:150–59.

Shaffern, Robert. 1994. "Christianity and the Rise of the Nuclear Family." *America* (May) 7:13–15.

Shah, Farida, and Melvin Zelnik. 1981. "Parent and Peer Influence on Sexual Behavior, Contraceptive Use, and Pregnancy Experience of Young Women." *Journal of Marriage and the Family* 43:339–48.

Shahar, Shulamith. 1990. *Childhood in the Middle Ages.* New York: Routledge, Chapman & Hall.

Shane, J. M., I. Schiff, and E. A. Wilson. 1976. "The Infertile Couple: Evaluation and Treatment." *Clinical Symposia* 28:5.

Shankman, Paul. 1998. "Margaret Mead, Derek Freeman, and the Issue of Evolution." *Skeptical Inquirer* 22:4.

Shapiro, Isaac, and Robert Greenstein.1999. "The Widening Income Gulf." *Center on Budget and Policy Priorities.* www.cbpp.org/9-4-99tax-rep.htm.

Sheehan, Michael M. 1978. "The Formation and Stability of Marriage in Fourteenth-Century England: Evidence of an Ely Register." *Medieval Studies* 32:228–63.

Sheehan, Nancy W., and Paul Nuttall. 1988. "Conflict, Emotional and Personal Strain Among Family Caregivers." *Family Relations* 37:92–98.

Sheets, Virgil L., and Sanford L. Braver. 1996. "Gender Differences in Satisfaction with Divorce Settlements." *Family Relations* 45:336–42.

Shehan, Constance L. 1984. "Wive's Work and Psychological Well-Being: An Extension of Gove's Social Role Theory of Depression." *Sex Roles* 11:881–99.

Shehan, Constance L., E. Wilber Bock, and Gary R. Lee. 1990. "Religious Heterogamy, Religiosity, and Marital Happiness: The Case of Catholics." *Journal of Marriage and the Family* 52:73–79.

Shelton, Beth Anne, and Daphne John. 1993. "Does Marital Status Make a Difference? Housework among Married and Cohabiting Men and Women." *Journal of Family Issues* 14:401–20.

Shelton, Beth Anne. 1992. *Women, Men and Time: Gender Differences in Paid Work, Housework, and Leisure.* New York: Greenwood Press.

Shepher, J. 1971. "Mate Selection among Second Generation Kibbutz Adolescents and Adults: Incest Avoidance and Negative Imprinting." *Archives of Sexual Behavior* 1:293–307.

Shephard, Jon M. 1993. *The Scientific Study of Social Structure.* Minneapolis: West.

Sheptycki, J. W. E. 1991. "Using the State to Change Society: The Example of 'Domestic Violence'." *Journal of Human Justice* 3:47–66.

Sherman, Lawrence W., and Richard A. Berk. 1984. "The Specific Deterrent Effects of Arrest for Domestic Assault." *American Sociological Review* 49:261–72.

Shihadeh, Edward S. 1991. "The Prevalence of Husband-Centered Migration: Employment Consequences for Married Mothers." *Journal of Marriage and the Family* 52:432–44.

Shore, R. Jerald, and Bert Hayslip, Jr. 1994. "Custodial Grandparenting: Implications for Children's Development." Pp. 171–220 in *Redefining Families: Implications for Children's Development*, edited by Adele Eskeles Gottfried and Allen W. Gottfried. New York: Plenum.

Shorter, Edward. 1975. *The Making of the Modern Family*. New York: Basic Books.

Shostak, Marjorie. 1981. *Nisa: The Life and Words of a !Kung Woman*. New York: Random House.

Siegel, Charles. 1998. "The Brave New World of Child Care." *New Perspectives Quarterly* 15(3):11–24.

Sieling, Mark. 1984. "Staffing Patterns Prominent in Female-Male Earnings Gap." *Monthly Labor Review* 107:29–33.

Sills, Yole G. 1994. *The AIDS Pandemic: Social Perspectives*. Westport, CT: Greenwood Press.

Silberstein, Lisa R. 1992. *Dual Career Marriage: A System in Transition*. Hillsdale, NJ: Lawrence Erlbaum Associates.

Silverman, Phyllis. 1988. "Research as a Process: Exploring the Meaning of Widowhood." Pp. 217–40 in *Qualitative Gerontology*, edited by S. Reinharz and G. Rowles. New York: Springer.

Silverstein, Merril. 2000. "The Impact of Acculturation on Intergenerational Relationships in Mexican American Families." *National Council on Family Relations Report* 45(2):F9.

Silverstein, Louise B., and Carl F. Auerbach. 1999. "Deconstructing the Essential Father." *American Psychologist* 54:397–407.

————. 2000. "Continuing the Dialogue about Fathers and Families." *American Psychologist* 55(6): 683–84.

Simon, Rita J. 1993. *The Case for Transracial Adoption*. Washington, DC: American University Press.

Simon, Robin W., and Kristen Marcussen. 1999. "Marital Transitions, Marital Beliefs, and Mental Health." *Journal of Health and Social Behavior* 40:111–25.

Simon, William, and John H. Gagnon. 1986. "Sexual Scripts: Permanence and Change." *Archives of Sexual Behavior* 15: 97–120.

————. 1987. "A Sexual Script Approach." Pp. 363–83 in *Theories of Human Sexuality*, edited by James H. Geer and William T. O'Donohue. New York: Plenum.

Simmons, Leo. 1945. *The Role of the Aged in Primitive Society*. New Haven, CT: Yale University Press.

Simmons, Ronald L., and Christine Johnson. 1998. "An Examination of Competing Explanations for the Intergenerational Transmission of Domestic Violence." Pp. 553–70 in *International Handbook of Multigenerational Legacies of Trauma*, edited by Yael Danieli et al. New York: Plenum Press.

Simmons, Wendy W. 2000. "When It Comes to Having Children, Americans Still Prefer Boys. *Gallup Poll,* December 26. http://www.gallup.com/poll/releases/pr001226.asp.

Singh, B. Krishna, and J. Sherwood Williams. 1981. "Childlessness and Family Satisfaction." *Research on Aging* 3:218–27.

Skinner, B. F. 1953. *Science and Human Behavior*. New York: Macmillan.

————. 1957. *Verbal Behavior*. New York: Appleton-Century-Crofts.

————. 1974. *About Behaviorism*. New York: Vintage.

Skolnick, Arlene. 1991. *Embattled Paradise*. New York: HarperCollins.

Skoloff, Gary N., Skoloff, and Wolfe. 1997. "Marriage Laws." P. 728 in *The World Almanac and Book of Facts, 1997,* edited by Robert Famighetti. Mahway, NJ: World Almanac Books.

Smelser, Neil. 1962. *Theory of Collective Behavior*. New York: Free Press.

Smith, Andrea B., Linda L. Dannison, and Tammy Vach-Hasse. 1998. "When 'Grandma' Is 'Mom'." *Childhood Education* 75(1):12–16.

Smith, Daniel Blake. 1978. "Mortality and the Family in the Colonial Chesapeake." *Journal of Interdisciplinary History* 8:403–27.

Smith, Donna. 1990. *Stepmothering*. New York: St. Martin's Press.

Smith, Dorothy. 1994. *Texts, Facts, and Femininity: Exploring the Relations of Ruling*. New York: Routledge.

————. 1998. *Writing the Social: Critique, Theory and Investigations*. Toronto: Univ. of Toronto Press.

Smith, Elsdon C. 1956. *Dictionary of American Family Names*. New York: Harper and Brothers.

Smith, Jack C., James A. Mercy, and Judith M. Conn. 1988. "Marital Status and the Risk of Suicide." *American Journal of Public Health* 78:78–80.

Smith, Ken R., and Cathleen D. Zick. 1986. "The Incidence of Poverty among the Recently Widowed: Mediating Factors in the Life Course." *Journal of Marriage and the Family* 48:619–30.

Smith, Robert J., and Ella L. Wiswell. 1982. *The Women of Suye Mura*. Chicago: University of Chicago Press.

Smith, Scott, and Kim M. Lloyd. 1992. "Marriage Opportunities and Family Formation: Further Implications of Imbalanced Sex Ratios." *Journal of Marriage and the Family* 54:440–51.

Smith, Thomas C. 1988. *Native Sources of Japanese Industrialization, 1750–1920.* Berkeley: University of California Press.

Smith, Tom W., and James Allan Davis. General Social Survey(s), 1972–1998. (Machine-readable data file). Principal investigators, Tom W. Smith and James A. Davis. Produced by the National Opinion Research Center, Chicago. Tape distributed by the Roper Public Opinion Research Center, Storrs, CT. Microcomputer format and codebook prepared and distributed by MicroCase Corporation, Bellevue, WA. Analysis by Gene H. Starbuck.

Snarey, John. 1993. *How Fathers Care for the Next Generation: A Four-Decade Study.* Cambridge: Harvard University Press.

Snyder, Barbara, and Kathy Keefe. 1985. "The Unmet Needs of Family Caregivers for Frail and Disabled Adults." *Social Work in Health Care* 10:1–14.

Software Toolworks Reference Library. 1990. Novato, CA: Software Toolworks.

Soldo, Beth J., and Emily M. Agree. 1988. "America's Elderly." *Population Bulletin* 43(September):1–53.

Solomon, Robert. C. 1981. *Love: Emotion, Myth, and Metaphor.* New York: Anchor.

Sommers, Christina Hoff. 1994. *Who Stole Feminism: How Women Have Betrayed Women.* New York: Simon and Schuster.

Sorenson, S. B., and C. A. Telles. 1991. "Self-Reports of Spousal Violence in a Mexican American and a Non-Hispanic White Population." *Violence and Victims* 6:3–16.

Sorokin, Pitrim. 1937. *Social and Cultural Dynamics, Vol. 5.* New York: E. P. Dutton.

Sorokin, Pitrim A., Carle C. Zimmerman, and C. J. Galpin. 1931. *A Systematic Sourcebook in Rural Sociology, Vol. 2.* Minneapolis: University of Minnesota Press.

South, Scott J. 1985. "Economic Conditions and the Divorce Rate: A Time-Series Analysis of the Postwar United States." *Journal of Marriage and the Family* 47:31–41.

South, Scott J., Kyle D. Crowder, and Katherine Trent. 1998. "Children's Residential Mobility and Neighborhood Environment Following Parental Divorce and Remarriage." *Social Forces* 77(2):667–693.

South, Scott J., and Kim M. Lloyd. 1995. "Spousal Alternatives and Marital Dissolution." *American Sociological Review* 60:21–35.

South, Scott J., and Glenna Spitze. 1994. "Housework in Marital and Nonmarital Households." *American Sociological Review* 59:327–47.

Spain, D., and S. M. Bianchi. 1996. *Balancing Act: Motherhood, Marriage, and Employment among American Women.* New York: Russell Sage.

Spanier, Graham B. 1976. "Measuring Dyadic Adjustment: New Scales for Assessing the Quality of Marriage and Similar Dyads." *Journal of Marriage and the Family* 38:15–28.

———. 1976. "Perceived Parental Sexual Conservatism, Religiosity, and Premarital Sexual Behavior." *Sociological Focus* 9:285–98.

Spanier, Graham B., and Paul C. Glick. 1981. "Marital Instability in the United States: Some Correlates and Recent Changes." *Family Relations* 30:329–38.

Spanier, Graham B., Robert A. Lewis, and Charles L. Cole. 1975. "Marital Adjustment Over the Family Life Cycle: The Issue of Curvilinearity." *Journal of Marriage and the Family* 37:263–75.

Spanier, Graham B., and R. L. Margolis. 1983. "Marital Separation and Extramarital Sexual Behavior." *Journal of Sex Research* 19:23–48.

Spanier, Graham B., and Linda Thompson. 1987. *Parting: The Aftermath of Separation and Divorce,* rev. ed. Newbury Park, CA: Sage.

Spector, Malcolm, and John I. Kituse. 1977. *Constructing Social Problems.* Menlo Park, CA: Benjamin Cummings Publishing.

Spellman, John W. 1964. "Introduction." Pp. 9–64 in *The Kama Sutra of Vatsyayana: The Hindu Treatise on Love and Social Conduct,* by Vatsyayana. Translated by Sir Richard F. Burton. New York: E. P. Dutton & Co.

Spiro, M. E. 1956. *Kibbutz: Venture in Utopia.* Cambridge: Harvard University Press.

———. 1958. *Children of the Kibbutz.* Cambridge: Harvard University Press.

Spitz, Rene A. 1945. "Hospitality: An Inquiry Into the Genesis of Psychiatric Conditions in Early Childhood." Pp. 53–72 in *The Psychoanalytic Study of the Child, Vol. 1,* edited by Anna Freud. New York: International Universities Press.

———. 1946. "Hospitalism: A Follow-Up Report." Pp. 113–17 in *The Psychoanalytic Study of the Child, Vol. 2,* edited by Anna Freud. New York: International Universities Press.

Spitze, Glenna. 1988. "Women's Employment and Family Relations: A Review." *Journal of Marriage and the Family* 50:596–618.

Spitze, Glenna A., and John R. Logan. 1992. "Helping as a Component of Parent-Adult Child Relations." *Research on Aging* 14:291–312.

Spitze, Glenna, John R. Logan, Glenn Deane, and Suzanne Zerger. 1994. "Adult Children's Divorce and Intergenerational Relationships." *Journal of Marriage and the Family* 56:279–93.

Spock, Benjamin. 1945. *Baby and Child Care*. New York: Simon and Schuster.

_____. 1989. *Dr. Spock on Parenting*. New York: Simon and Schuster.

Sprecher, Susan, and Diane Femlee. 1991. "Effects of Parents and Friends on Romantic Relationships: A Longitudinal Investigation." Paper presented at the American Sociological Association annual convention, Cincinnati, OH.

Sprecher, Susan, and Kathleen McKinney. 1993. *Sexuality*. Newbury Park, CA: Sage.

Sprecher, Susan, and S. Metts. 1989. "Development of the 'Romantic Beliefs Scale' and Examination of the Effects of Gender and Gender-Role Orientation." *Journal of Social and Personal Relationships* 6:387–411.

Sprey, Jetse. 2000. "Theorizing in Family Studies: Discovering Process." *Journal of Marriage and the Family* 62:18–31.

Stacey, Judith. 1993. "Good Riddance to 'The Family': A Response to David Popenoe." *Journal of Marriage and the Family* 55:545–47.

_____. 1996. *In the Name of the Family: Rethinking Family Values in the Postmodern Age*. Boston: Beacon Press.

Stacey, Judith, and Timothy J. Biblarz. 2001. "(How) Does the Sexual Orientation of Parents Matter?" *American Sociological Review* 66:159–183.

Stacey, William A., Lonnie R. Hazlewood, and Anson Shupe. 1994. *The Violent Couple*. Westport, CT: Praeger.

Stack, Carol B. 1974. *All Our Kin: Strategies for Survival in a Black Community*. New York: Harper & Row.

Stack, Steven. 1994. "The Effect of Geographic Mobility on Premarital Sex." *Journal of Marriage and the Family* 56:204–08.

_____. 1996. "The Effect of Physical Attractiveness on Video Dating Outcomes." *Sociological Focus* 29:1, 83–85.

Stack, Steven, and J. Ross Eshleman. 1998. "Marital Status and Happiness: A 17-Nation Study." *Journal of Marriage and the Family* 60:527–36.

Stafford, Laura, and Cherie L. Bayer. 1993. *Interaction between Parents and Children*. Newbury Park, CA: Sage.

Stan, Adele M., ed. 1995. *Debating Sexual Correctness: Pornography, Sexual Harassment, Date Rape, and the Politics of Sexual Equality*. New York: Delta.

Staples, Robert. 1988. "The Black American Family." Pp. 303–24 in *Ethnic Families in America: Patterns and Variations*, edited by Charles H. Mindel, Robert Habenstein, and Roosevelt Wright, Jr. New York: Elsevier.

_____, ed. 1991. *The Black Family: Essays and Studies*, 4th ed. Belmont, CA: Wadsworth.

Starbuck, Alexander. 1924. *The History of Nantucket County, Island, and Town: Including Genealogies of First Settlers*. Boston: C. E. Goodspeed & Co.

Starbuck, Gene H. 1980. *Models of Human Sexuality and Social Control*. Washington, DC: University Press of America.

_____. 1997. *A Community's Response to Domestic Violence*. Grand Junction, CO: Mesa State College Press.

Stark, Rodney, and Roger Finke. 1988. "American Religion in 1776: A Statistical Portrait." *Sociological Analysis* (Spring):39–51.

Stark, Rodney, and Lynne Roberts. 1998. *Contemporary Social Research Methods*. Bellevue, WA: MicroCase Corporation.

Statistical Abstract. *Statistical Abstract of the United States*. Washington, DC: U.S. Government Printing Office.

Stein, Peter J. 1976. *Single*. Englewood Cliffs, NJ: Prentice-Hall.

Steinfirst, Susan, and Barbara B. Moran. 1989. "The New Mating Game: Matchmaking via the Personal Columns in the 1980s." *Journal of Popular Culture* 22:129–40.

Steinmetz, Suzanne K. 1977–78. "The Battered Husband Syndrome." *Victimology: An International Journal* 2:499–509.

Steinmetz, Suzanne K., Sylvia Clavan, and Karen F. Stein. 1990. *Marriage and Family Realities: Historical and Contemporary Perspectives*. New York: Harper & Row.

Stephen, Timothy D. 1985. "Fixed-Sequence and Circular-Casual Models of Relationship Development: Divergent Views on the Role of Communication in Intimacy." *Journal of Marriage and the Family* 47:955–63.

Stephenson, Joan. 2000. "HIV Risk From Oral Sex Higher Than Many Realize." *JAMA: Journal of the American Medical Association* 283(10):1279.

Sternberg, Robert J. 1986. "A Triangular Theory of Love." *Psychological Review* 93:119–35.

_____. 1988. "Triangulating Love." Pp. 119–38 in *The Psychology of Love*, edited by Robert J. Sternberg and Michael L. Barnes. New Haven, CT: Yale University Press.

Stets, Jan E., 1991. "Cohabiting and Marital Aggression: The Role of Social Isolation." *Journal of Marriage and the Family* 53:669–80.

Stets, Jan E., and Murray A. Straus. 1990. "Gender Differences in Reporting Marital Violence and Its Medical and Psychological Consequences." Pp. 151–65 in *Physical Violence in American Families: Risk Factors and Adaptations to Violence in 8,145 Families*, edited by Murray A. Straus and Richard J. Gelles. New Brunswick, NJ: Transaction.

Stevenson, Brenda. 1996. *Life in Black and White: Family and Community in the Slave South*. New York: Oxford University Press.

Stewart, Abigail, Anne P. Copeland, Nia Lane Chester, and Janet E. Malley. 1997. *Separating Together: How Divorce Transforms Families.* New York: Guilford Press.

Stier, Haya, and Noah Lewin-Epstein. 2000. "Women's Part-Time Employment and Gender Inequality in the Family." *Journal of Family Issues* 21:390–410.

Stivers, Richard. 1976. *A Hair of the Dog: Irish Drinking and American Stereotype.* University Park: Pennsylvania State University Press.

Stodder, James. 1998. "Double-Surnames and Gender Equality: A Proposition and the Spanish Case." *Journal of Comparative Family Studies* 29:585–93.

Stolley, Kathy Shepherd, and Elaine J. Hall. 1994. "The Presentation of Abortion and Adoption in Marriage and Family Textbooks." *Family Relations* 43:267–73.

Stone, Lawrence. 1986. *The Family, Sex and Marriage in England, 1500–1800.* New York: Oxford.

Stossel, Scott. 1997. "The Man Who Counts the Killing." *Atlantic Monthly* (May).

Stout, Hilary. 1992. "Adequacy of Spending on AIDS Is an Issue Not Easily Resolved." *The Wall Street Journal,* April 26, Pp. A1, A6.

Straus, Murray A. 1971. "Some Social Antecedents of Physical Punishment: A Linkage Theory Interpretation." *Journal of Marriage and the Family* 33:658–63.

———. 1990. "The National Family Violence Surveys." Pp. 3–16 in *Physical Violence in American Families: Risk Factors and Adaptations to Violence in 8,145 Families,* edited by Murray A. Straus and Richard J. Gelles. New Brunswick, NJ: Transaction.

———. 1993. "Physical Assaults by Wives: A Major Social Problem." Pp. 67–87 in *Current Controversies on Family Violence,* edited by Richard J. Gelles and Donileen R. Loseke. Newbury Park, CA: Sage.

———. 1994a. "Corporal Punishment of Children and Depression and Suicide in Adulthood." In *Coercion and Punishment in Long-Term Perspective,* edited by Joan McCord. New York: Cambridge University Press.

———. 1994b. *Beating the Devil Out of Them: Corporal Punishment in American Families.* New York: Lexington Books.

Straus, Murray A., and Richard J. Gelles. 1986. "Societal Change and Change in Family Violence From 1975 to 1985 as Revealed in Two National Surveys." *Journal of Marriage and the Family* 48:465–79.

———. 1990. *Physical Violence in American Families: Risk Factors and Adaptations to Violence in 8,145 Families.* New Brunswick, NJ: Transaction.

Straus, Murray A., Richard J. Gelles, and Suzanne K. Steinmetz. 1980. *Behind Closed Doors: Violence in the American Family.* New York: Doubleday.

Straus, Murray A., Sherry L. Hamby, Sue Boney-McCoy, and David B. Sugarman. 1996. "The Revised Conflict Tactics Scale (CTS2): Development and Preliminary Psychometric Data." *Journal of Family Issues* 17:283–317.

Straus, Murray A., and Christine Smith. 1990. "Violence in Hispanic Families in the United States: Incidence Rates and Structural Interpretations." Pp. 341–68 in *Physical Violence in American Families: Risk Factors and Adaptations to Violence in 8,145 Families* edited by Murray A. Straus, and Richard J. Gelles. New Brunswick, NJ: Transaction.

Straus, Murray A., and Julie H. Stewart. 1999. "Corporal Punishment by American Parents: National Data on Prevalence, Chronicity, Severity, and Duration, in Relation to Child and Family Characteristics." *Clinical Child and Family Psychology Review* 2(2):55–70.

Street, Eddy. 1994. *Counselling for Family Problems.* Thousand Oaks, CA: Sage.

Strong, Bryan, and Christine DeVault. 1994. "Response to Stolley and Hall." *Family Relations* 43:274–76.

Stroup, Atlee L., and Gene E. Pollock. 1994. "Economic Consequences of Marital Dissolution." *Journal of Divorce and Remarriage* 22:37–54.

Stull, Donald E., Karen Bowman, and Virginia Smerglia. 1994. "Women in the Middle: A Myth in the Making?" *Family Relations* 43:319–24.

Suarez, Zulema E. 1993. "Cuban Exiles: From Golden Exiles to Social Undesirables." Pp. 164–76 in *Family Ethnicity: Strength in Diversity.* Newbury Park, CA: Sage Publications.

Sugarman, David B., and Gerald T. Hotaling. 1989. "Dating Violence: Prevalence, Context and Risk Markers." Pp. 3–32 in *Violence in Dating Relationships,* edited by Maureen Pirog-Good and Jan Stets. New York: Praeger.

Sweet, James, and Larry Bumpass. 1987. *American Families and Households.* New York: Russell Sage.

Sweet, James, Lawrence Bumpass, and Vaughn Call. 1988. "The Design and Content of the *National Survey of Families and Households.*" Working Paper NSFH–1. Madison, WI: Center for Demography and Economy, University of Wisconsin.

Swidler, Ann. 1980. "Love and Adulthood in American Culture." Pp. 120–47 in *Themes of Work and Love in Adulthood,* edited by Neil Smelser and Erik Erikson. Cambridge, MA: Harvard University Press.

_____. 1986. "Culture in Action: Symbols and Strategies." _American Sociological Review_ 51:273–86.

Szasz, Thomas. 1980. _Sex by Prescription_. Garden City, NJ: Anchor/Doubleday.

Szinovacz, Maximiliane E. 2000. "Book Review of _Husbands and Wives: Dynamics of Married Living_." _Journal of Marriage and the Family_ 62:855–56.

T

Takaki, Ronald. 1989. _Strangers from a Different Shore: A History of Asian Americans_. Boston: Little, Brown.

_____. 1994. "Japanese American Families." Pp. 146–63 in _Minority Families in the United States: A Multicultural Perspective_, edited by Ronald L. Taylor. Englewood Cliffs, NJ: Prentice-Hall.

Tanfer, Koray. 1987. "Patterns of Premarital Cohabitation Among Never-Married Women in the United States." _Journal of Marriage and the Family_ 49:483–97.

Taniguchi, Hiromi. 1999. "The Timing of Childbearing and Women's Wages." _Journal of Marriage and the Family_ 61:1008–19.

Tannahill, Reay. 1980. _Sex in History_. New York: Stein and Day.

Tapper, Nancy. 1991. _Bartered Brides: Politics, Gender, and Marriage in an Afghan Tribal Society_. New York: Cambridge University Press.

Tasker, Fiola L., and Susan Golombok. 1997. _Growing Up in a Lesbian Family: Effects on Child Development_. New York: Guilford.

Tavris, Carol. 1992. _The Mismeasure of Woman_. New York: Simon and Schuster.

Tavris, Carol, and Susan Sadd. 1977. _The Redbook Report on Female Sexuality_. New York: Dell.

Tavris, Carol, and Carole Wade. 1984. _The Longest War: Sex Differences in Perspective,_ 2nd ed. San Diego: Harcourt Brace Jovanovich.

Taylor, Robert Joseph, Linda M. Chatters, M. Bilinda Tucker, and E. Lewis. 1991. "Developments in Research on Black Families: A Decade Review." Pp. 275–96 in _Contemporary Families_, edited by Alan Booth. Minneapolis: National Council on Family Relations.

Taylor, Ronald L. 1994. "Black American Families." Pp. 19–46 in _Minority Families in the United States: Multicultural Perspective_, edited by Ronald L. Taylor. Englewood Cliffs, NJ: Prentice-Hall.

_____. 2000. "Diversity Within African American Families." Pp. 232–51 in _Handbook of Family Diversity_, edited by

David H. Demo, Katherine R. Allen, and Mark A. Fine. New York: Oxford University Press.

Teachman, Jay D. 1983. "Marriage, Premarital Fertility, and Marital Dissolution: Results for Blacks and Whites." _Journal of Family Issues_ 4:105–28.

Teachman, Jay D., Randal Day, Kathleen Paasch, Karen Carver, and Vaughn Call. 1998. "Sibling Resemblance in Behavioral and Cognitive Outcomes: The Role of Father Presence." _Journal of Marriage and the Family_ 60:835–48.

Teachman, Jay D., and Karen Polonko. 1990. "Negotiating Divorce Outcomes: Can We Identify Patterns in Divorce Settlements?" _Journal of Marriage and the Family_ 52:129–39.

Teachman, Jay D., Lucky M. Tedrow, and Kyle D. Crowder. 2000. "The Changing Demography of America's Families." _Journal of Marriage and the Family_ 62:1234–46.

Tenenbaum, Shelly. 1993. "The Jews." Pp. 769–81 in _Encyclopedia of American Social History, Vol. II_, edited by Mary Kupiec Cayton, Elliott J. Gorn, and Peter W. Williams. New York: Charles Scribner's Sons.

Terman, Louis M. 1938. _Psychological Factors in Marital Happiness_. New York: McGraw-Hill.

Terrell, John, and Judith Modell. 1994. "Anthropology and Adoption." _American Anthropologist_ 96:155–61.

Thomas, Jeanne L. 1986. "Age and Sex Differences in Perceptions of Grandparenting." _Journal of Gerontology_ 41:417–23.

Thomas, Mason P. 1972. "Child Abuse and Neglect: Historical Overview, Legal Matrix, and Social Perspectives." _North Carolina Law Review_ 50:344.

Thomas, Veronica G. 1990. "Determinants of Global Happiness and Marital Happiness in Dual-Career Black Couples." _Family Relations_ 39:174–78.

Thomas, W. I., and Florian Znaniecki. 1920. _The Polish Peasant in Europe and America_. Boston: Gotham Press.

Thompson, A. P. 1983. "Extramarital Sex: A Review of the Research Literature." _Journal of Sex Research_ 19:1–22.

Thompson, Elizabeth, and Ugo Colella. 1992. "Cohabitation and Marital Stability: Quality or Commitment." _Journal of Marriage and the Family_ 54:259–67.

Thompson, Linda. 1991. "Family Work: Women's Sense of Fairness." _Journal of Family Issues_ 12:181–96.

Thompson, Linda, and Alexis J. Walker. 1989. "Gender in Families: Women and Men in Marriage Work, and Parenthood." _Journal of Marriage and the Family_ 51:845–71.

Thompson, Ross S., and Paul R. Amato, eds. 1999. _The Postdivorce Family: Children, Parenting, and Society_. Thousand Oaks, CA: Sage.

Thompson, S. 1990. "Putting a Big Thing into a Little Hole: Teenage Girls' Accounts of Sexual Initiation." *Journal of Sex Research* 27:341–61.

Thompson, Warren. 1929. "Population." *American Journal of Sociology* 34(6):959–75.

Thorton, Arland. 1991. "Influence of the Marital History of Parents on the Marital and Cohabitational Experiences of Children." *American Journal of Sociology* 96:868–94.

Thurer, Shari L. 1994. *The Myths of Motherhood: How Culture Reinvents the Good Mother.* Boston: Houghton Mifflin.

Thurow, Lester C. 1987. "Tax Wealth, Not Income." Pp. 145–50 in *Structured Social Inequality: A Reader in Comparative Social Stratification*, edited by Celia S. Heller. New York: Macmillan.

Tichenor, Veronica Jaris. 1999. "Status and Income as Gendered Resources: The Case of Marital Power." *Journal of Marriage and the Family* 61:638–50.

Timberlake, Elizabeth M. 1980. "The Value of Grandchildren to Grandparents." *Journal of Gerontological Social Work* 3:63–76.

Tjaden, Patricia, Nancy Thoennes, and Christine J. Allison. 1999. "Comparing Violence over the Life Span in Samples of Same-Sex and Opposite-Sex Cohabitants." *Violence and Victims* 14(4):413–25.

Toliver, Susan D. 1998. *Black Families in Corporate America.* Thousand Oaks, CA: Sage.

Townsend, Aloen, and Patricia Gurin. 1981. "Re-Examining the Frustrated Homemaker Hypothesis." *Sociology of Work and Occupations* 8:464–88.

Townsend, John Marshall. 1989. "Mate Selection Criteria: A Pilot Study." *Ethology and Sociobiology* 10:241–53.

Trager, James. 1992. *The People's Chronology: A Year-by-Year Record of Human Events from Prehistory to the Present.* New York: Henry Holt.

Trattner, Walter I. 1979. *From Poor Law to Welfare State: A History of Social Welfare in America*, 2nd ed. New York: The Free Press.

Tregarthen, Timothy. 1988. "The Paradox of Poverty." *The Margin* (April):4–7.

Treiman, Donald J. 1977. *Occupational Prestige in Comparative Perspective.* New York: Academic Press.

Tribe, Lawrence H. 1990. *Abortion: The Clash of Absolutes.* New York: Norton.

Tschann, Jeanne M., Janet R. Johnston, and Judith S. Wallerstein. 1989. "Resources, Stressors, and Attachments as Predictors of Adult Adjustment after Divorce." *Journal of Marriage and the Family* 51:1033–46.

Tucker, M. Belinda. 2000. "Marital Values and Expectations in Context: Results from a 21-City Survey." Pp. 166–89 in *The Tie That Binds: Perspectives on Marriage and Cohabitation*, edited by Linda J. Waite. New York: Aldine de Gruyter.

Turnbull, Colin M. 1961. *The Forest People.* New York: Simon and Schuster.

Turner, R. Jay, and Franco Marino. 1994. "Social Support and Social Structure: A Descriptive Epidemiology." *Journal of Health and Social Behavior* 35:193–212.

Tuttle, Lisa. 1986. *Encyclopedia of Feminism.* New York: Facts on File Publications.

U

Udry, Richard. 1981. "Marital Alternative and Marital Disruption." *Journal of Marriage and the Family* 43:889–97.

United Nations. 1990. *Demographic Yearbook,* 42nd issue. New York: United Nations.

U.S. Bureau of the Census. 1965. *Statistical History of the United States from Colonial Times to the Present.* Washington, DC: U.S. Government Printing Office.

_____. 1980. *Census of the Population.* PC80-2-4C. Washington, DC: U.S. Government Printing Office.

_____. 1983. *Current Population Report.* Washington, DC: U.S. Government Printing Office.

_____. 1989. "Child Support and Alimony." *Current Population Reports* Series P–23, no. 129. Washington, DC: U.S. Government Printing Office.

_____. 1991. "Fertility of American Women: June 1990." *Current Population Reports* Series P–20, no. 454. Washington, DC: U.S. Government Printing Office.

_____. 1991a. "Marital Status and Living Arrangements: March 1990." *Current Population Reports, Special Studies* Series P–23, no. 173. Washington, DC: U.S. Government Printing Office.

_____. 1991b. *Statistical Abstract of the United States: 1992*, 112th ed. Washington, DC: U.S. Government Printing Office.

_____. 1991c. "The Hispanic Population in the United States: March 1991." *Current Population Reports* Series P-20, no. 455. Washington, DC: U.S. Government Printing Office.

_____. 1991d. *Population Profile of the United States 1991: Current Population Reports, Special Studies* Series P-23, no. 173. Washington, DC: U.S. Government Printing Office.

_____. 1992a. "Household and Family Characteristics: 1991." *Current Population Reports* Series P-20, no. 458. Washington, DC: U.S. Government Printing Office.

_____. 1992b. "The Black Population in the United States:

March 1991." *Current Population Reports* Series P-20, n. 464. Washington, DC: U.S. Government Printing Office.

————. 1992c. "Marital Status and Living Arrangements: March 1992." *Current Population Reports* Series P-20, no. 468. Washington, DC: U.S. Government Printing Office.

————. 1993. *Statistical Abstract of the United States: 1993*, 113th ed. Washington, DC: U.S. Government Printing Office.

————. 1995. "Who Receives Child Support?" http://www.census.gov/ftp/pub/socdemo/www/chldsupp.html.

————. 1996a. "Marital Status and Living Arrangements: March 1994." *Current Population Reports* (P20-484). Washington, DC: U.S. Government Printing Office.

————. 1996b. "Poverty Thresholds in 1995, by Size of Family and Number of Related Children Under 18 Years." http://www.census.gov/ftp.pub/hhes/poverty/thresh95.html.

————. 1996c. "Percentage of Women Who Have Had a Child in the Last Year Who Were Unmarried: June 1990 to 1994." http://www.census.gov/ftp/pub/population/socdemo/fertility/htab1.prn.

————. 1996d. "Number of Families Below the Poverty Level and Poverty Rate." http://www. census.gov/ftp/pub/hhes/poverty/histpov/histpov13.prn.

————. 1998. "Current Population Survey, March, 1998; Household and Family Characteristics." http://www.census.gov/prod/3/98pubs/p20-515u.pdf.

U.S. Department of Justice. 1985. *The Uniform Crime Reports for the United States.* Washington, DC: U.S. Government Printing Office.

U.S. Department of Justice. 1996. "National Crime Victimization Survey." http://www.ojp.gov/pub/bjs/press/ncvs95p.pr.

————. 1997a. *The Uniform Crime Reports for the United States.* http://www.fib.gov/pressrel/ucr.htm.

————. 1997b. *Criminal Victimization in the United States, 1994.* Bureau of Justice Statistics. Washington, DC: U.S. Government Printing Office.

————.2000. "USDOJ: 2001 Budget Summary." http://www.usdoj.gov/jmd/2001summary/vcrp-bs01.htm.

U.S. Department of Labor, Bureau of Labor Statistics. 1997. National Census of Fatal Occupational Injuries, 1997. Table 4. http://www.osha.gov/oshstats/bls/cftb0100.pdf.

U.S. House of Representatives Select Committee on Aging. 1987. *Exploring the Myths. Caregiving in America.* Washington, DC: U.S. Government Printing Office.

U.S. National Center for Health Statistics. 1990. "Advanced Report of Final Marriage Statistics, 1987." *Monthly Vital Statistics Report* 38(12)Supplement, April 3.

————. 1991a. "Annual Summary of Births, Marriages, Divorces, and Deaths: United States, 1990." *Monthly Vital Statistics Report* 39(13), August 18.

————. 1991b. "Advance Report of Final Divorce Statistics, 1988." *Monthly Vital Statistics Report* 40(4)Supplement 2, May 21.

Upchurch, Dawn M., Carol S. Aneshensel, Clea A. Sucoff, and Lene Levy-Storms. 1999. "Neighborhood and Family Contexts of Adolescent Sexual Activity." *Journal of Marriage and the Family* 61:920–33.

Usdansky, M. L. 1992. "Wedded to the Single Life: Attitudes, Economy Delaying Marriages." *USA Today*, July 17, P. A8.

Uttal, Lynet, and Mary Tuominen. 1999. "Tenuous Relationships: Exploitation, Emotion, and Racial Ethnic Significance in Paid Child Care Work." *Gender and Society* 13(6):758–80.

Utendorf, Kelvin R. 1998. "Recent Changes in Earnings Distributions in the United States." *Social Security Bulletin* 63:12–28.

V

Vaillant, Caroline O., and George E Vaillant. 1993. "Is the U-Curve of Marital Satisfaction an Illusion? A 40-Year Study of Marriage." *Journal of Marriage and the Family* 55:230–39.

Vandekerckhove, Lieven A. 1981. "The Role of Godparents: On the Integration of a Non-Familial Role in the Structure of the Kinship System." *Journal of Comparative Family Studies* 12:56–59.

Vandenheuval, Audrey. 1991. "In a Class of Our Own?" *Family Matters* 20:20.

Vanek, Joann. 1974. "Time Spent in Housework." *Scientific American* 231:116–20.

Van Gelder, L., and P. R. Brandt. 1996. *The Girls Next Door: Into the Heart of Lesbian America.* New York: Simon and Schuster.

Vannoy-Hiller, Dana, and William W. Philliber. 1989. *Equal Partners: Successful Women in Marriage.* Newbury Park, CA: Sage.

Vaughan, Diane. 1988. "Uncoupling: The Social Construction of Divorce." Pp 384–403 in *Social Interactions: Readings in Sociology*, 3rd ed., edited by Candace Clark and Howard Robbey. New York: St Martin's.

Vemer, Elizabeth, Marilyn Coleman, Lawrence H. Ganong, and Harris Cooper. 1989. "Marital Satisfaction in Remarriage Meta-Analysis." *Journal of Marriage and the Family* 51:713–25.

Vera, Herman, Donna H. Berardo, and Felix M. Berardo. 1985. "Age Heterogamy in Marriage." *Journal of Marriage and the Family* 49:553–66.

Visher, Emily B., and John S. Visher. 1988. *Old Loyalists, New Ties: Therapeutic Strategies with Stepfamilies*. New York: Brunner/Mazel.

Vivelo, Frank R. 1978. *Cultural Anthropology Handbook*. New York: McGraw-Hill.

Vogler, Carolyn, and Jan Pahl. 1994. "Money, Power and Inequality Within Marriage." *The Sociological Review* 42:263–88.

Voydanoff, Patricia. 1987. *Work and Family Life*. Beverly Hills, CA: Sage.

_____. 1989. "Work and Family: A Review and Expanded Conceptualization." Pp. 1–22 in *Work and Family*, edited by Elizabeth B. Goldsmith. Newbury Park, CA: Sage.

Voydanoff, Patricia, and Brenda W. Donnelly. 1999. "The Intersection of Time in Activities and Perceived Unfairness in Relation to Psychological Distress and Marital Quality." *Journal of Marriage and the Family* 61:739–51.

W

Wagner, Roland M., and Diana M. Shaffer. 1980. "Social Networks and Survival Strategies: An Exploratory Study of Mexican-American, Black, and Anglo Family Heads in San Jose, California." Pp. 173–90 in *Twice a Minority: Mexican-American Women*, edited by B. Margarita. St. Louis: C. V. Mosby.

Waite, Linda J. 1995. "Does Marriage Matter?" *Demography* 32:483–507.

_____. 2000. "Trends in Men's and Women's Well-Being in Marriage." Pp. 188–211 in *The Tie That Binds: Perspectives on Marriage and Cohabitation*, edited by Linda J. Waite. New York: Aldine de Gruyter.

Waite, Linda J., and Maggie Gallagher. 2000. *The Case for Marriage: Why Married People Are Happier, Healthier, and Better Off Financially*. New York: Doubleday.

Waite, Linda J., Gus W. Haggstrom, and David E. Kanouse. 1985. "Changes in the Employment Activities of New Parents." *American Sociological Review* 50:263–72.

Waite, Linda J., and Kara Joyner. 1996. "Men's and Women's General Happiness and Sexual Satisfaction in Marriage, Cohabitation and Single Living." Unpublished manuscript. Population Research Center, University of Chicago.

Waite, Linda J., and Lee A. Lillard. 1991. "Children and Marital Disruption." *American Journal of Sociology* 96:930–53.

Walby, Sylvia. 1990. *Theorizing Patriarchy*. Oxford: Basil Blackwell.

Walker, Alexis J. 1985. "Reconceptualizing Family Stress." *Journal of Marriage and the Family* 47:827–37.

_____. 2000. "Refracted Knowledge: Viewing Families Through the Prism of Social Science." *Journal of Marriage and the Family* 62:595–608.

Walker, Alexis J., Hwa-Yong Shin, and David N. Bird. 1990. "Perceptions of Relationship Change and Caregiver Satisfaction." *Family Relations* 39:147–52.

Walker, Alice, and Pratibha Parmar. 1993. *Warrior Marks: Female Genital Mutilation and the Sexual Blinding of Women*. New York: Harcourt Brace.

Walker, Lenore. 1979. *The Battered Woman*. New York: Harper & Row.

_____. 1984. *The Battered Woman Syndrome*. New York: Springer.

_____. 1989. *Terrifying Love: Why Battered Women Kill and How Society Responds*. New York: Harper Perennial.

Wallace, Pamela M., and Ian H. Gotlib. 1990. "Marital Adjustment During the Transition to Parenthood: Stability and Predictors of Change." *Journal of Marriage and the Family* 52:41–65.

Waller, Willard. 1937. "The Rating and Dating Complex." *American Sociological Review* 2:727–34.

_____. 1951. *The Family: A Dynamic Interpretation*. New York: Dryden.

Wallerstein, Judith S., and Sandra Blakeslee. 1989. *Second Chances: Men, Women, and Children a Decade After Divorce*. New York: Ticknor & Fields.

Wallerstein, Judith S., and Joan B. Kelly. 1976. "The Effects of Parental Divorce: The Experiences of the Child in Later Latency." *American Journal of Orthopsychiatry* 46:256–69.

_____. 1980. *Surviving the Breakup: How Children and Parents Cope With Divorce*. New York: Basic Books.

Wallerstein, Judith S., and Julia Lewis. 1998. "The Long-Term Impact of Divorce on Children: A First Report from a 15-Year Study." *Family and Concilliation Courts Review* 36(3):368–83.

Walsh, Anthony. 1996. *The Science of Love: Understanding Love and Its Effects on Mind and Body*. Buffalo, NY: Prometheus Books.

Walster, Elaine, Vera Aronson, Darcy Abrahams, and Leon Rottman. 1966. "Importance of Physical Attractiveness in Dating Behavior." *Journal of Personality and Social Psychology* 4:508–16.

Walster, Elaine, G. William Walster, and Ellen Berscheid. 1978. *Equity: Theory and Research*. Rockleigh, NJ: Allyn and Bacon.

Wandersee, Winifred. 1981. *Women's Work and Family Values, 1920–1940*. Cambridge, MA: Harvard University Press.

Waring, E. M., Betsy Schaefer, and Richard Fry. 1994. "The Influence of Therapeutic Self-Disclosure on Perceived Marital Intimacy." *Journal of Sex and Marital Therapy* 20:135–46.

Warner, W. Lloyd, and Paul S. Lunt. 1941. *The Social Life of a Modern Community: Yankee City Series, Vol. I.* New Haven: Yale University Press.

Watson, John. 1928. *Psychological Care of Infant and Child.* New York: Norton.

Watson, Rubie S., and Patricia Buckley Ebrey, eds. 1991. *Marriage and Inequality in Chinese Society.* Berkeley: University of California Press.

Wattenberg, Esther. 1993. "Paternity Actions and Young Fathers." In *Young Fathers: Changing Roles and Emerging Policies.* Edited by Robert I. Lerman and Theodora Ooms. Philadelphia: Temple University Press.

Weber, Claudia. 1999. "A Descriptive Study of the Relation between Domestic Violence and Pet Abuse." *Dissertation Abstracts International: Section B: The Sciences and Engineering* 59(8-B).

Weber, Max. [1925] 1964. *The Theory of Social and Economic Organization.* Translated by A. M. Henderson and Talcott Parsons. New York: Free Press.

————. [1904] 1958. *The Protestant Ethic and the Spirit of Capitalism.* Translated by Talcott Parsons. New York: Scribner's.

————. [?] 1949. *The Methodology of the Social Sciences.* Translated and edited by Edward H. Shils and Henry A. Finch. New York: Free Press.

Weeks, David L., and Joan Jurich. 1985. "Size of Community of Residence as a Predictor of Attitudes Toward Extramarital Sexual Relations." *Journal of Marriage and the Family* 47:173–78.

Weg, Ruth B. 1983. *Sexuality in the Later Years: Roles and Behavior.* New York: Academic Press.

Wegar, Katarina. 2000. "Adoption, Family Ideology, and Social Stigma: Bias in Community Attitudes, Adoption Research, and Practice." *Family Relations* 49:363–70.

Wegscheider, Sharon. 1981. *Another Chance: Hope and Health for the Alcoholic Family.* Palo Alto, CA: Science and Behavior Books.

Weigel, Daniel J., and Deborah S. Ballard-Reisch. 1996. "Relational Maintenance, Commitment, and Satisfaction in Marriages: Gender and Marital Life Course Issues." Paper presented at the annual conference of the Speech Communication Association, San Diego, CA.

————. 1999. "How Couples Maintain Marriages: A Closer Look at Self and Spouse Influences Upon the Use of Maintenance Behaviors in Marriages." *Family Relations* 48:263–69.

Weinberg, Martin S., Rochelle Ganz Swenson, and Sue Kiefer Hammersmith. 1980. "Sexual Autonomy and the Status of Women: Models of Female Sexuality in U.S. Sex Manuals from 1950 to 1980." *Social Problems* 30:312–24.

Weinberg, Martin S., and Colin J. Williams. 1980. "Sexual Embourgeoisment? Social Class and Sexual Activity: 1938–1970." *American Sociological Review* 45:33–48.

Weinberg, Martin S., Colin J. Williams, and Douglas W. Pryor. 1994. *Dual Attraction: Understanding Bisexuality.* New York: Oxford University Press.

Weis, David L. 1983. "Affective Reactions of Women to Their Initial Experience of Coitus." *Journal of Sex Research* 19:209–37.

Weiss, Robert S. 1975. *Marital Separation: Managing After a Marriage Ends.* New York: Basic Books.

Weitzman, Lenore. 1985. *The Divorce Revolution.* New York: Free Press.

————. 1996. "The Economic Consequences of Divorce Are Still Unequal: Comment on Peterson." *American Sociological Review* 61:537–38.

Welch, Charles E. III, and Paul C. Glick. 1981. "The Incidence of Polygamy in Contemporary Africa: A Research Note." *Journal of Marriage and the Family* 43:191–93.

Wells, Edward, and Joseph Rankin. 1991. "Families and Delinquency: A Meta-Analysis of the Impact of Broken Homes." *Social Problems* 38:71–93.

West, Candace, and Don H. Zimmerman. 1987. "Doing Gender." *Gender and Society* 1:125–51.

Westman, Jack C. 1994. *Licensing Parents: Can We Prevent Child Abuse and Neglect?* New York: Plenum.

Westoff, Charles F., and Noreen Goldman. 1988. "Figuring the Odds in the Marriage Market." Pp. 39–46 in *Current Issues in Marriage and Family,* edited by J. Gipson Wells. New York: Macmillan.

Wheelock, Jane. 1990. *Husbands at Home: The Domestic Economy in a Post-Industrial Society.* New York: Routledge.

Whitbeck, Les B., Kevin A. Yoder, Dan R. Hoyt, and Rand D. Conger. 1999. "Early Adolescent Sexual Activity: A Development Study." *Journal of Marriage and the Family* 61:934–46.

White, Burton L. 1985. *The First Three Years of Life,* rev. ed. Englewood Cliffs, NJ: Prentice-Hall.

White, Gregory. 1981. "Physical Attractiveness and Courtship Progress." *Journal of Personality and Social Psychology* 39:360–68.

White, Jacquelyn W., Paige Hall Smith, Mary P. Koss, and A. J. Figueredo. 2000. "Intimate Partner Aggression—What Have We Learned? Comment on Archer." *Psychological Bulletin* 126(5):690–96.

White, Lynn K. 1990. "Determinants of Divorce: A Review of Research in the Eighties." *Journal of Marriage and the Family* 52:904–12.

————. 1994. "Growing Up with Single Parents and Stepparents: Long-Term Effects on Family Solidarity." *Journal of Marriage and the Family* 56:935–48.

White, Lynn K., and Alan Booth. 1985a. "The Quality and Stability of Remarriages: The Role of Stepchildren." *American Sociological Review* 50:189–98.

————. 1985b. "The Transition to Parenthood and Marital Quality." *Journal of Family Issues* 6:435–49.

White, Lynn, and Bruce Keith. 1990. "The Effect of Shift Work on the Quality and Stability of Marital Relations." *Journal of Marriage and the Family* 52:453–62.

Whitebook, Marcy. 1999. "Child Care Workers: High Demand, Low Wages." *The Annals of the American Academy of Political and Social Science* 563:146–61.

Whitehead, Barbara Dafoe. 1996. "The Decline of Marriage as the Social Basis of Childrearing." Pp. 3–14 in *Promises to Keep*, edited by David Popenoe, Jean Bethke Elshtain, and David Blankenhorn. Lanham, MD: Rowman and Littlefield.

Whyte, Martin King. 1990. *Dating, Mating, and Marriage.* Hawthorne, NY: Aldine de Gruyter.

Wilkerson, Isabel. 1991. "Interracial Marriage Rises, Acceptance Lags." *New York Times*, December 2, Pp. A1, A11.

Wilkie, Jane Riblett, Myra Marx Feree, and Kathryn Strother Ratcliff. 1998. "Gender and Fairness: Marital Satisfaction in Two-Earner Couples." *Journal of Marriage and the Family* 60:577–94.

Wilkinson, Karen. 1980. "The Broken Home and Delinquent Behavior." Pp. 20–43 in *Understanding Crime*, edited by Travis Hirshi and Michael Gottfredson. Beverly Hills, CA: Sage.

Williams, Edith, and Norma Radin. 1999. "Effects of Father Participation in Child Rearing: Twenty-Year Follow Up." *American Journal of Orthopsychiatry* 69(3):328–36.

Williams, G. C. 1997. "Review of *Adaptation*, edited by Michael R. Rose and George V. Lauder." *Copeia* 1997:645–47.

Williams, Joan. 1999. *Unbending Gender: Why Family and Work Conflict and What to Do About It.* New York: Oxford University Press.

Williams, Norma. 1990. *The Mexican American Family: Tradition and Change.* Dix Hills, NY: General Hall.

Willie, Charles Vert. 1991. *A New Look at Black Families*, 4th ed. Dix Hills, NY: General Hall.

Wilson, Edward O. 1975. *Sociobiology, the New Synthesis.* Cambridge: Harvard University Press.

Wilson, Barbara Foley, and Sally Cunningham Clarke. 1992. "Remarriages: A Demographic Profile." *Journal of Family Issues* 13:123–41.

Wilson, James Q. 1983. *Thinking About Crime.* New York: Vintage.

Wilson, Kenneth, and Alehandro Portes. 1980. "Immigrant Enclaves: An Analysis of the Labor Market Experiences of Cubans in Miami." *American Journal of Sociology* 86:295–319.

Wilson, William Julius. 1978. *The Declining Significance of Race.* Chicago: University of Chicago Press.

————. 1987. *The Truly Disadvantaged: The Inner City, the Underclass, and Public Policy.* Chicago: University of Chicago Press.

————. 1996. *When Work Disappears: The World of the New Urban Poor.* New York: Alfred A. Knopf.

————. 2000. "Rising Inequality and the Case for Coalition Politics." *The Annals of the American Academy of Political and Social Science* 568:78–99.

Winch, Robert F. 1958. *Mate Selection.* New York: Harper.

————. 1971. *The Modern Family.* New York: Holt.

Wineberg, Howard. 1988. "Duration Between Marriage and First Birth and Marital Stability." *Social Biology* 35:91–102.

Wineberg, Howard, and James McCarthy. 1998. "Living Arrangements after Divorce: Cohabitation Versus Remarriage." *Journal of Divorce and Remarriage* 19(1–2):131–46.

Winton, Chester. 1995. *Frameworks for Studying Families.* Guilford, CT: Dushkin Publishing.

Wisensale, Steven K. 1993. "State and Federal Initiatives in Family Policy: Lesson From the Eighties, Proposals for the Nineties." Pp. 229–50 in *Family Relations: Challenges for the Future*, edited by Timothy H. Brubaker. Newbury Park: Sage.

Wojnilower, Albert. 1998. "Declining Economic Hegemony and Child Care." *New Perspectives Quarterly* 15(3):9–10.

Wolf, Arthur P. 1995. *Sexual Attraction and Childhood Association: A Chinese Brief for Edward Westermarck.* Stanford, CA: Stanford University Press.

Wolf, Arthur P., and Chieh-Shan Huang. 1980. *Marriage and Adoption in China, 1845–1945.* Stanford: Stanford University Press.

Wolf, Diane. 1992. *Factory Daughters: Gender, Household Dynamics, and Rural Industrialization in Java.* Berkeley: University of California Press.

Wolf, Margaret. 1988. "Marriage, Family, and the State in Contemporary China." Pp. 106–118 in *Family Relations: A Reader*, edited by Norval D. Glenn and Marion Tolbert. Chicago: Dorsey.

Wolf, Robin. 1996. *Marriages and Families in a Diverse Society.* New York: HarperCollins.

Wolff, Edward N. 1995. "How the Pie Is Sliced." *The American Prospect* 22:58–64.

Woll, Stanley B., and Peter Young. 1989. "Looking for Mr. or Ms. Right: Self-Presentation and Videodating." *Journal of Marriage and the Family* 51:483–88.

Women's Bureau. 1993. U.S. Department of Labor, Women's Bureau Fact Sheet. http://www.dol.gov/dol/wb/public/wb_pubs/ wagegap2.htm.

Wong, Morrison G. 1988. "The Chinese American Family." Pp. 230–57 in *Ethnic Families in America: Patterns and Variations*, 3rd ed., edited by Charles H. Mindel, Robert Wesley Habenstein, and R. Wright, Jr. New York: Elsevier.

Wood, Floris W. 1990. *An American Profile—Opinions and Behavior, 1972–1989.* Detroit: Gale Research.

Woodburn, James. 1966. "Population Control Factors: Infanticide, Disease, Nutrition, and Food Supply." Pp. 243–45 in *Man the Hunter*, edited by Richard B. Lee and Irven Devore. Chicago: Aldine.

Worthington, Rogers/Chicago Tribune. 1994. "Paternity Puts Challenge to Teen Fathers." *Salt Lake Tribune,* February 17, P.10A.

Wright, Carol L., and Joseph W. Maxwell. 1991. "Social Support During Adjustment to Later-Life Divorce: How Adult Children Help Parents." *Journal of Divorce and Remarriage* 15:21–48.

Wright, Carolyn, and Linda Stone Fish. "Feminist Family Therapy: The Battle against Subtle Sexism." Pp. 201–15 in *Subtle Sexism: Current Practice and Prospects for Change,* edited by Nijole Vaicaitis Benokraitis. Thousand Oaks, CA: Sage Publications.

Wright, Erik Olin. 1989. "Women in the Class Structure." *Politics and Society* 17:35–66.

Wright, Erik Olin, and Janeen Baxter. 1995. "The Gender Gap in Workplace Authority: A Cross-National Study." *American Sociological Review* 60:407–35.

Wright, James D. 1978. "Are Working Women Really More Satisfied? Evidence from Several National Surveys." *Journal of Marriage and the Family* 40: 301–13.

Wright, Robert. 1994. *The Moral Animal: Evolutionary Psychology and Everyday Life.* New York: Pantheon.

Wrong, Dennis H. 1987. "Social Inequality Without Social Stratification." Pp. 440–47 in *Structured Social Inequality: A Reader in Comparative Social Stratification*, 2nd ed., edited by Celia Heller. New York: Macmillan.

Wu, Zheng. 1995. "Premarital Cohabitation and Postmarital Cohabiting Union Formation." *Journal of Family Issues* 16:212–32.

WuDunn, Sheryl. "Divorce Rate Soars as Chinese Decide Love Is Part of Marriage." P.1B. *New York Times*, April 17.

X

Xiaohe, Xu, and Martin King White. 1990. "Love Matches and Arranged Marriages: A Chinese Replication." *Journal of Marriage and the Family* 52:709–72.

Xu, Xiaohe, Jianjun Ji, and Yuk-Ying Tung. 2000. "Social and Political Assortative Mating in Urban China." *Journal of Family Issues* 21:47–77.

Y

Yablonsky, L. 1979. *The Extra-Sex Factor: Why over Half of America's Married Men Play Around.* New York: Times Books.

Yamaguchi, Kazuo, and Linda R. Ferguson. 1995. "The Stopping and Spacing of Childbirths and Their Birth-History Predictors: Rational-Choice Theory and Event-History Analysis." *American Sociological Review* 60:272–98.

Yanagida, Kunio. 1957. *Japanese Manners and Customs in the Meiji Era.* Translated by Charles S. Terry. Tokyo: Obunsha.

Yankelovich, Daniel. 1994. "How Changes in the Economy Are Reshaping American Values." Pp. 16–53 in *Values and Public Policy*, edited by Henry J. Aaron, Thomas E. Bann, and Timothy Taylor. Washington, DC: The Brookings Institution.

Yllo, Kersti A. 1993. "Through a Feminist Lens: Gender, Power, and Violence." Pp. 47–62 in *Current Controversies on Family Violence*, edited by Richard J. Gelles and Donileen R. Loseke. Newbury Park, CA: Sage.

Yorburg, Betty. 1993. *Family Relationships.* New York: St. Martin's Press.

Young, Margaret H., Brent C. Miller, Maria C. Norton, and E. Jeffrey Hill. 1995. "The Effect of Parental Supportive Behaviors on Life Satisfaction of Adolescent Offspring." *Journal of Marriage and the Family* 57:813–22.

Z

Zabin, Laurie Schwab, Rebecca Wong, Robin M. Weinick, and Mark R. Emerson. 1992. "Dependency in Urban Black Families Following the Birth of an Adolescent's Child." *Journal of Marriage and the Family* 54:496–507.

Zal, H. Michael. 1992. *The Sandwich Generation.* New York: Plenum Press.

Zamyatin, Yevgeny. 1972. *We.* New York: Bantam.

Zaretsky, Eli. 1976. *Capitalism, the Family, and Personal Life.* New York: Harper & Row.

Zelnick, Melvin, John F. Kantner, and Kathleen Ford. 1981. *Sex and Pregnancy in Adolescence.* Beverly Hills, CA: Sage.

Zernike, Kate. 2001. "Program DAREs to Start Over Again." *The Denver Post,* February 18, P. 1ff. Denver, CO.

Zhangling, Wei. 1990. "The Family and Family Research in Contemporary China." *International Social Science Journal* 126:497.

Ziaxiang, A., L. Xinlian, and G. Zhahua. 1987. "The Causes of Divorce." Pp. 162–77 in *New Trends in Chinese Marriage and the Family*, edited by L. Jieqiong. Beijing: China International Book Trading.

Zimmerman, Shirley L. 1988. *Understanding Family Policy: Theoretical Approaches.* Newbury Park, CA: Sage.

Zimmerman, Shirley L. 1995. *Understanding Family Policy: Theories and Applications.* Newbury Park, CA: Sage.

Zinn, Maxine Baca. 1994. "Adaptation and Continuity in Mexican-Origin Families." Pp. 64–81 in *Minority Families in the United States: A Multicultural Perspective*, edited by Ronald L. Taylor. Englewood Cliffs, NJ: Prentice-Hall.

Zinn, Maxine Baca, and D. Stanley Eitzen. 1993. *Diversity in Families,* 3rd ed. New York: HarperCollins.

Zuska, Joseph J., and Joseph A. Pursch. 1988. "Long Term Management." Pp. 98–123 in *Alcoholism: a Practical Treatment Guide*, edited by E. Gitlow and Herbert S. Peyser. Philadelphia: Grune and Stratton.

Index